J. G. Fichte: *Foundation of the Entire Wissenschaftslehre* and Related Writings (1794–95)

DANIEL BREAZEALE was born in Houston, Texas, in 1945. After attending Austin College, he earned his PhD in Philosophy from Yale University in 1971. He then taught for many years at the University of Kentucky, where he is now Professor Emeritus of Philosophy. Breazeale has been a frequent recipient of research grants and fellowships from such sources as the National Endowment for Humanities and the Alexander von Humboldt Foundation. He is a co-founder of the North American Fichte Society and the author of many essays on Fichte, German idealism, and Nietzsche. He is also the translator of numerous volumes of Fichte's writings and the co-editor of a dozen volumes of collected essays on his philosophy.

J. G. Fichte: *Foundation of the Entire Wissenschaftslehre and Related Writings (1794–95)*

Edited and Translated by

DANIEL BREAZEALE

OXFORD
UNIVERSITY PRESS

Great Clarendon Street, Oxford, OX2 6DP,
United Kingdom

Oxford University Press is a department of the University of Oxford.
It furthers the University's objective of excellence in research, scholarship,
and education by publishing worldwide. Oxford is a registered trade mark of
Oxford University Press in the UK and in certain other countries

Published in the United States of America by Oxford University Press
198 Madison Avenue, New York, NY 10016, United States of America

British Library Cataloguing in Publication Data

Data available

Library of Congress Cataloging in Publication Data

Data available

ISBN 978–0–19–884290–3 (Hbk.)
ISBN 978–0–19–288222–6 (Pbk.)

To Viv,

Summoner and Sustainer

Table of Contents

III. OUTLINE OF WHAT IS DISTINCTIVE OF THE *WISSENSCHAFTSLEHRE* WITH REGARD TO THE THEORETICAL POWER

Preface

Early in 1801, having taken refuge in Berlin in the wake of the "Atheism Controversy," which led to the loss of his professorship in Jena, and convinced that his system of philosophy, the so-called "Doctrine of Scientific Knowledge" or *Wissenschaftslehre*, had been universally misunderstood, Fichte issued a *Crystal-Clear Report on the Most Recent Philosophy*, which bore the plaintive subtitle "an effort to force the reader to understand." This has served — with equal poignancy — as my personal motto over the several years I have labored over this translation and edition.

Having for many years studied, taught, and written about the texts translated in this volume, I remained only too well aware of how far I still was from truly "understanding" them, and I wanted to do something to remedy that situation. Fichte constantly challenged his own students and readers "to think the *Wissenschaftslehre*" for themselves and in their own way, and he added that only by doing so could anyone ever really succeed in "thinking *it*" — that is, the *Wissenschaftslehre* — at all. For me, that meant thinking it in English. Hence my decision to tackle a work described by a recent commentator as "the most difficult text to comprehend of all of those that have been produced in the history of philosophy since antiquity."[1]

This new English translation of the 1794/95 *Foundation of the Entire Wissenschaftslehre* is my effort to force *myself* to understand it, while at the same time helping others do the same. Accordingly, I have tried to produce an English version that is not only as accurate as I can make it but is as broadly accessible as possible. For this reason, I have supplemented my translations with rather extensive annotation and commentary, as well as with detailed outlines of the contents and structure of the *Foundation* and *Outline*. It is my hope that the latter will help orient readers who — like myself — sometimes find themselves rather lost in the wilderness of Fichte's complex "derivations."

After completing my translation of the *Foundation*, I realized that it really should appear, as Fichte himself had insisted, along with the shorter companion treatise of 1795, *Outline of What is Distinctive of the Wissenschaftslehre with Regard to the Theoretical Power*, as well as with the shorter *Concerning the Concept of the Wissenschaftslehre*, which Fichte published in May of 1794 as an introduction to his project for prospective students at the University of Jena. Though I first translated both of these texts more than thirty years ago,[2] they have been translated anew for

---

[1] Émil Jalley, "Présentation," in Fichte, *La Doctrine de la science (1794)*, Vol. 2, *Naissance et devenir de l'impérialisme allemand* (Paris: L'Harmattan, 2016), p.49.

[2] *Fichte: Early Philosophical Writings* (Ithaca, NY: Cornell University Press, 1988). I have subsequently translated and edited three more volumes of Fichte's writings: *Foundations of Transcendental Philosophy (Wissenschaftslehre) nova methodo* (Ithaca, NY: Cornell University Press, 1992); *Introductions to the Wissenschaftslehre and Other Writings* (Indianapolis, IN: Hackett, 1994) and, with Günter Zöller, *System of Ethics* (Cambridge: Cambridge University Press, 2005).

this volume, which also includes, as an Appendix, a translation of the transcriptions of the surviving portions of Fichte's lectures in Zurich during the first months of 1794. It was in these "Zurich lectures" that he made his very first effort to formulate and to articulate the system he would soon be presenting in printed form in his lectures in Jena.

I wish I could report that my experiment was a complete success and that I now truly understand every facet of this, Fichte's first and most influential presentation of the *Wissenschaftslehre*. I can make no such claim, however, though work on this project has certainly *advanced* my understanding of this remarkable thinker and of these challenging but rewarding texts. My sincere hope is that it may do the same for readers of this volume.

I first encountered these writings in graduate school, when I dropped out of a seminar on Fichte and Schelling taught by Miklos Vetö, because the key texts were then unavailable in English and because my German was not up to the challenge of reading the *Grundlage der gesamten Wissenschaftslehre*. I had more success with Alexis Philonenko's French translation, but even that was insufficient. I was therefore delighted when, shortly thereafter, Peter Heath published his English translation of the *Foundation*, in a volume that also included John Lachs' English version of Fichte's 1797 "Introductions" to the *Wissenschaftslehre*.[3] I have used Heath's translation in my graduate and undergraduate classes for many years, supplemented by an extensive list of "corrections and omissions," prepared and privately distributed by Fritz Marti.

Like many others, I have profited from Heath's work, as well as from Philonenko's, though I am not unaware of certain shortcomings in each. There are undoubtedly shortcomings in these new translations as well, though I hope they will not be debilitating. After completing the first drafts of my new translations, I compared them carefully and profitably with Heath's and Philonenko's versions, which allowed me to catch numerous errors and to improve my own translations. Regarding matters of translation, I also consulted with Joseph O'Neill, Erich Fuchs, and David W. Wood.

An invaluable resource for the annotation has been the comprehensive "commentary" on the *Foundation* prepared by Wolfgang Class and Alois Soller.[4] I have also benefited enormously from the substantial scholarly literature devoted to the *Foundation* and associated works, as indicated in the bibliography to this volume, as well as from the many scholarly conferences and symposia devoted to the early *Wissenschaftslehre* in which I have had the good fortune to participate over the years.

I am especially grateful to Reinhard Lauth, who fostered my budding interest in Fichte, and to Erich Fuchs, who has been a constant and reliable source of information and inspiration, as well as a dear friend. I am grateful too to my fellow Fichte scholars and friends around the world, with whom I have engaged for so long and

---

[3] *The Science of Knowledge,* trans. and ed. Peter Heath and John Lachs (NY, NY: Meredith, 1970; rpt. Cambridge: Cambridge University Press, 1982). There was also an earlier nineteenth-century translation, *The Science of Knowledge,* trans. and ed. A. E. Kroeger (Philadelphia: J. B. Lippincott, 1868; rpt. London: Trübner, 1889); however, the less said about this well-intended but utterly unreliable effort the better.

[4] Wolfgang Class and Alois K. Soller, *Kommentar zu Fichtes* Grundlage der gesamten Wissenschaftslehre (Amsterdam: Rodopi, 2004).

from whom I have learned so much. These include Tom Rockmore, Günter Zöller, Wayne Martin, Michael Vater, Fred Neuhouser, Claude Piché, Ives Radrizzani, Marco Ivaldo, Jacinto Rivera de Rosales, Mário Jorge de Carvalho, Jürgen Stolzenberg. Helmut Traub, Halla Kim, Violetta Waibel, Alois Soller, Faustino Fabianelli, Michael Gerten, Steven Hoeltzel, Jeffery Kinlaw, George Seidel, Marina Bykova, Alain Perrinjaquet, Yukio Irie, Elizabeth Millán Brusslan, Benjamin Crowe, Owen Ware, Gabriel Gottlieb, Kevin Zanelotti, Arnold Farr, Joseph Trullinger, Brett Fulkerson-Smith, Janet Roccanova, Yolanda Estes, and Carolyn Buchanan.

I would also like to thank my colleagues in the College of Arts and Sciences and Department of Philosophy at the University of Kentucky, who have granted me free reign to pursue my scholarly interests for half a century now, as well as to the generations of students who have gamely followed my instructions "to think the person who is thinking the wall." These students, many of whom were exposed to and helped improve earlier "beta versions" of these translations, were the readers I envisioned as I prepared these translations and notes.

I am indebted as well to the institutions and agencies that have generously supported my study of Fichte over the decades: the University of Kentucky, the National Endowment for the Humanities, and the Alexander von Humboldt Stiftung.

I am also grateful to Viviane Breazeale and David W. Wood for their diligent proofreading of this material and for their many valuable suggestions for improving both the accuracy and the readability of these texts.

I must also mention the highly professional editorial and production team at Oxford University Press, including the philosophy editor, Peter Momtchiloff, the project manager, Chandrasekaran Chandrakala, the copy-editor, Joy Mellor, and the proofreader Michael Janes—with all of whom it was a pleasure to work.

Thanks are due as well to Mitchell Nolte for his generous permission to reproduce his portrait of Fichte on the cover of this volume.

As a final thought regarding the daunting challenges of translating, understanding, and interpreting the original *Wissenschaftslehre*, allow me to misappropriate Fichte's own words:

Let us rejoice over the immense prospect that is ours to cultivate! Let us rejoice, because we feel our own strength—and because our task is endless![5]

Lexington, Kentucky
2020

[5] These are the concluding words of Fichte's fourth lecture concerning the vocation of the scholar, delivered in Jena in June of 1794 (*EVBG, GA,* I/3: 68; *SW,* VI, p. 346; *EPW,* p. 184).

Editor's Introduction

Genesis and First Presentation of the *Wissenschaftslehre* (1793–95)

In the summer of 1793, following the quite astonishing success of his first book, *Attempt at a Critique of all Revelation*,[1] and after publishing (anonymously) the "First Installment" of his even more controversial *Contribution toward Rectifying the Judgment of the Public concerning the French Revolution*, Fichte returned to Zurich, where he had previously spent a tumultuous year and a half as a private tutor, while also becoming engaged to Johanna Rahn, daughter of a well-to-do local official.[2] Having finally achieved a measure of public success and professional recognition, he was preparing to marry his fiancée later that year and looking forward to spending an extended period of time living with her in her father's house, while pursuing his burgeoning philosophical projects at a deliberate pace.

Fichte had been an enthusiastic admirer of Kant's philosophy ever since the moment of his first exposure to the same in the summer of 1790, and, on the strength of his treatise on revelation, he was already being hailed in some influential quarters as a new, rising star in the firmament of Kantian (or "Critical") philosophy. He was therefore invited to become a contributor to one of the more important organs associated with this new philosophical movement, the *Allgemeine Literatur Zeitung* (*A.L.Z.*), which was edited and published in Jena, the city and university most closely associated with these new advancements. Indeed, K. L. Reinhold, the best-known exponent of the effort to "improve" Kant's philosophy by providing it with a more systematic form and a deeper, more secure foundation, was a professor at Jena. An essential part of this endeavor, upon which Reinhold conferred the name *Elementarphilosophie* ("Elementary Philosophy" or "Philosophy of the Elements"), was Reinhold's effort to demonstrate

---

[1] Fichte had previously lived in Zurich from September of 1788 through March 1790.

The first edition of *VKO* was composed during his stay in Königsberg in the summer and early fall of 1791 and published—minus both its preface and the name of its author—in the spring of 1792. An expanded second edition, which included an important new "Doctrine of the Will," was prepared in Danzig during the winter of 1792–93 and appeared in April of 1793, a few months prior to Fichte's triumphal return to Zurich.

For the fascinating story of how Fichte's inaugural work happened to be published without the name of its author and the incalculable consequence this had for Fichte's reputation and career, as well as for additional information on Fichte's activities and writings up to 1800, see "Fichte in Jena," *EPW*, pp. 1–49.

[2] *Beitrag zur Berichtigung der Urtheile des Publikums über die französische Revolution.* The "First Installment" of Part One was composed in Danzig during the first months of 1793 and published (anonymously) in April of that year. Fichte wrote the "Second Installment" of Part One during the summer of 1793, immediately following his arrival in Zurich and prior to his marriage to Johanna Rahn (October 22, 1793). This "Second Installment" was published (also anonymously) in the first months of 1794. Under pressure from the authorities in Weimar and on the advice of friends, Fichte subsequently abandoned his plans to compose and to publish the projected Part Two of this work.

how the cognitive powers of intuition and understanding are both *grounded in* and hence *derivable from* a single, more fundamental mental power, the "power of representation" or *Vorstellungsvermögen*. This effort took the concrete from of a *philosophical system* in which all the results of the first *Critique* could allegedly be derived from a *single, foundational principle*: the so-called "Principle of Consciousness," according to which, in every state or moment of consciousness, the conscious subject *distinguishes* a mental representation both from itself and from the object to which that representation refers, while at the same time *relating* it to both the subject and the object. But Reinhold's project was even more ambitious; he also envisioned unifying Kant's theoretical and practical philosophy in the same way, by deriving both from a single foundational principle, though he did not manage to accomplish this before abandoning his own Elementary Philosophy for something even newer and more radical—namely, the system proposed by his successor in Jena, J. G. Fichte.

In the fall of 1793, however, there was as yet no "Fichtean" system of philosophy. Instead, he was preoccupied, first with defending and then with re-thinking his own allegiance not only to Kant, but also to Reinhold, of whose recent writings he had also become a sincere admirer and advocate. The re-examination in question was occasioned by a series of aggressive attacks upon the philosophies of both Kant and Reinhold. Of these criticisms, the ones that most affected Fichte were not those launched by defenders of older, now-threatened systems of philosophy, which he believed had already been adequately addressed by Kant himself. Instead, what profoundly shook Fichte's new philosophical commitments were the *skeptical* objections to the Critical philosophy raised by such authors as F. H. Jacobi, Salomon Maimon, and G. E. Schulze (a.k.a., "Aenesidemus").[3] Writing in 1795, he observed that "anyone who has not yet understood Hume, Aenesidemus (when he is correct), and Maimon and has failed to come to terms with himself concerning the points they raise, is not yet ready for the *Wissenschaftslehre*. It answers questions for him that he has not posed; it bandages him, where he has suffered no wound."[4] In contrast, Fichte's earlier commitment to transcendental idealism was indeed "wounded" in the second half of 1793, and he spent the rest of his life applying the bandage.

At the very moment that Fichte's philosophical commitments were being challenged, he found himself committed to reviewing three books for the *A.L.Z.*

---

[3] In the appendix to his 1797 work, *David Hume über den Glauben, oder Idealismus und Realismus,* Jacobi had criticized Kant's notion of "things in themselves" as incoherent and incompatible with his own transcendental idealism. Maimon's first book, *Versuch über die Transcendentalphilosophie* (1790), subjected Kant's *Critique of Pure Reason* to a withering examination and re-interpretation. Among other things, Maimon criticized Kant for having failed to demonstrate that pure, a priori concepts actually can and do—*in fact*—apply to sensible experience. Schulze's anonymously published work, *Aenesidemus oder über die Fundamente der von dem Herrn Professor Reinhold in Jena gelieferten Elementar-Philosophie* (1792), launched a full-bore skeptical attack not only upon both Kant's theoretical and practical philosophy, but also upon Reinhold's "new and improved" version of the same. For an excellent account of these skeptical assaults upon Kant and Reinhold, see chs. 2, 9, and 10 of Frederick C. Beiser's *The Fate of Reason: German Philosophy from Kant to Fichte* (Cambridge, MA: Harvard University Press, 1987).

[4] *Wer Hume, Aenesidemus, wo er Recht hat, u. Maimon noch nicht verstanden,* GA, II/3:389. This is a short unfinished manuscript from the spring of 1795.

The first two of these books were contributions to a then-raging debate concerning the implications of Kant's practical philosophy, especially regarding freedom of the will and the imputability of immoral actions. The first of these reviews, a review of Leonhard Creuzer's *Skeptical Reflections on Free Will*, was published anonymously (as was the custom at the *A.L.Z.*) October 30, 1793, with the second, a review of F. H. Gebhard's *On Ethical Goodness on the Basis of Disinterested Benevolence*, appearing in the next day's issue.[5] Taken together, these two reviews reveal how preoccupied Fichte was at this point with interpreting the Critical philosophy in a way that would permit him to reconcile the noumenal freedom of the will with empirical necessity, a project he now realized would require something still absent from the writings of both Kant and Reinhold: namely, a demonstration *that* reason is indeed practical, or capable of determining the will a priori.

The third volume was one that Fichte himself had originally requested to review, an anonymously published treatise by a self-proclaimed "Humean skeptic" entitled *Aenesidemus, or Concerning the Foundations of the Elementary Philosophy Propounded in Jena by Professor Reinhold, including a Defense of Skepticism against the Pretensions of the Critique of Reason*.[6] Fichte was at this point already acquainted with Jacobi's criticism of the kind of dogmatic Kantianism that affirms things in themselves, as well as with Salomon Maimon's more profound questioning of the *quid facti* supposedly underlying Kant's project of justifying the a priori application of pure forms of intuition and thinking to the sensory manifold. And he was, of course, quite familiar with (and already involved in) the debate surrounding the relation of free will to both natural determinism and moral obligation. But now he found his allegiance to Kant and Reinhold even more directly challenged by "Aenesidemus."[7] As he explained to the long-suffering editor of the *A.L.Z.*, "I have been thrown into an unforeseen labor by Aenesidemus' skepticism."[8]

---

[5] *Crev* and *Grev*. See Wayne Martin, "Fichte's Creuzer Review and the Transformation of the Free Will Problem," *European Journal of Philosophy* 26/2 (2018): 717–29.

[6] Though *Aenesidemus* was published anonymously, Fichte was aware of its author's identity, the same person he believed to have been the author of an anonymous and quite sarcastic review of *VKO*: namely, G. E. Schulze (1761–1833), Professor of Philosophy at Helmstedt and a former classmate of Fichte's at Pforta and Leipzig.

[7] For a detailed account of Fichte's encounter with and reply to such skepticism, see Breazeale, "The *Aenesidemus* Review and the Transformation of German Idealism," Ch. 2 of *TWL*; and "Reinhold/Schulze/Fichte: A Re-Examination," in *Krankheit des Zeitalters oder heilsame Provokation? Skeptizismus in der nachkantischen Philosophie*, ed. Martin Bondeli, Jiří Chotaš, and Klaus Vieweg (Paderborn: Fink, 2016), pp. 161–79.

[8] Fichte to C. G. Schütz, December 14, 1793, *GA*, III/2: 26. Fichte volunteered to review *Aenesidemus* early in 1793, and in a letter of May 25, 1793 to Schütz, editor of the *A.L.Z.*, he promised to submit his review "within a short time." In fact, he did not submit it until mid-January of the following year, and it finally appeared in the February 11 and 12, 1794, issues of the *A.L.Z.* Insight into the "unforeseen labor" mentioned by Fichte is provided by his correspondence during this period. See, for example, the draft of his November 1793 letter to L. W. Wloemer, *GA*, III/2: 4–17 and his mid-December letter to Henrich Stefani, *GA*, III/2: 27–9; *EPW*, pp. 370–1. See too his letters of November–December 1793 to J. F. Flatt, *GA*, III/2: 17–18; *EPW*, pp. 366–7, of December 6, 1793, to F. I. Niethammer, *GA*, III/2: 19–22; *EPW*, pp. 367–9, and of January 15, 1794, to H. V. Reinhard, *GA*, III/2: 39–41; *EPW*, pp. 372–4.

It was while working on this review that Fichte turned from simply questioning the adequacy of Kant's and Reinhold's presentations of transcendental philosophy to attempting to construct his own, radically new presentation of what he still took to be basically the same philosophical system. As he wrote in November of 1793, "I immediately began a book by a resolute skeptic, which led me to the clear conviction that philosophy is still very far from being a science. I was therefore forced to abandon my previous system and think of a tenable one."[9] He appears to have begun working seriously on the *Aenesidemus* review just after returning from his honeymoon in late October and to have continued working on it through the first few weeks of 1794. At the same time, and in close conjunction with his work on the *Aenesidemus* review, he began composing a long manuscript with the dual title "Personal Meditations on Elementary Philosophy/Practical Philosophy"—a work the editors of the new edition of Fichte's complete works describe as "a *Wissenschaftslehre in statu nascendi*,"[10] even though its author had at that point not yet decided upon that name for his emerging system.

By mid-December he had made great strides in developing his new ideas and could boast to his friend Heinrich Stephani that:

> [*Aenesidemus*] has overthrown Reinhold in my eyes and made me suspicious of Kant. It has overturned my whole system from the ground up. One cannot live under the open sky. It cannot be helped; the system has to be rebuilt. And this is just what I have been doing for the past six weeks or so. Come celebrate the harvest with me! I have discovered a new foundation, out of which it will be easy to develop philosophy in its entirety. Kant's philosophy is correct as such—but only with respect to its results, not its reasons. This singular thinker looks more marvelous to me every day. I believe he possesses a genius that reveals to him the truth without showing him why it is true. In short, I believe that in a few more years we shall have a philosophy that will be just as self-evident as geometry.[11]

When the *Aenesidemus* review finally appeared, in mid-February of 1794, Fichte's reservations concerning certain aspects of both Reinhold's Elementary Philosophy and Kant's Critical philosophy became public, along with the first tantalizing hints of his audacious new strategy for re-establishing transcendental idealism on a new, more secure foundation, one that would be immune to skeptical challenges, while at the same time resolving the controversies concerning the reality of human freedom and its relationship to dutiful action. This new foundational principle would be even deeper (or, if one prefers, even higher) than

[9] Fichte to L. W. Wloemer, November 1793 (draft), *GA*, III/2: 14.
[10] *GA*, II/3: 19. *Eigne Meditationen über ElementarPhilosophie/Practische Philosophie*, *GA*, I/3: 21–266. According to the editors of *GA* this manuscript was begun in early November 1793 and finished in mid-January 1794. See Reinhard Lauth, "Die Entstehung von Fichte's 'Grundlage der gesammten Wissenschaftslehre' nach den 'Eignen Meditationen über ElementarPhilosophie,'" in *Transzendentale Entwicklungslinien von Descartes bis zu Marx und Dostojewski* (Hamburg: Meiner, 1989), pp. 155–79.
[11] Fichte to Stefani, mid-December 1793, *GA*, III/1: 28; *EPW*, p. 371.

Reinhold's "Principle of Consciousness" and would be capable of grounding the practical as well as the theoretical part of the entire system. Unlike Reinhold's Principle of Consciousness, Fichte's new principle would not be grounded in *empirical reflection* upon "facts (*Tatsachen*) of consciousness"; instead, it would be based upon an *intellectual intuition* of that original act by means of which the I first posits itself for itself, an act which Fichte dubbed a *Tathandlung* or "F/Act." The new system would begin with a foundational principle asserting that "the I is *what* it is" purely and simply "*because* it is."[12]

Near the conclusion of the *Aenesidemus* review, while responding to Schulze's objections to Kant's moral theology and his effort to ground belief in God upon the alleged primacy of practical reason, Fichte provides his readers with what amounts to the first, rough public blueprint of the system he himself would spend the next few years expounding—first before a circle of friends and patrons in Zurich, next before his students in Jena, and then in a series of groundbreaking books based upon those same lectures.

> If, in intellectual intuition, the I is *because* it is and *is what* it is, then it is, to that extent, *self-positing*, absolutely independent and autonomous. The I that is present in empirical consciousness, however, the I as intellect, *is* only in relation to something intelligible, and is, to that extent, dependent. But the I that is thereby posited in opposition to itself is supposed to be not two, but one—which is impossible, for dependence contradicts independence. Since, however, the I cannot relinquish its absolute independence, this engenders a striving: the I strives to make what is intelligible dependent upon itself, in order thereby to bring the I that entertains representations of what is intelligible into harmony with the self-positing I. This is what it means to say that *reason is practical*. In the pure I, reason is not practical; nor is reason practical in the I as intellect. Reason is practical only insofar as it strives to unify these two. [...] Far from practical reason having to recognize the superiority of theoretical reason, the entire existence of practical reason is founded on the *conflict* between the self-determining element within us and the theoretical-knowing element, and practical reason itself would be abolished were this conflict to be eliminated.[13]

At the time he wrote this outline of the basic strategy for the foundational portion of his new version of transcendental philosophy, Fichte had still not yet hit upon the term "*Wissenschaftslehre*" and was continuing to refer simply to "my elementary philosophy," or, on one occasion, to his "philosophy of striving."[14] And of course he was still a long way from being able to provide a complete and adequate articulation—or, as he would put it, "presentation" (*Darstellung*)—of this new "philosophy of striving." Indeed, he fully expected to be spending the next few years in Zurich, patiently nourishing the seed planted in the *Aenesidemus* review. That, however, was not what happened.

---

[12] See *RA*, *GA*, I/2: 46-8 and 57; *SW*, I, pp. 9-10 and 16-17; *EPW*, pp. 64-5 and 70-1.

[13] *RA*, *GA*, I/2: 65-6; *SW*, I, pp. 22-4, *EPW*, pp. 75-6.

[14] *StrebungsPhilosophie*. *EM*, *GA*, II/3: 265.

"Zurich Lectures" Zurich, February–April 1794

At the very moment he was completing the *Aenesidemus* review and making major breakthroughs in his private efforts to clarify his new insights concerning the foundations, structure, and methods of transcendental philosophy as a whole, Fichte learned from sources in Weimar and Jena that he was being actively considered as Reinhold's replacement at the University of Jena, and shortly after the beginning of the new year he received an official offer from the university.[15]

This was, of course, not only a welcome surprise and yet another major stroke of good fortune, but also a remarkable honor for the 32-year-old author of the *Critique of all Revelation* and *Contribution toward Correcting the Judgment of the Public regarding the French Revolution*—two works that, albeit in different ways, were responsible for Fichte's reputation as both a political and a religious radical—an "enemy of throne and altar," as some put it. Nevertheless, as his correspondence with university officials and various intermediaries in Jena and Weimar reveals, Fichte made a determined effort to postpone his new appointment—first for "several years" and then for a single one—until he had time to develop adequately his new, as yet unnamed, system. As he wrote to his old Pforta classmate, Karl Böttinger, who was a member of the Consistory in Weimar and Director of the *Gymnasium* and who had been the first person to notify him of the forthcoming offer from Jena: "a discovery around the end of the fall made me wish for nothing more than a few years of independent leisure." Surely, he continued, the university authorities would prefer to have him assume his new position only *after* he had adequately worked out the details of his new system, which, he added, might well require "a few years of independent work."[16] He made a similar case in his response to C. G. Voigt, the Weimar official in charge of administrative matters at Jena, to whom he wrote as follows:

> To the extent that I have made any progress as an independent thinker, I have become more and more convinced that [...] philosophy, *thanks to the Critical attention it has received*, has come very near to its lofty goal of becoming a science possessed of certainty, though it has not yet attained that goal. One of the chief aims of the studies in which I am presently engaged (and to which

---

[15]   Reinhold, who was then at the pinnacle of his fame and who had a large and enthusiastic following among the students at Jena, notified the authorities sometime during the Fall Semester of 1793/94 that he would be leaving Jena for Kiel following the conclusion of that semester. On December 26, 1793, C. G. Voigt informed Fichte that an official offer would soon be arriving and stipulated that Fichte would be expected to assume his new professorial duties immediately following the Easter recess, that is, at the beginning of the Summer Semester of 1794. On January 5, 1794, Fichte received a letter from Gottlieb Hufeland, a Professor of Law at Jena, urging him to accept the forthcoming official offer and warning that any delay might result in an open competition for Reinhold's chair, giving Fichte's opponents time to make an issue of his rumored "democratism."

[16]   "The question is whether or not Jena wants to hinder a project that can be completed only in a period of independent leisure—whether they wish to have in me a quite ordinary professor, of the sort one can easily obtain, or whether they would prefer to see me enter upon my post with some distinction. If it is the latter, then I cannot start before Easter 1795—but then I will certainly have students" (Fichte to Böttiger, January 8, 1794, *GA*, III/2: 33–4).

I intended to dedicate the leisure I had acquired) was to determine whether this goal should be abandoned or what needed to be done in order to achieve it. Thanks to a stroke of good fortune, I have discovered—much sooner than I could have hoped—the path that, in my opinion, must lead in that direction. I have tested this path, and I think it is very likely to be the correct one. Had the avenue to another sort of activity [that is, the professorship in Jena] not become open to me at this point, I would have completely devoted a few years of my life exclusively to this project—one that can be properly accomplished only during a period of uninterrupted leisure. After making a rough estimate of the entire project, I calculate that it should be completely finished by Easter of 1795.

Apart from the interruption and perhaps complete discontinuation of this project (even if it should prove to be nothing more than a new experiment), another inconvenience would arise were I to have to begin my teaching duties by Easter of 1794. A teacher of philosophy has to have a system that is completely tenable (at least in his own eyes). At the moment I have no system that fully satisfies me, and I would therefore be unable to live up to the high expectations of me that have been raised by this honorable offer.[17]

When this request was rejected, Fichte was compelled—to borrow a term from horticulture—to "force" the growth of the new system upon which he was expected to begin lecturing in less than five months. Fortunately, he was at precisely that moment presented with yet another unexpected opportunity, one that greatly facilitated the accelerated development of the new system.

Fichte had never been particularly appreciated by the citizens of Zurich, for whom, in turn, he showed no particular affection. Nevertheless, once local rumors concerning his rising fame as a "Kantian" philosopher and his immanent departure for a prestigious university teaching position began to spread, he was approached by a small group of local clerics and officials, one of whom wrote that "it would be irresponsible of us to allow such a man to depart our city without having made some use of him." More specifically, they desired "to become more closely acquainted with this [Kantian] philosophy through oral lectures from a man who had caused such a great stir."[18] It was not long after this conversation, which reportedly took place in February of 1794, that Fichte was formally invited to deliver a series of lectures "on the Kantian philosophy" in the home of the person most responsible for organizing the Zurich lectures, the leading local pastor and noted physiognomist, Johann Kaspar Lavater.[19]

An important mediating role in this process was played by Jens Baggesen, the Danish-German poet and intimate friend of Reinhold. Baggesen was living in Switzerland during this period and first encountered Fichte in Bern in late

---

[17] Fichte to Voigt, January 8, 1794 (draft), *GA*, III/2: 42–3; *EPW*, p. 88.
[18] Georg Geßner, *Johann Kasper Lavaters Lebenbeschreibung* (Winterthur, 1803), p. 275 (as cited in *FiG*, I, p. 86). Geßner was a pastor in the nearby village of Waisenhaus and Lavater's son-in-law.
[19] Johann Kaspar Lavater is best remembered today as a leading proponent of the "science" of physiognomy. Fichte first became acquainted with Lavater during his earlier stay in Zurich as a private tutor in the home of the Ott family (1788–89).

October of 1793, during the latter's honeymoon. The two immediately became engaged in long and intimate philosophical conversations and correspondence, focusing upon Fichte's claim that Reinhold's Principle of Consciousness was not, in fact, the highest foundational principle of philosophy as a whole—though, according to Baggesen, Fichte was at this point claiming only that there *might be* some still-higher principle.[20] As a loyal friend of Reinhold, Baggesen resisted this suggestion, on the grounds that to seek a principle higher than the Principle of Consciousness would inevitably lead one into "pure egoism."

In early December, Baggesen visited Zurich and Fichte shared with him the results of his recent philosophical efforts, including his discovery of a new foundational principle for *philosophy as a whole*, not just for "theoretical" philosophy, that is, for the part of the system dealing with the conditions for the possibility of *cognition*. During these conversations Baggesen reports Fichte as wondering whether Kant

> possessed a genius like Socrates, one that told him what he did not know? Or is it perhaps Kant's low opinion of his own age, which has not risen to his own level, or is it modesty?—in any case, all that Kant writes is true—and all of his proofs are false. Philosophy still stands in need of a complete revolution.[21]

Reinhold too was criticized by Fichte: namely, for not going far enough. Distinguishing and relating—the two activities attributed by Reinhold to the "power of representation"—are not, insisted Fichte, the highest acts of the mind, and therefore the principle that expresses them cannot be the supreme foundational principle of all philosophy. There must therefore be a power of the human mind that is more fundamental than that of mere "representing," even if the latter is the proper starting point of the strictly *theoretical* portion of philosophy (the portion dealing with *cognition*). More fundamental than the proposition "I am engaging in representing" is the proposition "I am," and this, Fichte explained to Baggesen, must provide the absolutely first foundational principle. The original power of the mind—or, as Fichte will prefer to express it, of the I—is neither knowing nor willing; instead, it is the "thetic" power simply *to assert* or *to posit* (*Setzen*)—the power of the I to posit itself absolutely and unconditionally, as well as the power to posit itself as opposed by and reciprocally related to something it posited in opposition to itself.[22]

Baggesen was so impressed by this conversation that he took it upon himself to persuade Lavater to initiate and to host Fichte's lectures.[23] By early February, Fichte was able to send Lavater the following outline of the projected series:

---

[20] See Baggesen's letter to Reinhold, June 8, 1794 (*FiG*, I: 59).

[21] From Baggesen's *Tagebuch* (diary), December 7, 1793 (*FiG*, I: 67).

[22] This fascinating conversation is described in great detail in Baggesen's diary entry for December 7, 1793 (*FiG*, I: 67–8).

[23] As Baggesen wrote to Reinhold on June 8, 1794: "Fichte had no love for Lavater, and Lavater almost hated Fichte. I resolved to bring them together. In the case of Fichte, this was quickly accomplished. We shook hands, and he assured me that he was prepared to take the first step. Lavater was more difficult. From St. Gallen I sent him a letter describing my proposal, and behold, when I returned

My style of lecturing is always synthetic. I never throw out thoughts as they occurred to me in the privacy of my study. Instead, I think, discover, and develop them before the eyes of my audience and along with them. In doing so, I will endeavor, even in the smallest portions of the lecture, to follow the most strictly logical path. Since I will have almost everything written out, I rather hope to master this form of lecturing. This seems to me the sole foundation of all clarity. The only way to promote clarity further is by providing frequent examples (wherever the material permits) and by outlining the structure of the argument on the blackboard. It appears to me that the only way this aim can be combined with your wish that I complete something in its entirety [in this course of lectures] is as follows: I will have to devote two or three hours to prolegomena concerning the concept, the characteristic features, and the method of demonstration of philosophy, as well as the relation of this science to the other sciences with which it is confused. I will then develop—just as completely and as clearly as I can—the first foundational principles of *philosophy as a whole*, followed by the first foundational principles of *theoretical* philosophy, in order to show how one proceeds in the theoretical realm. I will then simply enumerate the remaining principles of theoretical philosophy, in order to provide a general survey of them and of their interconnection. This would take up the first month. In the second month I will present in detail and in a similar manner the first foundational principles of *practical* philosophy. The method of proceeding in this part of philosophy will be indicated, with particular reference to the highest foundational principles of practical philosophy. I can provide no more than an overview of the interconnection of the additional principles. I see no other means to combine the wish for clarity with the wish for completeness; for were I to lecture in detail merely upon practical philosophy, an entire year would hardly suffice. In a few years I will indeed present my entire system to the public. In any case, I would be honored if the same gentlemen who now join with me in oral conversation concerning these subjects should ever wish to engage with me in written dialogue concerning any points that might still remain obscure to them. If you approve of this expedient, then please be so kind as to inform the other gentlemen.[24]

---

from across the Alps Fichte was delivering philosophical lectures in Lavater's living room. They are now good friends" (*FiG*, I: 75). Erich Fuchs plausibly speculates that the animosity between Lavater and Fichte was very probably based on their considerable theological differences, and he calls attention to a later, disparaging remark of Fichte's regarding the "abominable consequences" of "Lavaterism" (*ZVau*, p. 60 n.).

Another influence upon Lavater may have been a letter he received from F. B. Meyer von Schauensee, a local francophone admirer of Fichte and translator of his book on the French revolution, chiding the citizens of Zurich for their failure to take advantage of the temporary presence in their midst of such a philosophical prodigy. Meyer reported as follows: "I am quite astonished by the fact that Zurich, which is so hospitable toward everything good and beautiful, has not taken advantage of this man. The time I have spent with him has been most agreeable. He sees things very clearly and feels them just as deeply. Humanity seems to him to be very important, and he strives eagerly to participate in the cause of humanity. People like this should always be important to us and have our respect" (Meyer von Schauensee to Lavater, January 29, 1794, as cited in *FiG*, 7, p. 1).

[24] Fichte to Lavater, beginning of February, 1794, *GA*, III/2: 60–1; *EPW*, pp. 374–5.

This letter makes it abundantly clear that what the "gentlemen in question" actually obtained from Fichte was much more than lectures "on the Kantian philosophy." Instead, they were present at the first public exposition of a radically new version of transcendental idealism, which Fichte, in the first lecture of the series, February 24, 1794, referred to for the very first time with the name "Doctrine of Science" or *Wissenschaftslehre*. It is therefore no exaggeration to describe Fichte's Zurich lectures as "the first *Wissenschaftslehre*," which is precisely how the manuscript of these lectures was later described by both Fichte's wife and Baggesen.[25]

As noted, Fichte commenced his series of lectures on Monday February 24 and continued them, with a few interruptions for holidays, five afternoons a week through April 26, for a total of approximately forty lectures. The lectures began at 5 p.m., and generally lasted for an hour, followed by an hour or so of conversation and refreshments. They were attended by a shifting cast of characters. Lavater was always present, since Fichte's lectures were held in his home. The average audience consisted of perhaps six or eight people, though more than twice that many appear to have been present for the final, festive oration on human dignity.

In several letters to his wife, Baggesen paints an attractive picture of the milieu in which the Zurich lectures were delivered:

> Around five o'clock I accompanied them to Lavater's house in order to visit him and attend Fichte's *collegium* in Lavater's living room. Just think of it! Lavater met me at the door, and I introduced him to Herbert, Erhard, and Rauscher. The room was already packed with listeners, with Fichte in their midst. Lavater brought in additional chairs, and people took their seats. Everyone was attentive, Lavater with his ears pricked, his eyes wide open, and his mouth ajar.
>
> Fichte was an excellent lecturer, but his lecture was so pure, so abstract, so rigorously logical, that surely only Erhard and Baggesen could completely comprehend what he was saying. [...] Following the *collegium* all six of us—Fichte, Lavater, Erhard, Herbert, Rauscher, and I—went for a walk along a new path, constantly engaging in philosophical discussion. We viewed the mountains and the sunset, and then lingered rather late into the evening, in heartfelt satisfaction.[26]

---

[25] In her unpublished memoir of her husband, Johanna Fichte writes: "after a four year absence from his bride he returned to Zurich, and, following the wedding, lived with his wife in her father's house, where he wrote the ["Second Installment"] of his *Letter on the French Revolution* [*sic*!] and his first *Wissenschaftslehre*, which he communicated in regular lectures to Lavater and several other local scholars" (*FiG*, I: 52).

Baggesen's reference to the status of the Zurich lectures occurs in a marginal remark in his copy of Fichte's *Crystal-Clear Report to the Public at Large* (1801), in which he boasts—to himself, apparently—that he is "perhaps Fichte's most sincere admirer and closest friend on earth," offering as evidence the fact that Fichte "gave him the original manuscript of his *Wissenschaftslehre*, as the person most worthy thereof" (as quoted by Heinrich Fauteck in "Die Beziehung Jens Baggesen zu Fichte," *Orbis Litterarum* 38 [1983], p. 319). Fauteck's article is illuminating for understanding the important role played by Baggesen in the development of Fichte's philosophy during this crucial period, since, as he observes, Baggesen "was nearly the only person who, as an immediate witness, shared with Fichte the experience of the genesis of the *Wissenschaftslehre*" (Fauteck, p. 314).

[26] Baggesen to his wife, April 26, 1794 (*FiG*, 6.1, pp. 43–4).

As was his customary practice, Fichte carefully composed the texts of his Zurich lectures in advance, and when he departed for Jena in mid-May, he left the complete manuscript of these "Zurich lectures" with his wife, who agreed to make two copies, one promised to Baggesen and another for one of Fichte's new in-laws, Johann Heinrich Rahn.[27] In addition, there appear to have been several *transcripts* of the Zurich lectures, as illustrated by Lavater's surviving transcriptions of the first five. Throughout his career, Fichte objected to the practice of taking notes during his lectures, so any "transcript" would have had to be made only following the lecture in question.[28]

As for the specific *content* of these forty or so Zurich lectures: to judge by the previously quoted outline of the same in Fichte's letter to Lavater, as well as other documentary evidence, including the surviving transcripts and copies of portions of the same and various comments in letters written by Fichte and others, one can plausibly reconstruct a rough outline of the entire series.[29]

The close parallels between the first five lectures (Lavater's transcription of which is almost all that survives today of Fichte's Zurich lectures) and *Concerning the Concept of the Wissenschaftslehre* are readily evident. Close parallels between the main body of the Zurich lectures and the *Foundation of the Entire Wissenschaftslehre* may also be inferred, not only from the comments concerning the same contained in the diary of Georg Geßner, who was present for nearly the entire series, and the brief excerpts contained in Baggesen's papers, but also from a remark in Fichte's July 14, 1794, letter to Lavater, in which he announces that "beginning today there will appear, in fascicles, a work I have written, a *Foundation of the Entire Wissenschaftslehre*. This is the series of lectures I had the

---

[27] Concerning these copies, see Johanna Fichte's letters to her husband of May [12]–17 and July 12, 1794, *GA*, III/2: 110 and 173. Baggesen still had his copy at the time he made the previously cited marginal boast in his copy of the *Sun-Clear Report*. Fichte's original mansuscript appears to have still been extant in 1830 when I. H. Fichte published his biography of his father, in which he reported that among his father's papers was the complete manuscipt of "the first presentation of the *Wissenschaftslehre*," which he says is "in structure and content similar to the first printed presentation and should actually be viewed as a preliminary study for the latter" (*J. G. Fichtes Leben und literarischer Briefwechsel* [Sulzbach: J. E. Seidel], 1830, Vol. I, p. 257). Neither Fichte's original manuscript nor either of the copies has survived—beyond, that is, the fragmentary transcripts translated below.

[28] As is confirmed by Geßner, no notes were taken during Fichte's Zurich lectures, though at least some of those present prepared transcripts of the lectures based on memory, and perhaps on conversations with others who had been present, or even with reference to Fichte's own manuscript. In his entry for March 6, Geßner writes: "This morning I wanted once again to finish my transcript of the *Wissenschaftselhre*, up to today's lecture, and I was able to do just that. [...] Then I attended the lecture for today, where we all just listened; no one wrote down anything, finding it preferable to write afterwards." (*ZVau*, p. 19; see too Fuchs, "J. K. Lavaters Nachschrift der Züricher Wissenschaftslehre," in *Der Grundansatz der ersten Wissenschaftslehre Johann Gottlieb Fichtes*, ed. Fuchs and Ives Radrizzani [Neuried: Ars Una, 1996], pp. 63–4).

In a later entry, Geßner mentions that he was able to fill in a gap in his own transcript thanks to Lavater who "dictated to me from the missing lectures by Fichte" (*ZVau*, p. 8). Note that the first part of the third lecture in Lavater's transcript is not in his own hand, but in that of someone else, most likely Geßner—further evidence that Lavater's transcript was not in fact composed during Fichte's lectures.

[29] For a detailed, day-by-day reconstruction of the contents, or at least the topics, of these lectures, based primarily upon the daily entries in Geßner's diary, see Fuchs' introduction to *ZVau*, pp. 18–23.

honor of delivering to you and your friends, revised and thought through for a second time, and here and there more precisely expressed."[30]

Pulling together all of this material, one can draw the following conclusions regarding the organization and content of the 40 Zurich lectures:

I. Prolegomena. This includes the five lectures transcribed by Lavater and corresponds roughly, though not exactly, to the content of *Concerning the Concept of the Wissenschaftslehre* (Lectures 1-5; Monday, February 24 - Friday, February 28).

II. Presentation of the Foundational Principles of Philosophy as a Whole. Presumably, these ten or so lectures corresponded to Part One of *Foundation of the Entire Wissenschaftslehre* (Lectures 5-15).

III. Presentation of the Foundational Principles of Theoretical Philosophy. Presumably, the next fourteen or so lectures corresponded to Part Two of *Foundation of the Entire Wissenschaftslehre* (Lectures 16-30).

IV. Presentation of the Foundational Principles of Practical Philosophy. Presumably, the next nine or so lectures corresponded to Part Three of *Foundation of the Entire Wissenschaftslehr* (Lectures 30-9).

V. Concluding Address. "Concerning Human Dignity." This privately published lecture corresponds to nothing in either *Concerning the Concept of the Wissenschaftslehre* or *Foundation of the Entire Wissenschaftslehre* (Lecture 40, Saturday, April 26).

Lavater's transcriptions of the first five lectures clearly represent the "Prolegomena" to the entire series and anticipate the "invitational" writing that Fichte was at that same time preparing for his prospective students in Jena.

Lecture I corresponds closely to the content of § 1 of *Concerning the Concept.* Both discuss the concept of philosophy as a science erected on the basis of a single, immediately certain foundational principle, and both emphasize the importance of systematic form as a means for transmitting certainty from the first principle to the theorems derived from it.

Lecture II is devoted to the relationship between philosophy and formal logic, as well as to defending the claim that the *Wissenschaftslehre* has to establish the certainty of the foundational principles of all the other, "special" sciences. As such, it corresponds to portions of §§ 2, 5, and 6 of *Concerning the Concept.*

Lecture III corresponds to portions of § 2 of *Concerning the Concept* and discusses the general nature of science as such and of philosophy as the supreme science. It also continues the examination of the relationship between the immediately certain foundational principle of the *Wissenschaftslehre* and the derived principles of the special sciences, as well as the peculiar relationship between philosophy and formal logic.

Lecture IV contains material to which nothing in *Concerning the Concept* corresponds: namely, a discussion of the relationship between geometrical and

---

[30] Fichte to Lavater, June 14, 1794, *GA*, III/2: 130.

philosophical *construction*. (Unsurprisingly, this is the portion of these lectures that has most attracted the attention of contemporary scholars.)

Lecture V corresponds to the longest section of *Concerning the Concept*, § 7, which considers the relationship of the *Wissenschaftslehre* to its *object*, the necessary actions of the human mind.

There is nothing in the Zurich lectures corresponding directly to §§ 3 and 4 of *Concerning the Concept*, which discuss strategies for demonstrating the consistency and completeness of any philosophical system.

What primarily distinguishes the Zurich lectures from *Concerning the Concept* and makes them of special interest is, above all, the special attention devoted to questions of philosophical *method*. This is evident, first of all, in the claim (in Lecture Four) that the supreme foundational principle, though not "demonstrable," can nevertheless be grounded and confirmed by means of "intellectual" or "pure" intuition," a claim repeated neither in *Concerning the Concept* nor in the *Foundation*,[31] where Fichte seems content to claim simply that the first foundational principle must be "purely and simply certain," "immediately certain," or "self-evident."

Lecture Four is of special interest in this respect, for it is there that Fichte explicitly confirms (*contra* Kant) that philosophy can and indeed must *construct* its own concepts a priori. But whereas geometry constructs its concepts by exhibiting them in empirical intuition, philosophy must exhibit its concepts within pure or intellectual intuition. These lectures also emphasize the "experimental" or "do it yourself" character of the *Wissenschaftslehre* even more strongly than *Concerning the Concept*.[32]

At the conclusion of the final lecture in the series, Fichte was presented with an honorarium[33] and a number of written testimonials. He subsequently arranged to have this concluding lecture privately printed and distributed to those who had attended his lectures, dedicating it to them "not as an inquiry, but rather as an

---

[31] Though the term "intellectual intuition" does not appear in the *Foundation*, this treatise does contain a (single) reference to "inner intuition," which Fichte will later, in *WLnm* for example, employ as a synonym for "intellectual intuition." See too *GWL, GA*, I/2: 253; below, p. 197.

[32] As Ives Radrizzani observes, "the most important changes all follow the same tendency. Fichte's first effort is to avoid coming into open conflict with Kant and Reinhold, his two famous precursors on the pathway of transcendental philosophy" (Radrizzani, "La 'Première' Doctrine de la Science de Fichte. Introduction et traduction," *Archives de Philosophie* 60 [1997]: 638).

The surviving transcripts of the first five Zurich lectures also reveal that Fichte was at that point still in the process of settling upon the appropriate *terminology* to employ for communicating his profoundly original philosophical *vision* and *project*. In these lectures, for example, he often employs the term *Darstellung* or "presentation" to designate what he would soon be calling *Setzen* or "positing," and he here describes what he had already (in the *Aenesidemus* review) identified as the original *Tathandlung* or "F/Act" of the I as the "absolute presentation" of the same. Following his arrival in Jena, however, he generally reserved the term "presentation" to designate the secondary or reflective copying of something—thus describing the *Wissenschaftslehre* itself as a "presentation" of the system constituted by the necessary acts of the mind, as derived from the I's original positing or F/Act.

[33] In his diary entry for April 23, written following his attendance at the thirty-seventh lecture in the series, Geßner notes that, following the lecture, in which "some propositions of practical philosophy struck me as very clear and applicable," he and Lavater went for a walk with a few other participants while discussing a present for Fichte, regarding which Geßner shrewdly—and, no doubt, accurately—commented, "I'd bet that he would basically prefer money" (Geßner, diary entry for April 23, 1794; as cited in *FiG*, 7, p. 7).

outpouring of enraptured feeling, in memory of the blissful hours that the author has passed with them in a common striving toward truth."[34]

Baggesen describes the scene as follow:

That evening, I, along with Ith and Stapfer, accompanied Fichte to Lavater's in order to hear the conclusion of his course of lectures, this one on the topic of human dignity. A very moving address, and there was also a poem from Geßner. After the others left, Lavater, Fichte (who had had his portrait drawn by Miss Pfenninger), Professor Voight (of whom I have become very fond), and the excellent Geßner assembled in the topmost room.—Tea and wonderful conversation concerning the nothingness of death in particular. I then accompanied Fichte as we visited Count Gorani—we enjoyed ourselves—animated conversation about revolution.[35]

Less than a week later Fichte departed for Jena.

Concerning the Concept of the Wissenschaftslehre
Zurich, April–May 1794

By mid-winter of 1794, Fichte had begun to assure his contacts in Jena and Weimar that he would indeed be able to expound his new system in his lectures during the Spring Semester. Less than a month after requesting a postponement in assuming his new duties, he could announce to Böttinger:

The success of this project is already as good as assured. Should it be that present circumstances will not permit this postponement, then I would at least wish to demonstrate through my lectures that I do possess such a system. Fortunately, since my last letter I have made so much progress in my work that I can now at least glimpse the conclusion shimmering before me, and therefore I could now lecture on philosophy with more confidence than when I last wrote. [...] At the same time, this new decision must alter my entire plan of studies; for, from now on, instead of continuing to pursue my dry speculations, I will have to plan to communicate them in my lectures.[36]

There can be no doubt that this change in plans was closely associated with the lectures Fichte was concurrently delivering in Zurich, which offered him exactly

---

[34] GA, I/1: 85. below, p. 458. "Concerning Human Dignity" appears to have been privately printed and distributed sometime in the spring of 1794. It was subsequently included in SW, I, pp. 412–16 (see GA, I/2: 86–9; below, pp. 458–60).

[35] Baggesen to his wife, April 27, 1794 (FiG, 6.1, p. 45). According to a record made by Böttinger of a conversation with Baggesen around March 15, 1795, Baggesen confided that, "concerning Fichte. He sometimes stimulates himself with strong drink. It was in such an ecstatic state that I heard him deliver the peroration of his Zurich lectures, which was subsequently published" (FiG, 6.1, pp. 138–9).

[36] Fichte to Böttiger, February 5, 1794. Karl August Böttiger, a schoolmate of Fichte's at Pforta, was the director of the Gymnasium in Weimar.

what he needed: an opportunity to rehearse his new ideas before a receptive, non-critical audience. He alludes to this in a letter to Reinhold of March 1, 1794, in which he writes "I have been lecturing on this subject for Lavater […] and several of Zurich's leading men. Of course, I cannot give them much more than a foretaste between now and the end of next month."[37]

Meanwhile, he enthusiastically welcomed a suggestion from Böttiger that, in lieu of the Latin "disputation," with which newly appointed professors customarily began their academic careers, he would instead prepare and have distributed to prospective students in Jena a brief "invitational" or "programmatic" text, written in German, in which he would address a few general questions concerning his new system.[38] He described the proposed work as follows in his March 1 letter to Böttiger:

> I had the material for such a work lying before me in nearly finished form. Without any further ado, I will have printed for this purpose a few lectures concerning the concept of philosophy and the first foundational principles of the same, which I am now delivering to some of the leading clergymen and statesmen of Zurich, with Lavater at their forefront.[39]

A week later he sent the manuscript of this "prospectus," now entitled *Concerning the Concept of the Wissenschaftslehre, or of so-called "Philosophy"* to Böttiger, who had agreed to see to its printing and distribution. As already noted, *Concerning the Concept* was very closely based upon the first five Zurich lectures, the ones he had described to Lavater as constituting the "prolegomena" to the entire *Wissenschaftslehre*.

In another letter from this same period, Fichte described the aim of this "programmatic" work as follows: it

> will establish the *concept* of philosophy in an entirely new manner and develop the first principles of the same up to Reinhold's Foundational Principle of Consciousness, for which it will furnish the proof—as well, perhaps, as establish the first foundational principle of an entirely new kind of practical philosophy.

He went on to explain that "for some time now I have been delivering lectures concerning philosophy as a whole to some of the leading statesmen and clerics of Zurich, and have therefore already had to think through these matters more than once."[40]

---

[37] *GA*, III/2: 80; *EPW*, pp. 377–8.

[38] Fichte's request was officially granted in a letter from G. C. Voigt, February 14, 1794. Another obstacle was presented by the fact that he had obtained no advanced degree. This problem was ultimately resolved on March 17, 1794, when Fichte was "granted" a doctorate by a family friend in Zurich, the Choirmaster and *comes palatinus* Prof. Johann Heinrich Rahn—a degree which, as the editor of *FiG* observes, "had very little prestige" (*FiG*, I, p. 100n.). See too the letter of May 21, 1794, from C. G. Henrichs, Prof. of History at Jena, to the Philosophical Faculty at Jena confirming receipt from Fichte of the fees required for conferring upon him the necessary degree (in *FiG*, 6.1, p. 48).

[39] Fichte to Böttiger, March 1, 1794, *GA*, III/2: 71.

[40] Fichte to Hufeland, March 8, 1794, *GA*, II/3: 82–3.

The intimate relationship between the first Zurich lectures and *Concerning the Concept* is further amplified in Fichte's April 2 letter to Böttiger, in which he complains that "it would indeed have been easy for me to write this [programmatic] text, had not my Zurich lectures, to which I have already committed myself, weighed so heavily upon my shoulders—though this is by no means counterproductive with respect to Jena." In this same letter he repeats his by now familiar claim that,

> though there is no further room for investigation beyond Kant's *spirit*, I am completely convinced that he laid at the foundation of his own investigations, albeit *obscurely*, the same foundational principles that I wish to establish *clearly* and *determinately*. I do, however, hope to be able to go beyond the *letter* of Kant's writings, and in doing so it seems to me that I will have achieved a degree of clarity that allows the *Zurichers* to comprehend me very well—which is saying something!

He also reveals that his aim in this "invitational" work was "to discuss speculative propositions that actually go a good deal deeper than Kant's, but to do so in an easygoing tone, just as if they were not deep speculations at all."[41]

The newly appointed *professor philosophiae ordinarius supernumerarius* arrived in Jena the evening of May 18, barely in time to celebrate his 32nd birthday the following day. Along the way, he stopped in Weimar to pick up a copy of *Concerning the Concept of the Wissenschaftslehre*, which had just become available in Jena to what Fichte rather hopefully described as "students of wisdom, hungry for instruction."[42] The term "*Wissenschaftslehre*" first appeared in print in the title of this short work.

Though he had predicted that it would be "easy" to write *Concerning the Concept of the Wissenschaftslehre*, this proved to be a longer and more challenging task than Fichte had imagined. He began in February, but did not send his manuscript to the printer until the end of April. In part, the reason for this delay was, as mentioned in his letter to Böttiger,[43] the fact that he was simultaneously writing *Concerning the Concept* and delivering the continuation of his Zurich lectures, which, unsurprisingly, he found to be a rather arduous task. But there were other reasons for this delay as well.

Karl Christian Erhard Schmid was a Professor of Philosophy and Theology at Jena and among the first generation of academic Kantians. Schmid had been the first professor to lecture on Kant at Jena, and he had enjoyed success both as an expositor of Kant and as a proponent of his own version of Kant's practical

[41] Fichte to Böttiger, April 2, 1794, *GA*, III/2: 89, 90, and 93.
[42] "*in den Händen der lehrbegierge WeisheitsSchüler*" Fichte to Böttiger, April 2, 1794, *GA*, III/2: 89.
[43] "It would have been easy for me to write this work, had not my Zurich lectures, to which I have committed myself, weighed so heavily upon my shoulders" (Fichte to Böttiger, April 2, 1794, *GA*, III/2: 89).

philosophy.[44] In his works on moral philosophy, Schmid at least appeared to take a very hard line regarding one of the more controversial issues associated with Kant's practical philosophy: namely, whether genuinely moral determinations of the will should be described as "free" or not. No, was Schmid's answer: the human will is thoroughly determined at both the empirical and the intelligible (or noumenal) levels.

The contemporary name for Schmid's position was "intelligible fatalism," a position that Fichte had rather sharply criticized in his earlier review of Creuzer's *Skeptical Reflections on Free Will*, a book that included a preface by none other than Schmid, whom Fichte singled out for sharp criticism at the conclusion of his review. Intelligible fatalism, he wrote, "utterly abolishes all morality"—and, what is worse, is thoroughly un-Kantian.[45] Though both the Creuzer and Gebhard reviews were published anonymously, Schmid was well aware of the identity of their author, as is indicated by his decision to include discussion of the Gebhard review in his response to the criticisms contained in the Creuzer review. This came in the form of an exceptionally sharp and personal "Declaration" published in the February 15, 1794, issue of the *Intelligenzblatt der A.L.Z.*—that is, *after* Schmid had become aware that the author of these hostile reviews was about to become his new colleague at Jena. In this "Declaration" Schmid not only defended his doctrine of intelligible fatalism and his understanding of Kant's writings, but he also complained loudly about the *tone* of the offending reviews and accused their author of impugning his character as well as his intellect. He also instructed the author to become better acquainted with the *letter* of Kant's writings before presuming to interpret the *spirit* of the same.[46]

True to form, Fichte was simply unable to allow Schmid's provocation to pass in silence and duly published his own "Counter-Declaration" (dated March 8, 1794) in the *Intelligenzblatt der A.L.Z.*,[47] in which he defended his interpretation of Schmid's position and complained, in return, about the bitter tone of *his* "Declaration." Despite this pointed public rejoinder to Schmid, Fichte was not unappreciative of the danger of unnecessarily provoking a senior scholar who would soon be his colleague. The same day his "Counter-Declaration" appeared in the *A.L.Z.* he wrote to Hufeland that the controversy with Schmid had opened his eyes to many things about the situation he would soon be entering upon and declared "I hope to show Mr. Schmid, and show him very soon, that I may very well have penetrated somewhat more deeply into the spirit of the Kantian

---

[44] See K. C. E. Schmid, *Kritik der reinen Vernunft im Grundrisse zu Vorlesungen nebst einen Wörterbuch zum leichtern Gebrauch der Kantischen Schriften* (1786). Schmid's next two books, *Versuch einer Moralphilosophie* (1790) and *Grundriss der Moralphilosophie* (1793), contained his explication of the doctrine of "intelligible fatalism."

[45] *RC, GA*, I/2: 13; *SW*, VIII, p. 416; *Crev*, p. 296.

[46] For Schmid's *Erklärung*, see *GA*, I/2: 75n.

[47] *Gegenerklärung über des Hn. Prof. Schmid Erklärung, GA*, I/2: 75–8. Despite Fichte's intention to win over his philosophical adversaries, including Schmid, the animosity between the two only increased over the next year. It finally culminated in the spring of 1796, when Fichte published in the *Philosophisches Journal* "A Comparison Between Prof. Schmid's System and the *Wissenschaftslehre*," a scathing essay which concluded with Fichte's notorious declaration of Prof. Schmid's "*non-existence as a philosopher,* as far as I am concerned" (*GA*, I/3: 266; *SW*, II, p. 456; *EPW*, p. 335).

philosophy than he himself has." But in this same letter he also apologized for the unduly harsh tone of certain passages in his own reviews and promised to be more circumspect in the future. He then added that he "has Schmid to thank" for forcing him to devote so much effort to composing his programmatic work, "which I might otherwise have written in somewhat of a hurry."[48]

As already noted, when we compare the texts of *Concerning the Concept of the Wissenschaftslehre* (and, to some extent, that of *Foundation of the Entire Wissenschaftslehre*) with the text of the *Aenesidemus* review and the five Zurich lectures, there are some striking differences. For example, the terms "intellectual intuition" and "F/Act" (or *Tathandlung*) feature prominently in the Zurich lectures and the *Aenesidemus* review, but both are conspicuously absent from *Concerning the Concept*, along with any mention of the need for "construction" in philosophy.

What explains these omissions? Surely they can be explained, at least to some extent, by what Ives Radrizzani has called Fichte's "politics of prudence."[49] He was, after all, under the (mistaken) impression that his prospective audiences at Jena would be filled with committed Reinholdians, and this may explain why he (briefly) eliminated the term *Tathandlung*, which he may have adopted, at least in part, as a polemical counterpart to Reinhold's *Tatsache* ("fact"). Whereas the Elementary Philosophy had claimed to be grounded upon "facts of consciousness," the *Wissenschaftslehre* would claim to be grounded upon something more fundamental: namely, that unconditioned and spontaneous F/Act in which the I posits itself "purely and simply." But there was no point in *emphasizing* or *belaboring* his differences with Reinhold, and this is probably why the explicit criticisms of Reinhold's "Principle of Consciousness," which figure prominently in the *Aenesidemus* review and the Zurich lectures, are dropped from the programmatic work. So too with the term *intellectual intuition* and the claim that the method of philosophy involves *construction*, both of which would be anathema to orthodox (or, as Fichte would put it, "dogmatic") Kantians, including Schmid. Why, he may have reasoned, provoke unnecessary conflict when the same notions could be communicated by means of less controversial terms, such as *insight* and *genetic method*? The public controversy with Schmid had warned him that at least some of his new colleagues, unlike the circle of friends present for his Zurich lectures, might be hostile, and he appears to have kept this in mind while composing *Concerning the Concept of the Wissenschaftslehre*.

A third reason why Fichte had to devote so much time and energy to this brief "programmatic" writing is the one he identified in a letter to his childhood friend and classmate, Friedrich August Weißhuhn, who had complimented him on the literary style of that work. To this Fichte responded:

The way this book, and especially the preface, was written was not something that happened so easily or immediately. In order for that to have been possible,

---

[48] Fichte to Hufeland, March 8, 1794, *GA*, III/2: 81–2.

[49] Ives Radrizzani, "La 'Première' Doctrine de la Science de Fichte," pp. 628 and 635–7. If Radrizzani's thesis is correct, this would certainly represent a rare departure from Fichte's more typical, rather imprudent mode of conduct during his first years in Jena.

one would have to have so completely mastered one's own system that one could toy with it and wear the chains of that system freely, just as if there were none. But I was not at that point the master of my own system, and it will be difficult for me ever to master it, for it is profound.[50]

Though Fichte had originally intended to include in *Concerning the Concept* a general outline of at least the "theoretical" portion of his new system, what he prepared instead for his prospective students was a series of observations and declarations concerning the task, the method, and the object of philosophical reflection, accompanied by some brief, vague hints concerning the *Wissenschaftslehre* itself as well as a discussion of the relationship of transcendental philosophy to other sciences. Like some of Fichte's later writings,[51] this short work is *about* Fichte's new system and not a systematic part of the *Wissenschaftslehre* itself. In the terminology proposed by Fichte himself in the Preface to the second, 1798, edition, it is a work of "critique" rather than of "philosophy" or "metaphysics." Its task is to investigate the possibility and meaning of "metaphysics" (in the post-Kantian sense of the term, i.e., transcendental philosophy) while at the same time specifying the method of such a science[52]—something that Fichte complained was lacking in Kant's own writings.[53]

Stipulating that philosophy is supposed to be a "science," *Concerning the Concept* commences by inquiring into the nature of science itself and into the relation of its "content" (namely, according to Fichte, "what is incontrovertibly true") and its "form" (namely, the systematic relationship between all the propositions included in that science). If there is to be one single unified science (which is still at this point no more than a hypothesis), then, argues Fichte, in a manner reminiscent of Reinhold, all scientifically valid propositions must ultimately rest upon a single *Grundsatz* or foundational principle, which is "purely and simply" (*schlechthin*) true: immediately certain, self-evident, and underived from any higher principle. It is, according to Fichte, the distinctive task of philosophy to carry out such an ambitious project of grounding all scientific knowledge as such, which is why philosophy should be called "the science of science" or *Wissenschaftslehre*.

---

[50] Fichte to Weißhuhn, July 1794, *GA*, III/2: 181. Weißhuhn and Fichte were classmates, first at the boarding school of Pforta and then again at the University of Leipzig. During the period of his most rapid philosophical development, Weißhuhn was one of Fichte's most valued philosophical correspondents and one of the first people with whom he had shared his growing excitement surrounding his "discoveries" during the fall and winter of 1793/94.

[51] See, for example, the two 1797 introductions to *VWL*, as well as *SB* (1801).

[52] "There can be a doctrine [*Lehre*] of transcendental philosophy, that is, of the *Wissenschaftslehre*, that is, a *theory* [*Theorie*] *of transcendental philosophy or of Wissenschaftslehre*, which considers how such a philosophy is to be brought into being—and with what justification—that is, with its *validity*, with what supports such a philosophy: my booklet, *Concerning the Concept of the Wissenschaftslehre*. Portions of the *Critique of Pure Reason*" (Fichte, *VLM, GA*, II/4: 53).

[53] Writing to Reinhold on July 4, 1797, Fichte suggests that the only reason Kant failed to arrive at Reinhold's insight that the power of representation is more fundamental than those of intuition and understanding is that "he appears to have philosophized far too little about his own philosophizing" (*GA*, III/3: 69; *EPW*, p. 420). This was an omission of which Fichte was determined never to appear guilty.

This is followed by a proposed strategy for demonstrating the consistency, uniqueness, and completeness of the proposed science of science—or, as Fichte often expresses this, the strategy for showing that the *Wissenschaftslehre* has actually "exhausted"—which is to say, *exhaustively* derived and delimited—the entire domain of human knowledge. As in the Zurich lectures, *Concerning the Concept* discusses the relationship of philosophy to the other sciences, and assigns to the former the task of deriving the foundational principles of the latter. Again, Fichte devotes special attention to the relationship between logic and the *Wissenschaftslehre* and provocatively maintains that the axioms of logic must all be derived from the foundational principles of the *Wissenschaftslehre*.

Perhaps the most innovative section of *Concerning the Concept* is § 7, in which Fichte declares the proper object of transcendental philosophy to be nothing other than the system made up of the "original" and "necessary" acts of the human mind, which underlie and make possible empirical consciousness but do not normally attain to consciousness at all, and of which philosophers are supposed to compose a "pragmatic history." In order to do this, however, they themselves must engage in freely initiated acts of "reflective abstraction" from our ordinary presuppositions concerning knowledge and reality. As in the Zurich lectures, Fichte here continues to emphasize the "experimental" character of his enterprise, as well as a certain unavoidable, but non-fatal, "circularity" that is implicit in such an undertaking.

Without mentioning Reinhold by name, Fichte concludes this section by declaring that representation may well prove not to be the supreme act of the human mind after all, but only the product of a still more fundamental action. But unlike in either the Zurich lectures or the *Aenesidemus* review, he here declines to identify this more fundamental action as a "*Tathandlung*" or "F/Act," just as he also here avoids the term "intellectual intuition."[54]

The first edition of *Concerning the Concept* concludes with a tantalizingly brief, two-page "Hypothetical Division of the *Wissenschaftslehre*," which, for all of its brevity, sheds light on the puzzling relationship between the three foundational principles established by the *Wissenschaftslehre* (or as Fichte here writes, between the "three absolutes") and illuminates the organization of the foundational portion of the system into "theoretical" and "practical" portions and the distinctive nature of each. Part Three also emphasizes what is perhaps Fichte's most distinctive philosophical innovation: namely, his audacious project of grounding an account of theoretical cognition upon an account of practical striving. Part Three concludes with an ambitious promise to derive from the practical part of the *Wissenschaftslehre* "new and improved" doctrines of the pleasant, the beautiful, the sublime, natural teleology, God, "the sense of truth," natural law, and morality—"the principles of which are material as well as formal."

---

[54] Another significant omission from the corresponding sections of the Zurich lectures is any mention of the *constructive* character of philosophy or any comparison between the methods of geometry and philosophy. One reason for this omission may have been that at this point Fichte was still emphasizing the continuity between Reinhold's Elementary Philosophy and the *Wissenschaftslehre*, and Reinhold's rationalist model of a philosophical system derived from a "single first principle" is difficult to reconcile with Fichte's actual method for constructing his "pragmatic history of the human mind."

Fichte eliminated Part Three when he authorized a second edition in 1798, on the grounds that it had been made redundant by the publication of *Foundation of the Entire Wissenschaftslehre*. However, *Concerning the Concept* continued to have a special claim on the affections of its author. As he wrote in 1797, "for those who have failed to understand the most accessible of my speculative writings, that is, the one concerning the concept of the *Wissenschaftslehre*, I can never write anything in the field of speculation that will be easier to understand."[55]

Foundation of the Entire *Wissenschaftslehre*, "First Installment" (Parts One and Two) Jena, Summer Semester 1794

A short announcement and description of the lectures Fichte intended to deliver during his first semester at Jena was appended to the published version of *Concerning the Concept of the Wissenschaftslehre*. Here he repeated what he had proposed in his April 2, 1794, letter to Böttiger: namely, two "private" courses of lectures on his new system, one on "theoretical philosophy" and one on "universal practical philosophy"—with the explanation that "in my system practical philosophy will be something quite different than it has been previously," plus a series of weekly "public" lectures on the theme "morality for scholars."[56]

By the time he arrived in Jena, however, Fichte—who had never before held an academic position—had amended his plans and had decided to offer only one set of private lectures during the Summer Semester, those on "theoretical philosophy" (corresponding to Parts One and Two of *Foundation of the Entire Wissenschaftslehre*), reserving his lectures on "Practical Philosophy" for the following semester. He explained this decision to his wife as necessary in order "not to make myself sick from studying" (even as he lamented that this would adversely affect their income).[57] And indeed, he had quite enough to do even without preparing additional lectures on "practical philosophy." As he complained to Goethe, "taking into account my public [as well private] lectures, I have had to fill at least three printer's sheets each week," and "just as soon as one sheet was finished, then the next one *had to* appear, and thus I *had to* let it go."[58]

---

[55] *ApT*, *GA*, I/4: 313n. *SW*, II, p. 481n. See too the similar remark in the preface to *GWL*, *GA*, I/2: 253; below, p. 197.

[56] Fichte to Böttiger, April 2, 1794, *GA*, I/2: 92. Compare this with the longer description appended to *BWL*, *GA*, I/2: 153-4; below, p. 191. As *professor philosophiae ordinarius supernumerarius* Fichte received a small salary, for which he was, among other things, expected to deliver occasional free "public" lectures, open to the entire academic community. In addition, he was permitted to offer one or more courses of "private" lectures each semester, for which he would be paid directly by the attending students—hence Fichte's expressed concern (in letters to his wife) about the disappointingly small enrollment for his private lectures.

[57] Fichte to Johanna Fichte, May 20, 1794, *GA*, III/2: 113.

[58] Fichte to Goethe, June 21, 1794, and September 20, 1794, *GA*, III/2: 143 and 203; *EPW*, p. 379. See the similar complaints in Fichte's July 2, 1795, letter to Reinhold: "Bear in mind that what you have received so far is a manuscript for the use of my listeners. It was hastily written along with my lectures (in the winter semester I had *three* lecture courses, all of which I had to work out almost completely)

Fichte was indeed exceptionally busy during his first semester in Jena. At this point he was living on his own in rented quarters (his wife and father-in-law would not arrive until after the conclusion of the Summer Semester) and enjoying a busy social and intellectual life with his new colleagues (and, in some cases, their wives), as well as with his students. He inaugurated a regular habit of taking his midday meals with a circle of likeminded colleagues and students. He also became intimately involved in helping some of his students establish a "Literary Society of Free Men," intended as a progressive alternative to the conservative and obstreperous student fraternities (or "orders") that then dominated student life at many German universities, but especially at Jena.[59]

At the same time, he was trying to make the best impression possible in his new environment, and even attempted (unsuccessfully) to win over Schmid and other perceived opponents on the faculty and in the court at nearby Weimar.[60] Sensitive to an undercurrent of opposition, based less upon his new philosophical ideas than upon his controversial and publicly stated views on religious and political matters, he prudently discontinued his plan to write the projected Second Part of his book on the French revolution.[61] Nevertheless, he soon found himself embroiled in a controversy arising from his public lectures, in which he was reported to have predicted the imminent demise of the aristocracy. Indeed, it was precisely in order to refute this charge that he published the first five lectures in this series as *Some Lectures Concerning the Scholar's Vocation*.[62] Despite his rather busy social life and the growing atmosphere of simmering controversy surrounding him, Fichte was able to complete Parts One and Two of *Foundation of the Entire Wissenschaftslehre* in his lectures by the final class of his first semester.

As soon as he learned that he would be unable to postpone his arrival in Jena and that he would be expected to lecture upon his new system, the recently baptized "*Wissenschaftslehre*," Fichte realized that he would not be able to base his

---

and alongside a thousand other diverse activities. I had to see to it that the written sheets were finished just as soon as the previous lecture concluded" (*GA*, III/2: 347; *EPW*, p. 401).

[59] "They say that Fichte's presence in Jena has already made a major impact, for it is said that the students are already expressing a rather enthusiastic predilection for democracy, i.e., for liberty and equality, a kind of philosophical (*vel quasi*) Jacobinism, which, if it should endure, may prove to be more than a bit awkward for our wise statesmen" (C. M. Wieland to Reinhold, June 27, 1794 [*FiG*, 1, p. 126]).

[60] See F. K. Forberg's May 30, 1794, letter to Reinhold, in which he reports that Schmid himself attended Fichte's first lecture and that Fichte had declared himself to be Schmid's friend (*FiG*, 6.1, p. 49).

[61] See Fichte's June 24, 1784, letter to Goethe, *GA*, III/2: 148. Though the two installments of Part One of his *Contribution toward Correcting the Public's Judgment of the French Revolution* had both been published anonymously, it was well-known in Jena that Fichte was the author. As he wrote to the French translator of Part One: "Unfortunately, everyone knows that I am the author of this work, and my invitation from Jena has in these circumstances raised God knows what concerns in certain weak minds. Many people imagine that the author of such a book must be a rough half-savage and cannibal. I must first allow such people to become accustomed to me, and then show them that I do not appear to be half as frightful as my writings make me appear to them to be" (Fichte to F. B. Meyer, April 19, 1794, *GA*, III/17: 157).

[62] See "Fichte in Jena," *EPW*, pp. 23–4.

lectures upon any existing textbook, and he therefore proposed a rather novel alternative, which he described as follows in his March 1, 1794, letter to Böttiger:

> I can now see for myself and have indeed known for a long time how inconvenient it is for both the instructor and the students to lecture without a textbook. This merely promotes the kind of thoughtless transcribing I would like to eliminate entirely, at least during my own lectures. I cannot employ for this purpose any of the available writings by Kant or Reinhold, nor can I write my own textbook between now and the end of next month. Consequently, I have hit upon the following expedient: What if I were to distribute my text in fascicles throughout the semester, *as a manuscript for the use of my listeners* (since I adamantly wish to delay for another year any public presentation of my system)? In doing so, I want to defy the usual disdain for printed materials that are supposed to be treated as manuscripts. Doesn't it amount to the same thing when a professor reads from his *own lecture notes*? In order to demonstrate that I am serious about this, the book must not become available in bookstores, but only to my listeners or to others I wish to receive it, through my own agent and only *with my authorization*. Since it may well be several years before I can publish "the *Wissenschaftslehre*" (the "*doctrine of science,*" and not the mere "*love of knowing*") as a proper textbook, and since I may therefore have to base my lectures on this manuscript for some time, a regular-sized edition might well be sold out.[63]

During his inaugural semester, Fichte delivered his private lectures on the foundations of the *Wissenschaftslehre* from six to seven every weekday morning,[64] reserving Friday afternoons for his public lectures on "Morality for Scholars." The first public lecture occurred on Friday, May 23, and the first private one the following Monday morning, May 26. Though he had promised to distribute the texts of his lectures to his students in printed form, there was a brief but understandable delay in obtaining from the printer the first fascicle. Consequently, the first weeks were devoted to what was described as "prolegomena" (which probably included lectures on the same material covered in the first five Zurich lectures and in *Concerning the Concept*). The "First Installment" of the printed text was distributed on June 14, two weeks after the beginning of the semester. Subsequent installments were then distributed on a weekly basis throughout the semester.[65]

---

[63] Fichte to Böttiger, March 1, 1794, *GA*, III/2: 71–2. This proposal was accompanied by a request that Böttiger help him find a local publisher who would be willing to print *GWL* in such a form and to distribute it under such conditions. It was Böttiger who put Fichte in contact with the Jena publisher and bookseller, C. E. Gabler.

[64] See his July 31, 1794 letter to Johanna Fichte, in which he complains about having to rise at 4 a.m. in order to prepare for his 6 a.m. lectures. In fact, Fichte had originally announced that his lectures on Theoretical Philosophy would begin at 8 a.m., but he was persuaded to offer them at an even earlier hour by students who had conflicts with other classes. (See the diary entry for May 20–2 by Johann Smidt, one of Fichte's most dedicated students [as cited in *FiG*, 7, p. 11].)

[65] See Fichte to Lavater, June 14, 1794, *GA*, III/2: 130.

Fichte's public lectures were immensely popular from the start,[66] but to his disappointment, his more esoteric private lectures on Theoretical Philosophy were, at first anyway, less well attended, beginning with only thirty-five students, though that number had nearly doubled by the end of the semester.[67] By that time, moreover, he seems to have won over a significant number of the more serious students of philosophy and to have attracted a circle of enthusiastic followers—a situation described as follows by one of his colleagues:

> Meanwhile, he has now enchanted all the easily excited young students in Jena, thanks to the utter novelty and originality of his speculations, the profundity of his lectures, in which he analyzes concepts in the most varied and surprising ways, the torrent of his eloquence, and his enthusiasm for republican freedom. With the minimum amount of philosophical talent with which nature has endowed me, I could in no way measure myself against these transcendental heroes. With each passing day I felt I was becoming more and more superfluous. It irritated me that the young people in my *conservatorium* spoke of nothing but the I and the Not-I and other Fichtean dogma, which I neither understood correctly nor knew how to incorporate into my own philosophical system.[68]

By the time he arrived in Jena, Fichte was already an accomplished orator, and his talents were on dazzling display in his Friday public lectures. But he also made a powerful, if somewhat different, impression upon the students enrolled in his private lectures, one of whom described them as follows:

---

[66] A few days following his inaugural public lecture, Fichte boasted to his wife that "the largest auditorium in Jena was still not large enough. Even the hallway and courtyard were packed. People were standing next to each other on tables and benches and standing atop one another's heads" (Fichte to Johanna Fichte, May 25, 1794, *GA*, III/2: 115). For a detailed description of the local reaction to these public lectures (the first five of which were published that September as *EVBG*), see "Fichte in Jena," Editor's Introduction to *EPW*.

[67] See Fichte's May 26, June 14–17, and July 31, 1794, letters to Johanna Fichte, *GA*, III/2: 115, 121, 133–4, and 177. In his May 26 letter he first expresses his disappointment with the small enrollment in his private lectures, which he blamed in part on the fact he had arrived only after many students had already enrolled in other classes, and in part on the fact that, like most of his colleagues, he had required his "private" students to pay the requisite lecture fee *in advance*. In an obvious effort to hide his disappointment, he announced to Johanna that "my celebrity is actually much greater than I had thought" and surmises that it might actually be a good thing not to have so many students his first semester "since otherwise this might have promoted envy" (*GA*, III/2: 114 and 116).
   In his June 14–17 letter, he writes that "I did not then know how things would go, since I did not have half as many students as Reinhold (even though I always had as many as most teachers). I began to doubt whether I would prevail.—But behold, in just four weeks I *have* prevailed. I deliver my public lectures in the largest auditorium in Jena, and yet there is still always a crowd of people outside the door. Last night, half the university honored me with festive music and a *vivat*, and it is quite plausible that I am now the most popular of all the current professors and that, already, they would not trade me for Reinhold. Consequently, my private lectures will in the future also be heavily attended" (*GA*, III/2: 124).
   According to the report of J. Rudolf Rahn's, a nephew of Fichte's who was studying medicine at Jena, by the end of June Fichte had between 200 and 300 in the audience for his public lectures and between fifty and sixty in his private lectures on Theoretical Philosophy (J. Rudolf Rahn to J. Henrich Rahn, ca. June 19, 1794, as cited in *FiG*, 6.1, p. 53).

[68] C. K. Forberg, *Lebenslauf eines Verschollenen* (1840), with respect to Jena 1794/95 (as cited in *FiG*, 1, p. 103).

Fichte's arrival in Jena struck those whose minds where similarly inclined like an electric shock. [....] From the time of his arrival, he made a brilliant appearance, and in his teaching he inspired the courage of the young by means of his exalted goal—while also nurturing their arrogance. His personality was, as a whole, an expression of the absolute, an expression of the most intense consciousness of the I. [....] The best minds attached themselves to him; and, in the confident seriousness of his assertions, the exalted aim of his inquiries, and the consistency of his demonstrations, a formless world seemed to be struggling to acquire new shape. [....] Fichte really was an impressive person. Jokingly, I used to call him the Bonaparte of philosophy, and there are many similarities between them. This small, broad-shouldered man did not stand calmly behind his lectern, like a secular sage; instead, he stood there, so to speak, fiercely and combatively, with his unkempt brown hair typically sticking out around his furrowed face—with the features of an old woman, as well as those of an eagle.[69]

Once the semester had commenced, Fichte began soliciting a broader readership than he had originally planned. He explained to Lavater precisely how interested parties in Zurich might either subscribe to the *Foundation* as it continued to appear in weekly fascicles throughout the rest of 1794 and the spring of 1795 or else place advance orders for the entire treatise, which would become available only after the lectures had been completed.[70] By the end of the semester, Fichte appears to have changed his mind about limiting the availability of the printed text of his lectures and authorized his publisher, C. E. Gabler, to make the bound fascicles publicly available as the "First Installment" of *Foundation of the Entire Wissenschaftslehre*.

The October 1, 1794, issue of the *A.L.Z.* included the following announcement of this "First Installment," an announcement composed for the publisher by Fichte's younger colleague, Friedrich Karl Forberg, though undoubtedly in close consultation with the author:

> It would be superfluous to introduce a work of Fichte's to the world with a letter of recommendation. The author of the *Critique of Revelation* guarantees a product that is most excellent and of the rarest originality. The present work (which is related to the author's invitational writing, *Concerning the Concept of the Wissenschaftslehre, or of so-called "Philosophy"*) is nothing less than an attempt to

---

[69] Johann Georg Rist, *Lebenerinnerungen I* (1880) (as cited in *FiG*, 1, pp. 221, 297, and 388). Rist was a student of Fichte's during the Winter Semester of 1795.

Compare this with the following report from Forberg's May 30, 1794 letter to Reinhold: "Fichte is here. I have visited him a few times and have found his conversation to be very informative. He is most open-hearted, but possesses little finesse. He is almost too self-aware, and yet he can also bear being contradicted. In his physiognomy I find much ugliness and very little wit. [...] I find much that is obscure in his programmatic writing and other things that are expressed paradoxically, but on the whole I find it to be uncommonly profound. Above all, I admire his consistency, but I fear that this might mislead him into one-sidedness. Unfortunately, he is now forced to work out his system as a professor. This is bound to accelerate this *periodum fatelem*. He works very quickly, and in doing so risks becoming pedantic—a danger that can be avoided by publishing only the results of one's meditations, rather than those meditations themselves, though this is not anything that can happen quickly" (as cited in *FiG*, 6.1, p. 49).

[70] Fichte to Lavater, June 14, 1794, *GA*, III/2: 130.

lead philosophy back to completely new and incontrovertible principles, and in this way to respond to a need that has been made palpable enough through the very *existence* of the writings of the more recent skeptics, such as Maimon and Aenesidemus, as well as through the discomfort that has for some time now been plaguing the heart of German philosophy, a discomfort occasioned, for the best of reasons, by Reinhold. Whether and to what extent the author has succeeded in this goal is, of course, not something that can be determined in advance of the appearance of the entire work. Nevertheless, even a hasty study of this work is sufficient to convince every competent reader that if any mortal is able to become for philosophy what Euclid has become for mathematics, then this is a task for Mr. Fichte.—The present *Foundation of the Entire Wissenschaftslehre* will be followed next Easter by a *detailed* system of the theoretical and practical *Wissenschaftslehre*. In addition, the author's respect for the public requires him to confess explicitly that the present work, which grew out of his lectures, is incomplete in his own eyes. It will still be a few more years before he can hope to be able to present this work to the public in a worthy form. Until then, he requests that this entire work be considered as nothing more than a manuscript, which he had printed only for the convenience of his listeners, since that is preferable to having them take detailed notes during his lectures; and it is for this reason that he is reluctant to see it brought before the tribunal of *public* critique.[71]

In his first semester lectures on "Theoretical Philosophy" Fichte succeeded in presenting Parts One and Two of the tripart "Foundation" of his new system, beginning with an immensely challenging presentation of "The Foundational Principles of the entire *Wissenschaftslehre*." The very title of Part One must have raised eyebrows among former students of Reinhold and others committed, as Fichte himself appeared to be, to developing a system of philosophy from a *single* foundational principle. In fact, the *Wissenschaftslehre* appears to have not one but three such principles: one asserting that the I posits itself absolutely (or "purely and simply"), another claiming that the I posits a Not-I in opposition to itself, and a third asserting that the I posits within itself a divisible I and a divisible Not-I. These are, respectively, the principles governing the I's originary acts of *thesis*, *antithesis*, and *synthesis* and are the bases of the so-called "qualitative" categories of *reality, negation*, and *limitation*.

The upshot of this discussion is that the first "purely and simply posited" foundational principle—viz., the I posits its own existence purely and simply—is impossible without the second, since in order to posit itself at all the I must also posit in opposition to itself a "Not-I" (inasmuch as all determination involves negation), and the only way to avoid the ensuing contradiction between the I and the Not-I is to posit both of them as occupying only *part* of the total realm of what is posited, within which each is what the other is not. The finite I and Not-I can therefore be said to "reciprocally determine" each other.

---

[71] *FiG*, 7, pp. 19–20. This same advertisement also appeared, on a separate sheet, at the conclusion of *EVBG*.

From this it follows that the original act of unconditioned and unconditional self-positing with which the *Foundation* commences—an act that Fichte here once again characterizes as a *Tathandlung* or F/Act (an "act" that is identical to its own product or "deed")—includes not just the absolutely self-positing I described in § 1, but also the positing of a Not-I in opposition to the I and of a divisible I that is united with a divisible Not-I by the concept of *limitation*. There is no temporal gap between these first three acts of positing; instead, they are all parts or aspects of one and the same original *Tathandlung* and can be distinguished from one another only in the artificial context of philosophical reflection. (Since everything else in this entire treatise—or system—is supposed to be derived from these same three, inseparably linked foundational principles, one might even say that the entire content of the *Foundation* is already implicit in the original F/Act with which it begins—or, more accurately perhaps, within the original synthesis of the limited I and limited Not-I with which Part One concludes.)

Part One is made even more difficult by Fichte's attempt to begin not with the F/Act in question, but instead with the abstract proposition that "A=A." His strategy in doing so is to begin with something no one could possible dispute (namely, the axioms or principles of formal logic) and then to demonstrate that these apparently "self-evident" truths are in fact *grounded in* (and thus derivable from) something even higher: not in any privileged "matter of fact" or "fact of consciousness" (as Reinhold would have it), but rather, in an utterly inexplicable and primordial *action* on the part of the I, by means of which it spontaneously posits itself *as* an I. But in order to accomplish this action, it must also posit (or posit in opposition to itself) everything else contained within the *Foundation*, which is *derived* from the foundational act of the I as a necessary condition for the occurrence of the same.

Most of the Summer Semester, however, was devoted to an exposition of the "theoretical" Part Two of the *Foundation*. Part One concluded with the deriv-ation of the reciprocally related divisible I and Not-I, leaving open the question concerning the precise character of their relationship. According to Fichte, there are only two possibilities: either the I posits itself as determined by the Not-I, or else it posits itself as determining the Not-I. The first alternative provides us with the foundational principle of the theoretical portion of the *Foundation*, which is certainly one of the most abstract and difficult texts in the history of philosophy. The basic task of Part Two is to find a way of thinking the proposition that the I posits itself as determined by the Not-I, without violating the "absolutely pos-ited" freedom of the I. In order to accomplish this task—or, as Fichte himself might put it, in order to conduct this experiment—he forged a method that would profoundly influence subsequent generations of philosophers. This con-sists of philosophical reflection upon a proposed synthesis—beginning with that of the (limited) I and the Not-I in the third foundational principle—in order, first, to uncover and to posit explicitly any *antitheses* or contradictions between the I and the Not-I implicit in this principle, and then to overcome that antithesis in a new, higher *synthesis*. This is what Fichte usually called "the synthetic method"[72] and has since been described, more accurately perhaps, as "the dialectical method" of philosophizing.[73] Employing this new, "dialectical" method, Fichte manages, in Part Two, to accomplish innovative deductions of the Kantian categories of quantity (*all, none, some*) and relation (*reciprocal* or *mutual determination, causal efficacy,* and *substantiality*).

The overall strategy of the theoretical portion of the *Foundation* was succinctly formulated more than half a year earlier in the following passage from the unpublished "Personal Meditations on Elementary Philosophy/Practical Philosophy":

> Intuition would first become possible only after we have demonstrated substantiality in the case of the subject, causal efficacy in the case of the object, and reciprocal interaction in the case of the representation. So these three points would constitute a part [of the projected treatise].—What a sublime prospect![74]

What a prospect indeed, for what this passage clearly indicates is that Fichte was willing to depart from Kant in more ways than one. He completely rejects the so-called "metaphysical deduction," in which Kant proposed to derive the pure categories of the understanding from the principles of formal logic, and instead derives them from the original self-positing of the I. Moreover, he also proposes to demonstrate that these same categories are conditions not merely for the possibility of *thinking* but also for the possibility of *intuiting*.

The I, that is, the original principle of subjectivity itself, asserts or posits itself absolutely and unconditionally. In this F/Act, it stakes a claim to *being* or *reality*. But it cannot make such a claim ("I am I") without at the same time positing in *qualitative* opposition to itself a Not-I, thus establishing the category of *nothingness* or *negation*. The glaring contradiction between the absolutely posited I and Not-I must be resolved, and it is resolved by positing both the I and the Not-I as *quantitatively limited by one another*, thus establishing the category of *determination* or *limitation*.

From the mutual limitation or determination of the I and the Not-I, Fichte obtains two subordinate principles: "the I posits itself as determined by the Not-I" and "The I posits itself as determining the Not-I," which are, respectively, the

---

[72] Here one must exercise caution, since Fichte also uses the same term ("synthetic method") to describe the quite different, proto-phenomenological or "genetic" method employed later in Parts Two and Three. On this topic, see Breazeale, "Transcendental Deduction or Pragmatic History? Methodological Reflections on Fichte's *Grundlage der gesammten Wissenschaftslehre*," in *New Essays on Fichte's* Foundation of the Entire Doctrine of Scientific Knowledge," ed. Daniel Breazeale and Tom Rockmore, pp. 19–36 (Amherst, NY: Humanity Books, 2001).

[73] See Thomas W. Seebohm, "Fichte's Discovery of the Dialectical Method," in *Fichte: Historical Contexts/Contemporary Controversies*, ed. Daniel Breazeale and Tom Rockmore, pp. 17–42 (Atlantic Highlands, NJ: Humanities Press, 1994); Gottfried Stiehler, "J. G. Fichtes synthetische Methode als Keimform der Dialektik." *Deutsche Zeitschrift für Philosophie* 10 (1962): 252–70; Werner Hartkopf, "Die Dialektik Fichtes als Vorstufe zu Hegels Dialektik," *Zeitschrift für philosophische Forschung* 21 (1967): 173–207; Klaus Hammacher, "Zur transzendentallogischen Begründung der Dialektik bei Fichte," *Kant-Studien* 79 (1988): 467–75; and Reinhard Lauth, "Der Ursprung der Dialektik in Fichtes Philosophie," in Lauth, *Transzendentale Entwicklungslinien von Descartes bis zu Marx und Dostojewski*, pp. 209–26 (Hamburg: Felix Meiner, 1989).

[74] *EM*, GA, II/3: 35.

foundational principles of Parts Two and Three of the *Foundation*. The former is the principle of cognition (in which the mind considers itself to be determined by an independently existing object) and hence of the "theoretical" part of the *Foundation*. This must precede the "practical" Part Three, in which the I strives to determine the Not-I, since before the I can posit itself as determining the Not-I it has to posit the reality of this same Not-I *for* the I.

The philosopher's task in Part Two is to determine, by means of successive, dialectically driven thought experiments, how it is possible to think of the I (which is, after all, always supposed to be thought of as "positing itself purely and simply") as *determined by* the Not-I. This occasions what is surely one of the most astonishing (as well as intellectually demanding) dialectical flights in the history of philosophy, as Fichte attempts to consider every possible alternative relationship between the limited I and Not-I and to do so under the rubric of the Kantian categories of relation: *causality, substantiality*, and *reciprocal determination*. All of these relationships turn out to be unstable. Whether the Not-I is considered to be a cause, of which the I is supposed to be the effect, or whether the I is considered to be a substance, of which the Not-I is supposed to be an accident, or whether the causally and substantially related finite I and Not-I are themselves supposed to be reciprocally related to one another: in each of these cases, no stable synthesis of I and Not-I appears to be possible, and yet such a synthesis is absolutely necessary if the I is to be able to posit itself as an I at all.

Fichte's surprising solution is to appeal to a *factum*, which can be shown to be a necessary condition for the possibility of such positing, though the *reality* or *occurrence* of such a *factum* can only be *presupposed*. The *factum* in question is an *Anstoß* or "check" that simultaneously obstructs the original activity of the I and "impels" it to engage in a series of additional cognitive acts, the upshot of which is consciousness of a *representation* of the Not-I. The acts in question all begin with what is arguably the most remarkable of all the acts assigned by Fichte to the I: *an act of creative synthesis on the part of the power of productive imagination*, which, as Fichte puts it, "oscillates between" the I and Not-I or "hovers above" the boundary separating them, thereby producing for the first time a *representation* (*Vorstellung*), by means of which the finite I (or intellect) is (finally) synthetically united with the Not-I.

To the question raised at the beginning of Part Two—How can the I posit itself as determined by the Not-I?—the answer is as follows: it does this whenever it thinks of or reflects upon itself as *entertaining representations*. "Representing" is an action of the intellect, made possible by the synthetic oscillation of the power of imagination between objectivity and subjectivity. Such an action presupposes both the original activity of the infinite or pure I and a theoretically inexplicable "check" upon that same activity. This is the process described in the separately titled "Deduction of Representation" with which Part Two concludes.

The "Deduction of Representation" also marks a major *methodological* shift on Fichte's part—from a series of dialectical thought experiments to what he calls "real philosophy." Such a philosophy traces the *genesis* of representation through a necessary series of interrelated mental acts, all of which occur only in consequence of the collision between the original activity of the I and the original limitation of the same. The philosopher is supposed to discover this series by *reflection* upon the actions of his own mind—as "purified" through *abstraction* from any external objects of the same.

Hence, just as the *Wissenschaftslehre* purports to provide a deduction of the categories of transcendental logic (Kant's concepts of pure understanding), which dispenses entirely with Kant's reliance upon the principles of formal logic and instead derives the latter from the former, so too does it purport to provide a deduction of what Reinhold presupposed as a simple "fact of consciousness"— namely, the fact of "representation"—along with the "principle" governing the same (Reinhold's "Principle of Consciousness").

The "Deduction of Representation" not only provides a deduction of representation itself, it also provides a genetic derivation of the I's essential cognitive powers or "faculties," a derivation that begins with the primordial synthetic power of productive imagination and then proceeds to derive the additional powers of sensation, intuition, representation, understanding, judgment, and reason. The latter, the power of "reason," is understood in this context purely theoretically: namely, as the intellect's ability to *abstract* entirely from all objects, thereby positing for the first time, explicitly and for itself, its own *freedom* to posit or not to posit—including the freedom to posit itself as determined by the Not-I, which was the starting point of Part Two.

Unlike the preceding, dialectical portion of Part Two, the method of the Deduction of Representation is purely *descriptive* or *phenomenological*, constituting, in Fichte's words, "a pragmatic history of the human mind." This method of "inner intuition" will become even more prominent in Part Three and will become the main method utilized by Fichte in later versions of his system, beginning with his lectures on *Wissenschaftslehre nova methodo* in 1796/97.[75]

The astonishing *originality* of Parts One and Two of the *Foundation* can hardly be over-emphasized. Though Reinhold was the first to propose a derivation of the Kantian powers of understanding and intuition from the more primitive "power of representation," Fichte proposes a deduction of "representation" itself from the sheer concept of subjectivity or "I-hood." And in order to accomplish this he deploys a novel, "dialectical" method of deriving the Kantian categories of the understanding, as well as a proto-phenomenological method of isolating (by means of abstraction and reflection) and then describing genetically the necessary and original acts of the human mind.[76]

Interspersed with these derivations, Part Two includes a running exchange between "idealism" and "realism," which become ever more refined and sophisticated in an effort to avoid the tensions and contradictions revealed by Fichte's analyses. This culminates, not in a victory for "idealism," but instead in a

---

[75] On this point, see Breazeale, "A Pragmatic History of the Human Mind," Ch. 4 of *TWL* and "The Synthetic-Genetic Method of Transcendental Philosophy: Kantian Questions/Fichtean Answers," in *The History of the Transcendental Turn*, ed. Sebastian Gardner and Matthew Grist (Oxford: Oxford University Press, 2015), pp. 74–95.

[76] He would subsequently employ this same mixed method in the *Outline of What is Distinctive of the Wissenschaftslehre with Regard to the Theoretical Power* in order to derive *the manifold of intuition* as well as the two a priori "forms" of the same, *space* and *time*.

synthesis of both: transcendental philosophy as "ideal-realism." Indeed, at the conclusion of Part Two, the balance still remains tipped in favor of realism, as is only appropriate in the *theoretical* portion of the *Wissenschaftslehre*, in accordance with the principle that the I posits itself *as determined by the Not-I.*

Fichte delivered his final lectures of the Summer Semester on Friday, September 26th, and shortly after that Gabler's "First Installment" of the *Foundation* became publicly available. Initial responses to this "First Installment," as well as general word of mouth in Jena and elsewhere, quickly convinced Fichte that he had been correct in initially restricting that text to his immediate listeners in Jena. Though the first reviews were still some months away, he was already becoming familiar with the blank incomprehension, if not outright ridicule, with which his work was being greeted in many quarters. "I will never attend Fichte's private lectures," wrote one of his in-laws, who was also a medical student at Jena in 1794.

> His lectures are so obscure, his courses are so abstract, that I could treat them only as a sideshow. If one wishes to understand Fichte, one has to make his classes the main event [….] There are also many medical students in all his lectures, and, even though they all complain that they have not understood them correctly, they still praise Fichte to the heavens![77]

Fichte's colleague and co-editor of the *Philosophisches Journal einer Gesellschaft Teutscher Gelehrten,* F. I. Niethammer, reported on this situation as follows:

> In the field of philosophy there are now all kinds of new works. The egoism, of which there is still such a disgraceful memory, has, as you know, recently been replaced by an I-ism [*Ichismus*], which is more consistent than its departed ancestor, but also even more unsavory. [….] Fichte has done with the subject what Spinoza did with the object. The latter placed everything in the object, the former places everything in the subject. The former made the object into the divinity, whereas the latter does the same for the subject.—I have not progressed very far in the results of my examination of the system of the *I* and *Not-I,* which is to me completely *empty.* […] Allowing oneself to engage in combat with an irrational skepticism necessarily produces something irrational. […] Before beginning my serious study of the Fichtean *Wissenschaftslehre* and out of fear of losing myself in the monstrous labyrinth of his chain of scholastic inferences, I established for myself a guiding light, which I could use to orient myself if need be. I asked myself the following question: what is the real task of philosophy?[78]

---

[77] J. Rudolf Rahn to J. Heinrich Rahn, December 1, 1794, *FiG,* 6.1, p. 86.

[78] Niethammer to J. B. Erhard, October 27, 1794, *FiG,* 6.1: 72–3. In his November 1794 letter to C. G. von Brinkman, Wilhelm von Humboldt remarks as follows concerning the recently published "First Installment" of the *Foundation:* "there has perhaps never before been anything more sharp-witted—as well, perhaps, as more over-subtle" (*FiG,* I, p. 169).

Compare this with Schiller's reaction, as reported in his October 29, 1794, letter to Goethe, in which he notes that Fichte has strong philosophical opponents in Jena, who criticize the *Wissenschaftslehre* as "subjective Spinozism," to which Schiller adds, "According to Fichte's oral remarks (though he has not reached this point yet in his book) the world is only a ball, which the I has

When the first review of the "First Installment" appeared, in February of 1795, this only increased Fichte's misgivings, inasmuch as its author, J. S. Beck, claimed that he had at first considered Fichte's new book to be nothing more than an exaggerated parody of a certain, currently faddish mode of philosophizing, but then realized that its first principle was simply a restatement of Spinoza's. Beck also singled out for ridicule Fichte's willingness to recognize the unavoidability within philosophy of certain kinds of circularity. Such circles, he smirked, "are magic circles, which, despite their circular form, possess great demonstrative power and are marvelously informative."[79]

In response to the growing chorus of criticism and incomprehension, Fichte explained to Reinhold that

> the conclusion of my programmatic work and the theoretical portion of *Foundation of the Entire Wissenschaftslehre* are extremely obscure. I know very well that the *Wissenschaftslehre* contains within itself an intrinsic element that makes it obscure and even incomprehensible to many people (though surely not to you). However, I hope that the Practical Part of the *Foundations,* together with a work of mine specifically devoted to theory, will help to make things clearer.[80]

Foundation of the Entire Wissenschaftslehre, "Second Installment" (Preface and Part Three) Jena, Winter Semester 1794/95

> Fichte is now the soul of Jena. And thank God he is. I know of no one else who possesses such spiritual depth and energy. To seek out and to determine the principles of even the most far-flung domains of human knowledge, as well as the principles of justice; to think, with the same mental power, the most distant consequences of these principles and to publish and lecture on them, despite the powers of darkness, and to do so with a fire and precision, the fusion of which would have perhaps seemed to this reader's poor soul to be an intractable problem: this [...] is surely a lot, and it is certainly no exaggeration to declare this about this man. I attend his lecturers every day and talk to him from time to time.[81]

tossed and then catches again by means of reflection. Hence he should actually have declared his own divinity—which is something we are currently expecting" (*FiG*, p. 160).

By December, even Baggesen was characterizing the published *Foundation* as nothing more than a "shadow play" or "spectacle," a farrago of thesis, antithesis, and syntheses, cobbled together to produce a mixture of "nonsense and sophistry," and ridiculing its author as a "hyperphilosophical" and "hypermetaphysical" "philosophical sorcerer" (Baggesen to Reinhold, December 25, 2014, *FiG*, I, pp. 210–11).

[79] *FiR*, I, pp. 276–7. Beck's review, which appeared in February 1795 in the *Annalen der Philosophie und des philosophischen Geistes* (and is reprinted in *FiR*, 1, pp. 264–78), was an omnibus review of *BWL* and the "First Installment" of *GWL*. Fichte appended excerpts from Beck's review to the second edition of *BWL*.
[80] Fichte to Reinhold, April 28, 1795, *GA*, III/2: 315; *EPW*, p. 390.
[81] J. C. F. Hölderlin to C. L. Neuffer, November 1794, *FiG*, I, pp. 161–2.

Thus wrote one of Fichte's most dedicated and infatuated students, Friedrich Hölderlin, in November of 1794.

Eventful as the first semester had been, it paled in comparison with the following one. Fichte's household now included his wife and father-in-law, as well as his childhood friend, F. A. Weißhuhn.[82] In addition, his weekly teaching load had more than doubled. During the Winter Semester of 1794-95 he composed and delivered three completely new courses of private lectures, which met daily from Monday through Friday. The first two of these new classes continued the presentation of the foundational portion of the *Wissenschaftslehre*, which had commenced during the Summer Semester, with Parts One and Two of the *Foundation*. One of these new courses of private lectures was on "Practical Philosophy" (originally announced for the preceding semester) and the other was on "Theoretical Philosophy" (which would not repeat anything from the preceding semester, but would instead supplement Part Two of the *Foundation*). In both classes Fichte continued his practice of distributing the printed text of his lectures to his students over the course of the semester in fascicles, and then, following the conclusion of that semester, making both sets of lectures publicly available: the first, as the "Second Installment" of *Foundation of the Entire Wissenschaftslehre* and the second as *Outline of What is Distinctive of the Wissenschaftslehre with Regard to the Theoretical Power.*[83]

The third new "private" class taught by Fichte during the Winter Semester of 1794/95 was officially described as "a propaedeutic to philosophy as a whole" and designed "to meet the needs of the students." As the description of this new course made clear, what Fichte was attempting to offer his students in these classes was nothing other than "preparation for transcendental philosophy."[84] As his text for this purpose, he chose Volume One of Ernst Plattner's *Philosophical Aphorisms, including some Guidance to the History of Philosophy*. He must have been quite satisfied with the results, since he continued to teach this same class every semester thereafter throughout his career in Jena and beyond, accumulating in the process hundreds of pages of remarkably interesting lecture notes.[85] As if this were not enough, it was also during this semester that Fichte inaugurated a regular

[82] Weißhuhn was in generally poor health and was invited by Fichte to join his family in the home he had just purchased in Jena. Weißhuhn was not afraid to criticize his friend's new system and, in the latter part of 1794 published in the *Philosophisches Journal für Moralität, Religion und Menschenwohl* (a journal edited by none other than Fichte's declared opponent, K. C. E. Schmid) a surprisingly critical review of *BWL*, which was the very first review of any of Fichte's writings on or presentations of the *Wissenschaftslehre* (reprinted in *FiR*, I, pp. 241–52). All too predictably, Weißhuhn's review provoked an indignant personal response from Fichte. Weißhuhn died in Fichte's home April 21, 1795.

[83] Both of these new publications became publicly available at the end of July 1795. The "Second Installment" of the *Foundation* also included a preface to the *Foundation* as a whole, as well as Part Three of the same.

[84] As cited in *FiG*, 7, p. 24n.

[85] *Philosophische Aphorismen nebst einigen Anleitungen zur philosophischen Geschichte. Ganz neue Ausarbeitung, Ersten Theil* (1793), which is reprinted in *GA*, II/4S. Fichte's copious notes for his Platner lectures are assembled and chronologically labelled in *GA*, II/4. Reinhold had previously lectured on "Logic and Metaphysics" at Jena, but he did so according to his own notes and without using Platner. It is likely that Fichte had attended Platner's lectures while studying at Leipzig, where Platner was a Professor of Physiology and Philosophy. His reasons for choosing this text by the skeptically inclined Platner are evident in the following report from Fichte's nephew: "Fichte is also lecturing on

Saturday afternoon *"conservatium philosophicum,"* for informal philosophical discussion with colleagues and students.[86]

In addition, he continued his series of public lectures on "morality for scholars" into the Winter Semester, beginning Sunday morning, November 9. In order to ensure the largest possible audience, he scheduled these public lectures at a time that would not conflict with other university events. Accordingly, he scheduled them for 9 a.m. Sundays, immediately following divine services at the local church and immediately preceding those at the university chapel.[87] To the surprise of no one but Fichte himself, this decision provoked an acrimonious dispute with the local authorities, which was eventually resolved only when Fichte reluctantly agreed to move his public lectures from Sunday morning to Sunday afternoon.[88]

During this brouhaha over his Sunday lectures, Fichte was becoming more and more embroiled in another, much more serious, controversy, this one provoked by his involvement in local efforts to disband the notoriously rowdy and secretive student "orders," which were, at least in his view, a blemish upon the entire university community. He spoke publicly against them and near the end of November agreed to help facilitate their dissolution. These efforts initially appeared to bear fruit, but they eventually failed—not, however, before provoking an escalating series of outrages, including students disrupting Fichte's classes, publicly insulting him and his family members on the street, and violently attacking his home. This culminated on the evening of April 9, when the windows of his home were destroyed and his father-in-law nearly killed by paving stones.

After appealing to the authorities for protection, Fichte finally decided that, for his own safety and that of his family, he would have to leave Jena. He took refuge in a rented country house in the nearby village of Osmannstedt, which is where he remained until the end of September, canceling his classes for the entire Summer Semester of 1795. While in Osmannstedt Fichte was actively exploring the possibility of leaving Jena for good. In the same letter to Baggesen in which he memorably described the *Wissenschaftslehre* as "the first system of freedom" and

---

Platner's *Aphorisms*—which he proposes to refute entirely, while overturning his entire system" (J. Rudolf Rahn to J. Heinrich Rahn, December 1, 1794; *FiG*, 6.1, p. 85).

[86] "I never failed to visit the *conservatorium* or *disputorium*, which Fichte held for his students, though I was there more as an observer than as a participant. At first, his explanations still eluded me, and my head would spin and reel like a millwheel whenever one or another listener would challenge the speculative propositions of the *Wissenschaftslehre*, employing a formal terminology with which I was not yet familiar" (Rist, *FiG*, I, p. 336).

[87] This meant that during the Winter Semester of 1794/95 Fichte was lecturing or teaching *seven days a week*: three different lecture courses each weekday, with the first beginning at 7 a.m. and the last ending at 7 p.m.; a "discussion section" or *conservatorium*, which he convened every Saturday afternoon, and a public lecture every Sunday. No wonder Wilhelm von Humboldt complained that he seldom had a chance to see Fichte "because of his enormous labors" (Humboldt to C. G. von Brinkman, November 1794, *FiG*, I, p. 169).

[88] Fichte had been forced to suspend his Sunday lectures while this new arrangement was being negotiated and did not resume them until January of 1795, only to cancel them almost immediately in the wake of the turbulent events surrounding his efforts to abolish the student "orders." For details concerning this serious controversy, see "Fichte in Jena" in *EPW*.

declared that "I am becoming more and more convinced that it will take half a lifetime to elaborate the *Wissenschaftslehre*—and one free of worry and work at that," he conveyed his eagerness to accept a lifetime pension from "the nation of France," along with his willingness to compose his works in "the universal language, Latin" (since his French was inadequate), while residing in Alsace "or some other German province of the republic."[89]

Needless to say, nothing came of such unrealistic plans, and Fichte spent the summer composing yet another public response to yet another public attack by Schmid, quarreling with Schiller over the latter's rejection of his most recent contribution to Schiller's new journal, *Die Horen*, and preparing new lectures on political philosophy, which he would begin delivering at Jena during the Winter Semester of 1795-96 and subsequently publish as *Foundation of Natural Right, according to the Principles of the Wissenschaftslehre*. The "Second Installment" of *Foundation of the Entire Wissenschaftslehre* (consisting of the Preface and Part Three) and *Outline of What is Distinctive of the Wissenschaftslehre with Regard to the Theoretical Power* were both published by Gabler in late July of that same summer of 1795,[90] as ongoing student unrest continued to disrupt life in Jena, eventually requiring military intervention. Even after his wife and father-in-law returned to Jena, Fichte remained in Osmannstedt until October 3.

On September 27, 1795, he wrote a letter to his wife, which testifies to the profoundly ambivalent situation in which he then found himself: On the one hand, he boasts about Reinhold's recent repudiation of his own system and conversion to the *Wissenschaftslehre*, and brags about receiving a letter from a visiting professor who plans to travel to Jena in order to study at his feet; but on the other, he concludes with the following declaration concerning the system he had spent the past two years conceiving and presenting to the public:

> I always insist *that one must be patient* and wait until a considerable portion of the whole is lying before one for inspection; but I also insist that, once this is the case, my system will be self-evident; and finally, I insist that I have not yet expressed a single letter of my system in the manner in which it should *remain*.[91]

---

[89] Fichte to Baggesen, April/May 1795 (Draft), *GA*, III/1: 297–301; *EPW*, pp. 385–6: "My system is the first system of freedom. Just as this nation [i.e., France] freed human beings from external shackles, so my system frees the human being from the fetters of things in themselves, which is to say, from that external influence with which all previous systems, including Kant's, have more or less crushed human beings. Indeed, the foundational principle of my system presents the human being as independent. During the very years France was using external force to win its political freedom I was engaged in an inner struggle with myself and with all of my own deeply ingrained prejudices, and this is the struggle that gave birth to my system. The French nation thus assisted in the creation of my system. Its valor encouraged me and supplied me with the energy I required in order to grasp my own system. Indeed, it was while writing about the French revolution that I was rewarded with the first hints and intimations of this system. In a certain sense, therefore, this system already belongs to that nation, and the question is only whether this nation wishes to claim my system externally and publicly by providing me with the wherewithal for developing it."

[90] This "Second Installment" consisted of Part Three plus a general preface to the *Foundation* as a whole. Unfortunately, it did not include the "illustrative plates," which, according to Forberg, Gabler had been urged to include (Forberg, *Fragmente aus meinen Papieren* (1796), entry for March 1795 [as cited in *FiG, I*, p. 253]).

[91] Fichte to Johanna Fichte, September 27, *GA*, III/2: 409.

Both Part Three of the *Foundation* and the entire *Outline* were composed under even more trying circumstances than the "First Installment" of the *Foundation*, as is evident from the rather hurried and somewhat skeletal appearance of the final portions of both of these works—composed and delivered, as they were, right in the midst of the ongoing public and private turmoil occasioned by the conflict over the dissolution of the student orders.[92] Nevertheless, each of these works makes essential and unique contributions to the project that commenced with the "First Installment" of the *Foundation*.

Part Three of the *Foundation*, titled "Foundation of the Science of the Practical," displays the same mixture of dialectical and proto-phenomenological methods that was employed in Parts One and Two, beginning with a dialectical derivation of the concept of *striving* from the foundational principle of Part Three: namely, the proposition that the I posits itself as determining the Not-I. This is accomplished by means of another "experiment in thinking," this one designed to overcome the tension between the finite, cognizing I (the subject of Part Two) and the absolute or pure or infinite I (the *Tathandlung*, which serves as the starting point of the entire *Foundation* and thus always possesses *regulative* validity for all that follows). The strategy for resolving this contradiction is to propose a certain sense in which the pure or absolute I determines or causes the divisible Not-I and thus indirectly determines the finite, cognizing I or intellect. And yet, if the absolute I were actually to exercise real causality in this case, that would eliminate the Not-I entirely; consequently, concludes Fichte, it can only *strive* to exercise such causality.

This dialectical derivation of striving is presented in terms of the interaction between two, equally essential features of the I: its original and absolute *self-positing* and its necessary *reflection* upon itself *as* self-positing (which Fichte characterizes, in terms borrowed from rational mechanics, as "centrifugal" and "centripetal" directions of the I's original activity). The basic idea is that the I must constantly reflect upon itself in order to determine whether it really does "fill up all reality," as would appear to be required by its initial self-positing. We already know from Part Two that it must always be found wanting in this respect, inasmuch as the I must always discover its original activity to be thwarted or checked—for that is a condition for the very possibility of any actual consciousness whatsoever.

But the *Anstoß* or "check" is merely one such condition; the other is that the I constantly *strives* to go beyond these same limits, and it is the task of Part Three to explain why—thereby proving precisely what Fichte had earlier claimed that no

---

[92] On April 1, 1795, Fichte's publisher issued a "clarification" in the *Annalen der Philosophie und des philosphischen Geistes*, in response to a complaint raised by J. S. Beck in his review of *BWL* and the "First Installment" of *GWL*, which had appeared in February in that same journal. Beck had wondered about the high price of such a relatively slim volume, to which Gabler replied by noting that the price mentioned was the price of the *complete* text of *GWL*, which he promised would became available at the time of the Easter book fair (though it fact, the "Second Installment" did not become publicly available until July). Gabler also noted that the price of the final, complete edition of *GWL* would be somewhat *lower* than the originally announced price, since "the text would not be as lengthy as the author had originally promised" (*FiG*, 7, p. 30). This suggests that Fichte may have been forced by circumstances beyond his control to abbreviate both works somewhat.

philosophy had yet succeeded in proving: namely, *that* reason indeed is and must be *practical.*[93] As in Part Two, Fichte then resumes his "pragmatic history of the mind" and proceeds to a genetic derivation of *feeling*, which is comparable to his earlier "Deduction of Representation." From this, in turn, he proceeds to a deduction of the I's positing of the *ideal*, of what *ought to be* but is not. In the course of this deduction, we move from *feeling* to *self-feeling*, from self-feeling to *longing*, and from longing to the *drive to modify the reality given through feeling*, a drive toward *different* feelings. The latter is revealed to be a drive aiming at *approval* and *satisfaction*—a drive that could be satisfied only when and only if the I posits itself as determining the Not-I (which, as in Part Two, represents a return to the foundational principle of this part of the *Foundation*).

Along the way, one encounters a derivation of the remaining Kantian categories: namely the modal categories of *actuality*, *possibility*, and *necessity*. The deduction of these categories had to be reserved for the "practical" portion of the treatise, since it is only there that one encounters what Fichte calls the I's basic power or faculty of reality: namely *feeling*. This is why the modal categories of reality could be derived only after those of quality, quantity, and relation.

This represents only the barest outline of the deductive scheme of Part Three, the most original and striking feature of which is the way in which it establishes what is sometimes (albeit misleadingly) called "the primacy of the practical."[94] In a major step beyond anything in Kant or Reinhold, Fichte now argues that we could not engage in *cognition*—indeed, could not be *conscious* at all—if we were not simultaneously engaged in *willing*, and hence engaged in *practical action in the world*, the ultimate (if unachievable) aim of which is to overcome the gulf between the I and the Not-I, which can now be more accurately reinterpreted as the gulf between the "pure I" and the concrete, finite, *existing* I.

Here is how one of Fichte's students—once again, Hölderlin—described what he took to be "the most distinctive feature" of Fichte's new system after having attended his lectures throughout the Winter Semester of 1794/95:

> Within every human being there is an infinite striving, an activity that forbids one from treating as permanent any limit whatsoever and permits absolutely no standstill, but aspires instead to become ever wider, freer, and more independent. This drive toward endless activity is limited. The activity, which is *unlimited with respect to its drive*, necessarily pertains to the nature of a conscious being (to an "I," as Fichte expresses it). But the *limitation* of this activity also pertains necessarily to the nature of a conscious being. From this it follows that if this activity were not limited, not deficient, then it would be everything, and nothing would

---

[93] Fichte first made this claim in the fall of 1793, in *RG*, in which he observed that "it is not a fact that reason is practical, nor that it has the power to produce the feeling of what is completely right." Consequently, "it must be proven *that* reason is practical" (*GA*, I/2: 26 and 28; *SW*, VIII, pp. 426 and 428; *Grev*, pp. 303 and 305).

[94] On this point, see Breazeale, "Der fragwürdige 'Primat der praktischen Vernunft' in Fichtes *Grundlage der gesamten Wissenschaftslehre*," *Fichte-Studien* 10 (1997): 253–71; and "The Theory of Practice and the Practice of Theory: Fichte and the 'Primacy of Practical Reason,'" *International Philosophical Quarterly* 36 (1996): 47–64.

lie outside it; nothing would lie outside us; we would have knowledge of nothing and would possess no consciousness; nothing would be *opposed* to us [*uns nichts entgegen*], and there would therefore be for us no *object* [*Gegenstand*]. But just as the limitation, i.e., the resistance (along with the state of being passively affected that is produced by such resistance), is necessary for consciousness, so is that infinite striving, which is limitless with respect to the drive, necessary in any conscious being. For if we did not strive to be infinite and free from all limits, then we would again feel nothing that might oppose this striving, and thus we would again feel nothing other than ourselves, would have knowledge of nothing, and would possess no consciousness.[95]

Fichte was clearly aware of the supreme importance of Part Three and in subsequent years frequently complained about what he viewed as the relative neglect of this—again, in his view—most important portion of the *Foundation*. As he lamented in 1805, "is there no one in Germany who has read § 5 of my *Wissenschaftslehre*, and not simply the first four §§?"[96] Or as he later wrote to Jacobi, "in § 5 of the *Wissenschaftslehre* striving, drive, revealed itself to be the actual vehicle of all reality. I suspect that those people who have tried so vigorously and for so many years to pin upon the *Wissenschaftslehre* a charge it does not deserve have never read as far as § 5."[97]

Outline of What is Distinctive of the Wissenschaftslehre with Regard to the Theoretical Power
Jena, Winter Semester 1794/95

Though the *Outline of What is Distinctive of the Wissenschaftslehre with Regard to the Theoretical Power* may not possess the same, truly revolutionary, import as Part Three of the *Foundation*, it too marks an important step in Fichte's ongoing advance beyond his predecessors and in his efforts to further articulate his own system. Just as, in Part Two of the *Foundation*, he had provided a deduction of what Reinhold took to be primitive and non-derivable (namely, representation, along with the power of the I to entertain representations), so here, in the *Outline*, he continues his effort to provide a deduction (or "genetic derivation") of matters

---

[95] Hölderlin to Karl Gok, April 13, 1795, *FiG*, I, p. 266. This entire paragraph is a single sentence in Hölderlin's original German.

[96] *Die Ausweisung zum seeligen Leben, GA*, I/9: 208. "The reigning view of the *Wissenschaftslehre* appears to be based on assertions by a few individuals, who have not even read § 5 of the old presentation, or who did not read it with the requisite attentiveness; for there they would at least have discovered that the *Wissenschaftslehre* is not a nihilism" (preface to an unwritten collection of essays [1808], *GA*, II/11: 7).

[97] Fichte to Jacobi, May 8, 1706, *GA*, III/5: 356. "For Berkeley, anyway, that divinity by means of which representations are produced in us was something supremely real. And many of those who have attempted to refute the *Wissenschaftslehre* appear to have taken it to be something similar to Berkeley's system. Perhaps they read only the First Installment of this system and were so wearied by this that they never read the Second. Had they done so, they would have discovered at the summit of everything else a certain *striving*, as the first object of any consciousness of what is real—and as mediating all other real consciousness" (*Neue Bearbeitung der W.L. 1800, GA*, II/5: 366).

that Kant, in the first *Critique*, had simply assumed. In Parts One and Two of the *Foundation*, Fichte had provided dialectical deductions of the Kantian categories of quality, quantity, and relation, and, in Part Three, a deduction of the modal categories. Here, in the *Outline*, he will offer a "deduction of intuition" corresponding to the Deduction of Representation at the conclusion of Part Two. This will require a transcendental derivation of three things that Kant, in the first *Critique*, had been content to treat as simply *given*: namely, the manifold of sensations and the pure a priori forms of that manifold, space and time.[98] Such a deduction will purport to establish that these same three things are *conditions for the possibility* of that act of pure—and "unconditioned"—self-positing with which Part One began.

The *Outline* appears to have been intended from the start not as an extension of the *Wissenschaftslehre* into the special sub-domain of *Naturphilosophie* or philosophy of nature,[99] but instead as an essential, systematic supplement to Part Two of the *Foundation*. This is strongly suggested by Fichte's insistence that the second edition of the *Foundation* appear in a single, consecutively page-numbered volume along with the *Outline*. Like Part Two of the *Foundation*, the *Outline* is exclusively concerned with the conditions for the possibility of *cognition*. Hence, it too is governed by the foundational principle governing the theoretical Part Two of the *Foundation*: in cognition the I posits itself as *determined by the Not-I*. The *Outline* advances the project of Part Two by further determining how this "independent" Not-I must be thought of in order for it to be posited as determining the finite I (or cognizing intellect).[100]

Limited as it is, the program of the *Outline* is still quite ambitious. In Part Two of the *Foundation* we discovered that the I can posit itself as determined by the Not-I only by spontaneously producing *representations* of the latter. Now, in the *Outline*, we will also discover that every representation must be *particular* and that no particular representation could ever exist apart from a *manifold* of other

---

[98] Regarding this point, Forberg provides the following anecdote: "I quickly realized that the Fichtean philosophy was utterly different than the Kantian. I disputed often with him concerning his absolute I, even though our views were not all that far apart. I too wanted to start with the I, but not with an absolute I; instead, I wanted to start with the empirical I, that is, with empirical consciousness of space and time, as Kant had done. So I then asked him, 'will you be able to deduce space from your absolute I?' And I feared that he would be no more successful in doing so than Reinhold had been in developing the manifold of matter from the concept of representation. 'If I cannot deduce space,' he replied, 'then I would sooner be a woodchopper than a philosopher'" (*FiG*, I, pp. 102–3).

[99] To the conclusion of his 1796/99 lectures on *Wissenschaftslehre nova methodo* Fichte appended a brief but indispensable sketch of the *entire system* of the *Wissenschaftslehre*, which was to consist of a "Foundational" portion or *prima philosophia*, followed by four systematic subdivisions: philosophy of nature, ethics, and what he calls "philosophy of the postulates," which, in turn, includes political or social philosophy ("philosophy of right") and philosophy of religion. While at Jena, Fichte presented two very different, but by no means incompatible, versions of the foundational portion of the system (*GWL* and *WLnm*), and he devoted considerable energy to developing ethics and philosophy of right (*SS* and *GNR*). He was preparing lectures on the philosophy of religion when he was publicly accused of atheism and lost his position at Jena in the ensuing "controversy." Other than some remarks concerning natural teleology in *SS*, he never developed his projected "philosophy of nature," neither during his career at Jena nor subsequently. (For at interpretation of the *Outline* in the context of Fichte's philosophy of nature, see Michael G. Vater, "Freedom's Body: Fichte's Account of Nature." In *The Bloomsbury Handbook to Fichte*, ed. Marina F. Bykova, pp. 101–17. [London and New York: Bloomsbury Academic, 2020.])

[100] However, in his letter of April 28, 1795, to Reinhold, Fichte did express hope that the *Outline* would also be clearer and more accessible than Part Two of the *Foundation*.

representations. We will observe as well how sensations, simply by being explicitly posited as such, become particular intuitions, which are always posited as part of a sensory manifold of interrelated intuitions. Finally, we will also discover precisely *how* these particular intuitions are necessarily related to one another: namely, alongside one another in *space* and before and after and simultaneous with one another in *time*. Only in this way can "particular" intuitions be posited at all. What the *Outline* purports to have accomplished, therefore, is to have *completed*—or at least to have advanced[101]—the *deduction*, already begun in the *Foundation*, of the very "facts of experience" that other philosophers—notably Kant and Reinhold—had been content to treat as simply *given*. This is precisely what Fichte emphasized to Reinhold:

> Perhaps the following will most clearly show the relationship of my system to yours and to Kant's. Kant seeks to discover the basis for that unity of the manifold [which is present] in the Not-I. How do you unite A, B, C, etc.—*which are already given*—into the unity of consciousness? [...] I believe it need only be said to be understood that this question presupposes another: "How do you first arrive at A and B and C?" They are *given*. In plain language this means, does it not, that you *do not know?* Very well then, either prove to me that and why you cannot know this, or else do not speak to me about philosophy as a science so long as you do not know it. At the proper time we will indeed inquire into how you may unite A and B, etc. But A *for itself* and the *subject* are also distinct, are they not? The first question, then, is how do you unite these? Once we know this, your second, subordinate question will be easy to answer. For you will undoubtedly assimilate B just as you assimilated A. And once A is within the subject and *B* is then assimilated into *that same subject*, then it undoubtedly follows that *B* will join A. This makes my path much easier and shorter than Kant's.
>
> The surprising result is now revealed (a result that is particularly illuminated by the deductions of time and space in my brief *Outline of What is Distinctive of the Wissenschaftslehre with Regard to the Theoretical Power*): namely, that there is no A that is absorbed first, nor can there be. Instead however high one ascends, something higher is always presupposed. For example, every intuition is necessarily posited in the *present* point in time, but there is no *present* point in time without a *past* one. Hence there is also no present intuition without a past intuition to which it is joined; and there is no first moment, no beginning of consciousness. This proves what Kant presupposed—that the Not-I is necessarily manifold. This also indicates why that great thinker, who surely penetrated those very same depths the *Wissenschaftslehre* is attempting to plumb, began his treatment of the Not-I precisely at the point he did. We, however, should no longer allow the matter to rest there.[102]

[101] In his July 2, 1795, letter to Reinhold, Fichte announced the imminent completion of the printing of the *Outline*, adding that "it is a fragment and proceeds only as far the deduction of time and space" (*GA*, III/2: 347; *EPW*, p. 401).

[102] Fichte to Reinhold, July 2, 1795, *GA*, III/2: 345–6; *EPW*, pp. 399–400.

Second edition of *Concerning the Concept of the Wissenschaftslehre*
Jena, 1798

The circumstances for publishing this second edition are clearly stated in the new Preface to the same: the first edition was sold out, but the author still wished to keep it available as "an introduction to this system," that is, to the *Wissenschaftslehre*. The second edition was entrusted to Gabler, publisher of the first edition, and included many minor textual changes, plus a few significant omissions from the first edition, including, most noticeably, the entire Part Three, or "Hypothetical Division of the *Wissenschaftslehre*." As Fichte explained in the Preface to the first edition of the *Foundation*:

> I have heard many complaints concerning the obscurity and unintelligibility of that portion of this book with which the public has become acquainted until now, as well as concerning the obscurity and unintelligibility of *Concerning the Concept of the Wissenschaftslehre*.
>
> Regarding objections to the latter, and especially to § 8 of the same, I may have been at fault in stating the foundational principles of the system—principles that are, in my case, determined by the entire system itself[103]—apart from that system, and in expecting my readers and critics to have the patience to leave everything just as indeterminate as I had left it. If, however, these objections concern the work as a whole, then I confess in advance that I will never be able to write anything in the field of speculation that will be intelligible to those who found *Concerning the Concept of the Wissenschaftslehre* to be unintelligible. Just as this work represents the limit of their ability to understand, so too does it represent the limit of my ability to make myself understood.[104]

The new edition also included, as an appendix, a reprint of an anonymous review of Schelling's *Concerning the Possibility of a Form for Philosophy as such*, and an excerpt from J. S. Beck's critical and condescending review of *Concerning the Concept* and the "First Installment" of the *Foundation*.[105] The new edition became available during the fall of 1798.

---

[103] This is a very significant admission. It means, for example, that one simply cannot hope to understand Part One of the *Foundation* apart from Parts Two and Three; for it is only very late in the game that the student of this treatise really grasps what is meant by and required for the possibility of "simply positing oneself."

[104] *BWL, GA,* I/2: 252–3; below, p. 197. The inclusion of the hostile review of Schelling's short work indicates that, at this point, Fichte considered him to be a reliable exponent of his own system.

[105] See *GA,* I/2: 165–72.

Second editions of *Foundation of the Entire Wissenschaftslehre* Berlin, 1802

Late in 1799, after having taken refuge in Berlin following the loss of his professorship in the wake of "Atheism-Controversy,"[106] Fichte apparently proposed to Gabler that they issue a new "revised, improved, and augmented" edition of the *Foundation*, that it should become available before the end of the year, and that the publisher should send Fichte the full honorarium in advance. While agreeing to this proposal, Gabler urged that the work not appear until the following spring, since the first edition was, in fact, not yet completely sold out.[107] After receiving a small partial advance from Gabler, Fichte began revising the *Foundation* and sent his revisions to the publisher, with the understanding that the new edition would appear in the spring of 1800. Gabler then proposed that Fichte obtain the cash balance due for the new edition from the Tübingen publisher, J. C. Cotta, who owed Gabler money and with whom Fichte had already contracted for a projected (but, in fact, never published) "new presentation" of the *Wissenschaftslehre*.[108] Following Fichte's rejection of Gabler's proposal there ensued a complex series of negotiations, which left Fichte with the impression that the previously agreed upon, joint plan for a new edition had been scrapped by both parties.

In May of 1801 a somewhat bewildered Cotta informed Fichte that he had seen an announcement of a new presentation of the *Wissenschaftslehre* to be published by Gabler, to which Fichte replied by explaining that what Gabler intended to publish was not a new *presentation* of the *Wissenschaftslehre*, but merely a new, revised *edition* of *Foundation of the Entire Wissenschaftslehre*. The older presentation, he explained to Cotta, "certainly should not be discarded, but only presented more clearly." Furthermore, he noted that in the new presentation (the one Cotta expected to publish) he would still need to refer to the older one, "since many matters are treated there with a patience and fluency that I would find it difficult to recapture now."[109] In this same letter he informs Cotta that, though he would prefer that Cotta himself publish the new edition of the *Foundation*, he felt obliged to consult further with Gabler before consigning the new edition to Cotta.

Meanwhile, Gabler had already advanced in his preparations for the new, revised edition, and, over and over again, requested Fichte's authorization to issue it—requests that were just as repeatedly denied. Finally, in August of 1801, Fichte informed Gabler that Cotta would be publishing a new, *unrevised* editions of both

---

[106] Regarding the circumstances of Fichte's dismissal from his position at Jena, see "Fichte in Jena," *EPW*, pp. 40–6, as well as Yolanda Estes' introduction to *J. G. Fichte and the Atheism Dispute (1798-1800)*, ed. Yolanda Estes and Curtis Bowman (Burlington, VT: Ashgate, 2010).

[107] See C. E. Gabler to Fichte, November 11, 1799. In his November 19, 1799, letter to his wife (*GA*, III/4: 157), Fichte assures her that payment from Gabler, along with his honorarium for the recently published *Vocation of Man*, should provide them with enough "to live on for a year" (*GA*, III/4: 146). Given his rather parlous circumstances at that point, it is difficult to resist the conclusion that one of Fichte's reasons for re-issuing the *Foundation*, despite the rather serious deficiencies to which he himself had already called attention, was the opportunity to earn some much-needed income.

[108] This would be the *Wissenschaftslehre* of 1801/02, which Fichte did indeed prepare for publication, but ultimately withdrew.

[109] Fichte to Cotta, May 9 and August 8, 1801, *GA*, III/5: 31–2 and 58.

the *Foundation* and the *Outline*. Moreover, he had instructed Cotta to publish both texts in a single volume with consecutively numbered pages and had provided him with a brief preface for the new, combined edition, which duly appeared early in January of 1802.

Meanwhile, Gabler was proceeding apace with publication plans for his new, revised, and expanded edition of the *Foundation*, and on January 8 sent copies to both Cotta and to Fichte, who, eight days after receiving Cotta's edition received Gabler's, accompanied by a friendly letter "as if nothing else had transpired between us, and he thought he could make a great friend of me."[110]

Over the next few months, Gabler tried to make amends with Fichte and proposed that Cotta assume the publication rights for all of Fichte's books previously published by Gabler, including the *Foundation of Natural Right* and *System of Ethics*.[111] Nothing came of this proposal, while Gabler continued to sell copies of his own new and now unauthorized edition of the *Foundation*. This prompted Fichte to publish an official "Declaration" that Cotta's edition was the only legal one and repudiating Gabler's.[112] Gabler responded with a "Counter-Declaration" of his own, accusing Fichte of failing to honor their prior agreement. Stung by what he considered to be Gabler's public slander (which omitted the fact that Gabler never paid Fichte in advance, as promised, and that he had later agreed not to publish his new edition), Fichte initiated against Gabler a rather Dickensian legal process, which endured for many years thereafter.[113]

Second edition of *Outline of What is Distinctive of the Wissenschaftselhre with Regard to the Theoretical Power* Berlin, 1802

Very little information is available concerning the circumstances of Gabler's new edition of the *Outline*. Though described on its title page as the "second improved edition" and dated 1802, the changes are all quite minor and mainly orthographic,

---

[110] This is according to Fichte's letter to Cotta of January 8, 1802, *GA*, III/5: 114, as well as according to the detailed "Instruktion für meinen Rechtsbestand in meiner Klage gegen den Buchhändler Gabler zu Jena" (*GA*, II/6: 383–401), instructions for a legal brief which Fichte prepared in the summer of 1803 for the use of his lawyer in his ongoing proceedings against Gabler. Fichte must at least have suspected that Gabler would in fact publish his new edition, since, in his November 28, 1801, letter to Cotta he urged him to hurry with his new, one-volume edition of the *Foundation* and *Outline*, since customers were asking for copies of the earlier, sold-out editions—and in order to prevent Grabler— "who," reported Fichte, "is up to no good"—from issuing his own "improved" second edition of the *Foundation* (*GA*, III/5: 95).

[111] Fichte to Cotta, February 8, 1802, *GA*, III/5: 118 and Fichte to K. F. E. Frommann, March 2, 1802, *GA*, III/5: 120.

[112] "*Erklärung*," signed "April 2, 1802" and published in the May 1, 1802, issue of the *A.L.Z.* (*GA*, II/8: 11). A month later (May 8, 1802), Gabler published in the same journal his own "Counter-Declaration," in which he accused Fichte of reneging on a contract they had made in 1799/1800.

[113] Fichte to F. I. Niethammer, Fall/Winter 1802, *GA*, III/5: 154. In his later "Instructions" for the attorney responsible for pressing his suit against Gabler, Fichte demanded damages for defamation, as well all income from any sales of Gabler's unauthorized edition of *GWL*—all remaining copies of which, he insisted, must "be burned, before witnesses, at his expense" (*GA*, II/6: 399). There seems to be no record of how Fichte's case against Gabler was eventually decided—if indeed it was ever decided at all.

which strongly suggests that most if not all of them were made by Gabler or perhaps by the printer and none by Fichte himself. Surprisingly, there is no mention of this unauthorized second edition of the *Outline* in any of Fichte's correspondence or in any of the (many) documents related to his subsequent legal proceedings against Gabler, which strongly suggests that he was unaware of this edition. In his February 6, 1806, letter to W. E. F. von Wolzogen, Fichte reports that "in the year 1804 I discovered he [i.e., Gabler] also re-issued my *Natural Right.*" However, there seems to have been no such second edition, so one might surmise that the rumor he had heard—or perhaps misheard—was really about Gabler's new edition of the *Outline*.

Subsequent Presentations of the Foundational Portion of the *Wissenschaftslehre* Jena, Berlin, Erlangen, Königsberg, and Berlin, 1796–1814

When, in the Winter Semester of 1796-97, Fichte once again offered lectures in Jena on the foundational portion of his new system, he did so according to a completely new strategy and method of presentation. This time, however, he did not have these lectures on the "Foundation of Transcendental Philosophy (*Wissenschaftslehre*) *nova methodo*" printed in advance and distributed to his students. Instead, he confined this new presentation to oral delivery—though he now permitted his students to take copious notes, with the result that several complete transcriptions of the *Wissenschaftslehre nova methodo* have survived.

His reluctance to publish new presentations of the foundational portion of the *Wissenschaftslehre* are evident in a remark he made some years later, when he observed that

> the text that appeared six years ago and was published as a manuscript for the use of my listeners, i.e., *Foundation of the Entire Wissenschaftslehre*, has, to the best of my knowledge, been understood by almost no one and been made use of by hardly anyone at all, apart from my own students. This is a text that does not appear to be readily able to dispense with oral assistance.[114]

---

[114] "['Seit sech Jahren…']" *GA*, I/7: 153; "Public Announcement of a New Presentation of the *Wissenschaftslehre*," *IWL*, pp. 186-7.

See the following anonymous report from a female acquaintance concerning the period 1794/95: "I had the good fortune to be standing next to [Fichte], and to find him very communicative. He would occasional pull from his pocket his notebook and read to me something concerning his philosophy of the I. It was all Greek to me. But once he realized that I was not understanding a single word, he took the trouble to explain every single comma and to ask me ten times on every page whether I had understood him, so that I finally had to understand something. One day he charged into our room, flushed, heated, and even more blustery than usual, crying 'it is abominable, abominable!' He had in his a hand a small piece of paper, and I asked 'What is it, Fichte, what has happened?'

"'Some stupid young people gave me this,' he said, and I asked 'How so? Calm down and explain yourself.'

"'Madam, you are a simple woman, and yet you understood what I read to you yesterday from my notebook, and then today I discovered on my lectern this note from my students, asking me to

Over and over again, he complained to his correspondents that readers of the *Foundation* were guilty of ignoring the fact that "this text was never intended for anyone but my own students, something that has been universally overlooked by friend and foe alike"[115]—though one can only wonder how he expected his readers to take this fact into consideration when he authorized Gabler to make those same texts available to the general public.

What kept him from publishing not only the *Wissenschaftslehre nova methodo* but *any* of his subsequent, fully—albeit quite variously—articulated presentations of the foundations of his system of philosophy was always the same fear, borne out of the initial public reception of the *Foundation*: namely, that he was incapable of producing a presentation capable of standing completely on its own and open to no misunderstanding whatsoever. He seems to have been determined to avoid having his philosophy once again become an object of ridicule.

After 1795, Fichte never again published a full-scale presentation of the all-important foundational portion of his own system, even though he continued to produce one new version of the same after another for the rest of his career, all of which were confined to his private lectures in Jena, Berlin, Erlangen, and Königsberg, until he had finally succeeded in producing more than a dozen completely different versions of the same—in addition to the Zurich lectures and the version published in 1794-95.[116] To be sure, he still dreamt of someday

explain—yet again—yesterday's lecture, since they had not understood me. Some people!'" (*Vertraute unpartheische Briefe über Fichtes Aufenthalt in Jena* [1799], as cited in *FiG*, I, p. 137).

[115] "What have you found unsatisfactory in my previous presentation of the *Wissenschaftslehre*? Surely not the principles? But if what you are dissatisfied with is the manner of derivation, and if what you are referring to is the published *Foundation*, then you are quite correct to find much that is unsatisfactory. This text was never intended for anyone but my own students, something that has been universally overlooked by friend and foe alike" (Fichte to C. E. Schmid, March 17, 1799, *GA*, III/3: 213; *EPW*, p. 426).

"I can easily believe that my *Wissenschaftslehre* was not understood, and that it is still not understood by those who believe that I am now making *different* claims. I realize very well that this is the fault of my presentation in that text, which was not intended for the public, but only for my own students, as the basis for my lectures. Consequently, no one understood the book nor gave me any credit at all. Instead, I was taken to be an idle chatterer, whose interference could only hinder the progress of science. From this people *concluded* that the system (which they knew perfectly well that they did not understand) *would* probably not be worth anything either. I know this and find it to be quite understandable. However, even though no scholar can be expected to know everything, he can at least be expected to know whether or not he understands something, and no honest person should be expected to judge something until he is conscious of understanding it" (Fichte to L. H. Jacob, March 4, 1799, *GA*, III/3: 206; *EPW*, p. 424).

[116] 1.) *Wissenschaftslehre nova methodo* (Jena, 1796-9). Unpublished lectures, repeated three times. A revised version of the first few lectures were published in 1797/98, as the two introductions and Ch. 1 of *VWL*; but the complete presentation of *WLnm* survives only in student transcriptions (*GA*, IV/2: 17-267; IV/3: 151-96 and 321-535; English translation, *FTP*).

2.) *Neue Bearbeitung der W.L.* (Berlin, 1800). Unpublished and unfinished manuscript, which began as an effort to revise the lectures on *WLnm* (*GA*, II/5: 331-402; partial English translation by David W. Wood, *New Version of the Wissenschaftslehre [1800]*, in *The Philosophical Rupture between Fichte and Schelling: Selected Texts and Correspondence (1800-1802)*, ed. and trans. Michael G. Vater and David W. Wood [Albany, NY: SUNY Press, 2012] pp. 93–118).

3.) *Darstellung der Wissenschaftslehre* (Berlin, 1801/2). Unpublished lecture manuscript, though prepared and revised for publication (*GA*, II/6: 129–324).

producing a truly adequate presentation of his system, one that would require no oral assistance and that could, in his own plaintive words "force the reader to understand,"[117] but he had serious doubts about his ability to do that[118] and, in any case, did not live to accomplish that goal.

Until the end of his life, moreover, he never stopped complaining about what he considered to be the well-nigh universal misunderstandings and caricatures of his first—and only published—full-scale presentation of the foundations of his system. He blamed these misunderstandings in part upon "the manner of philosophizing that then prevailed,"[119] as well as upon his own relative "immaturity" as an exponent of the *Wissenschaftslehre* in 1794,[120] but mainly upon the

4.) *Vorlesung der W.L.* (Berlin, Jan.-March, 1804). Unpublished lecture manuscript (*GA*, II/7: 66–235).

5.) *Die Wissenschaftslehre* (Berlin, April–June, 1804). Unpublished lecture manuscript, plus student transcription. (*GA*, II/8: 2–421; *SW*, X, pp. 89–314; English translation by Walter E. Wright, *The Science of Knowing: J.G. Fichte's 1804 Lectures on the Wissenschaftslehre* [Albany, NY: SUNY Press, 2005]).

6.) *3ter Cours der W.L. 1804* (Berlin, November–December 1804). Unpublished lecture manuscript (*GA*, II/7: 301–68).

7.) *4ter Vortrag der Wissenschaftslehre* (Erlangen, 1805). Unpublished lecture manuscript (*GA*, II/9: 179–311).

8.) *Wissenschaftslehre* (Königsberg, 1807). Unpublished lecture manuscript. (*GA*, II/10: 111–208).

9.) *Wissenschaftslehre* (Berlin, 1810). Unpublished lecture manuscript (*GA*, II/11: 293–392).

10.) *Die Wissenschaftslehre, in ihrem allgemeinen Umrisse dargestellt* (Berlin, 1810). A ten-page *published* pamphlet and by no means a full presentation of the foundations of the system. (*GA*, I/10: 335–45; *SW*, II, pp. 695–709); English translation by Walter E. Wright, "The Science of Knowledge in its General Outline [1810]," *Idealistic Studies* 6 [1976]: 106–17).

11.) *Wissenschaftslehre* (Berlin, 1811). Unpublished lecture manuscript (*GA*, II/12: 143–307).

12.) *Die Wissenschaftslehre* (Berlin, 1812). Unpublished lecture manuscript (*GA*, II/13: 43–189).

13.) *Die Wissenschaftslehre* (Berlin, 1813). Unpublished lecture manuscript; unfinished because of disruptions caused by war (*GA*, II/15: 133–68).

14.) *Wissenschaftslehre* (Berlin, 1814). Unpublished lecture manuscript; unfinished because of Fichte's death before the second first week of the semester (*GA*, II/17: 319–40).

[117] This is the subtitle of a metaphilosophical, or "critical," work Fichte published in 1801, *Sonnenklarer Bericht an das größere Publikum über das eigentliche Wesen der neuesten Philosophie. Ein Versuch, die Leser zum Verstehen zu zwingen*; *A Crystal-Clear Report to the General Public concerning the Actual Essence of the Newest Philosophy. An Attempt to Force the Reader to Understand*, trans. John Botterman and William Rasch, in *Fichte, Jacobi, and Schelling: Philosophy of German Idealism*, ed. Ernst Behler (New York: Continuum, 1987), pp. 39–115).

[118] "The reason for my misfortune as an author is that I am so incapable of placing myself in the literary public's frame of mind. I always assume many things to be self-evident, which hardly anyone else finds to be so" (Fichte to Reinhold, April 22, 1799; *GA*, III/3: 325; *EPW*, p. 428).

[119] "My published *Wissenschaftslehre* bears too many traces of the time in which it was written and of the manner of philosophizing that then prevailed. This made it less clear than a presentation of transcendental idealism needs to be" (Fichte to Friederich Johannsen, January 31, 1801; *GA*, III/5: 9).

[120] "I wish you would place less value on my treatment of the *Wissenschaftslehre*. I am certain about the main points, but once someone has grasped these he does far better to rely upon himself than upon this very immature presentation. How much more clearly do I understand this science now!" (Fichte to Reinhold, July 4, 1797; *GA*, III/2:69; *EPW*, p. 419).

Fichte had tried to persuade Reinhold of this same point even earlier, in his letter of March 21, 1797, in which he warned him that "your evaluation of *my* presentation, as it has appeared so far, is far too favorable. Or perhaps the content has permitted you to overlook the deficiency of the presentation. I consider it to be most imperfect. Yes, I know that it emits sparks, but it does not burn with a *single* flame" (*GA*, III/3: 57).

extraordinary circumstances surrounding the composition and publication of the *Foundation* and upon the fact that, in contrast to his practice in the lecture hall, he could not be present to answer questions raised by readers of the *Foundation* nor to address their apparent incomprehension.

Nevertheless, at the time of Fichte's death the *only* publicly available full-scale presentation of the foundations of the *Wissenschaftslehre* remained the one published in 1794/95. Despite its manifest difficulties and deficiencies, Fichte continued to cite and to endorse the *Foundation*, as for example, in the following passage from an unpublished "Report on the Concept of the *Wissenschaftslehre*" from 1806:

> Since I have just declared the previous presentation of the *Wissenschaftslehre* to be good and correct, then it goes without saying that no doctrine is ever to be expected from me other than the one I previously laid before the public. The essence of the previously published *Wissenschaftslehre* consists in the claim that the I-form (that is, the form of absolute reflection) is the ground and root of all knowing, and that everything that can ever be encountered within knowing—and as it can be encountered within knowing—can ensue only from the form of I-hood and from the analytic-synthetic exhaustion of this form, which proceeds from the middle point of a reciprocal interaction of absolute substantiality with absolute causality, and the reader will rediscover this character in an unaltered form in all our present and future declarations concerning the *Wissenschaftslehre*.[121]

Though the language here is no longer precisely that of 1794/95, the sentiment seems sincere. As Fichte explained to Reinhold, "my theory should be expounded in infinitely many ways. Everyone will have a different way of thinking it—and must have a different way of thinking it in order to think *it* at all."[122] Hence the sole purpose of any written "presentation" of the *Wissenschaftslehre* is precisely that: to help the reader to "think through" that system—on one's own and for oneself. Though the first Jena presentation may very well not have been the best, the most felicitous, or the most accessible presentation, it remains—as Fichte recognized—the only one we've got.[123] And, as the rich and varied reception of the *Foundation of the Entire Wissenschaftslehre* by generations of independent thinkers testifies, this is a work which, for all its manifest obscurities and acknowledged deficiencies, remains fully capable of serving that purpose.

---

[121] *Bericht über den Begriff der Wissenschaftslehre*" (1806), GA, II/10: 29; SW, VIII, p. 369.
[122] Fichte to Reinhold, March 21, 1796, GA, III/3: 57.
[123] This is not counting, of course, the many full-scale new versions that Fichte himself subsequently prepared but consistently refused to publish, all of which are now available in GA.

Contents and Outlines of *Foundation of the Entire Wissenschaftslehre* and *Outline of What is Distinctive of the Wissenschaftslehre with Regard to the Theoretical Power*

To the frustration of generations of readers and students, Fichte provided no table of contents for any of the editions of the *Foundation* and *Outline*. What follows are detailed outlines of the contents of each of these works, intended to help readers orient themselves in these all too frequently disorienting texts.

This outline follows Fichte's own textural divisions, but adds many additional divisions, subtitles, headings, and summaries. **Fichte's own titles and section numbers are always printed in bold type.** Everything else has been added by the editor/translator.

In order to make these outlines as broadly useful as possible, the running page numbers appearing in the left margins of these outlines refer to Volume One of *SW*. These same page numbers appear in most other editions of Fichte's writings, including *GA*, as well as in the margins of present volume.

Foundation of the Entire Wissenschaftslehre

Preface to the First Edition (1795)

Forward to the Second Edition (1802)

Part One: Foundational Principles of the Entire *Wissenschaftslehre*.

§ 1. First, Purely and Simply Unconditioned Foundational Principle.
"I am I." "The I posits itself purely and simply."
Deduction of the category of reality.

Prefatory remarks on method.

The path to the discovery of the first, utterly unconditioned foundational principle.

From self-consciousness as an empirical "fact" to self-consciousness as a self-positing "F/Act".

Further specification of the I as the self-positing "absolute subject" and the "necessary existence" of the same.

§ 2. Second Foundational Principle, Conditioned with Respect to its Content.
"I am not the Not-I." "A Not-I is purely and simply posited in opposition to the I." Deduction of the category of negation.

Prefatory remarks on method.

The path to the discovery of the second foundational principle of the Wissenschaftslehre.

§ 3. Third Foundational Principle, Conditioned with Respect to its Form.
"The I posits in the I a divisible Not-I in opposition to a divisible I."
Deduction of the category of determination or delimitation.

Provisional resolution of this contradiction by means of the synthetic concept of "divisibility."

B.) Derivation of the contradiction by means of the concept of "divisibility" and discovery of the third foundational principle of human knowledge: "Both the I and the Not-I are posited as divisible."

Confirmation of the correctness of the third foundational principle.

C.) Confirmation that act Y successfully unites the opposing propositions, which state that "the I is not posited in the I to the extent that the Not-I is posited" (= A,1, above) and that "the Not-I can be posited only insofar as the I is posited" (= A,2).

D.) *Conclusion*: We have now derived the only three possible foundational
principles of the *Wissenschaftslehre*. These constitute the total sum of what is
purely and simply certain and are summarized in the third foundational principle: "The I posits in the I a divisible Not-I in opposition to the divisible I."

Part Two: Foundation of Theoretical Knowledge.

§ 4. First Theorem.
"The I posits itself as determined by the Not-I."

A: Determination of the Synthetic Proposition to be Analyzed.

B. General Nature of the Synthesis of Terms Posited in Opposition to Each Other as Such in the Indicated Proposition (*viz., that the I posits itself as determined by the Not-I*).

Explication of the synthetic concept of reciprocal determination and deduction of the productive power of imagination.

C. Synthesis by Means of Reciprocal Determination of the Contradictions Implicit in the First of the Two Propositions Posited in Opposition to Each Other (*viz., in the "theoretical" proposition that the Not-I determines the I*).

Deduction of the synthetic concept of causal efficacy: "The Not-I has reality for the I only to the extent that the I is affected."

D. Synthesis by Means of Reciprocal Determination of the Opposing Propositions Contained in the Second of the Two Propositions Posited in Opposition to Each Other (*viz., in the proposition that the I posits itself as determining the Not-I*).

Deduction of the synthetic concept of substantiality: "Substance is all the reciprocal relations, taken generally; accident is a determinate reality that is related reciprocally to another one, which is reciprocally related to it."

E. Synthetic Unification of the Oppositions Occurring between the Two Indicated Types of Reciprocal Determination (*viz., in the concepts of cause and effect/substance and accident*).

Deduction of the synthetic concept of partial reciprocal determination, and hence of the synthetic principle that an independent activity is determined by reciprocally-related-acting-and-being-passively-affected, and reciprocally-related-acting-and-being-passively-affected is determined by an independent activity.

partially posits in itself a state of passive affection, but insofar as it posits activity in the Not-I it *partially* does not posit in itself a state of passive affection—and vice versa. Hence there is posited in both the I and the Not-I a second activity, an activity *independent* of the activity that is reciprocally related to any opposing state of passivity.

p. 149   III. The independent activities of the I and the Not-I are themselves only *partially* independent, since such independence contradicts the law of reciprocal determination. The independent activities must themselves be united by reciprocal determination, which is therefore valid only *partially*.

p. 150   IV. We have now deduced the following new synthetic principle: independent activity is determined by reciprocally-related-acting-and-being-passively-affected, and reciprocally-related-acting-and-being-passively-affected is determined by independent activity.

Analysis of the new synthetic principle.

p. 150   1.) The two independent activities of the I and Not-I can determine each other indirectly, by means of their reciprocal relationship.

p. 150   2.) The principle of reciprocal determination is valid for the relationship between independent and reciprocal activity, but not for the independent activities themselves.

p. 151   —Our new synthetic principle contains the following three propositions, to each of which one of the following sections of Part Two will be devoted:

       1.) An independent activity is determined by reciprocally-related-acting-and-being-passively-affected.

       2.) Reciprocally-related-acting-and-being-passively-affected is determined by an independent activity.

       3.) Both of these reciprocally determine each other, and it does not matter with which one begins.

I.

An independent activity is determined by reciprocally-related-acting-and-being-passively-affected.

pp. 151-3   1.) *Explication of the proposition that an independent activity is determined by reciprocally-related-acting-and-being-passively-affected.* An independent activity must be posited as the ground of the connection between the reciprocally related acting and being passively affected; hence the latter "determines" the former.

       2.) *Application of this principle to the two concepts that fall under it* (viz., the concepts of causal efficacy and substantiality).

       a.) *Application to the reciprocal concept of **causal efficacy**.*

p. 153   —The I's state of being passively affected is the *ideal ground* of the quantitatively opposed activity of the Not-I, in accordance with the category of limitation.

II.

Reciprocally-related-acting-and-being-passively-affected is determined by independent activity.

1.) *Explication of the proposition that reciprocally-related-acting-and-being-passively-affected is determined by independent activity.*

2.) *Application of this principle to the two reciprocal concepts that fall under it.*

a.) *Application to the concept of causal efficacy and derivation of the activity of "transferring" activity from the I to the Not-I.*

Not-I. This is an act of "positing by means of non-positing," from which we infer an independent activity of the Not-I, by means of which it affects the I.

b.) *Application to the concept of substantiality and derivation of the activity of "alienating."*

—By means of an independent activity, the I excludes or "alienates" from itself that activity which was posited as a limited quantum of its total activity, which therefore appears as a passive affection in comparison with the totality of the I's activity, thereby making possible the reciprocal-acting-and-being passively-affected characteristic of the concept of substantiality. The independent act of the I, which accomplishes such an act of "positing by means of non-positing," is called "alienating."

—Comparison of the I's independent acts of *transference* and of *alienation*.

Remark: Ambiguity of the term "accident."

III.

Reciprocally-related-acting-and-being-passively-affected and the independent activity reciprocally determine each other.

—The reciprocally-related-acting-and-being-passively-affected and the independent activity of the I must mutually determine one another.

1.) *General explication and analysis of this proposition as containing the following three subordinate propositions:*

α.) The activity independent of the form of the reciprocally-related-acting-and-being-passively-affected determines the activity independent of the content of the same, and vice versa.

1.) These two independent activities mutually determine each other. They are synthetically united and are one and the same.

2.) The transition in question occurs purely and simply because it occurs, and consciousness is impossible otherwise.

β.) The form of the reciprocally-related-acting-and-being-passively-affected determines the content of the same, and vice versa.

—Mutual encroachment (form) determines reciprocal relation (content) and vice versa. Form and content are synthetically united and are one and the same.

—The form and content of the reciprocally-related-acting-and-being-passively-affected mutually determine each other. If one is posited, so is the other.

γ.) Reciprocally-related-acting-and-being-passively-affected (understood as a synthetic unity of form and content) determines the independent activity (understood as a synthetic unity of form and content), and vice versa.

—These two synthetic unities of form and content—reciprocal-
acting-and-being-passively-affected (*mutual encroachment*) and
an independent activity of the I (*movement of transition*)—are
synthetically united and are one and the same.
—This entire process is grounded only in itself.

2.) *Application to the concepts of causal efficacy and substantiality.*

a.) *Application to the major synthesis of causal efficacy.*

pp. 171-3   α.) In the reciprocal relation of causal efficacy, the activity of the
form determines the activity of the content, and vice versa.
—In the reciprocally-related-acting-and-being-passively-affected
associated with causal efficacy, the activity of the form (transference) determines that of the content (independent activity of the
Not-I) and vice versa.
—The Not-I is active only insofar as its activity is posited by the I
(by means of a non-positing of its own activity); and, conversely,
the independent activity of the Not-I determines the passivity of
the I and hence the act of transference. No activity of the Not-I,
no positing by means of a non-positing.
Remarks:

pp. 173-4   —Reply to a commonsense objection and discussion of the
ambiguity of the verb "to posit."

p. 174   —For Critical idealism, real and ideal ground are one and the
same.

pp. 174-5   —Explanation of why the conclusion is so difficult for some
people to endorse.

pp. 176-7   *Conclusions*:
—The I must posit reality in the Not-I in order to posit itself.
—The activity of the I and of the Not-I are one and the same.
—The passive affection of the I and of the Not-I are one and the
same.
—The activity and passive affection of the I are one and the same.
—The activity and passive affection of the Not-I are one and the
same.

p. 178   *Remark*: On Critical idealism, and the relation between the theoretical and practical parts of *GWL*.

pp. 179-80   β.) In the reciprocal activity of causal efficacy the form of mere
reciprocity (viz., mutual encroachment: coming-to-be-through-
passing-away = mutual annulment) and the content thereof (viz.,
essential opposition of the components in question, the I and
Not-I) mutually determine each other.
—The form of the reciprocal-acting-and-being-passively-affected
in this case is *coming to be by passing away,* and the content consists in the *qualitative incompatibility* of its components.

—Since form and content are here synthetically connected, essential opposition is impossible apart from mutual encroachment, and vice versa.
—Ideal and real opposition are therefore one and the same.

γ) Synthetic unity of (α) the synthetic unity of the independent activity of the form and the independent activity of the content and (β) the synthetic unity of the form of reciprocally-related-acting-and-being-passively-affected and the content of the same in the concept of substance. Deduction of the synthetic function of the productive power of imagination and the indispensability of the "impulse" or "check."

pp. 205–6 —In the concept of substantiality, the independent activity, qua synthetic unity of opposites (subjective and objective) in the concept of determinability and the reciprocally-related-acting-and-being-passively-affected, qua synthetic unity (the relation of mutual exclusion, i.e., the coming together of opposites), mutually determine one another.

pp. 206–7 —The independent activity of the I which posits, opposes, and unites the reciprocally related components (i.e., what is subjective and what is objective, both of which are posited within the I) is the productive power of imagination.

pp. 207–8 —The *form* of the reciprocally-related-acting-and-being-passively-affected in this case is *mutual exclusion* of the components, and the *content* of the same is the *encompassing sphere* which embraces and thus unites both components. This form and content are united in the concept of mutual determinability.

p. 208 —Since these reciprocally related components are supposed to exclude each other, the boundary between them can only be produced and posited by the independent activity of the I: the "marvelous *power of imagination.*"

pp. 208–9 a.) The independent activity of the power of imagination determines the reciprocally-related-acting-and-being-passively-affected, and only by an absolute act of the I do the related components become components of this relationship.
—The coming together of the subjective and objective components is made possible *within the I* by the activity of the power of imagination, the activity of positing a boundary between these components.
—This is an "idealist" principle, but it fails to explain the presence within the I of something "objective."

pp. 210–11 b.) The reciprocally-related-acting-and-being-passively-affected determines the independent activity of the power of imagination.
—Only upon the occasion of an *impulse* or *check* upon its originally outgoing activity can the independent activity of the I (power of imagination) draw the requisite boundary between itself and the Not-I.
—The check does not *determine* the I; instead, it assigns it the task of determining itself by *positing* this check for itself.

—This is an (abstractly) "realistic" principle, but it fails to explain how the I can be aware of its own determinability.

c.) The independent activity of the power of imagination and the reciprocally-related-acting-and-being-passively-affected reciprocally determine each other.

Remarks:

Transition from an indirect, dialectical to a direct, genetic method of proof.
Beginning of the "pragmatic history of the human mind."

Deduction of Representation.

reflecting upon the product of its own productive activity of intuiting, what is intuited (the intuition itself) must first be "stabilized."

—This stabilization, which is required for the possibility of reflection
upon intuition, is made possible by the power of understanding,
which is a power intermediate between the I's powers of reason (its
thetic power to posit purely and simply) and imagination.

—Understanding is the power of the *actual*: there alone does *reality*
(which is a *product* of the power of imagination) *exist*, as something
given to the understanding.

Remark: On the relation of natural to philosophical reflection.

IV.) Further explanation of how what is intuited can be posited as such by the I.

1.) The I reflects upon its own intuiting activity as limited at the
point of the check (= C).

2.) In positing its own intuiting activity as limited at C, the I posits C
as the Not-I, and thereby posits itself (in opposition to the Not-I) as
an I, as the intuiting subject.

3.) The power of understanding apprehends an intuition (provided by
the reproductive power of imagination) of the I's own act of intuiting.

4.) In order for the intuiting subject to be determined as active, it
must be posited in opposition to an activity proceeding in the opposite direction, that is, from the Not-I (originating in the infinite realm
beyond C).

5.) The intuiting I intuits the opposing activity of the Not-I. This is
possible only if the original productive activity of the I, which posits
the Not-I in the infinite realm beyond C, is reflected back to the I as
the activity of the Not-I.

6.) What is intuited is posited by the I *as* what is intuited and posited
in opposition to the intuiting subject. What is intuited lies between C
and A and is apprehended by the power of understanding as something *real*.

Remark: On the reciprocal relationship between the intuiting subject
and what is intuited.

V.) Reciprocal determination of the objective and pure activities of
the intuiting subject.
—Absolute or pure activity (activity in general) is the condition of all
objective activity (the real ground of the same) and objective activity
(the activity of intuiting) is the ideal ground for determining any
activity as such.
—The boundary between these two activities must be posited. This
boundary, intuited by the power of imagination and stabilized in the
understanding, is the *condition* for the act of intuiting and its object.

VI.) The absolute and the objective activities of the I are distinguishable from each other only if there is a reciprocal relationship between
the intuiting subject and the intuited thing in itself.

—The condition of all objective activity is a state of being passively affected, which is intuited as a feeling of compulsion and stabilized in the understanding as *necessary*.

—Free (i.e., absolute) activity is intuited by the power of imagination as a wavering or oscillation between the performance and the non-performance of some act and apprehended by the power of understanding as *possible*.

—In intuition, objective and absolute activity are synthetically united: freedom and compulsion reciprocally determine each other. There is a mutual interaction between free self-affection (insofar as the I reflects upon itself) and affection from without.

pp. 240-1   VII.) The objective activity and the self-determining activity mutually determine each other. Self-determination occurs by means of thinking of an object, which is supposed to causally affect the intuiting subject.

—The objective or intuiting and the absolute or self-reverting activities of the I reciprocally determine each other.

—The intuited object is *thought of* by the intuiting subject as determining itself (in accordance with the category of causal efficacy) to produce a state of being passively affected in the intuiting subject.

pp. 241-3   VIII.) The power of judgment makes possible the activity of self-determination and is reciprocally related to the power of understanding. What is thought is therefore reciprocally related to what is thinkable.

—The self-determining activity of the I involved in determining the object of intuition is the *power of judgment*, the power either to reflect or to abstract from objects held fast in the power of understanding.

—Judgment and understanding must mutually determine each other.

—The object of thinking is determined by the reciprocal relation between the powers of judgment and understanding. The latter determines what is *thought* and the former what is *thinkable*.

—What is thinkable and what is thought reciprocally determine each other.

pp. 243-5   IX.) The self-reverting (or absolute or non-objective or reflective) activity of the I, which is supposed to determine the activity that posits objects as such (the power of judgment) can be posited by the I only if it possesses an absolute power to abstract from all objects as such and thereby to posit the pure I.

—The absolute power of abstraction (which is equivalent to theoretical *reason* as such) assigns us a mere rule: abstract from everything from which one can abstract, until all that remains is the pure, self-determining I or "subject."

—The I is what cannot be abstracted from; the Not-I is what can be abstracted from.

—Abstraction from determinate individuality is required for pure self-consciousness.

pp. 245-6   X.) This activity that determines the I (via abstraction) can itself be determined only by an absolutely non-determinate activity.
—Productive imagination is such an indeterminate activity, though it cannot be reflected upon (i.e., brought to consciousness) as such.
—In determining itself, the I is both the determining subject and what is determined.
—If the I reflects upon (and thus determines) itself, it must posit the Not-I as infinite and undetermined; and vice versa. The I and Not-I are here reciprocally related as finite and infinite.
Remark: On the source of Kant's antinomies.

p. 246   XI.) The I reciprocally interacts only with itself.
—At a still higher level of reflection, we can see that the I is absolutely determinate of everything—including the Not-I. Whether finite or infinite, the I is related to nothing but itself and is perfectly united with itself.

Part Three (§ 5): Foundation of the Science of the Practical.

§ 5: Second Theorem.
"The I posits itself as determining the Not-I."

Deduction of striving.

pp. 246-7   *Introduction to the "practical" part of GWL.*
—Relation of the foundational principle of Part Three, "The I posits itself as determining the Not-I" to the foundational principle of Part Two, "The I posits itself as determined by the Not-I."
—Methodological short-cut: Part Three will begin with the antithesis between the (limited) I as intellect and the (unlimited) "absolute" or self-positing I.

I.

The contradiction between the absolute I and the I as intellect can be overcome only by viewing the I as the cause of the Not-I. But this, in turn, harbors a new contradiction.

pp. 247-8   —The apparent contradiction between the absolute I and the I as intellect.
p. 249   —Unity of the I (in virtue of its own, unconditional self-positing).
p. 249   —The I as intellect is dependent upon a (theoretically inexplicable) "check" on its infinitely outgoing activity.
pp. 249-51   —Strategy for resolving the conflict between the absolute and the intelligent I: the Not-I (which is posited by the intellect as responsible for the check) must somehow be determined (i.e., caused) by the absolute I.

1.) We have now inferred a *determinate* activity of the I from its *absolute* activity.

2.) It follows that the Not-I must be viewed as a product of the absolute I.

pp. 251-2   —Consequently, in addition to the absolute, self-positing activity of the I (§ 1), we must also posit a determinate (practical) activity by means of which the absolute I simultaneously determines the Not-I and limits itself. The I is therby posited in opposition to and in conflict with itself, since it contains both the principle of positing itself and the principle of not-positing itself.

pp. 252-3   *Remark*: On the true meaning of the second foundational principle (§ 2).

—Absolute positing requires the positing of the limited I and limited Not-I, the possibility of which presupposes the first-hand experience of a certain *factum* of consciousness.

II.

The contradiction implicit in the claim that the I is the cause of the Not-I can be resolved only by positing an activity on the part of the I in addition to its act of self-positing.

p. 254   —The contradiction between the independence and the dependence of the I.

pp. 254-5   —Absolute opposition (and contradiction) between the I and Not-I.

p. 255   —The contradiction between the I and the Not-I can be reduced to an opposition (and contradiction) between the infinite and the finite I.

pp. 255-6   —The contradiction between the infinite and the finite I can in turn be reduced to a contradiction between the infinite (or pure) and finite (or objective) activities of one and the same I.

pp. 256-7   —The I is *finite* insofar as its activity is *objective* and is *limited* (i.e., is an activity that posits an object existing for itself) and *infinite* insofar as its activity is *pure* and self-reverting.

pp. 257-8   —Both activities are activities of one and the same I and are related to each other as *cause* to *effect*, with the pure activity understood as the cause of the objective activity in the sense that it is by means of the pure activity that the I determines itself to engage in the objective activity. In this way the pure activity is directly related to the I and indirectly related to the Not-I.

Deduction of the I's practical activity of striving.

p. 258   —The infinite activity cannot actually be the cause of the objective activity, since the I cannot limit itself.

p. 258   —Re-examination of what is involved in the I's "pure and simple" positing of the Not-I (§ 2): the I is free to posit the boundary between itself and the Not-I anywhere it wishes within the infinite domain posited in § 1. But it still cannot be responsible for limiting itself.

pp. 258-60 —Hence there must be *another activity* of the I, in opposition to which the activity of the object is posited. The positing of any actual object presupposes this new activity, which is what connects the pure and objective activities of the I.

p. 260 —This newly derived activity of the I cannot actually annul the object, though this is what is demanded by the absolute character of the pure I: the Not-I *ought to* conform to the I.
Footnote: On the pure I and the "categorical imperative."

p. 261 —In relation to a possible object, the pure, self-reverting activity of the I becomes, not a force, but a *practical tendency*, an *infinite striving*.

pp. 262-3 —This practical activity of the I is the condition for any positing of an object: *no striving, no object*.

p. 263 *Footnote*: On intelligible fatalism.

p. 264 *Remark*: It has now for the first time been *demonstrated* that "reason is practical."

p. 264 *Objection*: The activity of the object must be connected with the I's striving, but how is such a connection even possible? It cannot be purely and simply posited by the pure I, so what could be the ground of such a connection?

pp. 265-7 *Reply*: Though this cannot be demonstrated a priori, a "non-equivalence" with itself simply arises within the I when it encounters within itself an "alien element" in the form of a *check* upon its original activity. The I, qua intellect, spontaneously engages in reflection upon itself. It then compares this "discovered" limitation of its own activity (which it experiences as a subjective "*feeling*") with its original positing of its own, complete self-identity. It thereby becomes conscious of itself as limited and posits the Not-I as the cause of this limitation. The infinite and finite "states" of the I are thus already synthetically united.

Relation of the infinite objective activity of the I to its finite objective activity: ideal vs. actual objects.

p. 267 —In contrast to the pure, self-reverting activity of the pure I, striving is an objective, albeit infinite activity (infinite, because it extends infinitely beyond any encountered check upon the original activity of the I). This is in contrast to the finite (theoretical) objective activity involved in positing an object as the cause of a feeling.

pp. 268-9 —Every "objective" activity is *determinate* and has a determinate object. The objects of the finite objective activity are *actual* objects, and the objects of the infinite objective activity are *ideal* objects, that is, determinate *ends* or *goals* of activity—objects posited by the I rather than the Not-I.

pp. 269-70 —Though the goal aimed at by the infinite objective activity of striving is always determinate (and thus finite), the activity itself is infinite, since it can always be revised and extended.

p. 270 *Remark*: On the necessary idea of a "completed infinity" as an indication that we are "destined for eternity."

p. 270 *Conclusion*: The I is infinite with respect to its striving, but it could not strive if it were not also finite.

Genetic derivation of the I's endless striving (and hence of its capacity for being affected) from the concept of the I as such. Transition from an indirect, apagogic method of proof to a direct, genetic method. Resumption of the "pragmatic history of the human mind."

pp. 270-1 —The striving of the I is conditioned by an encounter with a determinate check upon its activity, a check that is resisted by the objective infinite activity (that is, by the *striving*) of the I. But the demand for absolute causality must itself be originally present within the I as such. What is the basis of this original, outgoing activity of the I, without which no object is possible?

pp. 270-1 —If anything is ever to have any influence upon the I, the possibility of such influence must already be present within the I itself; that is, some "difference" or "alien element" must already be present within the I.

pp. 271-2 —Since the I consists only in *activity*, the difference in question can only be a difference with respect to the activity of the I: namely, a difference in the *directions* of its activity.

p. 273 —Inwardly directed or self-reverting activity is "centripetal," and outwardly directed activity is "centrifugal."

pp. 273-4 —The I is supposed to be what it is *for itself*, and it must therefore originally contain the principle of *spontaneously reflecting upon itself.* Insofar as the I reflects upon itself, the direction of its activity is centripetal, but insofar as the I is the object of its own reflection, its activity is centrifugal and extends into infinity. These are not two distinct activities but two different directions of one and the same activity, distinguishable only in reflection.

pp. 274-5 —The reflection by means of which these two directions of the I's activity are distinguished requires some "third thing," to which they can each be related. This third thing is the *demand* (which the I makes upon itself) that it *reflect upon itself in order to determine whether or not it really does manage "to fill infinity,"* which is to say, whether it really has fully determined the Not-I. But if it were to accomplish this there would no longer be any distinction between the inward and outward directions of the I's activity, since there would be no "check" or "impetus" from the Not-I.

p. 275 *Remark*: On the incomprehensibility of God's self-consciousness.

pp. 275-6 —If any actual consciousness is to be possible, the centrifugal activity of the I must be *checked* at some point, and the I must at the same time *reflect upon itself* in order to determine if it does in fact fill out all reality and then recognize that it does *not* do so. In this case, reflection *distinguishes* the original outward direction of the I's activity, which is consistent with its demand to fill infinity, from the centripetal direction acquired by this same original centrifugal activity once it has been checked.

p. 276   *Conclusion*: The necessary reflection of the I upon itself, along with the demand that it discover itself to comprise all reality. Has now been shown to be the basis upon which the I proceeds beyond itself and strives for absolute causality. Since the I not only "posits itself" but "posits itself *as* self-posited," and thus is reciprocally related to itself, it opens itself to the discovery—within itself—of the influence of the Not-I and thus posits itself as limited (as well as unlimited).

pp. 277-8   *Remark*: On the differences between and ultimate unity of the "absolute," "practical," and "theoretical" I's.

p. 278   —Overview of the systematic moments constituting the essential nature of any finite rational being.

p. 278   *Footnote*: On the inability of stoicism to explain consciousness.
    Remarks:

pp. 278-9   1.) The reciprocal relation between the I and the Not-I and the necessity of the check or impetus for any actual consciousness.

pp. 280-1   2.) Realistic and idealistic aspects of the *Wissenschaftslehre*. Identity of the real and ideal grounds of the Not-I. The circle from which the human mind cannot escape.

pp. 281-2   3.) *Ideal-realism/real-idealism*. Interaction of the I's practical and ideal powers and, again, the circle from which the finite mind can never escape.

pp. 282-3   4.) The finite I and the Idea of the thing in itself. Yet again, the circle from which the human mind can never escape.

pp. 283-4   5.) Free exercise of the creative power of imagination is required for understanding the *Wissenschaftslehre*.

§ 6. Third Theorem. In the Striving of the I There Is Posited at the Same Time an Opposed Striving of the Not-I, which Counterbalances that of the I.

pp. 285-6   *Methodological remark*: On the differences between the methods and objects of inquiry of Parts Two and Three. The former deals with *how* things are posited by the I; the latter, with *what* is posited. Hence it is the practical portion of *GWL* that deals with metaphysics or "things in themselves."

pp. 286-7   *The striving of the I must be counterbalanced by the striving of the Not-I.*
    —The concept of striving is unintelligible apart from that of an opposing striving, which possesses the same force as the original striving.
    1.) Striving is a cause that is not a cause, and everything that strives for causality possesses force.
    2.) Striving possesses a determinate quantity; it is limited.
    3.) What strives is limited by a force outside itself.
    4.) This opposing force must itself be a striving to exercise causality, though it too fails to exercise such causality.
    5.) Consequently, these two opposed forces counterbalance each other.

§ 7. Fourth Theorem. The Striving of the I, the Opposed Striving of the Not-I, and the Equilibrium or Counterbalance between Them Must Be Posited.

Deduction of drive and feeling.

pp. 287-8   A.) The striving of the I is posited as something stabilized: i.e., as a *drive.*

1.) The striving of the I is stabilized as *something*. It is therefore posited not as an activity, but as something fixed and stabilized.

2.) Qua striving, this striving of the I is posited as a causality that exercises no effect upon the Not-I, but does affect the I itself: namely, by producing itself as such within the I. Such a determinate and stabilized self-produced striving is a *drive.*

—Analysis of the concept of a drive as (1.) grounded in the character of that to which it is attributed, and thus "self-produced," (2.) something fixed and enduring, and (3.) directed at exercising causality beyond itself, but unable to do so, qua mere drive. If a drive is to be posited, it must be posited in this manner.

p. 288   B.) An opposed striving of the Not-I must be posited in order to posit the striving of the I.

pp. 288-90   C.) The equilibrium between the striving of the I and the Not-I is posited as a *feeling* of *inability* or *coercion.*

Deduction of feeling.

—The I possesses both a real drive to fill infinity and a tendency to reflect upon itself, which it can do only if it finds this drive to be limited at some determinate point.

—The equilibrium between the striving of the I and the Not-I expresses itself within the I as a *feeling* of compulsion or inability.

—Analysis of "inability" as including (1.) a continued striving, (2.) a limitation of an actual activity through the presence *within the I* of something that limits the drive.

—Activity and limitation (passive affection) are combined in feeling.

—Feeling is a purely subjective state of the I, which the I "explains to itself" by positing something outside itself as the cause of the limitation in question.

Remarks:

pp. 289-90   1.) Objective validity and feeling, the necessary actions of the mind, and the impossibility of escaping the circle of the I.

pp. 290-1   2.) The differences between the standpoints of the philosophical observer and of the observed I.

§ 8. Fifth Theorem. Feeling Must Itself Be Posited and Determined.

pp. 291-2   *Preliminary remark*: Feeling both satisfies and fails to satisfy the I's drive to reflect upon itself as filling infinity.

1.) The I originally strives to fill infinity, in opposition to all objects.

2.) In order to determine whether it actually fills infinity, the I must reflect upon itself; but it can reflect only upon what is limited. What limits the I is the object, hence the I reflects upon itself as limited and as conditioned by the object.

3.) The limitation present in *feeling* both satisfies and fails to satisfy the I's drive to reflect upon itself.

a.) It is satisfied with respect to its form, since, in feeling, the I is indeed reflecting upon itself.

b.) It is not satisfied with respect to its content, since the I is supposed to "fill infinity," whereas the "feeling I" is always limited.

c.) The I's positing of its non-satisfaction with feeling is conditioned by its proceeding beyond the determinate limit that is present in feeling. Hence something infinite must be posited beyond the sphere of the I.

pp. 292-3   I.) Striving in the absence of reflection. *Example*: an elastic ball impacted by another ball.

a.) The first ball possesses an inner force, which strives to exercise causality upon itself (to expand), but it is unable to expand because of the opposing striving of the second ball. In this sense, it can be said to possess a "drive."

b.) A similar inner force and drive are present in the second ball.

c.) If the force of one ball is increased, then that of the second is diminished. But now they are in equilibrium.

p. 293   II.) The I's reflection upon its own striving.

—Unlike a lifeless body, the I is supposed to exercise causality upon itself, even if it is unable to exercise external causality (as in the case of a drive).

—The I accomplishes this by engaging in *reflection*, which is therefore an inner manifestation of the drive in question.

Remarks:

pp. 283-94   1.) Reciprocal interaction of striving and reflection. Neither is possible for the I without the other.

p. 294   2.) The necessary finitude of the I and the circuit of its functions: No restriction, no drive; no drive, no reflection; no reflection, no drive and no limitation.

p. 294   3.) The ideal and real activities of the I.

—The original striving or drive or force of the I is both ideal and real, directed both at the I itself and at something outside the I. It is then divided by the limitation encountered in its outward direction, which annuls the (real) force in that direction but not the inwardly directed, self-reverting, or *ideal* force.

p. 294   4.) The *drive to representation*, by means of which the I becomes an intellect, is a manifestation of the ideal activity of the I.

pp. 294-5   5.) All theoretical laws are grounded in the practical, moral law. Our system of representations depends upon our willing and acting, and not vice versa. Otherwise, fatalism would be unavoidable.

pp. 295-6   III.) The feeling of an inner drive or force is what separates what is living from what is lifeless.

pp. 296-7   IV.) The I's own inner, driving force determines an object for the ideal activity of the I, though the I possesses no feeling nor intuition of this object.

a.) The I discovers itself to be driven beyond and outside itself by this inner force.

b.) Though it cannot determine the real activity of the I, this drive does determine its ideal activity: it goes beyond the actual object of the limited ideal activity and posits an object that would be produced were this drive to possess causality.

c.) This act of production is not accompanied by any feeling or intuition of its object. We must therefore explain how the I can be driven toward something with which it is unacquainted.

pp. 297-8   V.) The I feels its own outgoing drive as a feeling of *compulsion* or *inability*.

—A drive can be felt only when an ideal activity is directed at the object of that drive, which requires some limitation of the real activity of the I.

—This produces the I's reflection upon—or rather, *feeling of*—itself as *limited*.

—The feeling in question thus includes feelings of the driving force and of the object of the same, neither of which manifests itself as such, plus a feeling of *compulsion* or *inability*.

§ 9. Sixth Theorem. Feeling Must Be Further Determined and Delineated.

Deduction of the I's feeling of itself.

pp. 297-9   I.) *The I posits itself for itself as a feeling subject.*

1.) The I that *feels itself* to be limited, or is limited "for itself," must spontaneously reflect upon itself with the goal of restoring—for itself—the activity that has been limited, thereby positing itself as free and unlimited.

—This act of reflecting upon the I that is already engaged in reflection occurs absolutely spontaneously.

Remark: There is a spontaneous *leap* from "life" to "intelligence." This is why philosophy must *begin* with the I and why materialism cannot explain consciousness on the basis of natural laws.

2.) The I spontaneously reflects upon itself as engaged in feeling.

—This spontaneous act on the part of the I is an *ideal* one and therefore must have as its object something present within the I, namely, a feeling. This act of reflection is directed at the I itself, insofar as it is already engaged in the kind of reflection associated with *feeling*. Consequently, the spontaneous act in question is a reflection upon a reflection or an action directed at an action.

—In this way, the feeling subject is posited as an I. But since an I is what determines itself, the feeling subject can be posited as an I only insofar as it is determined to engage in feeling by its own *drive*.

—What the I feels in this case is therefore itself and its own force. The I is the "feeling subject."

pp. 299–301 **II.** *As both the feeling subject and what is felt, the I is simultaneously passive and active and interacts reciprocally with itself.*

1.) In reflecting upon itself as engaged in feeling, the I is simultaneously active and passive.

2.) In this case, the I is active in relation to what is felt and passive in relation to its own externally directed drive.

3.) In this act of reflecting upon itself as engaged in feeling, the I posits itself as limited by the Not-I.

4.) The feeling subject is posited as actively producing the Not-I by means of ideal activity, but the I that reflects upon and thus feels the feeling subject is passively related to the Not-I, though these two I's are supposed to be one and the same.

5.) While engaged in feeling, the I never reflects upon its own ideal activity; it is therefore always related to the Not-I only passively and is therefore unaware of its own activity. Nevertheless, what is actually felt in this case is only the I itself.

p. 301 *Remark*: *Reality* is possible only through the relation of *feeling* to the I. Hence, only *belief* is possible with regard to reality.

§ 10. Seventh Theorem. Drive Itself Must Be Posited and Determined.

Deduction of the feeling of longing.

pp. 301–2 1.) In order to reflect upon and to posit the drive in question, it must manifest itself in some way within the I (since the I can reflect only upon itself).

p. 302 2.) The original drive of the I (which is what is hindered in "feeling") aims at real causality, but cannot achieve this, since the I's *striving* lacks causal efficacy and is restricted by the Not-I.

p. 302 3.) Because of its inner tendency to do so, the I must reflect whenever it is limited; hence it must reflect upon its own limited state as a feeling subject, and this produces a feeling of that state.

pp. 302–3 4.) The feeling in question is a feeling of an activity or drive that seems to have no object and reveals itself only as a *need*, which is felt as a *longing*.

The feelings of longing and compulsion must be distinguished from and reciprocally related to each other.

p. 303 5.) Since longing expresses itself only as a feeling, it can be determined only by determining this feeling, which can be determined only in relation to another feeling: the feeling of limitation or compulsion.

p. 303   6.) No feeling of compulsion, no feeling of longing; no feeling of longing, no feeling of compulsion.

—By means of this feeling of longing the I is *internally* driven beyond itself, and an external object reveals itself *within the I.*

p. 303   7.) Though synthetically united, *limitation* and *longing* are also posited in opposition to each other, since, in the feeling of limitation, the I is felt as *passively affected* and, in the feeling of longing, it is felt as *active.*

Longing and compulsion are manifestations of one and the same original drive.

pp. 303-4   8.) Longing and compulsion are manifestations of the same original drive, but directed at two different powers of the I. Directed at the theoretical power of reflection, this drive produces a feeling of compulsion; directed at the practical power of striving, it produces a feeling of longing.

p. 304   9.) Longing is therefore the original and independent manifestation of striving, which is not arrested by any limitation.

Remark: Longing is the vehicle of all practical laws, which must be derivable from it.

Longing and limitation are posited in opposition to and contradict each other.

p. 304   10.) With respect to the limitation of the I, longing is accompanied by a feeling of compulsion, related to a *real object.* With respect to the original striving of the I, longing is related to an *ideal object.* These real and ideal objects are posited in opposition to each other.

pp. 304-5   11.) As simultaneously limited and unlimited, finite and infinite, the I appears to contradict itself.

The ideal as the product of longing.

p. 305   12.) Longing determines the ideal activity to go beyond the limitations discovered through self-feeling, in which the external world reveals itself to the I *within the I itself.*

pp. 306-7   13.) The reality toward which longing is directed (i.e., the ideal) must be manifest through a feeling posited in opposition to the I's feeling of limitation and must be produced by the ideal activity of the I.

p. 306   14.) The object posited by the feeling of limitation is something real, which is posited in opposition to the object of longing, which is something ideal.

Deduction of the drive to determination.

pp. 306-7   15.) The I that freely reflects upon itself as engaged in feeling obtains a *feeling of itself* and thus posits itself both as what is determining (since, in this reflection, it determines itself for itself) and as what is determined. Hence it must possess an absolute *power of determining.*

p. 307   16.) Related to the I's power of self-determination, the original, outgoing activity of the I becomes a *drive to determine differently*, that is, a striving to *modify* that external reality that has already been given to the I through feeling as *determinable matter.*

p. 307   17.) This then is the object of longing: to *modify* an already given matter.

Limitation of the drive toward determination makes possible determination by means of the ideal activity.

p. 307   18.) The feeling of longing presupposes a limitation of the drive to determination, and this limitation must manifest itself as a distinctive feeling.

pp. 307–9   19.) The externally directed drive to determination encounters a limit and determines the ideal activity to posit an independent object as the ground of the I's limitation and to strive to determine this object. This results in a distinctive *feeling* of the *constitution* or *properties* of the object in question.

Deduction of the drive to representation.

pp. 309–12   20.) The relationship of the drive to determination to the ideal activity of the I.

a.) The ideal activity of the I drives its original, spontaneously self-determining activity outward.

b.) The task of the ideal, reflecting activity is to form *images* or *copies* of the object of reflection, whether that is the I or the Not-I, rather than to alter this object. It is therefore the *drive to representation.*

c.) The I can reflect only upon what is both determined and determining, a criterion it transfers from itself (as object of reflection) to the Not-I.

Example: Simple sensations, such as "sweet," are both determined and determining (i.e., not dependent upon other sensations), because such a sensation lies *within the I*, for which it is simple (i.e., both determined and determining), in accordance with the I's own law of limitation.

d.) In the case of reflection upon the I, the reflecting subject and the object of reflection are the same, which is not the case when one reflects upon the Not-I, even though the same law of determination applies in both cases.

e.) The drive to determination can determine only the ideal activity of the I, which is assigned the task of producing an image of an object that is given to it, but not of modifying that object.

A subjective determination of the I is transferred to an external thing.

pp. 312–15   21.) In opposition to itself as limited and *determinate*, the I encounters within itself resistance to its real activity. The limited real activity of the I is first posited as an inner, self-determining force or "intensive matter" and then projected outside of the I by the ideal activity, in accordance with the laws of the same, and attributed to the Not-I.

a.) Unable to determine the real activity of the I, the drive to determination determines its ideal activity and drives it to posit a Not-I, which is how consciousness of the I and of the Not-I are connected with one another.

b.) Every determinate thing of which we are conscious is something *particular*. Subjective feelings are transferred to objective things as properties of "matter," as the bearer of these properties; hence, all of our objective representations are grounded in subjective feelings. Matter too is originally something subjective, a product of the powers of imagination and thinking.

—*Reply to a possible objection*: This applies as well to tactile sensations.

The I must reflect upon itself while engaged in determining the object and must therefore interrupt its own activity of determining.

p. 315   **22.)** The drive to representation is directed at the I insofar as it is engaged in reflecting upon the limitation of its own real activity; hence the I here reflects upon itself as determining the object, and it must do so.

pp. 316   **23.)** In order to reflect upon itself in this manner, the I must interrupt its activity of determining the object in order to be able to reflect thereupon.

p. 316   **24.)** A *feeling* arises when the I reflects upon this interruption or limitation of its determining activity, and it ascribes this limitation to the object.

—The limitations in question are "limitations of intension," the kind that distinguish one feeling from another.

—A feeling is present only under two conditions: a *limitation* of the I's drive toward determination and spontaneous *reflection* upon this limitation.

—The I is not conscious of limiting its drive to determination by means of free reflection, however; instead, what is present is a feeling of being limited by the determinacy of the thing.

The distinction between feeling and intuition.

pp. 316-18 **25.)** In positing itself as intuiting a particular feeling (understood as an image of a particular object) the I posits itself as determining the boundary between itself and the object of this feeling, and hence as limiting that object and freely producing an image of the same.

—Such an image is therefore *contingent* in relationship to the I. But the I does not reflect upon its own reflection upon this feeling and instead attributes this contingency to the Not-I, which it views as contingent in relation to another Not-I.

—The "law of determination" is that everything determinate must be determined as such by itself.

—In its ideal activity the I at first hovers over the indeterminate boundary between itself and the Not-I, but, as actively engaged in intuiting, it must posit itself as *determined* by itself to posit a determinate boundary between itself and the object.

p. 318   26.) On the other hand, as an object of the I's intuition, this same object is supposed to be self-determined, which means that the I does not voluntarily produce its image of the object, which contradicts the preceding conclusion.

pp. 318-19   27.) The first step toward overcoming this contradiction is to distinguish *feeling* from *intuition*. The I's limitation at point X is only *felt*, whereas what is intuited (i.e., the object that is felt) is *freely posited*.

—Feeling *refers to reality*, but is *blind*; intuition *sees*, but is empty. Feeling and intuition must therefore be synthetically united.

Synthesis of feeling and intuition through reciprocal determination. Deduction of the drive to reciprocal determination.

pp. 319-20   28.) In addition to the object posited on the basis of feeling X, the ideal activity also freely posits in opposition to X another feeling (and another object) = Y. X and Y mutually exclude one another and are posited in consequence of the I's *drive to reciprocal determination*.

—It is the I's original drive toward determination that in this case determines its ideal activity to posit X and Y as reciprocally determining one another.

Deduction of the drive for change as such, as manifest in a longing for different feelings.

p. 320   29.) The boundary between the I and the Not-I, and thus object X, is posited by means of feeling. But this is also true of object Y, which commences at this same boundary point. Since both X and Y are related to feeling, so is the drive for reciprocal determination, which now reveals itself to be a drive for *different feelings* or for *change as such*.

—The I's drive for change as such manifests itself as a *longing* for "something else."

—Ideal activity and feeling are united in this drive for change as such, as are ideality and the I's drive toward reality.

—In longing, the I's (thwarted) external drive toward reality is merely *felt*, but it is then modified by the freely operating ideal activity of the I, in positing something beyond the present boundary of the object. This is an example of how a theoretical operation of the mind is grounded in a practical power of the I.

p. 321   30.) Every feeling depends upon the presence of some limitation, which cannot be produced by the I. This also applies to the new feeling that is posited by the drive for reciprocal determination in opposition to the feeling of limitation.

p. 321   31.) Longing is the feeling that underlies the positing of something in opposition to X. What is longed-for is thus determined as the feeling of "something other" than X.

pp. 321-2   32.) Whereas the present object is *felt*, the longed-for object can only be *intuited*, and intuited only negatively, as *not* involving the feeling associated with the present object. Feeling and intuition are synthetically united in longing.

—Since ideal activity cannot produce any feeling, it determines the longed-for object only negatively: as *not* being what is presently felt.

—Such negative determination continues into infinity, as is illustrated be simple sensations, which can be defined only negatively: "sweet" is "not sour," etc.

§ 11. Eighth Theorem. Feelings Themselves Must Be Capable of Being Posited in Opposition to Each Other.

pp. 322-3   1.) Ideal activity can determine feeling X only by relating it to another feeling, Y.

p. 323   2.) In order to do this, the ideal activity must posit X and Y in opposition to each other as well as unite them synthetically.

—This raises three questions: How is feeling possible? How are feelings posited as synthetically united? How are they posited in opposition to each other?

Feeling is posited as sensation.

p. 323   3.) Reflection upon the (unconscious) reflection involved in feeling results in the positing of this feeling by the ideal activity of the I as a *sensation* of matter.

Feelings are synthetically united by being posited as mutually limiting each other.

pp. 323-4   4.) The I is unable to reflect upon either of two opposed feelings without reflecting upon them both, since they mutually limit each other.

It is by means of feelings of approval and disapproval that feelings are posited in opposition to each other.

p. 324   5.) Since longing is connected with feeling X and thereby with a demand for another feeling (=Y), feeling Y is one that would be accompanied by *satisfaction*.

pp. 324-5   6.) Satisfaction of longing by the new feeling, Y, manifests itself as a feeling of *approval*: a feeling of harmony between drive and action. In feeling Y, the I reflects upon itself as both what determines and is determined by this feeling.

p. 325   7.) In the first feeling, X, the drive and the action of the I are not in harmony. Feeling X is therefore accompanied by a feeling of *disapproval* (in relation to feeling Y).

p. 325   8.) Objects X and Y are no longer distinguished merely as opposites; X is now determined as "producing a feeling of disapproval," and Y as "producing a feeling of approval."

—The "inner determinations" of things, as related to feelings, are the degrees to which they are capable of producing feelings of approval or disapproval.

Outline of What Is Distinctive of the Wissenschaftslehre with Regard to the Theoretical Power

§ 1. The Concept of the Particular in the Theoretical *Wissenschaftslehre*.

§ 2. First Theorem: The Indicated *Factum* [i.e., Feeling] Is Posited through Sensation, or, Deduction of Sensation.

§ 3. Second Theorem: The Sensing Subject Is Posited
through Intuition, or, Deduction of Intuition.

p. 340   —We must now determine how the I posits for itself sensation, as well as how it posits itself as the sensing subject.

pp. 340-1   I. The conflicted and therefore static objective activity of the I that is engaged in sensing must be posited in opposition to the unsuppressed actual activity of the I.
—What is sensed by the sensing I is its own conflicted and suppressed objective activity, which it regards as a static non-activity, that is, as the material substrate of an opposing force.

pp. 341-3   II. By mean of a new (ideal) activity of *intuiting*, the I freely ascribes to the Not-I the determinacy of the I's own constrained state of sensation.
—The real and objective activities of the I are synthetically united by a third, freely undertaken (ideal) activity of the I, the activity of *intuiting*.
—Intuiting is a *determinate, limited* ideal positing on the part of the I, which is therefore the *real ground* of intuiting.
—The (indirect) *ideal ground* of intuiting is the Not-I, which is supposed to explain the *determinacy* of the intuition.
—In intuiting, the ideal and real grounds coincide, inasmuch as the intuition is regarded as *both* posited by the I and posited by the Not-I.
—The I and the Not-I are here regarded as both independent of one another and in harmony with one another, and this presupposition is the foundation of all cognition.

pp. 343-4   *Remark*: On the method of this deduction, in which what is first viewed as an act of the I (an act that explains a certain product that is present for the I) is, in turn, shown to be the product of another act.

pp. 344-6   III. In sensation, the I actively determines its own passive state by means of limitation.
—In sensation, the I is simultaneously active and passive.
—In an *act of determining* an activity, the I is related to a state of passive affection, since what is to be determined—that is, *limited*—must be given to the I (which cannot limit itself).
—Hence the "third thing" that makes it possible to synthesize the I's activity and state of passive affection is *limitation*. In sensation, the I and Not-I reciprocally limit each other.
—The I becomes an *intellect* by freely crossing the boundary between itself and the Not-I and transferring to the Not-I something from itself, which is the same as absorbing into itself something from the Not-I.

IV. As an intellect engaged in intuiting its own state, the I posits itself as the limited, sensing subject and posits what it senses as "a sensation."

pp. 346-7   —Only if it is *limited* can the I be posited as the sensing subject.

pp. 347-8   A.) In sensation, the Not-I is *excluded* from the I.
             —In order to posit itself as limited (i.e., as the sensing subject), the activity of the I must extend beyond the boundary between the I and Not-I.
             —In order to posit itself as *limited* the I must also posit itself in opposition to its limited state as *unlimited*.
             —The activity of the I that is restricted at the boundary with the Not-I is its *real* activity, and the activity that extends beyond this boundary is an *ideal* activity. These activities reciprocally determine each other.
             —Ideality and reality are thus synthetically united; if nothing is ideal then nothing is real, and vice versa.

pp. 348-50   B.) In sensation, the restricted activity of the I is *related* to its pure activity.
             —What is related to the I in sensation is the activity lying between itself and its boundary with the Not-I, an activity that is both real (albeit restricted at this boundary) and ideal.
             —That to which the ideal, relating activity of the I is related is itself a (restricted) ideal activity of the I; consequently, this activity appears to the relating I not as an activity, but as a state of passive affection.
             —The proper name for the activity relating the I to its own limited ideal activity is *intuition*. What is intuited is the I that is engaged in sensing.
             —The subject responsible for relating this activity to the I is the I itself, which is, however, unaware of itself while engaged in intuiting, but is instead lost in its object.
             —With this, we obtain a *substrate* for consciousness: namely, the *being* of that pure activity of the I that is posited as independent of the Not-I, though it is posited in this manner only in consequence of something posited in opposition to the I.

pp. 350-4   V. When a sensation is posited by means of intuition, the boundary between the I and the Not-I is viewed as capable of indefinite extension beyond the actual boundary, thereby allowing the sensed object to be incorporated into the I and related to the sensation.

pp. 350-2   A.) *Derivation of the I's free act of limiting the Not-I by means of its unrestricted ideal activity.*
             —Sensation itself (and not just what is sensed) must be related to the I by means of limitation.
             —Since limiting is an act of the I, what is limited must be contained in the I.
             —What is sensed was related to the I by positing a contingent activity in opposition to the I, an activity the I is able either to

posit or not to posit; hence the I has the general ability to-posit-or-not-to-posit, which means that these acts of positing and non-positing are synthetically united.

pp. 352-3   B.) The connection between what is sensed and sensation.
—This synthetic act of positing and non-positing is what connects what is sensed with the sensation.
—In this synthetic act of positing and non-positing, the I posits the activity of the Not-I, but does not posit any determinate boundary between its own activity and that of the Not-I; instead, it is able to posit the Not-I at any point in chooses. This is therefore a free *act of limiting* on the part of the unrestricted ideal activity of the I.
—To this act of positing-and-non-positing there corresponds something that is simultaneously posited and not posited: namely, the activity of the Not-I, as the I extends the boundary between itself and the Not-I.

pp. 353-4   C.) *The boundary between the I and the Not-I, which is both real and ideal, is what permits what is sensed to be related to sensation.*
—This boundary is *real* insofar as it is posited by the Not-I and *ideal* insofar as it is posited by the I; hence, it is posited by both.
—This boundary is real insofar as it is ideal (i.e., posited by the I) and ideal insofar as it is real (i.e., posited by the Not-I).
—The I is related to what is sensed by means of this limit or boundary between itself and the Not-I, a limit that is simultaneously a real product of the Not-I and an ideal product of the I that posits it.
—In such an intuition the I "loses itself in its object" and does not refer the sensation to the sensing subject.

VI. Synthetic unity of the sensing subject and the object sensed.
pp. 354-5   —The unlimited, ideal activity of the I must determine its limited, real activity, and vice versa. How is this possible?

pp. 355-8   A.) The various activities of the I that are involved in intuition.
—The unlimited ideal activity of the I is a condition for the relation between the unlimited and limited activities of the I, but this relation is not a condition for the unlimited ideal activity, which must already be present within the I.
—This unlimited ideal activity must be posited as not limited by the boundary between the I and the Not-I, which limits the real activity of the I.
—This same boundary is related to the ideal activity, insofar as the latter extends beyond it.
—The boundary point and its ideal extension are synthetically united by being related to each other by another, as yet undisclosed, ideal activity of the I.

—Three activities of the I have now been discovered to be involved in intuition: one whose object is the unlimited ideal activity of the I; one whose object is the real, limited activity of the I; and one that moves the boundary point from the real to the ideal activity and extends it indefinitely.

pp. 358-61   **B.)** The I cannot posit itself for itself without positing itself as limited, thereby transcending or going beyond itself and positing a Not-I in order to explain to itself its own limitation.

—Our task is to find some basis for distinguishing the ideal from the real activity of the I, other than the limitation of one of these activities.

—The I cannot posit itself for itself without limiting itself, that is, without positing itself as limited.

—The I has an original tendency both to "fill up infinity" and to reflect upon itself in order to determine if it has accomplished this.

—The I cannot reflect upon itself, however, unless it is limited, that is, unless its striving to fill infinity is curbed at some point.

—When this occurs, the I feels itself and thus exists *for itself* as the passively affected subject.

—But the I is at this point not aware of itself as actively engaged in reflecting upon its own limited activity in accordance with the laws of its own nature, a reflection that is conditioned by something outside itself.

—The I now posits itself simply as passively affected or as limited by something outside itself.

pp. 361-2   *Remarks*:

1.) Concerning the thing in itself and the "circular thinking" engaged in by the transcendental dogmatist.

2.) The I is not ordinarily conscious of engaging in the act just deduced (which requires a much higher level of *philosophical* reflection), but there is a parallel between original self-consciousness and the way we attempt to orient ourselves whenever we awaken from a deep sleep.

pp. 362-5   **C.)** *Deduction of outer intuition.*

Postulate: When proceeding beyond point C (the boundary between the activities of the I and the Not-I), the I must reflect upon itself.

—In reflecting upon what lies beyond C, the I posits the product of this reflection as an active Not-I, though it is not at first conscious of doing this, since it has not yet reflected upon its own act of reflection.

—The I's very act of reflection limits the activity of the Not-I, which is now present only as a substrate of force, or as "matter."

—Since the I has not reflected upon the conflict between its own activity and the activity it attributes to the Not-I, no *consciousness* yet arises, neither of the sensed object nor of the sensing I.

VII. The I reflects upon its own activities and thereby posits itself both as what is reflected upon and as the subject engaged in reflecting.

Deduction of the "mediating intuition" that synthetically unites the image and its object.

pp. 365-87   —The I is finally in a position to observe or to reflect upon its own activities, including its own acts of reflection.

—It thereby discovers, for itself, the following products of its own actions: a limited, perceptible I; a limited, perceptible Not-I; and a point of contact or boundary between them.

—The I has an original tendency to reflect upon itself, a tendency that continues into infinity and is actualized whenever the I is limited (as it must be, if it is to posit itself as an I and hence if it is to be an I at all).

—The limitation of the I is first present to the I in the form of *feeling*, from which everything else pertaining to the theoretical portion of the *Wissenschaftslehre* must be derived.

—Unlike the previous "reflection" of the I's activity, which occurs necessarily and unconsciously whenever and because the I is limited by a feeling, this new reflection is one that arises *spontaneously* from the I itself. It is still *conditioned* by feeling, but not *necessitated* thereby.

—The following investigation will first consider the I reflected upon in this new reflection, then the I engaged in this act of reflecting, and finally, the synthesis of these two.

pp. 367-9   **A.)** *Synthetic unity of the I's feeling of compulsion and the attributes of the Not-I.*

—First, let us consider *the I that is reflected upon* in this new, spontaneous act in which the I reflects upon itself.

—The I explains to itself a determinate feeling of compulsion as caused by the determinate attributes or properties of the Not-I.

—Both the limited, *real* activity of the I and its spontaneous, *ideal* act of reflection upon itself as limited are acts of one and the same I, which ideally posits its real activity as limited by the attributes of the thing, as the ground of its feeling of compulsion.

pp. 369-71   **B.)** *Synthetic unity of the limited real and unlimited ideal activities of the I.*

—Let us now consider *the I that engages spontaneously in this new act of reflection.*

—As a condition for the possibility of the previously derived unity of a feeling and the properties of the Not-I, the I must reflect upon its own ideal activity and posit it as extending beyond the boundary between the I and the Not-I.

—The I can posit and reflect only upon what is limited; hence what it must posit is not this infinite, outgoing ideal activity itself, but is instead the *substrate* of the same (which is, of course, a product of the I's own absolute or productive activity).

—The I feels itself to be compelled to do this, but the productive activity of positing a substrate for the attributes of the Not-I has its ground solely in the I itself.

—Such a substrate of the properties of the Not-I is related to the feeling I by the *free and absolute activity* of the pure I itself; hence the I possesses within itself *the ground of the synthetic relationship* between its ideal and real activities, even though the feeling I is unaware of this.

p. 371   *Remark*: The point of unity between ideality and reality, representation and thing, is the unconditioned freedom of the self-positing I.

Footnote: On Diogenes and the practical, "common sense" proof of freedom.

C.) *The I posits the Not-I as its own product and does so by means of a "mediating intuition," which connects images and things.*

p. 372   —On the need for a higher synthesis of the preceding syntheses: namely, a synthesis of the I that is sensed and the I that senses.

—In the preceding synthesis A, the feeling I is limited and posits itself as limited; in synthesis B, it is free, and it (indirectly) posits itself as free by positing a substrate for the attributes of the object, a substrate that is a product of the intuiting I.

—In both syntheses, the I posits itself as both limited and limiting, but how is this possible?

—The following two, conflicting foundational principles can be derived from the two preceding syntheses:

pp. 372-3   1.) Active self-determination presupposes a state of passive affection, in which the object is given to the I prior to its acting.

—In order to posit itself as acting, the I must already have posited itself as not acting and posited its own force as limited by a given object.

p. 373   2.) In order to posit itself as limited, the I must already have posited the boundary between its own force and that of the Not-I and thus must already have posited itself as acting.

—Resolution of this contradiction by means of an *unconscious intuition*, which connects or "*mediates* between" an image and its object, each of which is impossible without the other.

pp. 373-4   —The sensing I does not realize that it is free; for itself, it is limited and compelled and does not realize that it itself, as engaged in intuiting, has produced that Not-I which it posits as limiting it.

—In freely reflecting upon its own activity of intuiting the Not-I, the I spontaneously "interrupts" and limits the latter, intuiting activity by means of its new activity of *reflecting*. But it cannot engage in such a spontaneous, self-determining activity unless there is another action of the I, one that is limited by this new action. Since nothing pertain to the I but activity, it can freely "determine itself" only by determining another of its own actions.

—By means of this new spontaneous act of *reflection*, which interprets its productive activity of intuiting, the I posits the Not-I as its own product.

—The I posits the Not-I as its own product only *indirectly*, however: namely, by positing this product as an *image* of what it takes to be a *contingent property* of the object.

—As a product of the I's own activity, the *image* is posited in opposition to a determinate "something," which is not a product of the I: namely, the *actual thing* that possesses these contingent properties and is the product of a prior act of intuiting.

—Since the image is supposed to be a *copy* of the thing, the thing must be contained in or accessible to the I after all. Consequently, a determinate, unconscious intuition of the thing lies at the basis of this relationship between the image and the thing.

pp. 375-7   *Remarks*:

—On the vital significance of that unconscious and immediate intuition that connects or "mediates between" an image and its object.

—When reflected upon, the productive activity of *intuiting* is interrupted, allowing the reflecting I to *form an image* of what it takes to be an *independent object*, which it does by reflecting upon the *intuition* it has just produced.

—The I is unable simultaneously to posit itself as forming images and as intuiting the object; instead, it is concerned only with forming an image of a product of its own, interrupted act of productive intuition, which it takes to be an independent Not-I.

—The I's immediate, unconscious productive intuition is the mediating link between the *image*, which is assigned to the I, and the *object*, which is assigned to the Not-I, or between "representations" and "things."

Deduction of a new law of the rational mind: the image and the thing reciprocally condition each other.

pp. 377-9   —The task is to explain why the I takes the (subjective) image it has formed to be an image of something outside itself, an (objective) Not-I.

—The image or representation is related to the I, since the I forms this image with complete freedom.

—This same image is supposed to be related to some external thing, which determines it as precisely *this* image.

—The conflict between the "subjective" and "objective" interpretations of the image is resolved by a law of the mind that asserts that the image and thing are synthetically connected and therefore inseparable.

Deduction of the relationship between a thing or substance and its properties.

pp. 379-81 —The task is to demonstrate that the relationship between a determinate image and its object is impossible unless that image is presupposed to be a *free creation of the mind.*
—Though the I is not immediately conscious of its own act of relating an image to its object, it is *indirectly* conscious of its own role in
this process, inasmuch as it posits the object as capable of being
otherwise, or as *contingent.*
—In a determinate image a particular property is attributed to an
object, which is determined thereby—that is, determined by the I's
assignment of this property to this object.
—The *contingency* of a thing's properties follows from the fact that
they were freely posited as such by the I.
—The power of imagination is responsible for assigning a set of contingent properties to an object, an object which, apart from such an
assignment, can be simple said *to be,* but not to be anything
determinate.
Conclusion: To posit the properties of any real thing or substance as
contingent is to posit them as products of the I, and hence to connect
them with the I.

Deduction of the categories of substantiality and causal efficacy.

pp. 381-4 —If "A+B" is the totality, then this totality must be simultaneously
determined and not determined by A and by B.
—The I posits itself as the totality, as self-determining, but in doing
so excludes from itself the Not-I.
—The question is whether the synthetic unity or totality of the
(limited) I and Not-I (A+B) is ultimately determined by the I (A) or
the Not-I (B), and the answer is that this totality is determined by A,
but only because A itself is at once equal and not equal to itself,
which is possible only because the power of imagination has the ability to unify the I.
—In forming an image, the I posits a determinate property in opposition to a still indeterminate image, and hence in opposition to the I
itself.
—Reflecting upon the determinacy of the property, which it has now
excluded from itself, the I posits itself (A or A+B) as determined by
something outside itself (B).
Remark: All the actions of the human mind that have been indicated
here occur *simultaneously,* in synthetic unity with one another.

pp. 384-6 —Reflecting further upon the determinacy of this same property,
while at the same time reflecting upon its own spontaneous reflection upon this property, the I attributes to this determinate property
the characteristic feature that relates it to the I: *contingency.*

Remark: The I cannot posit a limit without positing something as the ground of that limit. *Determining* and *producing* always go together, and this is the basis of the identity of consciousness.

—Consequently, the contingency in question is no longer attributed to the I; instead, it is attributed to another Not-I, which is posited as the necessary substrate of the contingent property.

—A property is contingent in relation to the substrate or thing of which it is a property, and this same substrate is necessary in relation to that property. This is the relationship of *substantiality*, in which a contingent Not-I (a property) is posited within the I's image and another, necessary Not-I (its substrate, the thing) is excluded from the I.

pp. 385-6   —Reflecting further upon its relation to the "necessary Not-I" (the substrate or thing), the I posits the latter as determining the property (the "contingent Not-I").

—Property and thing are now posited in opposition to each other, the former as *contingent* and the latter as *necessary*.

—Property and thing are synthetically united by another absolute act of the power of imagination, in which this *union* is itself posited as *contingent*, which is to say that the property is posited to be dependent upon the (necessary) thing or substrate.

—The I transfers the concept of *acting* from itself to the necessary Not-I, thus viewing the property in question as contingent upon the object, which is now viewed as an *actual thing*. Such a relationship is one of *causal efficacy*.

Remarks:

p. 386   1.) The powers of the mind involved in the operation just described are *imagination* and *intuition*.

pp. 386-7   2.) The *category* of causal efficacy is grounded in the power of imagination, but any determinate *rules* governing causal efficacy must be imposed by the power of understanding.

p. 387   3.) The Kantian categories are products of the power of imagination, and they arise along with the objects of experience.

pp. 387-8   4.) Objection to Maimon's characterization of the mind's imposition of the category of causality as a *deception*.

—The categories apply to objects because objects are products of the productive power of imagination.

pp. 488-9   5.) Reply to skeptical doubts concerning the "objective validity" of any a priori laws.

—It is only because we ourselves are the source of such laws that they possess such validity. Skepticism is rooted in an unfounded demand for cognition of "the thing in itself."

pp. 389-91   *Conclusion*: The harmony between the I and the Not-I in intuition.

—Insofar as the I posits the properties of its image to be determined by the necessary Not-I, it views itself as determined or *caused* by the thing, and thus not as an I at all.

—But since it is, after all, an I, the I necessary posits itself and thus posits itself in opposition to the contingent property of the image, and thus *in opposition to itself* insofar as posits such a property.

—We have now derived a distinction between a necessary I (the I "in itself") and a contingent I (determined by the Not-I), as well as between a necessary and a contingent Not-I.

—The necessary and contingent I are united by an absolute activity of the I, but the I is not conscious of this and posits it as a relationship of causal efficacy between itself and the Not-I.

—The I and Not-I each exist in themselves and act independently of each other, but they are also in harmony: the I must have an object and hence must posit the causal efficacy of the Not-I, and the Not-I cannot be a Not-I for the I unless the causal efficacy of the I is posited.

—What remains to be discovered is the ground of this harmony between the I and the Not-I.

—*Final definition of "intuition"*: The spontaneous, synthetic unity of the causal efficacy of the I and of the Not-I at a single *point.*

§ 4. The Intuition Is Determined in Time; What Is Intuited Is Determined in Space.

p. 391

—An intuition is an accident of the I, which must determine this intuition with respect to itself.

—We will here be concerned with how the I manages to relate *two* intuitions to each other in a synthetic unity of opposites and to relate both to itself.

Deduction of a common sphere for the causal efficacy of various objects of intuition.

pp. 392–3

I.) The contingent intuition and the necessary intuition occupy separate points.

—Every intuition is posited in opposition to another, in relationship to which the first intuition is *contingent* and the second *necessary*.

—Since these two intuitions occupy two distinct points, the "necessity" mentioned above is the necessity of being united with a certain point, whereas contingency is the lack of such necessity: another intuition might have occupied the first point, whereas the position of the second is wholly dependent upon that of the first.

—It must be possible to distinguish these two points from each other, independently of the intuitions with which they are united.

pp. 393–5

II.) Deduction of a common sphere for two opposed objects.

—The *objects* corresponding to these intuitions are themselves either necessary or contingent.

—The relationship between these two objects cannot be determined by their own, inner character, but is instead determined by something else, which is therefore an external condition for the possibility of intuition.

—What is required is that the two objects occupy a common, continuous sphere, within which they encounter each other at a single point.

—Such a sphere is a product of the power of imagination.

pp. 395–9   III.) This requisite common sphere is the common "sphere of causal efficacy" shared by opposed objects as expressions of their respective "free forces."

—The objects present in the I (i.e., the intuitions) are *appearances*, contingent expressions of the "free force" of those necessary objects (substances), which are posited by the I in opposition to the contingent images present in the I.

—These free forces express themselves with unrestricted causal efficacy and are posited in opposition to each other, one as contingent and the other as necessary in relation to the first, for which it is a necessary condition.

—What is required in order to unite these forces is a third thing: a common sphere in which they exercise their causality and within which each has its own exclusive sphere of efficacy, from which it excludes every other object.

—These forces or objects encounter one another contingently at a single point, without any reciprocal influence.

Deduction of space and of matter.

pp. 399–402 IV.) Space.

Deduction of space.

—What is in the I is determined by what lies outside it (the external *force* that produces *appearances* for the I).

—But when the I freely reflects upon itself, it recognizes that it was the I itself that posited this external substance and hence determined the Not-I.

—The I is free to choose which object to posit as occupying a particular sphere of efficacy, but this must be opposed by another such occupied sphere, which the I is not free to choose, since it is a necessary condition for the first (contingent) one.

—The name for this extended, connected, and infinitely divisible common sphere of causal efficacy is *space*, which is posited by the power of productive imagination.

Analysis of space.

1.) There is no empty space.

2.) Space is infinitely divisible and is posited as the sphere in which a force must necessarily express itself.

3.) Space cannot be separated from the products (of the external forces) that fill it, and vice versa.

4.) Things are (at this point) distinguishable from one another only spatially.

—The internal determinations of things are recognizable only by means of feeling and thus do not pertain to the theoretical part of the *Wissenschaftslehre*.

5.) Spatial determination and *the ideality of space.*

—Spatial determination requires two points, so that the place of one can be determined relative to that of the other.

—The fact that the I determines space by means of its own synthetic power of imagination shows the ideality of space.

6.) *The infinity of space*: every time we fill a space we posit another space.

Deduction of the manifold of outer (spatial) intuition.

pp. 402–4   V.) The I is free to choose which things in space to treat as necessary or determined (causes) and which as contingent or determinable (effects).

p. 404   VI.) The contingency of what is posited or exists reflects the spontaneity of the I's free determination of one thing as *determinable* and of another as *determinate* or *determined.*

—We can give no reason why the I posits a particular object as what is determinable (or as an effect); indeed, the *contingency* of the object consists precisely in its very existence in a certain space, its "being-there."

p. 405   VII.) Independence of the I and the Not-I.

—The inner forces of both the I and the Not-I operate with inner freedom and independently of each other.

—What exists in space is posited *idealiter* by the I and *realiter* by the Not-I.

—Space is the form or subjective condition for the possibility of outer intuition.

—We have now explained the *opposition* between the I and the Not-I, but not their *harmony.*

Deduction of Time.

pp. 405–9   VIII.) Time.

1.) Intuitions X and Y, which are supposed to be products of the free causal efficacy of the Not-I, are nothing *for the I* unless it exercizes its own free causal efficacy.

2.) The causal efficacy of the I and of the Not-I determine each other reciprocally when they meet at a synthetic point posited by the I as contingent, a point the I posits by means of its power of imagination.

3.) In order to posit the object of either intuition, the I must unite it with such a synthetic point and unite its causal efficacy with that of the Not-I.

4.) The I spontaneously determines whether it is object X or object Y that is to be united with this point.

5.) In order to posit the *possibility* of uniting either X or Y with the point in question, this point itself must be distinguished from the causal efficacies of X and Y.

6.) The point in question is a synthesis of the causal efficacies of X and Y, and thus it cannot be entirely separated from the causal efficacy of the Not-I; therefore, all that is separated from the point is a determinate object, X, while an undetermined product of the Not-I remains united with it.

7.) When the I spontaneously and synthetically unites the point in question with X, this excludes every other possible object or intuition from this same point.

8.) The synthetic unity of X and this point is posited by the I *spontaneously* and must therefore be posited as *contingent*, which means that another, *necessary* synthetic unity of *another* object or intuition with *another* point, must be posited in opposition to it.

9.) Both of these opposing points are synthetic unities of the causal efficacies of the I and the Not-I, but only the first is freely posited by the I (i.e., posited as contingent or capable of being different than it is).

10.) These two points of synthetic unity of the causal efficacies of the I and the Not-I are related to each other as contingent and necessary: if the first is posited to be contingent, then the second is posited as necessarily having already occurred (as a condition for the possibility of the first), but not vice versa.

11.) The contingently occurring synthetic point of unity is *dependent upon* the necessarily occurring one, but not vice versa.

12.) *Deduction of the temporal series.* Each of these points is, as such, contingent (as a point where the causal efficacies of the I and the Not-I confront each other); consequently, if either point is posited as contingent, then yet another point must be posited as necessary in relation to it, and so on ad infinitum. This irreversible series of dependent points is the *temporal series.*

13.) In relation to the past points, the *present* point is both dependent upon past points and contingent (since it is freely determined by the I).

14.) Regarded in their independence from the causal efficacy of the I, things exist in space *simultaneously*, but they can be perceived only *sequentially*, in a series in which each successive member is dependent upon the preceding one, which is not dependent upon it.

Remarks:

p. 409   **a.)** *On the ideality of time.*
—The past exists for us only when recalled in the present, for only then do we posit it.
—This should convince anyone of the ideality of time.

pp. 409-10   **b.)** In being conscious of time, the I is conscious of its own freedom and identity.
—There must be a past for us, since there can be no present moment without a past one, and because consciousness is possible only in the present moment.
—Consciousness is possible only if the I posits a Not-I in opposition to itself, which is possible only if it directs its ideal activity (reflection) at the Not-I.
—The characteristic feature of the present is that *any* perception might occur in the present, and in positing this contingency of the present moment, *the I becomes conscious of its freedom.*
—But the I cannot posit the present moment without positing it in opposition to another, past moment, one that is necessary and cannot be otherwise. In positing both moments, *the I is conscious of its identity.*
—For this reason, there can be no "first" moment of consciousness.

pp. 410-11   **c.)** Recall of the past.
—By reflecting that a different object could have been united with a past moment, one raises it to present consciousness (and views it as contingent).
—When one does this, one also posits the moment preceding this previously past moment as itself necessary.

p. 411   **d.)** Time is measured in terms of space, and vice versa.
—A determinate quantity of space exists *simultaneously*, but a determinate quantity of time exists *successively.*
—A determinate space is measured by the time it takes to traverse it, and a determinate time is measured by the space that a moving object can traverse during that time.

Concluding Remark

p. 411—   We have now established what is *distinctive* of the theoretical part of the *Wissenschaftslehre.*
—We have provided an a priori deduction of space, time, and the manifold of intuition as present to the I, all of which are *presupposed* by Kant in his *Critique of Pure Reason.*

Notes on the Translation

Though Fichte was an accomplished orator and could be an eloquent and persuasive author, the strictly "scientific" or theoretical writings collected here are composed in an extraordinarily dry and abstract style, modeled perhaps on Spinoza's *Ethics* and generally lacking in rhetorical charm or flourish. His sentences are sometimes impossibly long and ungainly, and his assertions are not infrequently obscure. Indeed, it is daunting to imagine how these same words could have galvanized their original audiences in the manner so widely reported. This undoubtedly had something to do with Fichte's habit of frequently interrupting his written lectures with extemporaneous explanations and illustrations. In an effort to provide the contemporary anglophone reader with something similar, the texts translated here have been supplemented with many editorial notes, including copious direct quotations from Fichte's *other* writings of the same period, which are included here as "commentary" on specific passages and claims.

If, despite my best efforts, these translations are still sometimes ungainly and obscure, one might argue that this is evidence of their fidelity to the originals. But I have done my best to avoid this. I have not hesitated to break up Fichte's sentences in the interest of clarity, though I have remained faithful to his paragraphing. I have generally followed his use of italics for emphasis (which, as is indicated in the footnotes, varies from edition to edition), except in the case of proper names, which usually appear in italics in the German texts but are not italicized in translation.

Everything within square brackets has been inserted by the editor/translator. This includes the occasional insertion of an original German word or phrase, as well as interpolations in the interest of clarity. I have also modernized the spelling of German words, other than in the original titles of earlier works. A few terms have been capitalized in order to indicate that they are here employed in a specific, rather technical sense: for example, "Critical (i.e., Kantian) philosophy" or "Idea" (in the sense of Kant's "Ideas of pure reason") or "Not-I."

These translations are all based on the first editions of the works in question, though all significant variants, omissions, and additions in later editions are provided in the footnotes. I have worked from the texts included in the monumental edition of Fichte's published and unpublished writings, lectures, correspondence, and transcriptions published under the auspices of the Bavarian Academy of the Sciences (= GA). The marginal page references refer not only to GA, but also to SW, the widely-available edition of Fichte's *Works* compiled by his son I. H. Fichte.

Fichte's Technical Vocabulary

Fichte boasted that he employed no special, technical vocabulary in his philosophical (or "scientific") writings, and even maintained that he had intentionally avoided "any fixed terminology" in his first presentation of the *Wissenschaftslehre*, since this "provides the easiest means for literalists to rob any system of its spirit and transform it into a desiccated skeleton."[124] Though technically true, this claim is nevertheless misleading, for he often employs ordinary German words—such as *"Ich," "setzen," "Anstoß," "reflectieren," "wechseln,"* and *"bestimmen"*—in rather extraordinary ways, while also making his own distinctive use of some rather uncommon words, such as *"Tathandlung."* One of the challenges for his translator is to preserve these unusual uses in English.

Another challenge is presented by the apparent ambiguity of certain key terms, the meaning of which is often difficult to pin down. Fichte was not unaware of this problem, and frequently advised his readers to understand such terms "in context" and to interpret single passages in terms of the larger whole of which they are a part.[125] He would certainly have endorsed the view that "meaning is use." As he explained to Reinhold:

> You should not assign to my expressions the same sort of weight that yours, for example, surely possess. […] My thoughts can be expressed in an infinite variety of ways, and it is to not to be expected (of me, in any case) that the first mode of presentation selected is also the most perfect. The body in which you clothe the spirit fits it very snugly. The body in which I clothe it is looser and can be easily cast aside. What I am trying to communicate is something that can neither be *expressed* nor *grasped by means of concepts,* but can only be *intuited.* My words are supposed to guide the reader in forming within himself the desired intuition. I advise anyone who wishes to study my writings to let words be words and simply try to enter my series of intuitions at one point or another. I advise the reader to continue reading, even if he has not completely understood what went before, until at some point a spark of light is finally struck.[126]

Despite this admonition, let us now consider a few specific terms that call for special comment.

der Anstoß ("check" or "impulse"). Like certain other key technical terms in the *Foundation*, this one is imported from rational mechanics or physics, in which an *Anstoß* is the force or "impulse' that sets a system in motion.[127] But it is also an

---

[124] Preface to *GWL*, *GA*, I/2: 252; below, p. 197.
[125] "The meaning of my words is always supposed to be explained by means of opposition and thus from the context" (Fichte, *Rückerinnerungen, Antworten, Fragen* [1799], *GA*, II/5: 186; *SW*, V, p. 373.
[126] Fichte to Reinhold, July 2, 1795, *GA*, III/2: 344; *EPW*, p. 398.
[127] Recent research suggests that Fichte's adoption of this term may in fact have been influenced by Jacobi's use of it, in a passage on the I (*Ich*) in his *Vermischte Schriften* (Carlsruhe: Schmieder, 1783), pp. 107-9. See Luis Fellipe Garcia, *La philosophie comme Wissenschaftslehre. Le projet fichtéen d'une nouvelle pratique du savoir* (Hildesheim, Zurich, and New York: Olms, 2018), p. 152, footnote 36; and David W. Wood, "Jacobi's Philosophy of Faith in Fichte's 1794 *Wissenschaftslehre*." In *Jacobi: Philosophy*

ordinary word for what resists, impedes, or "checks" a force. So too, in the *Foundation*, Fichte describes the *Anstoß* both as "the first mover outside the I" and as "a resistance."[128] It is important to keep this double meaning in mind, and in order to encourage this I often translated *Anstoß* as "check or impulse." It is also important to remember that this check or impulse is not a purely *passive affection* of the I. Only an active subject can be "checked," though it is equally true that if it is not checked it cannot posit itself as an I at all.[129]

bestimmen, die Bestimmung, bestimmt ("to determine," "determination," "determinate," or "determined.") The verb *bestimmen* means "to determine," in the sense of specifying or defining. A concept is *bestimmt* when one has determined what it means. Following Spinoza, Fichte was committed to the principle that all determination involves negation or limitation. To determine X (that is, to determine what X is) is the same as to determine what X is not, and thus to determine X is always to *limit* it. Of course, *Bestimmung* ("determination") also has another, rather different, meaning: namely, "calling" or "vocation" (as in the *Bestimmung des Gelehrten* or "Vocation of the Scholar"), which reminds us that there is a practical as well as theoretical kind of "determining."[130] With respect to the theoretical activity of cognition, the effort "to determine" X is an effort to *represent* X (to intuit it or to think it), whereas with respect to the practical activity of willing, the effort "to determine" X is an effort to *transform* it in accordance with normative criteria intrinsic to the I itself.

die Einbildungskraft ("power of imagination"). Unlike the English word "imagination," *Einbildungskraft* is a term that explicitly invokes the notion of unification: *ein—bilden*, "to form into (or picture as) one." Fichte follows Kant in distinguishing between the power of merely "reproductive" imagination and that of "productive"—or, as Fichte sometimes writes, "creative"—imagination. The productive power of imagination was identified by Kant as the faculty responsible for synthetically (and spontaneously) unifying the manifold of intuition. Fichte follows him in this usage, but applies it to an even more fundamental level, at which the power of imagination is responsible for overcoming the absolutely posited opposition between the finite I and Not-I, as described in the "deduction or representation" at the end of Part Two of the *Foundation*. The power of imagination thus lies at the foundation of the I's cognitive ability "to posit itself as determined by the Not-I"—that is, to possess objectively valid knowledge—and is responsible for spontaneously synthesizing the opposing realms of subject and object. Since

and Religion at the Crux of Modernity, ed. Alexander J. B. Hampton and George di Giovanni (Cambridge: Cambridge University Press, 2020).

[128] See *GA*, I/2: 411 and 358; below, pp. 342–43 and 296.
[129] For further discussion of the meaning of this important and often misunderstood term, see Breazeale, "*Anstoß*, Abstract Realism, and the Finitude of the I," Ch. 7 of *TWL*.
[130] "Fichte's employment of the term in its finitist-finalist double meaning addresses the tension between what is fixed or given in human existence and what is open and yet to be realized about it" (Günter Zöller, *Fichte's Transcendental Philosophy: The Original Duplicity of Intelligence and Will* [Cambridge: Cambridge University Press, 1998], p. 1. See too Ch. 3 of this same work, "Positing and Determining," pp. 43–54.

this synthetic power of productive imagination must occupy a position above or beyond both of the terms to be united, Fichte describes it as "hovering over" or "oscillating between" (*schweben*) these opposed factors—a description perhaps derived from Spinoza's account of the *fluctuations* of the power of imagination.[131]

das Factum, die Tatsache ("*factum*," "fact.") *Tatsache* was a neologism coined by J. J. Spalding to translate Joseph Butler's term "matter of fact," but it quickly became current and was adopted by philosophers such as Reinhold, who sought to ground their systems upon "the facts of consciousness." Fichte employs *Tatsache* in the sense of a "fact" that is simply *discovered to be the case*. In contrast, *factum* is a term imported from Latin and has its roots in *facere*, "to make," "to produce." Consequently, a *factum* is quite a different sort of "fact" than a *Tatsache*, since it has to be *produced* by the subject for which it is "a *factum*." The obvious antecedent for Fichte's use of this term is Kant's *Factum der Vernunft* or "fact of reason": namely, moral obligation, which is a "fact" only for one who freely imposes the moral law upon himself.[132] In order to preserve the quite significant difference between *factum* and *Tatsache*, I have translated the latter as "fact" and left the former in its original Latin.

der Grundsatz ("foundational principle"). A *Grund* is a basis, reason, or "ground," and the active of "grounding" is, in the case of philosophy, often that of basing or "grounding" one proposition upon another, "higher" one, from which the former may therefore be said to be *derived*. (Though Fichte also insists that all philosophical propositions must ultimately be based or grounded upon something that is not a proposition at all: namely, a self-evident intuition.) *Grundsatz* is a common German translation for "axiom," and the foundational principles of the *Wissenschaftslehre* are intended to function very much in the manner of Euclid's geometrical axioms. But there is nothing stipulative or hypothetical about a Fichtean *Grundsatz*. On the contrary, he insists that his three foundational principles are self-evidently certain, and indeed, are the ground of all further certainty.

das Ich, das Nicht-Ich ("the I," "the Not-I"). Talk about "the I" and "the Not-I" sounds just as odd in German as it does in English, and there can be no doubt that such language is at least partly responsible for the widespread—and stubbornly persistent—caricature of the *Wissenschaftslehre* as an unsound "subjective idealism," committed to outright egoism or even solipsism.[133] Fichte complained often about those who confused the "pure I," with which the *Foundation* begins,

---

[131] Spinoza, *Ethics*, Bk. II, Proposition 44, Corollary 1, Scholium. On this point, see Allen Wood, "Fichte on Freedom: The Spinozistic Background," in *Fichte and German Idealism*, ed. Eckart Förster and Yitzhak Y. Melamed (Cambridge: Cambridge University Press, 2012), pp. 126–8.

[132] In his 1805 lectures on the *Wissenschaftslehre*, Fichte explicitly replaces the term *Tathandlung* or "F/Act" with *factum* (*GA*, II/9: 253): "Where the I is, lives, and reigns, it exists absolutely as *factum*—and indeed, not as we have previously had it, as *facta*, as *factum et consummatum*, but as *factum fiens*, absolute *fiens*, act (*Tathandlung*)." At this point at least, *factum* is for Fichte a synonym for both *genesis* and *Tathandlung*.

[133] See, for example, Bertrand Russel's claim that Fichte "carried subjectivism to a point which seems almost to involve a kind of insanity" (*A History of Western Philosophy* [New York: Simon and Schuster, 1945], p. 718).

with their own concrete individual self (or "empirical I").[134] The Fichtean I is neither a substance nor an entity of any sort; it is a pure activity. It is Fichte's (perhaps ill-chosen) name for that spontaneously self-positing activity, which he claims can be shown to underly consciousness as a whole and to be necessarily instantiated—or, better, *embodied*—in finite human beings, which are the only *actually existing* I's. The pure I with which the *Foundation* commences is simply "the principle of subjectivity as such."[135] It is "nothing but the form of I-hood, self-reverting action,"[136] and it is identical to "reason as such."[137]

das Leiden ("being-passively-affected," "state of being affected," "passive affection," "affection"). This term designates an actual state of the I, a state of "*positive negation*,"[138] posited in opposition to the I's own active state. A stone could be described as "passive," but not as "passively affected" (or *leidend*) in the Fichtean sense. Indeed, he explicitly warns his readers not to associate this term with any sort of suffering or painful sensation and to think of "passive affection" in a strictly atemporal fashion, as the sheer negation—and hence as the suppression[139]—of activity.

schlechthin ("purely and simply"). *Schlechthin* is a term encountered on nearly every page of the *Foundation*. It is an ordinary adverb that means something like "*per se*" or "as such." The idea is that something is posited "*schlechthin*" if nothing else is required in order to posit it, in which case it might be said to be posited "unconditionally" or "absolutely."[140] An act that occurs *schlechthin* is one that does not presuppose any other acts. I have resisted translating this term as "absolutely," since that might suggest some special, spectral, or "philosophical" kind of positing, and have opted instead for the less graceful and more blunt "purely and simply."

setzen ("to posit," "positing"). The literal meaning of this verb is "to situate," and Fichte sometimes employs *setzen* in a purely logical sense corresponding to the Latin *ponere*, which has nothing do with conscious or unconscious mental activity, but only with formal entailment: if X is "posited," then Y is also posited. More frequently, however, he employs it to designate the fundamental activity of the I—which is to say, of reason as such. Though he may sometimes appear to suggest otherwise, to *posit* something is not to *create* it. It is, instead, to affirm or to assert it. This, moreover, may be accomplished in two different ways, and Fichte himself calls explicit attention to what he describes as the "double

[134] See, for example, section 9 of the Second Introduction to *VWL*.
[135] Fichte to Reinhold, April 28, 1795, *GA*, III/2: 314–15; *EPW*, p. 389.
[136] *VWL*, *GA*, I/4: 266; *SW*, I, p. 515; *IWL*, p. 100.
[137] "In the published *Wissenschaftslehre*, the pure I is to be understood as reason as such [*Vernunft überhaupt*], which is completely different than empirical I-hood" (*WLnmH*, *GA*, IV/2: 240; *FTP*, p. 393).
[138] *GWL*, *GA*, I/2: 293; below, p. 233.
[139] *GEWL*, *GA*, I/3: 155; below, p. 391.
[140] See *GWL*, *GA*, I/2: 313; below, p. 251, where Fichte explains that to posit anything *schlechthin* is to posit it "*without any ground.*" See too *GWL*, *GA*, I/2: 394; below, p. 327, where Fichte writes that the term *schlechthin* was chosen to emphasize the "spontaneity" of the pure or absolute I.

meaning" of the term *setzen*.[141] On the one hand, one may posit something "theoretically" (or in an "ideal" manner) simply by *thinking* it; on the other hand, one may also posit something "practically" (or in a "real" manner) by *intuiting* it—as is the case when the I originally "posits itself." "Positing" thus seems to be Fichte's most general name for the original activity of the I or for rational agency as such and is therefore integral to his project of unifying theoretical and practical reason.[142]

die Tathandlung ("F/Act"). Though it is often thought that Fichte coined this term, it was in fact in use long before him, and, indeed, predates the term *Tatsache* (or "fact"). *Tathandlung* is a compound word, which combines the word "deed" or "achievement" (*Tat*) with the word "action" (*Handlung*). *Tathandlung* had previously been employed in legal contexts to designate a violent or illegal act, and in religious and theological contexts to refer to the original, divine act of creation.[143] For Fichte, a *Tathandlung* is an act of the I in and through which it spontaneously becomes its own object and hence a subject. Only an I is capable of such a *Tathandlung*; indeed, this is what defines it as an I. Fichte frequently contrasts *Tathandlung* with *Tatsache* ("fact" or "matter of fact"), which, unlike a F/Act, is something simply *discovered* rather than also *accomplished* by the rational agent or I. Since no English word captures the meaning Fichte assigns to *Tathandlung*, I have coined the term "F/Act" for this purpose, despite the difficulty of pronouncing it.

wechseln, der Wechsel, die Wechselbestimmung, das Wechsel-Tun und Leiden ("to change," "alteration," "reciprocity," "reciprocal relationship," "reciprocally related components," "reciprocal determination," and "reciprocally-related-acting-and-being-passively-affected"). The verb *wechseln* and its substantive form *der Wechsel* mean "change," "exchange," "alteration," or "alternation." This is another example of an ordinary word to which Fichte assigns a special, technical meaning, inasmuch

---

[141] See *GWL, GA*, I/2: 325; below, p. 264. Regarding this "double meaning," see Claudio Cesa, "'…ein Doppelsinn in der Bedeutung des Wortes Setzen,'" in *Der Grundansatz der ersten Wissenschaftslehre Johann Gottlieb Fichtes*, ed. Erich Fuchs and Ives Radrizzani, pp. 34–44 (Neuried: Ars Una, 1996) and David W. Wood, "The 'Double Sense' of Fichte's Philosophical Language," *Revista de Estud(i)os sobre Fichte* 15 (2017).

[142] "Positing is neither a creative activity nor an affirmation of judgments. Rather, positing is the fundamental activity of rational agency in general. It is an activity articulated into existential commitment, predication, and inference. And it is an activity which forms the basis both of the ontological or transcendental forms of existential commitment and real inference, and of the logical forms of judgments and analytic inferences. Furthermore, since Fichte rejects any radical distinction between theoretical reasoning and practical reasoning, positing is an activity capable of both theoretical and practical inflections" (Paul Franks, "Fichte's Position: Anti-Subjectivism, Self-Awareness and Self-Location in the Space of Reasons," in *The Cambridge Companion to Fichte*, ed. David James and Günter Zöller [Cambridge: Cambridge University Press, 2016], p. 382).

[143] Regarding the origin and meaning of this controversial term, see Paul Franks, "Freedom, Tatsache and Tathandlung in the Development of Fichte's Jena *Wissenschaftslehre*," *Archiv für Geschichte der Philosophie* 79 (1997): 310–23; and David W. Wood, "Fichte's Absolute I and the Forgotten Tradition of *Tathandlung*," in *Das Selbst und die Welt—Beiträge zu Kant und der nachkantischen Philosophie*, eds. Manja Kisner, Giovanni Pietro Basile, Ansgar Lyssy, Michael Bastian Weiß (Würzburg: Königshausen & Neumann, 2019), pp. 167–92. Franks discusses the legal tradition for the use of this term, but the alternate, religious tradition, which appears to have been of much more importance for Fichte, appears to have been ignored by everyone but Wood.

as this is the term he employs to describe the complex relationship between two "opposed" but "reciprocally related" elements; hence, for Fichte, *wechseln* usually means "to be reciprocally related." In Part Two of the *Foundation*, he often uses *wechseln* simply as shorthand for the reciprocal relationship that has been established between, on the one hand, the action of the I and, on the other, its state of being passively affected: *Wechsel-Tun und Leiden* ("reciprocally-related-acting-and-being-passively-affected").

die Wissenschaftslehre (*Wissenschaftslehre*). *Wissenschaft* means "science" or "scientific knowing," and *Lehre* means "doctrine" or "theory." But the *Wissenschaftslehre* is by no means a "theory of science" in the contemporary sense. It is, instead, a systematic account of the conditions necessary for any rational account of both knowing and acting. *Wissenschaftslehre* should therefore be treated as a technical term. Though he did not coin this term, Fichte appropriated it as the designated name for his own distinctive version or presentation of what he took to be the same *transcendental* or *Critical* philosophy first propounded by Kant and then developed further by Reinhold and others. When he resumed his lectures on the foundational portion of his system in the Winter Semester of 1796/97, "according to a new method" of presentation, he explicitly identified "*Wissenschaftslehre*" and "transcendental philosophy."[144]

---

[144] See *WLnm*. The official title of these lectures, which Fichte repeated three times between 1796 and 1799, was "Foundation of Transcendental Philosophy (*Wissenschaftslehre*) *nova methodo.*"

German-English Glossary

abbilden	to portray
ableiten	to derive
die Absicht	intention (what one has in view), respect (as "in a certain respect")
die Absonderung	elimination
der Accident	accident, accidental property or feature
afficieren	to affect, to have an effect on
der Akt	act
andeuten	to indicate, to point out, to mention
anerkennen	to acknowledge, to recognize
die Anforderung	demand
anhalten	to arrest, to bring to a halt
anknüpfen	to attach, to connect, to hold together
die Anlage	aptitude, talent
die Annährung	approximation
annehmen	to assume, to recognize, to adopt
anschauen	to intuit
das Anschauen	intuiting, act of intuiting
das Anschauende	the intuiting subject
die Anschauung	intuition
die Ansicht	view, point of view, opinion, way of looking at, appearance, aspect
der Anstoß	check, impetus, impulse
der Antrieb	stimulus
die Art	kind, mode
aufbehalten	to preserve
auffassen	to grasp, to interpret, to construe, to apprehend
die Auffassung	apprehension
die Aufforderung	summons
der Aufgabe	task, assignment, problem
aufgehen	to be directed (at), to aim at
aufgestellt	established, indicated, "in question" (as in "the x in question")
aufhalten	to bring to a halt, to arrest
aufheben	to annul, to cancel
aufnehmen	to assimilate, to take up, to absorb, to accommodate
aufstellen	to establish, to present, to exhibit, to display, to describe, to put forward, to set up, to assert, to mention, to make (an assertion), to indicate, to propose, to state, to advance (a hypothesis)
aufweisen	to present
aufzeigen	to point to (or out), to show
ausdehnen	to extend
die Ausdehnung	extension
ausführlich	comprehensive
ausgehen (aus)	to proceed (from)
ausgehen auf	to be directed at, to aim at, to be bent on
ausschliessen	to exclude
das Ausschliessen	excluding, act of excluding, exclusion

(sich) äussern	to express, to manifest
die Äußerung	expression, manifestation
der Ausspruch	dictum, pronouncement
das Beabsichtigte	what is intended
bedingen	to condition
die Bedingung	condition (for the possibility of)
bedürftig	needy
die Befriedigung	satisfaction
die Befügnis	legitimacy
die Begebenheiten	what occurs
begehren	to desire
die Begierde	desire
begreifen	to comprehend, to grasp, to grasp in or by means of a concept
das Begreifen	(act of) comprehending, comprehension
das Begreifend	the comprehending subject
begrenzen	to limit, to delimit
die Begrenztheit	limited state
die Begrenzung	limitation, process of limiting
der Begriff	concept
beharrlich	constant
die Beharrlichkeit	constancy
der Beifall	approval
beimessen	to ascribe, to credit (to)
bekannt	well-known, familiar, known
die Beobachtung	observation
das Beruhen	(state of) rest
beschaffen	to constitute
die Beschaffenheit	structure, constitution, (set of) properties or attributes
beschränken	to restrict
die Beschränktheit	restricted state
die Beschränkung	restriction
beschreiben	to describe
bestehen	to subsist, to endure
das Bestehen	subsistence, endurance, continuing existence
für sich bestehend	self-subsistent
bestimmbar	determinable
die Bestimmbarkeit	determinability
bestimmen	to determine, to specify, to describe, to delineate
das Bestimmen	(act of) determining or specifying
bestimmt	determinate, determined, definite, specific
das Bestimmt	what is determinate, what is determined
die Bestimmtheit	determinacy, determinate state, precision
das Bestimmtsein	determinate being
betrachten	to observe
die Betrachung	observation
beweglich	movable, mobile, changeable
die Beweglichkeit	mobility
der Beweis	proof, argument
beweisen	to prove, to demonstrate
bewirken	to produce, to affect

das Bewirkte	effect, that which is brought about, product
das Bewusstsein	consciousness, act or state of consciousness
beziehen	to relate, to connect, to refer
die Beziehung	relation, connection
das Bild	image
bilden	to form or entertain images, to shape, to form
binden	to constrain, to bind
der Charakter	defining characteristic, character, nature
darstellen	to present, to expound, to exhibit, to portray
die Darstellung	presentation, exposition, portrayal
dartun	to subtantiate
das Dauerende	that which endures
dauern	to endure
die Denkart	way or manner of thinking
denken	to think, to conceive of
das Denken	thinking, act of thinking
das Denkende	the thinking subject
der Denkzwang	intellectual compulsion, feeling of being compelled to think in a certain way
die Differenz	difference
der Drang	impetus
die Eigenschaft	property
die Einbildungskraft	power of imagination, imagination
der Eindruck	impression
eingreifen	to encroach (upon one another)
das Eingreifen	encroachment, mutual encroachment
einig	unitary, united
einschränken	to limit
das Einschränken	limiting, act of limiting
die Einschränkung	limitation
das Eintreten	what enters (into)
einwirken	to have or to exercise an effect on, to influence, to act efficaciously, to affect
die Einwirkung	effect, influence, efficacious action
empfinden	to sense, to have a sensation
die Empfindung	sensation
der Endzweck	final goal
entäußern	to alienate
das Entäußern	act of alienating
die Entäußerung	alienation
das Entgegensein	being opposed, opposition
entgegensetzen	to posit in opposition, to oppose
entschließen	to resolve, to decide
der Entschluß	decision, resolve
das Entstehen	coming to be
entwerfen	to construct, to project, to originate
erblicken	to view, to catch sight of, to observe
sich ergeben	ensue
ergreifen	to apprehend
erkennen	to cognize, to recognize, to have a cognition of

das Erkennen	(act of) cognizing, cognition
die Erkenntnis	cognition
erweisen	to demonstrate, to show, to prove
die Erzählung	account
evident	self-evident, evident
die Evidenz	self-evidence, evidence
das Factum	*factum*
festhalten	to retain, to hold fast
das Festhalten	(act of) holding fast
festsetzen	to establish, to stipulate, to posit as fixed
feststellen	to ascertain, to establish
fixieren	to stabilize, to arrest
fixiert	fixed, stabilized, arrested
das Fixirtsein	fixedness
die Folge	sequence, consequence, result
die Folgerungsart	line of argument, (type of) inference
die Forderung	demand, requirement
fortdauern	to (continue to) endure
fortlaufen	to flow
fortleiten	to carry forward
das Fühlbar	what can be felt
das Fühlend	the feeling subject
für sich	for itself, by itself
gebunden	constrained, bound
die Gebundenheit	constraint, constrained state or condition
das Gedachte	the object of thought, what is thought of
das Gefühl	feeling
das Gefundene	what is found or discovered
der Gegensatz	opposite, opposing proposition, opposition.
gegenseitig	mutual, mutually
gegensetzen	to posit in opposition, to oppose
das Gegensetzen	(act of) positing in opposition, opposing, (act of) opposing
der Gegenstand	object
das Gegenstreben	opposed striving, counterstriving
das Gegenteil	opposite
der Gehalt	content
der Geist	mind, spirit
geistlich	mental, intellectual, spiritual
der gemeine Menschensinn	common sense
der gemeine Menschenverstand	ordinary human understanding
das Gemüt	mind
das Geschäft	operation
geschieden	separate, separated
geschloßen	self-contained, brought to a close, concluded
das Gesetztsein	posited-being, being-posited
der Gesichtspunkt	viewpoint
die Gewalt	power
die Glaube	belief, faith, confidence

glauben	to believe, to have confidence in, to trust
gleich	alike, identical, same, equal
das Gleichgewicht	counterbalance, equilibrium
die Gleichheit	identity
gleichsetzen	to posit as identical or the same
das Glied	component, element, member, link, factor
die Grenze	boundary, limit
die Größe	magnitude, quantity
der Grund	ground, reason, basis
gründen	to ground, to base upon, to found
die Grundlage	foundation
der Grundsatz	foundational principle
gültig	valid
die Haltbarkeit	tenability, stability
halten	to bring to a halt, to arrest, to restrain, to stabililize?
handeln	to act
das Handeln	acting, instance (mode or type) of acting
die Handlung	action
die Handlungsart	manner of acting
die Handlungsweise	way of acting
der Hauptsatz	chief principle
heben	to eliminate
hemmen	to curb, to obstruct
die Hemmung	obstruction
herabsetzen	to posit in diminished form
hervorbringen	to produce, to generate, to engender
hinausgehen	to extend, to go out
hinausgehend	outgoing
das Hinderniss	obstacle, hindrance
hineinscheiben	to interpolate
das Hinschauen	act of looking outwards toward, "ex-tuiting"
das Ich	the I
die Ichheit	I-hood
idealiter	*idealiter* (neo-Latin term meaning "ideally," or "in an ideal manner")
die Idee	Idea (capitalized in order to emphasize the technical, Kantian, sense of this term)
der Inbegriff	totality
die Intelligenz	intellect, intelligence
kennen	to be acquainted with, to be familiar with, to be aware of
die Kausalität	causality, causal influence
die Kenntniß	cognizance, acquaintance, awareness
die Körperwelt	corporeal world
die Kraft	force, energy
die Lehre	doctrine, theory, account
leiden	to be (passively) affected
das Leiden	being-passively-affected, state of passive affection, state of being passively affected, passive affection, affection, affecting
leidend	passively affected, passive
lenken (nach)	be directed or point (toward)

losreisen	to wrench away, to tear away
das Machen	productive activity, act of producing, productive act
das Machende	the productive subject or agent
die Macht	might
der Machtspruch	decree
das Mannigfaltige	manifold, multiplicity
die Mannigfaltigkeit	multiplicity
das Maß	measure
die Maßgabe	standard measure
das Material	material
die Materie	content, material
das Merkmal	characteristic feature, respect
der Mißfall	disapproval
mittelbar	mediated, mediate, mediately, indirect
die Mittelbarkeit	mediacy
das Mittelglied	mediating component
nachbilden	to copy
nachmachen	to imitate, to copy
nachweisen	to establish, to show
das Nicht-Ich	the Not-I
das Objekt	object
das Objektive	objective element, what is objective
das Prinzip	principle
räsonieren	to argue, to calculate, to reason
das Räsonnement	reasoning, line of reasoning, (line of) argument
realisieren	to realize, to make real, to bring into being
realiter	*realiter* (neo-Latin term meaning "really," or "in a real manner") [cf. idealiter]
das Recht	right, law, justice
reelle	real, genuine
reflectieren	to reflect (upon)
die Reflexion	(act of) reflecting, act of reflection
die Relation	relation, relationship
die Rücksicht	respect, aspect
die Ruhe	state of rest, state of repose
ruhend	in a state of repose, static
die Sache	content, matter, subject
der Satz	proposition, assertion, principle
schlecterdings	absolutely
schlechthin	purely and simply
die Schranke	limit
schranken	to limit
die Schwärmerei	fanaticism
schweben	to hover, to oscillate
das Sehnen	longing
der Sein	being
die Selbständigkeit	self-sufficiency
das Selbstgefühl	self-feeling, feeling of self
die Selbsttätigkeit	self-activity, spontaneous self-activity, spontaneity

die Sensibilität	sensibility
setzen	to posit, to suppose, to assume
das Setzen	act of positing, positing
das Setzend	the (actively) positing subject, the one who posits
der Sinn	sense
die Sinnenwelt	sensible world
sinnlich	sensible, sensory
die Sinnlichkeit	sensibility, sensuousness
die Sittlichkeit	ethics
stehend	stable
stetig	constant, continuous
die Stetigkeit	continuity
die Stimmung	mood, disposition
der Stoff	matter, material, stuff
der Stoß	impact, stimulus
streben	to strive
das Streben	striving, activity of striving
das Subjective	what is subjective, the subjective element
das Suchen	quest
die Tat	deed
die Tathandlung	F/Act
tätig	active
das Tätiges	the active subject, agent
die Tätigkeit	activity
die Täuschung	deception
der Teil	part, portion
trennen	to separate, to divide
der Trieb	drive
das Tun	acting, act, doing, instance or type of doing
die Übereinstimmung	agreement
der Übergang	transition
das Übergehen	movement of transition, transition, passage, movement
übersinnlich	supersensible
übertragen	to transfer
das Übertragen	act of transferring
die Übertragung	transference
der Umfang	range
umfassen	to comprise, to encompass
unbestimmbar	indeterminable
unbestimmt	indeterminate
die Unbestimmtheit	(state of) indeterminacy
ins Unendliche	ad infinitum, into the infinite
die Unendlichkeit	infinity, the realm of the infinite, infinite realm
unmittelbar	unmediated, immediate, immediately
die Unmittelbarkeit	immediacy
unterdrücken	to suppress
der Unterscheidungsgrund	ground of distinction
das Unvermögen	incapacity
die Ursache	cause

die Urteilskraft	power of judgment
verbinden	to connect
die Verbindung	connection, bond
verdrängen	to displace
vereinigen	to unite, to unify, to reconcile
die Vereinigung	unification, union
das Verfahren	way of proceeding, procedure
das Vergehen	passing away, vanishing
vergleichen	to compare
das Verhältniss	relation, relationship
verknüpfen	to connect, to tie together
vermindern	to diminish
die Verminderung	diminution
das Vermögen	power, ability
vermuten	to surmise
vernichten	to annihilate
die Vernunft	(power of) reason
die Verringerung	diminution, reduction
die Verschiedenheit	variety
das Verschwinden	disappearing
versinnlichen	to make sensible, to sensibilize
der Verstand	(power of) understanding
verstandlich	intelligible
die Verwandlung	transformation
verwechseln	to exchange
vollenden	to accomplish, to complete
das Vorbild	model, advance image, ideal prefiguration
das Vorhandsein	presence, being present
vorkommen	to occur
vornehmen	to undertake
vorschreiben	to prescribe
vorschweben	to hover before, to have (something) in mind
vorstellen	to represent, to have or to entertain representation
das Vorstellend	the representing subject
die Vorstellung	representation
wahrnehmen	to perceive
die Wahrnehmung	perception
der Wechsel	reciprocity, change, alteration, alternation, reciprocal relation, reciprocal relationship, reciprocally related components (Fichte often employs this term as shorthand for *Wechsel-Tun und Leiden*, or "reciprocally-related-acting-and-being-passively-affected")
die Wechselbestimmung	reciprocal determination
wechseln	to be related reciprocally, to determine each other (reciprocally), to change
die Wechselglieder	reciprocally related components
das Wechseln	reciprocal activity
das Wechseltun	reciprocal acting
das Wechsel-Tun und Leiden	reciprocally-related-acting-and-being-passively affected

wechselwirken	to interact, to stand in a relationship of reciprocal interaction
die Wechselwirkung	reciprocal causally effective operation, reciprocal interaction
wegfallen	to be suppressed
das Werden	becoming
das Wesen	essence, being, nature, creature, entity
der Widerstand	resistance
widerstreben	to strive in opposition
das Widerstreben	resistence, striving in opposition
widerstreiten	to oppose, to be in opposition to
wiederstehen	to resist
der Wille	will
die Willkür	choice, free choice, arbitrary choice, power of (free) choice
willkürlich	freely undertaken, arbitrary, voluntary
wirken	to act efficaciously, to operate, to have an effect upon, to affect
das Wirken	efficacious acting, accomplishment
wirklich	actual
die Wirklichkeit	actuality
wirksam	effective, effectively
die Wirksamkeit	causal efficacy, causality, efficacious power
die Wirkung	causally efficacious operation, effect
die Wirkungskreise	sphere of efficacy
wissen	to know
das Wissen	knowledge, knowing
die Wissenschaft	science
die Wissenschaftslehre	*Wissenschaftslehre* ("doctrine of scientific knowledge")
das Wollen	willing, act of willing
das Ziel	goal, object
das Zugestehen	admission
zuruckdrängen	to drive back
(in sich selbst) *zuruckgehend*	self-reverting
zurückwirken	to react
zusammenfassen	to combine
das Zusammenfassen	act of combining, combination
der Zusammenhang	combination, connection, context
zusammenhängen	to be connected, to cohere
zusammensetzen	to combine, to assemble, to posit together
zusammentreffen	to encounter
zuschreiben	to attribute
zusehen	to witness, to observe, to look at
der Zustand	state, situation
das Zutun	agency
der Zwang	compulsion
der Zweck	end, goal, aim, purpose
zweckmässig	purposeful, purposive
zwingen	to compel, to constrain

English-German Glossary

ability	*das Vermögen*
absolutely	*schlecterdings*
to absorb	*aufnehmen*
accident	*der Accident*
to accommodate	*aufnehmen*
to accomplish	*vollenden*
accomplishment	*das Wirken*
account	*die Erzählung, die Lehre*
to acknowledge	*anerkennen*
acquaintance	*die Kenntniß*
to be acquainted with	*kennen*
act	*das Tun, der Akt*
to act	*handeln*
act of alienating	*das Entäußern*
act of combining	*das Zusammenfassen*
to act efficaciously	*einwirken, wirken*
act of looking outwards toward	*das Hinschauen*
act of reflection	*die Reflexion*
act of transferring	*das Übertragen*
(instance of) acting	*das Handeln, das Tun*
action	*die Handlung*
active	*tätig*
the active subject	*das Tätiges*
activity	*die Tätigkeit*
actual	*wirklich*
actuality	*die Wirklichkeit*
ad infinitum	*ins Unendliche*
admission	*das Zugestehen*
to adopt	*annehmen*
advance image	*das Vorbild*
to affect or have an effect on	*afficieren, bewirken, einwirken, wirken*
to be (passively) affected	*leiden*
affecting	*das Leiden*
affection	*das Leiden*
agency	*das Zutun*
agent	*das Tätiges*
agreement	*die Übereinstimmung*
aim	*der Zweck*
to aim or be directed at	*ausgehen aus*
to alienate	*entäußern*
alienation	*die Entäußerung*
alike	*gleich*
alteration	*der Wechsel*
alternation	*der Wechsel*
to annihilate	*vernichten*
to annul	*aufheben*
appearance	*die Ansicht*
to apprehend	*auffasen, ergreifen*

apprehension	*die Auffassung*
approval	*der Beifal*
approximation	*die Annährung*
apptitude	*die Anlage*
arbitrary	*willkürlich*
to argue	*räsonieren*
argument	*der Beweis*
(line of) argument	*das Räsonnement*
to arrest or bring to a halt	*anhalten, aufhalten, fixieren, halten*
arrested	*fixiert*
to ascertain	*feststellen*
to ascribe	*beimessen*
to assemble	*zusammensetzen*
assertion	*der Satz*
to assimilate	*aufnehmen*
to assume	*annehmen, setzen*
aspect	*die Ansicht, die Rücksicht*
to attach	*anknüpfen*
to attribute	*zuschreiben*
(set of) attributes	*die Beschaffenheit*
to be aware of	*kennen*
awareness	*die Kenntniß*
to base upon	*grunden*
basis	*der Grund*
becoming	*das Werden*
being	*der Sein, das Wesen*
being opposed	*das Entgegensein*
being-passively-affected	*das Leiden*
being-posited	*das Gesetztsein*
being present	*das Vorhandsein*
belief	*die Glaube*
to believe	*glauben*
to bind	*binden*
bond	*die Verbindung*
bound	*gebunden*
boundary	*die Grenze*
to bring into being	*realisieren*
to bring to a halt	*aufhalten*
brought to a close	*geschloßen*
by itself	*für sich*
to calculate	*räsonieren*
to cancel	*aufheben*
to carry forward	*fortleiten*
causally efficacious operation	*die Wirkung*
to catch sight of	*erblicken*
causal efficacy	*die Wirksamkeit*
causal influence	*die Kausalität*
causal power	*die Causalität*
causality	*die Kausalität, die Wirksamkeit, die Ursache*
change	*der Wechsel*

to change	*wechseln*
changeable	*beweglich*
character	*der Character*
characteristic feature	*das Merkmal*
check	*der Anstoß*
chief principle	*der Hauptsatz*
(arbitrary) choice	*die Willkür*
(free) choice	*die Willkür*
cognition	*das Erkennen, die Erkenntnis*
cognizance	*die Kenntniß*
to cognize	*erkennen*
(act of) cognizing	*das Erkennen*
to cohere	*zusammenhangen*
combination	*das Zusammenfassen, der Zusammenhang*
to combine	*zusammenfassen, zusammensetzen*
coming to be	*das Entstehen*
common sense	*der gemeine Menschensinn*
to compare	*vergleichen*
to compel	*zwingen*
to complete	*vollenden*
component	*das Glied*
to comprehend	*begreifen*
(act of) comprehending	*das Begreifen*
the comprehending subject	*das Begreifend*
comprehension	*das Begreifen*
comprehensive	*ausführlich*
to comprise	*umfassen*
compulsion	*der Zwang*
to conceive (of)	*denken*
concept	*der Begriff*
concluded	*geschloßen*
condition (for the possibility of)	*die Bedingung*
to condition	*bedingen*
confidence	*die Glaube*
to connect	*beziehen, verbinden, verknüpfen*
to connect or hold together	*anknüpfen*
to be connected	*zusammenhangen*
connection	*der Zusammenhang, die Verbindung, die Beziehung*
(act or state of) consciousness	*das Bewusstsein*
consequence	*die Folge*
constancy	*die Beharrlichkeit*
constant	*beharrlich, stetig*
to constitute	*beschaffen*
constitution	*die Beschaffenheit*
to constrain	*binden, zwingen*
constrained	*gebunden*
constrained state or condition	*die Gebundenheit*
constraint	*die Gebundenheit*
to construct	*entwerfen*

to construe	*auffassen*
to contemplate	*betrachten*
content	*die Materie, die Sache, die Gehalt*
context	*der Zusammenhang*
continuing existence	*das Bestehen*
continuity	*die Stetigkeit*
continuous	*stetig*
to copy	*nachbilden, nachmachen*
corporeal world	*die Körperwelt*
counterbalance	*das Gleichgewicht*
counterstriving	*das Gegenstreben*
creature	*das Wesen*
to credit (to)	*beimessen*
to curb	*hemmen*
to decide	*enschließen*
deception	*die Täuschung*
decision	*der Entschluß*
decree	*der Machtspruch*
deed	*die Tat*
defining characteristic	*der Charakter*
definite	*bestimmt*
to delimit	*begrenzen*
to delineate	*bestimmen*
demand	*die Anforderung, die Forderung*
to demonstrate	*erweisen, beweisen*
to derive	*ableiten*
to describe	*aufstellen, beschreiben, bestimmen*
desire	*die Begierde*
to desire	*begehren*
determinability	*die Bestimmbarkeit*
determinable	*bestimmbar*
determinacy	*die Bestimmtheit*
determinate	*bestimmt*
(what is) determinate or determined	*das Bestimmt*
determinate being	*das Bestimmtsein*
determinate state	*die Bestimmtheit*
to determine	*bestimmen*
to (reciprocally) determine each other	*wechseln*
determined	*bestimmt*
(act of) determining or specifying	*das Bestimmen*
dictum	*der Ausspruch*
difference	*die Differenz*
to diminish	*vermindern*
diminution	*die Verringerung, die Verminderung*
to be directed at or point toward	*ausgehen auf, lenken (nach)*
disappearing	*das Verschwinden*
disapproval	*der Mißfall*
to displace	*verdrängen*
to display	*aufstellen*
disposition	*die Stimmung*

to divide	*trennen*
doctrine	*die Lehre*
(instance or type of) doing	*das Tun*
drive	*der Trieb*
to drive back	*zuruckdrängen*
effect	*die Einwirkung, die Wirkung, das Bewirkte*
effective(ly)	*wirksam*
efficacious acting	*das Wirken*
efficacious action	*die Einwirkung*
efficacious power	*die Wirksamkeit*
element	*das Glied*
to eliminate	*heben*
elimination	*die Absonderung*
to encompass	*umfassen*
to encroach (upon one another)	*eingreifen*
(mutual) encroachment	*das Eingreifen*
to encounter	*zusammentreffen*
end	*der Zweck*
endurance	*das Bestehen*
to endure	*dauern, bestehen*
to (continue to) endure	*fortdauern*
(that which) endures	*das Dauerende*
energy	*die Kraft*
to engender	*hervorbringen*
ensue	*sich ergeben*
entity	*das Wesen*
equal	*gleich*
equilibrium	*das Gleichgewicht*
essence	*das Wesen*
to establish	*aufstellen, festsetzen*
established	*aufgestellt*
ethics	*die Sittlichkeit*
(self-)evidence	*die Evidenz*
(self-)evident	*evident*
to exchange	*verwechseln*
to exclude	*ausschliessen*
excluding, act of excluding	*das Ausschliessen*
exclusion	*das Ausschliessen*
to exhibit	*aufstellen, darstellen*
exposition	*die Darstellung*
to expound	*darstellen*
to express	*(sich) äussern*
expression	*die Äußerung*
to extend	*ausdehnen, hinausgehen*
extension	*die Ausdehnung*
"ex-tuiting"	*das Hinschauen*
F/Act	*die Tathandlung*
fact	*die Tatsache, das Factum,*
factor	*das Glied*
factum	*das Factum*

faith	*die Glaube*
familiar	*bekannt*
to be familiar with	*kennen*
fanaticism	*die Schwärmerei*
feeling	*das Gefühl*
feeling of being compelled to think	*der Denkzwang*
feeling of self	*das Selbstgefühl*
the feeling subject	*das Fühlend*
final goal	*der Endzweck*
fixed	*fixiert*
fixedness	*das Fixirtsein*
to flow	*fortlaufen*
for itself	*für sich*
force	*die Kraft*
to form	*bilden*
to form or entertain images	*bilden*
to found or establish	*grunden*
foundation	*die Grundlage*
foundational principle	*der Grundsatz*
freely undertaken	*willkürlich*
to generate	*hervorbringen*
genuine	*reelle*
to go out	*hinausgehen*
goal	*das Ziel, der Zweck*
to grasp	*auffassen, begreifen*
ground	*der Grund*
to ground	*gründen*
ground of distinction	*der Unterscheidungsgrund*
to (bring to a) halt	*halten*
to have a cognition of	*erkennen*
to have confidence in	*glauben*
to have an effect upon	*wirken*
to have (something) in mind	*vorschweben*
to have or to entertain representations	*vorstellen*
to have a sensation	*empfinden*
hinderance	*das Hinderniss*
to hold fast	*festhalten*
(act of) holding fast	*das Festhalten*
to hover	*schweben*
to hover before	*vorschweben*
the I	*das Ich*
Idea (in the Kantian sense)	*die Idee*
ideal prefiguration	*das Vorbild*
idealiter	*idealiter*
ideally (in an ideal manner)	*idealiter*
identical	*gleich*
identity	*die Gleichheit*
I-hood	*die Ichheit*
image	*das Bild*
(power of) imagination	*die Einbildungskraft*

to imitate	*nachmachen*
immediacy	*die Unmittelbarkeit*
immediate(ly)	*unmittelbar*
impact	*der Stoß*
impetus	*der Anstoß, der Drang*
impression	*der Eindruck*
incapacity	*das Unvermögen*
indeterminable	*unbestimmbar*
(state of) indeterminacy	*die Unbestimmtheit*
indeterminate	*unbestimmt*
to indicate	*andeuten, aufstellen*
indicated	*aufgestellt*
indirect	*mittelbar*
(type of) inference	*die Folgerungsart*
infinite (realm)	*die Unendlichkeit*
infinity	*die Unendlickheit*
influence	*die Einwirkung*
to influence or have an influence on	*einwirken*
intellect	*die Intelligenz*
intellectual	*geistlich*
intellectual compulsion	*der Denkzwang*
intelligence	*die Intelligenz*
intelligible	*verstandlich*
(what is) intended	*das Beabsichtigte*
intention, respect	*die Absicht*
to interact	*wechselwirken*
interaction	*die Wechselwirkung*
to interpolate	*hineinscheiben*
to interpret	*auffasen*
to intuit	*anschauen*
intuiting, act of intuiting	*das Anschauen*
the intuiting subject	*das Anschauende*
intuition	*die Anschauung*
justice	*das Recht*
kind	*die Art*
to know	*wissen*
knowing	*das Wissen*
knowledge	*das Wissen*
law	*das Recht*
legitimacy	*die Befügnis*
limit	*die Grenze, die Schranke*
to limit	*einschränken, begrenzen, schranken*
limitation	*die Begrenzung, die Einschränkung*
limited state	*die Begrenztheit*
(act of) limiting	*das Einschränken*
(process of) limiting	*die Begrenzung*
line of argument	*die Folgerungsart*
link	*das Glied*
longing	*das Sehnen*
to look at	*zusehen*

to made sensible	*versinnlichen*
magnitude	*die Größe*
to make real	*realisieren*
to manifest	*(sich) äussern*
manifestation	*die Äußerung*
manifold	*das Mannigfaltige*
manner of acting	*die Handlungsart*
material	*das Material, der Stoff, die Materie, der Stoff, die Sache*
measure	*das Maß*
mediacy	*die Mittelbarkeit*
mediate(d)	*mittelbar*
mediately	*mittelbar*
mediating component	*das Mittelglied*
member	*das Glied*
mental	*geistlich*
to mention	*andeutung*
might	*die Macht*
mind	*der Geist, das Gemüt*
mobile	*beweglich*
mobility	*die Beweglichkeit*
mode	*die Art*
model	*das Vorbild*
mood	*die Stimmung*
moveable	*beweglich*
movement	*das Übergehen*
multiplicity	*das Mannifaltig, die Mannigfaltigkeit*
mutual(ly)	*gegenseitig*
nature	*das Wesen, der Character*
needy	*bedürftig*
the Not-I	*das Nicht-Ich*
object	*das Objekt, der Gegenstand, das Ziel*
the object of thought	*das Gedachte*
objective element	*das Objektive*
to observe	*erblicken, zusehen*
obstacle	*das Hinderniss*
to obstruct	*hemmen*
obstruction	*die Hemmung*
to occur	*vorkommen*
occurences	*die Begebenheiten*
to operate	*wirken*
operation	*das Geschäft*
opinion	*die Ansicht*
to oppose	*entgegensetzen, gegensetzen, widerstreiten*
opposed striving	*das Gegenstreben*
(act of) opposing	*das Gegensetzen*
opposing proposition	*der Gegensatz*
opposite	*das Gegenteil, der Gegensatz*
opposition	*das Entgegensein, der Gegensatz*
to be in opposition to	*widerstreiten*

ordinary human understanding	*der gemeine Menschenverstand*
to originate	*entwerfen*
to oscillate	*schweben*
outgoing	*hinausgehend*
part	*der Teil*
passage	*das Übergehen*
passing away	*das Vergehen*
passive	*leidend*
passively affected	*leidend*
to perceive	*wahrnehmen*
perception	*die Wahrnehmung*
to point to or point out	*aufzeigen*
portion	*der Teil*
to portray	*abbilden, darstellen*
portrayal	*die Darstellung*
to posit	*setzen*
to posit in diminshed form	*herabsetzen*
to posit as fixed	*festsetzen*
to posit as idential or the same	*gleichsetzen*
to posit in opposition	*gegensetzen, entgegensetzen*
to posit together	*zusammensetzen*
posited-being	*das Gesetztsein*
(act of) positing	*das Setzen*
(act of) positing in opposition	*das Gegensetzen*
the (actively) positing subject	*das Setzend*
the one who posits	*das Setzend*
power	*das Vermögen, die Gewalt*
power of (free) choice	*die Willkür*
power of judgment	*die Urteilskraft*
precision	*die Bestimmtheit*
to prescribe	*vorschreiben*
presence	*das Vorhandsein*
to present	*aufstellen, aufweisen, darstellen*
presentation	*die Darstellung*
to preserve	*aufbehalten*
principle	*das Prinzip, der Satz*
problem	*der Aufgabe*
procedure	*das Verfahren*
to proceed (from)	*ausgehen (aus)*
to produce	*bewirken, hervorbringen*
product	*das Bewirkte*
productive act or activity	*das Machen*
the productive subject or agent	*das Machende*
to project	*entwerfen*
pronouncement	*der Ausspruch*
proof	*der Beweis*
(set of) properties	*die Beschaffenheit*
property	*die Eigenschaft*
proposition	*der Satz*

to prove	*beweisen, erweisen*
purely and simply	*schlechthin*
purpose	*der Zweck*
purposeful	*zweckmässig*
purposive	*zweckmässig*
quantity	*dir Größe*
quest	*das Suchen*
range	*der Umfang*
to react	*zurückwirken*
real	*reelle*
realiter	*realiter*
to realize	*realisieren*
"really" (in a real manner)	*realiter*
reason	*der Grund, die Vernuft*
to reason	*räsonieren*
(line of) reasoning	*das Räsonnement*
reciprocal activity	*das Wechseln*
reciprocal causally effective operation	*die Wechselwirkung*
reciprocal determination	*die Wechselbestimmung*
reciprocal interaction	*die Wechselwirkung*
reciprocal relation(ship)	*der Wechsel*
reciprocally-related-acting-and-being-passively-affected	*das Wechsel-Tun-und-Leiden*
reciprocally related components	*die Wechselglieder, der Wechsel*
reciprocity	*der Wechsel*
to recognize	*anerkennen, erkennen, annehmen*
to reconcile	*vereinigen*
reduction	*die Verringerung*
to refer	*beziehen*
(act of) reflecting	*die Reflexion*
to relate	*beziehen*
to be related reciprocally	*wechseln*
relation	*das Verhältniss, die Relation, die Beziehung*
relationship	*das Verhältniss, die Relation*
to represent	*vorstellen*
representation	*die Vorstellung*
the representing subject	*das Vorstellend*
requirement	*die Forderung*
to resist	*wiederstehen*
resistance	*das Widerstreben, der Widerstand*
resolve	*der Entschluß*
to resolve	*entschließen*
respect	*die Aspect, die Rücksicht, das Merkmal*
(state of) rest	*das Beruhen*
to restrain	*halten*
to restrict	*beschränken*
restricted state	*die Beschränktheit*
restriction	*die Beschränkung*
result	*die Folge*

to retain	*festhalten*
right	*das Recht*
same	*gleich*
satisfaction	*die Befriedigung*
science	*die Wissenschaft*
(spontaneous) self-activity	*die Selbsttätigkeit*
self-contained	*geschloßen*
self-feeling	*das Selbstgefühl*
self-reverting	*(in sich selbst) zuruckgehend*
self-subsistent	*für sich bestehend*
self-sufficiency	*die Selbständigkeit*
sensation	*die Empfindung*
sense	*der Sinn*
to sense	*empfinden*
sensibility	*die Sensibilität, die Sinnlichkeit*
to sensibilize	*versinnlichen*
sensible	*sinnlich*
sensible world	*die Sinnenwelt*
sensory	*sinnlich*
sensuousness	*die Sinnlichkeit*
separate(d)	*geschieden*
to separate	*trennen*
sequence	*die Folge*
to shape	*bilden*
to show	*aufzeigen, erweisen, nachweisen*
simulus	*der Stoß*
situation	*der Zustand*
specific	*bestimmt*
to specify	*bestimmen*
sphere of efficacy	*die Wirkungskreise*
spirit	*der Geist*
spiritual	*geistlich*
spontaneity	*die Selbsttätigkeit*
stabilized	*fixiert*
stability	*die Haltbarkeit*
to stablize	*fixieren, halten*
stable	*stehend*
to stand in a relationship of reciprocal efficacy	*wechselwirken*
standard measure	*die Maßgabe*
state	*der Zustand*
to state	*aufstellen*
state of being passively affected	*das Leiden*
state of passive affection	*das Leiden*
state of repose	*die Ruhe*
in a state of repose	*ruhend*
state of rest	*die Ruhe*
static	*ruhend*
stimulus	*der Antrieb*

to stipulate	*festsetzen*
to strive	*streben*
to strive in opposition	*widerstreben*
(activity of) striving	*das Streben*
striving in opposition	*das Widerstreben*
structure	*die Beschaffenheit*
stuff	*der Stoff*
subject	*die Sache*
the subjective element	*das Subjective*
to subsist	*bestehen*
subsistence	*das Bestehen*
to substantiate	*dartun*
supersensible	*übersinnlich*
to suppose	*setzen*
to be supressed	*wegfallen*
to surmise	*vermuten*
to surpress	*unterdrücken*
to take up	*aufnehmen*
talent	*die Anlage*
task	*der Aufgabe*
to tear or wrench away	*losreisen*
tenability	*die Haltbarkeit*
theory	*die Lehre*
to think	*denken*
(act of) thinking	*das Denken*
the thinking subject	*das Denkende*
to tie together	*verknüpfen*
totality	*der Inbegriff*
to transfer	*übertragen*
transference	*die Übertragung*
transformation	*die Verwandlung*
(movement of) transition	*der Übergang, das Übergehen*
to trust	*glauben*
(power of) understanding	*der Verstand*
to undertake	*vornehmen*
unification	*die Vereinigung*
to unify	*vereinigen*
union	*die Vereinigung*
unitary	*einig*
to unite	*vereinigen*
united	*einig*
unmediated	*unmittelbar*
valid	*gültig*
vanishing	*das Vergehen*
variety	*die Verschiedenheit*
to view	*erblicken*
view, point of view	*die Ansich*
viewpoint	*der Gesichtspunkt*
voluntary	*willkürlich*

way of proceeding	*das Verfahren*
way of acting	*die Handlungsweise*
way or manner of thinking	*die Denkart*
well-known	*bekannt*
what is brought about	*das Bewirkte*
what is discovered	*das Gefundene*
what enters (into)	*das Eintreten*
what can be felt	*das Fühlbar*
what is found	*das Gefundene*
what is objective	*das Objective*
what is subjective	*das Subjective*
what is thought of	*das Gedachte*
will	*der Wille*
(act of) willing	*das Wolle*
Wissenschaftslehre ("Doctrine of Scientific Knowledge")	*die Wissenschaftslehre*
to witness	*zusehen*

Bibliography and Guide to Further Study

Collected Editions of Fichte's Writings

Johann Gottlieb Fichtes sämmtliche Werke, ed. I. H. Fichte. Berlin: Viet & Co., 1845–46 and *Johann Gottlieb Fichtes nachgelassene Werke*, ed. I. H. Fichte. Berlin: Viet & Co., 1834–35; photomechanical reprint in 13 vols., *Fichtes Werke*, ed. I. H. Fichte. Berlin: De Gruyter, 1971 [= *SW*].

Fichtes Werke. Auswahl in Sechs Bänden, ed. Fritz Medicus. Leipzig: Fritz Eckardt [Felix Meiner], 1908-12; photomechanical reprint, Darmstadt: Wissenschaftliche Buchgesellschaft, 1962 [= *FW*].

J. G. Fichte-Gesamtausgabe der Bayerischen Akademie der Wissenschaften, ed. Reinhard Lauth, Walter Jacobs, Hans Gliwitzky, and Erich Fuchs. Stuttgart-Bad Cannstatt: Frommann-Holzboog, 1962–2012 [= *GA*].

Editions of *BWL*

Ueber den Begriff der Wissenschaftslehre oder der sogenannten Philosophie, als Einladungsschrift zu seinen Vorlesungen über diese Wissenschaft. Weimar: Verlag des Industrie Comptoir, 1794.

Ueber den Begriff der Wissenschaftslehre oder der sogenannten Philosophie. Jena and Leipzig: Christian Gabler, 1798. This second edition of *BWL* included a new forward, as well as excerpts from two hostile reviews, one, by J. S. Beck, of *BWL* and the "First Installment" of *GWL*, and the other an anonymous review of Schelling's *Ueber die Möglichkeit einer Form der Philosophie überhaupt*. Part Three of the first edition is omitted, along with several controversial footnotes. There are numerous, generally minor alterations, omissions, and additions to the first edition text.

Ueber den Begriff der Wissenschaftslehre oder der sogenannten Philosophie, in *SW*, I, pp. 27–82. This edition is based on the second, 1798 edition and includes footnotes based on Fichte's handwritten marginalia in his personal copy of *BWL*, as well as material from the first edition, but not the two reviews originally appended to the second edition.

Über den Begriff der Wissenschaftslehre oder der sogenannten Philosophie, *FW*, I, pp. 155–215. This edition is based on the second, 1798 edition, but includes material from the first edition, as well as the marginalia included in *SW*. It also includes Part Three, but not the two reviews originally appended to the second, 1798 edition.

Ueber den Begriff der Wissenschaftslehre oder der sogenannten Philosophie, als Einladungsschrift zu seinen Vorlesungen über diese Wissenschaft, in *GA*, I/2: pp. 107-72. This complete edition is based on the first, 1794 edition, but includes all the variants and additions from the second edition, including the two reviews, as well as the marginalia included in *SW*.

Editions of *GWL*

Grundlage der gesammten Wissenschaftslehre als Handschrift für seine Zuhörer. Leipzig: Christian Gabler, 1794–95. [= *A*.] This first edition was originally issued sequentially in individual fascicles to students enrolled in Fichte's "private" lectures during the Summer Semester of 1794 and Winter Semester of 1794–95. The trade edition of *GWL* was originally published by Gabler in two installments. The first, consisting of Parts One and Two, was published at the end of September 1794; the second, consisting of Part Three and the preface to the whole (signed "Easter Fair, 1795"), appeared at the end of July 1795.

Grundlage der gesammten Wissenschaftslehre und Grundriß des Eigenthümlichen der Wissenschaftslehre, neue unveränderte Auflage. Tübingen: Cotta'schen Buchhandlung, 1802. [= *B*.] This combined edition of *GWL* and *GEWL* was published in January of 1802, with continuous pagination and a brief forward to the new edition. This edition of *GWL* is almost identical to *A*.

Grundlage der gesammten Wissenschaftslehre als Handschrift für seine Zuhörer, zweite verbesserte Ausgabe. Jena and Leipzig: Christian Ernst Gabler, 1802 [= *C*]. This new, unauthorized edition of *GWL* was published at almost the same moment as *B*. It includes many revisions, which Fichte had sent to Gabler in 1800, in anticipation of a new edition of *GWL*.

Grundlage der gesammten Wissenschaftslehre, als Handschrift für seine Zuhörer, in *SW*, I, pp. 83–324. This edition is based on *B*, but includes a few new passages and footnotes from *C* as well. It also includes additional footnotes based on Fichte's own handwritten marginalia in his personal copy of *GWL*.

Grundlage der gesammten Wissenschaftslehre als Handschrift für seine Zuhörer, in *FW*, I, pp. 275–519. This edition is based on *C*, but notes all differences with *A* and *B*, as well as the marginalia from *SW*.

Grundlage der gesammten Wissenschaftslehre als Handschrift für seine Zuhörer, in *GA*, I/2: 249–461. This complete edition is based on *A*, but includes all variations and additions from *B* and *C*, as well as the marginalia from *SW*.

Editions of *GEWL*

Grundriß des Eigenthümlichen der Wissenschaftslehre in Rücksicht auf das theoretischen Vermögen, als Handschrift für seine Zuhörer. Jena and Leipzig: Christian Ernst Gabler, 1795.

Grundlage der gesammten Wissenschaftslehre und Grundriß des Eigenthümlichen der Wissenschaftslehre, neue unveränderte Auflage. Tübingen: Cotta'schen Buchhandlung, 1802 [= *B*]. This combined edition of *GWL* and *GEWL* was published in January of 1802, with continuous pagination and a brief forward to the new edition. This ed. of *GEWL* is almost identical to the first.

Grundriss des Eigenthümlichen der Wissenschaftslehre in Rücksicht auf das theoretischen Vermögen, als Handschrift für seine Zuhörer, zweite verbesserte Ausgabe. Jena and Leipzig: Christian Ernst Gabler, 1802. This new, unauthorized edition of *GEWL* was published at almost the same moment as *B*. It includes some minor, mainly orthographic revisions.

Grundriss des Eigenthümlichen der Wissenschaftslehre in Rücksicht auf das theoretischen Vermögen, als Handschrift für seine Zuhörer, in *SW*, I, pp. 329–411.

Grundriss des Eigenthümlichen der Wissenschaftslehre in Rücksicht auf das theoretischen Vermögen, als Handschrift für seine Zuhörer, FW, I, pp. 522–603.
Grundriß des Eigenthümlichen der Wissenschaftslehre in Rücksicht auf das theoretischen Vermögen, als Handschrift für seine Zuhörer, in *GA, I/3,* pp. 139–208. This complete edition is based on the first, 1795 edition, but includes all the (minor) variations in the two later editions.

Editions of the "Zurich *Wissenschaftslehre*"

Züricher Vorlesungen über den Begriff der Wissenschaftslehre Februar 1794. Nachschrift Lavater. Beilage aus Jens Baggesens Nachlass: Exzerpt aus der Abschrift von Fichtes Züricher Vorlesungen. Ed. Erich Fuchs. Neuried: Ars Una, 1996 [= *ZVau*].
Züricher Vorlesungen über den Begriff der Wissenschaftslehre Februar 1794; Exzerpt aus Jens Baggesens Nachlass: Exzerpt aus der Züricher Vorlesungen über Wissenschaftslehre, Abschrift Baggesen. In *GA,* IV/3: 19–48. Same text as *ZVau*.

Additional Contemporary Works and Documents

Aus der Frühzeit des deutschen Idealismus. Texte zur Wissenschaftslehre Fichtes 1794–1894. Ed. Martin Oesch. Würzburg: Königshausen und Neumann, 1987.
Jacobi, F. H. *Über die Lehre des Spinoza,* 2nd revised edition. Breslau: G. Loewe, 1785.
Jacobi, F. H. *David Hume über den Glauben, oder Idealismus und Realismus.* Breslau: G. Loewe, 1787; photomechanical reprint with an introduction by Lewis White Beck, New York: Garland, 1983.
J. G. Fichtes Leben und literarischer Briefwechsel. Ed. I. H. Fichte. 2 vols. Sulzbach: J. E. Seidel, 1830.
J. G. Fichte in Gespräch. Berichte der Zeitgenossen. 7 vols. Ed. Erich Fuchs in cooperation with Reinhard Lauth and Walter Schieche. Stuttgart-Bad Canstatt: Frommann-Holzboog, 1978–2012.
J. G. Fichte in zeitgenössische Rezensionen. 4 vols. Ed. Erich Fuchs, Wilhelm G. Jacobs, and Walter Schieche. Stuttgart-Bad Canstatt: Frommann-Holzboog, 1995.
Maimon, Salomon. *Versuch über die Transzendentalphilosophie.* Berlin: Christian Friedrich Voß und Sohn, 1790.
Maimon, Salomon. *Streifereien im Gebiete der Philosophie.* Berlin. Wilhelm Vieweg. 1793.
Maimon, Salomon. *Über die Progressen der Philosophie.* Berlin: Wilhelm Vieweg, 1793.
Maimon, Salomon. *Versuch einer neuen Logik oder Theorie des Denkens, nebst angehängten Briefen von Philaletes an Aenesidemus.* Berlin: Ernst Felisch, 1794.
Reinhold, K. L. *Versuch einer neuen Theorie des menschlichen Vorstellungsvermögens.* Jena: Mauke, 1789.
Reinhold, K. L. *Beyträge zur Berichtigung bisheriger Missverständnisse der Philosophen,* Bd. I. Jena: Mauke, 1790.
Reinhold, K. L. *Ueber das Fundament des philosophischen Wissens.* Jena: Mauke, 1791.

Translations of Fichte's Early Writings

Attempt at a Critique of All Revelation. Trans. Garrett Green. New York: Cambridge University Press, 1978; reissued, with a new introduction by Allen Wood, 2010.

Contribution to the Correction of the Public's Judgments on the French Revolution. Ed. and trans. Jeffrey Church and Anna Marisa Schön. Albany: State University of New York Press, 2020.

A Crystal-Clear Report to the General Public concerning the Actual Essence of the Newest Philosophy. An Attempt to Force the Reader to Understand. Trans. John Botterman and William Rasch. In *Fichte, Jacobi, and Schelling: Philosophy of German Idealism.* Ed. Ernst Behler, pp. 39–115. New York: Continuum, 1987.

Early Philosophical Writings. Ed. and trans. Daniel Breazeale. Ithaca, NY: Cornell University Press, 1988.

Foundations of the Entire Science of Knowledge. Trans. Peter Heath. In *Fichte: Science of Knowledge (Wissenschaftslehre).* Ed. Peter Heath and John Lachs, pp. 89–286. New York: Appleton-Century-Crofts, 1970; reissued, with minor corrections, as *The Science of Knowledge.* Cambridge: Cambridge University Press, 1982.

Foundations of Natural Right. Trans. Michael Baur, ed. Frederick Neuhouser. Cambridge: Cambridge University Press, 2000.

Foundations of Transcendental Philosophy (Wissenschaftslehre) nova methodo. Ed. and trans. Daniel Breazeale. Ithaca, NY: Cornell University Press, 1992.

Introductions to the Wissenschaftslehre and Other Writings. Ed. and trans. Daniel Breazeale. Indianapolis, IN: Hackett, 1994.

J. G. Fichte and the Atheism Dispute (1798–1800). Trans. Curtis Bowman, ed. Yolanda Estes. Burlington, VT: Ashgate, 2010.

La doctrine de la science (1794). Vol. I. Trans. Marc Géraud. Paris: l'Harmattan, 2016.

"La 'Première' Doctrine de la Science de Fichte." Trans. and ed. Ives Radrizzani. *Archives de Philosophie* 60 (1997): 615–58.

Œuvres choisies de philosophie première. Trans. Alexis Philonenko. Paris: Vrin 1964; 2nd edition, 1972; 3rd edition. 1999.

"On the Linguistic Capacity and the Origin of Language." Trans. Jere Paul Surber. In Surber, *Language and German Idealism: Fichte's Linguistic Philosophy*, pp. 116–45. Atlantic Highlands, NJ: Humanities Press International, 1995.

The Philosophical Rupture between Fichte and Schelling: Selected Texts and Correspondence (1800–1802). Trans. and ed. Michael G. Vater and David W. Wood. Albany, NY: SUNY Press, 2012.

"Review of F. H. Gebhard, *On Ethical Goodness as Disinterested Benevolence.*" Trans. Daniel Breazeale. *The Philosophical Forum* 32 (2001): 297–310.

"Review of Leonhard Creuzer, *Skeptical Reflections on the Freedom of the Will.*" Trans. Daniel Breazeale. *The Philosophical Forum* 32 (2001): 289–96.

The Science of Knowledge. Trans. and ed. A. E. Kroeger. Philadelphia: J. B. Lippincott, 1868; reprint London: Trübner, 1889.

The Science of Knowledge. Trans. and ed. Peter Heath and John Lachs. New York: Meredith, 1970; reprint Cambridge: Cambridge University Press, 1982.

The System of Ethics. Trans. Daniel Breazeale and Günter Zöller. Cambridge: Cambridge University Press, 2005.

The Vocation of Man. Trans. Peter Preuss. Indianapolis, IN: Hackett, 1987.

About Fichte and the Early *Wissenschaftslehre*, and Works Cited

Acosta, Emiliano. "La deducción de las categorías en el *Fundamento de toda la doct-rina de la ciencia* de J. G. Fichte." In *Fichte en el laberinto del idealismo*, ed. Mariano L. Guadio and María Jimena Solé, pp. 111–56. Buenos Aires: RAGIF Ediciones, 2019.

Acosta, Emiliano. "*Wissenschaftslehre*." In *The Bloomsbury Handbook to Fichte*, ed. Marina F. Bykova, pp. 309–17. London and New York: Bloomsbury Academic, 2020.

Adamson, Robert. *Fichte*. Edinburgh: Blackwood, 1881.

Altman, Matthew C. "Fichte's Transcendental Idealism: An Interpretation and Defense." In *The Palgrave Handbook of German Idealism*, ed. Altman, pp. 320–43. Hampshire: Palgrave Macmillan, 2014.

Asmuth, Christoph. "'Das Schweben ist der Quell aller Realität.' Platner, Fichte, Schlegel, Novalis und die produktive Einbildungskraft." In *System and Context. Early Romantic and Early Idealistic Constellations*, ed. Rolf Ahlers, pp. 349–74. Lewiston, NY: Edwin Mellen Press, 2004.

Baumanns, Peter. *Fichtes ursprüngliches System. Sein Standort zwischen Kant und Hegel*. Stuttgart-Bad Cannstatt: Frommann-Holzboog, 1972.

Baumanns, Peter. *Fichtes Wissenschaftslehre. Probleme ihres Anfangs. Mit einem Kommentar zur § 1 der* Grundlage der gesammten Wissenschaftslehre. Bonn: Bouvier, 1974.

Baumanns, Peter. *J. G. Fichte: Kritische Gesamtdarstellung seiner Philosophie*. Freiburg and München: Karl Albert, 1990.

Beck, Lewis White. *Early German Philosophy: Kant and his Predecessors*. Cambridge, MA: Harvard University Press, 1969.

Beeler-Port, Josef. *Verklärung und Auges. Konstruktionsanalyse der ersten Wissenschaftslehre J. G. Fichtes*. New York: Lang, 1997.

Beiser, Frederick C. *The Fate of Reason: German Philosophy from Kant to Fichte*. Cambridge, MA: Harvard University Press, 1987.

Beiser, Frederick C. "Fichte's Critique of Subjectivism." Part II of *German Idealism: The Struggle against Subjectivism, 1781–1801*, pp. 215–345. Cambridge: Cambridge University Press, 1992.

Böhmer, Otto A. *Faktizität und Erkenntnisbegründung. Eine Untersuchung zur Bedeutung des Faktischen in der frühen Philosophie J. G. Fichtes*. Frankfurt: Rita G. Fischer Verlag, 1979.

Brachtendorf, Johannes. *Fichtes Lehre vom Sein. Eine kritische Darstellung der Wissenschaftslehren von 1794, 1798/99, und 1812*. Paderborn, Munich, Vienna, and Lund: Ferdinand Schonigh, 1995.

Breazeale, Daniel. "Certainty, Universal Validity, and Conviction: The Methodological Primacy of Practical Reason within the Jena *Wissenschaftslehre*." In *New Perspectives on Fichte*, ed. Daniel Breazeale and Tom Rockmore, pp. 35–59. Atlantic Highlands, NJ: Humanities Press, 1996.

Breazeale, Daniel. "The Theory of Practice and the Practice of Theory: Fichte and the 'Primacy of Practical Reason.'" *International Philosophical Quarterly* 36 (1996): 47–64.

Breazeale, Daniel. "Some Theses Concerning the Jena *Wissenschaftslehre*." In *Philosophie als Denkwerkzeug: Zur Aktualität transzendentalphilosophischer*

Argumentation, ed. Martin Götze, Christian Lotz, Konstantin Pollock, and Dorothea Wildenburg, pp. 49–58. Würzburg: Königshausen & Neumann, 1998.

Breazeale, Daniel. "Fichte's Abstract Realism." In *From Transcendental Philosophy to Metaphysics: The Emergence of German Idealism*, ed. Michael Baur and Daniel O. Dahlstrom, pp. 99–115. Washington, DC: Catholic University of America Press, 1999.

Breazeale, Daniel. "The Spirit of the *Wissenschaftslehre*." In *The Reception of Kant's Critical Philosophy: Fichte, Schelling and Hegel*, ed. Sally Sedgwick, pp. 171–98. Cambridge: Cambridge University Press, 2000.

Breazeale, Daniel. "*Der Satz der Bestimmbarkeit*: Fichte's Appropriation and Transformation of Maimon's Principle of Synthetic Thinking." *Internationales Jahrbuch des Deutschen Idealismus/International Yearbook of German Idealism* 1 (2003): 115–40.

Breazeale, Daniel. *Thinking Through the* Wissenschaftslehre: *Themes from Fichte's Early Philosophy*. Oxford: Oxford University Press, 2013.

Breazeale, Daniel. "Fichte's Project: The Jena *Wissenschaftslehre*." In *Kant, Fichte, and the Legacy of Transcendental Idealism*, ed. Halla Kim and Steven Hoeltzel, pp. 101–27. Lanham, MD: Rowman & Littlefiedl, 2015.

Breazeale, Daniel. "The Synthetic-Genetic Method of Transcendental Philosophy: Kantian Questions/Fichtean Answers." In *The History of the Transcendental Turn*, ed. Sebastian Gardner and Matthew Grist, pp. 74–95. Oxford: Oxford University Press, 2015.

Breazeale, Daniel. "Reinhold/Schulze/Fichte: A Re-Examination." In *Krankheit des Zeitalters oder heilsame Provokation? Skeptizismus in der nachkantischen Philosophie*, ed. Martin Bondeli, Jiří Chotaš, and Klaus Vieweg, pp. 151–79. Paderborn: Fink, 2016.

Breazeale, Daniel. "Fichte's Spinoza: 'Common Standpoint,' 'Essential Opposition,' and 'Hidden Treasure.'" *Internationales Jahrbuch des Deutschen Idealismus/ International Yearbook of German Idealism* 14 (2018): 103–38.

Breazeale, Daniel. "'The Summit of Kantian Speculation': Fichte's Reception of the *Critique of the Power of Judgment*." *Anuario Filosófico* 52 (2019): 113–44.

Breazeale, Daniel and Tom Rockmore (eds.). *New Essays on Fichte's* Foundation of the Entire Doctrine of Scientific Knowledge. Amherst, NY: Humanity Books, 2001.

Contents: Tom Rockmore, "Introduction," pp. 7-15; Daniel Breazeale, "Transcendental Deduction or Pragmatic History? Methodological Reflections on Fichte's *Grundlage der gesamten Wissenschaftslehre*," pp. 19-36; Steven Hoeltzel, "Fichte's Deduction of Representation in the 1794–95 *Grundlage*," pp. 39-59; Tom Rockmore, "Fichte on Deduction in the Jena *Wissenschaftslehre*," pp. 60-77; Michael Baur, "Self-Measure and Self-Moderation in Fichte's *Wissenschaftslehre*," pp. 81-102; Arnold Farr, "Reflective Judgment and the Boundaries of Finite Human Knowledge: The Path Towards Fichte's 1794–95 *Wissenschaftslehre*," pp. 103-21; C. Jeffery Kinlaw, "Imagination and Time in Fichte's *Grundlage*," pp. 122-37; Günter Zöller, "Positing and Determining in Fichte's *Foundation of the Entire Wissenschaftslehre*," pp. 138-52; Jere Paul Surber, "*Satz* and *Urteil* in Kant's Critical Philosophy and Fichte's *Grundlage der gesamten Wissenschaftslehre*," pp. 155-64; Pierre Kerszberg, "The Paradox of Primary Reflection," pp. 165-82; Michael G. Vater, "Schelling's *Vom Ich als Princip der Philosophie* as a

Reading of Fichte's *Grundlage der gesamten Wissenschaftslehre*," pp. 183–96; Vladimir Zeman, "Between Kant and Fichte: Fichte's *Foundation of the Entire Science of Knowledge*," pp. 197–209; Curtis Bowman, "Jacobi's Philosophy of Faith and Fichte's *Wissenschaftslehre* 1794–95," pp. 210–26; Dale Snow, "The Early Critical Reception of the 1794 *Wissenschaftslehre*," pp. 229–42; George Seidel, "Hegel's Early Reaction to the *Wissenschaftslehre*: The Case of the Misplaced Adjective," pp. 243–53.

Bruno, G. Anthony. "Genealogy and Jurisprudence in Fichte's Genetic Deduction of the Categories." *History of Philosophy Quarterly* 35 (2018): 77–96.

Les Cahiers de philosophie, "Le bicentenaire de la *Doctrine de la Science* de Fichte (1794–1994)." Numéro hors série, Printemps 1995.

Contents: Jean-Louis Vieillard-Baron, "Présentation: Le bicentenaire de la *Doctrine de la Science* de Fichte (1794–1994)," pp. 7–10; Claudio Cesa, "De la *Philosophie élémentaire* à la *Doctrine de la Science* de Fichte," pp. 11–27; Reinhard Lauth, "Le progrès de la connaissance dans la première *Doctrine de la Science* de Fichte," pp. 29–45; Jean-Christophe Merle, "La synthèse pratique de la seconde version de l'*Essai d'une critique de toute révélation*," pp. 47–67; Daniel Breazeale, "De la *Tathandlung* à l'*Anstoß* et retour. Liberté et facticité dans les *Principes de la Doctrine de la Science*," pp. 69–87; Jean-Christophe Goddard, "La *Doctrine de la Science* et l'Âge de l'Esprit," pp. 89–107; Pierre Kerzsberg, "Le futur comme problème transcendantal," pp. 109–22; Marc Maesschalck, "L'éthique des convictions chez Fichte de 1798 à 1805," pp. 123–36; Jean-François Marquet, "Fichte et le problème de la *Bestimmung*," pp. 137–48; Alain Perrinjaquet, "Le fondement de la philosophie pratique de Fichte en 1796–1799. *Doctrine de la Science nova methodo* ou *Fondements de toute la Doctrine de la Science*?" pp. 149–67; Alexis Philonenko, "Le devoir," pp. 169–79; Claude Piché, "L'esthétique a-t-elle une place dans la philosophie de Fichte?" pp. 181–202; Miklos Vetö, "L'action selon Fichte," pp. 203–10; Günter Zöller, "L'idéal et le réel dans la théorie transcendantale du sujet chez Fichte. Une duplicité originaire," pp. 211–25; Jacques D'Hondt, "Fichte en 1794," pp. 227–36); Ives Radrizzani, "La *Doctrine de la Science* et la Franc-Maçonnerie," pp. 237–52; Bernard Bourgeois, "*Cogito* kantien et *cogito* fichtéen," pp. 253–65; Jean-François Courtine, "Les débuts philosophiques de Hölderlin à Iéna et sa critique de Fichte," pp. 267–85; Alain Renaut, "Fichte aujourd'hui: actualité de la *Doctrine de la Science*," pp. 287–99; Tom Rockmore, "Fichte, le tournant subjectif et le rêve de Descartes," pp. 301–12); Jean-Louis Vieillard-Baron, "Remarques sur la critique hégélienne de Fichte," pp. 313–23; A. Perrinjaquet et I. Radrizzani, "Bibliographie fichtéenne," pp. 325–41.

Calkins, Mary Whiton. "Notes on Fichte's *Grundlage der gesamten Wissenschaftslehre*." *Philosophical Review* 3 (1894): 459–62.

Carvalho, Mario Jorge de. "What It Takes to Make a 'Thing' (Fichte, *Grundriss des Eigenthümlichen der Wissenchaftslehre*)." *La Revista de Estud(i)os sobre Fichte* No. 19 (Verano/Verão, 2019).

Cesa, Claudio. "Der Begriff 'Trieb' in der Frühschriften von J. G. Fichte (1792-1794)." In *Kant und sein Jahrhundert*, ed. C. Cesa and N. Hinske, pp. 165–86. Frankfurt a.M.: Peter Lang, 1993.

Claesges, Ulrich. *Geschichte des Selbstbewußtseins. Der Ursprung des spekulativen Problems in Fichtes Wissenschaftslehre von 1794–95*. Den Haag: Martinus Nijhoff, 1974.

Class, Wolfgang and Alois K. Soller. *Kommentar zu Fichtes* Grundlage der gesamten Wissenschaftslehre. Amsterdam: Rodopi, 2004.

Cohen-Maurel, Laure. "'(Toi.) (A la place du Non-Moi—Toi.' Jacobi, Fichte, Novalis." In *L'homme et la nature. Politique, critique et esthétique dans le romantisme allemand.* Berlina and Münster: LIT Verlag, 2020.

Da Cunha, João Geraldo Martins. "Analítica e dialética na primeira filosofia de Fichte." *Revista de Filosofia Aurora* 27 (2015): 759ff.

Dreschler, Julius. *Fichtes Lehre vom Bild.* Stuttgart: W. Kohlhammer, 1955.

Druet, Pierre-Phillippe, "L'*Anstoss*' fichtéen. Essai d'élucidation d'une métaphore. *Revue Philosophique de Louvain* 7 (1972): 384–92.

Dürr, Suzanne. "Fichtes Theorie der Subjektivität." In *Idealismus und Romantik in Jena: Figuren und Konzepte zwischen 1794 und 1807,* ed. Johannes Korngiebel, Klaus Vieweg, Johannes Korngiebel, and Michael Forster, pp. 25–38. Jena: Willhelm Fink, 2018.

Estes, Yolanda. "J. G. Fichte's Jena Wissenschaftslehre." In *Fichte en el laberinto del idealismo,* ed. Mariano L. Guadio and María Jimena Solé, pp. 157–82. Buenos Aires: RAGIF Ediciones, 2019.

Everett, Charles Caroll. *Fichte's Science of Knowledge: A Critical Exposition.* Chicago: Griggs, 1884.

Fauteck, Heinrich. "Die Beziehung Jens Baggesens zu Fichte." *Orbis Litterarum* [Copenhagen] 38 (1983): 312–37.

Ferrer, Diogo. "Paradox, Incompleteness and Labyrinth in Fichte's *Wissenschaftslehre.*" *La Revista de Estud(i)os sobre Fichte* No. 12. (Inv(i)erno 2016).

Fichte-Studien. "Die *Grundlage der gesamten Wissenschaftslehre* von 1794/95 und der transzendentale Standpunkt," ed. Wolfgang Schrader. *Fichte-Studien* 10 (1997):

Contents: Dominik Schmidig, "Sprachliche Vermittlung philosophischer Einsichten nach Fichtes Frühphilosophie," pp. 1–15; Thomas Sören, "Die *Grundlage der gesamten Wissenschaftslehre* und das Problem der Sprache bei Fichte," pp. 17–33; Jere Paul Surber, "Fichtes Sprachphilosophie und der Begriff einer Wissenschaftslehre," pp. 35–49; Holger Jergius, "Fichtes 'geometrische' Semantik," pp. 51–63; Günter Meckenstock, "Beobachtungen zur Methodik in Fichtes *Grundlage der gesammten Wissenschaftslehre,*" pp. 67–80; Hartmut Traub, "Wege zur Wahrheit. Zur Bedeutung von Fichtes wissenschaftlich- und populär-philosophischer Methode," pp. 81–98; Jürgen Stahl, "System und Methode—Zur methodologischen Begründung transzendentalen Philosophierens in Fichtes 'Begriffschrift,'" pp. 99–113; Kunihiko Nagasawa, "Eine neue Möglichkeit der Philosophie nach der *Grundlage der gesammten Wissenschaftslehre,*" pp. 115–23; Katsuaki Okada, "Der erste Grundsatz und die Bildlehre," pp. 127–41; Hisang Ryue, "Die Differenz zwischen 'Ich bin' und 'Ich bin Ich,'" pp. 143–56; Christian Klotz, "Der Ichbegriff in Fichtes Erörterung der Substantialität," pp. 157–73; Alois K. Soller, "Fichtes Lehre vom Anstoß, Nicht-Ich und Ding an sich in der *Grundlage der gesamten Wissenschaftslehre. Eine kritische Erörterung,*" pp. 175–89; Heinz Eidam, "Fichtes Anstoß. Anmerkungen zu einem Begriff der *Wissenschaftslehre* von 1794," pp. 191–208; Virginia López-Domínguez, "Die Deduktion des Gefühls in der *Grundlage der gesammten Wissenschaftslehre,*" pp. 209–18; Reinhard Loock, "Gefühl und Realität: Fichtes Auseinandersetzung mit Jacobi in der *Grundlage der Wissenschaft des Praktischen,*" pp. 219–37; Marek J. Siemek, "Wissen und Tun. Zur Handlungsweise der transzendentalen Subjektivität in der ersten Wissenschaftslehre

Fichtes," pp. 241–52; Daniel Breazeale, "Der fragwürdige 'Primat der praktischen Vernunft' in Fichtes *Grundlage der gesamten Wissenschaftslehre*," pp. 253–71; Marcin Poreba, "Das Problem der transzendentalen Freiheit in semantischer Formulierung (Dargestellt in Fichtes Jenaer Wissenschaftslehre)," pp. 273–83; Giuseppe Duso, "Absolutheit und Widerspruch in der *Grundlage der gesamten Wissenschaftslehre*," pp. 285–98; Manuel Jiménez-Redondo, "Der Begriff des Grundes in Fichtes Wissenschaftslehre," pp. 299–316; Helmut Girndt, "Das 'Ich' des ersten Grundsatzes der *Grundlage der gesamten Wissenschaftslehre* in der Sicht der *Wissenschaftslehre* von 1804²," pp. 319–33; Josef Beeler-Port, "Zum Stellenwert der *Grundlage* aus der Sicht von 1804. Eine Interpretation des Wechsels von analytische-synthetischer und genetischer Methode in § 5 der *Grundlage*," pp. 335–50.

Förster, Eckart. "Fichte's '*Complete* Revolution of the Mode of Thought' and 'Morals and Critique.'" In Förster, *The Twenty-Five Years of Philosophy: A Systematic Reconstruction*, trans. Brady Bowman. Cambridge: Harvard University Press, 2012, pp. 179–223.

Franks, Paul W. "Freedom, *Tatsache* and *Tathandlung* in the Development of Fichte's Jena *Wissenschaftslehre*." *Archiv für Geschichte der Philosophie* 79 (1997): 310–23.

Franks, Paul W. *All or Nothing: Systematicity, Transcendental Arguments, and Skepticism in German Idealism*. Cambridge, MA: Harvard University Press, 2005.

Franks, Paul W. "Fichte's Position: Anti-Subjectivism, Self-Awareness and Self-Location in the Space of Reasons." In *The Cambridge Companion to Fichte*, ed. David James and Günter Zöller, pp. 374–404. Cambridge: Cambridge University Press, 2016.

Fuchs, Erich. *Wirklichkeit als Aufgabe. Die doxischen Konstitutiva der theoretischen Konzeption des faktischen Gegenstandes in J. G. Fichtes "Grundlage der gesammten Wissenschaftslehre.* [I.D.] München: Salzer, 1973.

Fuchs, Erich and Ives Radrizzani (eds.). *Der Grundansatz der ersten Wissenschaftslehre Johann Gottlieb Fichtes*. Neuried: Ars Una, 1996.

Contents: Manfred Zahn, "Die Aktlehre in der späten Philosophie Kants und die Lehre vom Setzen in der Wissenschaftslehre Fichtes," pp. 13–41; Manfred Gawlina, "Die Aufgabe einer Deutung der 'transzendentalen Deduktion,'" pp. 43–55; Erich Fuchs, "J. K. Lavaters Nachschrift der Züricher Wissenschaftslehre," pp. 56–73; Alain Perrinjaquet, "Setzen, Endlichkeit und Selbstbeschränkung in der frühen Philosophie Fichtes," pp. 74–94; Daniel Breazeale, "Reflexives philosophisches und ursprüngliches Setzen der Vernunft. Über die Methode und Methodenlehre der frühen Jenenser Wissenschaftslehre," pp. 95–110; Liang Zhixue, "Die methodischen Probleme der ersten Wissenschaftslehre Fichtes," pp. 111–20; Reinhard Lauth, "Die konstituierenden Momente des Setzens in Fichtes erster Wissenschaftslehre," pp. 121–33; Claudio Cesa, "'…ein Doppelsinn in der Bedeutung des Wortes Setzen,'" pp. 134–44; Giuseppe Duso, "Absolutheit und Widerspruch in der Grundlage der gesamten Wissenschaftslehre," pp. 145–57; Alexis Philonenko, "Über die schöpferische Einbildungskraft bei Fichte," pp. 158–77; Günter Zöller, "Setzen und Bestimmen in Fichtes Grundlage der gesamten Wissenschaftslehre," pp. 178–92; Carla De Pascale, "Das Problem der Vereinigung: Intellektuelle Anschauung und produktive Einbildungskraft," pp. 193–204; Gaetano Rametta, "Setzen und Handeln im praktischen Teil der Grundlage der gesamten Wissenschaftslehre," pp. 205–15; Marco Ivaldo, "Setzen in praktischer Sicht: Überlegungen zu § 5 der Grundlage der gesamten

Wissenschaftslehre," pp. 216–29; Faustino Oncina Coves, "Das Setzen in der Rechtslehre," pp. 230–9; Ives Radrizzani, "Das Fichte-Bild von Main de Biran," pp. 240–57; Yashuhiro Kumamoto, "Die transzendentale Methode der ersten Wissenschaftslehre und die Seinslehre beim späten Fichte," pp. 258–65.

Fulkerson-Smith, Brett. "Fichte's Experiments with the Productive Imagination." In *Fichte and Transcendental Philosophy*, ed Tom Rockmore and Daniel Breazeale, pp. 103–27. New York: Palgrave Macmillan, 2016.

Garcia, Luis Fellipe. *La philosophie comme Wissenschaftslehre. Le projet fichtéen d'une nouvelle pratique du savoir*. Hildesheim, Zurich, and New York: Olms, 2018.

Gardner, Sebastian. "The Status of the *Wissenschaftslehre*. Transcendental and Ontological Grounds in Fichte." *Internationales Jahrbuch des Deutschen Idealismus/ International Yearbook of German Idealism* 5 (2007): 90–125.

Gaspar, Francisco Prata. "Wahrheit und Einbildungskraft: Erklärungsversuch einer Textstelle." *Fichte-Studien* 48 (2019): 25–44.

Girndt, Helmut. *Die Differenz des Fichteschen und Hegelschen Systems in der Hegelschen "Differenzschrift."* Bonn: Bouvier, 1965.

Goddard, Jean-Chrisophe. *Assise fondamentale de la doctrine de la science (1794)*. Paris: Ellipses, 1999.

Goh, Kienhow. "Drive (*der Trieb*)." In *The Bloomsbury Handbook to Fichte*, ed. Marina F. Bykova, pp. 399–407. London and New York: Bloomsbury Academic, 2020.

Gottlieb, Gabriel. "Fichte's Relational I: *Anstoß* and *Aufforderung*." In *The Palgrave Fichte Handbook*, ed. Stephen Hoeltzel, pp. 213–35. Cham: Palgrave Macmillan, 2019.

Goubet, J.-F. *Fichte et la philosophie transcendantale comme science. Étude sur la naissance de la première Doctrine de la Science (1793–1796)*. Paris: L'Harmattan, 2002.

Gueroult, Martial. *L'évolution et la structure de la doctrine de la science chez Fichte*. 2 vols. Paris: Société de l'édition, 1930.

Guyot, Laurent. "Le rôle de l'imagination productrice dans la genèse de la conscience de soi." *Fichte-Studien* 42 (2016): 121–34.

Haag, Johannes. "Fichte's Critique of Spinoza in the *Grundlage*." *Internationales Jahrbuch des Deutschen Idealismus/International Yearbook of German Idealism* 14 (2016): 139–63.

Haag, Johannes. "Imagination and Objectivity in Fichte's early Wissenschaftslehre." In *The Significances of the Imagination in Kant, Idealism, and Romanticism*, ed. Gerad Gentry and Konstantin Pollok, pp. 109–28. Cambridge: Cambridge University Press, 2019.

Hammacher, Klaus. "Zur transzendentallogischen Begründung der Dialektik bei Fichte." *Kant-Studien* 79 (1988): 467–75.

Hammacher, Klaus. "Fichte, Maimon und Jacobi. Transzendentaler Idealismus und Realismus." In *Transzendentalphilosophie als System*, ed. Alfred Mues, pp. 243–63. Hamburg: Meiner, 1989.

Hartkopf, Werner. "Die Dialektik Fichtes als Vorstufe zu Hegels Dialektik." *Zeitschrift für philosophische Forshung* 21 (1967): 173–207.

Henrich, Dieter. *Fichtes ursprüngliche Einsicht*. Frankfurt am Main: Klostermann, 1967; trans. David Lachterman, "Fichte's Original Insight," *Contemporary German Philosophy* 1 (1982) 15–52; reprint in *Debates in Nineteenth Century Philosophy:*

Essential Readings and Contemporary Responses, ed. Kristin Gjesdal, pp. 35–44. London: Routledge, 2015.

Henrich, Dieter. "Fichte." Part III of Henrich, *Between Kant and Hegel: Lectures on German Idealism*, ed. David S. Pacini, pp. 157–276. Cambridge, MA: Harvard University Press, 2003.

Hoeltzel, Steven H. "Fichte, Transcendental Ontology, and the Ethics of Belief." In *Transcendental Inquiry: Its History, Methods and Critiques*, ed. Halla Kim and Steven Hoeltzel, pp. 55–82. New York: Palgrave-Macmillan, 2016.

Hoeltzel, Steven H. "*Anstoß* and *Aufforderung* ('Check' and 'Summons')." In *The Bloomsbury Handbook to Fichte*, ed. Marina F. Bykova, pp. 353–61. London and New York: Bloomsbury Academic, 2020.

Hoeltzel, Steven H. "The Three Basic Principles (*drei Grundsätze*)." In *The Bloomsbury Handbook to Fichte*, ed. Marina F. Bykova, pp. 327–35. London and New York: Bloomsbury Academic, 2020.

Hogrebe, Wolfram (ed.). *Fichte's Wissenschaftslehre 1794. Philosophische Resonanzen*. Frankfurt a.M.: Suhrkamp, 1995.

Contents: Manfred Frank, "Philosophische Grundlage der Frühromantik," pp. 13–34; Rüdiger Bubner, "Von Fichte zu Schlegel," pp. 35–49; Wolfram Hogrebe, "Sehnsucht und Erkenntnis," pp. 50–67; Jürgen Stolzenberg, "Fichtes Begriff des praktischen Selbstbewußtseins," pp. 71–95; Marek J. Siemek, "Fichtes und Husserls Konzept der Transzendentalphilosophie," pp. 96–113; Werner Stelzner, "Selbstzuschreibung und Identität," pp. 117–40; Jürgen Mittelstraß, "Fichte und das absolute Wissen," pp. 141–61; Klaus Vieweg, "Fichtes Vorlesungen über die Bestimmung des Gelehrten von 1794," pp. 165–82; Klaus-Michael Kodalle, "Fichtes Wahrnehmung des Historischen," pp. 183–224; Odo Marquard, "Theodizeemotive in Fichtes früher Wissenschaftslehre," pp. 225–36.

Hohler, Thomas. "Fichte and the Problem of Finitude." *Southwestern Journal of Philosophy* 7 (1976): 15–33.

Hohler, Thomas. *Imagination and Reflection: Intersubjectivity. Fichte's* Grundlage *of 1794*. The Hague: Martinus Nijhoff, 1982.

Horstmann, Rolf-Peter. "Fichte's Anti-Skeptical Programme: On the Anti-Skeptical Strategies in Fichte's Presentations of the *Wissenschaftslehre* 1794 to 1801/2." In *The Transcendental Turn*, ed. Sebastian Gardiner and Matthew Grist, pp. 96–134. Oxford: Oxford University Press, 2015.

Horstmann, Rolf-Peter. "The Early Philosophy of Fichte and Schelling." In *The Cambridge Companion to German Idealism*, ed. Karl Ameriks, pp. 164–81. Cambridge: Cambridge University Press, 2017.

Imhof, Silvan. *Der Grund der Subjektivität. Motiv und Potenzial von Fichtes Ansatz*. Basel: Schwabe Verlag, 2014.

Imhof, Silvan. "Einsturz und Neubau. Fichtes erste Grundsatzkonzeption als Antwort auf den Skeptizismus." *Fichte-Studien* 43 (2016): 52–70.

Imhof, Silvan. "Realität durch Einbildungskraft. Fichtes Antwort auf Maimons Skeptizismus in der *Grundlage der gesammten Wissenschaftslehre*." *Fichte-Studien* 48 (2019): 3–24.

Inciarte, Fernando. *Transzendentale Einbildungskraft. Zu Fichtes Frühphilosophie im Zusammenhang des transzendentalen Idealismus*. Bonn: Bouvier, 1970.

Ivaldo, Marco. *Fichte*. Brescia: La Scuola, 2014.

Ivaldo, Marco. "Die praktische Konstitution des 'Setzens' nach der Wissenschaftslehre Fichtes." *Internationales Jahrbuch des Deutschen Idealismus/International Yearbook of German Idealism* 14 (2016): 165–86.

Jacobs, Wilhelm G. "Einleitung" [Editor's Introduction to] Fichte, *Grundriss des Eigentümlichen der Wissenschaftslehre*. Hamburg: Meiner, 1975, pp. vii–xvii.

Jacobs, Wilhelm G. *Johann Gottlieb Fichte. Eine Einführung*. Berlin: Suhrkamp, 2014.

Jalley, Emile. *La doctrine de la science (1794). Naissance et devenir de l'impérialisme allemand*, Vol. 2. Paris: l'Harmattan, 2016. [Vol. 1 of this set is a new translation of *BWL* and *GWL* by Marc Géraud.]

Jalloh, Chernor M. *Fichte's Kant-Interpretation and the Doctrine of Science*. Lanham, MA: University Press of America, 1988.

Janke, Wolfgang. *Fichte. Sein und Reflexion—Grundlagen der kritischen Vernunft*. Berlin: De Gruyter, 1970.

Kabitz, W. *Studien zur Entwicklungsgeschichte der Fichteschen Wissenschaftslehre aus der Kantischen Philosophie*. Berlin: Reuther & Reinhard, 1902.

Kárasek, Jindřich. "Reinhold's Principle of Consciousness and Fichte's Third Principle: An Attempt at a Reduction." In *Reinhold and Fichte in Confrontation: A Tale of Mutual Appreciation and Criticism*, ed. Martin Bondeli and Silvan Imhof, pp. 83–108. Berlin: De Gruyter, 2020.

Kim, Halla. "Abstraction in Fichte." In *Fichte and Transcendental Philosophy*, ed Tom Rockmore and Daniel Breazeale, pp. 143–62. New York: Palgrave-Macmillan, 2016.

Kim, Halla. "Fact/Act (*Tathandlung*)." In *The Bloomsbury Handbook to Fichte*, ed. Marina F. Bykova, pp. 345–52. London and New York: Bloomsbury Academic, 2020.

Kim, Halla. "Transcendental Method." In *The Bloomsbury Handbook to Fichte*, ed. Marina F. Bykova, pp. 337–44. London and New York: Bloomsbury Academic, 2020.

Kinlaw, C. Jeffery. "Self-Determination and Immediate Self-Consciousness in the Jena *Wissenschaftslehre*." In *Fichte and Transcendental Philosophy*, ed Tom Rockmore and Daniel Breazeale, pp. 176–89. New York: Palgrave-Macmillan, 2016.

Kinlaw, C. Jeffery. "Knowledge and Action: Self-Positing, I-Hood, and the Centrality of the Striving Doctrine." In *The Palgrave Fichte Handbook*, ed. Stephen Hoeltzel, pp. 163–87. Cham: Palgrave Macmillan, 2019.

Kinlaw, C. Jeffery. "Intellectual Intuition." In *The Bloomsbury Handbook to Fichte*, ed. Marina F. Bykova, pp. 371–80. London and New York: Bloomsbury Academic, 2020.

Kisser, Thomas. "Gradualität, Intensität, Subjektivität—Zur Struktur und Funktion der Qualitätskategorie bei Fichte und in ihrer Vorgeschichte." In *Intensität und Realität. Systematische Analysen Zur Problemgeschichte von Gradualität, Intensität und Quantitativer Differenz in Ontologie und Metaphysik*, ed. Thomas Leinkauf and Thomas Kisser, pp. 171–224. Berlin: De Gruyter, 2016.

Klotz, Christian. "Fichte's Explanation of the Dynamic Structure of Consciousness in the 1794–95 *Wissenschaftslehre*." In *The Cambridge Companion to Fichte*, ed. David James and Günter Zöller, pp. 65–92. Cambridge: Cambridge University Press, 2016.

Koch, Reinhard. *Fichtes Theorie des Selbstbewußtseins ihre Entwicklung von den "Eignen Meditationen über ElementarPhilosophie" 1793 bis zur "Neuen Bearbeitung der W.L."* Würzburg: Königshausen & Naumann, 1989.

Lang, Stefan. "Fichtes Programm einer Geschichte peformativen Selbstbewusstseins." In *System und Systemkritik um 1800. System der Vernunft*, ed. Christian Danz and Jürgen Stolzenberg, pp. 29–43. Hamburg: Felix Meiner, 2011.

Lauth, Reinhard. *Zur Idee der Transzendentalphilosophie*. Munich and Salzburg: Anton Pustet, 1965.

Lauth, Reinhard. "Nouvelles recherches sur Jacobi." *Archives de Philosophie* 34 (1971): 281–6.

Lauth, Reinhard. "Die Entstehung von Fichte's 'Grundlage der gesammten Wissenschaftslehre' nach den 'Eignen Meditationen über ElementarPhilosophie." In *Transzendentale Entwicklungslinien von Descartes bis zu Marx und Dostojewski*, pp. 155–79. Hamburg: Felix Meiner, 1989.

La Vopa, Anthony J. *Fichte. The Self and the Calling of Philosophy, 1762–1799*. Cambridge: Cambridge University Press, 2001.

Léon, Xavier. *Fichte et son temps*. 3 vols. Paris: Armand Colin, 1922–27.

Limnatis, Nectarios. "Fichte and the Problem of Logic: Positioning the *Wissenschaftslehre* in the Development of Germany Idealism." In *Fichte, German Idealism, and Early Romanticism*, ed. Daniel Breazeale and Tom Rockmore, pp. 21–40. Amsterdam: Rodopi, 2010.

Martin, Wayne E. "'Without a Striving, No Object is Possible.' Fichte's Striving Doctrine and the Primacy of Practice." In *New Perspectives on Fichte*, ed. Daniel Breazeale and Tom Rockmore, pp. 19–35. Atlantic Highlands, NJ: Humanities Press, 1996.

Martin, Wayne E. *Idealism and Objectivity: Understanding Fichte's Jena Project*. Stanford, CA: Stanford University Press, 1997.

Martin, Wayne E. "Fichte's Wild Metaphysical Yarn." *Philosophical Topics* 43 (2015): 87–96.

Martin, Wayne E. "Fichte's Creuzer Review and the Transformation of the Free Will Problem." *European Journal of Philosophy* 26 (2018): 717–29.

Martin, Wayne M. "Fichte's First Principle: Self-Positing and Gambit Normativity." In *The Bloomsbury Handbook to Fichte*, ed. Marina F. Bykova, pp. 319–26. London and New York: Bloomsbury Academic, 2020.

Metz, Wilhelm. *Kategoriendeduktion und produktive Einbildungskraft in der theoretischen Philosophie Kants und Fichtes*. Stuttgart-Bad Cannstatt: Frommann-Holzboog, 1991.

Metz, Wilhelm. "Fichtes genetische Deduktion vom Raum und Zeit in Differenz zu Kant." *Fichte-Studien* 6 (1994): 71–94.

Mittmann, Jörg-Peter. *Das Prinzip der Selbstgewißheit. Fichte und die Entwicklung der nachkantischen Grundsatzphilosophie*. Bodenheim: Athenäum-Hain-Hanstein, 1993.

Neuhouser, Frederick. *Fichte's Theory of Subjectivity*. Cambridge: Cambridge University Press, 1990.

Neuhouser, Frederick. "Fichte's Methodology in the *Wissenschaftslehre* (1794/95)." In *The Palgrave Handbook of German Idealism*, ed. Matthew C. Altman, pp. 300–19. Hampshire: Palgrave Macmillan, 2014.

Oberbeil, Fritz. *Die transzendentale Synthesis. Entwurf und Geschichte der Hauptfrage in Fichtes Jenenser Wissenschaftslehre*. Frankfurt: Peter Lang, 1985.

Oesch, Martin. *Der Handlungsproblem. Ein systemgeschichtlicher Beitrag zur erster Wissenschaftslehre Fichtes.* Hildesheim: Gerstenberg Verlag, 1981.

Perrinjaquet, Alain. "Some Remarks Concerning the Circularity of Philosophy and the Evidence of the First Principle in the Jena *Wissenschaftslehre*." In *Fichte: Historical Contexts/Contemporary Controversies*, ed. Daniel Breazeale and Tom Rockmore, pp. 71–90. Atlantic Highlands, NJ: Humanities Press, 1994.

Philonenko, Alexis. *La liberté humaine dans la philosophie de Fichte.* Paris: Vrin, 1966; 2nd edition, 1980.

Philonenko, Alexis. *L'Œuvre de Fichte.* Paris: Vrin, 1984.

Pippin, Robert J. "Fichte's Alleged Subjective, Psychological, One-Sided Idealism." In *The Reception of Kant's Critical Philosophy: Fichte, Schelling and Hegel*, ed. Sally Sedgwick, pp. 147–70. Cambridge: Cambridge University Press, 2000.

Radermacher, Hans. *Fichtes Begriff des Absoluten.* Frankfurt am Main: Vittorio Klostermann, 1970.

Radrizzani, Ives. "Der Übergang von der *Grundlage* zur *Wissenschaftslehre nova methodo*." *Fichte Studien* 6 (1994): 355–66.

Radrizzani, Ives. "Fichtes 'erste' Wissenschaftslehre." *Fichte-Studien* 16 (1999): 409–31.

Radrizzani, Ives. "La 'Première' Doctrine de la Science de Fichte." *Archives de Philosophie* 60 (1997): 615–58.

Rivera de Rosales, Jacinto. "The Methodological Singularity of the First Fichte." In *Fichte and Transcendental Philosophy*, ed Tom Rockmore and Daniel Breazeale, pp. 211–28. New York: Palgrave-Macmillan, 2016.

Rockmore, Tom. "Antifoundationalism, Circularity, and the Spirit of Fichte." In *Fichte: Historical Contexts/Contemporary Controversies*, ed. Daniel Breazeale and Tom Rockmore, pp. 96–112. Atlantic Highlands, NJ: Humanities Press, 1994.

Rockmore, Tom. "Fichte, Kant, and the Copernican Revolution." In *The Bloomsbury Handbook to Fichte*, ed. Marina F. Bykova, pp. 43–59. London and New York: Bloomsbury Academic, 2020.

Rodriguez, Gustavo Macedo. "La actividad infinita del yo en la Wissenschaftslehre de 1794–1795 de Johann Gottlieb Fichte." *Ideas y Valores* 66 (2017): 65–79.

Rohs, Peter. *Johann Gottlieb Fichte.* Munich: Beck, 1991.

Rosefeldt, Tobias. "Zwei Regresse des Selbstbewusstseins bei Fichte." In *Begriff und Interpretation Im Zeichen der Moderne*, ed. Jure Zovko, Dimitris Karydas, and Sarah Schmidt, pp. 63–76. Berlin: De Gruyter, 2015.

Ryue, Hisang. *Über Fichtes ersten Grundsatz "Ich bin." Kommentar zur § 1 der Grundlage der gesamten Wissenschaftslehre 1794/95.* München: Utz, 2000.

Schäffer, Dorothee. *Die Rolle der Einbildungskraft in Fichtes Wissenschaftslehre von 1794/95.* [I.D.] Köln: Guter und Hanson, 1967.

Schäffer, Rainer. *Johann Gottlieb Fichtes Grundlage der gesamten Wissenschaftslehre von 1794.* Darmstadt: Wissenschaftliche Buchgesellschaft, 2006.

Schmid, Jelscha. "'Es ist so, weil ich es so mache.' Fichtes Methode der Konstruktion." *Fichte-Studien* 48 (2019): 389–412.

Schmidt, Andreas. *Der Grund des Wissens. Fichtes Wissenschaftslehre in den Versionen von 1794/95, 1804/II, und 1812.* Paderborn: Ferdinand Schöningh, 2004.

Schmidt, Andreas. "Wahrnehmung und Anschauung. Über Fichtes Antwort auf Aenesidemus." In *Krankheit des Zeitalters oder heilsame Provokation? Skeptizismus in der nachkantischeen Philosophie*, ed. Martin Bondeli, Jiří Chotaš, and Klaus Vieweg, pp. 181–93. Paderborn: Fink, 2016.

Schmidt, Andreas. "Fichtes Begriff der 'Einbildungskraft' und seine Maimonschen Ursprünge." In *Idealismus und Romantik in Jena. Figuren und Konzepte zwischen 1794 und 1807*, ed. Johannes Korngiebel, Klaus Vieweg, Johannes Korngiebel, and Michael Forster, pp. 9–23. Jena: Willhelm Fink, 2018.

Schreiter, J. "Produktive Einbildungskraft und Außenwelt in der Philosophie J. G. Fichte." In *Der transzendentale Gedanke. Die gegenwärtige Darstellung der Philosophie Fichtes*, ed. Klaus Hammacher, pp. 120–7. Hamburg: Felix Meiner, 1981.

Schuhmann, Karl. *Die Grundlage der Wissenschaftslehre in ihrem Umrisse. Zu Fichtes "Wissenschaftslehren" von 1794 und 1810*. The Hague: Martinus Nijhoff, 1968.

Schüssler, Ingebourg. "Logik und Ontologie. Fichtes transzendentale Begründung des Satzes der Identität." In *Der transzendentale Gedanke. Die gegenwärtige Darstellung der Philosophie Fichtes*, ed. Klaus Hammacher, pp. 498–505. Hamburg: Felix Meiner, 1981.

Schwab, Phillip. "A = A. Zur Identätslogischen Systemgrundlegung bei Fichte, Schelling, und Hegel." *Internationale Jahrbuch des Deutschen Idealismus/ International Yearbook of German Idealism* 12 (2017): 261–89.

Seebohm, Thomas W. "Fichte's Discovery of the Dialectical Method." In *Fichte: Historical Contexts/Contemporary Controversies*, ed. Daniel Breazeale and Tom Rockmore, pp. 17–42. Atlantic Highlands, NJ: Humanities Press, 1994.

Seidel, George J. "Fichte." In *Activity and Ground: Fichte, Schelling, and Hegel*, pp. 41–87. Hildesheim and New York: Georg Olms Verlag, 1976.

Seidel, George J. *Fichte's Wissenschaftslehre of 1794: A Commentary on Part I*. Lafayette: Purdue University Press, 1993.

Seidel, Helmut. *Johann Gottlieb Fichte zur Einführung*. Hamburg: Junius, 1997.

Soller, Alois K. *Trieb und Reflexion in Fichtes Jenaer Philosophie*. Würzburg: Königshausen und Neumann, 1984.

Stadler, Christian Maria. *J. G. Fichtes Grundlegung des ethischen Idealismus, oder: Transzendentale Deduktion zwischen Wissen und Wollen*. Frankfurt: Peter Lang, 1996.

Stiehler, Gottfried. "J. G. Fichtes synthetische Methode als Keimform der Dialektik." *Deutsche Zeitschrift für Philosophie* 10 (1962): 252–70.

Stolzenberg, Jürgen. *Fichtes Begriff der intellektuellen Anschauung. Die Entwicklung in den Wissenschaftslehren von 1793/94 bis 1801/01*. Stuttgart: Klett-Cotta, 1986.

Stolzenberg, Jürgen. "Fichtes Satz 'Ich bin.' Argumentanalytische Überlegungen zu Paragraph 1 der *Grundlage der gesamten Wissenschaftslehre* von 1794/95." *Fichte-Studien* 6 (1994): 1–34.

Surber, Jere Paul. *Language and German Idealism: Fichte's Linguistic Philosophy*. Atlantic Highlands, NJ: Humanities Press International, 1995.

Talbot, Ellen Bliss. *The Fundamental Principle of Fichte's Philosophy*. New York: Macmillan, 1906.

Thomas-Fogiel, Isabelle. *Critique de la Représentation. Étude sur Fichte*. Paris: Vrin, 2000.

Thomas-Fogiel, Isabelle. "Le labyrinthe de l'idéalisme. Scepticisme, réalisme et idéalisme dans l'élaboration de la Doctrine de la science de 1794." *La Revista de Estud(i)os sobre Fichte* 13 (Verano/Verão 2016).

Thompson, Anna Boynton. *The Unity of Fichte's Doctrine of Knowledge*. Boston: Ginn, 1895.

Tillette, Xavier. "Fichtes Erfindung der Wissenschaftslehre." *Fichte-Studien* 9 (1997): 1–16.

Tse, Plato. "Die dreistufige Struktur der Kategoriendeduktion und ihr Sinn in Fichtes *Grundlage der gesammten Wissenschaftslehre* 1794/95." In *Das Selbst und die Welt—Beiträge zu Kant und der nachkantischen Philosophie*, eds. Manja Kisner, Giovanni Pietro Basile, Ansgar Lyssy, and Michael Bastian Weiß, pp. 193–213. Würzburg: Königshausen & Neumann, 2019.

Vater, Michael G. "Freedom's Body: Fichte's Account of Nature." In *The Bloomsbury Handbook to Fichte*, ed. Marina F. Bykova, pp. 101–17. London and New York: Bloomsbury Academic, 2020.

Vetö, Miklos. *Fichte: De l'Action à l'Image*. Paris: L'Harmattan, 2001.

Vrabec, Martin. "Verfügt das absolute Ich aus der 'Grundlage der gesamten Wissenschaftslehre' über ein Selbstbewusstsein?" *Fichte-Studien* 42 (2016): 95–105.

Waibel, Violetta L. "The Generation of Intuition and Representation through the Productive Imagination in the 1794/5 *Grundlage*." In *The Bloomsbury Handbook to Fichte*, ed. Marina F. Bykova, pp. 81–99. London and New York: Bloomsbury Academic, 2020.

Wallwitz, G. von. "Fichte und das Problem des intelligiblen Fatalismus." *Fichte-Studien* 5 (1999): 121–45.

Weischedel, Wilhelm. *Der frühe Fichte: Aufbruch der Freiheit zur Gemeinschaft*. Stuttgart-Bad Cannstatt: Frommann, 1973 [orig. 1939].

Wildfeuer, A. G. *Praktische Vernunft und System. Entwicklungsgeschichtliche Untersuchungen zur ursprünglichsten Kant-Rezeption Johann Gottlieb Fichtes*. Stuttgart-Bad Cannstatt, 1999.

Wilson, Eric Entrican. "Comment Fichte rompt avec la représentation." *Revue de Metaphysique et de Morale* 17 (2011): 333–41.

Wood, Allen W. "Fichte's Philosophical Revolution." *Philosophical Topics* 19 (1991): 1–28.

Wood, Allen W. "The I as Principle of Practical Philosophy." In *The Reception of Kant's Critical Philosophy: Fichte, Schelling and Hegel*, ed. Sally Sedgwick, pp. 93–108. Cambridge: Cambridge University Press, 2000.

Wood, Allen W. "Fichte's Absolute Freedom." In *The Free Development of Each: Studies in Freedom, Right, and Ethics in Classical German Philosophy*, pp. 164–93. Oxford: Oxford University Press, 2014.

Wood, David W. *"Mathesis of the Mind." A Study of Fichte's* Wissenschaftslehre *and* Geometry. Amsterdam: Rodopi, 2012.

Wood, David W. "The 'Double Sense' of Fichte's Philosophical Language." *Revista de Estud(i)os sobre Fichte* 15 (2017).

Wood, David W. "Fichte's Absolute I and the Forgotten Tradition of *Tathandlung*." In *Das Selbst und die Welt—Beiträge zu Kant und der nachkantischen Philosophie*, eds. Manja Kisner, Giovanni Pietro Basile, Ansgar Lyssy, Michael Bastian Weiß, pp. 167–92. Würzburg: Königshausen & Neumann, 2019.

Wood, David W. "Jacobi's Philosophy of Faith in Fichte's 1794 *Wissenschaftslehre*." In *Jacobi: Philosophy and Religion at the Crux of Modernity*, ed. Alexander J. B. Hampton and George di Giovanni. Cambridge: Cambridge University Press, 2020.

Wundt, Max. "Die Wissenschaftslehre von 1794." In *Fichte-Forschungen*, pp. 9–76. Stuttgart: Frommann, 1929.

Zimmer, Amie Leigh. "Fichte's Existential Logic." *Journal of Speculative Philosophy* 34 (2020): 201–23.

Zöller, Günter. "Thinking and Willing in Fichte's Doctrine of Subjectivity." In *New Perspectives on Fichte*, ed. Daniel Breazeale and Tom Rockmore, pp. 1–17. Atlantic Highlands, NJ: Humanities Press, 1996.

Zöller, Günter. *Fichte's Transcendental Philosophy: The Original Duplicity of Intelligence and Will*. Cambridge: Cambridge University Press, 1998.

Zöller, Günter. "From Critique to Metacritique: Fichte's Transformation of Kant's Transcendental Idealism." In *The Reception of Kant's Critical Philosophy: Fichte, Schelling and Hegel*, ed. Sally Sedgwick, pp. 129–46. Cambridge: Cambridge University Press, 2000.

Zöller, Günter. *Fichte lesen*. Stuttgart-Bad Canstatt: Frommann-Holzboog, 2013.

Zöller, Günter. "A Philosophy of Freedom: Fichte's Philosophical Achievement." In *The Palgrave Handbook of German Idealism*, ed. Matthew C. Altman, pp. 286–309. Hampshire: Palgrave Macmillan, 2014.

Zöller, Günter. "Fichte's Original Insight: Dieter Henrich's Pioneering Piece Half a Century Later." In *Debates in Nineteenth Century Philosophy: Essential Readings and Contemporary Responses*, ed. Kristin Gjesdal, pp. 45–56. London: Routledge, 2015.

Key to Abbreviations and Annotation

Abbreviations

(Unless otherwise indicated, the author of all the following is J. G. Fichte.)

A	First edition, of *GWL* [1794/95], first distributed to Fichte's students in individual fascicles and published in Leipzig by Ernst Gabler in two "installments."
ACR	*Attempt at a Critique of all Revelation* [1792/93], trans. Garrett Green (Cambridge: Cambridge University Press, 2010).
A.L.Z.	*Allgemeine Literatur-Zeitung.*
AP	*Appellation an das Publikum* [1799].
ApT	*Annalen des philosophischen Tons* [1797].
Arev	Review of *Aenesidemus* [1794], trans. Breazeale in *EPW*.
B	Authorized, combined second edition of *GWL* and *GEWL* [1802], published by the Tübingen publisher J. F. Cotta.
BM	*Die Bestimmung des Menschen* [1800].
BWL	*Ueber den Begriff der Wissenschaftslehre* [1794].
C	Unauthorized second, corrected edition of *GWL* [1802], published by the Leipzig publisher, Ernst Gabler [1802].
CCR	*A Crystal Clear Report to the General Public concerning the Actual Essence of the Newest Philosophy* [1801] , trans. John Botterman and William Rasch. In *Fichte, Jacobi, and Schelling: Philosophy of German Idealism,* ed. Ernst Behler, pp. 39–115 (New York: Continuum, 1987).
CPSW	*Comparison between Prof. Schmid's System and the Wissenschaftslehre* [1796], trans. Breazeale, in *EPW*.
Crev	Creuzer Review [1793], trans. Breazeale, *Philosophical Forum* 32 (2001): 289–96.
EM	*Eigene Meditationen über ElementarPhilosophie/Practische Philosophie* [1793-94].
EPW	*Fichte: Early Philosophical Writings*, ed. and trans. Daniel Breazeale (Ithaca, NY: Cornell University Press, 1988).
EVBG	*Einige Vorlesungen über die Bestimmung des Gelehrten* [1794].
FAD	*J. G. Fichte and the Atheism Dispute,* trans. Curtis Bowman, ed. Yolanda Estes (Burlington, VT: Ashgate, 2010).
FiG	*J. G. Fichte im Gespräch*, ed. Erich Fuchs, in cooperation with Reinhard Lauth and Walter Schieche (Stuttgart-Bad Cannstatt: Frommann-Holzboog, 1978).
FiR	*Fichte im Rezenzionen*, ed. Erich Fuchs, Wilhelm G. Jacobs, and Walter Schieche (Stuttgart-Bad Cannstatt: Frommann-Holzboog, 1995).
FNR	*Foundations of Natural Right* [1796/97], trans. Michael Bahr, ed. Frederick Neuhouser (Cambridge: Cambridge University Press, 2000).
FTP	*Foundations of Transcendental Philosophy (Wissenschaftslehre) nova methodo* [1796/99], trans. Breazeale (Ithaca, NY: Cornell University Press, 1992).
FW	*Fichtes Werke. Auswahl in Sechs Bänden*, ed. Fritz Medicus (Leipzig: Felix Meiner Verlag, 1910-12).
GA	*J. G. Fichte-Gesamtausgabe der Bayerischen Akademie der Wissenschaften*, ed. Reinhard Lauth, Walter Jacobs, Hans Gliwitzky, and Erich Fuchs (Stuttgart-Bad Cannstatt: Frommann-Holzboog, 1962-2012.)
GEWL	*Grundriss des Eigentümlichen der Wissenschaftslehre in Rucksicht des theoretischen Vermögen* [1795].

GNR   *Grundlage des Naturrechts* [1796/97].
Grev   *Gebhard Review* [1793], trans. Breazeale, *Philosophical Forum* 32 (2001): 297-310.
GWL   *Grundlage der gesamten Wissenschaftslehre* [1794/95].
IWL   *Introductions to the Wissenschaftslehre and Other Writings* [1797-1800], ed.
         and trans. Daniel Breazeale (Indianapolis, IN: Hackett, 1994).
K   Wolfgang Class and Alois K. Soller, *Kommentar zu Fichtes* Grundlage der gesa-
         mten Wissenschaftslehre (Amsterdam and New York, NY: Rodopi, 2004).
KrV   Kant, *Kritik der reinen Vernunft* [1787]. (Reference is always to the second or B
         edition, which has the same pagination as the third edition, which is the one
         utilized by Fichte.)
OC   *Œuvres choisies de philosophie première*, trans. A. Philonenko, 2nd edition
         (Paris: Vrin, 1972).
NBWL   *Neue Bearbeitung der W.L. 1800.*
PRFF   *The Philosophical Rupture between Fichte and Schelling: Selected Texts and
         Correspondence (1800-1802)*, trans. and ed. Michael G. Vater and
         David W. Wood (Albany, NY: SUNY Press, 2012).
RA   Rezension *Aenesidemus* [1794].
RC   Rezension *Creuzer* [1793].
RG   Rezension *Gebhard* [1793].
SB   *Sonnenklarer Bericht an das größere Publikum über das eigentliche Wesen der
         neuesten Philosophie* [1801].
SE   *System of Ethics* [1798], trans. Breazeale and Günter Zöller (Cambridge:
         Cambridge University Press, 2005).
SS   *Das System der Sittenlehre* [1798].
SW   *Johann Gottlieb Fichtes sämmtliche Werke*, ed. I. H. Fichte (Berlin: Viet & Co.,
         1845-46) and *Johann Gottlieb Fichtes nachglassene Werke*, ed. I. H. Fichte
         (Berlin: Viet & Co., 1834-35); photomechanical reprint in 13 vols., *Fichtes
         Werke*, ed. I. H. Fichte (Berlin: De Gruyter, 1971).
TWL   Daniel Breazeale, *Thinking through the Wissenschaftslehre: Themes from Fichte's
         Early Philosophy* (Oxford: Oxford University Press, 2013).
UGB   *Ueber den Unterschied zwischen des Geist und des Buchstabens in der Philosophie*
         [1794].
UGG   *Ueber den Grund unsers Glaubens an eine göttliche Weltregierung* [1798].
VKO   *Versuch einer Kritik aller Offenbarung* [first edition, 1792; second edition, 1793].
VLM   *Vorlesungen über Logik und Metaphysik. Zu Platners "Philosophischen Aphorismen"*
         [1794-1812].
VM   *The Vocation of Man* [1800], trans. Peter Preuss (Indianapolis: Hackett, 1987).
VSSW   *Vergleichung des von Herrn Prof. Schmid aufgestellten Systems mit der
         Wissenschaftslehre* [1796].
VSUS   *Von der Sprachfähigkeit und dem Ursprunge der Sprache* [1795].
VWL   *Versuch einer neuen Darstellung der Wissenschaftslehre* [1797/98].
WLnm   *Wissenschaftslehre nova methodo* [1796-99].
WLnmH   *Wissenschaftslehre nova methodo, Halle Nachschrift* [1797-98].
WLnmK   *Wissenschaftslehre nova method, Krause Nachschrift* [1798-99].
ZV   *Züricher Vorlesungen* [1794].
ZVau   *Züricher Vorlesungen über den Begriff der Wissenschaftslehre Februar 1794.
         Nachschrift Lavater. Beilage aus Jens Baggesens Nachlass. Excerpt aus der Abschrift
         von Fichtes Züricher Vorlesungen*, ed. Erich Fuchs (Neuried: Ars Una, 1996).

Annotation

Footnotes indicated by **symbols** (*, †, ‡, etc.) are Fichte's own footnotes to the various editions of these texts.

Footnotes indicated by **capital letters** contain all the significant changes and variants in the different editions of these same texts.

Endnotes are indicated by **Arabic numerals**.

Many endnotes consist of—sometimes lengthy—passages from Fichte's own writings from this period. These have been culled from his other publications, his lectures notes, and his personal correspondence. They are included here in an effort to allow Fichte himself to comment upon and illuminate various passages and difficulties in this, his first public presentation of the foundations of the *Wissenschaftslehre*.

Endnotes also include information concerning philosophical, historical, and biographical context; authors and texts to which Fichte alludes; philological matters; etc. For much of this material, I am indebted to Alois Soller and Wolfgang Class, authors of the indispensable *Kommentar* (= *K*) on the *Foundation of the Entire Wissenschaftslehre*.

Other endnotes provide cross-references to passages and texts in this volume and elsewhere.

TEXTS

I
CONCERNING THE CONCEPT OF THE *WISSENSCHAFTSLEHRE*, OR OF SO-CALLED "PHILOSOPHY"

Concerning the Concept
of the *Wissenschaftslehre*
or
of So-Called "Philosophy"[1]

As an Invitation to his Lectures on this Science

by

JOHANN GOTTLIEB FICHTE

Designated Regular Professor at the University of Jena

Weimar
Comptoire Industries
1794

Preface[A]

The author of this treatise has been convinced by his reading of the modern skeptics — especially Aenesidemus,[2] but also Maimon's excellent writings[3] — of something that even before this seemed to him to be very likely: namely, that philosophy itself has not yet been elevated to the rank of a self-evident science,[4] despite the efforts of the most perspicacious men. The author believes that he has discovered the reason for this. He also believes that he has discovered an easy way to satisfy fully all the quite well-founded demands made by the skeptic upon the Critical philosophy,[5] and he believes he can do so in a manner that will reconcile the conflicting claims of the dogmatic and Critical systems, just as the conflicting claims of the various dogmatic systems were reconciled by the Critical philosophy.* The author is not in the habit of speaking of things he has not yet accomplished, and he would either have executed his plan or forever held his silence on this subject,

[I, 30] were it not for the fact that the present occasion[6] seemed to call for him to give an account of how he has been employing his leisure until now and of the projects to which he intends to dedicate himself in the future.

[I/2: 110]   The following investigation pretends to no more than hypothetical validity, from which, however, it certainly does not follow that the author is able to base his assertions only upon unprovable hypotheses, nor that these claims are not supposed to be the results of a more profound and securely constructed system. To be sure, it will still be years before he will be able to promise to present this system to the public in a worthy form; but even now he expects people to be fair enough to postpone objections until they have examined the entire system.

The first aim of these pages was to permit students at the university to which the author has been called to decide whether to trust him to guide them along the path leading to the supreme science and to allow them to judge whether they can hope that he is able to shed sufficient light on this path to enable them to follow it without stumbling dangerously. Its second aim was to solicit the judgment of his patrons and friends regarding his project.

The following remarks are meant for readers who belong to neither of these groups, should this text come into their possession.

Until now, the author has been sincerely convinced that no human understanding can advance any further than that boundary upon which Kant stood, especially in the *Critique of the Power of Judgment*, and which he declared to be

---

[A] Preface to the first edition. [*2nd ed.*]

* The real controversy between the Critical philosophy and dogmatism may well concern *the connection between our cognition and a thing in itself*, a controversy in which the skeptics have quite correctly allied themselves with the dogmatists, and hence with healthy common sense (which certainly needs to be taken into consideration — not of course as a judge, but rather, as a witness summoned to bear testimony). Some future *Wissenschaftslehre* might be able to settle this controversy by showing the following: that our cognition is by no means connected with the thing in itself directly, by means of a representation, but is instead connected with it mediately or indirectly, by means of *feeling*; that, in any case, things are *represented only as appearances*, though they are *felt as things in themselves*; that no representation at all would be possible without feeling, but that things in themselves are cognized only *subjectively* — that is, only insofar as they have an effect upon our feeling.

the final boundary of finite knowing — even though he never determined this boundary for us.[7] The author realizes that he will never be able to say anything that has not already been indicated by Kant, directly or indirectly and with more or less clarity. He will leave it to future ages to fathom the genius of this man [1,31] who — often as if inspired from on high — drove philosophical judgment so decisively from the standpoint at which he found it toward its final goal. — He is just as sincerely convinced that, next to Kant's spirit of genius, nothing could make a greater contribution to philosophy than Reinhold's[8] systematic spirit, and he believes that he recognizes the honorable place that will always be accorded to Reinhold's Elementary Philosophy, despite the further progress that philosophy [I/2: 111] must necessarily make, no matter who is responsible for this progress. He has no malicious wish to misjudge nor to depreciate any [philosophical] contribution whatsoever. He realizes that every step ever attained by science had to be climbed before a higher one could be reached, and he really takes no personal credit for the fortunate accident of having been called to work only after being preceded by excellent workmen. He also realizes that scientific merit is not based upon the luck of discovery, but instead upon the integrity of the search, and hence that such merit is something everyone can only judge for and assign by himself. The author does not say this for the sake of these great men nor for the sake of those who would emulate them, but instead for the benefit of those other, not quite so great, men; nor was it intended for anyone who finds it superfluous.

In addition to these serious people, there are also facetious ones, who warn philosophers not to make themselves ridiculous by raising exaggerated expectations regarding their science. I have no wish to judge whether such people are really laughing sincerely, out of innate joviality, or whether there may not be among them some who are simply forcing themselves to laugh, as a means of spoiling, for unsophisticated inquirers, a project that they themselves — for comprehensible reasons — do not enjoy witnessing.* To the best of my knowledge, I have not yet nourished the humor of such people by saying anything to raise such high expectations; and perhaps I may therefore ask them to hold their laughter for the moment and to wait until this project has formally miscarried or been abandoned — not for the sake of philosophers and still less [1,32] for that of philosophy, but for their own sakes. Then they may ridicule our faith in humanity (to which they themselves belong) and our hopes regarding the great talents of human beings. Then, whenever they require consolation, they may repeat their consoling maxim: "Human beings are beyond help. This is how it always has been and always will be."

---

* *Malis rident alienis.* ["They smile at the misfortunes of others," Horace, *Satires*, II: 3, 72.]

[I, 32]
[I/2: 159]

Preface to the Second Edition

This booklet was out of print, and I needed it so that I could refer to it in my lectures. Furthermore, with the exception of some essays in the *Philosophisches Journal einer Gesellschaft Teutscher Gelehrten*,[9] it is the only work to date in which the *Wissenschaftslehre*'s distinctive manner of philosophizing is itself the object of philosophizing. It can therefore serve as an introduction to this system. For these reasons I have arranged for this new edition.

Despite its specific title and contents, even the aim and nature of this text have been frequently misunderstood. Consequently, on the occasion of this second edition I find it necessary to do something I thought to be quite unnecessary in the first edition: namely, to clarify these specific points[10] in a preface. — One can philosophize about metaphysics itself, which need not be a doctrine of alleged "things in themselves," but may instead be a genetic derivation of what appears in our consciousness.[11] One may investigate the possibility, the real meaning, and the rules governing such a science, which is very advantageous for the cultivation of the science of metaphysics itself. The philosophical name for a system of such inquiries is "critique." This, anyway, is all that ought [I, 33] to go by that name. Critique itself is not metaphysics, but lies beyond metaphysics. Critique is related to metaphysics in precisely the same way that metaphysics is related to the ordinary standpoint of natural understanding. Metaphysics explains the ordinary standpoint, and metaphysics is itself explained by critique. Genuine critique criticizes philosophical thinking. If philosophy itself is also supposed to be called "Critical," this can only mean that it criticizes natural [I/2: 160] thinking. — A pure critique is intermixed with no metaphysical investigations. The Kantian critique, which calls itself "critique," is by no means pure critique, but consists largely of metaphysics. Sometimes it criticizes philosophical thinking, and sometimes it criticizes natural thinking — which, taken by itself, would be no cause for reproach, if only the distinction between the two kinds of critique had been clearly indicated, as well as the kind of critique to which each of the individual investigations belonged. A pure metaphysics includes, as such, no additional critique beyond the critique that is supposed to be settled in advance.[12] Accordingly, none of the previous versions of the *Wissenschaftslehre*,[13] which identify themselves as metaphysics, are examples of pure metaphysics in this sense — nor could they have been, since this uncustomary manner of thinking could not have been expected to gain a hearing without the critical hints that accompanied it.

The nature of the following text has now been precisely indicated: it is a part of the critique of the *Wissenschaft*slehre, but it is by no means the *Wissenschaftslehre* itself, nor is it a part of the *Wissenschaftslehre*.

I described the present text as a part of this critique [of metaphysics]: specifically, it describes the relation of the *Wissenschaftslehre* to ordinary knowledge and to those sciences that are possible from the standpoint of ordinary knowledge, and it describes this in terms of the material or content [*Materie*] of knowledge. But there is another approach [to critique], one that contributes greatly toward forming a correct concept of our system, guards against misunderstanding, and provides a means of entry into this system: namely, consideration of the relationship of transcendental thinking to ordinary thinking in terms [not of the content of each mode of thinking, but rather] of its form — that is to say, a description of the [1,34] point of view from which the transcendental philosopher views all knowledge and of his state of mind while engaged in speculation. The author believes that he has explained himself with some clarity on these points in his two Introductions to a *New Presentation of the Wissenschaftslehre* (in the previously mentioned journal, 1797), especially in the Second Introduction.[14] — A science and the critique of that science mutually support and explain each other. It will not become easy to render a systematic and complete account of the *Wissenschaftslehre*'s manner of proceeding until it has become possible to provide a pure exposition of the *Wissenschaftslehre* itself. Until such time as he himself or someone else can accomplish this task, the author begs the public's forgiveness for the preliminary and incomplete character of this work!

All that has been altered in this second edition are a few phrases and expressions, which were insufficiently precise. Some footnotes, which embroiled the system in still avoidable polemical quarrels, have been omitted, as has the entire Third Part ("Hypothetical Division of the *Wissenschaftslehre*"), which, from the start, [I/2: 161] served a merely temporary purpose and the contents of which have since received much clearer and more ample expression in the *Foundation of the Entire Wissenschaftslehre*.

Since I am reissuing the text in which I announced my system for the very first time, I may perhaps be permitted to add some remarks concerning the history of this system's reception so far. Few people adopted the reasonable measure of remaining temporarily silent and reflecting a bit before offering an opinion. The majority betrayed their dumb astonishment at this new phenomenon and greeted it with idiotic laughter and tasteless ridicule. The more good-natured among them tried to excuse the author by treating the whole thing as nothing more than a bad joke, while others speculated in all seriousness that the author might soon be committed "to certain charitable institutions."[15] — It would be a most instructive contribution to the history of the human spirit were someone to recount the reception received by various philosophical theses when they first appeared. It is a genuine loss that we no longer possess the first, astonished contemporary judg- [I, 35] ments of some of the older systems. But there is still sufficient time to assemble a collection of the first reviews of the Kantian system — including, at the top of the list, the one that appeared in the renowned Göttingen *Gelehrten-Zeitung*[16] — in order to preserve them as curiosities for future ages. I myself wish to undertake this task on behalf of the *Wissenschaftslehre*,[17] and, as a first step, I am appending to this text two of the most remarkable hostile reviews of the *Wissenschaftslehre*[18] — and, of course, I do so without any further comment. That portion of the philosophical public which has now become better acquainted with my system requires no such comment, and as for the authors of these reviews, it is a sufficient misfortune for them to have said what they said.

Despite this terrible reception, soon afterwards this system nevertheless encountered a happier fate than may have been the lot of any other system. It has been enthusiastically [*mit Feuer*] adopted by many brilliant young thinkers, and,

after long and mature examination, a worthy philosophical veteran has given it his approval.[19] Thanks to the collective efforts of so many excellent minds, it is to be expected that this system will soon be described in multifaceted ways, that it will
[I/2: 162] be widely applied, and that it will achieve its aim of reforming philosophizing and thereby affecting scientific practice as such. There are similarities between the first reception of this system and the reception of the different and immediately preceding presentation of the same system — or, as some experts believe, of the different, immediately preceding system.[20] I have excellent reasons for claiming that my
[I, 36] system is simply a different version of the preceding one (but I hereby solemnly renounce any further dispute over this point[21]). Both systems were received similarly, though, as is to be expected from the Kantians, the reception given to the *Wissenschaftslehre* turned out to be much more coarse and vulgar than that given to Kant's writings. But despite their similar receptions, it is to be hoped that the two — whether two systems or two versions of the same system — will not share the same result: the generation of a swarm of slavish, brutal imitators. On the one hand, one would think that this sad, immediately preceding affair would deter the Germans from burdening themselves with the yoke of slavish imitation twice in a row. On the other, the form that has so far been selected for presenting this doctrine — a form that shuns the fixed letter — appears to have protected its inner spirit against such thoughtless imitators. Nor is it to be expected that friends of the *Wissenschaftslehre* would eagerly welcome such homage.

    This system still remains indescribably far from completion, and much still remains to be done. The foundation has scarcely been laid at this point. The construction of the building has barely begun, and the author wishes all of his previous writings to be viewed only as preliminary efforts. He previously feared that, for better or for worse, he would have to leave it to chance and bequeath his system — in the individual form in which it first presented itself to him and in dead letters — to some future age that might be able to understand it. Now, however, he can alter the plan he made when he first announced this system; for now he is obtaining agreement and receiving advice regarding this system, even from his own contemporaries. He is witnessing it acquire a more universal form through the shared labor of many persons, and he hopes to bequeath it as something liv-
[I/2: 163] ing within the spirit and the manner of thinking of his own age. To be specific, he will for the present discontinue the systematic extension of this system and instead will first attempt to elaborate what has already been discovered in a more multifaceted manner and make it evident to every impartial person. I have made a first step in this direction in the previously mentioned journal, and I will continue this project to the extent that my more pressing academic duties permit.[22]
[1,37] I have heard from several sources that many readers have found these essays to be illuminating, and if the public attitude toward the new doctrine has not been more widely altered, this might well be due to the fact that the journal in question seems not to have a very broad circulation. With the same aim in mind, I intend to publish a new attempt at a rigorous and strictly systematic presentation of the foundations of the *Wissenschaftslehre* just as soon as time permits.

Jena, Michaelmas, 1798

First Part

Concerning the Concept of the *Wissenschaftslehre* as Such

[I, 38]

[I/2: 112]

§ 1. Hypothetically Proposed Concept of the *Wissenschaftslehre*

The surest way to unite divided parties is by beginning with something on which they agree.

Philosophy is *a science*. All descriptions of philosophy are as unanimous on this point as they differ from one another regarding the object of this science.[B] But what if the source of this difference[C] were simply that the concept of science itself[D] was not completely developed? And what if the determination of this single feature[E] were sufficient to determine the concept of philosophy itself?

A science possesses systematic form. All the propositions of a science are connected in a single foundational principle, in which they unite to form a whole. This too is generally conceded, but is this enough to exhaust the concept of science?

Suppose that someone were to affirm a groundless and indemonstrable proposition: for example, that the air is inhabited by creatures with human desires, passions, and concepts, but with ethereal bodies; and suppose further that this person were to erect upon this proposition an ever so systematic natural history of these ethereal spirits — something which is, in itself, entirely possible. Would [I, 39] we consider such a system to be a science, no matter how strictly inferences are made within it and no matter how tightly its individual parts are linked to one another? On the other hand, when someone asserts a single theorem or fact[F] — a craftsman, perhaps, who affirms the proposition that there are right angles on either sides of a perpendicular to a horizontal line, or an illiterate farmer who asserts that the Jewish historian Josephus lived during the time of the destruction of Jerusalem.[G] — In such cases, everyone will admit that the person in question [I/2: 113] would possess scientific knowledge of what he asserts, even though the former cannot[H] systematically demonstrate his proposition from the principles of geometry and the latter cannot make a rigorous case for the historical credibility of his assertion, and even though they both have assumed this only on the basis of trust and belief.[I] But why do we refuse to call the system grounded upon an unproven and unprovable proposition a science? And why do we call "scientific" the

---

[B] All descriptions of philosophy are as unanimous on this point as they are divided from one another regarding the determination of the *object* of this science. [*2nd ed.*]

[C] and what if the source of this lack of unanimity [*2nd ed.*]

[D] the concept of science itself, which they all recognize philosophy to be [*2nd ed.*]

[E] this single feature on which everyone agrees [*2nd ed.*]

[F] asserts a single theorem [*2nd ed.*]

[G] who affirms the proposition that when a pillar is erected at a right angle to a horizontal surface it stands perpendicular and that, no matter how far it is extended, it will never incline toward either side (a proposition he may have first heard someone say and later discovered to be true in manifold experiences). [*2nd ed.*]

[H] even though he cannot [*2nd ed.*]

[I] even though he cannot systematically demonstrate his proposition from the principles of geometry. [*2nd ed.*]

cognition of the second person, which, as he understands it, is connected with no system?

The reason is undoubtedly because the former, despite its rigorous and methodologically correct form, contains nothing that could be known; whereas the latter, which completely lacks such a form, asserts something the persons in question actually *do and can know.*[J]

It follows that the essence of science lies in the character [*Beschaffenheit*] of its content, which — at least for the person who is supposed to be acquainted with this science — must be certain, something he can know.[K] Systematic form would therefore appear to be merely incidental to science — not its end, but merely a means to this end, as it were.

Suppose that[L] — for whatever reason — the human mind were able to know with certainly only very little, and that regarding everything else it could entertain only opinions, guesses, suspicions, and arbitrary assumptions. And suppose too — and once again, for whatever reason — that it really could not rest content [1,40] with limited or uncertain cognition. In this case its sole means for expanding its cognition and making it more certain would be by comparing what is uncertain with what is certain and then inferring the certainty or uncertainty of the former [I/2: 114] from its equivalence or nonequivalence to the latter.[M] If an uncertain proposition were the equivalent of one that is certain, then it could be safely assumed that it too would be certain. If the uncertain proposition were posited in opposition to the one that is certain, then we would know at once that the uncertain proposition is false. The mind would thereby be insured against being deceived any further by the false proposition. Even if it would not have attained truth, it would at least have attained freedom from error.

Allow me to make myself clearer. A science is supposed to be unified and whole. For a person who lacks any systematic acquaintance with geometry, the proposition that a perpendicular to a horizontal line makes two right angles or that Josephus lived during the time of the destruction of Jerusalem is undoubtedly[N] a single whole, and to this extent it is scientific knowledge.

But we also consider geometry as a whole to be a single science, even though it contains many propositions in addition to the one just mentioned. How then and by what means do many propositions, which in themselves differ greatly from each other, become a *single* science? How do they become one and the same whole?

This undoubtedly occurs because the individual propositions were not scientific propositions by themselves, but only became such in the context of the whole, through their position within and relationship to that whole. Simply by connecting parts, however, we can never produce anything that is not already

---

[J] the person in question actually *does and can know.* [*2nd ed.*]

[K] It would appear to follow that the essence of science lies in the character of its content and in the relation of this content to the consciousness of the person who is said to "know" something. [*2nd ed.*]

[L] We may provisionally consider the matter in the following way: Suppose that [*2nd ed.*]

[M] from its equivalence or nonequivalence (if I may make provisional use of these terms until I have the opportunity to explain them) to the latter. [*2nd ed.*]

[N] the proposition that a pillar erected at a right angle to a horizontal surface is perpendicular is undoubtedly [*2nd ed.*]

present in one of the parts of the whole. Consequently, if, among the propositions that were bound together, there had not been one that was certain, then the whole that was produced by binding them together would not be certain either.

From this it follows that at least one proposition must be certain, a proposition that subsequently communicates, so to speak, its certainty to the other propositions: so that if and insofar as the first proposition is certain, then a second one is as well; and if and insofar as this second proposition is certain, then a third [I, 41] one is as well, etc. This is how several propositions, which may perhaps be very different in themselves, could come to share a common certainty and thus constitute but a single science, since they would *all* possess *the same* certainty.

A proposition that is *certain* — and we have assumed that there is only one such proposition[O] — cannot derive its certainty merely from its connection with the other propositions [that constitute a systematic whole]. On the contrary, since nothing can arise from the union of several parts that is not present in any of those parts, the proposition in question must be certain prior to its connection [I/2: 115] with the other propositions, all of which must derive their certainty from that proposition. The latter has to be certain and agreed upon in advance of any connection with the other propositions. None of these others have to be certain in advance; they all become certain and are established for the first time through this association [with the proposition that is certain].

This also makes it clear that the assumption we have been making is the only correct one and that, in each science, there can be only one proposition that is certain and agreed upon prior to the connection [between the propositions that constitute that science]. Were there several such [certain] propositions, then they would either have no connection whatsoever with any other certain proposition (in which case these propositions would not be parts of the same whole, but would instead constitute one or more separate wholes) or else these certain propositions would be connected to each other. But the only way propositions are [in this case] supposed to be connected to each other is by sharing a common certainty, so that if one is certain then the other one must also be certain, and if one is uncertain then the other one must also be uncertain.[P] A proposition that is certain independently of other propositions could not be connected with them in this manner; if it is independently certain, then it will remain certain even if the others are not. Consequently, such a proposition would by no means be connected with the others via certainty. A proposition of this sort, one that is certain prior to its connection with others,[Q] is called a *foundational principle* [*Grundsatz*]. Every science requires a foundational principle. In fact, if we attend to the innermost character [1,42] of science, a science might well consist of only one proposition, one that is certain in itself (though naturally it would not be called a "foundational principle" in this case, since nothing else would be based upon it). Furthermore, a science can have

---

[O] We have just referred to a proposition (and we have assumed that there is only one such proposition) as purely and simply *certain*, and this proposition [*2nd ed.*]

[P] the other one must also be uncertain; all that is supposed to determine the connection between the two propositions is the relation of the certainty of the one to the certainty of the other. [*2nd ed.*]

[Q] prior to and independently of its connection [*2nd ed.*]

no more than one foundational principle, for if it had more than one it would be several sciences rather than one.

In addition to that proposition which is certain prior to its connection with the others, a science may also contain other propositions, which are recognized as certain only because of their connection with the foundational principle.[R] As was previously indicated, this connection between propositions is established by showing that if proposition A is certain, then proposition B must be certain as well, and that if proposition B is certain, then proposition C must also be certain, etc. This sort of connection is called the "systematic form" of the whole (that is, of the whole originating from the individual parts). — What is the point of connecting propositions in this manner? One does not do this simply in order to demonstrate one's virtuosity in the art of connecting; instead, one does this in order to confer certainty upon propositions that would possess no certainty in themselves. From this it follows that systematic form is not the aim of science but is only an inci-

[I/2: 116] dental means toward the achievement of that aim, a means that can be employed only if a science is supposed to consist of several propositions. Far from being the essence of science, systematic form is merely one of its incidental properties. — Imagine science as a building, the main object of which is stability [*Festigkeit*]. If we further assume that the foundation is secure, then once this foundation has been laid the main object of this building would have been achieved. Yet one cannot inhabit a mere foundation, which by itself provides protection neither against the willful attack of the enemy nor against the unwilled attacks of the weather, which is why one adds walls and a roof. All the parts of the building are connected to the foundation, as well as to all the other parts; in this way the entire building becomes stable. But no one constructs a stable building simply in order to have an opportunity to join things together. One joins things together in order to make the building stable, and the building is stable to the extent that all its parts rest upon a stable foundation.

The foundation [of our imaginary building] is stable. It is itself not grounded

[1,43] upon any additional foundation, but rather upon the solid, stable earth. — Upon what then do we propose to erect the foundation of our scientific structure? The foundational principles of our system should and must be certain in advance. Their certainty cannot be demonstrated within this system itself, since every proof that is possible within this system presupposes the certainty of these same foundational principles. If these foundational principles are certain, then of course everything derived from them is certain as well — but from what is the certainty of these principles themselves derived?[S]

Continuing in the construction of our theoretical building,[T] we can infer that *if* the foundational principle is certain, then so is another determinate individual proposition. But what is the basis for this "then"? What is the basis of this

---

[R] with the foundational principle and are recognized to be certain only in the same way and to the same degree that the foundational principle is recognized to be certain. [*2nd ed.*]
   [S] *but from what is the certainty of these principles themselves derived?* [*2nd ed.*]
   [T] After we have answered this question, do we not face a new and different one? — Continuing in the construction, [*2nd ed.*]

necessary connection between a proposition and a foundational principle, thanks to which the one is supposed to turn out to be just as certain as the other? What are the conditions for this kind of connection, and how do we know *that* they are the conditions in question and that they are the *exclusive* and *sole* such conditions?[23] And how do we ever come to assume that there is a necessary connection between different propositions and that this connection is governed by an exclusive and exhaustive set of conditions?

In short, how can the certainty of the foundational principle itself be established? And what is the warrant for that specific kind of inference by which we infer the certainty of other propositions from the certainty of the foundational principle?[U]

I call what is possessed by the foundational principle and is supposed to be [I/2: 117] communicated to all the other propositions within a science the *inner content* [*Gehalt*] of that foundational principle and [hence] of that science as such. I call the way in which this inner content is supposed to be communicated from this foundational principle to the other propositions the *form* of that science. The question, therefore, is this: How are the form and the content of a science possible in the first place? In other words, how is science itself possible?

An inquiry that would answer this question would itself be a science, *indeed, it would be the science of science as such.*

In advance of such an inquiry we cannot say whether it will or will not be possible to answer this question; that is, we cannot determine in advance whether our knowledge in its totality has a secure foundation,[V] or whether (at least so far [I, 44] as we can determine) it rests upon nothing at all, no matter how tightly its individual parts may be joined together. But if our knowledge is supposed to have a foundation,[W] then this question must be answerable, and there must be a science that answers it. If there is such a science, then our knowledge has a foundation.[X] Prior to our inquiry, therefore, we can say nothing about whether our knowledge is well-founded or groundless. The possibility of the requisite science can be demonstrated only by its actuality.

It is arbitrary what name we give to such a (still merely problematic) science. But suppose it could be shown that, in the wake of all previous experience, the field that remains available for scientific cultivation is already occupied by the respective sciences and that only a single uncultivated plot appears to remain, the one designated for the science of science as such. And suppose, too, that under a familiar name ("philosophy") one discovers the idea of a science — that is to say, the idea of something that wishes to be or to become a science, but which cannot decide where to take root. In such a case it would not be inappropriate to direct it to the empty plot we discovered, whether or not this is precisely what people have previously meant by the word "philosophy." Afterward, this science

---

[U] In short, how can *the certainty of the foundational principle in itself* be established? *And what is the warrant for that specific kind of inference by which we infer the certainty of other propositions from the certainty of the foundational principle?* [*2nd ed.*]

[V] has a recognizably secure foundation [*2nd ed.*]

[W] does have a foundation, for us [*2nd ed.*]

[X] our knowledge has a-recognizable foundation [*2nd ed.*]

[I/2: 118]

[1,45]

(if philosophy ever becomes a science) will be justified in shedding a few of the names it previously assumed out of (a by no means exaggerated) modesty: "esoteric amusement," "hobby," and "dilettantism." The nation that discovered this science would deserve to give it a name in its own language,* in which case it could be called "*science*, purely and simply" [*schlechthin* die Wissenschaft] or "doctrine of scientific knowledge" [*Wissenschaftslehre*]. What was previously called "philosophy" would therefore be called "*the science of science as such*."

[I/2: 119]

§ 2. Development of the Concept of the *Wissenschaftslehre*

[I, 46]

Nothing should be inferred from definitions. This means either that one should not, for no additional reason, infer that, simply because one is able to think without contradiction that a thing that is supposed to exist independently of our description of it possesses a certain property, it then follows that this same property must be encountered in the actual thing; or else it means that, in the case of a thing we ourselves are supposed to produce, in accordance with an image we have formed of its purpose, we should not conclude that, just because we can conceive of this purpose, it is therefore achievable in actuality. But this maxim certainly does not imply that one's mental or physical labors should have no purpose, or that one should not attempt to make this purpose plain, even before setting to work, but should instead leave the results of one's labors up to the play of one's imagination or fingers. Even before he knew whether he would discover a gas that could make his machine sufficiently lighter than the atmosphere, the inventor of the aerostatic spheres[25] could certainly calculate their size and the relation of the

---

* This nation would also deserve to coin in its language the other technical expressions to be employed in this science. This language itself, as well as the nation that speaks it, would thereby gain a decisive superiority over all other languages and nations.

[*Supplement to this footnote in the 2nd ed.*] There is even a system of philosophical terminology, which, with respect to all its derived parts, is necessary and must be proven to be so by proceeding in an orderly fashion and in accordance with the laws governing the metaphorical designation of transcendental concepts. All that has to be presupposed is an arbitrarily chosen fundamental term, since every language must begin with something arbitrary. Philosophy, which, with respect to its concept, is valid for all reason, would therefore become something quite national with respect to its terminology — something extracted from the innermost character of the nation that speaks this language and, in turn, something that perfects this national language by making it as specific as possible. However, this systematic-national terminology cannot be instituted in advance of the completion of the system of reason itself, both in its entire scope and in the complete development of all its parts. Terminological specification is the last task facing the philosophical power of judgment, one which, considered in its entire scope, may easily be too great for a single human lifetime.

This explains why the author has not yet accomplished what he seems to have promised in the preceding remark, but has instead made use of whatever technical terms were available, whether derived from German, Latin, or Greek. For the author, all terminology is merely provisional until such time as it can be established in a universal and permanently valid manner (whether this task be allotted to the author himself or to someone else). For the same reason, he has devoted little attention to terminology as such and avoided fixed definitions. For the same reason, he has made no personal use of certain apt remarks others have made concerning this point (e.g., a proposed distinction between "dogmatism" and "dogmaticism"[24]), since such remarks are relevant only to the present state of science. He plans to continue to employ paraphrase and variety of expression in order to give his presentations the clarity and specificity necessary to fulfill his intentions in each particular instance.

air within them to the atmosphere, and therefore their speed.[Y] And Archimedes could design that machine with which he wished to move the earth from its position, even though he was certain that he could discover no place beyond the earth's gravitational field from which he could actually operate this machine. — So too with the science we have just described: it is, as such, nothing that could exist independently of us and without our assistance. On the contrary, it can be produced only by the freedom of our mind, turned in a particular direction — supposing that such freedom exists,[Z] which is also something that we cannot yet know. Let us now specify in advance this direction [in which we must turn our attention in order to construct a *Wissenschaftslehre*], and let us produce for ourselves a clear concept of *what* our task is supposed to be. The question of whether or not we can actually produce the science in question will be decided by whether or not we actually do produce it. This, however, is not yet the issue at hand, which instead concerns what it is that we actually want to produce; and this is what will determine our definition [of so-called "philosophy" or *Wissenschaftslehre*].

1.) The science we have described is supposed to be, above all, a science *of science itself*. Every possible science has one foundational principle,[AA] which [I, 47] cannot be demonstrated to be true within that science itself, but must be certain [I/2: 120] in advance of it. Where then is this foundational principle supposed to be proven? Undoubtedly, this must be proved in that science which has to ground or establish the foundation of every possible science. — In this regard the *Wissenschaftslehre* has to accomplish two things. First, it has to establish the possibility of any foundational principles whatsoever and show how, to what extent, under what conditions, and perhaps to what degree anything at all can be certain, as well as show what the phrase "to be certain" means. Second, the *Wissenschaftslehre* has the specific task of demonstrating the foundational principles of all possible sciences, a task that cannot be accomplished within these sciences themselves.

Every science consisting not of one, single, isolated proposition, but rather of several propositions, which together constitute a whole, possesses systematic form.[BB] This form is the condition governing the connection between the derived propositions and the foundational principle, and it is this form that justifies our inferring from this connection that the derived propositions are necessarily just as certain as the foundational principle. So long as they retain their unity and do not concern themselves with matters not pertaining to them, the special sciences are quite unable to demonstrate this systematic form; instead,[CC] the possibility of their form is already presupposed by such sciences. A universal *Wissenschaftslehre* is obliged to ground the systematic form of all possible sciences.

[Y] and thus the speed with which his machine would move. [*2nd ed.*]

[Z] such mental freedom exists, [*2nd ed.*]

[AA] one *foundational principle* [*2nd ed.*]

[BB] possesses *systematic form.* [*2nd ed.*]

[CC] just as unable to demonstrate this systematic form as they are unable to demonstrate the truth of their foundational principles; instead, [*2nd ed.*]

2.) The *Wissenschaftslehre* is itself *a single science*. Therefore, it too must begin with one foundational principle,^{DD} one that cannot be proven within the *Wissenschaftslehre*, but has to be presupposed for that science to be possible.^{EE} But neither can this foundational principle be proven within any higher science. For in that case this higher science would itself be the *Wissenschaftslehre*, and that science whose foundational principle first had to be proven would not be the *Wissenschaftslehre*. Consequently, the foundational principle of the *Wissenschaftslehre*, which is thereby the foundational principle of all science and

[1,48] of all knowledge, simply cannot be proven.^{FF} That is to say, this foundational principle cannot be traced back to any higher principle, by comparison with which its own certainty would be illuminated. Yet this foundational principle is supposed to provide the foundation for all certainty. Consequently, it must surely be certain — certain in itself, for its own sake, and through itself. All other propositions will be certain because they can be shown to be in some respect equivalent to this foundational principle; but this principle has to be certain simply because

[I/2: 121] it is equivalent to itself. All other propositions will possess only an indirect certainty, derived from this foundational principle, which must be immediately certain. All knowledge is based upon this principle, and without it no knowledge whatsoever would be possible. It itself, however, is based upon no other knowledge; it is the principle of knowledge, purely and simply. — The foundational principle of the *Wissenschaftslehre* is purely and simply certain; i.e., it is certain *because* it is certain.^{GG} It is the foundation or ground of all certainty. That is to say, everything that is certain is certain because *this principle* is certain, and if *it* is not certain, then nothing is. It is the foundation of all knowledge. When one knows anything at all one knows what this principle asserts; one knows it immediately, just as soon as one knows anything at all. It accompanies all knowing, is contained in all knowing, and is presupposed by all knowing.

Insofar as the *Wissenschaftslehre* is itself a science and one that is supposed to consist of several propositions and not simply of its purely foundational principle — and simply from the fact that this doctrine has to establish the foundational principles of all the other sciences it follows that it must consist of several propositions — it must, I insist, possess systematic form. But it can borrow neither the specific character nor the validity of this form from any other science,^{HH} since the *Wissenschaftslehre* has to establish not just the foundational principles (and thereby the inner content) of all the other sciences, but also their form (and thereby the possibility of the connection between the various propositions within

[I, 49] these sciences). It follows that the *Wissenschaftslehre* must contain this form within itself and establish it through itself.

---

^{DD} with *one foundational principle* [*2nd ed.*]

^{EE} for it to be possible as a science. [*2nd ed.*]

^{FF} Consequently, this foundational principle — of the *Wissenschaftslehre* and thereby of all science and of all knowledge — simply cannot be proven [*2nd ed.*]

^{GG} Without contradicting oneself, one cannot question the basis of the certainty of this foundational principle. [Footnote in *SW*, based on Fichte's own handwritten marginalia.]

^{HH} it must possess *systematic form*. But it cannot call upon any other science for proof either of the *specific character* or of the *validity* of this form [*2nd ed.*]

We only need analyze this conclusion a bit in order to see what it actually says. — Let us provisionally call that about which one knows something the "content" of a proposition and what one knows about this something the "form" of a proposition. (In the proposition "gold is a body," what one knows about are gold and body, and what one knows about them is that they are in a certain respect equivalent, so that each of them may, to that extent, be posited in the place of the other. This is an affirmative proposition, and this [affirmative] relationship is the form of this proposition.)

No proposition is possible without both content and form. There must be something about which one has knowledge, and there must also be something one knows about this thing. It follows that the initial proposition of all *Wissenschaftslehre*[26] must have both content and form. This proposition is supposed to be certain immediately and through itself, which can only mean that its content determines its form and its form determines its content. This particular [I/2: 122] form can fit only this particular content, and this content can fit only this form. Any other form for this content or any other content for this form would annul the [absolutely first foundational] principle and, along with it, all knowledge. Hence the form of the absolutely foundational principle of the *Wissenschaftslehre* is not only provided by itself,[II] it is also put forward as purely and simply valid for the content of this [same] foundational principle. Should the *Wissenschaftslehre* turn out to have other foundational principles in addition to this absolutely first one, then these others could be only partially absolute, though they must [also] be partially conditioned by the first and supreme principle,[JJ] for otherwise there would not be one single foundational principle. — Consequently, the "absolutely first" element in any such additional foundational principle would have to be either its content or its form, and similarly, the conditioned element would have to be either its form or its content. Supposing the unconditioned element to be [1, 50] the *content*, then the *form* of this content would be conditioned by the absolutely first foundational principle, which, if it is supposed to be the absolutely first foundational principle, must condition something in this second principle. Accordingly, in this case the form of this additional foundational principle would be determined within the *Wissenschaftslehre* itself, determined through it and by means of its first foundational principle. Or supposing the reverse, that the form [of the additional foundational principle] is the unconditioned element. In this case the content of this principle would necessarily be determined by the [first] foundational principle, and hence its form would be indirectly determined by this first principle as well, insofar as it is supposed to be the form of a certain content. Thus, in this second case also, the form would be determined by the *Wissenschaftslehre*, and indeed, by its foundational principle. — But if an absolutely first foundational principle, as well as a *Wissenschaftslehre* and any system of human knowledge

---

[II] provided by itself, i.e., by this principle itself, [*2nd ed.*]

[JJ] This is because, in the first case they would not be foundational principles at all, but would instead be derived principles and, in the second case, etc." [Footnote in *SW*, based on Fichte's own handwritten marginalia.]

whatsoever are supposed to exist, then there cannot be any foundational principle that is determined neither in form nor in content by the absolutely first foundational principle. This is why there can be no more than three foundational principles: one determined absolutely and purely and simply by itself with respect both to its form and its content; one determined by itself with respect to its form; and one determined by itself with respect to its content. — If the *Wissenschaftslehre* contains any propositions in addition to these foundational principles, these additional propositions must all be determined by the foundational principle with respect both to their form and to their content. Consequently, a *Wissenschaftslehre* must determine the form of all its propositions, insofar as these are considered individually. But such determination of individual propositions is possible only insofar as these propositions reciprocally determine one another. Moreover, every proposition [in the *Wissenschaftslehre*] has to be *completely* determined: its form must fit only its content and no other, and this content must fit only the form in

[I/2: 123] which it is found and no other. Were this not the case, the proposition in question would not be equivalent in its certainty to the foundational principle (see above),[KK] and hence the proposition would not be certain. — Now if all the propositions of a *Wissenschaftslehre* are supposed to differ among themselves (which must be the case, since otherwise they would not be several different propositions, but would instead be repeated instances of one and the same proposition), then no proposition can be completely determined except insofar as it is deter-

[1, 51] mined as one proposition among many. In this manner, the entire series of propositions is completely determined and none can occupy a different position within the series than the one it does occupy. The position of every proposition in the *Wissenschaftslehre* is determined by another specific proposition and itself determines the position of a specific third one. The *Wissenschaftslehre* therefore determines its own form, by itself and in its entirety.

This form of the *Wissenschaftslehre* is necessarily valid for its content. This is because, if the absolutely first foundational principle were immediately certain (i.e., if its form suited only its content and its content suited only its form), and if all possible additional propositions were determined, directly or indirectly, either with respect to their form or with respect to their content, by this absolutely first foundational principle (if these additional propositions were already, so to speak, contained in the absolutely first foundational principle), then what is true of this absolutely first foundational principle would have to be true of these other propositions as well: their form would have to suit only their content, and their content would have to suit only their form. This applies to the individual propositions, but the form of the whole is nothing other than the form of the individual propositions, thought of in their unity with one another [*in Einem gedacht*]. What is valid for each individual proposition must also be valid for them all, considered as one.

The *Wissenschaftslehre*, however, is not only supposed to provide itself with its own form; it is also supposed to supply the form of all possible additional sciences,[LL]

[KK] equivalent in its certainty to the foundational principle (here one should recall what was just said on this topic), [2nd ed.]

[LL] is not only supposed to provide *itself* with its own form; it is also supposed to supply the form *of all possible additional sciences* [2nd ed.]

and it is supposed to establish the validity of this form for all the sciences. But this is conceivable only if everything that is supposed to be a proposition in another science is already contained in some proposition of the *Wissenschaftslehre* and is therefore already present in its own appropriate form within the *Wissenschaftslehre*. This offers us an easy path back to the content of the absolutely first foundational principle of the *Wissenschaftslehre*, concerning which we can now say more than we were previously able to say.

Suppose that "*to know with certainty*" means nothing other than this: to obtain insight into the inseparability of a particular content and a particular form (which [I/2: 124] is intended to be no more than a nominal definition, since a real definition[27] of knowing is quite impossible). From this it follows that, from the way in which the [I, 52] absolutely first foundational principle of all knowledge determines its form purely and simply through its content and determines its content purely and simply through its form, we can already see, at least to some extent, how the form of the entire content of knowledge might be determined — if, that is, this foundational principle includes all possible content. Accordingly, if our presupposition is correct and if there is one absolutely first foundational principle of all knowledge, it would then follow that the content of this foundational principle would have to contain within itself all possible content and would itself be contained in no other proposition. Such content would be content pure and simple, absolute content.

It is easy to see that whenever we presuppose that such a *Wissenschaftslehre* is possible at all and, more specifically, whenever we presuppose the possibility of its foundational principle, we are always already presupposing that human knowledge actually does constitute a system. If there is such a system, then it can also be shown (independently of our description of it in the *Wissenschaftslehre*) that there must be such an absolutely first foundational principle.

If there is no such system, then only two possibilities are conceivable. The first is that nothing whatsoever is immediately certain and that our knowledge consists of one or more infinite chains, in which every proposition is grounded in another, higher proposition, and this higher one, in turn, in a still higher one. We build our dwellings upon the earth. The earth rests upon an elephant. The elephant stands upon a tortoise. The tortoise? Who knows what it is standing on? And so on, ad infinitum. — If this is the actual state of our knowledge, then of course we cannot change this fact, but it also follows that we possess no secure knowledge. Perhaps we have traced the chain of propositions back to a specific one and have found everything to be secure so far.[MM] But who can guarantee that if we were to dig a bit deeper we would not discover that our knowledge is foundationless and therefore has to be abandoned? Our certainty would be begged and borrowed, and we could never be sure that it would remain certain tomorrow.

Or, in the second case, our knowledge would consist of several finite series, each ending in a foundational principle based only upon itself. But then there [I, 53]

[MM]   and have found everything to be stable so far. [*2nd ed.*]

would be several such foundational principles, completely isolated from and
[I/2: 125] unconnected with each other, since each grounds itself purely and simply and
independently of the others.[NN] There might, for example, be present within us
several innate truths, each of which is equally innate. But we could expect no
further insight into the interconnection of these innate truths, since this interconnection would be something lying beyond these individual truths. Or, to
take another example, perhaps things outside us contain a variety of simple
properties, which are communicated to us by means of the impressions they
make upon us. We, however, would not be able to penetrate to the connection
between these simple properties, since nothing can be more simple than the
simplest properties discovered in an impression. — If this is the actual state of
our knowledge, if human knowledge is in itself and essentially such a piecework
(as is the actual knowledge of many human beings), if our minds originally
contain several threads [of knowledge], which neither have nor can have any
point of connection: if this is our actual situation, then we are once again in no
position to struggle against our own nature. However far it extends, our
knowledge would indeed be certain, but it would not be *unified*. Instead, it
would constitute *many* sciences. — In this case, our dwelling would certainly be
stable, but it would not be a unified, coherent structure. Instead, it would be a
conglomeration of separate chambers, and we would be unable to pass from
one to the other. It would be a dwelling in which we would always be lost and
could never feel at home. It would contain no light, and we would remain poor
despite all our wealth, because we would never be able to make an estimate of
our wealth, consider it as a whole, and know what we actually possess. We could
never employ one portion of our dwelling to improve the others, because no
portion of the same would bear any relation to any other portion. Furthermore,
our knowledge would never be complete. Every day we would have to anticipate
that a new innate truth might express itself within us, or that experience might
present us with a new simple property. We would always have to be prepared to
pitch a new hut somewhere else. — In this case, no universal science would be
[I, 54] needed in order to provide the other sciences with a foundation. Each of these
sciences would be grounded upon itself, and there would be just as many
sciences as there are distinct, immediately certain foundational principles.

If, however, instead of one or more fragments of a system (as in the first case)
or several different systems (as in the second case), the human mind is supposed
to contain one complete and unified system [of knowledge], then there must
be such a supreme and absolutely first foundational principle. Though our
knowledge may radiate from this foundational principle in ever so many lines, from
each of which branch out still more, all of these lines must still cohere in one
single ring, which is itself attached to nothing, but, through its own power,
[I/2: 126] supports itself along with the entire system of knowledge. — Here we have a
planet that supports itself through its own gravity and irresistibly attracts toward
its center anything that is actually built perpendicular to and upon its surface,

---

[NN] since each grounds itself through itself, purely and simply and independently of the others
[*2nd ed.*]

and not, as it were, aslant and hanging in the air. Not even a single speck of dust can escape the gravitational field of this planet.

We cannot decide in advance of the inquiry whether or not there is any such system or any such foundational principle (which is the condition for the possibility of such a system). Not only is this foundational principle a proposition that is, as such, incapable of proof, it also cannot be proven that it is the foundational principle of all knowledge. Everything depends on the experiment.[28] Should we discover a proposition satisfying all the internal conditions necessary for the foundational principle of all human knowledge, we will then attempt to determine whether it also possesses the external ones: namely, whether we can trace everything we know or believe we know back to this proposition. If we succeed in this attempt, then we will have shown — by actually constructing it — that such a science is possible and that there is a system of human knowledge, which is portrayed by this science. If we fail in this attempt, then either there is no such system at all or else we have simply failed to discover it and must leave this discovery to our more fortunate successors. Simply to assert that such a system does not exist because we have failed[oo] to discover it is a presumption, the refutation of which does not deserve serious consideration.

[oo] *we have failed* [*2nd ed.*]

[I, 55]   **Second Part**

[I,2: 127]   **Explication of the Concept of the *Wissenschaftslehre***

§ 3.

To explicate[29] a concept scientifically (and it is clear that we are here concerned only with this highest type of explication) is to assign it a place in the overall system of the human sciences, that is, to show which concept determines its place and which other concept has its place determined by it. Yet the concept of the *Wissenschaftslehre* has no place in the system of the sciences, any more than knowledge in itself has any place in the system of knowledge as such. On the contrary, the *Wissenschaftslehre* is itself the locus of all scientific concepts and assigns all of them their places within itself and through itself. Clearly, we are here speaking only of a hypothetical explication. That is to say, the question is as follows: Assuming that there are already sciences and that these sciences contain truth (which is something one can by no means know prior to the universal *Wissenschaftslehre*), then what is the relationship between that *Wissenschaftslehre* which is supposed to be established and these [existing] sciences?

The answer to this question is also contained in the very concept of the *Wissenschaftslehre*. These existing sciences are related to the *Wissenschaftslehre* in the same way that something established is related to the foundation upon which it is established. The various sciences do not assign a place to the *Wissenschaftslehre*; instead, the *Wissenschaftslehre* assigns all them their places within[PP] and through itself. Therefore, all we have to do here is to develop this answer further.

The[QQ] *Wissenschaftslehre* is supposed to be the science of all the sciences. To
[I/2: 128] begin with, this raises the following question: How can the *Wissenschaftslehre* guarantee that it will provide the foundation, not merely for all the sciences discovered so far, those with which we are already acquainted, but for all possible
[I, 56] and discoverable sciences? How can it guarantee to exhaust completely the realm of knowledge?[RR]

In[SS] this respect, the *Wissenschaftslehre* is supposed to provide all the sciences with their foundational principles. From this it follows that all those propositions that serve as foundational principles of the various particular sciences are, at the same time, propositions contained within the *Wissenschaftslehre*. One and the same proposition must therefore be considered from two different points of view.[TT] Insofar as the proposition in question is contained within the *Wissenschaftslehre*, further inferences are there drawn from it; insofar as this same proposition is the foundational principle of a particular science, further inferences are also drawn

---

[PP] Not really within the *Wissenschaftslehre* itself, but nevertheless within that system of knowledge that the *Wissenschaftslehre* is supposed to portray. [Footnote in *SW*, based on Fichte's own handwritten marginalia.]

[QQ] 1.) The [*2nd ed.*]

[RR] This is in reply to Aenesidemus [Footnote in *SW*, based on Fichte's own handwritten marginalia.]

[SS] 2.) The [*2nd ed.*]

[TT] considered from two different points of view: as a proposition contained within the *Wissenschaftslehre*, but also as a foundational principle standing at the pinnacle of some particular science. [*2nd ed.*]

from it within that science. Now either the same inference is drawn from the same propositions in both the *Wissenschaftslehre* and in the particular sciences, or else different inferences are drawn in each case. In the first case, the *Wissenschaftslehre* would include not only the foundational principles of the particular sciences, but also all the [additional] propositions inferred [from these principles] within those sciences, in which case the latter would not be particular sciences at all, but merely parts of one and the same *Wissenschaftslehre*. The second case — namely, that different inferences are drawn from one and the same proposition within the *Wissenschaftslehre* and within a particular science — is likewise impossible, since the *Wissenschaftslehre* is supposed to supply all the sciences with their form.[30] The alternative is that something else (something that can, to be sure, be obtained only from the *Wissenschaftslehre*) must be added to a mere proposition of the *Wissenschaftslehre* if this same proposition is to become the foundational principle of a particular science. This raises the question, What is the "something else" that is added in this case? Or, since this "something else" constitutes the difference in question [between the same proposition qua contained in the *Wissenschaftslehre* and qua foundational principle of a particular science], Where lies the precise boundary between the *Wissenschaftslehre* as such and every particular science?

In[UU] this same respect, the *Wissenschaftslehre* is also supposed to determine the form of all the sciences. We have already indicated how this might be accomplished. Now, however, we are confronted by another science called "*logic*," which makes this same claim [to determine the form of all the sciences]. The *Wissenschaftslehre* has to be distinguished from logic, and we must therefore examine the relationship between them.

The[VV] *Wissenschaftslehre* is itself a science, and we have already specified what it has to accomplish qua science. Yet simply because it is a science — that is, a [I, 57] type of knowledge (in the formal sense)—, it is a science of something. It has an object, and it is clear from what has already been said that this object can be [I/2: 129] nothing other than the system of human knowledge as such.[WW] This raises the question, What is the relationship between this science, qua science, and its object as such?[31]

§ 4. To What Extent Can the *Wissenschaftslehre* Be Sure That It Has Exhausted Human Knowledge as Such?

Human knowledge in its entirety is not the same as what has truly been known or has been imagined to have been truly known *so far*. Suppose that a philosopher had really mastered the latter and was able to prove by means of a complete induction that his system includes all that is known so far; he would nevertheless

---

[UU]   3.) In [*2nd ed.*]
[VV]   4.) The [*2nd ed.*]
[WW] Since this science (1) asks how is science possible at all, and (2) claims to have exhausted human knowledge, which is supposed to be based upon a single foundational principle. [Footnote in *SW*, based on Fichte's own handwritten marginalia.]

still be a long way from having accomplished his task.^{XX} For how would he demonstrate by means of his induction from previous experience that there could also be no future discovery that would not fit into his system?— Nor would it be any more thoroughgoing for him to excuse himself by saying, for example, that he only intended to exhaust the knowledge that is possible in the present sphere of human existence. For were his philosophy valid only for this present sphere, then he would be acquainted with no other possible sphere, and thus he would also be unacquainted with the limits of that sphere his philosophy is supposed to exhaust. He has arbitrarily drawn a boundary, the validity of which he can scarcely demonstrate except by appealing to past experience, which could always be contradicted by future experience, even within the same purported sphere of human existence. To say that human knowledge in its entirety is supposed to be exhausted means that one has to determine, unconditionally and purely and simply, not [1,58] only what a human being is capable of knowing at his present level of existence, but what he is capable of knowing at any possible and conceivable level of his existence.^{YY}

[I/2: 130]   Such an exhaustive determination of human knowledge is possible only if it can be shown, first, that the asserted foundational principle is exhausted, and, second, that no other foundational principle is possible.

A foundational principle has been exhausted when a complete system has been erected upon it, that is, when the principle in question necessarily leads to *all* the propositions that are asserted [within this system] and when *all* these propositions necessarily lead back to that foundational principle. The negative proof that our system includes no superfluous propositions^{ZZ} is that no proposition occurs anywhere in the entire system that could be true if the foundational principle were false — or could be false if the foundational principle were true. This is the negative proof that our system contains no superfluous propositions, because a proposition not belonging to the system could be true even if the foundational principle of the system were false, or false even if it were true. If the foundational principle is given, then *all* of the [other] propositions must be given as well. Each individual^{AAA} proposition is given in and through the foundational principle.

---

^{XX} from having accomplished the task of philosophy. [*2nd ed.*]

^{YY} Reply to a possible objection, which could be made only by a popular philosopher:^{32} [*2nd ed:* Reply to a possible objection:] — The actual tasks of the human mind are certainly infinite, both in number and in scope. They could be completed only in a completed approximation to infinity — something that is, in itself, impossible. But these tasks are infinite only because they are immediately given *as* infinite tasks. There are infinitely many radii in an infinite circle whose center is given; but when this center is given, so too is the whole infinite circle with its infinite number of radii. To be sure, one end of each radius lies at infinity, but its other end lies in that center that every radius has in common. This center is given and so is the direction of the radii (for they are supposed to be straight lines). Thus all the radii are given. (Among this infinite number of radii, which ones are actually to be drawn is *determined* by the impression made by the Not-I. [*2nd ed.*: is *determined* by the gradual development of our original limitation.] But these radii are not *given* [by such impressions]; they are *given* along with the center of the circle.) Human knowledge is infinite in *scope* [*Graden*], but its *nature* [*Art*] is wholly determined through its own laws and can be exhausted [i.e., exhaustively described and delimited].

[The tasks lie before us and confront us, and they must be exhaustively described, even though they are not and cannot be completed (Footnote to this footnote in *SW*, based on Fichte's own handwritten marginalia.)]

^{ZZ} no *superfluous* propositions [*2nd ed.*]

^{AAA} Each particular [*2nd ed.*]

From what has already been said concerning the interconnection of the individ- [1,59] ual propositions of the *Wissenschaftslehre*, it is clear that this science would immediately include — in and through itself — the negative proof in question. This negative proof will demonstrate that our science is *systematic*, i.e., that all its parts cohere in one single foundational principle. — Furthermore, the science is a *system* (or is complete) when no additional propositions can be inferred from its foundational principle, and this furnishes the positive proof that the system does not include any more propositions^BBB than it should. The only question remaining is, When and under what conditions can no additional proposition be inferred? Obviously, nothing is proven by the merely relative and negative cri- terion that *I* cannot see how anything further could be inferred from this founda- [I/2: 131] tional principle. I may well be followed by another person, one who is able to see something where I can see nothing. In order to be able to demonstrate purely and simply and unconditionally that nothing more can be inferred [from this founda- tional principle] we need a positive criterion. This criterion can only be this: that the foundational principle from which we began is our final result.^CCC In that case it would be clear that we could proceed no further without retracing the path we had already taken. In some future exposition of the *Wissenschaftslehre* it will be shown that this doctrine really does complete this circuit and that it leaves the inquirer at precisely the point where he began, and thus that the *Wissenschaftslehre* also includes within and through itself this second, positive proof [that it has exhausted its foundational principle].*

Yet even if the asserted foundational principle is exhausted and a complete system is erected upon it, it still does not by any means follow that the exhaus- tion of this principle involves the exhaustion of human knowledge as such — unless, that is, one has already presupposed what needs to be proven: namely, [I, 60] that the foundational principle of this science is also the foundational principle of human knowledge as such. It is true that nothing more can be added to or subtracted from this completed system^DDD [of human knowledge], but what is there to prevent broader future experience from perhaps adding to human con- sciousness propositions not based upon the foundational principle in question, propositions which therefore presuppose one or more additional foundational principles (even if no traces of such new propositions should be presently observable)? In short, in addition to this system that has been completed, why should not one or more different systems be capable of existing in the human mind? Admittedly, these systems would not have the least connection with each other or have the smallest point in common either with each other or with that

---

^BBB any fewer propositions [*2nd ed.*]
^CCC is itself at the same time our final result. [*2nd ed.*]
   * The *Wissenschaftslehre* thus possesses absolute totality. Within it, each thing leads to every- thing, and everything leads to each thing. It is, however, the only science that can be completed. Completeness is therefore its distinguishing feature. All the other sciences are infinite and can never be completed, for they do not return to their foundational principles. The *Wissenschaftslehre* must demonstrate that this is the case and show why it is so.
   [*Error!* (Footnote to this footnote in *SW*, based on Fichte's own handwritten marginalia.)]
^DDD from *this* completed system [*2nd ed.*]

first system, but then they are not supposed to have such points in common if they are supposed to constitute several systems rather than one. Hence, in order

[I/2: 132] to prove satisfactorily the impossibility of such new discoveries, it must be shown *that* there can be only one system in human knowledge. — But since the proposition that this system is the only such system is itself supposed to be part of human knowledge,[EEE] this proposition can be based only upon the foundational principle of all human knowledge[FFF] and can be demonstrated only on the basis of this foundational principle. For the time being, we would at least have established the following: namely, if, at some future time we were to become conscious of another foundational principle, this new foundational principle could not simply be *another one, distinct from* the one proposed; it would have to be a proposition *posited precisely in opposition* to the previous

[I, 61] foundational principle.[GGG] The reason for this is as follows: It was presupposed above that the foundational principle in question includes the proposition, "there is a single system in human knowledge." Consequently, any proposition we suppose not to be included in this unified system would not merely differ from this system but would be posited in opposition to it, since this system is supposed to be the only system. Such a proposition would therefore have to be based on a foundational principle containing the proposition, "human knowledge is *not* a single system." If one continued to make reverse inferences,[33] one would have to arrive at a foundational principle squarely opposed to the previously proposed foundational principle. If, for example, the first one asserted that "I am I," then the other one would have to assert that "I am Not-I."[HHH]

We neither can nor should directly conclude from this contradiction that such an additional principle is impossible. If the previous foundational principle includes within itself the proposition, "there is a single system of human knowledge," then, of course, it also includes within itself the proposition "nothing must contradict this single system," and both of these propositions are first inferred from this foundational principle itself. Consequently, when we assume that

---

[EEE] But since the proposition that all human knowledge constitutes but one, single, internally consistent [system of] knowledge must itself be part of human knowledge, [*2nd ed.*]

[FFF] can be based only upon that proposition which has been proposed as the foundational principle of all human knowledge [*2nd ed.*]

[GGG] it would have to stand in contradiction to the form of the previous foundational principle [*2nd ed.*]

[HHH] Consequently, any proposition we suppose not to be included in this unified system would not merely differ from this system, but even the mere existence of such a proposition would contradict the system in question, since this system is supposed to be the only one possible. The supposed additional foundational principle would contradict a proposition derived [from the previously proposed foundational principle], the one that asserts the unity of the system. And since *all* of the propositions in this system are inseparably connected with each other (so that if any one of them is true, then they are necessarily all true, and if any one of them is false, then they are necessarily all false), this new proposition would contradict every single proposition of that system — and, more specifically, it would contradict the foundational principle of that system. If we also presuppose that this proposition alien to our system should itself have a systematic basis in consciousness in the manner described above, then it follows merely from the formal contradiction which its existence represents that the system to which this alien proposition is said to belong would also materially contradict the entire previous system and would therefore have to be based upon a foundational principle posited in direct opposition to the foundational principle of the first system. Thus, for example, if the foundational principle of the first system were the proposition "I am I," then that of the second would have to be "I am Not I." [*2nd ed.*]

everything that follows from this foundational principle is absolutely valid, we are already assuming that the foundational principle in question is the absolutely first [I/2: 133] and only foundational principle and that it governs human knowledge purely and simply. There is therefore a circle here from which the human mind can never escape, and one does well to concede its presence explicitly, in order to avoid being confused by its unexpected discovery at some later time. This circle is as follows: If proposition X is the first, the supreme, and the absolute foundational principle of human knowledge, then there is only a single system of human knowledge, for this is a conclusion that follows from proposition X. However, since human knowledge is supposed to constitute a single system, it follows that proposition X, which (according to the proposed science) is actually the founda- tion of a system, is the foundational principle of human knowledge as such and [I, 62] that the system grounded upon X is the single system of human knowledge.

There is no reason to be embarrassed by this circle. To desire its abolition would be too desire that human knowledge should completely lack any founda- tion at all — that nothing should be purely and simply certain and that all human knowledge should instead be only conditional, that no proposition should be valid in itself, but instead, that every proposition should be valid only on the con- dition that the proposition from which it follows is valid.[III] Whoever wishes to do so can always ask himself what he would know if his I were not an I — that is, if he did not exist and if he were unable to distinguish any Not-I from his I.

§ 5. What Is the Boundary Separating the Universal *Wissenschaftslehre* from the Particular Sciences Based Upon It?

We have already discovered (in § 3) that one and the same proposition cannot be, in one and the same respect, both a proposition within the universal *Wissenschaftslehre* and the foundational principle of a particular science; instead, something else must be added in the latter case. — This "something else" can be obtained only from the universal *Wissenschaftslehre*, since this includes all possible human knowledge. Yet this additional element must not already be contained in the same [I/2: 134] proposition that is supposed is to be elevated to the status of *Wissenschaftslehre*[JJJ] by the addition of this "something else"; for if this were the case, then this propos- ition of the *Wissenschaftslehre* would already be the foundational principle [of a particular science] that it is supposed to become, and there would be no bound- ary separating the particular sciences and the divisions of the universal *Wissenschaftslehre*. Some individual proposition of the *Wissenschaftslehre* must therefore be, so to speak, united with that proposition which is supposed to become the foundational principle [of a particular science]. The objection we are here dealing with does not arise directly from the concept of the *Wissenschaftslehre* itself, but instead arises from the presupposition that there really are other

---

III from which it follows is valid. In a word, it is to claim that there is no immediate truth at all, but only mediated truth — but *without anything by which it could be mediated.* [*2nd ed.*]
JJJ to the status of being the foundational principle of some particular science [*2nd ed.*]

[1, 63] sciences in addition to and separate from the *Wissenschaftslehre*. Consequently, this objection can be answered in turn only by means of another presupposition. For the moment it will suffice if we can simply indicate some possible way of drawing the boundary. We cannot, nor should we, here demonstrate that the boundary in question is the true boundary, though it well might be.

Accordingly, let us make the following assumptions: that the *Wissenschaftslehre* includes all of those specific actions that the human mind is necessarily forced to perform — whether conditionally or unconditionally; that, at the same time, the *Wissenschaftslehre* proposes that the ultimate explanatory ground for these necessary actions is the mind's purely and simply free and uncoerced ability to determine itself to act at all; and therefore, that the *Wissenschaftslehre* provides for both a necessary and a non-necessary or free mode of acting. The *Wissenschaftslehre* would therefore be able to determine the actions of the human mind insofar as it acts out of necessity, but not insofar as it acts freely. — If it is further assumed that the free actions of the mind are also to be determined on the basis of some ground, then this determination could not occur within the *Wissenschaftslehre* itself. Yet since we are here dealing with *determination* [*Bestimmung*] this must occur within [the domain of] *science* and therefore must occur within the particular sciences. Now the object of these [free] actions can only be what has been furnished by the *Wissenschaftslehre* as necessary (since nothing is present except what the *Wissenschaftslehre* has provided, and the *Wissenschaftslehre* provides nothing at all except what is necessary). It would therefore have to be the case that in the foundational principle of any particular science an action that had been permitted to remain free within the *Wissenschaftslehre* becomes determined. In this case, the *Wissenschaftslehre* would furnish the foundational principle in question with necessity and freedom as such, whereas the particular science in question would determine this freedom in a specific way. With this, we have discovered the sharp boundary-line we were

[I/2: 135] seeking: as soon as an action that is in itself free has been assigned a specific
[1, 64] direction, we have moved from the domain of the universal *Wissenschaftslehre* into that of some particular science. — Allow me to make myself clear by means of two examples.

The *Wissenschaftslehre* furnishes us with space as necessary and with the point as an absolute boundary, but it leaves the power of imagination completely free to posit this point wherever it likes. As soon as this freedom becomes determined — for example, by moving the point toward the boundary of the unbounded space and thereby generating a line* — we are then no longer within the domain of the

* A question for the mathematician: — Is the concept of straightness not already included in the concept of a line? Is there any kind of line other than a straight one? Is a so-called curved line anything other than a stringing together of infinitely many points, which are infinitely close to one another? This conclusion seems to me to be vouched for by the fact that the curved line is originally the boundary line of infinite space. (An infinite number of infinite radii are drawn from the I as their center. But our limited power of imagination must assign a terminus to each of these radii. Considered in their unity [*als Eins*], these terminal points constitute the original curved line.) This makes it clear *that* and *why* the task of measuring the circumference of a circle by means of a straight line is an infinite task, one that could be accomplished [only] in a completed approximation to infinity. This also makes it clear why the straight line cannot be defined. [This footnote appeared only in the first edition.]³⁴

Wissenschaftslehre, but are instead within the territory of a particular science called "geometry." The foundational principle of geometry is the general task of limiting space in accordance with a rule, or the task of spatial construction. Geometry is in this manner sharply separated from the *Wissenschaftslehre.*

The *Wissenschaftslehre* furnishes us with a Not-I, which is purely and simply independent of the laws governing mere representations, just as it also provides us with the laws governing how this Not-I should and must be observed,^{KKK} and it provides these necessarily. It also furnishes (again, as something necessary) the laws according to which nature should and must be observed.* But the [1, 65] power of judgment still retains its complete freedom to apply these laws to all or not to apply them. It also retains the freedom to select from the multiplicity of [I/2: 136] laws, as well as of objects, whichever law it chooses for application to whatever object it chooses. It is free, for example, to consider the human body as raw matter, as organized matter, or as animate matter. But as soon as the power of judgment has been assigned the task of observing a particular object according to a particular law,^{LLL} in order to determine thereby whether and to what extent the object in question conforms or fails to conform to this law, the power of judgment is then no longer free, but is subjected to a rule. Accordingly, we are no longer within the *Wissenschaftslehre,* but are instead within the domain of another science called "natural science." The foundational principle of natural science is the overall task of comparing every object of experience to every law of nature present in our mind. Natural science consists entirely of experiments (and does not consist in a passive relationship to the unregulated effects upon us of nature). We conduct these experiments voluntarily, and nature may or may not correspond to them. In this manner, natural science is sufficiently distinguished from the *Wissenschaftslehre* as such.

Thus (though we take note of this only in passing) we can already see why only the *Wissenschaftslehre* will possess absolute totality and why all the particular [1,66] sciences will be infinite. The *Wissenschaftslehre* contains nothing but what is

---

^{KKK} The *Wissenschaftslehre* furnishes us with nature as something which, both in its being and in its specific determinations, has to be viewed as independent of us, as well as with the laws in accordance with which it should and must be observed. [Footnote added in *2nd ed.*]

* Strange as this may seem to many natural scientists, it will nevertheless be shown in due course that the following can be strictly demonstrated: viz., that the scientist himself has imposed upon nature all of those laws that he believes he learns by observing nature, and that all of these laws — the most specific as well as the most general, the laws governing the construction of the smallest blade of grass as well as those governing the movements of the heavenly bodies — must be derivable from the first principle of all human knowledge, in advance of all observation. It is true that we cannot become *conscious* of any law of nature nor of any law whatsoever unless some object is given to which the law in question can be applied. It is true that not all objects necessarily have to conform to these laws, nor do they all have to conform to them to the same extent. It is true too that no single object does or can conform to these laws totally and completely. But for precisely these same reasons it is also true that we do not learn these laws of nature by observation, but instead that they underlie all observation. They are not so much laws governing a nature independent of us as they are laws for ourselves, that is to say, laws governing the manner in which we have to observe nature. [This footnote appeared *only* in the first edition.]

^{LLL} For, example, determining whether animal life can be explained purely on the basis of what is inorganic, or whether crystallization might perhaps be the transition from chemical bounding to organized structure, or whether magnetic and electrical forces are essentially the same or are different, etc. [Footnote in *SW*, based on Fichte's own handwritten marginalia.]

necessary. If what is necessary is necessary in every respect, then its quantity is also necessary — that is to say, it is necessarily limited. All the other sciences begin with freedom — the freedom of our mind as well as the freedom of Not-I,[MMM] which is purely and simply independent of us. If this is to be actual freedom, purely [I/2: 137] and simply subject to no law, then no sphere of efficacy can be prescribed for it, for such a prescription could be made only in accordance with a law. The spheres of efficacy of the particular sciences are therefore infinite. — An exhaustive *Wissenschaftslehre* thus represents no threat to the human mind's infinite progress toward perfectibility. The *Wissenschaftslehre* does not abolish this infinite progress; on the contrary, this progress is posited with complete security and is beyond all doubt, and it assigns to the human mind a task it cannot complete in all eternity.

§ 6. How Is the Universal *Wissenschaftslehre* Related to Logic in Particular?

The *Wissenschaftslehre* is supposed to establish the form of all possible sciences. According to a common opinion, which may contain some truth, logic does the same thing. How then are these two sciences related to each other, particularly in regard to this enterprise which both presume to undertake?[NNN] An easy path into this highly important inquiry is to recall that logic is supposed to furnish every science with nothing but its mere form, whereas the *Wissenschaftslehre* is supposed to furnish them with content as well as form. Form is never separated from content nor is content ever separated from form in the *Wissenschaftslehre*; content and form are intimately united in every proposition of the *Wissenschaftslehre*. If the propositions of logic contain merely the form of possible sciences, without their content, then these logical propositions are not at the same time propositions of the *Wissenschaftslehre*, but are distinct from them; consequently, the entire science [I, 67] of logic is neither the *Wissenschaftslehre* itself nor even a part of this doctrine. No matter how odd it may sound to say this, given the present state of philosophy, logic is not a philosophical science at all; instead, logic is a separate science in its own right, which, however, should not detract in the least from its dignity.

If this is what logic is, then it must be possible to indicate a determination of freedom by means of which the boundary between logic and universal [I/2: 138] *Wissenschaftslehre* is drawn[OOO] In the *Wissenschaftslehre*, content and form are necessarily united. Logic is supposed to establish nothing but form, separated from content. In itself, this separation is not necessary; instead, it occurs only by means of freedom. In logic, therefore, freedom must be determined to undertake

---

[MMM] the freedom of nature [*2nd ed.*]

[NNN] [The *2nd ed.* introduces a paragraph break at this point.]

[OOO] then it must be possible to indicate a determination of freedom by means of which scientific activity crosses from the realm of the *Wissenschaftslehre* into that of logic — a movement that establishes the boundary between the two sciences. Such a determination of freedom is then easy to indicate. [*2nd ed.*]

such a separation.[PPP] The name for such an act of separation is *abstraction*; accordingly, the essence of logic consists in abstraction from the entire content of the *Wissenschaftslehre*.

From this it would follow that the propositions of logic would possess only form. This, however, is impossible, since, according to the concept of a proposition as such, every proposition must have content as well as form (see § 1). Consequently, the content of logic would have to be what was merely form in the *Wissenschaftslehre*. This content would once again acquire the universal form of the *Wissenschaftslehre*, though this form would here be thought of specifically as the form of a logical proposition. This second free action, by means of which form[QQQ] becomes the form of form itself, as its content,[RRR] is called *reflection* No abstraction is possible without reflection, and no reflection is possible without abstraction. Considered separately, each of these actions is an action of freedom; if, however, they are reciprocally related to each other, then, if one of them occurs, [I, 68] the other must necessarily occur as well.[SSS]

The special relationship between logic and the *Wissenschaftslehre* follows from what was just said. Logic does not provide the foundation for the *Wissenschaftslehre*; it is, instead, the latter which provides the foundation for the former. It is purely and simply the case that the *Wissenschaftslehre* cannot be demonstrated from logic. Prior to the *Wissenschaftslehre*, one may not presuppose the validity of a single proposition of logic — including the law of contradiction. On the contrary, every single logical proposition, as well as logic in its entirety, must be demonstrated from the *Wissenschaftslehre*. What has to be shown is that the forms established within logic actually are the forms of a particular content in the *Wissenschaftslehre*.

Neither is the *Wissenschaftslehre* conditioned and determined[TTT] by logic; instead, it is logic that is conditioned and determined by the *Wissenschaftslehre*. The *Wissenschaftslehre* does not somehow obtain its form from logic. It possesses [I/2: 139] its form within itself and establishes it for a possible [subsequent] free act of abstraction. The *Wissenschaftslehre* is the condition for applying logic; the forms established by the *Wissenschaftslehre* may not be applied to any content not already contained in the *Wissenschaftslehre*.[UUU] These forms do not necessarily have to be applied to the entire content they contain within the *Wissenschaftslehre*, for in

---

[PPP] separated from content. Since form and content are not originally separated, this act of separation can only occur by means of freedom. Logic would therefore come into being through this free separation of sheer form from content. [*2nd ed.*]

[QQQ] by means of which form as such (*überhaupt*) [Footnote in *SW*, based on Fichte's own handwritten marginalia.]

[RRR] by means of which form becomes its own content and turns back upon itself [*2nd ed.*]

[SSS] is impossible without abstraction. When separated from each other and considered by themselves, these actions are actions of freedom; if, thus separated, they are related to each other, then each is the necessary condition for the other. For synthetic thinking, however, they both constitute but one and the same action, viewed from two different sides. [*2nd ed.*]

[TTT] *conditioned* and *determined* [*2nd ed.*]

[UUU] The *Wissenschaftslehre* is the condition for the validity and applicability of logical propositions. The forms established by logic may not, in the ordinary business of thinking and in the particular sciences, be applied to any content other than that content they already contain within themselves in the *Wissenschaftslehre*. [*2nd ed.*]

that case no particular science [of logic] would arise, and we would instead have nothing but a repetition of portions of the *Wissenschaftslehre*. Nevertheless, these logical forms must necessarily be applied to a portion of the content of the *Wissenschaftslehre*, to a content included within the content of the latter. If this condition is not met, then the science produced thereby is nothing more than a castle in the air.^{VVV, WWW}

[I, 69]   Finally, the *Wissenschaftslehre* is necessary — not, to be sure, as a clearly thought-out and systematically established science, but rather as a natural predisposition. Logic, on the other hand, is an artificial product of the freedom of the human mind. No knowledge nor science whatsoever would be possible without the *Wissenschaftslehre*;[35] without logic, all of the sciences could still have come into being, only somewhat later. The former is the exclusive condition for all the sciences; the latter is a highly beneficial discovery for securing and facilitating scientific progress.

I will now provide examples illustrating what has just been scientifically derived.

"A = A" is undoubtedly a logically correct proposition, and insofar as it is this, it means "*if* A is posited, then A is posited." This raises two questions: Is A posited? And *if* A is posited, to what extent and why is it posited? I.e., how are this *if* and this *then* connected at all?

Suppose that the A in the previous proposition meant "I," and thus that it possesses its own specific content. In this case, the proposition [*if* A is posited, then A is posited] would mean first of all "I am I" or "*If* I am posited, then I am posited." But since the subject of this proposition is the absolute subject, the subject purely and simply, then, in this single case, the proposition's inner content is posited along [I/2: 140] with its form: "I am posited, *because* I have posited myself. I am, *because* I am."— Whereas logic asserts that "*if* A is, then A is," the *Wissenschaftslehre* asserts that "*because* A is, then A is."^{XXX} The first question, "Is A posited?"^{YYY} would therefore be answered as follows: It is posited, *because* it is posited.^{ZZZ}

Suppose that the A in our original proposition did not mean "I," but anything else instead. In that case, what was just said is sufficient to provide us with insight into the condition under which one could say "A is posited" and into what justifies the inference "if A is posited, then A is posited". — This inference is justified because the proposition "A = A" is originally valid *only for* [1,70] *the I* and is a proposition derived from the proposition "I am I," which is a proposition of the *Wissenschaftslehre*. From this it follows that all the content to which the proposition "A = A" is supposed to be applicable must be contained and included within the I. A can therefore be nothing but *something that is posited in the I*, and the proposition in question would now read, "What is posited in the I is posited." If A is posited in the I, then A is posited (to the

---

^{VVV}   then the particular science produced thereby is nothing more than a castle in the air, no matter how logically correct the inferences within this science may be. [*2nd ed.*]

^{WWW}   This is what happened in the case of the pre-Kantian dogmatic systems, which propounded a false concept of "thing." [Footnote in *SW*, based on Fichte's own handwritten marginalia.]

^{XXX}   *because* A (this specific A = I) is [*2nd ed.*]

^{YYY}   Is A (this specific A) posited?, [*2nd ed.*]

^{ZZZ}   *because* it is posited. It is posited unconditionally and purely and simply. [*2nd ed.*]

extent, that is, that it is posited as something possible, actual, or necessary) and hence is incontrovertibly true, so long as the I is supposed to be I. — Furthermore, if the I is posited because it is posited, then everything posited in the I is also posited because it is posited; and so long as A is something posited in the I, then A is posited, if it is posited. Our second question has therefore been answered as well.

§ 7. How Is the *Wissenschaftslehre* Related to Its Object?[AAAA]

Every proposition of the *Wissenschaftslehre* has form and content. One knows something, and there is something about which one possesses knowledge. But of course the *Wissenschaftslehre* is itself the science of something, and not this "something" itself. Consequently, the *Wissenschaftslehre* as such, along with all its propositions, would be the form of a certain content, which is present in advance of this doctrine. How is the *Wissenschaftslehre* related to this content, and what follows from this relationship?

The object of the *Wissenschaftslehre* is, by all accounts, the system of human knowledge. This knowledge exists independently of the science of the same, though it is by means of this science that such knowledge is established in a sys- [I/2: 141] tematic form. What then is this new form, and what distinguishes it from that form which must be present prior to this science? And how is this science as such distinguished from its object?

We may call what exists in the human mind independently of the science in question "the actions of the mind." These actions constitute *what* is present in advance. They occur in certain specific ways, and this serves to distinguish one [1, 71] action from another, which is *how* these actions are present in the mind. Both content and form are therefore originally present in the human mind prior to our knowledge and are inseparably connected with each other. Every action occurs in a specific way, in accordance with a law, and this law determines that action. If all the actions of the mind are interconnected and are subject to uni-versal, specific, and individual laws, then they also present a system for any pos-sible observer.

With respect to their sequence,[BBBB] however, it is by no means necessary that these actions actually occur in our mind in this systematic form, one after another.[CCCC] It is not necessary that we should first become conscious of that action under which all others are subsumed and which furnishes the highest law, and that we should next become conscious of that action under which fewer actions are sub-sumed, etc. Nor does it by any means follow that we encounter all of these actions in their pure and unmixed state. Several actions, which another possible observer

---

[AAAA] Note that we have entirely abstracted from this question until now and hence that everything that has been said so far will need to be modified in the light of the answer to this question. [Footnote in *SW*, based on Fichte's own handwritten marginalia.]

[BBBB] With respect to their temporal order [*2nd ed.*]

[CCCC] in this systematic order, in which they are derived as dependent upon one another [*2nd ed.*]

might well be able to distinguish from one another, might well appear to us to be only a single action. For example, the highest action of the human mind is supposed to be that of positing its own existence,[DDDD] but it is by no means necessary that this be (temporally) the first action of the mind of which we become clearly conscious. Nor is it even necessary that we ever obtain pure consciousness of this action of self-positing, or that the intellect be capable of thinking purely and simply, "*I am*," without thinking at the same time that something else is *not* I.[EEEE]

These actions of the human mind constitute the entire material of any possible *Wissenschaftslehre*, but not this science itself. In order to bring such a science into existence, an additional action of the human mind is required, one not included among all of these [necessary] actions: namely, the mind's action of becoming conscious of its own mode of acting as such. Since this new action is not supposed to be included among all of those actions of the mind which are necessary — and which exhaust the necessary actions of the mind — , it must be a free action. —

[I/2: 142] This, therefore, is precisely how the *Wissenschaftslehre*, qua systematic science, comes into being: like all possible sciences, it arises by means of a specific deter-

[I, 72] mination of freedom, and in this case the specific determination of freedom is the free action of raising to consciousness the manner in which the human mind as such acts.[FFFF] All that distinguishes the *Wissenschaftslehre* from the other sciences is this: the object of these other sciences is itself a free action, whereas the object of the *Wissenschaftslehre* are necessary actions.

By means of this free action, something that in itself is already form (i.e., the necessary action of the human mind[GGGG]) is incorporated as content into a new form (the form of knowing or consciousness). The action in question is therefore one of reflection. These necessary actions are torn from that sequence in which they themselves might have occurred and presented in a pure, unmixed form. This same action is therefore also one of abstraction. It is impossible to reflect without having engaged in abstraction.

That form of consciousness in which the human mind's necessary manner of acting[HHHH] is supposed to be incorporated is itself undoubtedly included among its necessary modes of acting, and the intellect's mode of acting will undoubtedly be incorporated into the form of consciousness in precisely the same way that any-thing else is incorporated into this form. It should therefore not be difficult to answer the question concerning from where, for the purposes of a possible *Wissenschaftslehre*, this form is supposed to come. Yet if one thereby avoids the question of form, then all the difficulties are transferred to the question of content. — In order to incorporate the human mind's necessary manner of acting[IIII] within the form of consciousness, we would have to be already acquainted with this manner of acting as such, which means that this manner of acting would already

---

[DDDD] the highest action of the intellect is supposed to be that of self-positing. [*2nd ed.*]

[EEEE] that we ever obtain consciousness of this action of self-positing in a pure form, or that the intellect be capable of thinking purely and simply "*I am*," without thinking at the same time of some-thing else, something that *is not the intellect itself.* [*2nd ed.*]

[FFFF] in which the intellect acts [*2nd ed.*]

[GGGG] the necessary action of the intellect [*2nd ed.*]

[HHHH] the intellect's necessary manner of acting [*2nd ed.*]

[IIII] the intellect's necessary manner of acting [*2nd ed.*]

have to be incorporated within the form of consciousness. We would therefore be caught up in a circle.

According to what has been said, this manner of acting is supposed to be separated as such from all that it is *not*, and this separation is supposed to be accomplished by an act of reflective abstraction. This abstraction occurs freely. The human mind is not led to engage^{JJJJ} in such abstraction by any blind compulsion. The entire difficulty is thus contained in the following question: What rules guide freedom when it is engaged in this act of separating [the necessary actions of the human mind from those that are not necessary]? How does the human [I, 73] mind know what it is supposed to *accept* and what it is supposed to ignore?^{KKKK}

This is something it simply cannot know, insofar anyway as it is not already [I/2: 143] conscious of what it is supposed to be raising to consciousness (which is self-contradictory). It follows that this activity is governed by no rule at all and that there can be no such rule. The human mind makes various attempts. By blindly groping, it succeeds in reaching the dawn, and only then does it emerge into the bright light. At first it is led by obscure feelings* (the origin and reality of which the *Wissenschaftslehre* has to disclose).³⁷ And if we had not begun with obscure feelings concerning things that we did not clearly recognize until later, we would, to this day, still have no clear concepts and would still remain that lump of clay which first wrenched itself from the earth. — This then is the history of philosophy,^{LLLL} and we have now indicated the real reason why it is only after much aimless wandering that a few people have been able to become conscious of something that nevertheless lies there openly in every human mind and that anyone can easily grasp once it has been presented to him. All philosophers have begun with the [1, 74] same goal; they all wished to employ reflection in order to separate the manner of acting that is necessary to the human mind^{MMMM} from any accidental conditions of the same, and all of them have actually accomplished such a separation — only more or less purely or completely. On the whole, however, philosophical judgment has always progressed and advanced toward its goal.

---

^{JJJJ} The power of philosophical judgment is not led to engage [*2nd ed.*]

^{KKKK} How does the philosopher know *what* he is supposed to accept as pertaining to the intellect's necessary mode of acting and what he should ignore as accidental? [*2nd ed.*]

* This makes it clear that the philosopher requires an obscure feeling for what is right, or genius, to no less an extent than does, for instance, the poet or the artist. The difference lies in the type [of this obscure feeling.] The poet or artist needs a sense of beauty; the philosopher needs a sense of truth. Certainly, such a sense does exist. [Footnote in both editions; the words *beauty* and *truth* are emphasized in the *2nd ed.*, which also adds the following *supplement* to this footnote.]

I am not quite sure how and why, but an otherwise admirable philosophical author³⁶ has become a bit agitated over the innocent assertion contained in the foregoing note. "One would," he says, "prefer to leave the empty word 'genius' to tightrope walkers, French chefs, 'beautiful souls,' artists, and others. For sound sciences it would be better to advance a theory of discovery." — To be sure, one indeed ought to advance such a theory, and that will certainly happen just as soon as science as such has arrived at the point from which it is possible to discover such a theory. But where is the contradiction between such a project and the assertion made above? — And how will such a theory of discovery be discovered? Perhaps by means of a theory of the discovery of a theory of discovery? And [how shall we discover] this?

^{LLLL} This is then also confirmed by the history of philosophy [*2nd ed.*]

^{MMMM} The manner of acting that is necessary to the intellect [*2nd ed.*]

[I/2: 144]   Yet this act of reflection also belongs to the human mind's necessary manner of acting[NNNN] — not insofar as such reflection does or does not occur (for in this respect it is free), but rather, insofar as reflection occurs in accordance with laws,[OOOO] and insofar as the specific manner in which such reflection occurs is something determined (on the condition that it occur at all). From this it follows that the overall system of the human mind's manner of acting[PPPP] must include within itself the laws governing such reflection. Afterwards, once this science has been completed, one can then of course check to see whether or not one has succeeded sufficiently in including within it the laws governing such reflection. For this reason, one might believe that a self-evident proof of the correctness of our scientific system would be possible, at least after the fact.

Yet those same laws of reflection,[QQQQ] even if they are in agreement with those rules we hypothetically presupposed at the outset of our enterprise, are nevertheless themselves results of their own previous employment. Here a new circle reveals itself: we have presupposed certain laws of reflection, and now, in the course of our science, we discover these same laws; hence [we conclude that] these are the only possible laws.[RRRR] Had we begun with other presuppositions, then we would undoubtedly, in the course of our science, also have discovered other laws.[SSSSS] The only question is whether or not these laws would have agreed with the ones we presupposed. If not, then we could be sure that either the laws we presupposed or the laws we discovered (or, most likely, both) were false. Thus we cannot prove anything after the fact by means of the indicated type of faulty [I, 75] circular inference. Instead, we infer the correctness of the system from the *agreement.*[TTTT] But this is only a negative proof, which establishes mere probability. If the reflections we discover do *not* agree with those we presupposed, then the system is surely false. If they do agree, then it may be correct; but it does not necessarily have to be correct.[UUUU] For even though it is true that, if there is only one system in human knowledge, then there is but *one* way in which such agreement can be *correctly inferred,* it nevertheless always remains possible to produce [I/2: 145] such agreement accidentally, by means of two or more *incorrect inferences,* which together produce such agreement. — It is as if I were to make an attempt to test division by means of multiplication. If I fail to obtain the desired sum as the product of this multiplication and obtain instead any other number, then I have certainly erred at some point in my calculations. If I obtain the desired results, then it is probable that I have calculated correctly, but it is still no more than probable, for I might have made the same mistake in multiplying that I did in dividing. I might, for example, have said that 5 x 9 = 36 in both cases, in which case this agreement

---

[NNNN] belongs to the intellect's necessary manner of acting [*2nd ed.*]

[OOOO] occurs *in accordance with laws,* [*2nd ed.*]

[PPPP] system of the intellect's manner of acting [*2nd ed.*]

[QQQQ] Yet these same laws of reflection, which, in the course of the *Wissenschaftslehre,* we discover to be the only possible laws by means of which a *Wissenschaftslehre* could come into being [*2nd ed.*]

[RRRR] we discover these same laws to be the only ones possible; our presupposition was therefore quite correct, and our system is correct with respect to its form. [*2nd ed.*]

[SSSS] also have discovered other laws, as the only correct ones. [*2nd ed.*]

[TTTT] from the *agreement* between what we presupposed and what we discovered. [*2nd ed.*]

[UUUU] then it *may* be correct; but it does not necessarily *have to be* correct. [*2nd ed.*]

would prove nothing. — So it is with the *Wissenschaftslehre*: it is not merely a rule; it is at the same time the calculation [in accordance with this rule]. Someone who doubts the correctness of our product does not doubt the eternal validity of the law requiring one to posit one of the factors just as many times as the same unit is contained in the other factor. Such a person may well be just as convinced of this law as we are and simply doubts whether we have correctly followed the law in question.

Thus, even if we establish that supreme systematic unity, which is the negative condition for the correctness of our system, something more is still required, something that can never be strictly demonstrated, but which can only be assumed to be probable: namely, that this unity itself has not been produced accidentally, by means of incorrect inference. Several strategies may be employed in order to increase this probability. If the series of propositions [included in the *Wissenschaftslehre*] is no longer present in one's memory, one may review this series several times; or one may proceed in the opposite direction and infer the [1,76] foundational principle from the results; or one may reflect upon one's own reflections, etc. In this way the probability becomes ever greater, but it never becomes certainty. If a person is simply conscious of having pursued his inquiries with honesty* and without having presupposed the results,^{VVVV} then he may very well [I/2: 146] be content with this probability; and if someone doubts the tenability of our system, we may demand that he point out to us the error in our reasoning,^{WWWW} but one may never claim infallibility. — That system of the human mind which is supposed to be portrayed by the *Wissenschaftslehre* is absolutely certain and infallible. Everything based upon this system is purely and simply true. It never errs, and anything that has ever been or ever will be necessarily present within a [1,77] human soul is true. If human beings have erred,^{XXXX} the mistake did not lie in what was necessary; instead, the mistake was made by the free power of reflective judgment, when it substituted one law for another. If our *Wissenschaftslehre* is an accurate portrayal of this system of the human mind, then, like this system itself,

* The philosopher requires not merely a sense of truth, but a love of truth as well. By this I do not mean that he should eschew any attempt to establish previously assumed results by means of what he himself recognizes to be sophistry, even if he were to believe that none of his contemporaries would discover this. In such a case, he himself would know that he does not love truth. Yet everyone is his own judge in this matter, and no one has the right to accuse another of this kind of dishonesty, unless the evidence for it is glaringly obvious. But the philosopher must also guard against those involuntary instances of sophistical reasoning, to which no investigator is more prone than the investigator of the human mind. It is not enough that he have an obscure feeling that he is seeking the truth; he must become clearly conscious of this and must elevate it to his supreme maxim, so that he would welcome even the truth that there is no truth at all — provided only that this were true. He must not be indifferent to any proposition, no matter how dry or overly subtle it may appear to be. They must all be equally sacred in his eyes, for they are all parts of the same single system of truth, and each supports all the others. He must never ask, "What consequences will this have?" but must proceed straight along his path, no matter what the consequences may be. He must shirk no effort and yet must always be prepared to abandon the most strenuous and profound endeavors the moment someone shows him or he himself discovers that they are unfounded. And suppose that he has made a mistake in his reasoning? What more would this be than the common fate of every thinker so far?

^{VVVV} the results he wished to discover [*2nd ed.*]
^{WWWW} we may demand *that that person point out to us the error in our reasoning* [*2nd ed.*]
^{XXXX} If *human beings* have erred, [*2nd ed.*]

it too is purely and simply certain and infallible. But the question is precisely whether and to what extent our portrayal is accurate,[YYYY] and this is something that we can never show by means of strict proofs, but only by means of proofs [I/2: 147] that establish probability. Our portrayal contains truth only on the condition and only insofar as it is accurate. We are not the legislators of the human mind, but are instead its historians. We are not, of course, journalists, but are instead writers of pragmatic history.[38]

[1,78]   Pertinent to this also is the fact that a system can actually be on the whole correct, even if its individual parts lack complete self-evidence. It may contain faulty inferences, here and there intermediate propositions may be omitted or demonstrable propositions may be advanced without proof or be proven incorrectly; nevertheless, the most important results may still be correct. This would appear to be impossible. It would seem that the tiniest deviation from the straight line must necessarily lead to an infinitely increasing deviation. And this would certainly be the case if the human being were only a thinking being and not a feeling one as well.[ZZZZ] The deviation would grow and grow if feeling did not often compensate for the previous deviation by producing a new deviation from the straight path of argumentation, thereby leading one back to a point to which one would never have been able to return by means of correct inference.

Consequently, even if a universally valid *Wissenschaftslehre* were to be established, the power of philosophical judgment would always still have to work

[YYYY] The modesty of this remark has been contrasted with the alleged great immodesty that its author has subsequently displayed. It would certainly have been impossible for him to have foreseen the sorts of objections with which he would have to deal or the form these would take. And of course he was not at that time nearly so well acquainted with the majority of philosophical authors as he is now. Otherwise, he would not have failed to anticipate those objections that have actually been made and respond to them. Meanwhile, he finds nothing in the above remark that would contradict his conduct since writing it. The above remark was concerned only with objections to his *inferences*. His opponents, however, have not yet reached that point. They are still quarreling over the foundational principle, i.e., over his entire view of philosophy. It is, however, the author's innermost conviction, then as well as now, that there can be no quarrel whatsoever concerning this point, so long as one knows what is at issue, and in fact he never counted upon such a dispute. He is speaking of objections that have at least the appearance of being well-grounded, that is, of *proving* and *establishing* something. Those who have supposedly been struck by his alleged immodesty have not offered such objections. — Here is the explanation [for the author's allegedly immodest response to his critics], an explanation he could not have then supposed would be necessary: Rubbish of this sort — that is, the sort of rubbish that is spoken by those who have not acquired the necessary preliminary knowledge nor conducted the necessary preliminary exercises and who show that they do not even know what is at issue, the sort of rubbish that is uttered in a howling and spiteful tone, the sort of rubbish that cannot have sprung from any zeal for the progress of science and must therefore have sprung from less worthy motives, such as petty jealousy, vindictiveness, thirst for glory, desire for money, and other similar motives — such rubbish does not deserve the slightest forbearance, and in replying to such rubbish one is by no means governed by the rules of *scientific* dispute. Why do these commentators fail to draw the only appropriate conclusion: namely, that the tone that displeases them so much owes its origin solely to their own tone? [Footnote added in *2nd ed.*]

[ZZZZ] a feeling being as well. What would happen if human beings had to arrive at all that they know by means of clear thinking, and if it were not far more often the case that one is unconsciously governed by the fundamental tendency of reason operating within oneself, which, by means of new deviations from the straight path of formal and logically correct argumentation, leads one back to the only result that is materially true — a result at which one would never have been able to arrive by drawing correct inferences from incorrect intermediary propositions. [*2nd ed.*]

toward its continual perfectibility. There will always remain gaps to be filled, proofs that need improvement, and determinations that need to be more precisely determined.

I have two remarks to add to the foregoing.   [I/2: 148]

The *Wissenschaftslehre* presupposes that the rules of reflection and abstraction [I, 79] are familiar and valid. It must necessarily make this presupposition, and there is no reason to be ashamed of this or to make a mystery of it and conceal this fact. Like any other science, the *Wissenschaftslehre* is permitted to express itself and to draw direct conclusions. It may presuppose all the rules of logic and may employ whatever concepts it requires. But it presupposes these merely in order to be able to make itself intelligible, and it presupposes them without drawing from this any conclusions. Everything provable must be proven. Except for that first and highest foundational principle, all the propositions [in the *Wissenschaftslehre*] must be derived. Thus, for example, neither the logical principle of positing in opposition (i.e., the principle of contradiction, which is the basis of all analysis) nor the principle of sufficient reason [*Satz des Grundes*] (i.e., "no two things are positing in opposition to each other unless they are equivalent in some third thing, and no two things are equivalent unless they are posited in opposition to some third thing," which is the basis of all synthesis) is derived from the absolutely foundational principle; however, both of these logical principles are derived from the two foundational principles that are themselves based upon the absolutely first foundational principle. These two principles are indeed foundational principles, but not absolute ones, for they each contain only something absolute. Accordingly, these propositions [i.e., the two foundational principles containing something absolute], along with the logical principles based upon them, must indeed be derived, though not proven.[39]— Let me make myself even clearer. What is established by the *Wissenschaftslehre* is a proposition that has been thought and expressed in words. Such a proposition corresponds to an action of the human mind, an action that, in itself, does not necessarily have to have been *thought of* at all. Nothing has to be presupposed for this action, other than that without which it would not be possible *as* an action, and this is not something that is tacitly presupposed; instead, it is the business of the *Wissenschaftslehre* to establish this clearly and definitely *as* that without which the action in question would be impossible, If, for example, action D is the fourth action in a series, then another action, C, must precede it and must be proven to be the exclusive condition for its possibility.[AAAAA] C, in turn, must be preceded by action B. Action A, however, is purely and simply possible; it is totally unconditioned, and therefore action A neither may nor should presuppose anything whatsoever. However, the act of *think-* [I, 80] *ing* of action A is an entirely different action than A itself and presupposes far more. If we suppose that the thought of A is itself action D in the sequence of actions we have to establish, then it is clear that it presupposes for its possibility [I/2: 149] actions A, B, and C; indeed, it is also clear that A, B, and C must be tacitly presupposed, since the first task of the *Wissenschaftslehre* is to think this first act of the

---

[AAAAA] the exclusive condition for its possibility (that is, for the possibility of action C). [*2nd ed.*]

mind. It is only when we arrive at proposition D that these presuppositions [A, B, and C] are proven, but by then we have again presupposed several additional actions. The form of the science is therefore constantly surging ahead of its material, and this is the previously indicated reason why this science, as such, can possess no more than probability. What is portrayed and the portrayal of the same belong to two different series. In the first series, nothing unproven is presupposed, whereas the second series is impossible unless some things are necessarily presupposed, which cannot be proven until later.

The kind of reflection governing the entire *Wissenschaftslehre*, insofar as it is a science, is an *act of representing* [*ein Vorstellen*]. From this it by no means follows that everything reflected *upon* is also nothing but an act of representing. In the *Wissenschaftslehre* the I *is represented*; but from this it by no means follows that it is represented merely *as* representing — that is, merely as an intellect. Other features[BBBBB] may well be discoverable in this I. Qua philosophizing *subject*, the I is indisputably only a representing I, but it might well be more than this qua *object* of philosophizing.[CCCCC] Representing is the highest and absolutely first act of the philosopher as such, but the absolutely first act of the human mind might well be something else. Even in advance of all experience, it is already probable that this is so, since representation is something that can be completely exhausted[40] and that operates in a thoroughly necessary manner. The necessity of representation must therefore have an ultimate foundation, one which, qua ultimate foundation, can be based upon nothing further. Assuming this to be true, it would follow that a science based upon the concept of representation might indeed be a very useful propaedeutic to our science, but could not be the *Wissenschaftslehre* itself.[41]— Something that certainly does follow from what has

[I, 81] been said here is that we can become conscious of all of the intellect's manners of acting (which are supposed to be exhaustively described by the *Wissenschaftslehre*) only in the form of representation, that is, only insofar as and in the manner that they are represented.

[BBBBB] that it is represented merely *as* representing. Other features [*2nd ed.*]

[CCCCC] Qua philosophizing subject, the I is indisputably only a representing I, but it might well be more than this qua object of philosophizing. [*2nd ed.*]

Third Part   [I/2: 150]

Hypothetical Division of the *Wissenschaftslehre* ^{DDDDD}

The absolutely first foundational principle must be shared by all parts of the *Wissenschaftslehre*, since it is supposed to provide the foundation, not merely for a portion of human knowledge, but for knowledge in its entirety. Division is possible only by positing in opposition elements [*Glieder*] that must both be equivalent to some third element.

Let us posit the I as the highest concept, to which a Not-I is posited in opposition. It is clear that the Not-I cannot be posited in opposition to the I unless this Not-I is *posited*, and indeed, posited within the highest thing we can conceive of — that is, posited within the I. In this case it would be necessary to consider the I in two different respects: as that *within* which the Not-I is posited and as *what* is posited in opposition to the Not-I, and is hence itself posited within the absolute I. This latter I is supposed to be equivalent to the Not-I, in the sense that they are both posited in the absolute I, and, at the same time and in the same respect, it is supposed to be posited in opposition to the Not-I. This, however, is conceivable only if the I includes some third element, in terms of which the I and the Not-I would be equivalent, and this third element is the concept of quantity. The I and the Not-I would each possess a quantity, a quantity determinable by what is posited in opposition to each of them.* The first possibility is that the quantity of the I is determined by the Not-I. To this extent, the I is dependent and its proper name is "intellect." This dependent I is dealt with in the Theoretical Part of the *Wissenschaftslehre*, which is based upon the concept of representation as such, a concept that is supposed to be derived from — and hence demonstrated by means of — the foundational principles.

The I, however, is supposed to be absolute and is supposed to be determined purely and simply by itself; but if it is determined by the Not-I, then it is not self-determined — which contradicts the highest and absolutely first foundational principle. In order to avoid this contradiction, we must assume that the Not-I that [I/2: 151] is supposed to determine the intellect is itself determined by the I, which in this case would not be engaged in representing, but would instead possesses absolute causality. — But such causality would completely annul the opposing Not-I and, along with it, all of those representations that depend upon this Not-I. Consequently, the assumption of such an absolute causality would contradict the second and third foundational principles. It follows from this that we have to represent this absolute causality *as* something that contradicts representation, as something that *cannot be represented*, as a causality that is not a causality. The concept of a causality that is not a causality is, however, the concept of *striving*.

---

^{DDDDD} [This entire "*Hypothetische Eintheilung der Wissenschaftslehre*" was omitted from the 2nd ed., for reasons explained in the Preface to the second edition. It is also omitted from *SW*, which follows the text of the *2nd ed.*]

* The only absolutely a priori concepts are the concept of the I, the concept of the Not-I, and the concept of quantity (limitation). All other pure concepts are derived from these three by positing them in opposition to and by equating them with [other concepts].

Such a causality is conceivable only under the condition of a completed approximation to infinity — which is itself inconceivable. — This concept of striving (the necessity of which has to be proven) provides the foundation for the second part of the *Wissenschaftslehre*, which is called the Practical Part.

Considered in itself, this second part is far and away the most important. To be sure, the first part is no less important, but only as the foundation of the second part and because this second part is purely and simply unintelligible apart from it. It is in the second part that the theoretical part is first given its precise delimitation and its secure foundation. This is because the necessary striving that is established [in this second part] makes it possible to answer the following questions: Why, given the occurrence of an affection, must we have any representations at all? What warrants our referring the representation in question to something outside of us as its cause? What warrant do we have for even assuming the existence of a power of representation[42] that operates fully in accordance with laws (laws which are themselves not represented as laws of the power of representation, but rather as laws of the striving I, the applicability of which is conditioned by the effect upon feeling of the counter-striving Not-I)? In this second part, the foundations are laid for new and fully elaborated doctrines of the pleasant, the beautiful, and the sublime, of the lawfulness of nature in its freedom, of theology [*Gotteslehre*], of so-called common sense or the natural sense of truth — and finally, for new doctrines of natural law and morality, the principles of which are material as well as formal. All of this follows upon the establishment of three absolutes: an absolute I, which is governed by laws it gives itself and which can be represented only under the condition of an affection by the Not-I; an absolute Not-I, which is free and independent of all of our laws and which can be represented only as expressing these laws, either positively or negatively, but always to a finite degree; and an absolute power within ourselves to determine ourselves

[I/2: 152] purely and simply according to the effects of both the Not-I and the I, a power that can be represented only insofar as it distinguishes an affection by the Not-I from an effect of the I, or from a law. No philosophy can go beyond these three absolutes.

[Announcement of the author's Jena lectures for the Summer Semester of 1794][43, EEEEE]

You, the citizens of that academic community of which I too will soon become a [I/2: 153] fellow citizen, are familiar from the catalog with the lectures[44] I intend to deliver on that science, the concept of which I have here attempted to develop. I have nothing further to say to you on this topic, other than this: that I hope to be able to place into your hands a printed guide to both parts of this science, as *a manuscript for my students*.[45, FFFFF] Following my arrival [in Jena], I will announce the hours of my lectures at the usual location.[46]

I still owe you an explanation of just one point. As all of you undoubtedly realize, the sciences were not invented as an idle mental occupation to meet the demand for a more refined type of luxury. Were this all they were, then the scholar [*Gelehrte*] would belong to the same class as all of those living tools of a luxury that is no more than a luxury; indeed, the scholar would be a contender for the top of this class. All our inquiries must be directed toward achieving humanity's highest goal, which is the improvement of our species; and humanity, in the highest sense of the word, must radiate around students of the sciences, as around its own center. Every addition to the sciences increases the duties of its servants. It thus becomes increasingly necessary to take most seriously to heart the following questions: What is the proper vocation of the scholar? What is the place of the scholar in the larger scheme of things? What is the relationship of scholars to one another and to people at large? More specifically, what is the rela- [I/2: 154] tionship of scholars to the various classes [*Stände*] of human beings? How and by what means can they most expeditiously execute the duties that have been imposed upon them by these relationships, and how can they develop the skills required in order to accomplish this? These are the questions I shall be attempting to answer in the series of public lectures I have announced under the title *Morality for Scholars*.[47] You should not expect any systematic science to be developed in these lectures. The scholar more frequently falls short in his acting than in his knowing. Grant instead, that, like a society of friends united by more than a single bond, we will dedicate ourselves to employing these hours together in order to kindle within ourselves a lofty and ardent sense of our common duties.

[EEEEE] [For obvious reasons, this brief announcement was not included in the 2nd ed.]

[FFFFF] I say this not in order to infringe upon the rights of critique, but in order to show my respect for critique and its representatives, the public.

II

FOUNDATION OF THE ENTIRE
WISSENSCHAFTSLEHRE

Foundation
of the
Entire *Wissenschaftslehre*

as a
Manuscript for His Listeners[1]

by

JOHANN GOTTLIEB FICHTE

Leipzig
Christian Ernst Gabler
1794

Preface* ²

In the preface to this book, which was really not intended for the general public, I would have had nothing to say to that public were it not for the fact that this text, though incomplete, had been brought to the attention of a portion of this public in the most indiscreet manner.³ For the time being, however, this is all that should be said about such matters.

I believed, and I believe still that I have discovered the path that philosophy must follow in order to raise itself to the status of a self-evident science.⁴ I modestly announced this discovery† and explained how I originally intended to develop this idea and how, as a result of my altered circumstances,⁵ I would have to develop it instead. As was only natural, I then set to work executing my plan. It was just as natural that other experts and practitioners of this science should have examined, tested, and passed judgment on my idea and that, if they were displeased with the manner in which I wished to pursue this science, they should have sought to refute me, whether on the basis of internal or external grounds. But what cannot be comprehended is the point of straightaway rejecting my claims without the least examination — or, at most, merely taking the trouble to distort my claims and seizing every opportunity to ridicule and to denounce them in the most vehement manner.⁶ What could have so thoroughly rattled these judges? Was I supposed to speak respectfully of mere parrotry⁷ and superficiality, even though I have no respect whatsoever for such things? Why should I have had any duty to do so — particularly since I had other things to accomplish? And indeed, I might well have allowed every incompetent bumbler to proceed peacefully along his own path, had they not forced me to clear a space for myself
[I, 87] by exposing their incompetence.

Or is there perhaps yet another reason for their hostile behavior? The following remarks are meant for honorable persons, to whom alone they will make any
[I/2: 252] sense: Whatever my doctrine might be, whether it is genuine philosophy or fanatical nonsense,⁸ this has no effect upon me personally, so long as I have conducted my inquiry honestly. I would no more think that my own personal worth was increased by the good fortune of having discovered the genuine philosophy than I would think it lessened by the misfortune of having piled new errors upon those of the past. I am not in the least concerned with my own person; but I care passionately about the truth, and I will always proclaim what I consider to be true as forcefully and as decisively as I am able.

In the present book, taken together with the *Outline of the What is Distinctive of the Wissenschaftslehre with Regard to the Theoretical Power*, I believe I have developed my system to the point that every expert can completely survey not

---

* In the first edition, this Preface appeared along with the *second installment*, i.e., with *Part III* of *Foundation of the W.L.*, which was printed somewhat later and subsequently published at the same time as *Outline of the What is Distinctive of the W.L.* [namely, in July of 1795]. [Footnote added in *C*.]

† In the book *Concerning the Concept of the Wissenschaftslehre, or of So-Called Philosophy* (Weimar: Industrie Comptoir, 1794). [In *C*, this footnote is expanded to read "*second, corrected and expanded edition*, Leipzig and Jena: Gabler, 1798."]

only the foundation [*Grund*] but also the scope of the same, as well as the manner in which one must build further upon this foundation. My present situation[9] does not permit me to make any specific promise about *when* and *how* I will continue to elaborate my system.

I myself consider this presentation to be extremely imperfect and defective. In part, this is because I needed it for my lectures and therefore had to publish it in fascicles for the use of my listeners, in which case it could be supplemented by oral presentation. And in part this is because I have sought to avoid, as much as possible, any fixed terminology — which provides the easiest means for literalists[10] to rob any system of its spirit and transform it into a desiccated skeleton. I will continue to observe this same maxim in presenting future versions of my system, until I have finally arrived at the final and complete presentation of the same.[11] Here, however, I will make no additions to it; instead, I wish only to invite the public to join me in calculating what needs to be constructed in the future. Before one can precisely determine any individual proposition [within this system], one must first explain its connection [to the other propositions in the system] and obtain an overview of the whole — a method that admittedly presupposes that [I, 88] one possesses the good will to do justice to the system rather than the intention merely to discover errors in it.

I have heard many complaints concerning the obscurity and unintelligibility of that portion of this book with which the public has become acquainted until now,[12] as well as concerning the obscurity and unintelligibility of *Concerning the Concept of the Wissenschaftslehre*.

Regarding objections to the latter work, and especially to § 8 of the same,[13] I [I/2: 253] may have been at fault in stating the foundational principles [*Grundsätze*] of the system — principles that are, in my case, determined by the entire system — apart from the system itself and in expecting my readers and critics to have the patience to leave everything just as indeterminate as I had left it. If, however, these objections concern that work as a whole, then I confess in advance that I will never be able to write anything in the field of speculation that will be intelligible to those who found *Concerning the Concept of the Wissenschaftslehre* to be unintelligible. Just as this work represents the limit of their ability to understand, so too does it represent the limit of my ability to make myself understood. This limit separates my mind from theirs, and I beseech such readers not to waste their time on my writings. — Whatever the reason for this failure of understanding on their part, the *Wissenschaftslehre* contains within itself a reason why it must always remain unintelligible to certain readers: namely, because it presupposes the free power [*Vermögen*] of inner intuition.[14] — Moreover, every philosophical author can justifiably expect his reader to hold fast to the thread of his argument and not to forget the previous step just as soon as he has arrived at the subsequent one. So far as I know, there is nothing in these works that cannot, under this condition, be understood — and indeed, must necessarily be understood correctly; and I believe as well that the author of a book should also have a voice in answering this question [concerning the intelligibility of his work]. — Whatever has been thought with complete clarity is intelligible; and I am conscious of having thought everything through with such complete clarity that, were I to have enough time and space, I would be able to elevate each of my claims to any desired level of clarity.[15]

[I, 89]   I consider it especially necessary to add that I do not say everything, but instead would like to leave something for my readers to think about as well. To be sure, I anticipate many misunderstandings, which I might have prevented with a few words. I have not added these few words, however, because I wished to encourage independent thinking. The *Wissenschaftslehre* should by no means *force* itself upon the reader, but should be a *necessity* for him, just as it was for its author.

I ask future critics of this text to consider it as a whole and to view each of the individual thoughts from the point of view of the whole.[16] The reviewer from

[I/2: 254] Halle expresses his suspicion that I was simply trying to deliver a joke,[17] and other critics of *On the Concept of the Wissenschaftslehre* also seem to have believed this — at least to judge from how lightly they pass over the issues and from the jocular tone of their remarks, as if they had to answer jokes with jokes.

On the basis of my own experience in working through this system three times[18] and finding that each time my thoughts concerning individual propositions of the same were modified in various ways, I can also expect that, as I continue to reflect upon it, my thoughts will always continue to change and to undergo further development. I myself will work as diligently as possible on this task and will welcome every useful suggestion from others. — In addition, no matter how inwardly convinced I may be that the foundational principles upon which this entire system is based cannot be overturned, and no matter how strongly I may here and there have expressed this conviction (as I am fully entitled to do), it nevertheless remains a possibility — even if it is one that I have so far found to be unthinkable — that these principles might be overturned after all. I would welcome this as well, since truth would thereby be the winner. So please, simply examine these foundational principles and try to overturn them.

What my system actually is and how it should be classified — whether it is, as *I* believe, genuine and thoroughgoing Criticism,[19] or whatever else one might wish

[I, 90]   to call it — is irrelevant. I have no doubt that various names will be found for it and that it will be accused of many, mutually contradictory heresies.[20] One may do this, of course, but one should not censure me by referring to older refutations; refute me on your own instead.

Jena

Easter Fair 1795[21]

Forward to the Second Edition[22]

[I, 85]

[I/2: 461]

In the course of preparing a new presentation of the *Wissenschaftslehre*[23] it has once again become clear to the originator of this science that, for the time being anyway, no new presentation will be able to make this first one completely super-fluous and dispensable. The majority of the philosophical public still does not seem so well prepared for this new perspective that they would not find it useful to have the same content available in two very different forms and be able to rec-ognize this content as the same in both cases. Furthermore, the method that will be employed in the new presentation (one that has been devised to assure greater comprehensibility) is one that leads one back to the path followed in the present presentation — which, pending the eventual appearance of a rigorously scientific presentation of the *Wissenschaftslehre*, will always be a very good thing. Finally, several important points are presented in this presentation with a degree of detail and clarity that the author has no hope of ever being able to surpass. The new presentation will need to make reference to several such passages.

For all of these reasons we have issued this new, unaltered reprint of the first presentation, which was out of print.

The new presentation will appear next year.[24]

Berlin
August 1801

Fichte

[I, p. 91]
[I/2: 255]

Part One

Foundational Principles of the Entire *Wissenschaftslehre*

§ 1. First, Purely and Simply Unconditioned Foundational Principle

We have to *seek out* the absolutely first, purely and simply [*schlechthin*] unconditioned foundational principle[25] of all human knowledge.[26] If this is the
absolutely first foundational principle, then it cannot be *proven* or *determined*[27]
[by anything else].[28]

    This foundational principle is supposed to express that *F/Act* [*Tathandlung*][29]
which neither appears nor can appear among the empirical determinations of our
consciousness, but instead lies at the basis of all consciousness and alone makes
consciousness possible.[A] In presenting this F/Act the danger is not so much that
one will, so to speak, *fail* to think what one is thereby supposed to think (this is
something that has already been taken care of by the very nature of our mind) as
that one will thereby think what one is not supposed to think. It is therefore necessary to *reflect* upon what one can initially consider to be this F/Act and to
abstract from everything that does not really pertain to it.[30]

    Even by means of such an act of abstracting reflection, however, that which is
[I, 92] not in itself a fact of consciousness can never become a fact of consciousness.[31]
Instead, such an act of abstracting reflection leads one to recognize that one must
necessarily *think* of this F/Act as the foundation of all consciousness.

    The laws[B] in accordance with which one simply must think of this F/Act as the
foundation of human knowledge — or, what amounts to the same thing, the rules
in accordance with which this act of reflection is accomplished — have not yet
been shown to be valid, but they are tacitly presupposed to be familiar and
agreed-upon.[32] Only later will these rules be derived from the foundational principle, which can be correctly established only on the condition that these same
[I/2: 256] rules are correct. This constitutes a circle, though an unavoidable one (see § 7 of
Concerning the Concept of the Wissenschaftslehre[33]). Since, however, this circle
cannot be avoided and is openly admitted, one may employ all the laws of general
logic in establishing the highest foundational principle.

    In order to engage in that act of reflection we are supposed to perform, we
must begin with some proposition that everyone will concede without objection.
There may well be several such propositions. Reflection is free, and it does not
matter from which point it starts. Let us select that proposition from which the
shortest path leads to our goal.

    If this proposition is conceded, then that proposition upon which we wish to
base the entire *Wissenschaftslehre*, as the foundation of the same, must be also be
conceded, as a F/Act, and reflection must reveal *that* this F/Act must be admitted

---

    [A] This has been overlooked by everyone who has pointed out either that the first foundational
principle *does not occur* among the facts of consciousness or else that it *contradicts* these facts.
[Footnote added in *C*.]
    [B] The laws (of general logic). [Added in *C*.]

as such, *along with the proposition in question.* — So let us propose any fact what-soever of empirical consciousness and then remove from it one empirical deter-mination after another, until nothing is left but what purely and simply cannot be thought away and from which nothing further can be removed.[34]

1.) Everyone will concede the proposition "*A is A*"[35] (which means the same thing as "A = A," since this is the meaning of the logical copula) and will do so without giving it the least thought. One recognizes this proposition to be com-   [I, 93] pletely certain and agreed-upon.

   If, however, someone should request a proof of this proposition, one would certainly not embark upon the task of providing such a proof, but would instead maintain that this proposition is *purely and simply* certain — that is to say, *certain for no further reason*[36] and insofar as one responds in this manner (undoubtedly with universal approval), one ascribes to oneself the power *to posit something purely and simply.*[37]

   2.) In asserting that the above proposition is certain in itself one is *not* positing that A *exists.* The proposition "*A is A*" is by no means equivalent to the proposi-tion "*A is*" or "*there exists an A.*" ("*To be,*" when posited without any predicate, means something altogether different than "to be" with a predicate. For further discussion of this point, see below.[38]) Suppose that A signifies a space enclosed by two straight lines: even in this case, the proposition[C] ["A is A"] remains correct, even though the proposition "*A exists*" would obviously be false.

   What one *posits* here, however, is that "*if* A exists, *then* A exists."[39] Whether A   [I/2: 257] exists or not is thus by no means the question. What is in question is not the *con-tent* of the proposition, but merely its *form.* It is not a question of that *about which* one possesses knowledge, but rather, a question of *what* one knows about any object whatsoever, no matter what it may also be.

   What is posited[40] in the claim that the above proposition ["if A, then A"] is purely and simply certain is therefore *this*: that there is a necessary connection between that "*if*" and this "*then.*" What is posited *purely and simply* and *without any ground* in this case is the *necessary connection between the "if" and the "then."* I will provisionally designate this necessary connection as "X."

   3.) Nothing is yet posited thereby regarding *whether* A itself exists or does not exist. This raises the question: under what condition does A *exist*?
   a.) X is at least contained *in* the I and is posited *by* the I, since the I is that which judges in the case of the above proposition — and indeed, does so in accordance with X, considered as a law. X is therefore given to the I as a law, and, since X is asserted purely and simply and without any further   [I, 94] ground, this law must be given to the I by the I itself.[41]
   b.) *Whether* and *how* A is posited at all is something we do not know. But since X is supposed to designate a connection between an act (with which we are unacquainted) of positing A and an absolute positing[42] of this same

---

[C] the first proposition [Added in C.]

A (on the condition of the previous act of positing A), then A, like X itself, is posited *in* and *through* the I, *at least insofar as this connection is posited.* — X is possible only in relation to some A; but X is actually posited in the I, and thus A must also be posited in the I, insofar as X is related to A.

c.) X is related to that A which occupies the logical position of the subject in the above proposition, just as it is also related to that A which is in the predicate;^D for both of these A's are united by X. Both are therefore posited in the I, insofar as they are posited at all; and the A in the predicate position is purely and simply posited, on the condition that the A in the subject position is posited. Accordingly, the above proposition can also be expressed as follows: "if A is posited *in the I*, then *A is posited* — and therefore *exists*."

4.) It is by virtue of X, therefore, that the I posits that *A exists purely and simply for the judging I, and it exists at all only because it is posited in the I as such.* In other words, what is posited is that whatever the I may be doing — whether it is positing or judging or doing anything else — there is something [= X] in the I that is constantly self-identical, constantly one and the same; and this X that is posited purely and simply can also be expressed as follows: "I = I" or "I am I."

5.) By means of this operation⁴³ we have already arrived, albeit without notic-ing it, at the proposition "I am" (though not, to be sure, as expressing a *F/Act* [*Tathandlung*], but rather as expressing a *fact* [*Tatsache*]).

[I/2: 258]

For X is purely and simply posited: this is a fact^E of empirical consciousness. But X is equivalent to the proposition, "I am I," and thus the latter is also posited purely and simply.

The proposition "I am I" has quite a different meaning, however, than the proposition "A is A," for only under a certain condition does the latter proposition

[I, 95] have any content. *If* A is posited, then of course it is posited *as* A, that is, with predicate A. But this proposition by no means settles the question of *whether* A is posited at all and hence whether it is posited with any particular predicate. In contrast, the proposition "I am I" is valid unconditionally and purely and simply, for it is equivalent to the proposition X.^F It is valid not only with respect to its form, but also with respect to its content. In this proposition, the I is posited with the predicate of self-identity, and it is not the case that it is posited only under a certain condition; instead, it is posited purely and simply. The I *is* therefore pos-ited, and this proposition can therefore be expressed as follows: "*I am.*"

This proposition "I am" has so far been based merely upon a fact and has no validity beyond that of a fact. If the proposition "A = A" (or, more precisely, if that which is purely and simply posited in this proposition — i.e., X) is certain, then the proposition "I am I" must also be certain.⁴⁴ It is indeed a fact of empirical

---

^D which occupies the position of the predicate; [As emended in *C.*] which stands for the position of the predicate; [As emended in *SW.*]

^E is a *fact* [Emphasis added in *C.*]

^F To express this in a more popular form: I — that is, the I who posits A in the predicate position *because it was posited in the subject position* — necessarily know about my own positing of the subject and thus necessarily possess knowledge of myself. I then intuit myself anew and am, for myself, the same as what I now intuit myself to be. [Footnote added in *C.*]

consciousness that we are required to consider X to be purely and simply certain, and hence we are also required to consider that proposition upon which X is grounded — namely, the proposition "I am" — to be purely and simply certain as well. That the I itself is posited prior to every act of positing that occurs within the I is, therefore, the explanatory ground of all the facts of empirical consciousness.[45] — ("Of *all* the facts," I say, though this depends upon the proof of the proposition that X is the highest fact of empirical consciousness, a fact that underlies all the other facts of empirical consciousness and is contained in them all — something that might well have been granted without any proof at all, despite the fact that the entire *Wissenschaftslehre* is concerned with showing this.)

6.) We now return to the point from which we started.
a.) The proposition "A = A" is a *judgment*. However, according to the testimony of empirical consciousness, all judging is an action of the human mind, for judging satisfies all the conditions for being an action within empirical consciousness,[46] conditions that must be familiar and settled for the sake of reflection.
b.) This acting [i.e., judging that A = A] is based upon something that is not based upon anything higher: namely, X = "I am."
c.) What is *purely and simply posited* and *based upon itself* has therefore been shown to be the basis [*Grund*] of *a particular* act of the human [I, 96] mind (and the entire *Wissenschaftslehre* will show that it is the basis of *all* acting by the human mind), and therefore it is the basis of the pure character of the human mind — the pure character of activity in itself, in [I/2: 259] abstraction from the particular empirical conditions[47] of the same.
    The I's positing of itself through itself is therefore the pure activity of the I. — The I *posits itself*,[48] and by virtue of this sheer positing by itself it *is*; and conversely: by virtue of its sheer being, the I *is*, and it *posits* its being.[49] — The I is at the same time the acting subject and the product of this action, what is active and what is brought about by means of this activity.[50] Action and deed are [here] one and the same, and this is why [the proposition] "I am" expresses a F/Act,[51] though this is also the only possible F/Act,[52] as must be shown by the entire *Wissenschaftslehre*,

7.) Now let us consider yet again the proposition "*I am I.*"
a.) The I is purely and simply posited. Let us assume that what is *purely and simply posited* in this proposition is the I that occupies the position of the formal subject*[53] and that the I that occupies the predicate position is *what exists* [*das seyende*]. It follows that what is expressed — or purely and

---

* This, at any rate, is what is expressed in the logical form of every proposition. In the proposition "A = A," the first A is the A that is posited in the I — either, like the I itself, posited purely and simply or else, like every determinate Not-I, posited on the basis of some ground or another. In doing this, the I behaves as an absolute subject, and thus one calls the first A "the subject." The second A designates what the I that makes itself into an object of reflection discovers to be *posited* within itself, because it *has first posited* it within itself. The judging I predicates something, not actually of A, but of itself: namely, that it

simply posited — in the purely and simply valid judgment that both I's are completely one and the same [*Eins*] is this: the *I* is, *because* it has posited itself. Hence:

b.) The I in the first [subject] sense and the I in the second [predicate] sense are supposed to be purely and simply the same [*gleich*]. One can therefore reverse the preceding proposition and say that the I posits itself purely and simply *because* it *is*. It *posits* itself through its mere being, and it *is* through its mere being-posited [*Gesetztseyn*].

[I, 97]

And this makes completely clear the sense in which we are here using the term "I" and leads us to a determinate explanation of the I as absolute subject. *The being (essence)* [*Seyn (Wesen)*] of the I qua absolute subject *consists simply in positing itself as existing [als seyend].*[54] It is as it *posits* itself to be, and it *posits* itself as it *is*. Consequently, the I exists purely and simply and necessarily for the I. Anything that does not exist for itself is not an I.[55]

[I/2: 260]

(Explication. One certainly hears the question, "*what* then was I before I arrived at self-consciousness?"[56] To this, the natural answer is, "I was nothing at all, since I was not an I. The I exists only insofar as it is conscious of itself." — The possibility of such a question is based upon confusing the I as *subject* with the *I* as *object* of reflection on the part of the absolute subject and is in itself completely illegitimate. The I produces a representation of itself [*stellt sich selbst vor*], and in doing so assimilates itself to the form of representation, and only now is it *something*, an object. In this form, consciousness obtains a substrate that *exists*, even without actual consciousness, and is thought of as corporeal as well. One thinks up such a situation and asks, "*What* was the I then? That is to say, what is the substrate of consciousness?" But in doing this, one *also* thinks, without noticing it, of the *absolute subject*, as intuiting this substrate. In doing so one tacitly adds in thought precisely that from which one professed to have abstracted and thereby contradicts oneself. One cannot think of anything whatsoever without thinking as well of one's I, as conscious of itself. One can never abstract from one's self-consciousness, and this is why all questions of the preceding sort are unanswerable, since they cannot even be raised — at least not if one understands oneself correctly.[57])

8.) If the I exists only insofar as it posits itself, then it also exists only *for* the positing subject and posits [itself] only for the existing subject [*das seyende*]: *the I exists for the I.*[58] However, if it posits itself purely and simply, just as it is, then it posits itself necessarily and necessarily exists for the I. *I exist only for myself, yet for myself I exist necessarily.* (In saying "*for myself,*" I already posit my being.)

[I, 98]

9.) When applied to the I, *self-positing* and *being* are completely equivalent. The proposition, "I am because I have posited myself" can therefore also be expressed as follows: "*I exist purely and simply because I exist.*"[59]

discovers within itself an A. This second A is therefore called the "predicate." Thus, in the proposition "A = B," A indicates what is now posited and B indicates something that has already been encountered as posited. "*Is*" expresses the I's transition from positing to reflection upon what is posited.

Furthermore, the self-positing I and the existing I are completely identical, one and the same. The I is *what* it posits itself to be, and it posits itself as *that* which it is. Consequently, *I am purely and simply what I am.*[60]

10.) The immediate expression of the F/Act we have now elaborated could be expressed in the following formula: *I exist purely and simply,* i.e., *I am purely and simply **because** I am, and I am purely and simply **what** I am — and I am both only for the I.*   [I/2: 261]

If one were think of the account[61] of this F/Act as standing at the summit of a *Wissenschaftslehre,* then it would perhaps have to be expressed as follows: *The I originally* [62] *posits its own being purely and simply.*[G, 63]

We began with the proposition "A = A," not as if the proposition "I am" could be demonstrated from "A = A," but because we had to start from something given as *certain* within empirical consciousness. However, in the course of our explication it became evident that the proposition "A = A" is not the ground of the proposition "I am"; on the contrary, it is the latter that grounds the former.[64]

If one abstracts from the determinate content of the proposition "I am," that is, if one abstracts from the I, all that remains is the sheer form that is given along with this content, *the form of the inference from being-posited to being,* which is [I, 99] what must occur for the sake of logic (see *Concerning the Concept of the Wissenschaftslehre,* § 5), one thereby obtains the *foundational principle of logic,* namely, the proposition "A = A," which can be demonstrated and determined only through the *Wissenschaftslehre. Demonstrated:* A is A, because the I, which has posited A, is identical to that in which A is posited. *Determined:*[65] everything[H] that exists does so only insofar as it is posited in the I, and there is nothing beyond the I. In the preceding proposition [A = A] no possible A (no thing) can be anything but something posited in the I.

If one then abstracts from all judging, as a determinate acting, and attends purely to the human mind's overall *mode* of acting,[66] which is given through this form,[67] then one obtains the *category of reality.*[68] Everything to which the proposition "A = A" is applicable possesses reality [only] *insofar as that proposition is applicable to it.* Whatever is posited through the mere positing of any thing (a thing posited in the I)[69] possesses reality and belongs to the essence of the I.

(Maimonian skepticism[70] is ultimately based on a question concerning our right to apply the category of reality.[71] This cannot be derived from any other [I/2: 262] right; instead, we are purely and simply entitled to apply this category. Instead, we must derive all our other possible rights to apply categories from this one; and even Maimonian skepticism tacitly presupposes this right, because it recognizes

---

[G] To express all of this in other words, which I have subsequently employed to express the same point: the *I* is the necessary identity of subject and object, a subject-object, and it is this purely and simply, without any further mediation. This, I say, is what this means, even if this [newly formulated] proposition is not as easy to grasp nor is its high importance, which was thoroughly neglected prior to the *Wissenschaftslehre,* as easy to evaluate. For this reason, the preceding explication is not dispensable. [Footnote added in *C.*]

[H] Reading, with *GA,* "*alles*" for "*ist.*"

the correctness of general logic. — But we can point to something from which this[I] category is itself derived: namely, the I, as absolute subject. For everything else to which this category of reality could possibly be applied, it must be shown that reality is transferred to it[72] *from the I* — that it must exist insofar as the I exists.)

———————————

Kant, in his deduction of the categories, gestured toward our proposition as the foundational principle of knowledge, but he never established it determinately *as a foundational principle*. Before him, Descartes had asserted something similar, *cogito ergo sum* ["I think therefore I am"], which need not be interpreted as the

[I, 100] minor premise and conclusion of a syllogism, the major premise of which is *quodconque cogitate, est* ["whatever thinks exits"].[73] Instead, he may very well have considered this to be an immediate fact of consciousness, in which case it means the following: *cogitans sum, ergo sum* ["I am a thinking subject, therefore I am"] (or, as we would put it, *sum, ergo sum* ["I am, therefore I am"]). But in this case the addition of *cogitans* is quite superfluous; it is not the case that if one exists then one necessarily thinks, but rather that one necessarily exists if one thinks. Thinking by no means constitutes the essence [of the I's being], but is only a specific determination of its being, in addition to which there are many other determinations of our being.[74] — Reinhold establishes the Principle of Representation;[75] and, expressed in the Cartesian form, his foundational principle would read as follows: *repraesento, ergo sum* ["I engage in representing, therefore I am"], or, more correctly, *repraesentans sum, ergo sum* ["I am a subject engaged in representing, therefore I am"]. He goes considerably farther than Descartes,[76] but — assuming that he intends to establish not merely the propaedeutic to the science [of philosophy], but also that science itself[J] — he does not go far enough, for even representing is not the essence of the being [of the I], but only a particular deter-

[I/2: 263] mination of the same, in addition to which there are still other determinations of our being,[77] *even if they must pass through the medium of representation in order to attain to empirical consciousness.*

Spinoza goes beyond our proposition, understood in the sense indicated. Spinoza does not deny the unity of empirical consciousness, but he completely denies pure consciousness.[78] According to him, the entire series of representations entertained by an empirical subject is related to the one single pure subject in the same way a single representation is related to a series of representations. For him, the I (i.e., that which he calls *his* I or I call *my* I) does not exist purely and simply *because* it exists, but because *something else* exists. — According to Spinoza, the I does indeed exist *for* the I; but he [also] asks what the I would be for something outside the I. Such a being "outside the I" would similarly have to be an I, of which the posited I (e.g., *my* I), along with all the I's that could possibly be posited, would be modifications. He separates *pure* from *empirical* consciousness. He posits the former in God, who is never conscious of himself, since pure consciousness never attains to consciousness; and he posits the latter in the particular

---

[I] Reading, with K, "*jene*" for "*jede*."
[J] Omitting, with K, the *nur* in Fichte's phrase, *wenn er nur die Wissenschaft selbst.*

modifications of the Deity. Set up in this manner, his system is completely consistent [I, 101] and irrefutable, because he is on his own turf, where reason cannot pursue him any further; but his system is groundless, for what justifies his proceeding beyond that pure consciousness that is given in empirical consciousness? — It is indeed possible to indicate what drove him to his system: namely, the necessary striving to produce the highest unity in human cognition. This unity is present in his system, the error of which consists only in the fact that he believed that he was inferring on the basis of theoretical, rational grounds, when he was in fact driven by a practical need, and that he believed he had established something actually given, when in fact he established merely an aspirational ideal, which could never be achieved.[79] In the *Wissenschaftslehre* we will rediscover Spinoza's highest unity, [I/2: 264] not as something that *exists*, but rather as something that *ought* to be but *cannot* be produced by us. — One further remark: if one oversteps the *I am*[80] then one must necessary arrive at Spinozism. In a very readable treatise, *Concerning the Progress of Philosophy*,[81] Salomon Maimon has shown that Leibniz's system, thought through in its entirety, is nothing other than Spinozism and that there are only two fully consistent systems: the Critical system, which recognizes this limit, and the system of Spinoza, which oversteps it.

§ 2. Second Foundational Principle, Conditioned with Respect to its Content

For the same reason that the first foundational principle could be neither proven nor derived, neither can the second foundational principle. Thus, here again, as above,[82] we will proceed from a fact of empirical consciousness, and we will deal with this in the same way and with the same justification.

1.) Everyone will undoubtedly recognize that the proposition "−A is not = A" is completely certain and settled, and it is hardly to be expected that anyone would demand a proof of this proposition.[83]

2.) If, however, such a proof were to be possible, then in our system (the inherent correctness of which is, to be sure, merely problematic so long as the *Wissenschaftslehre* remains incomplete) it could be derived only from the proposition "A = A."

3.) Such a proof, however, is impossible. This is true for the following reason: even [I, 102] if one were to make the extreme assumption that the proposed proposition is fully equivalent to the proposition "−A = −A,"[84] and hence completely equivalent to some Y that is posited in the I[85] (in which case the proposition in question would mean no more than "*if* the opposite [*Gegenteil*] of A is posited, *then* it is posited"), then what would in that case be posited purely and simply would be the same connection [*Zusammenhang*] (= X) that was posited above.[86] Hence the proposition "−A is not = A" would not have been derived from the proposition "A = A," but would instead be [I/2: 265] that proposition itself. (And in this case the form of this proposition, insofar as it is a purely logical proposition, would actually stand under the highest form, that of *formability*[87] *as such* — the form of the unity of consciousness.)

4.) This has no bearing whatsoever on the question, *Is the opposite of A then posited, and under which condition of the form of sheer action does this occur?*[88] This condition is what would have to be derived from the proposition "A = A" if the previously proposed proposition ["−A is not = A"] were a derived proposition. But a condition such as this can by no means result from the proposition "A = A," inasmuch as the form of positing in opposition [*Gegensetzen*] is by no means contained in the form of positing, but is, on the contrary, posited in opposition [*entgegengesetzt*] to it. Accordingly, the form of positing in opposition is itself posited purely and simply and is not conditional upon anything. —A is posited *as* such purely and simply *because* it is posited.[89]

Thus, just as surely as the proposition "−A is not = A" occurs among the facts of empirical consciousness, there occurs among the actions of the I an act of positing in opposition; and this act of positing in opposition is, with respect to its mere *form*, an act that is purely and simply possible, conditional upon nothing and possessing no higher ground.

(The *logical* form of this proposition *as* a proposition, when formulated as "−A = −A," is conditional upon the identity of the subject and predicate — that is, upon the identity of the I *that is engaged in representing* and the I *that is represented as* engaged in representing. See the remark on p. 203 above. But even the possibility of positing in opposition presupposes the identity of consciousness, and the acting I that posits itself in this function [of positing in opposition] [I, 103] actually proceeds as follows: A (that is, that which is posited purely and simply) = A (that which is reflected upon). By means of an absolute action, −A is posited [by the I] in opposition to this A that is an object of reflection, and then it is judged that this −A is also posited in opposition to that A which is posited purely and simply [i.e., it is now posited in opposition to the first rather than to the second A in the proposition "A = A"]. This is because the first A is equivalent to the second one, an identity [*welche Gleichheit*] grounded in the identity [*die Identität*][90] of the positing I and the I that is reflected upon; see § 1. — Moreover, it is also presupposed that the I that acts in and judges *both* of these acts is the same I. Were it possible for this I to be posited in opposition to itself in both acts, then −A would be = A. From this it follows that the transition from positing to positing in opposition is also possible only by means of the identity of the I.[91])

5.) It is thus by means of this absolute action and purely and simply through it that [I/2: 266] what is posited in opposition, insofar as it is posited *in opposition* (that is, insofar as it is posited as a sheer opposite as such), is posited. Every opposite, insofar as it is an opposite, is so purely and simply, thanks to an action of the I and for no other reason. Being posited in opposition is, as such, posited by the I purely and simply.[92]

6.) In order for any −A to be posited, an A must be posited. Accordingly, the action of positing in opposition is, in another respect, also conditioned. Whether such an act is possible at all is something that is dependent upon another action. Consequently, this act [of positing in opposition] is, insofar as it is an instance of acting at all, conditioned with respect to its content [*Materie*]; it is a way of acting that is related to another way of acting. That one has acted in precisely *this*

manner and not some other is unconditioned; the *form* of the action is unconditioned (i.e., it is unconditioned with respect to its *how*[93]).

Positing in opposition is possible only under the condition of the unity of consciousness on the part of the one who engages in [both] positing and positing in
opposition. Were consciousness of the first action not connected with consciousness of the second, then the latter would not be an act of positing *in opposition*,
but would be purely and simply an act of positing. Only in relation to an act of
positing does it become an act of positing in opposition.[94]

7.) Until now we have been considering action merely *as* action and have been
speaking about the *manner* of action. Let us now turn to a consideration of the
product of this act [of positing in opposition] = −A.   [I, 104]

Once again, we can distinguish between two things in −A: namely, its *form* and
its *content*. It is the form of −A that determines that it is an opposite at all (the
opposite of some X). If −A is posited in opposition to a determinate A, then it
possesses *content* — it is not what some determinate something is.

8.) The *form* of −A is determined purely and simply by the act [of positing in
opposition]; −A is an opposite because it is the product of an act of positing
in opposition. The *content* of −A is determined by A; −A is not what A is, and its
entire essence consists in this: that it is not what A is. — Concerning −A, I know
that it is supposed to be the opposite of some A or another. But concerning that
thing *of* which I know this [namely, that it was posited in opposition to something
else], I can know *what* this thing may or may not be only if I am acquainted with A.

9.) Nothing is originally posited but the I, and it alone is posited purely and
simply (§ 1). Thus it is only to the I that anything can be posited in opposition
purely and simply. But that which is posited in opposition to the I = *Not-I*.[95]

10.) As surely as the unconditioned admission of the certainty of the proposition
"−A is not = A" occurs among the facts of empirical consciousness, *so is a Not-I
surely posited purely and simply in opposition to the I*. Everything that we have said
about positing in opposition as such is derived from this original act of positing
[a Not-I] in opposition [to the I] and is therefore originally valid for the latter.
The form of this original positing in opposition is therefore purely and simply
unconditioned and its content conditioned. And in this way the second founda- [I/2: 267]
tional principle of all human knowledge would be discovered as well.[96]

11.) As a consequence of the sheer act of positing in opposition, the opposite of
everything that pertains to the I must pertain to the Not-I.[97]

(According to the usual opinion, the concept of the Not-I is a discursive
concept,[K] obtained by means of abstraction from everything that is represented.
But it is easy to show the superficiality of this explanation. In order to obtain a
representation of anything at all, I must posit it in opposition to the representing
subject. Consequently, the object of representation can and must contain some X,[98]
by means of which it reveals itself as what is to be represented and not as the

---

[K] is merely a universal concept, [Added in C.]

[I, 105] representing subject. But no object [*Gegenstand*][99] can teach me *that* everything in which this X lies is not the representing subject but is instead something to be represented; on the contrary, there is such an object at all only on the presupposition of this law.[L])

The purely formal, logical proposition "A = A" arose from the material[100] proposition "*I am*" by means of abstraction from the content of the latter. The logical proposition "–A is not = A," which I would like to call the *principle of positing in opposition*,[101] is obtained by means of a similar abstraction from the [material principle] established in the present § [namely, "I *am not* the Not-I"]. For reasons that will become evident in the following §, this is not yet the proper place to determine this principle or even to express it verbally. If one finally abstracts completely from any determinate action of judging and attends merely to the form of the inference from being posited in opposition to not-being, one then obtains the *category of negation*.[102] Here again, clear insight into this will become possible only in the following §.

§ 3. Third Foundational Principle, Conditioned with Respect to its Form

With every forward step we take in our science we draw nearer to that domain in which everything can be demonstrated.[103] In the case of the first foundational principle, nothing at all should or could be demonstrated; it was unconditioned with respect both to its form and its content, and it was certain independently of [I/2: 268] any higher foundation. In the case of the second foundational principle, the act of positing in opposition could indeed not be derived; but since what was posited unconditionally was only the form of this principle, it could then be rigorously demonstrated that *what was posited in opposition* must be = Not-I. The third foundational principle is almost completely susceptible of proof, because, unlike the second, it is not determined with respect to its content, but instead, with respect to its form; and, again unlike the second principle, it is determined not by one, but by two [preceding] principles.

To say that the third foundational principle is determined with respect to its form and unconditioned only with respect to its content means that the two preceding principles determine the task posed for the action[M] established by means of this principle, though these preceding principles do not determine how this

---

[L] but is instead something to be represented. In order to be able to posit any *object* whatsoever, I must already know this [i.e., I must be acquainted with this X that makes possible the distinction between the representing subject and the represented object and be able to recognize the latter as Not-I]; therefore, this X must lie within me myself, the representing subject, originally and in advance of all experience. — And this remark is so obvious that anyone who understands it and is not elevated thereby to [the standpoint of] transcendental idealism must unquestionably be mentally blind. [Added in C.]

[M] the *task posed for action* [Emphasis added in C.]

task is to be resolved. Such a resolution occurs unconditionally and purely and [I, 106] simply by means of a decree [*Machtspruch*] of reason.

We will therefore begin with a deduction,[N] and we will continue this deduction as far as we are able. The impossibility of continuing it any farther will undoubtedly indicate where we will have to break off our deduction and call upon that unconditional decree of reason which ensues from the aforementioned task.

A.)

1.) Insofar as the Not-I is posited, the I is not posited, for the I is completely annulled by the Not-I.[104]

    The Not-I is now posited *in the I*, for it is posited in opposition [to the I]. But all positing in opposition presupposes the identity of the I,[105] in which something is posited and something else is posited in opposition to what was posited.

    It follows that, insofar as the Not-I is posited in the I, the I is not posited in the I.

2.) However, the Not-I can be posited only insofar as and to the extent that there is posited in the I (in the identical consciousness) an I to which the Not-I can be posited in opposition.

    The Not-I is now supposed to be posited within [this same] identical consciousness.

    Consequently, insofar as the Not-I is supposed to be posited, the I must also be posited within [this same] identical consciousness.

3.) These two conclusions stand in opposition to each other. Both have been arrived at by means of an analysis of the second foundational principle, and therefore both are contained within this principle. Consequently, the second foundational principle is posited in opposition to and annuls itself.

4.) But the second foundational principle annuls itself only insofar as and to the extent that what is posited is annulled by what is posited in opposition, i.e., only insofar as this principle is valid. But this same principle is now supposed to be annulled by itself and to possess no validity.   [I/2: 269]

    Hence it does not annul itself.

    The second foundational principle annuls itself and does not annul itself. [I, 107]

5.) If this is the situation with the second foundational principle, then it is also the situation with the first one: it too annuls itself and does not annul itself.

    If I = I, then everything in the I is posited.

    But now the second foundational principle is supposed to be posited in the I and also not posited in the I.

[N] a deduction, from which the task in question will be derived, [Added in C.]

Consequently, the I is not = I; instead, I = Not-I and Not-I = I.[106]

B.) All of these inferences have been derived from the foundational principles established above, and derived from them in accordance with the laws of reflection, the validity of which is presupposed. Hence these inferences must be correct. But if they are correct, then the identity of consciousness, which is the sole, absolute foundation of our knowledge, is nullified. We must therefore discover some X that will allow all these inferences to be correct without nullifying the identity of consciousness.

1.) Both of the opposites that are supposed to be united lie within the I, qua consciousness. Consequently, X must also lie within I.[107]

2.) The I and the Not-I are both products of the original actions of the I, and consciousness itself is a product of the first, original action of the I — the action of positing the I through itself.[108]

3.) However, according to the preceding inferences, that action which produces the Not-I, i.e., the action of positing in opposition, is by no means possible without X. X itself must therefore be a product, and indeed a product of an original action of the I. Consequently, there is an action of the human mind = Y, the product of which is X.

[I, 108]

4.) The form of this action is completely determined by the task indicated above. The task in question is to unify and equate the I and the Not-I, which have been posited in opposition to each other, and to do so in such a way that they do not mutually annul each other. The preceding opposites are supposed to be assimilated to the identity of a single [*des einigen*] consciousness.

5.) This statement of our task, however, by no means determines *how* this [unification of the I and the Not-I] could occur and in which way it would be possible. The answer to the question is not contained within the task and can by no means be derived from it. Accordingly, as was the case above, we must conduct an experiment[109] and ask, How can A and −A, being and non-being, reality and negation, be thought together in a manner that does not annihilate and annul them?

[I/2: 270]

6.) It is not to be expected that anyone will answer this question in any way other than as follows: A and −A will mutually *limit* each other. Therefore, if this is the correct answer, action Y would be *an action of limiting* [*ein Einschränken*] each of these terms posited in opposition to one another and limiting each by means of the other, and X would designate those *limits* [*Schranken*] [that are the products of action Y].

(One should not understand me to be claiming that the concept of limits is an analytic concept, contained in the union of [the concepts of] reality and negation and derivable therefrom. To be sure, the concepts posited in opposition to each other are provided by the first two foundational principles, and the demand that they be united is contained in the first principle. But the way in which they might be united is not contained in these principles; instead, it is determined by a *special* law of our mind, a law that is supposed to be raised to consciousness by means of the experiment we are now conducting.)

7.) But the concept of limits contains more than the X we are seeking, for this concept also contains the concepts of reality and negation, which are to be unified. Thus, in order to obtain the pure concept of X we must engage in an additional act of abstraction.[110]

8.) *To limit* something means to nullify its reality by means of negation, not *entirely* but only in *part*. Consequently, the concept of a limit contains, in addition to the concepts of reality and negation, that of *divisibility* [*Teilbarkeit*] (the category of *quantifiability* [*Quantitätsfähigkeit*] as such,[111] not that of any *determinate* quantity[112]). This concept of divisibil-   [I, 109] ity is the X we have been seeking, and therefore action Y is that action by means of which *the I as well as the Not-I are purely and simply posited as divisible.*[113]

9.) *The I as well as the Not-I are posited as divisible.*[114] This is because action Y cannot *succeed* the act of positing in opposition; that is to say, it cannot be viewed as having first become possible in consequence of the latter action, since, according to the preceding proof, without the action in question [= Y, the action that makes it possible to posit I and Not-I as divisible], the action of positing in opposition would annul itself and therefore be impossible. Moreover, Y cannot *precede* the action of positing in opposition, since action Y was undertaken precisely in order to make possible the act of positing [I and Not-I] as opposed to each other; and divisibility is nothing without something divisible. Consequently, the act of positing in opposition occurs immediately in and along with action Y; both actions are one and the same and are distinguishable from each other only in reflection. Insofar as the Not-I is posited in opposition to the I, the I (*that to which* something is posited in opposition) and the Not-I (*that which is*   [I/2: 271] posited in opposition) are posited as divisible.[115]

C.) All that remains to be investigated is whether the indication action [= Y, the action of limiting] actually resolves our task and whether all the mutually opposed propositions have been united.

1.) The first conclusion[116] is now determined as follows: The I is not posited in the I insofar as and to the extent that a part of reality is posited in the Not-I. A part of reality is annulled in the I: namely, the part assigned to the Not-I. This proposition is not contradicted by the second proposition [viz., A,2: "the Not-I can be posited only insofar as and to the extent that there is posited in the I (in the [self-]identical consciousness) an I to which the Not-I can be posited in opposition."]. Insofar as the Not-I is posited, the I must also be posited; as such, they are both posited as divisible with respect to their reality.

Now for the first time, by means of the indicated concept [of divisibility], one can say of both [the I and the Not-I] that they are *something*.[117] The absolute I[118] of the first foundational principles is not *something* (it neither possesses nor can possess any predicate); it is purely and simply *what* it is, and this can be explained no further. Now, by means of this concept [of divisibility], *all* reality is included in consciousness,[119] and that portion of it that does not pertain to the I pertains to the Not-I, and

[I, 110]   vice versa. Both are something: the Not-I is what the I is not, and vice versa. When posited in opposition to the absolute I (to which anything can be posited in opposition only insofar as the absolute I is represented and not insofar as it is in itself — as will become evident in due course), the Not-I is *purely and simply nothing*; but when it is posited in opposition to the restrictable I, the Not-I is a *negative magnitude*.

2.) The I is supposed to be self-identical [*sich selbst gleich*] and yet it is also supposed to be posited in opposition to itself. However, it is self-identical with respect to consciousness; consciousness is unitary [*einig*]. But in this consciousness the absolute I is posited as indivisible, whereas, in contrast, the I that is posited in opposition to the Not-I is posited as divisible. Consequently, insofar as it is posited in opposition to a Not-I, the I itself is posited in opposition to the absolute I.

In this manner the opposing propositions are united without any damage to the unity of consciousness; and this constitutes, so to speak, evidence that the concept in question [namely, the concept of limiting] is the correct one.

D.) According to our presupposition (which can be demonstrated only through the completion of the *Wissenschaftslehre*), there is only one purely and simply unconditional foundational principle, only one foundational principle conditioned with respect to its form, and only one conditioned with respect to its content; and there can be no additional foundation principles beyond these [three]

[I/2: 272]   that have now been established.[120] Hence the sum of that which is unconditioned and is purely and simply certain has now been exhausted, and I would like to express this in the following formula: *the I posits in the I a divisible Not-I in opposition to the divisible I.*[121]

No philosophy can go beyond this cognition; but every well-grounded philosophy should return to it, and insofar as a philosophy does this it becomes *Wissenschaftslehre*.[122] From now on, anything that is supposed to appear within the system of the human mind must be derivable from what has here been established.[123]

1.) By means of the concept of divisibility we have united the I and the Not-I, which are posited in opposition to each other. If we abstract from the determinate content [of the third foundational principle], i.e., from the I

[I, 111]   and the Not-I, so that all that remains is the *sheer form of unification* — by means of the concept of divisibility — of terms posited in opposition to each *other,* we then obtain the logical principle that has been known hitherto as the "*grounding* principle" or "principle of sufficient *reason*" [*Satz des Grundes*].[124] This principle states that "A is, in part, = −A, and vice versa ["−A is, in part, = A"]." Everything posited in opposition to something else is, with respect to one characteristic feature [*in Einem Merkmale*] = X, like its opposite, and everything that is like something else is, with respect to one characteristic feature = X, different from it.[125] Such a characteristic feature = X is called the "ground." In the first case, it is the ground of the *relation* or *connection* [*Bezihungs-Grund*] between the opposed terms, and in the second, it is the ground of the *distinction* [*Unterscheidungs-Grund*] between the equated terms, for to posit opposed terms as the same, i.e., to compare them, is called *relating* or *connecting* them to each other, and to posit in opposition to each other terms that have been connected or posited as the same is called "*distinguishing*" them.[126] This logical principle is *demonstrated* and *determined* by the material foundational principle we have established.[127]

Demonstrated, because:

a.) Every −A that is posited in opposition is posited in opposition to an A, and this A is posited.

To posit −A is to annul A, and at the same time not to annul it [since in positing −A one also posits A]. Consequently, A is now annulled only in part; instead of that X which has not been annulled in A, what is posited in −A is X itself (rather than −X), and thus, in X, A = −A.[128] This was the first point.

b.) Everything that is posited as the same (=A, =B) is the same as itself, by virtue of its being-posited in the I. A = A. B = B.

But B is now posited as = A, and thus B is not posited by means of A; for, if that were that the case, then B would = A and not = B. (Two terms would not have been posited, but only one.)

If, however, B is not posited by positing A, then, to this extent, B = −A, and, by positing both as the same, neither A nor B is [I/2: 273] posited; what is posited instead is some X that is = X and = A and = B. This was the second point.

This shows how the proposition A = B can be valid, even though, in itself, it contradicts the proposition A = A. X = X, A = X, and B = X. Therefore A = B, insofar as each = X [the ground of connection]; but A = −B insofar as each = −X [the ground of distinction].

Terms that are the same are posited in opposition to each other in only *one* respect [*Teil*], and the same is true of things that are [I, 112] posited in opposition to each other: they are opposite in only one respect. For if they were posited in opposition to each other in several respects — that is, if the terms posited in opposition to each other each contained characteristic features that were posited in opposition to each other — then one of these opposed characteristics would belong to that wherein the compared terms are the same, and thus they would not be posited in opposition to each other, and vice versa. Accordingly, every well-grounded judgment contains only one ground of connection and only one ground of distinction. If it contains several, then it is not one, but many judgments.

2.) The logical grounding principle [or principle of sufficient reason] is *determined* by the preceding material foundational principle. I.e., its validity is itself limited; it is valid only for a portion of our cognition.[129]

Only under the condition that various things are, as such, either posited as the same or posited in opposition to each other will they be posited either as opposites or as the same with respect to any particular characteristic feature. This however is by no means to claim that it is purely and simply and unconditionally the case that everything that can appear within our consciousness must be posited as the same as something else and posited in opposition to some third thing. A judgment concerning something that can neither be posited as the same as nor in opposition to anything else is by no means governed by the principle of sufficient reason, for such a judgment does not satisfy the conditions for the valid employment of this principle. Such a judgment is not grounded in anything; instead, it itself grounds all possible judgments. It possesses no ground, but it itself provides the ground for everything that is grounded. The object of such a judgment is the absolute I, and all judgments that have as their subject the absolute I are valid purely and simply and without any ground.[130] We will have more to say about this below.[131]

3.) That action in which one, in comparing two items, seeks the characteristic feature through which they are *posited as opposites* is called the *antithetic* way of proceeding. This is commonly called the *analytic* way of proceeding, though this term is less apt than "antithetic," in part because the term "analytic" may give rise to the opinion that something can be developed out a concept that one has not first placed there by means of *synthesis,* and in part because the designation "antithetic" more clearly indicates that this way of proceeding is the opposite of the synthetic way of proceeding. The *synthetic* way of proceeding consists precisely in the fact that one is seeking to discover in things posited in opposition to each other that characteristic feature in which they are *the same.* In accordance with their sheer logical form, which abstracts completely from the entire content of cognition, as well from the manner in which one obtained a cognition, judgments brought about in the first way are called antithetic or negative judgments, and judgments brought about in the second way are called synthetic or affirmative judgments.

[I, 113]
[I/2: 274]

4.) If the logical rules governing all antithesis and synthesis are derived from the third foundational principle of the *Wissenschaftslehre,* then one's legitimate right to engage in all acts of antithesis and synthesis is derived from this principle as well. But in our presentation of this third foundational principle we have observed that the original action that it expresses — the action of connecting terms posited in opposition to each other in a third term — was not possible without the action of positing in opposition, and that the action of positing in opposition was, in turn, impossible without that of connecting, and therefore that these two actions are, in fact, inseparably connected and can be distinguished only in reflection. From this it also follows that neither of those logical actions, which are originally grounded in the actions of connecting and separating and are actually nothing but particular, finer determinations of those actions, is possible apart from the other. No antithesis is possible without a synthesis, for [the method of] antithesis consists in seeking out, in terms that are the same [*in Gleichen*], that characteristic feature that is posited in opposition [i.e., that distinguishes them from each other]; but these terms that are the same would not be the same had they not first been posited as the same by means of a synthetic act.[132] In sheer antithesis one abstracts from the fact that these terms were first posited as the same through such a synthetic action. They are purely and simply taken to be the same, without any inquiry into why this is the case. Reflection is here directed only upon what is posited in opposition within them, which is thereby raised to clear and distinct consciousness. — Conversely, it is equally the case that no synthesis is possible without an antithesis. Terms posited in opposition are supposed to be united. But they would not be posited in opposition to each other except by means of an action of the I; in synthesis, however, one abstracts from this fact, simply in order to raise the ground of their [I, 114] connection to consciousness by means of reflection. — Thus, with respect to content, there are no purely analytic judgments, and by means of such judgments not only does one, as Kant puts it, not get very far; one makes no headway whatsoever.[133]   [I/2: 275]

5.) The celebrated question placed by Kant at the head of the *Critique of Pure Reason* — "How are synthetic judgments possible *a priori*?"[134] — has now been answered in the most universal and satisfactory way.[135] In our third foundational principle we have achieved a synthesis of I and Not-I, which are posited in opposition to each other, by means of the posited divisibility of both. One cannot inquire any further concerning the possibility of this [act of synthesis]; it is purely and simply possible and one is entitled to it without any further ground. All other syntheses that are supposed to be valid must be contained in this [original] synthesis [of the limited I and the limited Not-I], a synthesis that must be achieved in and along with these other syntheses. Accordingly, the proof of this original synthesis is the most convincing proof that these other syntheses are just as valid as the original one.[136]

6.) *All of these other syntheses must be contained in the original, highest synthesis* [of the limited I and limited Not-I], and this points in the most definite manner to the path we must pursue in our science. — It should be one of syntheses, and thus our entire way of preceding from now on will be synthetic (at least in the theoretical part of the *Wissenschaftslehre*, since our procedure in the practical part is just the reverse, as will become evident in due time). Every proposition will contain a synthesis. — And yet no synthesis is possible without a preceding antithesis, from which, however, we abstract, insofar as it is an action, and seek only to discover the product of this act of antithesis: namely, the terms that are posited in opposition to each other. In the case of every proposition [in the theoretical part of our science] we must therefore begin by pointing out the terms posited in opposition [in that proposition], which are the terms that are supposed to be united. — All the syntheses [to be] established are supposed to be contained in the highest synthesis, which we have just undertaken, and they are supposed to be capable of being developed from it. Thus we must seek out in the I and Not-I — which are connected through this highest synthesis, and

[I 115]   insofar as they are connected through this synthesis — any remaining characteristic features posited in opposition to each other. Then we must connect these features to each other by means of a new ground of connection, which must, in turn, be contained in the supreme ground of connection [that is, in the highest synthesis, that of divisibility]. And then — in the terms posited in opposition to each other but bound together in this first synthesis — we must once again seek out new terms posited in opposition to each other, in order to connect them by means of a new ground of connection, a ground that is also contained in the first synthesis we have derived. And we must continue in this manner so long as we are able, until we finally arrive at terms posited in opposition to each other that do not permit of any further and complete connection, and in this way we will make the transition [from the theoretical] to the practical part [of our science].[137] Our way

[I/2: 276]   forward is therefore fixed and secure and is prescribed by the subject-matter itself, and we can know in advance that we cannot go astray so long as we maintain the appropriate degree of attentiveness to our path.

7.) Just as antithesis is not possible without synthesis nor synthesis without antithesis, so are both impossible without thesis — that is, without an act of positing that occurs purely and simply and by means of which an A (the I) is neither posited as the same as anything else nor posited in opposition to anything else, but is posited purely and simply.[138]

In its relation to our system, this [act of] thesis is what furnishes this whole [that is, the *Wissenschaftslehre*] with tenability and completeness. It must be a system and a single one.[139] Terms posited in opposition to one another must be connected so long as such opposites remain, until absolute unity has been produced — which, to be sure, could be accomplished only through a completed approach to the infinite,[140] which is in itself impossible (as will become evident in due course[141]). — The necessity of positing terms in opposition and connecting them in a specific way follows immediately from the third foundational principle. The overall necessity of connecting things follows from the first, highest, and purely and simply posited foundational principle. The *form* of the system is grounded in the highest synthesis [i.e., in the third foundational principle]; *that* there is supposed to be any system at all is grounded in the absolute thesis [i.e., in the first foundational principle].

This is enough concerning the application of the preceding remark to our system as such, but there is another, even more important application of this remark to the form of judgment, which, for various reasons, may not here be dispensed with. Just as there were antithetic and synthetic judgments, so, by analogy,[142] there also ought to be thetic judgments, [I, 116] which are, with respect to a certain determination, posited in direct opposition to the two other forms of judgment. This is because the correctness of the first two types of judgments presupposes some ground, and indeed a double ground, one of connection and one of distinction.[143] Both of these grounds can be indicated, and they must be indicated if the judgment is to be proven. (E.g., "a bird is an animal." Here the ground of connection, which is what is reflected upon in this case, is the determinate concept of an animal: namely, that it consists of matter, of organized matter, and of animated living matter; and the ground of distinction, which is what is abstracted from in this judgment, consists in the specific differences between various kinds of animals — whether they have two feet or four, feathers, scales, or a hairy skin. Or consider the judgment, "a plant is not an animal." Here the ground of distinction, which is what is reflected upon in this case, is the specific difference between a plant and an animal, and the ground of connection, which is what is abstracted from in this judgment, is organization as such.) In contrast, a thetic judgment would [I/2: 277] be one that posits something that is not equal to anything else nor posited in opposition to anything else, but is simply posited as equal to itself. Such a judgment cannot, therefore, presuppose any ground of connection nor any ground of distinction; instead, the third term in question, which is logically required and has to be presupposed, would simply be the *task* of finding a ground.[144] The original and supreme judgment of this type is "I am," a judgment that says nothing whatsoever about the I, but instead leaves open the predicate position for a possible determination of the I, into infinity. All judgements subsumed under this one, that is, all judgements contained in the absolute positing of the I, are of this type (even if they do not always actually have the I as their logical subject), as is the case, for example, in the judgment "the human being is free."[145] Either one considers this to be a positive judgment, in which case it would assert "human beings belong to the class of free beings," which means that there should be some ground of the connection between a human being and a free being, which, as the ground of freedom, would have to be contained in the concept of a free being as such, as well as in the concept of a human [I, 117] being in particular. But, far from it being the case that any such ground is available to us, we cannot even point to a class of free beings. Alternately, one can consider this same judgment to be a negative one, in which case the human being would be posited in opposition to all beings bound by the laws of natural necessity. But in this case the ground for distinguishing between what is necessary and what is not necessary must be available, and one must be able to show that the ground of this connection is not contained in the concept of the human being, but instead in a concept posited in opposition thereto. At the same time, it must be possible to indicate a characteristic feature common both to the concept of a free being and to that of a human being. But a human being — to the extent that the predicate "freedom" can validly be applied to a human being, that is to say, insofar as a human being is an absolute and not a represented nor representable subject — has nothing whatsoever in common with a natural being and is therefore also not posited in opposition to such a being. Yet, in accordance with the logical form of the judgment, which is that of a positive judgment, both concepts [viz., "human being" and "freedom"] are supposed to be united. They cannot, however, be united in any concept whatsoever, but only in the Idea[146] of an I whose consciousness is determined by nothing whatsoever outside itself, but instead itself determines everything outside itself by means of its own sheer consciousness. But such an Idea is itself unthinkable, inasmuch as, for us, it harbors a contradiction. Nevertheless, it is established as our supreme practical goal. A human being should infinitely approach unattainable freedom. —

[I/2: 278]

Or consider the judgment of taste, "A is beautiful" (which is to say, the proposition that A contains some characteristic feature which is also contained in the ideal of the beautiful). This is a thetic judgment, because I am unable to compare this feature with the ideal, since I am not familiar with this ideal. Instead, this judgment sets a task for my mind, the task of discovering such an ideal, a task assigned by my mind's absolute self-positing and one that could be accomplished only by means of a completed approximation to infinity. — For this reason, Kant and his followers have

[I, 118]

quite correctly called such judgments "*infinite*,"[147] though to the best of my knowledge no one has explained them in a clear and definite manner.

8.) From what has just been said it follows that no ground can ever be adduced for any determinate thetic judgment; instead, the manner in which the human mind proceeds in the case of all thetic judgments is grounded in the positing of the I purely and simply through and by itself.

It is useful and will provide us with the clearest and most definite insight into the distinctive character of the Critical system to compare this way of grounding thetic judgments with the way in which antithetic and synthetic judgments are grounded.

All terms$^{\circ}$ posited in opposition to each other in any concept that expresses the ground of the distinction between the two terms are brought into agreement with each other in a *higher* (more universal, more comprehensive) concept, which is called the concept of the species [*Gattungsbegriff*].[148] This presupposes a synthesis comprising both terms, precisely to the extent that they are the same. (Thus, e.g., gold and silver, insofar as they are the same, are contained in the concept "metal," which does not contain those concepts in which gold and silver are posited in opposition to each other, e.g., the concept of a determinate color.) This is the source of the logical rule governing definition: namely, that every definition must include both the species-concept, which contains the ground

---

$^{\circ}$ *All* terms [Emphasis added in *SW*.]

of connection, and the specific difference, which contains the ground of distinction. — In contrast, all terms posited as alike are posited in opposition to each other in a *lower* concept, which expresses some special determination of each term, which was abstracted from in the judgment expressing their identity. That is to say, every synthesis presupposes a preceding antithesis. For example, the concept "body" abstracts from the varieties of color, specific weight, taste, smell, etc. Hence everything that fills space, is impenetrable, and has some weight is a body, even though these same things are posited in opposition to one another with respect to these same features. (The *Wissenschaftslehre* will determine *which* determinations are more general or more specific and thereby determine *which* concepts are higher or lower. The fewer the number of intermediate concepts required in order to derive any concept from the supreme concept, that of "reality," the higher the concept; the greater the number of intermediate concepts required, the lower the concept. Y is surely a lower concept than X if X occurs in the series that constitutes the derivation of Y from the highest concept, and vice versa.) [I/2: 279] [I, 119]

The situation is quite different in the case of what is purely and simply posited, the I. Insofar as a Not-I is posited in opposition to the I, it is immediately posited as like the I; — but not [as synthesized or unified] in a *higher* concept (which would perhaps contain both the I and the Not-I, and which would presuppose a [still] higher act of synthesis, or at least of thesis), which is the case with all other comparisons. Instead, , the Not-I is posited as like the I in a *lower* concept. The I itself is posited in diminished form [*herabsetzt*] in a lower concept, that of divisibility, so that it can be posited as like the Not-I; and, in this same concept [of divisibility], the I is posited in opposition to the Not-I. In this case, therefore, there is no *upward* ascent, which is otherwise the case with every act of synthesis, but instead a *downward* descent. Insofar as they are posited by means of the concept of mutual limitability as both alike and opposed to each other, both the I and the Not-I are, so to speak, something (namely, accidents) contained in the I (understood as a divisible substance) and posited by the I (understood as the absolute, unrestrictable subject, to which nothing is equal nor posited in opposition). — For this reason, all judgments that have as their logical subject either the limitable, determinable subject or something restricting the I must themselves be restricted or determined by something higher. But all judgments that have as their logical subject the absolute, indeterminable I[149] cannot be determined by anything higher, since the absolute I is not determined by anything higher; instead, such judgments are grounded purely and simply through themselves.[150]

This constitutes the essence of the *Critical* philosophy: that an absolute I is put forward [*aufgestellt*] as purely and simply unconditioned and determinable by nothing higher, and if such a philosophy infers consistently from this foundational principle it then becomes *Wissenschaftslehre*.

In contrast, a philosophy is *dogmatic* if it views the I as something equal to and posited in opposition to something else, which is accomplished through what is supposed to be the higher concept of a *thing* (*ens*), a concept that is at the same time advanced quite arbitrarily as what is purely and simply highest.[151] In the Critical philosophy, a thing is what is posited by the I; in dogmatic philosophy a thing is that within which the I itself is posited. Criticism is for this reason *immanent*, because it posits everything in the I, whereas dogmatism is *transcendent*, because it proceeds beyond the I. Insofar as dogmatism can be consistent, Spinozism is its most consistent product. If, as one should, one deals with dogmatism in accordance with its own foundational principles, one should ask the dogmatist why he assumes his thing in itself with no higher ground, since he demands such a higher ground in the case of the I. Why is it valid to treat the thing in itself as absolute, when the I is not supposed to be absolute? He cannot justify doing this, and we are therefore justified, in accordance with his own foundational principles, in demanding that he assume nothing without a reason or ground and thus that he specify in turn a [still] higher species-concept for the concept of a thing in itself, and then specify in turn a still higher genus-concept for this species-concept, and so on ad infinitum.[152] Hence, if it is not to contradict itself, any thoroughgoing dogmatism must deny that our knowledge possesses any ground whatsoever and therefore must deny that there is any system whatsoever in the human mind.[153] A thoroughgoing dogmatism is a skepticism that despairs over the fact that it doubts, for such a philosophy must annul the unity of consciousness and, along with this, logic as a whole. It is therefore not dogmatism after all, and it contradicts itself insofar as it claims to be this.*

[I, 120]

[I/2: 280]

[I, 121]

[I/2: 281]

(Accordingly, Spinoza posits the ground of the unity of consciousness in a substance that is necessarily determined with respect both to its content — the determinate series of representations — and its form of unity. I would, however, ask him the following question: What, in turn, contains the ground of the necessity of this substance, with respect both to its content — the various series of representations contained in this substance — and to its form — in accordance with which it is supposed to exhaust *every possible* series of representations and to constitute a complete *whole*? But he provides me with no higher ground for this necessity; instead, he asserts that this is purely and simply the case. Spinoza says what he says because he is forced to assume something as absolutely primary, a supreme unity. If that is what he is looking for,

---

* There are only two systems [of philosophy], the Critical and the dogmatic. Skepticism, as described above, would not be a system at all, since it denies the very possibility of any system whatsoever. But it can deny this only systematically; hence it contradicts itself and is quite irrational. The nature of the human mind has seen to it in advance that skepticism is also impossible. No one has yet been such a skeptic in earnest. The critical skepticism of Hume, Aenesidemus, and Maimon, which exposes the inadequacy of the grounds that have been offered heretofore and, in doing so, indicates where more tenable ones may be discovered, is something else. Science profits from such critical skepticism, if not always with respect to its content, then certainly with respect to its form; and anyone who denies the perspicacious skeptic his due respect exhibits a poor understanding of what is to the advantage of science.

however, then he should have stuck with that unity given to him in consciousness and would not have needed to fabricate a still higher one, when
nothing compelled him to do so.)

There would simply be no way to explain either how any thinker could
ever be able to go beyond the I, or how, once he had done this, he could
ever be able to halt [his search for a ground] at any point, were it not for
an encounter with a practical datum, which completely explains this phenomenon. What drove the dogmatist beyond the I is not, as some seem to
believe, a theoretical datum; it was a practical one: namely, the feeling that
our I, to the extent that it is practical,[154] is dependent upon a Not-I, which
is by no means subject to our legislation and is to that extent free. But
what forced the dogmatist to come to a halt at some point [in his search
for a ground] was also a practical datum: namely, the feeling that it is necessary to subordinate and to unify under the practical law of the I everything that is Not-I. But, as will become evident in due course,[155] this
[necessary subordination of the Not-I to the practical law of the I] is by no
means something that exists, as it were, as the object of a concept, as
something present, but as the object of an Idea, something that *ought* to
be present and ought to be brought about by us.

Finally, this makes it evident that dogmatism, as such, is not at all what
it claims to be and that our preceding arguments against the dogmatist [I, 122]
were unjust and that the dogmatist would be unjust to himself were he to
accept them. Dogmatism's supreme unity is in fact nothing other than the
unity of consciousness, and it cannot be anything else; and its thing in
itself is the substrate of divisibility as such, or the supreme substance, [I/2: 282]
within which are posited both I and Not-I (Spinoza's "intellect" and
"extension"). But by no means does dogmatism elevate itself to the pure
absolute I, let alone go beyond this I. When it proceeds the farthest (as in
Spinoza's system), it extends only to our second and third foundational
principles, but not to the first, purely and simply unconditioned principle,
though dogmatism ordinarily fails by a wide margin to elevate itself even
that high. It was reserved for the Critical philosophy to make this final
step and thereby to complete the science [of philosophy]. As will become
evident in due course, the theoretical part of our *Wissenschaftslehre* —
which is also developed only from the second and third foundational
principles, since, in this part, the first foundational principle possesses
only regulative validity — is a systematic Spinozism, with the proviso that
every I is itself the sole supreme substance.[156] To this theoretical part,
however, our system adds a practical part, which grounds and determines
the theoretical part. The entire science is thereby brought to completion,
and the contents of the human mind are completely exhausted.[157] In this
way ordinary human understanding, which was insulted by all pre-Kantian
philosophy[158] and which, to judge simply from our own theoretical
philosophy, still remains separated from philosophy with no hope of
reconciliation, is completely reconciled with philosophy.[159]

9.) If we abstract completely from the *determinate* form of a judgment — that is, from whether it is one in which the terms are *posited in opposition to each other* or in which they are *compared to each other* and whether it is based on a ground of *distinction* or on a ground of *connection* — until all that remains is what is universal in this mode of acting, namely, the limiting of one term by the other, we thereby obtain the category of *determination* [*Bestimmung*] (delimitation [*Begrenzung*], or, for Kant, limitation [*Limitation*][160]). Hence the act of positing any quantity at all, whether a quantity of reality or of negation, is called "determination."

PART TWO^A

Foundation of Theoretical Knowledge

§ 4. First Theorem

Before we embark upon our path, a brief reflection upon it is in order. — We now have three logical foundational principles: the principle of *identity*, which grounds all other foundational principles, as well as two others, the principle of *positing in opposition* and the *grounding principle* or *principle of sufficient reason*, which are themselves mutually grounded in the first principle.[161] It is the latter two foundational principles that make the synthetic way of proceeding possible at all. They establish and ground the form of the synthetic way of proceeding. Consequently, in order to be sure of the formal validity of the way we are proceeding in our reflection, we need nothing more than these two principles. — Similarly, the first synthetic action, that is, the foundational synthesis [*Grundsynthesis*] (that of the I and Not-I [in the third foundational principle, as presented in § 3]), establishes a content for all possible future syntheses, and for this reason we also require nothing more from this side [, i.e., that of content]. From this foundational synthesis it must be possible to develop everything else that should be included in the *Wissenschaftslehre*.

But if something is to be developed from this synthesis, then the concepts united in it [viz., the concepts of the I and the Not-I] must also contain other concepts, concepts that have not yet been established; and our task is to discover these. We will accomplish this by proceeding as follows. — According to § 3, all synthetic concepts arise from the union of terms posited in opposition to each other. The first thing we must do, therefore, is seek out those characteristic features [*Merkmale*] that have been posited in opposition to each other within the concepts established [in § 3] (in this case, the concepts of the I and the Not-I, insofar as these are posited as mutually determining each other). This search is conducted [I/2: 284] by means of reflection, which is a freely undertaken action of our mind: — I said, *to seek out*, which presupposes that these features are already present and not something that we have, as it were, fabricated artificially, by means of our own [I, 124] reflection (which is something reflection is quite unable to accomplish). In other words, we are here presupposing an original and necessary antithetic action on the part of the I.[162]

It is the task of reflection to exhibit [*aufzustellen*] this antithetic action, and it first approaches this task analytically, since to raise to clear consciousness terms that have been posited in opposition to each other within a specific concept (= A) — as opposed to each other — is to "analyze" that concept. Here however, one must take particular note of the following: in this case, the concept we

---

^A In the first edition, Part Two was preceded by a title page identifying it as the *Second Installment of the Foundation of the Entire Wissenschaftslehre*.

are analyzing by means of reflection is by no means one that has already been given to reflection; on the contrary, it is a concept that is supposed to be first discovered by means of reflection. Hence, until we have completed our analysis, the concept we are seeking will be termed "X." This raises the question; how can one analyze an unknown concept?

No antithetic action of the kind that is presupposed for the very possibility of analysis is possible without a synthesis, and therefore no specific antithetic action is possible without a specific synthetic one (§ 3). These two actions are intimately united; they constitute one and the same action and can be distinguished only in reflection. This means that one can infer the antithesis from the synthesis. Similarly, the third term, in which the two terms that were posited in opposition to each other are united, cannot be established as a product of reflection but as something discovered thereby. But it is discovered as the product of that original synthetic action of the I which, for this reason, and like the actions already established, need not rise to the level of empirical consciousness *as* an act. From now on, therefore, we will be encountering nothing but synthetic actions, actions that, unlike the first ones, are not purely and simply unconditioned. Nevertheless, our deduction will reveal that these are indeed actions — and actions of the I. That is to say, they are actions of the I just as surely as the first synthesis from which they are developed and with which they are one is itself an action of the I; and this first synthesis is an action of the I, just as surely as the highest F/Act of the I, through which the I posits itself, is an action of the I.—The actions to be established are [I, 125] *synthetic*; but the reflection by means of which they are established is *analytic*.

These antitheses, however, which must be presupposed for the possibility of reflective analysis, must be thought of as having preceded[163] such reflection, inasmuch as the possibility of the synthetic concepts that are to be established[164] depends upon these antitheses. But no antithesis is possible without a synthesis. [I/2: 285] Hence a higher synthesis is presupposed to have already occurred, and our first task must be to seek out this higher synthesis and exhibit it clearly. In fact, this synthesis must actually have been established in the preceding §. Nevertheless, a few additional remarks on this topic were perhaps appropriate, inasmuch as we are now making the transition into an entirely new part of the *Wissenschaftslehre*.

A. Determination of the Synthetic Proposition to be Analyzed

The I as well as the Not-I are each posited by [*durch*] the I and posited in the I as *mutually* restrictable [*beschränkbar*] *by each other*; that is to say, they are posited in such a way that the reality of the one annuls that of the other and vice versa.[165] (§ 3.)

This principle contains the following two propositions:

1.) *The I posits the Not-I as restricted*[166] *by the I.* For the moment, it would at least seem that we can make no use whatsoever of this proposition, though it will in the future play a large role in the practical part of our science. This is because the Not-I is nothing so far; it possesses no reality, and thus we are utterly unable to imagine how the I could annul any reality in the Not-I, which possesses no reality, or how the Not-I could be limited [*eingeschränkt*], since it is nothing. So long, therefore, as reality has not been ascribed in some manner to the Not-I, this [first] proposition seems entirely useless. To be sure, the proposition under which this proposition is subsumed, namely, that the I and Not-I mutually limit each other, is indeed posited; but whether the proposition just indicated [viz., "the I posits the Not-I as restricted by the I"] is also posited through this former proposition and contained in it remains utterly problematic. It might also be the case that the I can be limited in relation to the Not-I purely and exclusively insofar as it has first limited the Not-I—that is, insofar as the act of limiting has its origin in the I. Perhaps the Not-I does not limit the I in itself at all, but limits only the limiting [I, 126] activity of the I. In this case, the preceding proposition [viz., "the I posits the Not-I as restricted by the I"] would still remain true and correct, and there would be no need to ascribe absolute reality to the Not-I nor to subsume this problematic proposition under the proposition that "the I and Not-I mutually limit each other."

2.) This proposition [viz., the third foundational] principle also includes the following proposition: *the I posits itself as restricted by the Not-I.*[167] This is a proposition that can be put to use. Moreover, it must be accepted as certain, since it can [I/2: 286] be derived from the proposition previously established.

The I is first posited as absolute [§ 1], and then it is posited as a limitable reality capable of quantity, and indeed, as capable of being limited by the Not-I [§ 3]. All of this, however, is posited by the I and these are therefore the elements [*Momente*] of our proposition.

(It will become evident:

1.) that the proposition "the I posits itself as restricted by a Not-I" grounds or provides the foundation for the theoretical part of the *Wissenschaftslehre*—though this will not become evident until we have completed the theoretical portion,[168] which must be the case with any synthetic presentation.[169]

2.) that the (still problematic) proposition, "the I posits the Not-I as restricted by the I," grounds or provides the foundation for the practical part of the *Wissenschaftslehre*. But since this proposition is at this point problematic, so too is the possibility of such a practical part. From this it becomes evident:

3.) why reflection must begin with the theoretical part, even though it will eventually become evident that it is not the theoretical power [*Vermögen*][170] that makes possible the practical power [of the I], but just the reverse; it is the practical power that first makes possible the theoretical power. (It will become evident that reason in itself is purely practical and first becomes theoretical through the application of its laws to a Not-I that limits it.) — Reflection must proceed in this manner, because the thinkability of the practical foundational principle is grounded in the thinkability of the theoretical foundational principle. Thinkability, after all, is always what concerns reflection.

4.) It follows that our division of the *Wissenschaftslehre* into theoretical and [I, 127] practical parts is purely problematic (which is why we mention this division only in passing and are unable to draw any sharp boundary, since we do not yet recognize any such boundary). We do not yet know whether we shall be able to complete the theoretical part nor whether we might yet stumble upon a contradiction

that is purely and simply beyond resolution. Even less can we know whether we
[I/2: 287] will be driven from the theoretical part into a distinctively practical one.)

B. General Nature of the Synthesis of Terms Posited in Opposition to Each Other as Such in the Indicated Proposition

The proposition "*the I posits itself as determined by the Not-I*" has just been derived from the third foundational principle. If that principle is valid, then so is this proposition; and that foundational principle must be valid, just as surely as the unity of consciousness is not supposed to be annulled and the I is not supposed to cease to be an I (§ 3). Hence the validity of this proposition must be just as certain as it is certain that the unity of consciousness should not be annulled.

The first thing we must do is analyze this proposition, i.e., discern if it contains any terms posited in opposition to each other — and, if so, which ones.

The I posits itself *as determined by the Not-I*. To that extent, the I is not supposed to be engaged in any act of determining, but is supposed *to be* determined, and the Not-I is supposed to be engaged in determining, in setting boundaries to the reality of the I. It follows that our proposition contains the following propositions:

The Not-I (actively) *determines the I* (which is, to that extent, affected[171]). By means of absolute activity *the I posits itself* as determined. So far as we can see, all activity must proceed from the I. It is the I that has posited itself, posited the Not-I, and posited both in [the concept of] quantity. But to say that the I posits itself as determined is obviously to say that *the I determines itself.* Hence the proposition in question [viz., "the I posits itself as determined by the Not-I"] also includes the following proposition:

[I, 128]   *The I determines itself* (by means of absolute activity).

For the moment, let us abstract entirely from the question of whether each of these two propositions might contradict itself, contain an internal contradiction, and thereby nullify itself. In any case, this much is immediately evident: these two propositions mutually contradict each other, since the I cannot be active when it is supposed to be passively affected, and vice versa.

(To be sure, the concepts of *activity* [*Tätigkeit*] and *being passively affected* [*Leiden*] have not yet been derived and developed as posited in opposition to each other, but nothing further should be inferred from the fact that these concepts are posited in opposition to each other. We have here employed these terms merely for the purposes of clarity. This much is obvious: that one of them implies and affirms what the other denies, and vice versa, and this certainly constitutes a contradiction.)

If two propositions contained in one and the same proposition contradict and therefore annul each other, then the proposition that contains them both annuls itself. This is what happens in the case of the proposition established above [viz., the proposition that the I posits itself as determined by the Not-I]; therefore, it annuls itself.

But this proposition is not supposed to annul itself, at least not if the unity of
[I/2: 288] consciousness is not to be annulled. Hence we must attempt to unify [*zu vereinigen*]

these propositions that have been posited in opposition to each other. (As was observed above, we should not, when engaged in reflection, artificially fabricate a point of union for these propositions; instead, this point of union must already be present within our consciousness, since the unity of consciousness has been posited — posited, however, along with the proposition that threatens to annul it. And our task in reflecting is simply to seek out this point of union. We have just analyzed a synthetic concept = X, which is actually present; and, from the opposition discovered by means of this analysis, we are now supposed to infer what kind of concept this unknown X is supposed to be.)

Let us now proceed to our task.

One of our propositions affirms what the other denies. It is therefore reality and negation that in this case [both] annul each other and are not supposed to annul each other, but be united, and this union is supposed to occur (§ 3) by means of restriction or determination. [I, 129]

The absolute totality of reality is ascribed to the I insofar as it is asserted that the I determines itself. The I can determine itself only as reality, since it is posited as reality purely and simply (§ 1), and no negation whatsoever is posited in the I. Nevertheless, the I is supposed to be determined[172] by itself, and this cannot mean that it annuls a [portion of] reality within itself, for in that case it would immediately be placed in contradiction with itself. Instead, this can only mean that the I determines [this] reality and, in doing so, determines itself. It posits all reality as an absolute quantum, beyond which there is no reality at all. This reality is posited in the I. The I is therefore determined to the extent that reality is determined.[173]

It must also be observed that this [act of determining its reality] is an absolute act of the I, the same act that occurred in § 3, in which the I posits itself as quantity, and which, for the sake of what follows, has to be established precisely and clearly at this point.

The Not-I is posited in opposition to the I. Just as the I contains reality, the Not-I contains negation. If the absolute totality of reality is posited in the I, then the totality of negation is necessarily posited in the Not-I, and this negation must itself be posited as an absolute totality.

Both the absolute totality of reality in the I and the absolute totality of negation in the Not-I are supposed to be united through determination. Accordingly, the I *determines* itself *in part* and *it is determined in part.*[B] [I/2: 289]

These are both supposed to be thought of, however, as *one* and *the same*; i.e., the I is supposed to be determined precisely insofar as it determines itself and to determine itself in precisely the same respect in which it is determined.

The I *is* determined: this means that reality is abolished in it. Hence, if the I posits only *a part* of the absolute totality of reality in itself, it thereby annuls in itself the rest of this totality. By means of the act of positing in opposition (§ 2) and by virtue of the equivalence of quantity to itself,[174] the I posits in the Not-I a quantity of reality equal to that which was nullified in the I (§ 3). A degree is always a degree, whether a degree of reality or of negation. (Divide, for [I, 130]

[B] *In part.* Hence this proposition is to be taken with a *double* meaning, each of which must nevertheless be able to subsist alongside the other. [Added in C.]

example, the whole of reality into ten equal parts, and then posit five of these in the I; from this it follows that five parts of negation are necessarily posited in the Not-I.)

The I posits in the Not-I just as many parts of reality as it does parts of negation in itself, and this reality in[175] what is posited in opposition [to the I] also nullifies reality in the I itself. (Thus, for example, if five parts of negation are posited in the I, then five parts of reality are posited in the Not-I.)

Accordingly, the I posits negation within itself insofar as it posits reality in the Not-I, and it posits reality in itself insofar as it posits negation in the Not-I. It therefore posits itself as [both] *self-determining* (insofar as it *is* determined) and as *becoming* determined (insofar as it *determines* itself). And with this, we have accomplished our task, insofar as it was assigned above.[176]

("Insofar as it was assigned above": this is because we have still not answered the question concerning how the I could posit negation or reality in the Not-I, and until we have answered this question we have accomplished next to nothing. This is merely a reminder that no one should take exception to the apparent emptiness and inadequacy of our resolution of this task.)

We have therefore undertaken a new synthesis. The concept exhibited in this synthesis is contained under the higher genus-concept of *determination*, since it is by means of determination that quantity is posited. But if this is really to be a different concept, and if the synthesis to which it points is to be a new one, then it must be possible to point to the specific difference that distinguishes this concept from that of determination as such; i.e., it must be possible to indicate the ground of the distinction between these two concepts. — Without asking how or in what way this occurs, let us agree that *determination*, as such, serves only to *establish*
[I/2: 290]   *quantity*. By means of the synthetic concept we have now established, the quantity of *the one* is posited *through the quantity of what is posited in opposition to it*, and vice versa. Determining the reality or the negation of the I determines at the same time the negation or the reality of the Not-I, and vice versa. I can start with either
[I, 131]   of these two terms posited in opposition to each other that I choose; either way, I would, through my act of determining, have determined the other at the same time. Analogously with the term "reciprocal interaction" [*Wechselwirkung*], this more determinate kind of determining can rightly be called "*reciprocal determination*" [*Wechselbestimmung*]. This is the same as what Kant calls "*relation*."[177]

C. Synthesis by Means of Reciprocal Determination of the Contradictions Implicit in the First of the Two Propositions Posited in Opposition to Each Other

It will become evident that synthesis by means of reciprocal determination makes no noticeable contribution to resolving the chief difficulty in itself.[178] We have nevertheless gained a firm footing for our method.[179]

If the major principle stated at the beginning of this § [namely, "The I as well as the Not-I are each posited by the I and are posited in the I as *mutually* restrictable *by each other*"] contains all of the opposing propositions that are here supposed to

be united (and, according to the preceding remark on method, they are all supposed to be posited in it), and if, moreover, these opposing propositions are
somehow supposed to be united with one another by means of the concept of
reciprocal determination, then the propositions posited in opposition to each
other in the previously unified general propositions [viz., "the Not-I (actively)
determines the I" and "the I determines itself"] must already be indirectly united
through reciprocal determination.^C Just as these particular opposing propositions
are contained in the previously established, general opposing propositions, so too
must the synthetic concept that unites them[180] be contained in the previously
established general concept of reciprocal determination. We must therefore proceed with this concept precisely as we proceeded with the concept of *determination* as such. We determined^D the latter concept; that is, we limited the sphere of
its domain to a lesser quantity by adding the condition that the quantity of one
term is supposed to be determined by what is posited in opposition to it, and
vice versa. This is how we obtained the category of reciprocal determination. [I/2: 291]
According to the demonstration just completed, we must now determine this
concept more narrowly; i.e., we must limit its sphere by adding a specific
additional condition. In this way, we will obtain [new] synthetic concepts subsumed under the higher concept of reciprocal determination.   [I, 132]

We will therefore find ourselves in the position of determining these concepts
[we are seeking: namely, those of causality and substantiality] by means of the
sharp boundary between them, so that the possibility of confusing them with one
another and straying from the domain of one into the domain of the other will be
utterly eliminated. Any error will reveal itself immediately by its lack of sharp
determination.

The Not-I is supposed to determine the I; i.e., the Not-I is supposed to annul
reality in the I. This, however, is possible only on the condition that the Not-I
possesses within itself that portion of reality it is supposed to annul in the
I. Accordingly, *the Not-I possesses reality in itself.*

However, *all reality is posited in the I*. But the Not-I is posited in opposition to
the I; therefore, no reality is posited in the Not-I, but only negation. All [that is]
Not-I is negation; accordingly, *the Not-I possesses no reality whatsoever in itself.*

These two propositions mutually annul each other. Both are included in the
proposition, "the Not-I determines the I,"[181] which therefore annuls itself.

Yet this proposition is included in the major proposition we have just established, the principle of the unity of consciousness. If the former proposition is
annulled, then so is the major principle in which it is included, along with the
unity of consciousness, which includes this major principle. It follows that this
proposition cannot annul itself and that the terms posited in opposition to each
other within it must instead be capable of being united.^E

1.) This contradiction has not, so to speak, already been resolved through the
concept of reciprocal determination. Were we to posit the absolute totality of

---

^C *must already be indirectly united by means of reciprocal determination.* [Emphasis added in C.]
^D We *determined* [Emphasis added in C.]
^E [This entire paragraph is excised in C.]

reality as *divisible*, that is, as something that can be increased or decreased (and we have yet to derive even the justification for doing this), then of course we could arbitrarily remove parts of this totality, which, under this condition, we would have to posit in the Not-I. This much is achieved by means of the concept of reciprocal determination. But how then are we able to arrive at the point of removing parts

[I/2: 292]   from the reality of the I?[F] This is a question that has not yet been touched upon. To be sure, reflection, [which operates] in accordance with the law of reciprocal determination, posits that the same reality that has been annulled in one term is posited

[I, 133]   in the term posited in opposition to it, and vice versa — but only *if* reflection has first annulled reality in one of the terms. But what justifies or requires reflection to undertake [an act of] reciprocal determination in the first place?

Let us clarify this point further. Reality is purely and simply posited in the I. In the third foundational principle and again just now, the Not-I was specifically posited as a *quantum*. But every quaum is *something* and therefore possesses *reality*. Yet the Not-I is supposed to be a negation — and is therefore, as it were, a real negation (a negative magnitude).

According to the concept of sheer relation, however, it makes no difference to which of the two items posited in opposition to each other one chooses to ascribe reality and to which one ascribes negation. This depends upon with which of the two objects one begins one's reflection. And this is actually the case in mathematics, which abstracts completely from all qualities and attends only to quantity. It makes no difference whether I choose to call a step forward or a step backward "positive" magnitude; this depends solely upon whether I wish to establish as my final result the sum of the former or the sum of the later. So too in the *Wissenschaftslehre*, what is negation in the I is reality in the Not-I, and vice versa. This much and no more is prescribed by the concept of reciprocal determination. Whether I now wish to call what is in the I reality or negation depends upon my own arbitrary choice [*Willkür*]. This is a matter of merely relative* reality.

This reveals an ambiguity implicit in the concept of reality itself, an ambiguity that was introduced through the concept of reciprocal determination. If this ambiguity cannot be eliminated, then the unity of consciousness is nullified: [for

[I, 134]   in that case] the I is reality, and the Not-I is reality as well, and both are no longer posited in opposition to each other, and the I is not = I, but = Not-I.

2.) If the previously indicated contradiction is to be resolved satisfactorily, then before we do anything else we must eliminate this ambiguity, since it could perhaps be concealing the contradiction in question, in which case it would not be a true but only an apparent contradiction.

[I/2: 293]   The source of all reality is the I.[G] The concept of reality is first given through and along with the I. But the I *is* because it *posits itself*; and it *posits itself because*

[F]   But *then how are we able to arrive at the point of removing parts from the reality of the I?* [Emphasis added in C:]]

*   It is remarkable that in ordinary linguistic usage the word "*relative*" is always used correctly and is always employed to designate things that can be distinguished from one another merely through their quantity and nothing more, and that one nevertheless connects with the word *relation* no determinate concept from which this word stems.

[G]   is this I, for this is posited immediately and purely and simply. [Added in C.]

it *is*. *Self-positing* and *being* are therefore one and the same. But the concepts of *self-poisiting* and *activity* as such are also one and the same. All reality is therefore *active*, and everything that is *active* is reality. Activity is *positive* reality^H (in contrast with merely *relative* reality¹⁸²).

(In this case, it is very necessary that one think of the concept of activity quite purely.¹⁸³ This concept designates nothing that is not contained in the absolute positing of the I by itself, nothing not immediately contained in the proposition "*I am*." This makes it clear that one must abstract completely not only from all *temporal conditions*, but also from every *object* of activity. Inasmuch as it posits its own being, the F/Act of the I is by no means directed at an object, but reverts into itself [*geht in sich selbst zurück*].¹⁸⁴ Only when the I is engaged in representing itself¹⁸⁵ does it first become an object [of consciousness]. — It is difficult for the power of imagination to refrain from contaminating the pure concept of activity with the latter characteristic feature, namely, that of an object.^I However, it is sufficient that one be alerted to this deception on the part of the power of imagination, so that, in one's inferences, one might at least abstract from everything that could stem from such contamination.¹⁸⁶)

3.) The I is supposed to be determined; this means that reality — or, as this concept has now been determined, *activity* — is supposed to be annulled in the I. It follows that the opposite of *activity* is posited in the I. But the opposite of activity is called *being passively affected [Leiden]*. Being passively affected is *positive* negation^J and is to this extent posited in opposition to purely *relative* negation.¹⁸⁷

(One wishes that the term "being passively affected" had fewer associated connotations. It surely goes without saying that in the present case one should not [I, 135] be thinking of any kind of painful sensation. But it should perhaps be noted that what one is supposed to be thinking of in this case is something that is not only abstracted from all *temporal conditions*, but abstracted as well, at least up to this point, *from all activity* in what is posited in opposition [to the I] as *producing the [I's] state of being passively affected. Being passively affected* is the mere negation of the previously established pure concept of activity; and indeed, it is the *quantitative* [negation of activity], since the concept of activity is itself quantitative; for the sheer negation of activity, in abstraction from quantity, would be = 0, i.e., *a state of repose [Ruhe]*. Everything in the I that is not immediately included in the "*I am*" and is not posited immediately by the positing of the I through itself is, for the I, a state of being passively affected (*affection as such*).¹⁸⁸

4.) If the absolute totality of reality is supposed to be preserved when the I is in a state of being passively affected, then, by virtue of the law of reciprocal determination, the same degree of activity must necessarily be transferred [*über-* [I/2: 294] *tragen*] to the Not-I.^K

---

^H is *positive*, absolute reality. [Added in C.]
^I of the object to which activity is directed. [Added in C.]
^J is *positive absolute* negation. [Added in C.]
^K transferred to the Not-I, according to the preceding. [Added in C.]

With this, the preceding contradiction[189] is resolved. The *Not-I*, as such, *possesses no reality in itself; but it does possess reality insofar as the I is passively affected*, which follows in accordance with the principle of reciprocal determination. The following proposition is very important for all that follows: so far as we can see at this point at least, *the Not-I possesses reality for the I only to the extent that the I is affected, and in the absence of such an affection of the I, the Not-I possesses no reality whatsoever.*

5.) The synthetic concept [of causality] just derived is subsumed under the higher concept of reciprocal determination, for in this latter concept the quantity of the one term, the Not-I, is determined by the quantity of the term posited in opposition to it, the I. But our new concept is specifically distinguished from the latter concept [of reciprocal determination]; for in the concept of reciprocal determination it was a matter of complete indifference which of the two opposed terms was determined through the other — that is to say, to which of them reality was ascribed and to which of them negation was ascribed. Quantity was determined [through the concept of reciprocal determination], but nothing more than mere quantity. — In the present synthesis [of causality], however, such a substitution of one term for the other is not a matter of indifference; instead, it is determined
[I, 136]   to which of the two terms reality and not negation is to be ascribed and to which negation and not reality is to be ascribed. By means of the present synthesis [of causality], therefore, *activity* is posited; and indeed, the degree of activity posited in the one term is the same as the degree of *affection* posited in the term posited in opposition to the first term, and vice versa.

This synthesis [of activity and affection] is called the synthesis of *causal efficacy* (causality) [Wirksamkeit (*Kausalität*)].[190] That to which *activity* is ascribed and which is, to that extent, *not affected* is called "the *cause*" [*die Ursache*] (primordial reality, positive, purely and simply posited reality, which is aptly expressed by this same term[191]). That to which *the state of being passively affected* is ascribed and which is, to that extent, *not activity* is called "that which *is brought about*" (the effect) [*das* bewirkt (*der Effect*)]. It is thus something that depends upon something else and is therefore not a primordial reality). Thought of in combination with each other, cause and effect are called "*a causally effective operation* [*eine Wirkung*]." One should never call an effect a causally effective operation.[192]

(In the concept of causal efficacy, as just deduced, one must abstract completely from any *temporal conditions*,[193] and this concept can be easily thought of apart from such conditions. In part, this is because time has not yet been deduced, and we are therefore certainly not justified in employing that concept here, and in part
[I/2: 295]   this is because it is by no means true that one must think of the cause *as such* — that is, insofar as it is actively engaged in a specific causally effective operation — as preceding the effect in time, which is how it will appear later when we discuss the schematism.[194] By virtue of [their] synthetic unity, cause and effect should be thought of as one and the same. For reasons that will subsequently become apparent, what precedes the causally effective operation in time is not the cause, as such, but the substance to which causal efficacy is ascribed. But in this respect the affected substance also precedes in time that which is brought about or affected within it.)

D. Synthesis by Means of Reciprocal Determination of the Opposing Propositions Contained in the Second of the Two Propositions Posited in Opposition to Each Other

The second proposition established as contained in our major principle [in Part Two] — viz., "The I posits itself as determined; i.e., it determines itself" — itself [I, 137] includes propositions posited in opposition to each other and therefore annuls itself. But since it cannot annul itself without also immediately annulling the unity of consciousness, we must unite the opposing propositions contained within this principle by means of a new synthesis.

a.) The I determines itself; it is the *determining subject* [*das* bestimmende],[L] and is therefore active.

b.) The I determines itself; it is that *which is becoming determined* [*das* bestimmte werdende], and it is therefore passively affected.[M] Consequently, in one and the same action, the I is both active and passively affected. Reality and negation are ascribed to it at the same time, which is undoubtedly a contradiction.

This contradiction is supposed to be resolved by means of the concept of reciprocal determination,[195] and it would certainly be completely resolved if the former proposition could be thought of as follows: *the I determines its activity by means of its passive affection,*[196] *or it determines its passive affection by means of its activity.* In this case, it would be both active and passively affected in one and the same state. The question is only *whether* and *how* such a proposition can be thought.

Some standard must be established if any determinacy whatsoever (any measurement) is to be possible. But this standard can be nothing but the I itself, for only the I is originally posited purely and simply.   [I/2: 296]

Reality, however, is posited in the I. From this it follows that the I must be posited as the *absolute totality* of reality (and thus as a quantum containing all quanta and able to serve as the standard of measurement for all quanta). And it must be posited as such purely and simply, if the hypothetically proposed synthesis is to be possible and if the contradiction is to be resolved satisfactorily. Consequently:

1.) For no reason [*Grund*] whatsoever and quite unconditionally, the I posits purely and simply the *absolute totality of reality,* and it posits this as a quantum, beyond which no greater quantum is possible; and purely and simply by virtue of this positing it posits this absolute maximum of reality *within itself.* — Everything posited in the I is reality, and all reality that exists is posited in the I (§ 1). But this reality in the I is a quantum, and indeed a quantum that is posited purely and [I, 138] simply (§ 3).

2.) The quantity of what lacks reality (the state of being passively affected) is supposed to be determined through and with reference to this purely and simply posited standard measure. But what is lacking is nothing, and what lacks is

---

L it is the *determining subject* (that is, the verb is here employed in the active voice). [Added in C.]

M it is *determined* and therefore affected. (In accordance with its inner meaning, determinacy always indicates a state of being passively affected, a loss [*Abbruch*] of reality.) [Added in C, which also replaces "that *which is becoming determined*" with "that which is *determined*."]

nothing.[N] What is lacking can therefore be determined only insofar as the *remainder of reality* is determined. Consequently, the I can determine only the limited quantity of its own *reality*, and, in determining this, it at the same time determines the quantity of *negation* (by means of the concept of reciprocal determination).

(Here once again we are abstracting entirely from the determination of negation in the I as the opposite of *reality in itself*,[197] and we are directing our attention solely to the determination of a quantum of reality which is less than the totality.)

3.) A quantum of reality that is not equal to the totality of the same is itself a *negation*, namely, *negation of the totality*. It is posited in opposition to the totality as a limited quantity of the same; but anything posited in opposition is the negation of that to which it is opposed. Every determinate quantity is a non-totality.

4.) If, however, such a quantum is to be *posited in opposition* to the totality and thereby *compared* to it (in accordance with the rules governing all synthesis and antithesis), then some ground of connection between the two must be present, and it follows that this is the concept of *divisibility* (§ 3). The absolute totality contains no parts, but it can be compared to and distinguished from [such] parts, and the previously mentioned contradiction[198] can be satisfactorily resolved in this manner.

5.) In order to obtain clear insight into this point, let us reflect upon the concept of reality. The concept of reality is equivalent to that of totality. To say that all [I/2: 297] reality is posited in the I means that all activity is posited in the I; and conversely, to say that everything in the I is reality is to say that the I is *only* active. It is [an] [I, 139] I only insofar as it is active; and insofar as it is not active it is Not-I.

All passive affection is non-activity. Consequently, affection can be determined only if it is related to activity.

This corresponds precisely to our task, according to which an affection is supposed to be determined through activity, by means of reciprocal determination.

6.) A state of passive affection can be related to activity only on the condition that it possesses some ground of connection to the latter. This, however, can be nothing other than the general ground of the connection between reality and negation: namely, quantity. To say that it is by means of quantity that passive affection can be related to activity means that *passive affection is a quantum of activity*.[199]

7.) In order to be able to think of a quantum of activity, one must possess a standard measure of activity, that is, a measure of *activity as such* (which was spoken of above as the totality of reality). The quantum [of activity posited in the I] is, as such, the measure in question.

8.) If *all* activity is posited in the I as such, then to posit a quantum of activity[O] is to diminish activity; and, insofar as it does not constitute *all* activity, such a quantum is an affection, even though *in itself* it is still activity.

[N]   is nothing. (Non-being cannot be perceived.) [Added in C.]
[O]   then to posit a *quantum of activity* [Emphasis added in C.]

9.) Accordingly, an affection is posited by positing a quantum of activity — by positing the latter in opposition, not to *activity as such*, but to *all* activity.[200] That is to say, this quantum of activity, *as* such, is itself posited as an affection and is *determined* as such.

("*Determined*": All affection is a negation of activity. A quantum of activity negates the totality of the same, and, insofar as this occurs, this quantum pertains to the sphere of affection. — If this quantum of activity is considered as nothing but activity [and not as a determinate quantum of the same], then it does not belong *within* the sphere of affection, but is excluded from it.)

10.) We have now indicated an X[201] that is at the same time reality and negation, activity and affection.

a.) X is *activity* [*ist* Tätigkeit] insofar as it is related to the Not-I, since X is [I, 140] posited in the I — that is, in the I that posits and acts.

b.) X is *a state of being passively affected* [*ist* Leiden] insofar as it is related to the totality of acting. It is not acting as such, but is a *determinate* acting, a particular [I/2: 298] way of acting, which is included in the sphere of acting as such.

(Draw a circle = A and note how the enclosed surface of the same = X is posited in opposition to an infinite surface in an infinite space, which is what is excluded [from X]. Now draw another circle = B inside circle A. In this case the surface excluded from B = Y. Y is, in the first place, included within the surface circumscribed by A and is, along with A, posited in opposition to the endless surface excluded from A. To that extent, Y is completely the same as X. But, to the extent that surface Y is thought of as enclosed within B, Y is posited in opposition to an excluded infinite surface, including that portion of surface X which does not lie within B. Space Y is thereby posited in opposition to itself, for it is, on the one hand, a part of surface X and, on the other, it subsists on its own as surface Y.)

"*I think*"[P] is, first of all, an expression of activity; the I is posited as *thinking* and to that extent as *acting*. In addition, "*I think*" is an expression of negation, of limitation, of affection; for thinking is a particular determination of being, and the concept of thinking excludes all other types of being.[202] The concept of thinking is therefore posited in opposition to itself, inasmuch as it indicates an activity (when it is related to the object of thought) but [also] indicates an affection (when it is related to being as such), for being must be limited if thinking is to be possible.

Every possible predicate of the I indicates a limitation of the I. The subject — that is, the I — is what is purely and simply active or what exists [*seiende*] purely and simply. Any predicate (e.g., "I engage in representing," "I strive," etc.) encloses [I, 141] this activity within a restricted sphere. (How and by what means this occurs is a question that has not yet arisen.)

11.) One can now see with complete clarity how the I, through and by means of its own activity, determines its own affection and how it can be active and affected at the same time. It is *engaged in determining* insofar as it posits itself with absolute spontaneity as occupying a determinate sphere — a sphere that is only one of all those that constitute the absolute totality of the I's realities[203] — and insofar as what is reflected upon is nothing but this absolute act of positing,

---

[P] For example, "*I think*" [Added in C.]

abstracting from the boundaries of the same. The I is *determinate* insofar as it is considered to be posited within this determinate sphere, in abstraction from the spontaneity of the act of positing.

[I/2: 299]

12.) We have now discovered the original synthetic action of the I by means of which the contradiction in question is resolved, and in this way we have discovered a new synthetic concept,[204] which we must investigate somewhat more closely.

Like the previously discovered concept of causal efficacy, our new concept is a further specification of the concept of reciprocal determination, and we will obtain the clearest insight into both concepts [i.e., causal efficacy and the new concept we are trying to elucidate, i.e., the concept of substance] by comparing them with one another.

In accordance with the general rules of determination,[205] (1) both concepts must be the same as the concept of reciprocal determination; (2) both must be posited in opposition to the concept of reciprocal determination; (3) these two concepts must be the same, insofar as both are posited in opposition to reciprocal determination; (4) each of these two concepts must be posited in opposition to the other.

a.) These concepts are the same as that of reciprocal determination in the sense that in both them, as in the concept of reciprocal determination, activity is determined through affection and (which amounts to the same thing) reality is determined through negation, and vice versa.

b.) Both concepts are posited in opposition to the concept of reciprocal determination. This is because the concept of reciprocal determination posits only reciprocity [*Wechsel*][206] as such, but does not determine this relationship. It remains completely open whether there is supposed to be a transition from reality to negation or from negation to reality. In the two syntheses derived above, however, the order of reciprocity is fixed

[I, 142]   and determined.

c.) The concepts are the same in the sense that this order is fixed in both.

d.) They are posited in opposition to each other with respect to this same order of reciprocity. In the concept of causality, activity is determined by affection; in the concept just derived [viz., that of substance], affection is determined by activity.[207]

13.) Insofar as the I is viewed as comprising the entire, purely and simply determined domain [*Umfang*] of all reality, it is *substance*. Insofar as it is posited in a sphere (contained within the domain of all reality) that is not determined purely and simply (though how and by what means this sphere is determined is a question that remains for the moment uninvestigated), it is something *accidental*; i.e., *an accident is present in the I*. The boundary separating this particular sphere from the entire domain [of reality] is what makes an accident an accident. This boundary is the basis for the distinction between substance and accident. This boundary lies within the domain [of all reality], and therefore the accident exists in and in relation to [*in, und an*] the substance;[208] it excludes something from this entire domain, which is why what is excluded is an accident and not a substance.[209]

14.) No substance is thinkable without a relation to an accident, for the I first becomes substance by positing possible spheres within the absolute domain [of all reality]. It is through possible accidents that *realities* first arise, for otherwise all reality would be purely and simply one. The realities of the I are its ways of acting, and   [I/2: 300] the I is substance insofar as all possible ways of acting (ways to be) are posited in it.

No accident is thinkable apart from substance, since in order to recognize something as a *determinate* reality, I must relate it to *reality as such*.[210]

Substance is *all the reciprocal relations* [*Wechseln*], *taken generally*; [an] accident is a *determinate reality that is related reciprocally to another one, which is reciprocally related to it*.[211]

There is originally only one substance, the I.[212] All possible accidents, and therefore all possible realities, are posited in this one substance. — In due time, we will see how several accidents, *which are the same with respect to some characteristic feature*, collectively comprise the unified substance, and can themselves be thought of as substances, whose accidents are determined *by the differences between* [*other*] *characteristic features* [of these accidents considered as substances], features present alongside those features that make them the   [I, 143] same.[213]

> *Remark.* Several matters remain uninvestigated and utterly obscure, including that activity of the I by means of which it distinguishes substance and accident within itself and relates these to each other, as well as what occasions the I to engage in this action, which, so far as we can surmise on the basis of the first synthesis [viz., the synthesis of causal efficacy], might very well be an effect of the Not-I.
>
> Thus, as is normally the case in every synthesis, everything is correctly united and joined together in the middle, but not at the two extremes.[214]
>
> The remark illuminates a new aspect of the *Wissenschaftslehre*'s manner of proceeding: it will continue to insert new intermediate components [*Mittelglieder*] between those components posited in opposition to each other; however, the contradiction will not be completely resolved in this way, but only displaced and posited anew. If a new intermediate component is inserted between two components that have been united, but which further investigation has revealed to be not completely united, then, to be sure, this eliminates the contradiction in question. But in order to accomplish this one had to introduce new extremes [*Endpunkte*], which are once again posited in opposition to each other and must be united anew.
>
> The genuinely highest task and the one under which all others are subsumed is to answer the following question: How can the I have any immediate effect upon the Not-I or the Not-I upon the I, since they are supposed to be posited in complete opposition to each other? One inserts between them some X, upon which both have an effect and by means of which each therefore has a mediated or indirect effect upon the other. Nevertheless, one quickly discovers that this X must, in turn, also contain some point at which I and Not-I come into immediate contact [and thus contradict each other]. In order to prevent this, one avoids this sharp boundary by inserting a new intermediate component = Y. But it soon becomes evident that, just as in the   [I, 144] case of X, Y also must contain some point in which the two components   [I/2: 301] posited in opposition to each other come into immediate contact. And

things would continue in this manner forever were the knot not loosened but severed by means of an absolute decree of reason, not a decree pronounced by the philosopher himself, but one to which he merely calls attention: namely, that since there is no way in which the Not-I can be united with the I, *there ought to be* no Not-I at all.[215]

One can also view this matter from another angle, in the following way: — To the extent that it is limited by the Not-I, the I is finite; but in itself, that is, to the extent that it is posited through its own absolute activity, the I is infinite. These two aspects of the I, its finitude and its infinitude, are supposed to be united. But [as we will see in section E] such a union is impossible in itself. To be sure, the conflict may be ameliorated for a long time by introducing new intermediate components [*durch Vermittelung*]: the infinite restricts the finite. In the end, however, the complete impossibility of the sought-for unification will reveal itself, and therefore finitude must be overcome as such. All limits must disappear, the infinite I alone must remain as one and all.[216]

Posit *light* at point m in the continuous space A, and posit *darkness* as point n. Since space is continuous and there is no gap between m and n, there must necessarily be some point o, lying between m and n, which is at the same time both light and darkness, which is a contradiction. — Between light and darkness let us posit an intermediate component, *twilight*. If twilight stretches from points p to q, then at p it shares a boundary with light and at q with darkness. In this manner, however, one obtains only a postponement, and the contradiction has not been satisfactorily resolved. Twilight is a mixture of light and darkness. But clear light can share a boundary with twilight at point p only if p is at the same time light and twilight, and, since twilight can be distinguished from light only if twilight is also darkness, this boundary is possible only if p is simultaneously light and darkness. And the same is true of point q. — Consequently, this contradiction can be resolved only if light and darkness are not posited in opposition to each other as such, but can be distinguished from each other only in degree. Darkness is merely a very small quantity of light. — This is precisely the relationship between the I and the Not-I.

[I, 145]

[I/2: 302]

E. Synthetic Unification of the Oppositions Occurring between the Two Indicated Types of Reciprocal Determination.[217]

The I posits itself as determined by the Not-I. This was the major principle with which we began, one that could not be annulled without at the same time annulling the unity of consciousness.[218] Nevertheless, this principle harbored contradictions, which we had to resolve. The first question to arise was this one: How can the I be at once *determining* and *determined*? This question was answered as follows: by virtue of the concept of reciprocal determination, *determining* and being *determined* are one and the same. Accordingly, insofar as the I posits within itself a determinate quantum of negation it at the same time posits in the Not-I a determinate quantum of reality, and vice versa. But this raised another question:

Where should reality be posited, in the I or in the Not-I? This question was answered as follows by means of the concept of causal efficacy: Negation or a state of being passively affected is supposed to be posited in the I, and, in accordance with the general rule of mutual determination, the same quantum of reality or activity is supposed to be posited in the Not-I. — But this raised a new question: How can a state of being passively affected ever be posited in the I? And this question was answered as follows by means of the concept of substantiality: In the I, being passively affected and activity are one and the same, since being passively affected is simply a diminished quantum of activity.   [I, 146]

These answers, however, have sent us winging in a circle. *If* the I posits within itself a smaller degree of activity, then, to be sure, it thereby posits within itself a state of being passively affected and posits an activity in the Not-I. But the I cannot possess any ability purely and simply to posit a lower degree of activity within itself, inasmuch as, in accordance with the concept of substantiality, it posits all activity in itself and posits nothing within itself but activity. Accordingly, an activity of the Not-I must precede the positing of a lesser degree of activity in the I, and this activity of the Not-I must have first actually destroyed a portion of the activity any of the I before the I could posit within itself a smaller portion of the same. But this is equally impossible, since, in conformity with the concept of causal efficacy, an activity can be ascribed to the Not-I only insofar as a state of being passively affected is posited in the I.[219]

Let us explain more clearly the chief point at issue here, even if we cannot yet do so in an entirely rigorous manner.[220] If I may presuppose for this purpose a familiarity with the concept of time, [let us consider the following two cases]: In the first [I/2: 303] case, in conformity with the sheer concept of causal efficacy, suppose that the limitation of the I proceeds only and alone from the activity of the Not-I. Imagine that at moment A the Not-I does not exercise any effect upon the I, in which case all reality lies within the I, which contains no negation at all; in that case, according to the above, no reality is posited in the Not-I. Now imagine that at moment B the Not-I exercises an effect upon the I with three degrees of activity; it then follows, in conformity with the concept of reciprocal determination, that three degrees of reality are annulled in the I and three degrees of negation posited there instead. But in this case, the I comports itself purely passively. The degrees of negation are admittedly posited in the I, but they *are* also merely *posited* — i.e., they are present only *for some intelligent being* external to the I, an intelligence that observes the I and the Not-I in this causally efficacious operation and judges in accordance with the rule of reciprocal determination. The degrees of negation are not, however, present *for the I itself.* For this, the I would have to compare its state at moment A with its state at moment B and be able to distinguish the different quanta of its activity at both moments, and it has not yet been indicated how this might be possible. In the case we have here been considering, the I would certainly be limited, [I, 147] but it would not be conscious of its limitation. To employ the terminology of our proposition, the I would indeed be *determined* but *it would not posit itself* as determined, though some being external to the I could posit it as determined.

Or, in the second case, in conformity with the pure concept of substantiality, suppose that the I possesses the ability to posit a lesser quantum of reality within itself and to do so voluntarily [*willkürlich*], purely and simply, and independently of any influence by the Not-I. This is the presupposition of transcendent[Q] idealism[221] and, more specifically, of the [doctrine of] pre-established harmony, which is such an idealism.[222] Here we are abstracting completely from the fact that this presupposition already contradicts the absolutely first foundational principle [of the *Wissenschaftslehre*].[223] In addition, suppose that the I possesses the ability to compare this diminished quantity [of reality] with the absolute totality [of reality] and to measure itself by the latter. Under this presupposition, suppose that at moment A the I possesses two degrees of diminished reality and at moment B three degrees. In this case it is easily understandable how the I could judge itself to be limited at both moments and more limited in moment B than in moment A. But it is by no means evident how the I could refer this limitation to something in the Not-I, as the cause of the same. On the contrary, it would have to consider

[I/2: 304] itself to be the cause of this limitation. Employing the terminology of our proposition, the I would then certainly posit itself as determined, but not as determined *by the Not-I*. (Of course, the idealist[R] denies the legitimacy of this reference to a Not-I, and he is consistent in doing so; but he cannot deny the fact of such referring, nor has it yet occurred to anyone to deny this fact. But the [transcendent] idealist still must at least explain this admitted fact, quite apart from the legitimacy of the same. But he cannot do this on the basis of his presupposition, and his philosophy is therefore incomplete. If, however, he also assumes the existence of

[I, 148] things outside us, as happens in the case of pre-established harmony,[S] then he is inconsistent as well.)

Employed separately, both of these syntheses thus fail to explain what they are supposed to explain, and the contradiction of which we previously complained remains: if the I posits itself as determined, then it is not determined by the Not-I; if it is determined by the Not-I, then it does not posit itself as determined.

I. Let us now exhibit this contradiction quite precisely.

The I cannot posit within itself a state of being passively affected without also positing activity in the Not-I; but it cannot posit any activity in the Not-I without positing within itself a state of being passively affected. It can posit neither without the other. It can posit neither of these purely and simply,[224] and therefore it can posit neither of them. Consequently:

    1.) The I does not posit a state of being passively affected in itself insofar as it posits activity in the Not-I; nor does it posit activity in the Not-I insofar as it posits within itself a state of being passively affected. It [therefore] does not posit at all. (It is important to note that what is denied is not the *condition* [*die* Bedingung] but *what is conditioned* [*das* Bedingte].) What is called into question is not the rule of reciprocal determination as such, but rather, the very application of the same to the present case.) This is what was just demonstrated.

  [Q] Reading, with *C* and *GA*, "*transcendenten*." *A*, *B*, and *SW* all have "*transcendentalen*," which is obviously an error.

   [R] the dogmatic idealist [Added in *C*.]

   [S] pre-established harmony, at least on the part of some Leibnizians. [Added in *C*.]

2.) But the I is supposed to posit within itself a state of being passively affected, and, to this extent, it is supposed to posit activity in the Not-I, and vice versa. This follows from the propositions that were previously posited purely and simply.[225]

II. The first proposition denies what the second affirms.

These two propositions are therefore related to one another as negation is related to reality. But negation and reality are united by means of quantity. Both propositions must be valid, but each must be valid only *partially.* They must [therefore] be thought of in the following manner:

1.) *Insofar* as the I posits activity in the Not-I, it *partially* posits in itself a state of being passively affected; but *insofar* as it posits activity in the Not-I, the [I/2: 305] I *partially* does *not* posit in itself a state of being passively affected, and vice versa.[T]

2.) Insofar as the I posits activity in the I, it posits a state of passive affection in the Not-I, but only *partially;* and insofar as it posits activity in the I, the I [I, 149] *partially* does *not* posit a passive affection in the Not-I. (This can be formulated as follows: There is posited in the I an activity that is not posited in opposition to any state of passivity whatsoever in the Not-I, and there is posited in the Not-I an activity that is not posited in opposition to any state of passivity whatsoever in the I. For the time being and until we have become more closely acquainted with it, let us call such activity the *independent* activity [of the I and of the Not-I].[226])

III. But such an independent activity in the I and the Not-I contradicts the law of positing in opposition, which has now been more narrowly determined as the law of reciprocal determination; therefore, such an activity specifically contradicts the concept of reciprocal determination, which governs our present investigation.

All activity in the I determines a state of being passively affected in the Not-I, and *vice versa.*[U] This is in accord with the concept of reciprocal determination. — But we have just established the following proposition:

A certain activity in the I determines no state of being passively affected in the Not-I;[V] and a certain activity in the Not-I determines no state of being passively affected in the I. This proposition is related to the preceding one as negation is related to reality. Consequently, these activities [that is, the independent activity, which does not determine a state of passive affection in the I or the Not-I, and the independent activity that does determine such a state] must be united by means of [reciprocal] determination; i.e., each can be valid only partially.[227]

The previously mentioned proposition, the one that was contradicted, is the principle of reciprocal determination. This principle is [therefore] supposed to be

---

[T] and vice versa. (More clearly expressed: the [law of] reciprocal determination *is in a certain respect* valid and applied, but *in a certain other respect* it is not applied.) [Added in C.]

[U] in the Not-I ([that is, it] permits such a state of being passively affected to be inferred), and vice versa. [Added in C.]

[V] in the Not-I (does not permit such a state of being passively affected to be inferred); [Added in C.]

valid only partially; i.e., it is itself supposed to be determined; its validity is supposed to be limited to a certain domain by means of a rule.

Or, to express this in another way: the independent activity of the I and the independent activity of the Not-I are independent only *in a certain sense*. This will become clear at once, since:

[I, 150]   IV. According to what was said above, there is supposed to be in the I an activity that determines and is determined by a passive state of the Not-I; and conversely, there is supposed to be in the Not-I an activity that determines and is determined by the I's state of being passively affected. The concept of reciprocal determination is applicable to [the relationship between] this activity and this state of passive
[I/2: 306]   affection.

At the same time, both the I and the Not-I are supposed to contain an activity that is not determined by any passive state of the other, as was just posited in order to resolve the indicated contradiction.

These propositions are supposed to be compatible with each other; therefore, it must be possible, by means of a synthetic concept, to think of them as united in one and the same action. The concept in question, however, can be no other than that of reciprocal determination. The proposition in which both of these propositions would be thought of as united would be the following:

The independent activity is determined by reciprocally-related-acting-and-being-passively-affected [*durch Wechsel-Tun, und Leiden*] (that is, by acting and being passively affected, understood as mutually determining each other by means of reciprocal determination); and conversely, *reciprocally-related-acting-and-being-passively-affected is determined by the independent activity.*[W]

If this proposition is affirmed, it becomes clear

1.) in what sense the independent activities of the I and of the Not-I mutually determine each other and in what sense they do not. They do not determine each other immediately or directly [*unmittelbar*]; instead, they do so mediately or indirectly [*mittelbar*],[X] by means of their acting and being passively affected, conceived of as reciprocally related.

2.) [It also becomes clear] how the principle of reciprocal determination can simultaneously be valid and not valid. It is applicable to [the relationship between] reciprocal activity and independent activity; but this principle is not applicable to independent activity, nor is it applicable to the independent activity in itself.[228] Both reciprocal and independent activity are governed by the principle of reciprocal determination, but this principle does not apply to independent activity, nor does it apply to the independent activity.[Y]

[W] *independent activity.* (What pertains to the sphere of reciprocity [*Wechsel*] does not pertain to that of independent activity, and vice versa. Thus each of these spheres allows itself to be determined by the sphere posited in opposition to it.) [Added in *C.*]

[X] They do not determine each other *immediately* or *directly*; instead, they do so *mediately* or *indirectly*. [Emphasis added in *C.*]

[Y] nor does it apply to independent activity in itself. ["in itself" added in *B* and *C.*]

Let us now reflect upon the meaning the proposition just established. It contains [I, 151]
the following three propositions:

1.) An independent activity is determined by reciprocally-related-acting-and-being-passively-affected.

2.) Reciprocally-related-acting-and-being-passively-affected is determined by an independent activity.[229]

3.) Each of these reciprocally determines the other, and it does not matter whether one proceeds from reciprocally-related-acting-and-being-passively-affected to independent activity or, conversely, proceeds from the independent activity to reciprocally-related-acting-and-being-passively-affected.

I.

In the case of the first proposition, we must begin by asking what it really means [I/2: 307]
to say that an independent activity is determined by a reciprocally-related-acting-and-being-passively-affected. Following that, our task will be to apply this proposition to the cases before us.[230]

1.) Reciprocally-related-acting-and-being-passively-affected determines an independent activity as such.[Z] — Recall that we are concerned to determine the concept of reciprocal activity itself, i.e., to restrict[AA] its validity by means of a rule. *Determining,* however, involves indicating the ground [of a distinction or relation]. Thus, insofar as the ground for the application of this proposition is indicated, then the proposition itself is at the same time restricted.

That is to say that, in conformity with the principle of reciprocal determination, in positing an activity in one of the two terms, a state of being passively affected is immediately posited in opposition thereto in the other, and vice versa. The principle of positing in opposition makes it perfectly clear that, *if* any state of being passively affected is supposed to be posited *at all,* then this passive state must be posited in what is posited in opposition to what is active. But the question still remains unanswered, *Why* must any state of being passively affected be posited *at all*? Why not simply stop with activity on the part of one [of the two opposed terms]? That is to say, why should any reciprocal determination occur at all? — Being passively affected and activity are, *as such,* posited in opposition to each other; yet a state of being passively affected is supposed to be immediately posited by means of activity, and vice versa. Consequently, in [I, 152] accordance with the principle of determination,[231] they must be alike [*gleich sein*] in some third thing = X. (This third thing, X, makes possible the transition from the state of being passively affected to that of activity, and vice versa, without which the unity of consciousness would be

---

[Z] Reciprocally-related-acting-and-being-passively-affected determines an independent activity *as such* (i.e., a determinate *quantity* of reciprocally-related-acting-and-being-passively-affected is *posited*). [Emphasis and parenthetical clause added in *C.*]

[AA] i.e., *to restrict* [*zu beschränken*] [Emphasis edded in *C.*]

destroyed, and it must do this without, if I may put it in this way, producing any hiatus within consciousness.) This third thing is the *ground of the
relation or connection* [*Beziehungsgrund*] between doing and being passively affected in their reciprocal relationship to one another.

This ground of connection is not dependent upon the reciprocal determination [of acting and being passively affected]; instead, the latter is
dependent upon the former. The reciprocal determination [of these two
terms] does not make possible the ground of their connection; instead, it
is this ground that first makes possible the reciprocal relationship in question. Accordingly, though this ground of connection is indeed *posited* in
reflection[232] by means of the reciprocal determination [of activity and
being passively affected], it is posited in reflection as independent of this
reciprocal relationship and of the terms reciprocally related thereby.

Furthermore, this ground of connection is *determined* in reflection by
means of the reciprocal relation;[BB] i.e., if the reciprocal determination is
posited, then the ground of the connection [between the reciprocally
related terms] is posited within the same sphere as the sphere of reciprocal determination. This ground of connection, so to speak, expands the
circumference of the sphere of the reciprocal relationship in order to
establish the latter securely by means of this ground. The ground of connection completely occupies the sphere of determination, whereas the
reciprocal relation occupies only a portion of this sphere. This should be
clear from what has already been said, but it needs to be recalled here for
the purposes of reflection.

This ground [of connection between the reciprocally related terms] is a
reality, or, if one thinks of reciprocal determination as an action, it is an
activity. — An independent activity is therefore determined through
reciprocal determination as such.

(From what has been said it is also evident that the absolute totality of
reality is the ground of all reciprocal determination. This may never be
annulled, and this is why the quantum of reality that is annulled in one
[reciprocally related] term must be posited in the term posited in opposition to it.)

2.) Let us now apply this general principle to the particular cases that fall
under it, which is what we are now considering.

a.) Through the I's state of being passively affected, an activity of the
Not-I is posited, and this occurs by means of the reciprocal concept
of *causal efficacy* [*Wirksamkeit*]. This is a reciprocal relationship of
the type we have been discussing, by means of which an independent
activity is supposed to be posited and determined.

The reciprocal determination [in this case] proceeds from the state
of being passively affected. The state of passive affection *is* posited,

[I/2: 308]

[I, 153]

[BB] *determined in reflection* (aseigned its place in reflection) by means of the reciprocal relation
[Emphasis and parenthetical remark added in C.]

and activity is posited through and by means of this state of being passively affected. The state of being passively affected is posited *in the I*. It is completely grounded in the concept of reciprocal determination that *if* an activity is to be posited in opposition to this state of passivity, then this activity must be posited in that which is posited in opposition to the I, that is, in the Not-I. — In this transition there of course is and must be some connecting link or ground, which is in this case a ground of connection. As we know, this is [the concept of] *quantity*, which remains equal to itself in the I and in the Not-I, in the state of passive affection and in activity. This is the ground of the relationship [between the state of being passively affected and the activity], and it can appropriately be called the *ideal* ground of the same. The I's state of being passively affected is therefore the ideal ground of the activity of the Not-I.[233] — The operation we have now examined was completely justified by the rule of reciprocal determination.

A more difficult question[CC] is the following: Should the rule of reciprocal determination be applied in this case at all, and if so, why? It will be readily conceded that [in this case] activity is posited in the Not-I,[DD] but why is activity posited at all? This question must not be [I/2: 309] answered by appealing to the principle of reciprocal determination, but instead by an appeal to the higher grounding principle or princi- [I, 154] ple of sufficient reason.[234]

A state of being passively affected *is posited* in the I; that is to say, a quantum of its activity is annulled.

This state of passive affection, or this *diminution* of activity, must have *a ground*, since what is annulled is a *quantum*, and every quantum is determined by another quantum, thanks to which it is neither a smaller nor a larger quantum, but is precisely the quantum that it is. This follows from the principle of determination (§ 3).

The ground of this diminution cannot lie within the I,[EE] for the I posits within itself only activity and not a state of being passively affected. It posits itself only as existing [*seiend*] (§ 1). From this it follows that the ground in question does not lie within the I, a proposition that — thanks to [the law of] positing in opposition, according to which that which does not pertain to the I pertains to the Not-I (§ 2) — means that the ground of the diminution [of activity in the I] lies in the Not-I.

Here we are no longer talking about mere *quantity*; instead, we are concerned with *quality*. The state of being passively affected is posited in opposition to the essence [*Wesen*] of the I, insofar as this

CC An entirely different question [As altered in C.]
DD in the Not-I, once a state of being passively affected is posited in the I [Added in C.]
EE within the I (it cannot proceed immediately from the I, from the original essence of the same) [Parenthetical remark added in C.]

consists in being [*Sein*], and only to this extent could and must the ground of this passive affection be posited not in the I but in the Not-I. The state of being passively affected is posited as a quality opposed to reality, viz., as negation (and not merely as a lesser quantum of activity: see B, in the present section IV).[235] But the ground of a quality is called a *real ground*.[236] The real ground of the [I's] state of being passively affected is an activity of the Not-I, an activity that is independent of reciprocity and is already presupposed for the possibility of the same. And this independent activity if the Not-I is posited so that the passive affection of the I might have a real ground. — By means of the reciprocal relation discussed above [between the activity of the Not-I and the passive affection of the I] there is therefore posited an activity of the Not-I, which is independent of this reciprocity and presupposed by it.

(Partly because we have now arrived at a vantage point from which we can very conveniently survey the entire system, and partly in order to avoid providing dogmatic realism, even for a moment, with any confirmation that it might draw from the preceding proposition, let us once again explicitly note that the [preceding] inference to a real ground in the Not-I is based upon the fact that the I's state of being passively affected is something *qualitative* — which is something one must assume in reflecting upon the mere principle of causal efficacy — and that the validity of this inference therefore extends no farther than the validity of this presupposition.[237] — When we examine the second reciprocal concept, that of substantiality, we will see that, in reflecting upon this concept, the state of passive affection can be thought of only as something *quantitative*, that is, as a mere diminution of activity, and by no means as something *qualitative*. Accordingly, we will see in this reflection that when the ground disappears so does that which is grounded upon it, and the Not-I will again become a purely ideal ground. — To put the point succinctly: If the explanation of representation, i.e., speculative philosophy[238] in its entirety, proceeds from the fact that the Not-I is posited as the cause of representation, which is posited as the effect of the same, then the Not-I is the real ground of everything; it exists purely and simply because it exists and as what it is: Spinoza's *fatum*.[239] The I itself is [in this case] merely an accident of the Not-I and by no means a substance. In this manner we obtain a materialistic Spinozism,[240] which is a form of dogmatic realism, a system that presupposes the absence of the highest possible abstraction, namely, abstraction from the Not-I, and is completely baseless and ungrounded, since it fails to establish the ultimate ground. — If, on the other hand, the explanation of representation proceeds from the I as the substance of representation and from representation as a mere accident of the I, then the Not-I is by no means the real ground of the representation, but only its ideal

[I/2: 310]

[I, 155]

ground, and therefore the Not-I possesses no reality whatsoever apart from the representation. The Not-I is not a substance, not something self-subsistent nor posited purely and simply; instead, it is merely an accident of the I. Such a system, however, can provide no ground whatsoever for the limitation of reality in the I, i.e., for that affection through which representation arises. Any inquiry into the same is completely blocked in this case. Such a system would be a form of dogmatic idealism,[241] which has indeed engaged in the highest abstraction and is therefore thoroughly grounded, but which is still incomplete, inasmuch as it fails to explain everything that needs to be explained. From this it follows that the true point of contention between realism and idealism concerns the path one should take in [I, 156] order to explain representation. It will become evident that this question remains completely unanswered in the theoretical part of our *Wissenschaftslehre*; or rather, it is there answered by claiming that both paths are correct: under a certain condition one is required to proceed along one path and under another, opposing condition, one is required to proceed along another path. In this manner, human reason — which is to say, all finite reason — falls into contradiction with itself and is caught in a circle. A system that arrives at this [I/2: 311] conclusion is a form of Critical idealism,[242] which has been most consistently and completely established by Kant. This conflict of reason with itself must be resolved, even if it should turn out to be impossible to do so in the theoretical *Wissenschaftslehre*; and, since the absolute being of the I cannot be sacrificed, the conflict must be decided to the advantage of the second-mentioned manner of inference, just as in dogmatic idealism — with the difference that our idealism is not dogmatic but practical; it does not determine what *is*, but what *ought to be*. But this must be accomplished in a manner that explains what needs to be explained, which is something dogmatism is unable to accomplish. The diminished activity of the I must be explained on the basis of [*aus*] the I itself; the ultimate ground of this diminution must be posited in the I. Such an explanation proceeds as follows: the I, which is in this respect practical, is posited as something that *ought* to contain within itself the ground of the existence of that Not-I which diminishes the activity of the intelligent I.[243] This is an infinite Idea,[244] which cannot be thought of as such. By means of such an Idea one does not so much explain what needs to be explained as show *that* and *why* it cannot be explained. The knot [represented by this contradiction] is therefore not so much untied as it is posited into infinity). [I, 157]

An independent activity of the Not-I was *posited* through the reciprocal relationship between the I's state of being passively affected and the activity of the Not-I. This independent activity is also *determined* by the same reciprocal relationship; it is posited in order to provide a ground for the I's state of being passively affected. Hence the domain of this independent activity extends no farther than that of the I's state of passive affection. For the I, there is by no means any original reality and activity of the Not-I, except insofar as the I discovers itself to be in a state of being passively affected. No passive affection in the I, no activity in the Not-I. And this is also true even when what one is referring to is this activity [of the Not-I] considered as an activity independent of the concept of causal efficacy and hence as the real ground [of such causal efficacy]. Even the thing in itself exists only insofar as there is posited in the I at least the possibility of a state of being passively affected: this is a canon[245] that will first receive its complete determination and obtain applicability in the practical part.)

b.) By means of the concept of substantiality, the activity of the I posits and determines, in this very same I, a state of being passively affected.[FF] This activity and state of passive affection are grasped as reciprocally related to each other. Their mutual determination is the second of the two types of reciprocal determination mentioned above; and in this case as well, an activity independent of and not contained in this reciprocal relationship is also supposed to be posited and determined by means of this reciprocal relationship.

[I/2: 312]

The state of being passively affected and activity are, as such, posited in opposition to each other; and, as we saw above, through one and the same action in which a determinate quantum of activity is posited in the one term, an equal quantum of passive affection is surely posited in the term posited in opposition thereto, and vice versa. But it is contradictory to claim that, by means of one and the same action, a state of being passively affected and activity are both posited in one and the same thing, rather than in things posited in opposition to each other.

[I, 158]

This is precisely the contradiction that was previously annulled by deducing the concept of substantiality as such, inasmuch as being passively affected, considered in itself and in accordance with its quality, is supposed to be nothing whatsoever but activity, whereas, with respect to its quantity, passive affection is supposed to be a quantity of activity less than the totality of the same. In this way it is easy enough to comprehend, in a general manner, how a diminished quantity measures itself against an absolute totality and can be posited *as* a diminished quantity, since it is not equal to this totality with respect to its quantity.

The ground of connection between the two is, in this case,[246] activity. The totality as well as the non-totality of both is activity.

[FF] the activity of the I (accident of the I) posits and determines, in the this very same I, a state of being passively affected (a negation). [Parenthetical additions in C.]

But activity — and indeed, in this case as well, an activity that is not equal to the totality of activity, but is limited — is also supposed to be posited in the Not-I as well. This raises the question, How is a limited activity of the I to be distinguished from a limited activity of the Not-I? That is to say, how, under this condition, are the I and the Not-I still to be distinguished from each other as such, now that we have eliminated as a ground of their distinction the claim that the I is supposed to be active and the Not-I is supposed to be passively affected?[GG]

If it is impossible to distinguish the I and the Not-I, then the requisite reciprocal determination is also impossible, and none of the determinations derived from this reciprocal determination are possible at all. The activity of the Not-I is determined by the I's state of being passively affected; the I's state of passive affection, however, is determined by that quantity of *its* activity which remains following the diminution [of the totality of activity]. In this case, it is indeed presupposed for the possibility of any connection to the absolute [I/2: 313] totality of the I that the diminished activity is an activity of the I[HH] — and an activity of precisely the same I in which the absolute total- [I, p. 159] ity is posited. — Diminished activity is posited in opposition to the totality of activity. This totality, however, is posited in the I; hence, in accordance with the preceding rule of positing in opposition, what is posited in opposition to the totality, namely, the diminished activity, should be posited in the Not-I. But if it were to be posited in the Not-I, then there would be no ground of connection which would bind it to the absolute totality, in which case the reciprocal determination would not occur and everything derived so far would be annulled.

Consequently, the diminished activity, which, qua *activity as such*, would not be capable of being connected with the totality, must retain a character that is capable of furnishing the ground for such a connection. In this way, it would become an activity of the I and by no means of the Not-I. The character of the I, however, which can certainly not be ascribed to the Not-I, is that of *positing*[II] *purely and simply and without any ground* (§ 1). This diminished activity must therefore be *absolute*.

"Absolutely and without any ground" means (§ 3) "entirely unrestricted"; yet this action of the I is supposed to be restricted. The response [to this implicit contradiction] is as follows: Only insofar as it is an instance of acting at all, and no further, is this action of the I supposed to be restricted by no ground or condition. The I can act or not act; this action, as such, occurs with absolute spontaneity. But

---

[GG] (a point I beg the reader not to overlook). [Added in *C*.]
[HH] activity *of the I* [Emphasis added in *C*.]
[II] *positing and being-posited* [edded in *C*.]

insofar as this same action is supposed to be directed at some object, it is restricted. The I could have not acted[JJ] (if, that is, one is for a moment willing to think of such an affection as occurring without being reflectively appropriated by the I). But *if* the I ever does act, then its action *must* be directed precisely at this object and no other.[247]

In this manner, an independent activity [of the I] is *posited* through the indicated reciprocal determination. That is to say, the activity that is involved in the reciprocal relationship is itself independent — not insofar as it is *involved in this reciprocal relationship*, but only insofar as it is *activity*. Insofar as it is enters into this reciprocal relationship, it is limited, and to this extent it is in a state of being passively affected.[KK]

This independent activity is further determined by means of reciprocity: namely, in pure reflection. In order to make this reciprocal relationship possible, the activity must be taken to be absolute. What is established thereby is not *absolute activity as such,* but an *absolute activity that determines a reciprocal relationship.* (As we will see later, this absolute activity is called the power of imagination [*Einbildungskraft*].[248]) Such an activity, however, is posited only in order to determine[249] a reciprocal relationship, and its domain is therefore determined by that of this reciprocal relationship itself.

[I, 160]

[I/2: 314]

II.

Reciprocally-related-acting-and-being-passively-affected is determined by an independent activity: This is the second proposition we have to explicate.

1.) Our first task is to explain this proposition as such and carefully distinguish its meaning from that of the preceding proposition.[250]

The previous proposition proceeded from the reciprocal relationship between activity and being passively affected, which it presupposed. Hence it was by no means concerned with the form of this relationship, qua a merely reciprocal relationship (a movement of transition from one term to the other), but with the *content* [*Materie*] of the same, that is, with the content of the components involved in the reciprocal relationship.[251] It was inferred that, if a reciprocal relationship between activity and being passively affected is present, then the components [*Gliedern*] that can be exchanged [*verwechselt*] must be capable of being present as well. How are these components possible? It was in order to answer this question that we indicated an independent activity as the ground of this reciprocal relationship.[252]

In the present case, however, we will not begin with the reciprocal relationship, but instead with what first makes this reciprocal relationship possible *as* a reciprocal relationship, and we will be considering this with respect to its *form*, as a movement of transition [*Übergehen*].[LL]

[JJ] could also have not acted [Added in C.]
[KK] affected. It is considered in two different respects. [Added in C.]
[LL] as a *movement of transition* [Emphasis added in C.]

From this we will proceed to the reciprocally-related-acting-and-being-passively-affected. In the previous section, we were concerned with the [I, 161] ground of the *content* of the reciprocal relationship; here we will be concerned with the ground of its *form*. In this case as well, the formal ground of this reciprocal relationship is supposed to be an independent activity,[253] a claim we now have to demonstrate.

If we are willing to reflect upon our own reflection, we can make the ground of the distinction between the form and the content of the reciprocal relationship even clearer.

In the first case,[254] the reciprocal relationship is presupposed as *occurring*; hence we abstract completely from the way in which it might have occurred and reflect only upon the possibility of the components that are involved in this reciprocal relationship.—The magnet attracts the iron; the iron is attracted by the magnet: these two propositions are reciprocally related to each other [*die mit einander wechseln*]; i.e., each is posited by the other. This is presupposed *as an established factum*.[255] Consequently, we do not ask *who* posits one of these components by means of the other, or *how* this positing of one of them by means of another is supposed to occur in the first place. Instead, we only ask why [I/2: 315] the sphere of these propositions, each of which could be posited in the place of the other, includes *precisely both of these components*. They must each contain something that makes them capable of being placed in a reciprocal relationship with each other. This — that is, the content that makes them reciprocally related propositions — is what we are seeking to discover.

In the second case,[256] we will be reflecting upon the *occurrence* of the reciprocal relationship and therefore abstracting completely from the propositions involved in this relationship. The question is no longer, what justifies the claim that *this* proposition is reciprocally related to another? Instead, the question is now, *How* is a reciprocal relationship possible at all? And it will then become evident that there must be present some intelligent being, external to the iron and the magnet, who observes both, unites in its consciousness the concepts of them both, and is forced to assign to one of these concepts a predicate posited in opposition to a predicate assigned to the other ("attracts"/"is attracted").[257]   [I, p. 162]

The first case involves a simple reflection upon what appears — a reflection conducted by the observer. The second case involves a reflection upon the first reflection — a reflection, conducted by the philosopher, upon the character of the first observation.

If it is agreed that the independent activity we are seeking is supposed to determine the form and not merely the content of the reciprocal relationship,[258] then nothing prevents us from conducting our investigation according to a heuristic method[259] and proceeding in our reflections from the reciprocal relationship, since this will make our investigation much easier.

2.) Let us now apply the proposition we have just explained in a general way to the individual cases subsumed under it.

a.) In the reciprocal relationship of *causal efficacy* an activity is posited in the Not-I by means of a state of being passively affected in the I; i.e., a certain activity is *not* posited in the I, but is instead removed from the I and *posited* instead in the Not-I. In order to obtain the mere form of this reciprocal relationship, we must abstract not only from *what* is posited (that is, from the activity), but also from those components in which something is not posited as well as posited (that is, from the I and the Not-I). Nothing then remains but the pure form: *a positing by means of a non-positing,*MM i.e., *an act of transferring* [*Übertragen*]. This, therefore, is the formal character of the reciprocity involved in the synthesis of causal efficacy and hence the material character of that activity which reciprocates [*welche wechselt*] (in the active sense of accomplishing the reciprocal relationship).260

[I/2: 316]

This activity is independent of the reciprocal relationship it makes possible and accomplishes. It is not first made possible by this reciprocal relationship.

This activity is independent of the components of the reciprocal relationship *as such*, since it is by means of this activity that they both become reciprocally related components, and it is this activity [of transference] that places them into a reciprocal relationship with each other. Each of these components may very well exist apart from this independent activity; for this, it is sufficient that they be isolated and not be reciprocally bound to each other in any way.

[I, 163]

Positing, however, is characteristic only of the I; consequently, this activity of transference, which is a condition for the possibility of determination by means of the concept of causal efficacy, is an activity that pertains *to the I*. The I transfers activity from the I to the Not-I. To this extent, it annuls activity within itself, and this, according to what was said above, means that the I, by means of an [independent] activity, posits in itself a state of being passively affected. The Not-I is in a state of being passively affected to the extent that the I is actively engaged in transferring activity to the Not-I: activity *becomes* transferred to the Not-I.

(For the moment, one should not be disturbed by the fact that this proposition explicitly contradicts the first foundational principle,261 from which, through our effort to explicate the immediately preceding proposition,262 we have now inferred an independent activity of the Not-I, an activity independent of any reciprocal relationship (see above, pp. 247). It is sufficient that this conclusion follows just as correctly from established premises as does the proposition that contradicts it.

MM *non-positing* (an attribution by means of a denial), [Added in C.]

At the appropriate time, the ground of the unity of both propositions will become evident, without the need for any ad hoc contributions on our part.[263]

One should not fail to take note of our previous claim that the activity in question is independent of the reciprocal relationship it makes possible.[NN] This means that there might well be another reciprocal relationship, one that is not first made possible by this independent activity.[264]

Despite all the restrictions to which the proposition in question may be subjected, we have obtained from it at least this much: that the I, insofar as it is in a state of being passively affected, must *also* be active, even if it is not *purely* active. And this may very well prove to be a most important result and one that will richly repay all of our investigative labors.)

b.) In the reciprocal relationship of *substantiality*, activity is supposed to be posited as restricted by absolute totality; that is to say, what is excluded from this absolute totality by a limit [*Grenze*] is posited as [I/2: 317] *not* posited by the positing of the restricted activity, and hence posited as absent from this restricted activity. The purely formal charac- [I, 164] ter of this reciprocal relationship is therefore a *non-positing* by means of a positing. What is absent is posited in the absolute totality, but it is *not* posited in the restricted activity. It is posited *as* not posited in the reciprocal relationship. In accordance with the previously established concept of substantiality, we have proceeded from positing purely and simply, and indeed, from a positing of the absolute totality.

From this it follows that the material character of that action which posits this reciprocal relationship itself must likewise be a non-positing by means of a positing — and indeed, by means of an absolute positing. We will here refrain entirely from any inquiry concerning the origin of the non-posited-*being* [*nicht-gesetzt*-sein] that is present in the restricted activity and can thus be considered to be already given, as well as from any inquiry concerning the ground of such non-posited-being.[265] We are presupposing that the restricted action[OO] is present, and in doing this we are not asking how it may exist or be present in itself. Instead, we are merely asking how it may enter into a reciprocal relationship with what is unrestricted [*mit der Unbegrenztheit*].

All positing as such, and absolute positing in particular, pertains to the I. The action posited by the preceding reciprocal relationship [of substantiality] itself proceeds from absolute positing and is therefore an action of the I.

[NN] from *that* reciprocal relationship *which it makes possible* [Emphasis added in *C*.]
[OO] the restricted activity [Changed in *C* from *begrenzte Handlung* to *begrenzte Tätigkeit*.]

This action or activity of the I is completely independent of the reciprocal relationship that is first posited through the [independent] action in question. This [independent] action purely and simply posits one component of the reciprocal relationship, namely, absolute totality [of action] — and in doing so it first posits the other component of this relationship *as diminished* activity, as less than the totality [of action]. We are not asking where this activity, as such, may come from; for this activity *as such* is not a component of the reciprocal relationship. It is such a component only as *diminished* activity, and it first becomes diminished activity through the positing of the absolute totality and by being related thereto.

The independent activity in question proceeds from positing; however, what it actually achieves is a non-positing. We could therefore describe such an activity as *an act of alienating [ein Entäußern]*. A determinate quantum of the totality is excluded from the activity posited as diminished; it is viewed as not contained in this activity, but as situated outside it.

[I, 165]

The characteristic difference between this *act of alienating* and the previously established *act if transferring* should not go unnoticed. By means of the latter, something is certainly also eliminated from the I; but one abstracts from this and reflects only upon the fact that what is eliminated from the I is posited in what is posited in opposition to the I. — Here, in contrast, [in the case of alienation], something is merely excluded, and in this case, anyway, we are not concerned with whether it is posited in something else or with what this something else might be.[266]

[I/2: 318]

A state of being passively affected must be posited in opposition to the indicated activity of alienating, and this is indeed the case: a portion of the totality *becomes* alienated, *becomes* posited as not posited. The activity [of alienating] possesses an object, and this object is a portion of the totality. The substrate of reality to which this diminution of activity or this state of being passively affected pertains, whether to the I or to the Not-I, is here of no concern to us, and it is very important not to make any inferences at this point other than those that follow from the proposition in question and that one grasp the form of this reciprocal relationship in its full purity.

(Every thing is what it is and possesses those realities that are posited when it is posited. A = A (§1). To say that something is an accident of something else is to say that it is not posited through the positing of the latter; it does not belong to the essence of what is posited and is excluded from the original concept [*Urbegriff*] of the same. This is the meaning of the term "accident" as we have now explained. There is, however, another sense of this term, one in which the accident can be ascribed to the thing in question and posited in it. At the appropriate time we will see what this implies.[267])

III.   [I, 166]

Reciprocally-related-acting-and-being-passively-affected [*das Wechsel*] and the activity independent thereof are supposed to determine each other reciprocally. Just as before, we must begin by investigating the general meaning of this proposition and then apply it to the particular cases subsumed under it.

1.) In both the independent activity and the reciprocally-related-acting-and-being-passively-affected we have once again distinguished two things: we have distinguished the form of the reciprocally-related-acting-and-being-passively-affected from its content; and, in conformity with this distinction, we have [also] distinguished an independent activity that determined the form of the reciprocally-related-acting-and-being-passively affected from another independent activity, one that is determined in reflection by the content of the reciprocally-related-acting-and-being-passively-affected.[268] For this reason, we cannot immediately investigate the proposition we are attempting to elucidate in the form in which we have expressed it, since [I/2: 319] any talk about reciprocally-related-acting-and-being-passively-affected is now ambiguous, depending upon whether we are attending to the form or to the content of the same, and the same is true of the independent activity. Consequently, the first thing we must do is unite form and content, [both in reciprocally-related-acting-and-being-passively-affected and in the independent activity], and this can be accomplished only by means of the principle of reciprocal determination [*Satz der Wechselbestimmung*]. The proposition that reciprocally-related-acting-and-being-passively-affected and the independent activity reciprocally determine each other must therefore contain, in turn, the following three propositions:

α.) The activity independent of the form of the reciprocally-related-acting-and-being-passively-affected determines the activity independent of the content of the reciprocally related terms, and vice versa; in other words, these two independent activities mutually determine each other and are [therefore] synthetically united.

β.) The form of the reciprocally-related-acting-and-being-passively-affected determines the content of the same, and vice versa; in other words, they mutually determine each other and are synthetically united. Only now, for the first time, can we understand and explicate the following proposition:

γ.) Reciprocally-related-acting-and-being-passively-affected (understood as a synthetic unity [of form and content]) determines the independent activity (understood as a synthetic unity [of form and content]), and vice versa; in other words, they mutually determine each other and are themselves synthetically united.

α.) The activity that is supposed to determine the *form* of the reciprocally-related-acting-and-being-passively-affected, that is, the activity that is supposed to determine the latter *as* a reciprocally-related-acting-and- [I, 167] being-passively-affected while remaining an utterly independent activity, is a *transition* from one of the components comprised in the reciprocally-related-acting-and-being-passively-affected to the other, understood *as* an act of transition (and not, as it were, as an action in general). The independent activity that determines the *content* of the reciprocally-related-acting-and-being-passively-affected is an activity that posits in the components something that makes possible a transition from one component to the other. — The latter [independent] activity [i.e., the one that determines the content of the reciprocally-related-acting-and-being-affected] is the activity that provides us with the X we were previously seeking (above p. 245–6), an X that is included in both the reciprocally related components, and is included *only in both* and not in just one of them.[269] This X is what makes it impossible to be satisfied with positing one component (whether reality or negation), but requires us to posit the other at the same time, inasmuch as it reveals the incompleteness of either apart from the other. It is this Xupon which the unity of consciousness depends and must depend, if no hiatus is to arise within consciousness. X is, as it were, the *guide* [*Leiter*] of consciousness.[270] The first [independent] activity [i.e., the activity that determines the form of the reciprocally-related-acting-and-being-passively-affected] is consciousness itself, insofar as it depends upon this X, in addition to the reciprocally related components. This activity is one [*Eins*], even though it changes its objects (i.e., these reciprocally related components), and it necessarily must do so if it is to be one.

[I/2: 320]

To say that the first [independent activity] determines the second would mean that what undergoes transition is grounded in the movement of transition itself, that transition is made possible simply by transition itself.[A, 271] To say that the second [independent] activity determines the first would mean that the transition is grounded in that which undergoes transition qua action, that the transition itself is immediately posited simply by positing what undergoes transition.[B] To say that these independent activities mutually determine each other would be to say that the mere transition posits within the reciprocally related components that [X] which makes any movement of transition possible, and it also means that something is immediately reciprocally exchanged [*gewechselt*] between them simply by positing them as reciprocally related components. What makes the transition possible is the fact that it occurs, and it is possible only insofar as it actually does occur.[272] It is grounded in and through itself and occurs purely and simply because it occurs. The transition in question is an absolute action, with no determining ground or any external conditions. — The ground of the transition from one reciprocally related component to the other lies within consciousness itself and not outside of consciousness.[273] Consciousness, purely and simply because it is consciousness, must be engaged in a movement of transition; and were it not so engaged, there would arise within consciousness a hiatus, which would

[I, 168]

A (an idealist claim) [Added in C.]
B (a dogmatic claim) [Added in C.]

occur purely and simply because it would not, in this case, be consciousness at all.

β.) The form of the reciprocally-related-acting-and-being-passively-affected
and the content of the same are supposed to determine each other
reciprocally.

As was just observed, the *reciprocally-related-acting-and-being-passively-
affected* is distinguished *from the [independent] activity that it presupposes*
by abstracting from the latter (e.g., abstracting from any observing intellect, which posits — in its own mind — the components of this recipro-
cally-relating-acting-and-being-passively-affected as components that
are supposed to reciprocally determine each other). Instead, one must
here think of the components as reciprocally determining each other on
their own; [and in doing this] we are transferring to the thing something
that may perhaps lie entirely within ourselves. At the appropriate time we
will see to what extent such an abstraction is or is not valid.

Considered in this manner, the components reciprocally determine each
other on their own. The *form* of their reciprocity is their mutual *encroachment* [*Eingreifen*] and being encroached upon; the *content* of their reciprocity is the *acting-and-being-passively-affected* that immediately occurs
in both as a result of this encroachment and of this openness to being
encroached upon [*Eingreifen lassen*]. For brevity's sake, let us call this the
mutual *relationship* of the components that reciprocally determine each
other. This encroachment is supposed to determine the relationship of
the components and do so immediately and by means of nothing but the
encroachment — purely by means of the encroachment *as such*, without
any additional determination. Conversely, the relationship of the components that reciprocally determine each other is supposed to determine the [I/2: 321]
encroachment; i.e., it is posited that they encroach upon each other solely
through their [mutual] relationship, without any additional determination. Their [mutual] encroachment is already posited simply through their
relationship, here thought of as determining them *prior* to their reciprocally-
related-acting-and-being-passively-affected. (This encroachment is not, as
it were, an accident of the components, without which they could also
continue to exist.) At the same time, moreover, their relationship is also [I, 169]
posited through their encroachment, here thought of as determining
them prior to their relationship. Their (mutual) encroachment and (mutual)
relationship are one and the same.[C]

1.) These components are related to each other in such a way that
they reciprocally determine each other [*daß sie wechseln*], and apart
from this reciprocal determination they have no mutual relationship
whatsoever. If they are not posited as reciprocally determining each
other, then they are not posited at all. 2.) At the same time, the content
of this reciprocally-related-acting-and-being-passively-affected, that is

---

[C] [No paragraph break at this point in C.]

to say, its content — that is, the quantity[D] of acting and being-passively-affected, etc., posited through it — is completely determined,[E] without the need for any additional contribution, simply by the fact that, with respect to its mere form, a reciprocal relationship is posited as such between them.[F] — They necessarily *determine each other reciprocally*, and they can do so in only one possible way, which is determined purely and simply by the fact *that* they determine each other reciprocally. — If they[G] are posited, then a determinate reciprocally-related-acting-and-being-passively-affected is posited; and if a determinate reciprocally-related-acting-and-being-passively-affected is posited, then they[H] are posited. These components and a determinate reciprocally-related-acting-and-being-passively-affected are one and the same.

γ.) The independent activity (as a synthetic unity [of form and content]) determines the reciprocally-related-acting-and-being-passively-affected (as a synthetic unity [of form and content]), and vice versa. In other words, they reciprocally determine each other and are synthetically united.

As a synthetic unity, the [independent] activity is an absolute *movement of transition*, and the reciprocally-related-acting-and-being-passively-affected is an absolute *encroachment*, which is completely determined through itself. To say that the former determines the latter would mean that the encroachment of the reciprocally determined components is posited simply through the fact that the transition occurs. To say that the latter determines the former would mean that the [independent] activity must necessarily make a transition from one component to the other simply insofar as these components encroach upon each other. To say that the transition and the encroachment determine each other mutually would mean that insofar as the one is posited so is the other, and vice versa. From either of the contrasting components one can and must make a transition to the other. Everything is one and the same. — The whole, however, is posited purely and simply; it is grounded upon itself.

[I, 170]
[I/2: 322]

In order to clarify this proposition and indicate its importance, let us now apply it to the propositions subsumed under it.

The [independent] activity that determines the form of the reciprocally-related-acting-and-being-passively-affected determines everything that occurs in the latter; and conversely, everything that occurs in the latter determines the former. With respect to its form (i.e., the mutual encroachment of the components), the mere reciprocally-related-acting-and-being-passively-affected is impossible within the action of transition, since the mutual encroachment of the components is posited precisely by means of

[D] *quantity* [Emphasis added in *C.*]
[E] completely *determined* [Emphasis added in *C.*]
[F] *with respect to* their mere *form*, a reciprocity *as such* is posited between them. [Emphasis added in *C.*]
[G] If *they* [Emphasis added in *C.*]
[H] then *they* [Emphasis added in *C.*]

the movement of transition. Conversely, the transition is posited by the mutual encroachment of the reciprocally related components; insofar as they are posited as encroaching upon each other, there necessarily occurs a movement of transition. No encroachment, no transition; no transition, no encroachment: these are one and the same and can be distinguished from each other only in reflection. In addition, the same [independent] activity [that determined the form also] determines the content of the reciprocally-related-acting-and-being-passively-affected. The reciprocally related components are first posited *as such* only through the necessary movement of transition, and, since they are posited *only* as such, it is only through this transition that they are first posited at all; and conversely, the activity that engages and is supposed to engage in the movement of transition is posited [only] insofar as the reciprocally related components are posited as such. One can therefore proceed from whichever of the moments that have been distinguished [in reflection] one wishes; insofar as one of them is posited, then so are the other three. The activity that determines the content of reciprocally-related-acting-and-being-affected determines this as a whole. This activity posits those components that can and — precisely for this reason — must be involved in the transition; therefore, this activity [that determines the content also] posits the activity of the form[274] [that is, the independent activity that determines the form of the reciprocally-related-acting-and-being-passively-affected] and thereby posits everything else.

The [independent] activity therefore reverts into itself by means of the reciprocally-related-acting-and-being-passively-affected, and the reciprocally-related-acting-and-being-passively-affected reverts into itself by means of the activity. Everything reproduces itself,[275] and no hiatus is possible in this case; from any of the components one is driven to all the others. The activity of the form [i.e., the independent activity that determines the form of the reciprocally-related-acting-and-being-passively-affected] determines the activity of the content, which, in turn, determines the content of the reciprocally-related-acting-and-being-passively-affected, which determines the form of the reciprocally-related-acting-and-being-passively-affected, and this form determines the activity of the form, etc. They all constitute one and the same synthetic condition [I, 171] [*Zustand*]. The action reverts into itself through a circular movement.[276] But what is posited purely and simply is the whole circular movement. It is because it is, and no higher ground for this movement can be indicated.

The application of this proposition will first become evident in what follows.

2.) The proposition that the reciprocally-related-acting-and-being-passively-affected and the activity that has until now been considered to be independent of this reciprocally-related-acting-and-being-passively-affected are supposed to determine each other mutually must now be applied to the particular cases that are subsumed under it,[277] beginning with the following:

a.) [This proposition must first be applied] to *the concept of causal efficacy* [*Wirksamkeit*]. — Let us investigate the synthesis posited in this concept in accordance with the schema we have just established: α) In the reciprocal relation of causal efficacy the activity of the form[278] determines the activity of the content, and vice versa. β) In the reciprocal activity of causal efficacy the form of the reciprocal relation determines the content of the same, and vice versa. γ) The synthetically united [independent] activity determines the synthetically united reciprocal relation of causal efficacy, and vice versa; they are themselves synthetically united.

α.) Considered simply with respect to its form, the [independent] activity in question — namely, the activity that had to be posited as a condition for the possibility of the reciprocal relation that was posited in the concept of causal efficacy — is an activity of *transference* [*Uebertragen*], *a positing by means of non-positing*. Inasmuch as something is (in a certain respect) *not* posited, something [else] is (in a certain other respect) *posited*. This activity *of the form* is supposed to determine the activity *of the content*. The latter was an independent activity of the Not-I, which first made possible that component [of the reciprocal relation of causal efficacy] from which this relation proceeded: namely, a passive affection in the I. To say that the activity of the content is determined, grounded, and posited[279] by the activity of the form is obviously to say that what is posited by the activity of the form, by virtue of its function of positing, is this very activity of the Not-I, which is posited only *insofar* as something [else] is not posited. (This is not the place to investigate what

this non-posited being might be.[280]) — A limited sphere is thereby prescribed for the Not-I; and this sphere is [a product of] the activity of the form. The Not-I is active only insofar as it is posited as active by the I (to which the activity of the form pertains), and this occurs by means of a non-positing. — If there is no positing by means of a non-positing, then there is no activity of the Not-I. Conversely, the activity of the content, and therefore the independent activity of the Not-I, is supposed to ground and determine the activity of the form and thereby determine the [act of] transference (the positing by means of a non-positing). According to everything said above,[281] this obviously means that the activity of the content is supposed to determine the transference as a *transference*; it is supposed to posit that X[282] which indicates the incompleteness of one of the components [involved in the reciprocal relation of causal efficacy] and thereby make it necessary to posit it as a *reciprocal* component — and, in doing this, makes it necessary to posit a second component as well, to which the first is reciprocally related. This [first] component is a state of being passively affected *as such* [*das Leiden* als *Leiden*]. In this manner, the Not-I grounds the *non*-positing and thereby determines and conditions the activity of the form. The activity of the form posits by means of a non-positing and purely and simply in no other way; but non-positing is conditional upon an activity of the Not-I, and the entire postulated action is therefore conditional upon this as well. Positing by means of a non-positing is confined to the sphere of an [independent] activity of the Not-I. — [I/2: 324] No activity of the Not-I, no positing by means of a non-positing.

(Here we are once again in the vicinity of the same conflict we objected to above,[283] albeit in a somewhat mitigated form. The result of the first sort of reflection[284] establishes a dogmatic idealism: *all the reality of the Not-I is nothing more than a reality that has been transferred from the I.* The result of the second sort of reflection[285] establishes a dogmatic realism: *there can be no transference unless an independent reality of the Not-I, a thing, is already presupposed.* The task of the synthesis that must now be established is no less than this: to resolve this conflict and to indicate a middle path between [I, 173] idealism and realism.)

These two propositions must be synthetically united, which is to say that they must be viewed as one and the same. This occurs in the following way: by virtue of the principle of reciprocal positing, that which is activity in the Not-I is, in the I, a state of being passively affected, which is why we could posit a *passive affection of the I* instead of an activity of the Not-I. By means of the postulated synthesis, therefore, passive affection of the I and activity of the I — non-positing and positing — are completely one and the same in the concept of causal efficacy. In the concept of causal efficacy, the proposition that the I does not posit something in itself and the proposition that the I posits something in the Not-I assert exactly the same thing. These propositions do not refer to distinct actions but to one and the same action. Neither grounds the other, nor is either grounded in the other, for they are one and the same.

Let us reflect further upon this proposition. It contains the following claims: a) The I does not posit something in itself; i.e., it posits this same thing in the Not-I. b) That which is thereby posited in the Not-I is precisely what[I] is *not* posited or negated by what is not posited in the I.[286] This action reverts into[287] itself: insofar as it is *not* supposed to posit something in itself, the I is itself the Not-I; but since the I is nevertheless supposed to exist, it must posit,[288] and since [in this case] it is not supposed to posit [something] in the I, it must posit it in the Not-I. Yet no matter how rigorously this proposition may now have been demonstrated, ordinary human understanding[289] nevertheless continues to object to it. We wish to discover the ground of this resistance, in order to quiet the demands of ordinary human understanding, at least until we can actually satisfy [I/2: 325] these demands by indicating the domain in which they hold sway.

[I] *is precisely what* [Emphasis added in C.]

The two propositions just established obviously contain an ambiguity regarding the meaning of the word "*to posit.*"[290] Common sense[291]

is sensitive to this ambiguity, and this explains its resistance. —

[I, 174]

The Not-I does *not* posit something in the I; in other words, it negates it. This means that, for the I, the Not-I is not engaged in positing at all, but only in annulling. Accordingly, the Not-I is posited in opposition to the I only with respect to its *quality*[292] and is the *real ground* of a determination of the I. — But the proposition that the I does not posit something in the I does not mean that the I is not engaged in positing at all; [for] it is indeed engaged in positing, since not positing something posits it as negation. Instead, this proposition means that the I is engaged in not positing only *in part*. It follows that the I is posited in opposition to itself not with respect to its quality but only with respect to its *quantity*;[293] it is therefore the *ideal ground*[294] of a determination within itself. — The I does *not* posit something within itself, and it posits this same thing within the Not-I: these two propositions mean the same thing. The I is therefore the ground of the reality of the Not-I in the same way that it is the ground of a determination within itself, the ground of its own state of being passively affected; it is the purely *ideal ground* [of both].

What has now been posited purely ideally [*idealiter*] in the Not-I is supposed to become the real [*realiter*][295] ground of a passive affection in the I; the ideal ground is supposed to become a real ground, and this is a claim common sense will never accept.[J] — Were we to concede that the Not-I should be understood in the sense in which it is understood by common sense and take it to be a real ground, which affects the I without any contribution from the latter (as a kind of stuff, as it were, which would indeed first have to be created[296]), we could then cause common sense great embarrassment by asking how this real ground is ever supposed to become an ideal ground[297] — which must occur if any passive affection is ever supposed to be posited in the I and raised to consciousness by means of this representation. As with the previous question,[298] the answer to this one also presupposes the immediate encounter [*Zusammentreffen*] of the I and the Not-I, and this is a question to which common sense and all its champions will never give us a well-grounded answer. —

[I, 175]

Both questions are answered by means of our [present] synthesis, and they can be answered only by means of a synthesis, which means that each question can be answered only by means of the other.

[I/2: 326]

The deeper meaning of the above synthesis[299] is therefore as follows: *the ideal and the real ground are one and the same in the concept of causal efficacy*[300] (and therefore everywhere, since a real ground is first present in the concept of causal efficacy). People do not wish to

---

[J] and this is something that cannot be grasped by the dogmatic tendency within human beings. [As revised in C.]

endorse this proposition, which grounds Critical idealism and thereby unites idealism and realism. And the reason for this reluctance is their inability to engage in abstraction.[301]

That is to say, when various things outside of us are related to one another in accordance with the concept of causal efficacy, a distinction is made between the real ground of the relatability [*Beziebarkeit*] of these things and the ideal ground of this relatability. (Whether this is legitimate or not will become evident in due time.)[302] There is supposed to be something in the things in themselves, independent of our representations [of them], thanks to which these things encroach upon one another without any assistance from us. But the fact that *we* relate them to one another is something that is supposed to have its ground within us, perhaps in our sensation. In doing this, we then also posit our own I outside ourselves, as[K] a thing that exists without any assistance from us — though who knows how. And now, without any assistance from us, some other thing is supposed to have an effect upon this I, just as a magnet, for example, has an effect upon a piece of iron.*   [I, 176.]

But the I is nothing outside of the I; instead, it is itself the I. If the essence of the I consists purely and simply in the fact that it posits itself, then *self-positing* and *being* are one and the same for the I. In the I, real ground and ideal ground are the same, — conversely, *not positing* oneself and *not being* are, for the I, also the same. The real [I/2: 327] ground and the ideal ground of negation are the same as well. Part of what this means is that the proposition "the I *posits* something or other [as] *not* in itself" is, once again, one and the same proposition as "the I is *not* something or other."

Accordingly, the proposition that something *is not* posited in the I (*realiter*) obviously means the same as the proposition that the I does not *posit* it in itself (*idealiter*), and vice versa: to say that the I does *posit* something [as] not in itself means that it is not posited in the I.

The Not-I is supposed to have an effect upon the I; it is supposed to annul something in the I. This obviously means that the Not-I is supposed to annul a positing in the I; it is supposed to see to it that

<hr>

[K] outside of ourselves, qua *positing subject*, as an *I, as* [As revised in *C.*]

* The following remark is intended less for my own listeners than for other learned and philosophical readers who may have somehow come across this book. — Most human beings would rather consider themselves to be a piece of lava in the moon that an *I.* This is why they have not understood Kant and have no inkling of the spirit of his philosophy. For the same reason, they will also fail to understand this presentation, even though it begins by reviewing the conditions for all philosophizing. Anyone who is not yet in agreement with himself on this point will be unable to understand any well-grounded [*gründliche*] philosophy and requires no such philosophy. Nature, whose machine he is, will surely guide him in all he must do, without any assistance from him. Philosophizing demands self-activity, and this is something one can acquire only from oneself. — If we have no eyes, we should not wish to see; but we also should not claim that our eyes can see.

[Addition to this footnote, in *C*:] Following its first appearance, this footnote was ridiculed by many individuals in the author's circle, who felt that it was directed at them. I would have preferred to remove it from this new edition, but, unfortunately, I am reminded that it is still apt.

the I does not posit something in itself. If what is supposed to be affected in this case is actually supposed to be an *I*, then the only causally effective operation that can possibly by exercised upon it is one that produces in the I a non-positing.

Conversely, a Not-I is supposed to exist for the I, and this can mean only that the I is supposed to posit reality in the Not-I, since there is and can be for the I no other reality than that which is posited by the I.

The activity of the I and the activity of the Not-I are one and the same: this means that the I is able *not* to posit something in itself only insofar as it posits it in the Not-I and that it can posit something in itself only insofar as it does *not* posit it in the Not-I. But, just as surely as it is an I, the I must always be engaged in positing [*überhaupt setzen muß*]; it does not, however, have to posit [everything] precisely *in itself.* — Passive affection of the I and passive affection of the Not-I are also one and the same. To say that the I does *not* posit something in itself is to say that it is posited in the Not-I. The activity and the passive affection of the I are one and the same, for insofar as the I does *not* posit something in itself, it posits it (i.e., it posits the very same thing in the Not-I).[L] The activity and the passive affection of the Not-I are one and the same. Insofar as the Not-I is supposed to have an effect upon the I and to annul something in it, the I posits this same thing in the Not-I. With this, the entire synthetic unity has been clearly presented. None of the moments in question is the ground of any of the others; instead, they are all one and the same.

[I, 177]

It follows that the question, what is the ground of the I's state of being passively affected?, can by no means be answered, and least of all can it be answered by presupposing an activity of the Not-I qua thing in itself; for there is no purely passive affection in the I. But another question does indeed remain: namely, what then is the ground of the reciprocally-related-acting-and-being-passively-affected that has now been established, taken in its totality? It is impermissible to claim that this reciprocal-acting-and-being-passively-affected is posited purely and simply as such, without any ground, and that the judgment that posits the presence of this reciprocal-acting-and-being-passively-affected is a thetic judgment; for only the I is posited purely and simply, and the pure I contains no such reciprocally-related-acting-and-being-passively-affected. It is, however, immediately clear that such a ground is incomprehensible in the context of the theoretical [portion of] the *Wissenschaftslehre*. This is because the ground in question is not subsumed under the first principle of the theoretical *Wissenschaftslehre*[303] — namely, "the I posits itself as determined by the Not-I" — but is instead presupposed by this principle. Consequently, if it should nevertheless be

[I/2: 328]

[L] it posits the very same thing in the Not-I. [As emended in *C*.]

possible to discover such a ground, it must lie beyond the boundaries of the theoretical *Wissenschaftslehre*.

With this, Critical idealism, which holds sway over our theory,[304] [I, 178] has been definitively established. Our theory is dogmatically opposed to both dogmatic idealism and dogmatic realism, inasmuch as it demonstrates both that the pure activity of the I is not the ground of the reality of the Not-I and that the pure activity of the Not-I is not the ground of the passive affection of the I. Regarding the question posed to Critical idealism — namely, what is the ground of the reciprocal relationship that has been assumed to exist between the I and the Not-I?[305] — Critical idealism confesses its ignorance and indicates that inquiry into this ground lies beyond the boundaries of theory.[306] In providing an account of representation, Critical idealism proceeds neither from an absolute activity of the I nor from an absolute activity of the Not-I, but from a determinate being [*Bestimmtsein*] that is at the same time an act of determining [*Bestimmen*], because nothing else is immediately contained in nor can be contained in consciousness. What may further determine this determination is something that remains completely undecided in the theoretical portion of the *Wissenschaftslehre*, and this incompleteness will drive us beyond the theoretical to the practical part of the *Wissenschaftslehre*.

At the same time, our frequent references to the "*diminished, limited, and restricted activity of the I*" become perfectly clear. This expression designates an activity directed at something in the Not-I, at an *object* and is therefore an objective acting. The I's acting as such, i.e., its positing, is by no means restricted and cannot be restricted; but its positing *of the I* is restricted, inasmuch as it must posit a Not-I [in order to posit itself].

β.) In the concept of causal efficacy, the form and content of sheer reciprocal-acting-and-being-passively-affected mutually determine each other.

We discovered above that it is only by means of reflection that [I/2: 329] sheer reciprocally-related-acting-and-being-passively-affected is distinguishable, as such, from an activity independent of it. If [on the other hand] the reciprocal activity is posited in the reciprocally-related components themselves, then one has abstracted from the [independent] activity and the reciprocally-related-acting-and-being-passively-affected is being considered purely in itself and as [I, 179] reciprocal-acting-and-being-passively-affected. At the appropriate time it will become evident which mode of reflection is correct, or perhaps that neither of them, employed on its own, is correct.[307]

Here again, in reciprocally-related-acting-and-being-passively-affected as such, the form of this reciprocity can be distinguished from its content. The form of reciprocally-related-acting-and-being-passively-affected is nothing but the mutual intrusion of the components of the same upon each other. The content is that within each component that makes their mutual intrusion possible and necessary.[308] — In the case of causal efficacy, the characteristic form of reciprocal-acting-and-being-passively-affected is a *coming to be by means of* a *passing away* (a becoming by means of a disappearing). — (It is vital to note that we are here abstracting completely from the substance that is affected, that is, from the substrate of passing away, and hence from all *temporal conditions*. If this substance is posited, then of course coming to be is, *in relation to this substance,* posited in time.[309] Nevertheless, no matter how difficult this may be for the power of imagination,[310] one must abstract from substance, since substance is not involved in the reciprocally-related-acting-and-being-passively-affected. Nothing pertains to the reciprocally-related-acting-and-being-passively-affected but what *enters into this reciprocal relation* [*das Eintreten*] and what is, as a result, *displaced* [*verdrängt*] and *annulled*. And this is all that concerns us here: namely, what enters into this reciprocal relation, insofar as it does so. For example, X negates −X. To be sure, −X was present *in advance, before* it was negated, and if it is to be regarded as something that exists, then it must certainly be posited in the preceding time, whereas X, in contrast, is posited in the ensuing time. In the present case, however, −X is not supposed to be thought of as existing, but rather as *not existing.* The existence of X and the non-existence of −X, moreover, by no means occur at different times, but at *the same moment.* It follows that, if nothing else is present which forces us to posit this moment within a series[M] of moments, then they simply do not occur in time.) The content of the reciprocally-related-acting-and-being-passively-affected we are investigating is *essential opposition* [*wesentliches Entgegensein*] (in accordance with a qualitative incompatibility).

[I,180]

[I/2: 330]

The form of this reciprocally-related-acting-and-being-passively-affected is supposed to determined its content. This means that the components are posited in essential opposition to each other because and to the extent that they mutually annul each other. The (actual) mutual annulment determines the sphere of essential opposition. If they do not annul each other then they are not essentially opposed (*essentiliter opposita*). — This is a paradox, which again and again provokes the previously mentioned misunderstanding, in which, on the basis of first appearances, one believes that we are here inferring something essential from something contingent. It is true that we do infer essential opposition from the annulment in question,

[M] as a *series* [Emphasis added in C.]

but not the converse: we do not infer the annulment in question from essential opposition. In order to make the latter inference, an additional condition would be required: namely the immediate influence of each essentially opposed component upon the other (e.g., in the case of bodies, the condition that they are present in the same space). Both items that have been posited in essential opposition to each other might well exist in isolation from each other and apart from any connection with each other, in which case they would still be posited in essential opposition; but they would not annul each other, since they are not connected. — The source of this misunderstanding, as well as the means to correct it, will soon become evident.

The content of this reciprocally-related-acting-and-being-passively-affected is supposed to determine its form. This means that being posited in essential opposition determines the mutual annulment, but only on the condition that the components are posited in essential opposition, and only insofar as they are so posited can they mutually annul each other. — If the annulment in question is indeed posited within the sphere occupied by the opposing terms as such, but is not supposed, as it were, to completely fill this sphere, but to fill only a smaller sphere within this larger one, the boundaries of which are determined by the additional condition that there is an actual influence [of one component on another]: if this is granted, then everyone will concede this proposition[311] without objection, and the paradox in question could be merely that we at first explicitly propounded it as a paradox. However: The content and the form of the reciprocally-related-acting-and-being-passively- [I, 181] affected are supposed to determine each other mutually; that is to say, their mutual annulment, and thus also their [mutual] encroachment and immediate influence [upon each other], is supposed to follow simply from their opposition to each other; and their opposition is supposed to follow from their mutual annulment. Both are one and the same; they are, in themselves, posited in opposition; they mutually annul each other. Their influence [upon each other] and their being posited in essential opposition are one and the same.   [I/2: 331]

Let us reflect even further upon this result. What is actually posited by means of this synthesis is the necessity of the connection between the components of the reciprocally-related-acting-and-being-passively-affected.[312] This is the X that indicates the incompleteness of one of the two components, and this is something that can be contained only in both. The possibility of separating a being in itself or on its own [of either of the components] from the reciprocally-related-acting-and-being-passively-affected is thereby denied: both are posited as reciprocally related components, and they are not posited at all outside of this reciprocally-related-acting-and-being-passively-affected. — That the components are posited in opposition to each other — that they are ideally opposed — is inferred from their being really opposed to each other, and vice versa. Being opposed to each other really and ideally are one and the same. — The offence[313] taken by ordinary human understanding at this result disappears as soon as one realizes that one of the components of this reciprocally-related-acting-and-being-passively-affected is the I, to which nothing *is* opposed except what the I *posits* in opposition to itself, and that the I itself *is* opposed to nothing to which it has not *posited* itself in opposition. This new result is therefore simply the previous one under a new guise.[314]

γ.) In [the synthetic concept of] causal efficacy the [independent] activity, thought of as a synthetic unity, and the reciprocally-related-acting-and-being-passively-affected, thought of as a synthetic unity, mutually determine each other, and these two synthetic unities constitute a synthetic unity.

We can call the [independent] activity, considered as a synthetic unity, an *indirect or mediate positing*[N] (the latter term being taken in the affirmative sense — a positing of reality by means of a non-positing of reality[315]). Sheer reciprocally-related-acting-and being-passively-affected, considered as a synthetic unity, consists in the *identity of essential opposition and real annulment.*

[I, 182]

1.) To say that the [independent] activity is determined by reciprocally-related-acting-and-being-passively-affected is to say that the *mediacy* of positing (which is what is actually involved here) is the condition and ground of the complete identity of essential opposition and real annulment. Being posited in opposition to each other and [reciprocal] annulment are one and same because and insofar as the positing [of the components] is a *mediated* positing.[316] — a.) Were there to occur an *unmediated* or *immediate* positing of the components that are supposed to be reciprocally related to each other, then being opposed and annulment would be distinct from each other. Suppose that the components of the reciprocally-related-acting-and-being-passively-affected are A and B, and suppose that, to begin with, A = A and B = B, but that subsequently, that is, after a determinate quantity [of time], A is also equal to −B and B equal to −A. In this case, both A and B, taken in their first meaning, could be posited without annulling each other. Here we would be abstracting from that aspect in which they are opposed. They would therefore not be posited as essentially opposed (that is to say, their essence would not be posited as consisting purely in their being posited in opposition to each other) and as mutually annulling each other; and this is because they were *immediately* posited, each independently of the other. But in this case, they would also not be posited merely as reciprocally related components but as realities in themselves (A = A, § 1). Reciprocally related components can

[I/2: 332].

[N]   *mediate positing* (a mediating attribution) [addition in C.]

be posited only *mediately*: A is equal to −B and is purely and simply nothing more than this, and B is equal to −A and is purely and simply nothing more than this. The essential opposition as well as the mutual annulment, as well as the identity of essential opposition and mutual annulment, follows from this mediacy of positing. b.) This is because, if A is posited only as the opposite of B and as capable of no other predicate whatsoever (including that of being *a thing*, which is a predicate that the power of imagination, not yet accustomed to rigorous abstraction, is always ready to add to the mix) — that is, if A is posited as real only insofar as it is not B, and if B is posited [as real] only inso-   [I, 183] far as it is not A — , then their common essence consists in the fact that each is posited by means of the *non-positing* of the other, and they are therefore posited *in opposition*. Moreover, if one abstracts from an active intellect, which posits, abstracts, and reflects only upon the reciprocally related components, then their common essence consists in the fact that they mutually annul each other. Accordingly, their essential opposition and mutual annulment are identical, insofar as and to the extent that each component is posited purely by means of the non-positing of the other and purely and simply in no other way.

According to what was said above, this is the case with the I and the Not-I. The I (here considered as absolutely active) can transfer reality to the Not-I only insofar as it does *not* posit this reality in itself, and conversely, the I can transfer reality to itself only insofar as it does not posit it in the Not-I. (Upon further determination of this last point it will become evident that it does not contradict the previously established absolute reality of the I.[317] Indeed, this is already clear to some extent, since what concerns us here is a *transferred* and by no means an *absolute* reality.) It follows that the essence of the I and the Not-I, insofar as they are supposed to be reciprocally related to each other, consists solely in the fact that they mutually oppose and annul each other. Accordingly:

The *mediacy* of positing (which, as will become evident, constitutes the law of consciousness: *no subject, no object; no object, no subject*) and it alone grounds the essential opposition of the I and the Not-I and thereby grounds   [I/2: 333] all the reality of the Not-I as well as of the I — insofar as the I is posited merely *as* posited,[318] or posited as an ideal reality. For what is absolute is not lost thereby; it lies in *the subject that is engaged in positing*. So far as we have advanced in our synthesis, this mediacy of positing is not supposed to be grounded in turn in what it grounds, nor can it be so grounded in accordance with the lawful employment of the principle of sufficient reason or grounding principle.[319] Accordingly, the ground of this mediacy lies in neither of the indicated components, neither in the reality of the Not-I nor in the ideal reality of the I [*in der idealen des Ich*]. It must therefore lie in the absolute I,   [I, 184] and this mediacy must itself be absolute; that is to say, it must be grounded through and in itself.

This inference, which is here quite correct, leads to a new variety of idealism, one even more abstract than the preceding one.[320] In the latter, an activity, which was posited in itself, was annulled by the nature and essence of the I. This activity, which was quite possible in itself, was annulled purely and simply and without any further ground, thereby making possible an object and a subject, etc. In this previous sort of idealism, representations develop *as* such from the I in a completely unknown and inaccessible manner, in accordance, perhaps, with a consistent and purely idealistic pre-established harmony.[321]

In the kind of idealism we are now considering, however, the activity, as such, contains its law immediately within itself: it is a mediate activity and purely and simply no other kind of activity; and it is so absolutely because it is so. No activity whatsoever is thereby annulled in the I; the mediate [activity] is present and there is not supposed to be any immediate [activity] at all. Everything else however — the reality of the Not-I, and, to that extent. the negation of the I; the negation of the Not-I, and, to that extent, the reality of the I — can be completely explained on the basis of the mediacy of this activity. According to this sort of idealism, representations develop from the I in accordance with a determinate and cognizable law of its own nature. A ground for these representations can be indicated, but not for this law.[O]

This latter kind of idealism necessarily annuls the previous kind, for it actually explains, on the basis of a higher ground, what was for the latter inexplicable.[322] The previous kind of idealism can [thus] even be refuted in an idealistic manner. The foundational principle of such a system [that is, of this new kind of idealism] would read as follows: *The I is finite purely and simply because it is finite.*

[I/2: 334]

Whether such an idealism ascends higher or not, it certainly does not ascend as high as we are supposed to ascend: that is, to what is posited purely and simply and unconditionally. To be sure, a state of finitude is supposed to be posited purely and simply; but everything finite is, in accordance with its very concept, restricted by what is posited in opposition to it, and absolute finitude is a self-contradictory concept.[323]

[I, 185]

In order to distinguish this from the preceding kind of idealism, which annuls something that has been posited in itself, and is called *qualitative* idealism, I shall call this new kind of idealism, which originally posits a restricted quantity, *quantitative* idealism.[324]

2.) The mediacy of positing is determined by the fact that the essence of the reciprocally related components consists in sheer opposition, which is the condition for the possibility of mediate positing. If the essence of the reciprocally related components consists in anything other than their sheer opposition, then it is immediately clear that through the non-positing of one of the components in its entire essence the other component would by no means be posited in its entire essence, and vice versa. If, however, the essence of the components consists in nothing other than their sheer opposition, then, if they are to be posited at all, they can be posited only mediately, as follows from what was just said.

[O] A ground for these *representations* can be indicated, but not a ground for this *law*. [Emphasis added in *C*.]

Here, however, [that is, in this section,] essential opposition, opposition in itself, is established as the ground of the mediacy of positing. The essential opposition in question occurs purely and simply^P and cannot be further explained; the mediacy of positing is grounded in essential opposition.

Just as the first kind of inference established a quantitative idealism, so this [new] inference establishes a quantitative realism, which must certainly be distinguished from the previously established qualitative realism.[325] According to the system of qualitative realism, the I receives an impression [*Eindruck*] from an independent Not-I,[326] which possesses reality in itself, and, by means of this impression, the activity of the I is, in part, driven back into itself. The purely quantitative realist confesses his ignorance concerning this point and recognizes that the positing of reality in the Not-I first occurs for the I in accordance with the law of the ground; but he claims that *a limitation of the I is really present*, without any help from the I itself, whether by means of its absolute activity (as in the case of the qualitative idealist) or in accordance with a law contained in the I's own nature (as in the case of the [I, 186] quantitative idealist). The qualitative realist affirms the reality of *something engaged in determining* independently of the I, whereas the quantitative realist affirms the reality of a mere *determination*. A determination of the I is present, the ground of which is not to be posited in the I; for the quantitative realist, this is a *factum*. He has no way of inquiring into the ground of this determination *in itself*; in other words, this determination is, for the quanti- [I/2: 335] tative realist, something that is purely and simply present, without any ground. To be sure, he must, in accordance with the law of the ground, which lies within himself, relate this determination to something in the Not-I, as its real ground, though he knows that this law lies only within himself and is not deceived by it. It should be immediately obvious to everyone that such a realism is the same as what was established above as Critical idealism, just as it should also be obvious that Kant established nothing else but this — nor could he have wished to do so, given the level of reflection at which he situated himself.* [I/2: 336]

The previously described [quantitative] idealism differs as follows from the [quantitative] realism just described: though both assume the finitude of the I, for the quantitative idealist this finitude is posited purely and simply,

---

^{P} occurs purely and simply in this system [Added in *C*.]

* Kant demonstrates the ideality of objects from the presupposed ideality of time and space. Conversely, we will demonstrate the ideality of time and space from the demonstrated ideality of objects. He needs ideal objects to fill space and time. We need space and time to be able to situate ideal objects. It follows that our idealism, which is not a dogmatic but a Critical idealism, goes a few steps further than his.

This is not the place to show that Kant also *knew* very well what he did not *say* (something that can, incidentally, be very plainly shown) nor to indicate the reasons why he could not say nor wish to say all that he knew. The principles that have been and will be established here obviously provide the ground for his principles, as anyone who familiarizes himself with the *spirit* of his philosophy can convince himself (though in order to do this one must also possess spirit). He said several times that in his *Critiques* he intended to establish only the propaedeutic to the science [of philosophy] and not the science itself, and it is hard to grasp why his imitators do not want to believe him on this single point.[327]

[I, 187]   whereas for the quantitative realist it is something contingent, which cannot
be further explained. Quantitative realism annuls qualitative realism as
ungrounded and superfluous, and it does this by completely explaining —
independently of qualitative realism, though it repeats the same error —
what it is supposed to explain: the presence of an object within consciousness.
I said that it commits the same error; namely, it simply cannot explain how a
real determination can become an ideal one, how a determination that is
present *in itself* can become a determination *for the positing I.* — To be sure,
it has now been shown how the mediacy of positing is determined and
grounded by positing in essential opposition. But what is the ground of positing as such^Q? *If* positing is supposed to occur, then of course it can occur
only mediately; but positing as such is, nevertheless, an absolute action of the
I, which, in this function [of positing], is utterly undetermined and undeterminable. This system [of quantitative realism] is therefore burdened by a
difficulty frequently mentioned above: the impossibiliyy of any transition
from what is restricted to what is unrestricted. [Quantitative] idealism^R does
not have to address this difficulty, since it completely annuls such a transition. On the other hand, however, quantitative idealism is annihilated by an
obvious contradiction: namely, that it purely and simply posits something
finite. — It is to be expected that our investigation will follow the same course
as before and that, by means of a synthetic unification of both syntheses, a
Critical quantitative idealism will reveal itself to be the middle path between
both modes of explanation.[328]

3.) Mediacy of positing and essential opposition mutually determine each other;
they occupy one and the same sphere[329] and are one. It is immediately clear
[I, 188]   how this must be thought of if it is to be thought of as possible: namely, *being*
and *being-posited*, ideal and real relationship, being opposed and being posited in opposition must be one and the same. Moreover, the condition under
which this is possible is also immediately clear: namely, what is posited to be
in a relationship and that which posits this are one and the same. In other
[I/2: 337]   words, what is posited to be in a relationship is the I. — The I is supposed to
stand in a relationship with some X (which must, to this extent, be a Not-I),
in accordance with which it can be posited only through the non-posited-
being of the other, and vice versa. Now the I, just as surely as it is an I, can
stand in a certain relationship only insofar as it posits itself as standing in this
relationship. Consequently, when one is speaking of the I, it is all the same
whether one says, "it *is posited* in this relationship" or "it *posits itself* in this
relationship." The I can be placed in such a relationship (*realiter*) only insofar
as it posits itself (*idealiter*), and it can posit itself in such a relationship only
insofar as it is placed therein. This is because no such relationship is posited

---

^{Q} *positing* as such [*das* Setzen *überhaupt*] [Emphasis added in C.]
^{R} *Quantitative* idealism [Added in C.]

by the sheer, purely and simply posited I, for such a relationship is in contradiction with the purely and simply posited I.

Let us now develop the important content of our [new] synthesis even more clearly. — Constantly presupposing the major principle of all theoretical operations, as established at the beginning of § 4,[330] from which we have developed everything else, but also presupposing nothing more this, I maintain that it is a law for the I that both the I and the Not-I are to be posited only mediately.[331] That is to say, the I is to be posited only by means of the non-positing of the Not-I, and the Not-I is to be posited only by means of the non-positing of the I. (In every case, the I is thus purely and simply *that which is engaged in positing* [*das setzende*], though we are abstracting from this in our present inquiry. The I is *what is posited* [*das gesetzte*] only on the condition that the Not-I is posited as not posited, that it is negated.[332]) — To express this in more ordinary language: the I, as it is here being considered, is purely the opposite of the Not-I and nothing more, and the Not-I is purely the opposite of the I and nothing more. No thou, no I; no I, no thou.[333] For the sake of clar- [I, 189] ity, we will, from this point on and in *this* respect (but in no other), refer to the Not-I as *object* [*Objekt*] and to the I as *subject,* even though we cannot yet indicate the appropriateness of these appellations.[334] The Not-I that is independent of this reciprocally-related-acting-and-being-passively-affected should not be called an object, and the I that is independent of it should not be called a subject. — Subject is therefore what is not object, and object is what is not subject, and up to this point no further predicates apply to either.

If one employs this law[335] as the ground for an explanation of representation, without inquiring any further concerning the ground of this law itself, then, first of all, one requires no influence of the Not-I (which is what the qualitative realist assumes) in order to provide a ground for the passive affection present in the I — and, secondly, one does not require even this [I/2: 338] passive affection (determination)[336] (which is what is presupposed by the quantitative realist) in order to explain representation. — Let us assume that the I, by virtue of its very essence, must be engaged in positing as such, which is a proposition that will be proven in the major synthesis that follows.[337] In this case, it can posit nothing but the subject or the object, and it can posit either of these only mediately. Suppose it posits the object: it then necessarily annuls the subject, and there arises within the latter a passive affection, which it necessarily refers to a real ground in the Not-I. In this way there arises the representation of a reality of the Not-I, independent of that of the I. — Or suppose that the I posits the subject: it then necessarily annuls the posited object, and once again there arises a passive affection [of the object], which, however, is referred to the activity of the subject; and this produces the representation of a reality of the I independent of that of the Not-I. (This is a representation of the freedom of the I, which, in the context of our present manner of inference is, of course, a *purely represented* freedom.) — Proceeding from the mediating component [*Mittelglied*],[338] we have completely explained and grounded the (ideal)[339] passive affection and the

[I, 190]   (ideal) independent activity of the I, as well as of the Not-I, which is certainly how such an explanation should be accomplished, in accordance with the law of synthesis.

The law in question, however, is obviously a *determination* (of the activity of the I, *as* such), and it must therefore possess some *ground*, and the *Wissenschaftslehre* has to indicate this ground. But if one does not introduce a new mediating component by means of a new synthesis (which is precisely what needs to be done), then the ground in question can be sought only in the factors [*Momenten*] *immediately restricting this determination* — that is, either in the *act of positing* or in the passive *affection* of the I. The quantitative idealist takes positing to be the determining ground [of the activity of the I in this case], thereby making the law governing the I's positing into the law of positing as such, whereas the quantitative realist derives the law of such positing from the passive affection of the I. According to the quantitative idealist, this is a subjective and ideal law, which is grounded purely in the I; according to the quantitative realist, it is an objective and real law, which is not grounded in the I. — But there is no way to investigate where the ground of this law may lie or even if it possesses any ground at all. To be sure, the passive affection of the I, which is described as inexplicable, must be referred to a reality in the Not-I, which is responsible for this affection, but this occurs purely in consequence of an explicable law of the I, one that is explained precisely by means of this passive affection.[340]

The result of the synthesis just described is that both the quantitative idealist and the quantitative realist are wrong[341] and that the law in question is neither a purely subjective and ideal nor a purely objective and real one, but that the ground of this law must lie at once in both the object and the subject. For the moment, however, we have no way of investigating how this it is possible for this ground to lie in both the object and subject, and we confess our ignorance concerning this matter. This is the position of Critical quantitative idealism, which we promised to establish above.[342] Since, however, the previously assigned task[343] has not yet been completed, and since many more syntheses still lie before us, we may in the future have something more specific to say about this kind of grounding.[344]

[I/2: 339]

b.) We will now deal with the concept of substantiality in precisely the same
[I, 191]   way we dealt with the concept of causal efficacy: that is to say, we will synthetically unite the [independent] activity of the form and that of the content; then we will unite the form of the mere reciprocally-related-acting-and-being-passively-affected with its content; and, finally, we will synthetically unite the two synthetic unities produced in this way.

α.) Let us begin with the [independent] activity of the form and the [independent] activity of the content (presupposing that one is familiar from the foregoing with the sense in which these terms are here being employed).

Our chief concern in this section, as well as in those that follow, is to grasp accurately and determinately *what is characteristic* of [the concept of] substantiality.[S]

According to the preceding, the [independent] activity of the form in this particular reciprocal relation [viz., that of substantiality] is an act of non-positing by means of an act of absolute positing: positing something as *not posited* by positing something else as *posited*, negation by means of affirmation.[345] — What is not posited is nevertheless still supposed to be posited: it is supposed to be posited as not posited. Accordingly, it is not supposed to be completely *annihilated*, as is the case in the reciprocal relation of causal efficacy; instead, it is simply supposed to be *excluded* from a determinate sphere.[346] It is negated, therefore, not by *positing as such* but only by a *determinate* positing. By means of this positing — which is determined in this, its proper function, and hence is also, qua objective activity,[347] engaged in determining — , what is posited (as posited) must likewise be determined; i.e., it must be posited within a determinate sphere, as filling the same. And this makes it evident how, by means of such positing, something else can be posited as *not* posited: it is only *in this sphere* that the latter is not posited, and precisely in this way it is posited as not posited in this sphere; i.e., it is excluded from it, since what is posited in this sphere is supposed to *fill* it. — Hence, by means of this action, what is excluded is not yet by any means posited in any determinate sphere, and the sphere of what is excluded acquires in this manner no predicate whatsoever other than a negative one: it is *not this sphere*. What sphere it may [I/2: 340] occupy, or whether it occupies any determinate sphere at all, is something that remains completely undecided purely by means of this positing [by means of not positing]. — Consequently, *the* [I, 192] *determinate character of the formal activity involved in reciprocal determination by means of substantiality is exclusion from a determinate and filled sphere, which, to this extent, includes the totality* (of what is contained therein).

The difficulty in this case obviously lies in the fact that what is excluded = B[348] is nevertheless posited, and it is *not posited* only within the sphere of A. But the sphere of A is supposed to be posited as absolute totality, from which it would follow that B could not be posited at all. Consequently, the sphere of A must be posited as at once totality and non-totality: it is posited as totality with respect to A, and it is posited as non-totality with respect to the excluded B. Yet the sphere of B is itself not determined; it is determined only negatively, as the sphere of Not-A.[349] Taking all of this into account, A would be posited as a determinate and, to this extent, total and

---

[S] (on account of its opposition to [the concept of] causal efficacy). [Added in *C.*]

complete part of an indeterminate and, to this extent, incomplete whole. The positing of such a *higher sphere, one encompassing within itself both what is determinate and what is indeterminate,* would therefore be that activity which makes possible the previously indicated formal activity [, that is, the independent activity of the form in the reciprocal relationship of substantiality]. This activity [through which a higher sphere is posited] would therefore be the activity *of the content*, which is what we are seeking.

(Consider a determinate piece of iron that moves[350] = C. Now posit this [piece of] iron purely and simply as = A, as an absolute totality, which is how it is posited through its sheer concept (conforming to the principle A = A, see §1). Movement = B is not to be found within this sphere. In positing A, you therefore exclude B from the sphere of A. Nevertheless, you do not annul the movement of the piece of iron = C. You by no means intend to deny utterly the possibility of movement; hence you posit this movement outside the sphere of A, in an indeterminate sphere, since you simply do not know under what condition and for what reason the piece of iron = C is capable of moving.[T] Sphere A is the totality of the piece of iron, and yet it is also not the totality, inasmuch as this sphere does not include the movement of C, which is surely also iron. You must therefore draw a higher sphere around both, a sphere that includes within itself both the iron that moves and the unmoved iron. The iron is a substance insofar as it fills this higher sphere (not, as one usually but erroneously thinks, insofar as it fills sphere A as such; in this respect [i.e., with respect only to A] it is a thing in itself[351, U]), and movement and non-movement are its accidents.[352] At the appropriate time we will see that non-movement pertains to it in a different sense that does movement, as well as why this is the case.[353])

The [independent] activity of the form determines that of the content:[354] this means that a more encompassing, albeit indeterminate, sphere can be posited only insofar as something is excluded from the absolute totality and is posited as not contained therein. A higher sphere is possible only on the condition of the occurrence of an actual act of excluding. No excluding, no more comprehensive sphere; i.e., no accident in the I, no Not-I.[355] The meaning of this proposition is clear at once, and we will simply add a few words concerning its application. — The I is originally posited as *self-positing*, and to this extent *self-positing* fills the sphere of the I's absolute reality. If it posits an object, this objective positing must be excluded from

[I, 193]

[I/2: 341]

[T] *since you simply do not know under what condition and for what reason the piece of iron = C is capable of moving.* [Emphasis added in C.]

[U] it is a thing that is determined for itself, through its own sheer concept, in accordance with the proposition A = A. [Added in C.]

this sphere and posited in a sphere posited in opposition thereto, that of *non-self-positing*. Positing an object is the same as not positing oneself. The present line of argument proceeds from this action: it asserts that the I posits an object, or excludes something from itself, purely and simply because it excludes it and for no higher reason. It is by means of this act of exclusion that the higher sphere of *positing as such* becomes possible (abstracting from whether what is posited is the I or the Not-I). — It is clear that this kind of inference is idealistic and coincides with the previously established quantitative idealism,[356] according to which the I posits something as a Not-I purely and simply because it posits it. Accordingly, in such a   [I, 194] system the concept of substantiality must be explained precisely as it was just explained. — In addition, it here becomes clear in a general way that, in relation to quantity, *self-positing* occurs in a double manner: once as absolute totality and once as a determinate part of an indeterminate magnitude — a proposition that may in the future prove to have supremely important consequences.[357] — It is furthermore clear that what is indicated by the term "substance" is not *that which endures* but rather *that which is all-encompassing*.[358] The distinguishing feature of endurance applies to substance only in a very derivative sense.[359]

The [independent] activity of the content determines and conditions the [independent] activity of the form.[360] This means that the more encompassing sphere — as a more encompassing sphere (which therefore embraces the subordinate spheres of the I and the   [I/2: 342] Not-I) — is purely and simply posited; and it is only thereby that the act of exclusion first becomes possible as an actual action (though only under a condition that remains to be added). — It is clear that this line of argument leads to realism, and indeed to a qualitative realism.[361] I and Not-I are posited as posited in opposition to each other: the I, as such, is everywhere engaged in *positing* [*überhaupt setzend*]. It is contingent that, under a certain condition — namely, when it does *not* posit the Not-I — it posits itself, and this is determined by the ground of positing as such, which does not lie within the I.[362] — According to this line of argument, the I is a being engaged in representing [*ein vorstellendes Wesen*], which must conform itself to the constitution of things in themselves.[363]

But neither of these two lines of argument is supposed to be valid; instead, they are supposed to modify[364] each other reciprocally. Because the I is supposed to exclude something from itself, a higher sphere is supposed to exist and be posited; and because a higher sphere exists and is posited, the I must exclude something from itself. More succinctly: there is a Not-I because the I has posited something in opposition to itself, and the I posits something in opposition to itself because a Not-I exists and is posited.[365] Neither   [I, 195] is the ground of the other; instead, they are both one and same action of the I, and they can be distinguished from each other only in reflection. — It is immediately clear that this result is equivalent to the previously established proposition that the ideal and real ground are one and the same[366] and that this result can be explained by that proposition. Critical idealism is therefore established by the present proposition, just as it was established by the previous one.

β.)   In the case of substantiality, the form and the content of the reciprocally-related-acting-and-being-passively-affected are supposed to determine each other mutually.

The *form of reciprocal-acting-and-being-passively-affected* consists in reciprocally related components mutually excluding and being-excluded by each other.[367] If A is posited as absolute totality, then B is excluded from A's sphere and posited in the indeterminate but determinable sphere, B. — Conversely, insofar as B is posited (that is, insofar as it is reflected upon as posited), then A is excluded from the absolute totality.[V] This means that sphere A is no longer absolute totality,[W] but is, along with B, part of an undetermined but determinable sphere. — It is important to take note of this last point and to grasp it correctly, since everything depends upon it. — It follows that the form of reciprocally-related-acting-and-being-passively-affected is mutual exclusion of the components from absolute totality.

[I/2: 343]

(Posit [a piece of] iron as such and in itself:[368] in doing so, you obtain a determinate and complete concept, which fills its sphere. Now posit the iron as moving: in doing so, you obtain a characteristic feature [*Merkmal*] [of this piece of iron] that is not contained in your [previous] concept and is, accordingly, excluded from it. But insofar as you nevertheless ascribe this movement to the iron, then the previously determined concept of iron is no longer determinate or determined,[369] but merely determinable.[X] It is lacking a determination that will, at the appropriate time, be determined as the ability to be attracted by a magnet [and hence, to move].[370])

With respect to the *content of the reciprocally-related-acting-and-being-passively-affected*, it is clear at once that in the form of this reciprocal relationship, as expounded above,[371] it remains undetermined which [of the two components] constitutes actual totality. If B is supposed to be excluded, then the totality fills sphere A; if, on the contrary, B is supposed to be posited, then the entire indeterminate but determinable totality occupies both spheres, that of B and that of A. (Here we are abstracting completely from the fact that the latter sphere, that of A and B, remains to be determined.) This

[I, 196]

[V]   *from absolute totality* [Emphasis added in C.]
[W]   This means that sphere A is no longer subsumed under the concept of the same [i.e., absolute totality]; sphere A is no longer absolute totality, but [As emended in C.]
[X]   no longer as determined but merely as determinable [As emended in C.]

indeterminacy cannot be allowed to remain. The totality is a totality in each case.[372] Were each of them to possess a distinguishing feature in addition to this [viz., totality], by means of which they could be distinguished from each other, then the postulated reciprocal relationship would be completely impossible; for in that case there would be but one totality [*ist die Totalität Eins*], and there would be only one reciprocal component, and thus no reciprocal relationship at all. (To express this in a more comprehensible, albeit less stringent manner: — Think of yourself as the observer of this reciprocal excluding. If you are unable to distinguish these two totalities, between which the reciprocal relationship oscillates,[373] then, for you, there is no reciprocal relationship. But you could not distinguish [these components] were there not, outside of them both, insofar as they are nothing but totality, some X, according to which you oriented yourself.[374]) Accordingly, the *determinability* of the totality, as such, must be presupposed for the sake of the possibility of the postulated reciprocally-related-acting-and-being-passively-affected. It is presupposed that one can distinguish these totalities from each other in some respect or another, and this determinability *is the content of the reciprocal relationship,* that which supports and underlies the reciprocal-acting-and-being-passively-affected [*dasjenige woran der Wechsel fortläuft*], and the one and only means by which it can be stabilized.

(Consider the [piece of] iron in itself, perhaps in the way in which it is given in ordinary experience, without any educated acquaintance with physics[375] — that is to say, as isolated and without any noticeable connection with anything outside itself and as, among other things, enduring in its place. When you posit it in this manner, [I/2: 344] movement does not pertain to its concept. And even if the iron is given within experience as moving, you are quite right in ascribing this movement to something outside the iron.[376] But when you nev- [I, 197] ertheless ascribe the movement to the iron, which you are equally correct in doing, then your previous concept is no longer complete, and you must determine it further in this respect and, for example, posit attractability by a magnet within your concept of the iron. — This makes a difference. When you proceed from the first concept [of totality], duration in place is essential to the iron, and movement is only contingent with respect to it.[Y] If, in contrast, you proceed from the second concept [of totality], then duration is just as contingent[Z] as movement,[AA,377] since the former stands just as much under the condition of absence of a magnet as the latter stands

[Y] *duration in place* is *essential* to the iron, and *movement* is only *contingent* with respect to it [Emphasis added in C.]

[Z] *duration* is *just as contingent* [Emphasis added in C.]

[AA] as *movement* [Emphasis added in SW.]

under the condition of its presence. You will therefore be disoriented, unless you can provide some reason why you must proceed from the first and not from the second concept, or vice versa — that is to say, you will be generally disoriented unless there is some way to determine upon which totality one has to reflect — whether upon the determinate totality that is posited purely and simply or upon the determinable totality that arises from this totality along with what is excluded [from it], or whether one should reflect upon both.)

The form of the reciprocal-acting-and-being-passively-affected determines its content. This means that it is mutual excluding that determines totality in the sense just indicated; i.e., it is mutual excluding that determines which of the two totalities is the absolute one, from which we must proceed. That component which excludes another from the totality is, insofar as it does this, the totality, and vice versa, and beyond this there is no further ground whatsoever for determining totality. — If B is excluded by A (which is posited purely and simply), then, *to this extent*, the totality is A; and if B is reflected upon (in which case A is not considered to be the totality), then, *to this extent*, A + B, which is in itself indeterminate, is the determinable totality. What is determinate or what is determinable is the totality, depending upon how one takes them up.[378] — To be sure, it seems that there is nothing new in this result, which appears to assert precisely what we already knew prior to this synthesis. Previously, however, we still harbored the hope of discovering some determining ground [of the totality in question]. But this hope is completely stifled by the present result, which has a negative meaning and informs us that no determining ground whatsoever is possible except by means of relation.

[I, 198]

[I/2: 345]

(In the preceding example, one can proceed from the purely and simply posited [determinate] concept of the iron, in which case what is essential[BB] is duration in place, or one can proceed from the determinable concept of iron, in which case duration in place is an accident.[CC] Both are correct, depending on how one takes them up, and there can be no rule determining where one should start. The distinction [between these two ways of proceeding] is purely relative.)

The content of reciprocal-acting-and-being-passively-affected determines its form: this means that mutual excluding is determined by the determinability of the totality (in the sense explained above), *which is therefore posited*, since it is supposed to determine something else.[379] (That is to say, the determination is actually possible and occurs in accordance with some X, the discovery of which does not concern us here.[380]) One of these two — either what is

---

[BB] what is *essential* [Emphasis added in C.]
[CC] it is an *accident* [Emphasis added in C.]

determinate or what is determinable — is absolute totality, which the other is therefore not; hence there is also something that is absolutely excluded: namely, what is excluded by this totality. If, for example, what is determinate is absolute totality,^{DD} then what is excluded thereby is what is absolutely excluded. — The upshot of the present synthesis is therefore this: there is an absolute ground of totality, a ground that is not merely relative.^{EE}

(In the preceding example, it is not a matter of indifference whether one proceeds from the determinate or from the determinable concept of iron nor whether one wishes to consider duration in place to be essential to iron or, instead, to be something contingent. Assuming that, for some reason or another, one must proceed from [I, 199] the determinate concept of iron, then only movement is an absolute accident, but not duration.)

Neither the form nor the content [of the reciprocal-acting-and-being-passively-affected] should determine the other; instead, they should mutually determine each other: this means — to get to the point without a lengthy detour — that the absolute and relative ground³⁸¹ for determining totality are supposed to be one and the same; the relation [*die Relation*] is supposed to be absolute, and the absolute is supposed to be nothing more than a relation.

Let us try to make this supremely important result clear:^{FF} Determining the totality at the same time determines what is to be excluded, and vice versa. This is also a relation, but there is no question concerning this one. The question is, which of these two possi- [I/2: 346] ble modes of determination should be adopted and affirmed? From the perspective of the first mode of determination [viz., "the form of the reciprocal-acting-and-being-passively-affected determines its content"], the answer would be: neither of them. Here there is no determinate rule other than this: if one adopts one of the components, then one cannot adopt the other, and vice versa. But one cannot affirm *which* of the two should be adopted. In the case of the second mode of determination [viz., "the content of reciprocal-acting-and-being-passively-affected determines its form"], this question would be answered as follows: one of the two must be adopted, and thus there must be some rule for doing so. But what this rule may be is, naturally, a question that must remain undecided, since *determinability* rather than *determination* is supposed to be the determining ground of what is to be excluded.

Both propositions are united in the present one, for what it asserts is that there should of course be a rule, but not one that establishes either of the two modes of determination; instead, it

---

^{DD} what is determinate is *absolute* totality [Emphasis added in *SW*.]
^{EE} there is an *absolute ground* of totality, a ground is *not* merely relative [Emphasis added in *SW*.]
^{FF} Clear. — The determination [Dash added in *C*.]

should establish them both, *as reciprocally determined by each other.* —
Neither of the totalities we have considered so far is the totality we
are seeking; instead, this totality is first constituted by the two of
them reciprocally determined by each other. What we are concerned
with, therefore, is *a relation of the two modes of determination* —
determination by means of relation and absolute determination,

[I, 200]

and the totality we are seeking is first established by this relation. A
is not supposed to be absolute totality, nor is A + B; instead, absolute totality is A determined by A + B. What is determinable is
supposed to be determined by what is determinate, and what is determinate is supposed to be determined by what is determinable. The
unity that arises in this manner is the totality we are seeking. — It is
clear that this must be the result of our synthesis, but it is somewhat
more difficult to understand what this implies.

What is determinate and what is determinable are supposed to
determine each other reciprocally. This obviously means that the
determination of what is to be determined consists precisely in
this: that it is something determinable. It is *something determinable*
and nothing more; this constitutes its entire essence. — This determinability is therefore the totality we have been seeking; i.e.,
determinability is a determinate quantum; it possesses its own
boundaries, beyond which no additional determination occurs,
and all possibility determinability lies within these boundaries.

Let us apply this result to the preceding case,[382] which will make
everything immediately clear. — The I posits *itself.* [= A]. The
purely and simply posited reality of the I consists therein, and this

[I/2: 347]

exhausts the sphere of this reality and therefore contains the absolute totality (of the purely and simply posited reality of the I).[383] The
I posits *an object* [= B]. This objective positing must necessarily be
excluded from the sphere of the I's self-positing. Yet this objective
positing is still supposed to be ascribed to the I, and in this way we
obtain the sphere A + B as the (as yet unlimited[384]) totality of the I's
actions. — According to the present synthesis, these two spheres are
supposed to determine each other reciprocally. A contributes what it
possesses: an absolute boundary;[385] A + B provides what it possesses:
content [*Gehalt*]. To the extent that *it posits itself* as positing[386] in
accordance with this rule, the positing I is now an object, and therefore
not the subject; or it is a subject, and therefore not the object. — In
this way the two spheres collapse into one another; only as united do

[I, 201]

they occupy a single *limited* sphere, and to this extent the determination of the I consists in its determinability by means of subject
and object.[387]

Determinate determinability is the totality we have been seeking,
and such a totality is called a *substance.*[388] — No substance is possible
as such unless there is a movement beyond[389] what is purely and simply posited, which in this case is the I that *posits* only *itself.* That is to

say, no substance is possible unless something is excluded from the self-positing I, in this case a posited Not-I or object. — However, a substance that is, as such, supposed to be nothing more than determinability, albeit a determinate, stabilized, and firmly established determinability, remains indeterminate. It is no substance (i.e., nothing *all*-encompassing) if it is not further determined by what is purely and simply posited, in this case by *self-positing*. The I *posits itself* — either as *self-positing*, which it accomplishes by excluding the Not-I,[GG] which it accomplished by excluding itself. — "*Self-positing*" here occurs twice over here, but in two very different respects: the first kind of self-positing is an *unconditioned* positing, whereas the second is a *conditioned* positing, determinable by excluding the Not-I.[390]

(If the determination of the [piece of] iron in itself is *duration in place*, this means that alteration of place is thereby excluded. The iron is, to this extent, *not substance*, since it is *not determinable*. Alteration of place is nevertheless now supposed to be ascribed to the iron. This is not possible in the sense that duration in place is supposed to be completely annulled thereby, since the iron itself, in the sense in which it is posited, would thereby be annulled; and the alteration of place would therefore not be ascribed to the iron, which contradicts what is requested.[391] It follows that duration can be annulled only in part, and that alteration of place becomes determined and bounded by duration, which is to say that alteration of [I/2: 348] place occurs only within the sphere dependent upon a certain condition — e.g., the presence of a magnet — and does not occur out- [I, 202] side this sphere. Outside this sphere there is once again duration. — Who cannot see that the term "duration" is here employed in two very different senses: first as unconditioned and then as conditional upon the absence of a magnet?)[HH, 392]

Let us continue our discussion of the application of the foundational principle just established.[393] Just as A + B is determined by A, so is B itself determined [by A], since it lies within the circumference of the now determinate determinable [totality]; and, as we have just shown, A itself is now determinable. Now insofar as B is itself determined, A + B can also be determined by B, and it *must* be determined by B, since an absolute relation occurs, which alone is supposed to occupy the totality we have been seeking. *Consequently, when A + B is posited, and when A is, to this extent, posited within the sphere of what is determinable, then A + B is, in turn, determined by B.*

This proposition will become clear at once if we apply it to the preceding case. — The I is supposed to exclude something from

---

[GG] *or as positing the Not-I* [Emphasis added in C.]
[HH] *conditional upon the absence of a magnet* [Emphasis added in C.]

itself: this is the action that we have, until now, considered to be the first moment[394] of the entire reciprocally-related-acting-and-being-passively-affected we are investigating. I will now proceed to a further inference — which I am entitled to do, since we are now in the space of reason:[395] if the I is supposed to exclude something from itself, then this must be posited as lying within the I prior to the act of excluding, i.e., *independently* of the same. Since we can indicate no higher ground for this positing [within the I of what will subsequently be excluded from it], it must here be posited purely and simply. Proceeding from this point, *the I's act of excluding* is something that is not posited in what is posited purely and simply, insofar as it is purely and simply posited, and it must be excluded from the sphere of the latter as inessential thereto.[396] (When, in order to make possible its exclusion from the I, an object is immediately posited in the I — albeit in a manner that is, for us, completely incomprehensible — and to the extent that it is indeed supposed to be an object: in that case it is *contingent* that it is excluded [from the I] and that, in consequence of this act of excluding, it is *represented*, as will become evident later.[397] In itself — not outside the I, but within it — this object would be present if this act of excluding had not occurred. The object as such — in this case, B — is what is determinate; what is excluded by the subject — in this case, B + A — is what is determinable. The object can be excluded or not excluded; in either case it remains an object in the sense indicated above.[398] — The posited being of the object here appears twice over, but who cannot see the difference between these two appearances: in one case its appearance is *unconditioned* and occurs purely and simply, and in the other it appears *under the condition of being-excluded by the I.*)

[I, 203]

[I/2: 349]

(Movement is supposed to be excluded from the [piece of] iron that has been posited as enduring. Movement was not posited in the iron in accordance with the concept of the same; but now it is supposed to be excluded from the iron, so it must be posited independently of this excluding; indeed, in consequence of its not-being-posited by the iron, it must be posited purely and simply. [^{II}To express this same point in a more easily comprehended albeit less stringent manner: in order for one to posit the movement of the iron in opposition to the iron itself, one must already be acquainted^{JJ} with it. One is not, however, supposed to have become acquainted with movement by means of the iron.^{KK} Thus one must be familiar with it from elsewhere,^{LL} and, since we are here considering nothing else whatsoever except for iron and movement, it follows that we must be acquainted with movement purely and simply.]

^{II} [These square brackets are Fichte's.]
^{JJ} *acquainted* [Emphasis added in C.]
^{KK} [*durch das Eisen*] *by means of the iron* [Emphasis added in C.]
^{LL} from *elsewhere* [Emphasis added in C.]

Proceeding from this concept of movement,[MM] it is contingent to movement whether it also pertains to, among other things, iron. It[NN] is what is essential, and for it the iron[OO] is what is contingent. Movement is what is posited purely and simply. As enduring in place, the [piece of] iron is excluded from the sphere of movement. Duration is now annulled, and movement is ascribed to the iron. — The concept of movement here appears twice-over: the first time as unconditioned and the second time as conditional upon annulment of the iron's duration.)

Thus — and this was the previously established synthetic proposition — totality consists purely in the complete relation,[399] and [I, 204] there is absolutely nothing fixed, which could determine this relation. Totality consists in the completeness of a *relation*, and not [in the completeness] of a *reality*.[400]

(Considered separately, the components of the relation are the *accidents*, and the *substance* is the totality of these accidents, as was already asserted above. — All that needs to be added here is to make explicit to those who are not able to draw such an easy inference for themselves that nothing whatsoever is to be thought of in a substance as stabilized [*fixiert*], but purely as a reciprocal-acting-and-being-passively-affected. As has already been sufficiently explained, if a substance is *determined* or if something *determinate is thought of as substance*, then of course reciprocal-acting-and-being-passively-affected must proceed *from one or another of the components*, which [I/2: 350] is stabilized *insofar as* the reciprocal relationship is supposed to be determined. It is not, however, *absolutely* stabilized, since I can just as well proceed from the component posited in opposition to this one, in which case the same component that was previously essential, stabilized, and firmly established is now contingent, as is illustrated by the preceding examples. Synthetically united, the accidents are the substance, which contains nothing whatsoever except these accidents. An analysis of the substance yields the accidents, and, following a complete analysis of the substance, nothing at all remains but the accidents.[PP, 401] Here one should not think of an enduring substratum, of a possible bearer of accidents.[402] Whatever the accident, it is in every case the bearer *of itself*, as well of those accidents *posited in opposition to it*,[QQ, 403] and it has no additional need for any special bearer [of accidents].[404] — By means of its most wonderful power (one that we shall determine more closely at the appropriate time[405]), the positing I brings the vanishing accident to a halt and

---

[MM] from *this* concept of movement [Emphasis added in *C.*]
[NN] *It* [Emphasis added in *C.*]
[OO] *the iron* [Emphasis added in *C.*]
[PP] Nothing whatsoever is left, other than the accidents [As emended in *C.*]
[QQ] the bearer *of itself*, as well of those accidents *posited in opposition to it* [Emphasis added in *C.*]

[I, 205]

stabilizes it until it has compared it with the accident that displaces it. — This power is almost always misunderstood, but it is the power that combines into a unity things constantly posited in opposition to each other, the power that intervenes between moments that would have to mutually annul each other, and retains both. It is this power alone that makes possible life[406] and consciousness, and, in particular, consciousness as a continuous temporal series.[407] It accomplishes all this only because it continually carries forward [*fortleitet*] within itself accidents that possess no *common* bearer, nor *can* they possess one, since in that case they would mutually annul each other.[408])

γ.) The [independent] activity, as a synthetic unity, and reciprocally-related-acting-and-being-passively-affected, as a synthetic unity, are supposed to determine each other reciprocally and should themselves constitute a synthetic unity.

The activity in question, as a synthetic unity, is most briefly described *as an absolute act of combining and retaining factors posited in opposition to each other* — one subjective,[409] the other objective — *in the concept of determinability*,[410] an absolute act of combining factors that are nevertheless also posited in opposition to each other. (In order to expound and secure a higher, more comprehensive standpoint, let us compare the synthesis we are now describing with the previously established unification of the I and Not-I as such by means of quantity (in § 3[411]). Just as in that case the I was, with respect to its quality, first posited purely and simply as absolute reality,[412] so now the I becomes *something*, i.e., something determined with respect to its *quantity* as purely and simply posited in the I: the I is purely and simply posited as a *determinate quantity. Something* subjective is posited as utterly subjective. This way of proceeding is a *thesis*,[413] and indeed a quantitative thesis, as distinct from the previous qualitative thesis.[414] But all the I's modes of acting must proceed from a thetic way of proceeding.[415] [RRBecause of the limitation [*Begrenzung*] we have here prescribed for ourselves through our foundational principle,[416] we cannot make any further progress, and this is why there is a thesis within the theoretical part of the *Wissenschaftslehre*, even though, were we ever to break through this boundary, it might become evident that it too is a synthesis, which can be traced back to the supreme thesis].[417] Just as a Not-I was previously posited in opposition to the I as such, (I, 206) as an opposed *quality*,[418] here something objective is posited in opposition to what is subjective; and this occurs purely by means of its exclusion from the sphere of what is subjective, and thus purely through and by means of *quantity* (by means of limitation, by means of determination). This way of proceeding is a quantitative antithesis, just as the previous way of

[I/2: 351]

RR [These square brackets are Fichte's.]

proceeding[419] was a qualitative antithesis. In the present case, however, neither is what is subjective supposed to be annihilated by what
is objective nor is what is objective supposed to be annihilated by
what is subjective — just as, previously, neither was the I as such
supposed to be annulled by the Not-I nor was the Not-I supposed to
be annulled by the I, but both were supposed to subsist alongside
each other. What is subjective and what is objective must therefore
be synthetically united, and this occurs by means of a third factor,
with respect to which they are the same: determinability. Both of
these — neither the subject in itself nor the object in itself, but
instead, what is subjective and what is objective,[420] as posited by
means of thesis and antithesis — are reciprocally determinable by
each other, and only insofar as this is the case can they be combined
and retained by the power of the I that is active in this synthesis
(namely, the power of imagination). — Just as before,[421] however,
this antithesis is [with respect to its content] impossible without a
thesis, because something can be posited in opposition only to
something that has [already] been posited. But even the thesis
required here[422] is, with respect to its content, impossible without
the content of the antithesis.[423] This is because before anything can
be determined purely and simply — that is, before the concept of
quantity can be applied to it — it must be present with respect to its
quality. Consequently, something or other must be there, something
in which the active I marks out a boundary for what is subjective
and leaves the rest to what is objective. — Just as previously, how- [I/2: 352]
ever, this antithesis is, with respect to its form, impossible without a
synthesis, since otherwise what is posited would be annulled by the
antithesis, in which case it would not be an antithesis but would
itself be a thesis. Hence all three actions[424] are only one and same [I, 207]
action, and the individual moments of this one action can be distinguished from one another only by reflecting upon them.[425]

Concerning the sheer reciprocal-acting-and-being-passively-
affected: if the form of the same (reciprocal exclusion of the components) and its content (the encompassing sphere, which contains
both components as excluding each other) are to become synthetically united, then reciprocal excluding is itself the sphere in which
they are included; i.e., the reciprocally-related-acting-and-being-
passively-affected consists in the sheer relation, and nothing else is
present other than reciprocal excluding, which is the determinability
just described.[426] — It is easy to see that this must be the mediating
component [*Mittelglied*], but, in the case of sheer determinability, a
sheer relation, without something that stands in this relation, it is
somewhat more difficult to imagine anything that is not absolutely
nothing. (Here and throughout the theoretical part of the
Wissenschaftslehre one must abstract entirely from this "something"[427]). Let us offer the power of imagination the best guidance

we can.[428] — Consider A and B. (We already know[429] that what is designated by this is A + B determined by A and this same A + B determined by B, but we can abstract from this for our present purposes and can call them simply A and B.) A and B are thus posited in opposition to each other. If one is posited then the other cannot be posited; and yet they are supposed to stand alongside one another — and, indeed, not merely *in part*, as was previously required,[430] but entirely, and to stand together *as* posited in opposition to each other — without reciprocally annulling each other. Our task is to think this [relation]. But the reciprocally related components cannot be thought of together in any way whatsoever and with any possible predicates, except *insofar as they reciprocally annul each other*. What is to be thought of here is neither A nor B, but their conjunction, the mutual encroachment[SS, 431] of both, and this alone is their point of union.

[I, 208]

[I/2: 353]

(At physical point[432] X, posit light at temporal moment A and darkness at the immediately ensuing moment: light and darkness are then sharply distinguished from each other, as they are supposed to be. But moments A and B immediately border one another, and there is no gap between them. Now imagine the sharp boundary between them = Z. What is contained in Z? Not light, since this is at moment A, and Z is not A; and not darkness either, since this is at moment B. Thus, neither light nor darkness [is present in Z]. — But I could just as well say that both light and darkness are present in Z, since, if there is no gap between A and B, then neither is there one between light and darkness; therefore, they come into immediate contact with each other in Z.[433] — One could say that in the preceding inference I employed my power of imagination to expand Z, which was supposed to be nothing but a boundary, and to transform it into a moment in its own right; and this is correct.[TT] [[UU]Moments A and B have themselves arisen in no way other than through such an expansion by means of the power of imagination.] I therefore *can* expand Z by means of the sheer power of imagination, and I *must* do so if I wish to think the immediate limitation of moments A and B. With this, we have, at the same time, begun an experiment with our own marvelous power of productive imagination,[434] which will soon be explained and without which nothing whatsoever in the human mind can be explained — and which may very well prove to be the foundation of the entire mechanism of the human mind.)

a.) The activity we have just explained[435] determines the reciprocal-acting-and-being-passively-affected [of subject and object],

---

[SS] the *conjunction*, the *mutual encroachment* [Emphasis added in C.]
[TT] *and this is correct* [Emphasis added in C.]
[UU] [These square brackets are Fichte's.]

which we have also explained.[436] This means that the coming together of reciprocally related components, as such, is conditional upon an absolute activity of the I,[437] by means of which the I posits something subjective and something objective[438] in [quantitative] opposition to each other and unites them both. Only in the I, and only by means of this action of the I, are these components reciprocally related; only in and only by means of this same action of the I do they come together.[439]

The proposition in question is clearly idealistic.[440] If the indi- [I, 209] cated activity is taken to exhaust the essence of the I, insofar as it is an intellect[441] (and this is indeed how it must be taken, albeit with certain limitations[442]), then the activity of representing [*Vorstellen*] consists in this: that the I posits something subjective and posits in opposition to this something else, something objective, etc.[443] With this we glimpse the beginning of a series of representations in empirical consciousness. We previously established a law regarding the mediacy of positing,[444] [I/2: 354] and according to this law (which remains valid here as well) nothing objective can be posited unless something subjective is annulled, and nothing subjective can be posited without annulling something objective, and this law would have been sufficient to explain the alternation [*Wechsel*] of representations. But now, however, we have added an additional determination, since the two terms [what is subjective and what is objective] are supposed to be synthetically united, and both are supposed to be posited by one and the same act of the I. This will allow us to explain the unity of that which encompasses the reciprocal-acting-and-being-passively-affected, even as the reciprocally related components are being-posited-in-opposition-to-each-other, which is something that could not be explained by the law of the sheer mediacy [of positing]. We would in this way obtain an intellect, along with all of its possible determinations, purely and exclusively by means of absolute spontaneity. The I would be constituted in just the way it posits itself to be constituted, in just the way it posits itself, and just because it posits itself as constituted in this way.[VV] — Though one may go back as far as one wishes in this series, one must always finally arrive at something already present in the I, in which something is determined as subjective and something else is posited in opposition to this as objective. To be sure, the presence of what is supposed to be subjective can be explained purely and simply

---

[VV] *in just the way* it posits itself to be constituted, in just the way it posits itself, and *just because* it posits itself as constituted in this way. [Emphasis added in *C.*]

[In *SW*, the emphasis is as follows:] *in just the way* it posits itself to be constituted, in just the way it posits *itself*, and *just because* it posits itself as constituted in this way

through the I's positing of itself purely and simply; but this does not explain the presence of what is objective, for this is something that is not posited purely and simply by the positing of the I. — The proposition in question does not, therefore, fully explain what is supposed to be explained.

b.) Reciprocal-acting-and-being-passively-affected determines the [independent] activity: this means that what makes the I's activity of positing in opposition and conjoining possible is by no means the real presence of components posited in opposition to each other, but rather their sheer coming together or coming into contact with one another in consciousness, as this was just explained.[445] This coming together is the condition for this activity of the I. It is simply a matter of understanding this correctly.

The following objection was just made to this idealistic mode of explanation: If something in the I is determined as subjective, and, by this same act of determination, something else is excluded from the sphere of the I as what is objective, then one must explain how what is to be excluded can be present in the I; and this is something that this idealistic mode of inference cannot explain. This objection is answered as follows by the present proposition. The objective element that is supposed to be excluded does not have to be present at all; all that

needs to be present for the I is — if I may express myself in this way — a check or impulse [*Anstoß*].[446] That is to say, what is subjective must, for some reason [*Grund*] lying beyond the activity of the I, be unable to extend any further.[447] Such an impossibility of further extension would therefore constitute the previously described sheer reciprocal-acting-and-being-passively-affected, or the sheer encroachment; it would not limit the I, qua active; instead, it would assign it the task of limiting itself. But all limitation occurs by means of opposition; consequently, the I, precisely in order to satisfy this task, would have to posit something objective in opposition to the subjective factor that is supposed to be limited and then synthetically unite both [the objective and subjective factors], as was indicated above. It would be possible to derive the entire representation in this manner. It is immediately obvious that this mode of explanation is realistic, though it is based upon a kind of realism that is much more abstract than any of those considered hitherto.[448] This is because this kind of realism does not assume that there is a Not-I present outside the I, nor does it assume that there is a determination present within the I, but only that the I has the

task of undertaking a determination within itself; that is to say, all it assumes is the *sheer determinability* of the I.

One might for a moment believe that this task of determination is itself a determination and that the present reasoning is in no way different from that associated with the previously established quantitative realism,[449] which assumed the presence of a determination. It is, however, very illuminating to display the difference between them. In the case of quantitative realism, the determination is given; here, it is supposed to be spontaneously accomplished by the active I. (If it is permissible to anticipate what is still to come, then the difference between these two types of realism can be described even more precisely. We will see in the practical part [Part Three] that the determinacy we are now speaking of is a feeling. Now a feeling is certainly a determination of the I, but not of the I as intellect, that is, of that I which posits itself as determined by the Not-I, though this is the only I with which we are here concerned.)[WW] It follows that this task of [producing a] determination [of the I] is not the determination itself.

The present line of reasoning commits the error of all realism, inasmuch as it treats the I purely as a Not-I, and this is why it is unable to explain what is supposed to be explained: the transition from the Not-I to the I. If we grant what was requested, then the determinability of the I — or the I's task of becoming determined — is, to be sure, posited, albeit without any assistance from the I. From this one can certainly explain how the I [I/2: 356] could be determinable through and for something outside the I,[XX] but not how the I could be determinable through and for the I,[YY] even though the latter is what was required. In accordance with its essence, the I is determinable only insofar as it posits itself as determinable, and it can determine itself only to that extent. The present line of reasoning cannot explain how it is possible for the I to accomplish this.

c.) These two inferences are supposed to be synthetically united. This means that the [independent] activity and the reciprocal- [I, 212] acting-and-being passively-affected are supposed to determine each other reciprocally.

It could not be assumed that the reciprocal-acting-and-being-passively-affected, or a sheer check or impulse that occurs without any assistance from the positing I,[450] assigns the I the

---

[WW] [Following *K* in moving this closing parenthesis to this point, instead of placing it at the end of the following sentence, which is where it appears in all three editions.]

[XX] *for something outside the I* [Emphasis added in *C*.]

[YY] but how the I *could be determinable for the I* (how this task of determination could ever become part of the I's scientific knowledge [*je zu seiner Wissenschaft gelangen könne*], so that it could subsequently determine itself on the basis of such knowledge), yet [Emphasis and parenthetical remark added in *C*.]

task of restricting itself. This is because the *explanandum* does not, in this case, lie within the *explanans*.[451] It must, therefore, be assumed that the impulse or check in question would not be present without the assistance of the I; instead, it would occur to the activity of the I precisely in the act of positing itself — which is to say that the I's activity of striving beyond itself would be, so to speak, driven back into itself (reflected[452]). The I's self-limitation would then follow very naturally from this [reflection], and from this self-limitation everything else that was required would follow as well.

In this manner, the reciprocal-acting-and-being-passively-affected and the [independent] activity would, in fact, be mutually determined through each other and synthetically united, which is what was required by the course of our inquiry. The impulse or check (which is not posited by the positing I) would happen to the I insofar as it is active, and it would therefore be a check only insofar as the I is active. The possibility of such a check is conditional upon this activity: no activity of the I, no impulse or check. Conversely, the I's [independent] activity of determining itself would be conditional upon the check: no impulse or check, no self-determination.[453] — Furthermore, no self-determination, nothing objective, etc.

Let us now try to become better acquainted with the supremely important final result we have now discovered. The I's activity of combining items posited in opposition to each other and the coming together of these items posited in opposition to each other (considered in itself and in abstraction from the activity of the I) are supposed to be united and to be one and the same. The chief difference here is the difference between *combining* and *coming together* [*Zusammenfassen und Zusammentreffen*].[454] Accordingly, we will penetrate most deeply into the spirit of the proposition in question by reflecting upon the possibility of uniting the combining and the coming together [of the components posited in opposition to each other].

It is easy to see that the coming together [of the components], as such, is and must be conditional upon an act of combining.[455] The components posited in opposition to each other are, as such, posited in complete opposition to each other and have nothing in common whatsoever. They come together only insofar as the boundary between them is posited, a boundary that is posited neither by the positing of the one nor by the positing of the other of these components; instead, this boundary must be specifically posited.[456] — But this boundary is then also nothing more than what they have in common; hence, to posit their boundary means to combine them. But this act of combining them is also possible only by positing

[I/2: 357]

[I, 213]

their boundaries.^{ZZ} They come together only under the condition of an act of combining, an act accomplished for and by means of the subject that combines them.^{AAA}

The act of combining — or, as we can now express this more precisely, the positing of a boundary — is conditional upon a coming together; or, since (according to what was said above) the subject that actively accomplishes the limitation in question is supposed to be one of the components that comes together — and indeed, it is supposed to be this only *as* active — , the act of combining or the positing of a boundary is conditional upon a check upon the activity of the subject that posits the boundary. This is possible only on the condition that the activity of this subject extends^{BBB} into the domain of what is unlimited, undetermined, and undeterminable, that is, into the infinite. Were it not to extend endlessly, then a check upon the activity of this subject would not follow from a limitation of that activity. The limitation could in that case be one posited through the mere concept of this subject (which is what must be assumed by a system that purely and simply establishes a finite I^{457}). In that case, it might be merely a matter of new limitations within the bounds of those [already] established through the concept of this subject, new limitations that permit one to infer an impulse or check from outside [the subject], a check that would have to be determined in some other way [than by the original concept of the subject]. From the [first] limitation as such, however, one could [in such a case] draw no inferences at all — though this is something we have nevertheless managed to do here.

(The components posited in opposition to each other, which is what we are here discussing [namely, the boundary between, on the one hand, the two components posited in opposition to each other and, on the other, the infinitely outgoing activity of the I], are supposed to be posited in opposition to each [I/2: 358] other purely and simply; there is supposed to be no point of union whatsoever between them. But no finite things are pos- [I, 214] ited purely and simply in opposition to each other; they are [also] alike with respect to the concept of determinability and are completely determinable through each other.^{458} This is a distinguishing feature of everything finite. It is also a distinguishing feature of everything infinite. To the extent that there can be several infinities, they too are alike with respect to the concept of determinability. Hence the only things that can be posited as completely opposed to each other and not alike in any

---

^{ZZ} by positing their boundary [Emendation in *C.*]
^{AAA} accomplished *for* and *by means of* the subject that combines them. [Emphasis added in *C.*]
^{BBB} only on the condition that the activity of the subject, in and for itself and left entirely to itself, extends [Added in *C.*]

respect at all are the finite and the infinite, and these must therefore be the terms posited in opposition to each other, which is what we are now discussing.)

Both [the coming together of the components and the combining of them by the subject] are supposed to be one and the same. This means, briefly: *no infinity, no limitation; no limitation, no infinity; infinity and limitation are united in one and the same synthetic component.*[459] — If the activity of the I did not extend into the infinite [= B], it could not limit its own activity. It could posit no boundary [= A] for its activity, which it is nevertheless supposed to do. The activity of the I consists in unrestricted self-positing, in opposition to which there occurs some resistance.[460] If the activity of the I were to give way to this resistance, then the activity lying beyond the boundary of this resistance would be utterly annihilated and annulled; and, to this extent, the I would posit nothing whatsoever [B determined by A]. But of course, the I is supposed to engage in positing beyond this boundary-line. It is supposed to restrict itself; and, to this extent, it is supposed to posit itself as not positing itself. In this domain [A + B], the I is supposed to posit the undetermined, unlimited, and infinite boundary[461] (= B, above), and, in order to do this, it must be infinite [A determined by B]. — Furthermore, were the I not to limit itself, it would not be infinite. — The I is only what it posits itself to be. To say that it is infinite means that it posits itself as infinite: it *determines* itself by means of the predicate "infinity," and in doing so it limits itself (the I) as the substrate of infinity.[462] It distinguishes itself from its own infinite activity (though it and its infinite activity are, in themselves, one and the same), and this is how the I must comport itself if it is to be infinite [A + B determined by B]. — The activity that extends into the infinite, which the I distinguishes from itself, is supposed to be *its* activity; it is supposed to be ascribed to the I. Consequently, the I must, in a single, undivided and indivisible action,[463] assimilate this infinite action to itself once again, (A + B determined by A). But if the I assimilates this infinite activity to itself, it is determinate, and thus not infinite. But it is supposed to be infinite, and therefore this infinite activity must be posited outside the I.[464]

[I, 215]

[I/2: 359]

The I posits itself as both finite and infinite at the same time and thus stands in a reciprocal relationship in and with itself — a reciprocal relation that, as it were, contradicts itself and thereby reproduces itself, inasmuch as the I wants to unite components that cannot be united — first attempting to assimilate the infinite to the form of the finite and then driven back to positing the infinite beyond the finite and, in the same moment, once again attempting to assimilate it to the form of the finite.

This reciprocal relationship of the I with itself is the *power of imagination* [*das Vermögen der Einbildungskraft*].

Coming together and the act of combining are, in this way, completely united with each other. This coming together, or the boundary, is itself a product of the apprehending subject and is produced in and in order to facilitate the act of apprehending[CCC] [the boundary in question] (absolute thesis of the power of imagination, which, to this extent, is utterly productive). Insofar as the I and this product of its activity [viz., the boundary between the finite and the infinite] are posited in opposition to each other, the components that come together are themselves posited in opposition to each other, and neither of them is posited at the boundary (antithesis of the power of imagination). Insofar, however, as both are once again posited as united — a productive activity that should be ascribed to the I — , the components that limit each other are themselves combined at the boundary (synthesis of the power of imagination, which, in its antithetic and synthetic operations is reproductive, all of which will be made clearer at the appropriate time).

The components posited in opposition to each other are supposed to be combined in the concept of sheer *determin-* [I, 216] *ability* (and by no means in that of determination). This was a cardinal moment of the required [process of] unification, and we still must reflect upon this moment as well, a reflection that will completely determine and clarify what was just said. Suppose that the boundary posited between components posited in opposition to each other (one of which is itself the subject that posits the opposed components, whereas the other, with respect to its existence, lies completely outside of consciousness and is posited only for the sake of the necessary restriction) is posited as a firm, fixed, and unchangeable [I/2: 360] boundary, in which case the two components would be united by *determination* and not by *determinability*. In that case, however, the totality required for the reciprocal relationship of substantiality would not be filled. (A + B would be determined only by the determinate A and not, at the same time, by the indeterminate B.) Consequently, the boundary in question must not be taken to be a firm one, nor is this how it is taken in the preceding explication of the power of imagination, which is what is active in this process of limitation. For the sake of determining the subject, the power of imagination posits an infinite boundary, as a product of its activity which

---

[CCC] is produced *in* and *in order to facilitate* the act of apprehending [Emphasis added in C.]

precedes into infinity. It seeks to ascribe this activity to itself (to determine A + B by A), but were it actually to accomplish this, the subject would no longer be *this* [infinite] activity; instead, since this activity is posited in a determinate subject, it would itself be determined and therefore not infinite. The power of imagination is thereby driven back, as if into the infinite (it is assigned the task of determining A + B by B). What remains, therefore, is nothing but determinability, the Idea of determination (which cannot be achieved in this manner), but no determination itself. — The power of imagination posits no fixed boundary at all, for it itself possesses no fixed standpoint. Only [the power of] reason posits something fixed, and it does so by first stabilizing the power of imagination. The power of imagination oscillates or hovers [*schwebt*] in the middle between determination and non-determination, between the finite and the infinite. It is therefore by means of this power

[I, 217]

that A + B is determined *at the same time* by the determinate A and by the indeterminate B, and this is the very synthesis of the power of imagination we were just discussing. — This hovering characterizes the power of imagination by means of its product,[465] which is, as it were, produced by the power of imagination in the course of and by means of its oscillation or hovering.

   (As we shall see later,[466] it is this hovering or oscillating of the power of imagination between components that cannot be united, this conflict of the power of imagination with itself, that extends the state of the I in this oscillation and conflict[467] to a moment of *time*.[468] — For pure reason alone, everything is simultaneous; time exists only for the power of imagination. — The power of imagination does not sustain this oscillation for long, for no longer than a moment — except in the feeling of

[I/2: 361]

the sublime, in which there arises *astonishment* and in which the reciprocal-acting-and-being-passively-affected in time comes to a standstill. Reason intervenes, thereby producing a reflection, and determines the power of imagination to assimilate B into the determinate A — that is, into the subject [B determined by A]. But now, yet again, the determinately posited A must be restricted by an infinite B [A determined by B]. In the case of theoretical reason, the power of imagination deals with this infinite B in just the same way as before, and it continues in this way until it has achieved the complete self-determination of reason, at which point no limiting B, other than reason itself, is required by the power of imagination. That is to say, it continues *until* [it has produced] *a representation of the representing subject*.[469] In the practical field, the power of imagination extends into the infinite, until it arrives at the utterly undeterminable Idea of supreme unity, something that would be possible only after a completed infinite, which is itself impossible.)

*   *

*

1.) Without the infinity of the I — without an absolute productive power of the I, which extends into the domain of what is unrestricted and unrestrictable — it is not possible to explain even the possibility of representation. This absolute productive power has now been derived synthetically from the postulate that there is a representation, a postulate [I, 218] contained in the proposition, "the I posits itself as determined by the Not-I."[470] We can see in advance, however, that this power will be traced back to a still higher one[471] in the practical part of our science.[472]

2.) All the difficulties that stood in our way have now been satisfactorily resolved. The task was to unite two terms posited in opposition to each other, the I and the Not-I. They can be completely united by the power of imagination, which unites items posited in opposition to each other. — The Not-I is itself a product of the self-determining I,[473] and by no means anything absolute and posited outside the I. An I that posits itself *as* self-positing, or as a *subject*, is impossible without an object that has been produced in the manner now described. (The determination of the I, its reflection upon itself as something determinate, is possible only on the condition that it limit itself by means of something posited in opposition to it.) — The only question that cannot be answered here is, How and by what means does that check or impulse, which had to be assumed in order to explain representation, happen to the I? This is a question that lies [I/2: 362] beyond the boundary of the theoretical part of the *Wissenschaftslehre*.

3.) The proposition with which the theoretical *Wissenschaftslehre* commences — *the I posits itself as determined by the Not-I* — is now completely exhausted, and all the contradictions it harbors have been overcome. The I can posit itself in no other way than as determined by the Not-I. (No object, no subject.) To this extent, it posits itself as determined. At the same time, it also posits itself as engaged in determining, because what limits it in the Not-I is its own product. (No subject, no object.) — The requisite reciprocal interaction [between the I as determined by the Not-I and as determining the Not-I] is not merely *possible*; what is required by the indicated postulate [namely, that the I is determined by the Not-I] is not even thinkable apart from such a reciprocal interaction. What was previously only problematically valid now possesses apodictic certainty. — At the same time, it has thereby been proven that the theo- [I, 219] retical part of the *Wissenschaftslehre* is concluded. For every science is concluded when its foundational principle has been exhausted, and the foundational principle is exhausted when, in the course of the investigation, one returns to it.[474]

4.) If the theoretical part of the *Wissenschaftslehre* is supposed to be exhausted, then all the moments necessary for explaining representation must have been established and grounded; therefore, all we have to do from now is apply what has now been proven and tie it all together.

Before we pursue this path, however, it is useful and has important implications for full insight into the entire *Wissenschaftslehre* to reflect upon this path itself.

5.) Our task was to investigate how and under what conditions the problematically established proposition, "the I posits itself as determined by the Not-I," is thinkable.[475] We have exhaustively examined all the possible determinations of this proposition and have done so by means of a systematic deduction of these determinations. By isolating what is untenable and unthinkable, we have confined what is thinkable within a smaller and smaller circumference; and in this way we have, step by step, drawn ever closer to the truth, until we have finally discovered the only possible way to think what we were supposed to think. If this proposition [that the I posits itself as determined by the Not-I] is now true as such, which is to say, apart from any of the particular determinations it has now acquired — and that this is the case is a postulate based upon our supreme foundational principle [in Part Two] — then, according to the preceding deduction, it is true in *this way* alone. The proposition in question is, therefore, at the same time *a factum originally present in our*

[I/2: 363]

mind.[476] — Allow me to make myself clearer: All the thought-possibilities established in the course of our investigation, which we thought of and which we were conscious of thinking, were also *facta* of our consciousness — insofar as we were engaged in philosophizing. But these were *artificial* [*künstliche*] *facta*, engendered by the spontaneity of our power of reflection in accordance with the rules of reflection. Following the elimi-

[I, 220]

nation of all that has been proven to be false, the only remaining thought-possibility is, first and foremost, just such a spontaneously generated artificial *factum*; it is this insofar as it was raised to the consciousness (of philosophers) by means of reflection — or, to be more precise, what is an artificially generated *factum* is the *consciousness* of this *factum*.[477] But the assertion with which this inquiry began[478] is now supposed to be true, which means that something in our mind is supposed to correspond to it. Furthermore, it is supposed to be capable of truth only in the *one* way indicated; consequently, something in our mind must correspond to this kind of thinking, originally and independently of our reflection; and it is in this higher sense of the word that I call what has here been established a "*factum*," whereas the other thought-possibilities we have indicated are not *facta* in this sense. (For example, in the course of our inquiry we certainly encountered the realistic hypothesis that the content of a representation may perhaps be given from without. This hypothesis is something that had to be thought, and the thought of it was a *factum* of reflecting consciousness. Upon closer examination, however,

we discovered that such an hypothesis contradicts the foundational principle in question, since anything to which content would be given from
without would not be an I, which it is nevertheless supposed to be,
according to the requirement[479] [implicit in the first principle of Part
One], but would instead be a Not-I, We also discovered that, for the
same reason, nothing outside of itself could correspond to such a
thought, which is completely empty and must be rejected as a thought
pertaining to a transcendent rather than to a transcendental system.)

It should be noted in passing that *facta* are certainly established in the
Wissenschaftslehre, and this is what distinguishes it, as a system of real
thinking[480] from all empty and purely formulaic philosophy.[481] Here,
however, it is not permissible straightaway to postulate something to be
a *factum*; instead, one must offer a proof *that* it is a *factum*, as we have
done in the present case. Reliance upon *facta* lying within the purview of
ordinary conscious, unguided by any philosophical reflection, produces (if [I, 221]
one is only consistent and is not already in possession of the results that
are supposed to be based on these *facta*) nothing but a deceptive popular
philosophy,[482] which is no philosophy at all. If, however, the *facta* in [I/2: 364]
question are supposed to lie beyond the purview of ordinary consciousness, then one must indeed know how one has arrived at the conviction
that they are present as *facta*. One must also be able to communicate this
conviction, and such a communication of conviction is certainly proof
that these *facta* are *facta*.

6.) It is surely to be expected that such a *factum* must have some consequences
within our consciousness. If it is supposed to be a *factum* of which an *I* is
conscious, then the I must first posit this *factum as* present within its consciousness. And since this may present certain difficulties and be possible
in only one way, perhaps we can indicate the manner in which the I posits
this *factum* within itself. — To express this more clearly, the I must explain
this *factum*, but it can explain it only in conformity with the laws of its
own nature, which are the same laws that have guided our preceding
reflection. From now on, the object of our philosophical reflection will be
the manner in which the I processes [*bearbeitet*], modifies, and determines
this *factum* within itself, its entire way of dealing with this *factum*.[483] — It
is clear that, from this point on, all our reflection occurs at a very different
level and possesses a very different meaning.[484]

7.) The preceding series of reflections and the ensuing series of reflections are
to be distinguished from each other, first of all, by their objects. Previously,
we were reflecting upon thought-possibilities. It was the spontaneity of the
human mind that produced the object of reflection — namely, these same
thought-possibilities, though it produced them in conformity with the
rules of an exhaustive, synthetic system — and also produced the form of
reflection, that is, the very act of reflecting. It turned out that what we were [I, 222]
reflecting upon did indeed contain within itself something real, but mixed
with empty dross, which had to be gradually eliminated, until nothing

remained except what was sufficiently true for our purposes, that is, for the purposes of the theoretical *Wissenschaftslehre*. — In the future series of reflections, we will be reflecting upon *facta*. The object of this reflection is itself a reflection, namely the reflection of the human mind upon the datum established within it. (To be sure, this deserves to be called a datum [*Datum*] only insofar as it is the object of this mental reflection upon it; otherwise, it is a *factum*.[485]) In the future series of reflections, therefore, the object of reflection is not first *produced* by means of this same reflection, but is simply *raised to consciousness* thereby. From this it also follows that, from now on, we will no longer be dealing with mere hypotheses, in which the small amount of true content must first be separated from the empty dross; instead, reality can legitimately be ascribed to everything established from now on. — The *Wissenschaftslehre* is supposed to be a pragmatic history of the human mind.[486] We have been laboring until now only to secure entry into this pragmatic history, simply in order first to be able to point to an indubitable *factum*. We have discovered this *factum*, and from now on our perception — which is, to be sure, not blind but engaged in conducting experiments[487] — can peacefully follow the course of events [*dem Gange der Begebenheiten*].[488]

[I/2: 365]

[I, 223]

8.) These two types of reflection also differ in their directions. For the time being, let us abstract completely from artificial philosophical reflection and attend only to the original and necessary reflection the human mind engages in with respect to this *factum* (which will from now on become the object of a higher, philosophical reflection). It is clear that this same human mind is unable to reflect upon the given *factum* in any way other than in conformity with the very same laws in conformity with which this *factum* was discovered — that is, in accordance with the laws that have directed our own previous reflection, and not in conformity with any other laws. This reflection preceded from the principle, "the I posits itself as determined by the Not-I," and then followed a path leading to the *factum* in question. The present, natural reflection, which is to be established as a necessary *factum*, starts with this *factum* and must then continue until it has arrived at the principle [with which Part Two began], since the application of the foundational principles that have been established cannot be concluded until this principle [that the I posits itself as determined by the Not-I] has confirmed itself as a *factum* (that is, until the I posits itself *as* positing itself as determined by the Not-I). Consequently, the new series of reflections will follow this same path, albeit *in the opposite direction*; and philosophical reflection must necessarily proceed in the same direction, even though it can only follow this path and not subject it to any laws.

9.) If reflection precedes from now on in the opposite direction, then the indicated *factum* is at the same time the turning point for reflection.[DDD]

[DDD] the turning point for the reflection undertaken by a person engaged in philosophizing; [Added in C.]

This *factum* is the point at which two completely different series are linked, and in which the end of the first reflection is attached to the beginning of the second. Hence, the basis for distinguishing the preceding reflection from the one that will be valid from now on must be contained in this point. — Our way of proceeding was synthetic, and it will remain so throughout. The *factum* in question is itself a synthesis. To begin with, this synthesis unites two components posited in opposition to each other in the first series [of reflection]. This, therefore, would be [I/2: 366] how this synthesis [represented by the *factum* in question] is related to the first series. — This same synthesis must also include two components posited in opposition to each other for the second series of reflection, for the purposes of a possible analysis and a synthesis following therefrom. Since no more than two terms posited in opposition to each other can be united in this synthesis, the components united in it at the conclusion of the first series must be precisely the same as those that are supposed to be yet again separated from each other in order to begin the second series. But if they are really the very same components, then the second series is not a second series at all, but simply the reverse of the first one, and our procedure is no more than a repetitive dissolution [*Auflösen*], [I, 224] which serves no purpose, in no way increases our knowledge, and fails to advance our inquiry a single step. Hence the components of the second series, insofar as this is what they are, must nevertheless differ in some way from those of the first series, even though they are supposed to be the same. And they can have acquired this difference purely and solely by means of the synthesis and in the course, as it were, of accomplishing it. — It is worth the effort to become properly acquainted with this difference between the two components posited in opposition to each other, insofar as they are components either of the first or of the second series, and this will shed the clearest light on the most important and characteristic aspect of the present system.

10.) In both cases, the components posited in opposition to each other are what is subjective and what is objective, but they are present as such in the human mind [*Gemüt*] in very different ways *before* the synthesis and *after* it. *Prior to* the synthesis, they are simply posited in opposition to each other and nothing more; the first is what the second is not, and the second is what the first is not. They indicate a sheer relation and nothing more. They are something negative and are purely and simply nothing positive (just as, in the previous example,[489] light and darkness were both negative at point Z, if this is considered to be a boundary that is merely *thought*). These components are mere thoughts, lacking any reality; moreover, they are the thought of a mere relation. — When one makes an entrance, the other is annihilated; but the first component cannot make an entrance at all, since it can do so only with the predicate of being different than the second, and therefore the concept of the other enters along with that of the first — and annihilates it. It follows that nothing whatsoever is present, nor can anything be present; our consciousness is not filled, and absolutely nothing is present in it. (To be sure, we could not have undertaken any of our previous inquiries without a beneficent deception on the part of the power of imagination, which tacitly provided each of the terms posited purely in opposition to each other with a substrate; otherwise, we would have been unable to think these components, since they were absolutely nothing, and one cannot reflect upon nothing. This deception could not be prevented, nor should it have been; its product should simply be deducted and excluded from the sum of our conclusions, which is what actually occurred.) *Following* the synthesis, these same components can be grasped by and held fast in consciousness and can, so to speak, fill it. (They are now *for reflection* — with the favor and permission of reflection — what they previously were as well, to be sure, though only tacitly and in the face of persistent objections on the part of reflection.) — Just as, previously,[490] light and darkness, as *extended to a moment by the power of imagination*, were certainly something in point Z, something that did not absolutely annihilate itself.

[I, 225]
[I/2: 367]

The components undergo this transformation insofar as they, so to speak, undergo the synthesis, and it must be shown how and in what way this synthesis is able to communicate to these components anything they did not already possess. — It is the task of the power of synthesis [i.e., the power of imagination] to unite components posited in opposition to each other, to *think* of them as one (since this demand is initially addressed, as was previously always the case, to the power of thinking [*Denkvermögen*].) But the power of thinking is unable to satisfy this demand, even though the task still remains. There therefore arises a conflict between this demand and this inability. The mind abides in this conflict and oscillates between the demand and the impossibility of fulfilling it, and in this state — but in it alone — it holds fast to both the demand and the inability — or, which means the same thing, it transforms them in such a way that both can be grasped and held fast at the same time.[491] — In this way, that is, by coming into contact with these components, again being driven away from them, and then again coming into contact with them, the mind endows them with a certain content *in relation to itself* as well as with a certain extension. (At the appropriate time, this extension will reveal itself to be a manifold[492] in time and space.[493]) The name for this state of mind is *intuiting* [*Anschauen*]. The power active in this state has already been identified above[494]: it is the productive power of imagination.

[I, 226] 11.) We can now see that the very same situation that threatened to eliminate the possibility of any theory [*Theorie*] of human knowledge here provides us with the only condition under which such a theory can be erected. We could not foresee how we were ever supposed to be able to unite components posited in opposition to each other. Now, however, we see that it is simply impossible to explain anything that occurs in our mind without reference to components posited in absolute opposition to each other. This is because the power underlying all these occurrences, the productive power of imagination, would by utterly impossible in the absence of components posited in absolute opposition to each other, that is, posited as not to be united and as completely unsuited to the I's power [I/2: 368] of apprehension. At the same time, this provides illuminating proof that our system is correct and that it is has exhaustively explained what needed to be explained. What was presupposed can be explained only in terms of what is discovered, and what is discovered can be explained only in terms of what is presupposed.[495] Hence, the entire mechanism of the human mind follows from components posited in absolute opposition to each other, and this entire mechanism can be explained in no other way than by means of an absolute being-posited-in-opposition.

12.) At the same time, this fully illuminates a previous assertion, which has not yet been fully clarified: namely, how ideality and reality[496] could be one and the same,[497] how they are distinguished from each other only by differences of perspective [*verschiedene Art sie anzusehen*], and how the one can be inferred from the other. — Prior to the synthesis, the components posited in absolute opposition to each other (what is finitely subjective and what is infinitely objective) are mere objects of thought and [therefore] "ideal," in the sense in which we have here consistently employed this term. When they are supposed to be unified by the power of thought, but cannot be unified in this way, they acquire reality through the oscillation or hovering of the mind (which, in this function, is called the power of imagination), because they thereby become intuitable. That is, they thereby acquire reality as such, for there is no kind of reality other than by means of intuition, nor can there be any other kind of reality. [I, 227] When, however, one abstracts once again from intuition — something that can certainly be done with regard to the sheer power of thinking, but not with regard to consciousness as such (see above, pp. 303–4)[498] — , this reality becomes, in turn, something purely ideal; it possesses a being that has arisen purely through the laws governing the power of representation.[499]

13.) The lesson to draw from this is, therefore, that all reality — reality *for us*, as goes without saying, since reality cannot be understood in any other way in a system of transcendental philosophy[500]— is generated by the power of imagination. One of the greatest thinkers of our age, who, so far as I can see, teaches the same lesson,[501] calls this a *deception* [*Täuschung*] on the part of the power of imagination. But every deception must posit truth in opposition to itself; it must be possible to avoid every deception. [I/2: 369] Thus, when it has been proven, as it is supposed to have been proven in our system, that the possibility of our consciousness, of our life, and of our being for ourselves — that is to say, the very possibility of our being as an I — is based upon this action by the power of imagination, then this action cannot be eliminated, unless we are supposed to abstract from the I [as well], which is self-contradictory, since the subject engaged in the act of abstracting cannot possibly abstract from itself. Consequently, this action on the part of the power of imagination does not deceive us, but provides us with truth, and the only possible truth. To assume that it deceives us is to establish a skepticism that teaches one to doubt one's own being.[502]

Deduction of Representation

I.) Let us begin by situating ourselves securely at the point at which we have arrived. A check happens to the infinitely outgoing activity of the I, an activity within [I, 228] which, precisely because it extends into the infinite, nothing can be distinguished [from anything else]. But this activity of the I is by no means supposed to be annihilated by the check in question; instead, it is reflected, driven inward. It acquires a direction directly opposite of its original direction.

One can represent this infinitely outgoing activity with the image of a straight line proceeding from A to B to C, etc. The check could occur either prior to C or beyond C, but let us assume that it occurs at C and that, in accordance with what was said above,[503] the reason [*Grund*] for this lies not in the I, but in the Not-I.

[I/2: 370]   Under the condition posited, the direction of the activity of the I proceeding from A to C is reflected from C to A.

Just as surely as the I is supposed to be an I, nothing can have any effect whatsoever upon it without producing a reactive efficacy [*ohne daß dasselbe zurückwirke*]. Nothing in the I, including the direction of its activity, allows itself to be annulled. Consequently, the activity reflected back toward A, *insofar as it is reflected*,[504] must, at the same time, *have a reactive efficacy* extending to C.

We thereby obtain between A and C a doubled direction of the I's activity, an activity in conflict with itself, in which the direction from C to A can be viewed as a passive affection [*Leiden*] and the direction from A to C as a sheer activity, though both are one and the same state of the I.

This state, in which [activities in] totally opposed directions are unified, is precisely the activity of the power of imagination, and we have now completely determined what we were previously seeking:[505] an activity that is possible only by means of a passive affection and a passive affection that is possible only by means of an activity. — The activity of the I between A and C is a *resisting* [*widerstehende*] activity; but such an activity is impossible unless the activity of the I is reflected, since all resistance presupposes something that is being resisted. Insofar as the original direction of the I's activity is reflected, this is a state of being passively affected; but no [activity in a certain] direction can be reflected if it is not present as this direction, and indeed, present as such along all points of the same. Both directions [that is, the activities in both directions], the one proceeding [I, 229] from A and the one proceeding from C, must be the same, and this is precisely what resolves the previous problem.[506]

Insofar as its activity lies between A and C, the state of the I is one of intuiting [*ein Anschauen*],[507] for intuiting is both an activity that is impossible without a state of being passively affected [*ein Leiden*] and a state of being passively affected that is impossible without an activity. — Intuiting has now been determined for philosophical reflection, but only for philosophical reflection. As an accident of the I [qua substance], it still remains completely indeterminate from the stand-point of the subject, since, in order for it to be determined, it must be possible to distinguish it from other determinations of the I, and this is not yet possible. Intuiting is equally indeterminate from the standpoint of the object, for, in order for it to be determined, it must be possible to distinguish something intuited, as such, from something that is not intuited, which is likewise not yet possible.

(It is clear that the activity of the I, when restored to its first and original direction, also extends beyond C. But insofar as it extends beyond C, it is not striving in opposition to anything, since the check does not occur past C; consequently, this original activity is not one of intuiting. It follows that both the intuition and what is intuited are limited at C. The activity extending beyond C is not intuition, [I/2: 371] and the object of this activity is nothing intuited. At the appropriate time, we will see what these may be.[508] Here we wish only to call attention to the fact that we have left some matters undiscussed and that we intend to take them up later.)

II.) The I is supposed to be engaged in intuiting; but if the intuiting subject is actually supposed to be an I, then this means that *the I is supposed to posit itself as intuiting,* since nothing pertains to the I except insofar as it ascribes it to itself.[509]

The I posits itself as intuiting: this mean, first of all, that it posits itself as *active* in the intuition. What else this might also mean will become evident in the course of our inquiry. Now insofar as the I posits itself in the intuition as active, it posits something in opposition to itself, something that is passive rather than active in the intuition.

In order to orient ourselves in this investigation we need merely recall what [I, 230] was said above[510] concerning the reciprocal relation [between activity and being passively affected] contained in the concept of substantiality. The two compo-nents posited in opposition to each other — the activity and the state of being passively affected — are not supposed to annihilate and annul each other; instead, they are supposed to continue to exist alongside each other; they are simply sup-posed to exclude each other mutually.

It is clear that something intuited has to be posited in opposition to the subject that is actively engaged in intuiting.[511] The question is simply this: how and in what way might what is intuited be posited?[512]

Something intuited, which, insofar as it is intuited, is posited in opposition to the intuiting I, is necessarily a Not-I. From this it follows, first of all, that the action of the I that posits such an intuited something is *not an act of reflection*, not an inwardly but rather an outwardly directed activity;[513] consequently, so far as we are now able to see, it must be an act of production. What is intuited is, as such, something produced.[514]

It is also clear that the I cannot be conscious of its own activity in producing what is intuited, as such. This is because such an activity is not reflected and is not ascribed to the I.[515] (This activity is credited to the I only in the course of the philosophical reflection in which we are currently engaged, which must always be carefully distinguished from the ordinary kind of reflection.)

The productive power [of the I] is always the power of imagination. Consequently, the positing of what is intuited occurs by means of the power of imagination, and this positing is itself an intuiting.[EEE, 516]

[I/2: 372]

[I, 231]

This intuition is now supposed to be posited in opposition to an activity involved in the intuition, an activity the I ascribes to itself. In one and the same action [of intuiting] there are supposed to be present at the same time an activity of intuiting, which the I ascribes to itself by means of a reflection, and another activity, which it does not ascribe to itself. The latter is a sheer intuiting, which the former activity is supposed to be as well, though it is supposed to be reflected. The question is, how does this activity occur and what follows from it?

As an activity, the act of intuiting is directed toward C. Yet it is an act of intuiting only insofar as it strives in opposition [*widerstrebt*] to [another activity proceeding in] the opposite direction, toward A. If it does not strive in opposition, it is no longer an act of intuiting, but an activity pure and simple.[517]

Such an activity of intuiting is supposed to be reflected; i.e., the activity of the I (which is always one and the same activity) proceeding toward C is supposed to be redirected toward A, and indeed to be so directed *as* striving in opposition to [an activity aiming in] the opposite direction (for otherwise it would not be *this* activity; that is, it would not be the activity of intuiting).

This involves the following difficulty: By means of the impulse or check from outside, the activity of the I has already been reflected toward A; and now it is supposed to be yet again reflected in the same direction, but this time by means of absolute spontaneity (since the I is supposed to posit itself as intuiting purely and simply because it is an I).[518] But if these two directions are not distinguished, then no intuition whatsoever will be reflected; instead, the intuition will simply be repeated a second time in the same way, since the activity is the same. It is one and the same activity of the I, and it has the same direction as well — from C toward A. From this it follows that, if the required reflection is to be possible, these two activities must be distinguishable from each other. Consequently, before we can proceed any further we must determine how and by what means these two activities can be distinguished from each other.

III.) Let us determine our task more narrowly. — Even in advance of the investigation one can vaguely see how the first direction of the I's activity toward A might be distinguished from the second activity in the same direction. This is because the first is reflected by a sheer check or impulse from without, whereas the second is reflected [toward A] by means of absolute spontaneity. From our level of philosophical reflection, at which we have voluntarily situated ourselves from the beginning of our inquiry, we can now catch a glimpse of this [distinction]. Our task, however, is to demonstrate precisely this distinction, which must be

[I, 232]

[EEE] is itself an intuiting, an act of looking *outwards toward* [*ein Hin*schauen] (in the active sense of this term) an indeterminate something. [Addition in C.]

presupposed for the possibility of any philosophical reflection.[FFF] The question [I/2: 373]
before us is this: How does the human mind originally arrive at this distinction
between a reflection of an activity proceeding from outside itself and one proceeding from within? It is this distinction that is supposed to be derived as a
factum, and it is supposed to be demonstrated precisely by means of this
derivation.

The I is supposed to be determined as the subject engaged in intuiting[GGG]
and thereby distinguished from what is intuited. This was the requirement with
which we began, and we could not have proceeded from any other. As the subject of intuition, the I is supposed to be posited in opposition to its object and
thereby distinguished, first of all, from the Not-I. It is clear that we would have
no fixed point for making this distinction [between the I and Not-I], but would
be forever turning in a circle, were the intuition not first stabilized [*fixirt*] in
itself and as such.[519] Only then can the relation of the I as well as of the Not-I to
the intuition be determined. Consequently, the possibility of satisfying the previously assigned task depends upon the possibility of stabilizing the intuition
itself and as such.[520]

This task is equivalent to the one just indicated — viz., making the activity
directed toward A distinguishable from the second activity in that same direction
— , and the solution to the latter task will satisfy the former as well. If the intuition
itself is ever stabilized, then it already contains within itself the first reflection
toward A; consequently, not only can the [activity in the] first direction be
reflected toward A, but so can the intuition as such — without any fear of confusion or mutual annulment.

The intuition is supposed to be stabilized as such, so that it can be grasped as
one and the same intuition. But the act of intuiting is, as such, by no means stabilized; instead, it is an oscillation of the power of imagination between conflicting
directions. To say that this is to be stabilized is to say that the power of imagination should no longer oscillate or hover, which would mean that the intuition   [I, 233]
would be utterly annihilated and annulled. This, however, is not supposed to
occur; consequently, the intuition must retain at least some product of this state
[of oscillation], some trace of the opposing directions, consisting of neither but
assembled from both.[521]

Three elements are involved in such a stabilization of intuition, by means of
which an intuition first becomes an intuition: [1.] First, there is the act of stabilizing or positing as fixed [*festsetzen*]. The entire process of stabilization occurs
spontaneously,[HHH] for the sake of reflection; and, as we shall soon see, it occurs
by means of the spontaneity of reflection itself. Consequently, this act of stabilizing is accomplished by that power of the I which posits purely and simply, the
power of reason.[522] — [2.] Then there is what is determined or becoming deter-   [I/2: 374]
mined, and this, as we know, is the power of imagination, for the activity of which

---

[FFF] is to exhibit [*darzulegen*] precisely this distinction, which must be presupposed as an original
factum of natural consciousness. [As amended in C.]
  [GGG] determined as the *subject engaged in intuiting* [Emphasis added in C.]
  [HHH] *spontaneously* [Emphasis added in C.]

a boundary is posited. — [3.] Finally, there is what comes into being by means of this determination: the product of the power of imagination in its oscillation. It is clear that, if the required holding fast [*Festhalten*] is to be possible, then there must be some power that accomplishes it, and neither the determining power of reason nor the producing power of imagination is such a power. The power in question must therefore be an intermediate one, lying between the powers of reason and imagination. This is the power by means of which what is changeable *endures* [*besteht*] and becomes, as it were, *understandable* [*verständig*],[523] and[III] this power is therefore rightfully called the *power of understanding* [*Verstand*].[524] — The power of understanding is such only insofar as something is stabilized therein, and everything that is stabilized is stabilized only in the understanding. The power of understanding can be described either as the power of imagination stabilized by the power of reason or as the power of reason provided with objects by the power of imagination. — Despite what may have been said from time to time concerning the actions of the power of understanding,[525] it is a dormant, inactive power of the mind, the mere receptacle for what is produced by the power of imagination and for what is determined or remains to be determined by the power of reason.

[I, 234]   (Only in the understanding *is* there reality; it[JJJ] is the power of *what is actual*;[526] it is in[KKK] the understanding that what is ideal becomes real. [[LLL]Consequently, the term "*to understand*" also expresses a relationship to something that is supposed to come from outside, with no assistance from us.[MMM]] The power of imagination produces reality, but there *is* in it no reality. The product of the power of imagination becomes something real only when it is apprehended and comprehended by the power of understanding.[527] — We assign no reality to what we are conscious of as being a product of the power of imagination; but we do indeed assign reality to what we discover to be contained in the understanding, to which we ascribe no productive power at all, but only that of preservation. — It will become evident that, in reflection[NNN] and in consequence of the laws of reflection, we can go back no further than to the understanding, in which one certainly encounters something that is *given* to reflection as the content [*Stoff*] of representation, though one is not conscious of the way in which this enters the understanding. This is why we are firmly convinced of the reality of things existing outside ourselves, without any assistance from us: because we are not conscious of the power by means of which they are produced. Were we, in ordinary reflection, nevertheless able to become conscious of what we are conscious of in philo-

[I/2: 375] sophical reflection — namely, that what we are conscious of first enters the

---

[III] becomes *understandable* (brought to a stand-still, as it were), and [Addition in *C.*]
[JJJ] reality (although [this is] first [produced] by means of the power of imagination); it [Addition in *C.*]
[KKK] it is *in* [Emphasis added in *C.*]
[LLL] [These square brackets are Fichte's.]
[MMM] with no assistance from us, though this is always only indicated and intimated [*durchaus aber lediglich gedeutet, und vernommen werden*] [addition in *C.*]
[NNN] given to natural reflection, which is posited in opposition to artificial, transcendental, philosophical reflection [addition *C.*]

understanding by means of the power of imagination — , then we would once again describe everything as a deception, and in doing so we would be just as incorrect as we were when we described things as existing outside of and without any assistance from ourselves.)

IV.) Let us once again pick up the thread of our investigation where we left it dangling, since it was impossible to follow it any further.

[1.] The I reflects upon its activity proceeding toward C when it is engaged in intuition.[528] For the reasons indicated above,[529] this activity cannot be reflected upon as resisting an activity in the opposite direction, from C to A. Nor can this same activity be reflected simply as an activity proceeding outwardly as such; for in that case it would be the entire infinite activity of the I, which cannot be reflected and is not the activity involved in intuition, which is indeed supposed to be reflected upon. From this it follows that the intuiting activity of the I must [I, 235] be reflected upon as proceeding to C, as limited and determined by C. This would be the first point.

[2.] Accordingly, the intuiting activity of the I is limited at C by the absolute activity operative in reflection. — But this intuiting activity is a purely reflecting one and is not itself reflected upon (except in our present, philosophical reflection), and for this reason the limitation at C is posited in opposition to the I and ascribed to the Not-I. A determinate product of the absolutely productive power of imagination is posited in the infinite realm lying beyond C, and this occurs by means of an obscure, unreflected intuition. This product does not attain to determinate consciousness, but limits the power of reflected intuition and does so precisely in accordance with the same rule and for the same reason[530] that the first, indeterminate product was posited at all. This would be the second point. — This product is the Not-I, and it is by positing the Not-I in opposition to itself that, for our present purposes, the I first determines itself *as* an I at all. This is how the logical subject of the proposition "the I is engaged in intuiting" becomes possible.

Determined in this manner,[531] the activity of the intuiting I is posited as fixed, at least with respect to its determinations, and is comprehended by the power of understanding for the sake of further determination. Otherwise, the conflicting activities of the I would thwart and mutually annihilate each other.

[3.] This activity[of intuiting] proceeds from A to C and is supposed to be apprehended as proceeding in this direction by a reflecting activity of the I, which proceeds from C to A. — It is clear that opposing directions are present in this act of apprehension, and thus it is clear that this apprehension occurs by means of the power of positing opposites [*das Vermögen des Entgegengesetzen*], the power of imagination, and therefore must itself be an intuition. This would [I/2: 376] be the third point. In its present function, the power of imagination does not produce anything; instead, it simply apprehends something that has already been produced [by the productive power of imagination] and comprehended by the understanding (and it does this so that it can be posited in the understanding, and not, as it were, in order to preserve it). For this reason it is called the reproductive power of imagination.[532]

[4.] The intuiting subject must be determined;^{OOO} moreover, it must be
[I, 236] determined as such, that is, as active. Another activity must be posited in opposition
to^{PPP} this active subject, an activity that is *not the same* as the first one, but is
another activity.[533] Activity, however, is always activity; and until now we have
been able to distinguish nothing in activity except its direction.[534] But the direction
from C to A is such an opposing direction, which originates from being externally
reflected [*durch das Reflektirtseyn von aussen entstanden*] and is preserved in the
understanding. This would be the fourth point.

[5.] Insofar as what is present in intuition is supposed to be determined by this
[activity in an] opposing direction, this [activity in the] opposing direction must
be intuited. Accordingly, the determination of the intuiting subject must always
be accompanied by an unreflected intuition of what is intuited.^{QQQ, 535}

If, however, what is intuited is supposed to be posited in opposition to the
intuiting subject, then what is intuited must itself be determined *as* something
intuited; and this is possible only by means of reflection. The question is simply
this: Which of the externally directed activities is supposed to be reflected
upon? It must be one of these externally directed activities that is reflected
upon; but the activity involved in intuiting, the activity proceeding from A to C,
provides [only] an intuition of the intuiting subject.

It was observed above that, for the sake of limiting the intuition as such at C,
the productive activity of the I must extend beyond C into the realm of the indeterminate. This activity is reflected from infinity to A,[536] passing through C along
the way. But from C to A there [also] lies the first [activity in this] direction, a
trace of which is preserved in the understanding. This is the activity against which
the activity from A to C (which is ascribed to the I in intuition) strives and which,
in relation to the same, must be assigned to what is posited in opposition to the I,
to the Not-I. This activity posited in opposition is intuited as posited in opposition [to the I], and this would be the fifth point.

[6.] What is intuited must be determined as such and, moreover, determined
as something intuited and posited in opposition to the intuiting subject; i.e., it
must be determined by something that is not intuited, but is still supposed to be
a Not-I. But anything of this sort, lying beyond C, is an absolute product of the
[I/2: 377] activity of the I.^{RRR, 537} What is intuited, however, lies between C and A, and, in
[I, 237] accordance with its determination in the understanding, this is apprehended as
something real.[538] This would be the sixth point.

The intuiting subject and what is intuited are reciprocally related to each
other as activity and a state of being passively affected (relation and negation)
are related to each other; they are therefore united by reciprocal interaction:
if nothing is intuited, there is no intuiting subject, and *vice versa*. Similarly,
when and insofar as something is posited as intuited, an intuiting subject is
also posited, and *vice versa*.

---

^{OOO} *be determined* [Emphasis added in C.]
^{PPP} *in opposition to* [Emphasis added in C.]
^{QQQ} of *what is intuited* [Emphasis added in C.]
^{RRR} activity of the I (the thing in and for itself, qua noumenon. This is the source of the natural
distinction between a representation and the thing represented thereby). [Addition in C.]

Both must be determined, since the I is supposed to posit itself as the intuiting subject and, to that extent, posit itself in opposition to the Not-I. In order to do this, however, it requires some firm ground for distinguishing the intuiting subject from what is intuited. But according to the preceding explication of their reciprocal interaction, there is no such ground of distinction.[539]

Insofar as *either* of these two components is further determined, the *other* is also determined thereby, precisely because they stand in a relationship of reciprocal determination. — For the same reason, however, one of the two must be determined *through itself* and not through the other, since otherwise we would never escape from the circle of reciprocal determination.

V.) Considered in itself — that is, as an activity — the intuiting subject is already determined by the fact that it is in a relationship of reciprocal determination. It is an activity to which there corresponds in what is posited in opposition thereto[540] a state of being passively affected, an *objective* activity. Such an activity is further determined by a non-objective, and therefore *pure*, activity — activity purely and simply and as such.

These two activities are posited in opposition to each other and must be synthetically united; that is, they must be reciprocally determined by each other: (1.) Objective activity must be determined by pure and simple activity. Activity as such is the condition of all objective activity; it is the real ground of the latter. (2.) Activity as such is by no means supposed to be determined by objective activity, except insofar as objective activity is posited in opposition to activity as such: namely, as a state of being passively affected. Consequently, activity as such is determined by the object of activity and hence by objective activity. Objective activity is the ground of the determination, or the ideal ground, of activity as such. (3.) Each activity is determined by the other, and this means that the bound- [I, 238] ary between them must be posited. This is the transition from pure to objective activity, and vice versa, and this is a *condition* [*Bedingung*] that can either be reflected [upon] or abstracted from.

This condition, as such — that is, the boundary between pure and objective activity — is intuited by the power of imagination and stabilized in the under- [I/2: 378] standing, both of these operations occurring in the manner described above.[541]

Intuition is an objective activity under a certain *condition*. Were it unconditioned, it would not be an objective activity but a pure one.

Since it is determined through reciprocal interaction, it is also the case that what is intuited is something intuited only under a certain condition. Apart from this condition it would not be something intuited, but would instead be something posited purely and simply, a thing in itself — purely and simply a state of being passively affected, as the opposite of pure and simple activity.[542]

VI.) For both the intuiting subject and what is intuited,[SSS] intuition is something conditioned. Accordingly, they cannot yet[TTT] be distinguished from each

---

[SSS] in relationship to both the intuiting subject and to what is intuited [As emended in *C.*]
[TTT] Accordingly, the intuiting subject and what is intuited cannot yet [As emended in *C.*]

other with reference to this distinguishing feature,[543] and hence we must now determine them further. — We are trying to determine the condition for [the possibility of] intuition in both cases and whether they may not perhaps be distinguishable thereby.[544]

To say that, under the condition in question, the absolute activity becomes an objective activity is obviously to say that absolute activity is annulled and annihilated as such, and what is present, in its stead, is *a state of being passively affected*. It follows that a state of being passively affected is the condition of all objective activity.

This state of being passively affected must be intuited.[545] But such a state can be intuited only as the impossibility of any activity [on the part of the I] in opposition to this state of passive affection, as a feeling of being compelled to engage in a specific, determinate action — an intuition[546] that is, indeed, always possible for [I, 239] the power of imagination. This compulsion is stabilized in the understanding as necessity.[UUU, 547]

The opposite of this activity conditioned by a state of being passively affected is a free activity. Such an activity is intuited by means of the power of imagination as an oscillation of the power of imagination between performing and not performing one and the same action, an oscillation between apprehending and not apprehending one and the same object by means of the power of understanding. Such an object is grasped by the understanding as a possibility.[VVV]

Both types of activity, which are in themselves opposed to each other, are synthetically united. (1.) Compulsion is determined by freedom. The free activity determines itself to act in a determinate way (*self-affection*[548]). (2.) Freedom is determined by compulsion. Only if it is already determined by being passively affected can that spontaneous self-activity [*Selbsttätigkeit*],[549] which is always free when one determines oneself, determine itself to act in a determinate way. (Spontaneity [*Spontaneität*] can engage in reflection only under the condition that a reflection occasioned by an impulse or check from outside has already [I/2: 379] occurred; but even under this condition, it is not *required* to reflect. (3.) In intuition, both [compulsion and freedom] determine each other reciprocally. Reciprocal interaction between the self-affection of the intuiting subject and an affection from outside is the condition under which the intuiting subject is an intuiting subject.

With this, we have at the same time also determined what is intuited. The thing in itself[WWW] is an object of intuition on the condition that there is a relationship of reciprocal interaction [between the intuiting subject and the intuited thing]. Insofar as the intuiting subject is active, what is intuited is passively affected; and insofar as what is intuited (which, to this extent, is a thing in itself) is active, the intuiting subject is passively affected. Furthermore, insofar as the intuiting subject is active, it is not passively affected, and vice versa. So too, in the case of what is intuited. But this provides us with no firm determination, and we therefore cannot escape from our circle in this way. Hence we must continue our

UUU as *necessity* [Emphasis added in C.]
VVV as a *possibility* [Emphasis added in C.]
WWW the thing in and for itself [As emended in C.]

process of determination. That is to say, we must attempt to determine what each of the two components, considered on its own, contributes to the reciprocal interaction in question.

VII.) The activity of the intuiting subject, to which there corresponds in the [I, 240] object a state of being passively affected and which is therefore included with this in the previously mentioned reciprocal interaction,[550] is posited in opposition to another activity, to which there corresponds in the object no state of being passively affected. The latter activity (which is the activity involved in self-affection) is therefore directed at the intuiting subject itself. The activity of the intuiting subject must be determined by the latter activity.

Such a determining activity must be intuited by means of the power of imagination and stabilized in the understanding, just as was the case with the other kinds of activity discussed up this point.

It is clear that the objective activity of the intuiting subject can also have no ground other than the activity of self-determination.[551] Accordingly, if the latter activity were to be determined, then so would the former, and with it the contribution of the intuiting subject to the reciprocal interaction would be determined, which it turn would determine the contribution of what is intuited to this reciprocal determination.

These two activities must determine each other reciprocally: (1.) As was just indicated, the self-reverting activity must determine the objective activity.[XXX] (2.) The objective activity must determine the self-reverting activity.[552] The determination of the object requires just as much self-determining activity as objective activity. But the objective activity is determinable by the determination of the object, and thus the activity involved in self-determination is determinable by this as well. (3.) Accordingly, these two activities reciprocally determine each other, as has now been shown; and, once again, we have no firm point for determining them.

To the extent that the activity of what is intuited in this reciprocal determi- [I/2: 380] nation is directed at the intuiting subject, this activity is similarly determined by the self-reverting activity, through which it determines itself to affect the intuiting subject.

According to our previous explication,[553] the activity of self-determination is a determination of a stabilized product of the power of imagination in the understanding by means of reason; it is therefore an *act of thinking*. The intuiting subject determines itself to *think* of an object.

Insofar as the object is determined by thinking, it is something thought [*ein Gedachte*].   [I, 241]

In this way, the object has now been determined as determining itself[YYY] to affect the intuiting subject. This determination was made possible, however, only because a state of being passively affected was supposed to be determined in the intuiting subject, which is posited in opposition to the object. No passive affection in the intuiting subject, no original, self-reverting activity in the object, qua an

---

XXX The *self-reverting* activity must determine the *objective* activity [Emphasis added in C.]
YYY as *determining itself* [Emphasis added in C.]

activity that is thought. No such activity in the object, no passive affection in the intuiting subject. According to the preceding explication, however, such reciprocal determination occurs by means of *causal efficacy*.[554] Consequently, the object is thought of as the *cause* of a passive affection in the intuiting subject, which is thought of as its *effect*. — The inner activity of the object, by means of which it determines itself to causal efficacy, is something merely thought (a *noumenon*, if, as one must, one employs the power of imagination to provide this activity with a substrate[555]).

VIII.) The activity of self-determination for the purpose of determining a determinate object[zzz] must be further determined, since we still have no firm point [by means of which to determine it]. However, this activity is determined by an activity of the intuiting subject that determines no object as a determinate something (= A) and is directed at no determinate object. (It is therefore directed, so to speak, at an object as such, a sheer object.)

Through self-determination, such an activity must be capable of furnishing itself with either A or −A as its object. This same activity would, therefore, be completely undetermined, or free, with respect to A or −A; it would be free either to *reflect upon* A or to *abstract from* it.

Such an activity must, first of all, be intuited by means of the power of imagination; but since it oscillates in the middle between terms posited in opposition to each other, between apprehending and not apprehending A, this activity must also be intuited *as* the power of imagination, that is, it must be intuited in its freedom of oscillating from one to the other (as when one views a *law* — with which, to be sure, we are as yet unacquainted[556] — as the mind's deliberation with itself). — Yet one of these two, either A or −A, must be apprehended by means of
[I/2: 381]   this activity. (A is posited either as what is to be reflected upon or as what is to be
[I, 242]   abstracted from.) For this reason, this activity must also be intuited as the power of understanding. — Both of these [the power of imagination and the power of understanding], reunited by means of a new intuition and held fast in the understanding, constitute *the power of judgment*.[557] Judgment is the, until now, free power to reflect upon or to abstract from objects already posited in the understanding and, on the basis of this reflection or abstraction, to posit these objects in the understanding with additional determinations.

Both of these activities — the sheer power of understanding, as such, and the power of judgment, as such — must again determine each other reciprocally. (1) The power of understanding must determine that of judgment. Understanding already contains within itself those objects from which the power of judgment abstracts or upon which it reflects, and it is therefore the condition for the possibility of any power of judgment at all. (2.) The power of judgment must determine that of understanding; it determines any object whatsoever as an object for the power of understanding. Without the power of judgment, there would be no reflecting at all. Without it, therefore, nothing would be stabilized in the understanding, since this is something first posited by means of and for the purposes of reflection. Hence there would also be no power of understanding at all without

---

[zzz] a *determinate* object [Emphasis added in C.]

the power of judgment; and the power of judgment is therefore, in turn, the condition for the possibility of the power of understanding. (3.) Consequently, these two determine each other reciprocally. If nothing is present in the understanding, there is no power of judgment; if there is no power of judgment, there is nothing present in the power of understanding *for the power of understanding*, no thought of what is thought of, as such.

The object too is now determined in accordance with this reciprocal determination. As the object of thinking — and as, to this extent, passively affected — , what is thought is determined by something that is not thought, and thus by something that is merely thinkable (which possesses the ground of its thinkability within itself, and not in the thinking subject, and is therefore, to this extent, active, and in relation to which the thinking subject is supposed to be passively affected). Both of these, what is thought and what is thinkable, are now reciprocally determined by each other: (1.) everything that is thought is thinkable, and (2) everything thinkable is thought of as thinkable and is thinkable only insofar as it is thought to be thinkable. If nothing is thinkable, then nothing is thought; and if nothing is thought, then nothing is thinkable. — What is thinkable and thinkability as such are objects of the power of judgment alone.

Only what has been judged to be thinkable can be thought of as the cause of an [I, 243] intuition.

The thinking subject is supposed to determine itself to think of something as thinkable, and to this extent what is thinkable would be passively affected. On the other hand, what is thinkable is supposed to determine itself to be thinkable, and, to this extent, the thinking subject would be passively affected. This presents us, yet again, with a reciprocal interaction in thinking, an interaction between the thinking subject and what is thought. But since this pro- [I/2: 382] vides us with no firm point of determination, we must determine the judging subject still further.

IX.) The activity that determines any object whatsoever is determined by an activity that has no object at all, that is, by an activity that is not in the least objective and is posited in opposition to the objective activity. The question is simply this: How can such an activity be posited, and how can it be posited in opposition to the objective activity?

Just as we have now deduced the possibility of abstracting from any determinate^AAAA object (= A), we are here postulating the possibility of abstracting from any object whatsoever.^BBBB If the required determination[558] is supposed to be possible, then there must be such an absolute power of abstraction; and it must be possible, if any self-consciousness and any consciousness of a representation are supposed to be possible.

Such a power of abstraction must, first of all, be capable of being intuited. — By its very nature, the power of imagination oscillates constantly [*überhaupt*] between the object and what is not an object. [Suppose that] it is stabilized as

---

^AAAA from any *determinate* [Emphasis added in C.]
^BBBB *from any object whatsoever* [Emphasis added in C.]

having no object: this means the (reflected upon) power of imagination is completely annihilated, and this annihilation, this non-being of the power of imagination, is itself intuited by the power of imagination (which in this case is not reflected upon, and therefore does not attain to clear consciousness). (The intuition in question is the obscure representation present within us whenever we are

[I, 244] reminded, for the sake of pure thinking, to abstract from any contribution from the power of imagination, and this is an intuition that is frequently present for the thinker.) — The product of such a (non-reflected) intuition is supposed to be stabilized in the understanding; and yet this product is supposed to be nothing. It is not supposed to be any object at all, and therefore it cannot be stabilized. (An example of this is the obscure representation of the thought of a sheer relationship, apart from any related components.) Accordingly, nothing remains but the very rule of reason as such, which tells us to abstract — the sheer law governing a determination that can never be realized (by means of the power of imagination and understanding, which is what is required for clear consciousness). This absolute power of abstraction is therefore reason itself.CCCC

If everything objective is annulled, there remains at least that which *determines itself* and *is determined by itself:* the pure I, or the subject. Subject and object are determined by each other in such a way that either of them is utterly excluded by the other. If the I determines only itself, then it determines nothing outside itself; and if it determines something outside itself, then it does not determine only itself. But the I has now been determined as that which remains following the

[I/2: 383] annulment of all objects by means of the power of abstraction, and the Not-I has been determined as that from which this power of abstraction can abstract. With this, we have finally obtained a firm standpoint, on the basis of which we can distinguish between the object and the subject.

(This, therefore, is actually the obvious source of all self-consciousness, a point that can no longer be misunderstood once it has been pointed out. Anything from which I can abstract and which I can think away — even if this does not occur all at once, but nevertheless in such a way that I can subsequently abstract from what I left remaining and then leave remaining that from which I am now abstracting — is not my I, and I posit it in opposition to my I only by considering it to be something from which I am able to abstract. The more of himself a determinate individual is able to think away, the closer his empirical self-consciousness comes to pure self-consciousness — from the child who leaves his cradle for the first time and thereby learns to distinguish it from himself, to the popular philosopher, who entertains idea-pictures and inquires concerning the seat of the soul,[559] and finally, to the transcendental

[I, 245] philosopher, who at least thinks for himself the rule for thinking of a pure I[560] and then acts in accordance with this rule.)

X.) This activity, which determines the I by abstracting from it everything that can be abstracted from it, must itself be determined in turn. But nothing

---

CCCC is therefore *reason* itself. (*Pure* reason, in the theoretical sense, without the power of imagination; this was what Kant took as his object in the *Critique of Pure Reason.*) [Emphasis and parenthetical remark added in *C.*]

remains to be further determined in that *from* which nothing can be abstracted and *in* which there is nothing from which one could abstract (which is why the I is judged to be *simple*[561]). For this reason, the determining activity in question can be determined only by a purely and simply posited, non-determining activity, and what is determined by this activity[562] is determined by what is utterly undetermined.

To be sure, such a power of what is utterly undetermined, which is the condition [for the possibility] of all that is determined, has now been attributed to the power of imagination by means of the [preceding] inferences. But such a power can by no means be raised to consciousness, for then it would have to be reflected and thus determined by the understanding, in which case it would no longer remain undetermined and infinite.

It follows that when the I is engaged in self-determination it must be considered to be at once determining and determined. If, by means of the present, higher determination, one reflects upon the fact that what determines what is purely and simply determined must itself be purely and simply undetermined, as well as upon the fact that the I and Not-I are purely and simply posited in opposition to each other, then, if what is viewed as determined is the I, what is determining and undetermined is the Not-I; and, in contrast, if the I is viewed [384] as determining, then it itself is what is undetermined, and what is determined thereby is the Not-I. From this there ensues the following conflict:

If the I reflects upon itself and, in doing so, determines itself, then it is the Not-I that is infinite and unlimited. If, on the other hand, the I reflects upon the Not-I as such (upon the universe) and thereby determines it, then it is the I itself that is infinite. In representation, therefore, the I and the Not-I reciprocally interact with each other:[564] if the one is finite, then the other is infinite, and vice versa. [I, 264] But one of the two is always infinite. — (This is the basis of Kant's *antinomies*.[565])

XI.) If, by means of a still higher reflection, one reflects upon the fact that the I itself is what is purely and simply determining and therefore also what purely and simply determines the preceding reflection (the reflection upon which the conflict in question depends), then the Not-I is, in any case, once again what is determined by the I. And this is so no matter whether the Not-I is explicitly determined for reflection or whether it is left undetermined in reflection, in order that the I may determine itself. Consequently, since it can be either finite or infinite, the I interacts reciprocally only with itself — a reciprocal interaction in which the I is completely united with itself and beyond which no theoretical philosophy can go.

Part Three

Foundation of the Science of the Practical[565]

§ 5. Second Theorem

The proposition ensuing from the three foundational principles of the entire *Wissenschaftslehre* was as follows: *the I and Not-I determine each other reciprocally.* This is a proposition that includes within itself the following two propositions: first, *the I posits itself as determined by the Not-I*, a proposition we have now explicated, while also discovering that *factum* in our mind which has to correspond to this proposition;[566] second, *the I posits itself as determining the Not-I.*

As we were beginning the preceding § we could not yet know whether we would ever be able to assign any meaning to the second proposition, since it presupposes the *determinability* and therefore the *reality* of the Not-I, an assumption [I, 247] for which we could at that point provide no basis. Now, however, thanks to and presupposing this postulated *factum*,[567] we have at the same time postulated the reality of the Not-I — its reality *for* the I, as goes without saying, since the entire *Wissenschaftslehre*, as a transcendental science, cannot go beyond the I, nor should it. With this, the precise difficulty that hindered us from assuming this second proposition has been eliminated. If the Not-I possesses reality for the I and (which means the same thing) if the I posits the Not-I as real (and both the possibility and the character of this kind of positing have now been displayed), then it follows that, if any additional determinations of this same proposition are to be thinkable (which, to be sure, is something we cannot yet know), then the I can certainly also posit itself as determining (limiting, setting a boundary to) this [additionally] posited reality.

In explicating the proposition that the I posits itself as determining the Not-I, we could precede as we did in explicating the proposition that the I posits itself as determined by the Not-I. Like the latter, the former proposition contains many components posited in opposition to each other. We could seek these out, unite them synthetically, and then synthetically unite, in turn, the concepts arising from this synthesis, and then synthetically unite any concepts arising from the latter synthesis, should these turn out to be posited in opposition to each other, etc.[568] By employing such a simple and thoroughgoing method, we would be [I/2: 386] certain of completely exhausting our proposition. There is, however, a shorter yet no less exhaustive way of explicating it.

To wit: this proposition [that the I posits itself as determining the Not-I] contains a major antithesis, which embraces the entire conflict between the I, as intellect (and hence, to that extent, limited) and this same I as posited purely and simply (and hence, to that extent, possessing an unlimited nature), and this antithesis will require us to assume, as a means for uniting the components of this antithesis, that the I possesses a practical power. Our first task is to seek out the antithesis in question, the components of which are posited in opposition to each other, and unite them.[569] The remaining antitheses will then reveal themselves on their own and will be all the easier to unite.

I.

In order to seek out the antithesis in question we will take the shortest path. This will enable us to prove, from a higher standpoint, that we are permitted to assume the chief principle of the entire practical *Wissenschaftslehre* and that this proposition possesses, right from the start, a greater validity than any merely problematic proposition. The chief principle in question is this: *the I posits itself as determining the Not-I.*

The I is, as such, I. It is absolutely one [*schlecterdings Ein*], and this is because it is posited through itself (§1).

Now, to be sure, insofar as the I is specifically *engaged in representing* (or is an *intellect*), it is, *as such*, also one [*Eins*]: a power of representation governed by necessary laws. To this extent, however, it is by no means one and the same as the absolute I, which is posited purely and simply through itself.

The reason for this is as follows: The I as intellect, *insofar as it is already this*, is indeed determined by itself with respect to its particular determinations within this sphere [of representation], and there is also nothing within this sphere except what the I posits within itself. Our theory[570] directly contradicts the opinion that something enters the I, something to which the I is related only passively.[571] Considered in itself and as such, however, *this sphere* itself [that is, the sphere of representations posited by the I] is not posited within the I by the I itself [as intellect], but by something outside the I. The *mode* and *manner* of [such] representing are surely determined, as such, by the I; but, as we have seen, the fact *that* the I is engaged in representing at all is not determined by the I, but by something outside it. The only way we could think representation to be possible as such was by presupposing that a check or impetus [*Anstoß*] occurs to the undetermined and infinitely outgoing activity of the I. It follows that the I as *intellect* is *as such* [I/2: 387] dependent upon an undetermined and, until now, utterly undeterminable, Not-I and that it is an intellect only through and by means of such a Not-I.*

And yet the I, along with all its determinations, is supposed to be[572] posited purely and simply by the I itself, and it is therefore supposed to be completely [I, 249] independent of any possible Not-I.

Consequently, the absolute I and the intelligent I (if it is permissible to express oneself as if these constituted two I's, even though they are supposed to constitute only one) are not one and the same; instead, they are posited in opposition to each other, which contradicts the absolute identity of the I.[573]

This contradiction must be eliminated, and this can be accomplished only as follows: The intelligence of the I as such, which is what provokes this

---

* Any reader who attaches profound meaning to this assertion and is able to anticipate its far-reaching implications is one I welcome wholeheartedly, and such a reader may from now on continue to draw inferences from this proposition in his own way. — A finite [rational] being is finite only as an intellect; the practical legislation that such an intellect is supposed to have in common with the infinite I is not dependent upon anything external to the I.

[In contrast,] those readers who have acquired the facility of suspecting at least atheism (if not worse) on the basis of an incomplete outline of a completely new system, one that they are unable to absorb in a single glance, are invited to stop with this explanation and see what they may be able to make of it.

contradiction, cannot be annulled without once again placing the I in a new contradiction with itself. This is because, if an I is ever posited and a Not-I is posited in opposition to it, then, according to the entire theoretical [portion of the] *Wissenschaftslehre*, a power of representation is also posited, along with all of its determinations. As we have just observed and as has been demonstrated in the theoretical part, insofar as the I is already posited as an intellect, then it too is determined purely through itself. But the *dependence* of the I, qua intellect, is supposed to be annulled, and this is conceivable only under the following condition: namely, *that the I determines through itself this Not-I, which has until now remained unknown*[574] and to which there is ascribed that check or impetus by means of which the I becomes an intellect. In this way, the Not-I that is to be represented would be *immediately* determined by the absolute I, whereas the representing I would — thanks to that determination [by the check] — be *mediately* or *indirectly* determined by the absolute I. The I would be dependent solely upon itself; that is

[I, 250] to say, it would be completely determined by itself. It would be what it posits itself
[I/2: 388] to be and purely and simply nothing else, and the contradiction would be satisfactorily eliminated. We would thereby have demonstrated, in a preliminary manner, at least the second half of the proposition in question: the I determines the Not-I (inasmuch as the I is the determining subject and the Not-I is that which becomes determined).[575]

The I as intellect was causally related to the Not-I, to which the postulated check is attributed; this check was produced [*bewirkt*] by the Not-I, as its cause. This is because the causal relationship consists in this: owing to the limitation of the activity of one of the [causally related] components (or to a quantity of being passively affected in that component), an equal quantity of activity is posited in what is posited in opposition to this first component, in accordance with the law of reciprocal determination. If the I is supposed to be an intellect, however, then a portion of the I's infinitely outgoing activity must be annulled and then posited in the Not-I, in accordance with the law in question. Since, however, the absolute I is quite incapable of being passively affected and is supposed to be absolute activity and nothing whatsoever but activity, it must be assumed, as was just indicated, that this postulated Not-I is also determined and therefore passively affected. And the activity posited in opposition to this state of being passively affected must be posited in what is posited in opposition thereto, that is, in the I — not indeed in the I as intellect, since this is itself determined by the Not-I, but rather, in the absolute I. But the relationship that must thereby be assumed is a causal one. Consequently, the absolute I is supposed to be the *cause* of the Not-I, insofar as the latter is the ultimate ground of all representation; and, to this extent, the I as intellect is the product of the absolute I.

1.) The I is purely and simply active and is nothing but active: this is the absolute presupposition. From this there is inferred, first of all, a state of being passively affected by the Not-I, insofar as the latter is supposed to determine the I as intellect. The activity posited in opposition to this state of being passively affected is posited in the absolute I and posited there as a *determinate* activity, as precisely that activity which determines the

Not-I. A certain *determinate activity* of the I is thus inferred from the *abso-* [I, 251]
lute activity of the I.

2.) Everything that has just been said serves at the same time to make the
preceding inference[576] even more illuminating. A representation as such
(and not, as it were, a particular determination of that representation) is
incontrovertibly a product of the Not-I. But there can simply be nothing
whatsoever in the I that is supposed to be a product of the Not-I, since
the I is what it posits itself to be, and there is nothing in the I that it does
not posit in itself. Consequently, this Not-I[577] must itself be a product
[*ein bewirktes*] of the I, and indeed, of the absolute I.[578] (In this case, therefore, there would be no effect [*Einwirkung*] upon the I from outside, but [I/2: 389]
merely a causally efficacious operation [*Wirkung*] of the I upon itself —
an operation that, admittedly, takes a roundabout route,[579] for reasons
which are still unrecognizable, though they will perhaps become visible
in the future.[580])

The absolute I is therefore supposed to be the cause of the Not-I, considered in
and for itself; it is the cause only of what remains in the Not-I after one has
abstracted from it every demonstrable form of representation. The absolute I is
the cause of that to which the check upon the infinitely outgoing activity of the
I is attributed, whereas those particular determinations of what is represented
as such — those determinations of which the intelligent I is, in accordance with
the necessary laws of representing, supposed to be the cause — are displayed in
the theoretical [portion of the] *Wissenschaftslehre*.

[Yet] the I cannot be the cause of the Not-I in this same way,[581] that is, by
means of absolute positing.

The I posits itself purely and simply and for no additional reason [*Grund*], and
it *must* posit itself if it is supposed to posit anything else. This is because what
does not *exist* can posit nothing; the I exists (for the I) purely and simply and
exclusively through its own positing of itself.

The I cannot posit the Not-I without limiting itself. This is because the Not-I is
posited in utter opposition to the I: what the Not-I is, the I is not. Consequently,
insofar as the Not-I is posited (that is, insofar as the predicate "being-posited" is
assigned to it), the I is not posited. Were the Not-I perhaps to be posited with no [I, 252]
quantity, and thus as unlimited and infinite, then the I would not be posited at all;
its reality would be completely annihilated, which contradicts what was said
above. — Consequently, the Not-I must be posited with a determinate quantity,
and the reality of the I must therefore be limited in accordance with the quantity
of reality posited in the Not-I. — As has been demonstrated in the theoretical
Wissenschaftslehre the expression "*to posit a Not-I*"[A] is completely equivalent to
the expression "*to limit the I*."

According to what we are here presupposing,[582] the I is supposed to posit a
Not-I *purely and simply* and without any reason or ground, which is to say that it
is supposed to limit itself — and, thus, to not posit itself, in part — purely and

---

[A] "*to posit* a Not-I" [Emphasis removed in C.]

simply and without any ground.[583] It must therefore contain within itself that ground on the basis of which it does not posit itself. The principle [*Princip*] of positing itself and the principle of not positing itself must both reside in the I. In this case, the I would, by its very nature [*in seinem Wesen*], be posited in opposition to itself and in conflict with itself. It would contain within itself a two-fold principle opposed to itself — an assumption that contradicts itself, since in that case it would contain no principle whatsoever. The I would be [I/2: 390] nothing at all, since it would annul itself.

(We have arrived at a point from which we can display more clearly the true meaning of our second foundational principle, *a Not-I is posited in opposition to the I*, and this will allow us to display the true meaning of our system more clearly than has been possible until now.

This second foundational principle contains only some components that are absolute, but it contains others that presuppose a *factum*, which can by no means be demonstrated a priori, but only through each person's own experience.

In addition to the positing of the I through itself, there is also supposed be another act of positing. From the a priori standpoint, this is merely an hypothesis.[584] *That* such an act of positing occurs can be demonstrated only by means of a *factum* of consciousness. Every person must demonstrate it [viz., the reality of this second act of positing] to himself through such a *factum*, and no one can demonstrate it to anyone else on rational grounds. — To be sure, by adducing rational grounds, one might trace some [other] *factum*, which the other person concedes, back to this [I, 253] supreme *factum*, but such a proof would do no more than lead this person to recognize that, in conceding the first *factum*, he has also conceded the second. — It is, however, absolutely and purely and simply grounded in the nature of the I that, *if* there is such a [second] act of positing, it must be one of *positing in opposition*, and what is posited in opposition must be *a Not-I*. — No higher ground can be adduced from which one might derive how it is possible for the I to distinguish anything whatsoever from itself; instead, this distinction itself [between the I and the Not-I] underlies and grounds all derivation and grounding. It is purely and simply certain that this act of positing, which is not an act of positing the I, must be an act of positing something in opposition [to the I]. That such an act of positing occurs is something that anyone can demonstrate to himself only through his own experience. This is why the argument of the *Wissenschaftslehre* is valid purely and simply a priori; it establishes only those propositions that are certain a priori. But the *Wissenschaftslehre* first obtains reality only through experience. This entire science would have no content and would be empty for anyone unable to become conscious of this postulated *factum* — though one can be sure that this will not be the case for any finite rational being[585] — , even though such a person would still have to concede the formal correctness of this science.

The *Wissenschaftslehre* is therefore possible a priori, whether or not it is supposed to apply directly to objects. The object is not a priori; instead, it is first given to the *Wissenschaftslehre* in experience. Objective validity is furnished to everyone [only] by means of his own consciousness of the object, a consciousness that can only be postulated a priori but not deduced. — Simply as an example:

Our science would possess no content for the deity — that is, for a consciousness in which everything would be posited simply by virtue of the I's being-posited —, even though the concept of such a consciousness is, for us, unthinkable. This is [I/2: 391] because no positing whatsoever would occur in such a consciousness other than the positing of the I.[586] Nevertheless, even for God our science would still possess formal correctness, since its form is that of pure reason itself.)

II. [I, 254]

We have observed that the required causal influence of the I upon the Not-I, which was supposed to resolve the indicated contradiction between the independence of the I, as an absolute being [als absoluten Wesen], and the dependence of the I, as an intellect, itself harbors a contradiction. The first contradiction [between the independence and dependence of the I] must nevertheless be resolved, and it can be resolved only by means of the requisite causality. We must therefore attempt to resolve the contradiction implicit within this requirement and will now turn to this second task.

In order to accomplish this, let us first seek to obtain a somewhat deeper understanding of the true meaning of the contradiction in question.

The I *is supposed to exercise a causal influence upon the Not-I*,[587] and it is supposed to first produce the Not-I for a possible representation of the Not-I. This is because nothing can pertain to the I that it does not itself posit within itself, either directly or indirectly, and because the I is supposed to be all that it is purely and simply through itself. — The demand for causality [on the part of the I] is therefore grounded in the absolute essence [*Wesenheit*] of the I.

The I *can exercise no causal influence upon the Not-I*, for the Not-I would then cease to be Not-I (that is, it would cease to be what is posited in opposition to the I) and would itself become I. But it was the I itself that posited the Not-I in opposition to itself; therefore, this positing in opposition cannot be annulled, unless something posited by the I is supposed to be annulled at the same time. In that case, however, the I would have to cease to be an I, which contradicts the identity of the I. It follows that the contradiction implicit in the required causal influence [of the I upon the Not-I] is grounded in the fact that a Not-I is purely and simply posited in opposition to the I and must remain posited in opposition to it.

The contradiction in question is therefore a contradiction between two different aspects of the I. These are what contradict each other, and our task is to discover some intermediary between them. (No such contradiction would arise with respect to an I in opposition to which nothing is posited, in the unthinkable idea of the deity.) Insofar as the I is absolute, it is *infinite* and *unlimited*. It posits [I/2: 392] all that is, and what it does not posit does not exist. (That is to say, it does not exist [I, 255] *for* it, and there is nothing *outside* this absolute I.) But everything that it posits, it posits as I, and the I posits this as all that it posits. In this respect, therefore, the I contains within itself everything, i.e., an infinite and unlimited reality.[588]

Insofar as the I posits a Not-I in opposition to itself, it necessarily posits *limits*[589] (§ 3) and posits itself within these limits. It divides the totality of all posited being whatsoever between itself and the Not-I; and to this extent it therefore necessarily posits itself as *finite*.

These two, very different actions [of the I] can be expressed through the following two propositions: First, the I posits itself purely and simply as *infinite* and *unlimited*;[590] second, the I posits itself purely and simply as *finite* and *limited*. A still higher contradiction would thereby be posited within the essence of the I itself, inasmuch as this essence manifests itself through both its first and second actions [of positing]. This, therefore, is the source of the present contradiction. If the former [contradiction within the essence of the I] is resolved, then so is the latter contradiction between the absolute and limited I], which is based upon the former.

All contradictions are resolved [*vereinigt*] by more closely determining the propositions that contradict each other, and this is the case here as well. The I must have been posited as in one sense *infinite* and in another *finite*. Were it posited as both infinite and finite in one and the same sense, then the contradiction would be irresolvable; the I would be not one but two, and we would be left with no solution other than the one proposed by Spinoza: namely, to displace the infinite by positing it outside us. In that case, however, it would remain forever unknown how even the *idea* of the infinite could ever arise within us. (On account of his dogmatism, Spinoza himself could not even pose this question.)

In what sense, then, is the I posited as infinite, and in what sense is it posited as finite?

Both infinitude and finitude are credited to the I purely and simply. The ground of its infinity is its sheer action of positing, and the same is true of its finitude. In [I, 256] either case, simply by positing something the I posits itself in what it has posited; that is, it ascribes this to itself. All we have to do, therefore, is discover the difference between the actions involved in these two different acts of positing, and we will thereby have accomplished our task.

Insofar as the I posits itself as infinite, its activity (of positing) is directed at [I/2: 393] itself and at nothing other than the I. Its entire activity is directed at the I, and this activity constitutes the ground and scope of all being. The I is therefore *infinite insofar as its activity reverts into itself*.[591] To this extent, its activity is also infinite, since its product, the I, is infinite. (Infinite product, infinite activity; infinite activity, infinite product. This is a circle, but not a vicious one, because it is that circle from which reason cannot escape, since it expresses what is purely and simply certain through itself and for its own sake. The product, the activity, and the active subject are here one and the same — see § 1[592] — , and we distinguish them simply in order to express ourselves.) Nothing is infinite but the *pure activity* of the I, and the *pure I alone* is infinite. Pure activity, however, is an activity that has no object whatsoever, but reverts into itself.

Insofar as the I posits limits and, in accordance with what was just said, posits itself within these limits, its activity (of positing) is not directed immediately at itself, but at a Not-I posited in opposition to itself (§§ 2-3). Such activity is therefore no longer pure; instead, it is *objective* activity (which posits an object for itself. The word "object" [*Gegenstand*] nicely designates what it is supposed to designate. Every object of an activity, insofar as it is such an object, is necessarily something posited in opposition to that activity, something standing *in resistance* or *in opposition* to it.[593] If no resistance is present, then this activity also has no object [*Objekt*] at all, and no objective activity whatsoever is present. Instead, if it is still supposed to be an activity, it is a pure, self-reverting one. The very concept of objective activity already indicates that such an activity is resisted and therefore restricted.) It follows that the I is finite insofar as its activity is *objective*.   [I, 257]

Considered in both these respects — whether as reverting upon the active subject itself or as directed at an object outside the I — , the activity in question is supposed to be one and the same activity, the activity of one and the same subject, which posits itself as one and the same subject in both respects. There must therefore be some bond of unity between these two kinds of activity, which conducts consciousness from the one to the other; and the requisite causal relationship is such a bond. That is to say, the self-reverting activity of the I is related to the objective activity in the same way that a cause is related to its effect: By means of the first [pure] activity, the I determines itself to engage in the second [objective] activity. Accordingly, the first activity is directed *immediately* at the I, but it is *mediately* or *indirectly* directed at the Not-I, by virtue of the determination of [I/2: 394] the I itself which occurs thereby, according to which the I is what determines the Not-I. The requisite causal influence [of the I upon the Not-I] would thereby be realized.

The first requirement, therefore, is that the action of the I through which it posits itself (an action that was established in our first foundational principle) be related to that action by means of which it posits a Not-I (an action that was established in our second foundational principle) in the same way a cause is related to what it produces. Generally speaking, however, such a relationship cannot be evinced [in this case]; on the contrary, it has been found to be completely contradictory. This is because such a relationship would require that the I, in positing itself, posit at the same time the Not-I, and thus not posit itself; and this is a conclusion that annuls itself. — It has been explicitly asserted that the I posits something in opposition to itself purely and simply and without any ground,[594] and it is only in consequence of the unconditional character of this action that the proposition that expresses it can be called a foundational principle. It was noted at the same time, however, that at least something in this same action must be conditioned: namely, the product of the same. This means that what must arise by means of this act of positing in opposition [to the I] must necessarily be a Not-I, and could be nothing else. Let us now delve more deeply into the meaning of this [I, 258] remark.

The I *purely and simply* posits an object (a Not-I, which stands over against and is posited in opposition to the I). In this *sheer act of positing* the Not-I, the I is dependent only upon itself and upon nothing outside itself. If any *object* whatsoever is posited, and if, by means of this, the I is posited as *limited* in any way, then this achieves what was desired. In this case, one should not think of any *determinate* limit; the I is now limited purely and simply. But where does this limit lie? Inside or outside point C?[595] And by means of what could such a point be determined? This is something that continues to depend solely upon the spontaneity of the I, a spontaneity that is posited through the expression "purely and simply" [*schlechthin*]. The boundary-point [between the I and the Not-I] lies wherever the I posits it within the domain of the infinite. Since it is supposed to be limited, the

I is finite; but within this finitude, it is infinite, since the limit in question can always be posited further out within the infinite domain.[596] With respect to its finitude, the I is infinite; and with respect to its infinitude, it is finite. — The I is therefore not limited by this absolute positing of an object, except insofar as it limits itself purely and simply and without any ground. But such an absolute limitation contradicts the absolutely infinite nature of the I and is therefore impossible, as would be the entire act of positing a Not-I in opposition [to the I, were the limitation in question absolute].

[I/2: 395] Furthermore, the I posits an *object* wherever it may wish within the infinite domain,[597] and in doing so it posits an activity that is independent of its own activity (of positing) but is instead posited in opposition to that activity. To be sure, there is a certain (here unexamined) sense in which this activity posited in opposition must *lie within the I*, inasmuch as it is posited in the I. There is, how-ever, another (equally unexamined) sense in which this same activity must *lie within the object*. Insofar as it lies within the object, this activity [of the object] is supposed to be posited in opposition to some activity or other (= X) of the I — but not in opposition to that activity by means of which activity X is posited in the I, since this is the same activity [that was involved in positing the activity of the object]. Consequently, it [that is, the activity attributed to the object] must be

[I, 259] posited in opposition to *some other activity* [of the I]. From this it follows that, insofar as an object is supposed to be posited — and as a condition *for the possi-bility of such positing* — an activity (= X) distinct from the activity of positing must be present within the I. What activity is this?

To begin with, this is the kind of activity that *is not annulled* by the object, since it is supposed to be posited in opposition to the activity of the object. Accordingly, both activities are supposed to be positing as subsisting alongside one another. Hence the kind of activity we are now discussing is one whose being is independent of the object, just as the object is, in turn, independent of it. — Furthermore, such an activity must be purely and simply grounded in the I, because it is independent of the positing of all objects, which are, conversely, independent of it. The activity in question is therefore posited through the abso-lute action of the I, that action by which it posits itself. — Finally, according to the preceding, the object should be capable of being posited beyond the I, into the domain of the infinite. Therefore, the activity of the I that resists the activity of the object must itself extend into the domain of the infinite, beyond all possible objects; and this activity must itself be infinite. — But just as surely as our second foundational principle is valid, an object must be posited. — Consequently, X is the infinite activity that is posited within itself by the I, and this activity is related to the objective activity of the I in the same way that the ground of some possibil-ity is related to what is grounded thereby. The object is posited only insofar as an [infinite] activity of the I is resisted: no such activity of the I, no object. — This infinite activity, which is posited by the I within itself, exerts itself like the deter-mining subject in relation to what is determined. An object can be posited only *insofar as* this activity is resisted, and insofar as it is not resisted there is no object.

Let us now consider this activity with respect to its relation to the activity of the object. — Considered in themselves, both of these activities are independent

of each other and posited completely in opposition to each other. There is no connection or relation between them. But if, in accordance with what is demanded,
an object is to be posited, then these two activities must be connected with each
other by the I that posits an object.[598] The positing of any object at all also depends
upon this connection: insofar as an object is posited, these activities are con-   [I, 260]
nected to each other, and insofar as they are not connected, no object is posited. —
In addition, since the object is posited absolutely, purely and simply, and without
any ground[599] (by the act of positing, considered simply as such), then the connec-   [I/2: 396]
tion between these two activities is also established purely and simply and without
any ground. Only now has the extent to which the positing of the Not-I is supposed to be absolute been fully explained: it is absolute insofar as it is grounded
upon this connection [between the infinitely outgoing, but resisted activity of the I
and the activity attributed to the object], a connection that is solely dependent
upon the I.[600] To say that these activities are purely and simply connected is to say
that they are purely and simply posited as the same.[601] However, just as surely as an
object is supposed to be posited, these activities are not the same; and therefore all
one can say is that their likeness is purely and simply demanded: they *ought* to be
purely and simply the same. — Since, however, they are not the same, the question
always remains: which of the two should conform to the other, and which of them
is supposed to contain the ground for equating them? — It is immediately obvious
how this question must be answered. Insofar as the I is posited, all reality is posited; everything ought to be posited in the I. The I ought to be purely and simply
independent, and everything ought to be dependent upon it. What is demanded,
therefore, is the conformity of the object with the I.[602] It is the absolute I that
demands this, and it demands it precisely for the sake of its own absolute being.*

(Let us assume the occurrence of activity Y, an activity of what will   [I, 261]
henceforth be posited as the object, though it here remains unexamined *how*
and by *which power* of the subject this activity of the object is posited. An
activity of the I is *connected* to activity Y; in this case,[603] therefore, one must
think of an activity outside the I (= −Y), an activity that would be the same as
this activity of the I. What is the ground of the connection [*Beziehungsgrund*]
between these two activities in this case? It obviously lies in the demand that
all activity be equivalent to the activity of the I, a demand grounded in the
I's absolute being. −Y lies in a *world* in which all activity would *actually* be   [I/2: 397]
equivalent to the activity of the I; this is an ideal. But Y is not in agreement
with −Y; instead, it is *posited in opposition* to −Y. This is why Y is ascribed to an

---

* Kant's categorical imperative. If it is anywhere clear that Kant, in his Critical undertaking,
assumed — albeit only tacitly — precisely the premises established by the *Wissenschaftslehre*, it is here.
How else could he ever have been able to encounter a categorical imperative, as an absolute postulate
of conformity with the pure I, without presupposing the absolute being of the I, through which everything would be posited, and, insofar as it *is* not posited, at least *ought* to be posited? — The majority of
Kant's followers seem merely to parrot what this great man says concerning the categorical imperative,
but they do not appear to have yet achieved clarity regarding the basis for the authority of an absolute
postulate.[604] — Only *because* and *insofar as* the I is itself absolute does it have the right to postulate
absolutely, and this right then extends no further than the right to postulate this, its own absolute
being, from which, to be sure, much else may then be *deduced*. — A philosophy that appeals to a fact
[*Tatsache*] of consciousness whenever *it* cannot make any further progress is hardly better grounded
than the discredited Popular Philosophy.

object, and without this connection and the absolute demand[604] upon which it is based there would be no object for the I, which would instead be the all in all[605] — and, for precisely this reason, the I would be nothing, as we shall see below.[606])

The absolute I therefore connects itself purely and simply to a Not-I (the −Y in question), which, as it seems, is supposed to be a Not-I with respect to its form (insofar as it is something utterly external to the I) but not with respect to its content (insofar as it is supposed to be in complete harmony with the I). But the Not-I cannot be in harmony with the I, inasmuch as it is also, simply with respect to its form, supposed to be a Not-I. Consequently, the activity of the I that is connected to the Not-I is by no means an act of determining [the Not-I] (so that it is actually equivalent to the I); instead, it is merely a *tendency* [*Tendenz*], a *striving* [*Streben*][607] toward determination [of the Not-I by the I], which is nevertheless fully warranted, since it is posited by the absolute positing of the I.

The conclusion of our investigation up to this point is therefore as follows:[608] Considered *in its connection with a possible object*, the pure, self-reverting activity of the I is a *striving*, and indeed, according to the preceding proof, *an infinite* [I, 262] *striving.* This infinite striving, extending endlessly outward, is the *condition for the possibility of any object*: no striving, no object.

We can now see the extent to which this conclusion, which has been arrived at by means of additional foundational principles, satisfies the task we have set ourselves and can determine the extent to which the contradiction in question[609] is resolved thereby. — Considered as an intellect as such, the I is dependent upon a Not-I, and it is an intellect only insofar as there is a Not-I; yet the intelligent I is nevertheless supposed to depend solely upon the I. In order to find this to be possible, however, we again had to assume that, insofar as the Not-I is supposed to be the object of the intelligent I, the I exercises a causal influence upon and determines the Not-I. At first glance, and taking the word "causality" in its full scope, such causality annulled itself:[610] if it is presupposed, then either the I or the Not-I is not posited, and there can therefore be no causal relationship between them. We tried to resolve this contradiction by distinguishing between two activities of the I posited in opposition to each other — namely, its pure and objective activities — and by presupposing that the pure activity might be immediately related to the objective activity as a cause is related to what it produces, and that the objective activity might be immediately related to the object as a cause is related to what it produces. Hence, we presupposed that the pure activity of the I might be allowed to stand at least *mediately* or *indirectly* in a causal relationship with the object (a [I/2: 398] relationship mediated by the objective activity). To what extent has this presupposition now been confirmed, and to what extent has it not been confirmed?

To begin with, to what extent has the pure activity of the I proven itself to be the cause of the objective activity? First of all, no object can be posited if no activity of the I is posited in opposition to the activity of the object. This activity of the I must necessarily occur in the subject itself, prior to all objects, purely and simply and exclusively by means of the subject; therefore, it is the pure activity of the subject. To this extent, consequently, the pure activity of the I is, as such, a *condition for any activity that posits an object*. [Secondly,] this pure activity is [I, 263] originally directed at no object whatsoever and must be completely independent of any object, just as the object is independent of this pure activity. To this extent, therefore, this pure activity must be connected to and compared with the activity of the object (which is, to this extent, not yet posited as an *ob*-ject [Ob-*jekt*]), and this connecting and comparing occurs by means of an equally absolute action of the I.* To be sure, this action is, with respect to its *form* (i.e., with respect to its actual occurrence), *absolute*.[611] (The absolute spontaneity of reflection, as discussed in the theoretical portion of the *Wissenschaftslehre,* and the absolute spontaneity of the will, as will be discussed in the practical portion of the same, are both grounded in the absolute being of this action.) Nevertheless, this same absolute action is, with respect to its *content* (that is, with respect to the fact that it is *an act of connecting* [*ein Bezeihen*] and that it demands the equivalence and subordination [to the activity of the I] of that which will subsequently be posited as an object) conditioned by the absolute being-positing of the I as the sum of all reality. In this respect, the pure activity of the I is a *condition for the act of connecting,* without which it is impossible to posit any object. — Insofar as the pure activity is connected to a (possible) object by means of the action just indicated, it is, as we said, an act of striving. The reason the pure activity is posited as connected to any object at all does not lie within the pure activity itself; but the pure activity does contain within itself the reason why, *if* it is posited in connection to an object, it is posited as a *striving.*   [I/2: 399]

(This demand, that everything be in harmony with the I, that all reality ought to be posited purely and simply through the I, is a demand of what is rightfully called "practical reason."[612] Such a practical power of reason has previously been   [I, 264] postulated, but not demonstrated.[613] The challenge that was from time to time issued to philosophers — namely, to demonstrate *that* reason is practical — was therefore entirely justified. — Moreover, such a proof must be conducted in a manner that satisfies theoretical reason itself, which cannot be dismissed simply by fiat [*durch einen Machtspruch*]. This is possible only in the manner indicted: namely, by showing that reason itself could not be theoretical were it not practical. No intellect is possible for a human being unless that human being also possesses a practical power. The possibility of all representation is grounded upon the latter. And this is what has just been shown, inasmuch as it has now been demonstrated that no object whatsoever would be possible without a striving.)

Yet we still have another difficulty to address, a difficulty that threatens to overturn our entire theory and concerns the requisite connection between the tendency on the part of the pure activity and the activity of the future object. Whether this connection is supposed to occur immediately or by means of an

---

* The claim that the pure activity [of the I], *in itself* and *as such*, is connected to an object, and that no additional, specifically absolute action of connecting is required for this purpose, would be the transcendental foundational principle of *intelligible fatalism*,[613] which was the most consistent system of freedom possible prior to the establishment of a *Wissenschaftslehre*. And, on the basis of this foundational principle, one was certainly justified in drawing the conclusion that no pure activity can be posited within a finite creature, since no such activity manifests itself [in such a creature], and that a finite creature is posited as purely and simply finite — posited, as goes without saying, not by itself, but by something outside it. The system of intelligible fatalism would be valid for the deity, that is, for a creature whose objective activity would also be immediately posited by its pure activity, were it not the case that, for us, such a concept would be extravagant.

ideal projected in accordance with the Idea of this pure activity, it is in either case impossible, unless the activity of the object is somehow supposed to be already given to the I that makes this connection. If we permit the activity of the object to be given to the I that makes this connection in the same way [that the pure activity of the I is given to it] — that is, by connecting it with the tendency of the I's pure activity —, then our explanation is circular, and we simply obtain no first ground whatsoever for the connection in question. But there is supposed to be such a first ground, and hence this is something that must be indicated — albeit only in an Idea, as goes without saying.

The absolute I is purely and simply equivalent to itself; everything in it is one and the same I and pertains (if it is permissible to express oneself so improperly) to one and the same I, within which nothing can be distinguished and nothing is manifold. The [pure] I is all and nothing, because it is nothing *for itself* and can distinguish within itself neither a positing subject nor anything posited. — By virtue of its own essential nature, the I *strives* (which, once again, is said improperly and merely with respect to a future connection [to an [I, 265] objective activity]) to assert itself in this condition. — A non-equivalence [*eine* [I/2: 400] *Ungleichheit*], and therefore something alien, arises within the I. (*That* this occurs is not something that can be demonstrated a priori; instead, this is a claim that everyone can confirm only through his own experience. At the moment, we can say nothing further about this alien element, other than that it *cannot* be derived from the inner nature of the I, since in that case nothing at all would be distinguishable therein.)

This alien element necessarily conflicts with the I's striving to be purely and simply self-identical; and if we think of the I is observed in these two different states by some intelligent being external to it, such an I would, *for such an external being*, appear to be limited and its force [*Kraft*][614] driven back — just as we assume happens, for example, in the physical world.

The intellect that is supposed to posit this limitation is, however, not a being external to the I, but is the I itself. In order to resolve the difficulty before us, therefore, we must take a few additional steps. — If the I is equivalent to itself, and if it necessarily strives toward complete identity with itself, then it must immediately restore this striving that it itself did *not* interrupt. In this way it would be possible for the I to compare its limited state with that state in which the [I's infinite] striving, which was curbed,[615] is restored — a sheer connection of itself with itself, therefore, without any contribution from the object, so long as it is possible to indicate a ground connecting these two states [of the I].

Suppose that the striving activity of the I proceeds from A to C[616] without encountering any check; in this case, nothing can be distinguished up to C, since the I cannot be distinguished from the Not-I, and nothing at all occurs between A and C of which the I could become conscious. This striving activity of the I, which contains the primary ground of all consciousness, would be curbed at point C, though the I would never obtain any consciousness of it. By virtue of its own inner nature, however, this activity cannot be curbed; hence it continues beyond C; [I, 266] but it does so as an activity that has been externally curbed and maintains itself *only* through its own inner force, and it therefore continues to a point where it no longer encounters any resistance — to D, for example. [^Ba.) Beyond D, this activity can no longer be an object of consciousness, just as it cannot be an object of consciousness between A and C, and for the same reason. b.) It is not claimed here that the I itself posits its activity as curbed and then maintains it only through itself, but only that an intellect external to the I would be able to posit it in this way.]

For the sake of clarity, let us continue to examine what has just been presupposed. — An intellect [external to the I] is supposed to posit what is required, [I/2: 401] correctly and in accordance with the situation — and the intellect in question is precisely we ourselves as presently engaged in scientific reflection. Moreover, this intellect must necessarily posit this activity as that of an *I* — that is, as the activity of a self-positing being, to which nothing pertains that it does not posit within itself. Consequently, just as surely as this activity that is curbed and then restored is supposed to be the activity of an I, this I must posit within itself both the curb upon its activity and the restoration of the same. *But this activity can be posited as restored only insofar as it is posited as curbed, and it can be posited as curbed only insofar as it is posited as restored.* According to what was said, these reciprocally determined each other. Consequently, the states of the I that are to be united are already synthetically united in and for themselves; they cannot be posited at all unless they are posited as united. But *that* they are posited at all is inherent in the sheer concept of the I and is postulated along with the latter. It follows that all that has to be posited in and by the I is the curbed activity, which, however, must certainly be posited and must therefore be restored.

All positing of the I would therefore proceed from the positing of a purely subjective state,[617] and all synthesis would proceed from a synthesis with what is posited in opposition — a synthesis that is, in itself, necessary and occurs within the subject alone.[618] This purely and exclusively subjective element will subsequently reveal itself to be *feeling* [*Gefühl*].[619]

Furthermore, an activity of the object is now posited as the ground of this [I, 267] feeling.^C Hence, as required above, this activity would indeed be given by means of feeling to the subject that makes the connection, and therefore the requisite connection to an activity of the pure I is now possible.

So much for resolving the difficulty in question. Let us now return to the point from which we began. No infinite striving of the I, no finite object in the I: this was the result of our investigation, and this appears to have annulled the contradiction between the finite, conditioned I, as intellect, and the infinite, unconditioned I. Considering this matter more closely, however, we discover that, though we have indeed removed this contradiction some distance from the point at which we encountered it as a contradiction between the intelligent and non-intelligent I, it has only been further displaced, and higher foundational principles have now been brought into conflict.

---

^B [These are Fichte's square brackets.]
^C as the condition for the possibility of this feeling [An alteration in *SW*, based upon Fichte's own marginal correction.]

That is to say, we had to resolve the contradiction between an infinite and a finite activity of one and the same I; and we accomplished this in such a way [I/2: 402] that the *infinite* activity is supposed to be only self-*reverting* and purely and simply not objective, whereas the *finite* activity is supposed to be *objective*. Now, however, the infinite activity, as a *striving*, is itself connected to the object, and to this extent it is itself an objective activity. But since this activity is nevertheless supposed to remain infinite, and since the first, finite activity is supposed to continue to exist alongside it, this leaves us with an infinite and a finite activity of one and the same I,[620] an assumption that, once again, contradictions itself. The only way this contradiction can be resolved is by showing that the infinite activity of the I is objective, albeit in a sense different from the sense in which its finite activity is objective.

Undoubtedly, the first thing anyone would suspect is that the finite objective activity of the I is directed at an *actual* object, whereas its infinite striving is directed at a merely *imagined* one, and this suspicion will indeed be confirmed. [I, 268] But this would mean that we have provided a circular answer to our question, since we would have already presupposed a distinction[621] that is made possible only by distinguishing these two activities from each other. We must, therefore, investigate this difficulty somewhat more deeply.

Just as surely as it is supposed to be an object, every object is necessarily a determinate one; and insofar as it is determinate, it is supposed to determine the I, and its determining of the I is itself determinate (has its boundary). Consequently, every objective activity, just as surely as it is an objective activity, is a determining one; and, to this extent, it is also determinate[622] and therefore finite as well. It follows that even this infinite striving can be infinite only in a certain sense, whereas in another sense it must be finite.

An objective finite activity is now *posited in opposition* to this infinite striving. This objective finite activity must therefore be finite in the same sense in which the striving is infinite, and the activity of striving is infinite to the extent that this objective activity is finite. Striving does indeed possess an end or goal [*Ende*]; it simply has a different end than the objective activity. The question is, What is the end of this striving?

For the sake of its own act of determining, the finite objective activity already presupposes an activity of the I, an activity that is posited in opposition to the infinite activity of the I, and it is this activity posited in opposition to the infinite activity of the I that is subsequently supposed to be determined as the object.[623] This objective activity is dependent, limited, and finite — not, to be sure, insofar as it is an activity as such (since, according to what was said above,[624] it is, to this extent, absolute), but insofar as it posits the *determinate* boundaries of an object (which resists the I to precisely this extent, neither more nor less). The ground of its determining, and hence also of its own being-determined, lies outside of this activity.[625] — An object that is determined by an activity that is, to this extent, limited is an *actual* object.

[I/2: 403] In this respect, the activity of striving is not finite; it proceeds beyond the boundary that has been indicated and determined in advance by the object, and, according to the preceding,[626] it must proceed beyond this boundary if there is supposed to be any such determination of this same boundary. It does not determine the actual world, which is dependent upon an activity of the Not-I that interacts reciprocally with the activity of the I; instead, it determines a world as it [I, 269] would be were all reality to be posited purely and simply through the I. Hence, what this activity determines is an ideal world, a world posited only by the I and purely and simply by no Not-I.

To what extent, however, is the activity of striving nevertheless finite as well? It is finite to the extent that it is directed at any object whatsoever and insofar as it must posit boundaries for this object, just as surely as it supposed to be an object at all. In the case of an actual object, what was dependent upon the Not-I was not the action of determining as such, but rather, the boundary of the determination. In the case of an ideal object, however, both the action of determining and the boundary [of the determination] are dependent solely upon the I, which stands under no condition other than the condition that it must posit some boundary or another, a boundary it can extend into infinity, since such an extension depends solely upon the I.

The ideal is an absolute product of the I, which can be elevated ever higher, into infinity; but at any determinate moment, this ideal possesses a limit of its own, which by no means has to remain the same at the next determinate moment. Indeterminate striving is, as such, infinite — though, admittedly, it should not, to this extent, be called "striving," since it has no object (though we neither possess nor could possess any designation for such indeterminate striving, which lies beyond all determinacy). But this indeterminate and infinite striving does not attain, as such, to consciousness; nor can it attain to consciousness, since consciousness is possible only by means of reflection and reflection only by means of determination. Just as soon as this infinite striving is reflected upon, it necessarily becomes finite. When the mind becomes aware that this striving is finite, it extends it further; but just as soon as it poses for itself the question, "is it now infinite?," it becomes finite, and this occurs precisely as a result of posing this question — and so it continues, ad infinitum.[627]

Combining *infinite* and *objective* is thus itself a contradiction. That [activity] which is directed at an object is finite; and that [activity] which is finite is directed at an object. The only way to eliminate this contradiction would be to eliminate the object, but the object is never eliminated except in a completed infinity. The I can extend the object of its striving to infinity; but were it at any determinant [I, 270] moment to be extended to infinity, then it would no longer be an object at all, and the Idea of infinity would be realized — which, however, is itself a contradiction.

Nevertheless, the Idea of such a completed infinity hovers before us and is contained in our innermost nature, which demands that we resolve this contradiction, despite the fact that we are presently unable to conceive of the possibility [I/2: 404] of its resolution and can foresee that we will continue to be unable to think this to be possible at any moment of our existence, extending into eternity.[628] This, however, is precisely a sign that we are destined for eternity.[629]

The nature of the I has therefore now been determined, to the extent that it can be determined, and the contradiction contained in the I has now been resolved, to the extent that it can be resolved. The I is infinite, but only with respect to its striving; it strives to be infinite. But the very concept of striving already contains finitude, for anything that is not *resisted* is not a striving. Were the I more than striving, if it possessed an infinite causality, then it would not be an I, would not posit itself, and would therefore be nothing. Were it not endowed with this infinite striving, then, once again, it would be unable to posit itself, since it could not posit anything in opposition to itself; consequently, it would also not be an I, and it would therefore be nothing.

In order to make completely clear the concept of striving, which is of supreme importance for the practical part of the *Wissenschaftslehre*, we will now present what has just been deduced in another way.

According to the preceding exposition, there is a striving of the I, which is a striving only insofar as it is resisted and insofar as it can possess no causality. This, therefore, is a striving that, insofar as it is such, is also conditioned by the Not-I.

Note that I said "insofar as it can possess no causality." Such causality is therefore [only] demanded. That such a demand for absolute causality must be originally present in the I has been shown to follow from the irresolvable contradiction between the I as an intellect and as an absolute being [*Wesen*]. [I, 271] This proof was therefore apagogic:[630] it was shown that the identity of the I must be abandoned if one does not accept the demand for absolute causality.

It must be possible to provide a direct, genetic[631] proof of this demand.[632] It must reveal itself to be worthy of belief, but not merely by appealing to higher principles, which would contradict each other without this demand; instead, the demand for absolute causality on the part of the I must itself be *deducible* from these higher principles, so that one can gain insight into *how* such a demand arises within the human mind. — It must be possible to indicate the presence, not of a mere striving for a determinate causality (conditioned by a determinate Not-I), but of a striving toward causality as such, which is the basis of the former, determinate causality. — An activity that goes beyond the object becomes a striving precisely inasmuch as and because it goes beyond the object; therefore, it becomes a striving only on the condition that an object is present. It must be possible to [I/2: 405] indicate the basis or ground of the I's activity of going beyond itself, an activity by means of which an object first becomes possible. This outgoing activity of the I, which precedes every activity that resists it[633] and grounds the possibility of such activity as related to the I, must be grounded purely and exclusively in the I; and this provides us for the first time with the true point of union between the absolute I, the practical I, and the intelligent I.

Let us explain ourselves even more clearly regarding the actual point at issue:[634] — It is clear that the I, insofar as it posits itself purely and simply — insofar , that is, as it posits itself to be and posits itself to be as it is — must be absolutely identical to itself; and it is also clear that, to this extent, nothing whatsoever that is different[635] can appear within the I. From this, of course, it follows at once that *if* anything foreign were to appear within the I, it would have to be posited by a Not-I. But if the Not-I is supposed to be at all capable of positing anything in the I, *then the conditions for the possibility of such a foreign influence* must be grounded *within the I itself, within the absolute I*, in advance of any actual foreign influence.

The I must originally and purely and simply posit within itself the possibility that
something might have an influence upon it. Without any detriment to its absolute   [I, 272]
self-positing, it must, as it were, hold itself open to another positing. Consequently,
if any difference [*Verschiedenheit*] is ever supposed to be able to enter the I, a difference must already be present within the I itself; indeed, this difference must be
grounded in the absolute I as such. — The apparent contradiction contained in
this presupposition will, at the appropriate time, resolve itself, and its inconceiv-
ability will vanish.

Our investigation can most conveniently begin from the following point: namely,
that the I is supposed to encounter within itself something heterogeneous and
foreign, something that has to be distinguished from itself.

And yet, this alien element is supposed to be encountered *in the I*, and it must
be encountered therein.[D] Were it to lie *outside the I*, it would then be nothing for
the I, and nothing would result from it for the I. It must therefore be, in a certain
respect, *similar* [*gleichartig*] to the I; it must be ascribable to the I.[636]

The essence of the I consists in its activity; accordingly, if this heterogeneous
element is also supposed to be ascribable to the I, then it simply has to be an
activity of the I. Such an activity cannot, as such, be foreign to the I, but is perhaps
foreign to it only with respect to its *direction*,[637] which [in this case] is grounded
not in the I but outside of it. — If, in accordance with our frequently invoked presupposition, the activity of the I proceeds into the infinite, but is checked at a certain point, yet not annihilated thereby, but only driven back upon itself: then, in
this case, the activity of the I, insofar as this is what it is, always remains an activity of the I, and all that is foreign and opposed to the I is the fact that this activity   [I/2: 406]
is driven back upon itself. Remaining unanswered at this point are only the following, difficult questions, in answering which, however, we will also penetrate
into the innermost essence of the I: namely,[638] How does the I come to direct its
activity *outwardly* into infinity? How can the I distinguish the outward direction
of its activity from its inward direction? And why is the activity that is driven   [I, 273]
back in an inward direction viewed as foreign, rather than as grounded in the I?

The I posits itself purely and simply, and insofar as it does this its activity is
self-reverting. The direction of this activity is purely *centripetal* — if it is permissible to presuppose something that has not yet been derived, simply in order to
make ourselves understandable and if it is furthermore permissible to borrow
from the natural sciences a term that, as will become evident at the appropriate
time, first enters the natural sciences precisely from the present transcendental
point.[639] (*A single* point determines no line; two points are always required for the
possibility of determining a line, even if the second point were to lie at infinity
and to indicate nothing but a sheer direction. Similarly, and for precisely the same
reason, there is no direction if there are not two, and indeed two directions posited in opposition to each other. The concept of direction is a purely reciprocal
concept; *one* direction is no direction at all and is purely and simply inconceivable. Consequently, we can assign a direction to the absolute activity of the I, and
a centripetal direction at that, only under the tacit presupposition that we will

---

[D] and it can be encountered only therein [Addition in *SW*, from Fichte's own marginalia.]

also discover another, centrifugal direction of the I's activity. Taken most rigorously, the image of the I in the present mode of representation[640] is that of a self-constituting mathematical point, in which there is no direction and within which nothing at all can be distinguished, a point that is *entirely where* it is and whose contents [*Inhalt*] and boundary — its content [*Gehalt*] and form — are precisely one and the same.) If the essential nature of the I includes nothing more than this constitutive activity, then the I is for us what every body is for us. We also ascribe to a body (in accordance with the principle, A = A) an *inner* force, posited through its very being. If, however, we philosophize in a purely transcendental manner, and not, so to speak, transcendently, we must then assume that it is posited *by us that* this force is supposed to be posited by the very being of this body (for us), but not that it is posited *by and for the body itself that* this force is sup-

[I, 274] posed to be posited. This is why such a body is, for us, lifeless and soulless and is not an I.[641] The I [however] is not supposed to posit itself only for some intellect outside itself; instead, it is supposed to posit itself *for itself*; it is supposed to posit itself *as* posited by itself. Just as surely as it is an I, therefore, it is supposed to

[I/2: 407] contain the principle of life and consciousness solely within itself. Accordingly, just as surely as it is an I, the I must contain within itself, unconditionally and without any ground, the principle of reflecting upon itself. Hence we originally consider the I in two aspects: on the one hand, insofar as it is engaged in reflecting, in which case the direction of its activity is centripetal; on the other hand, insofar as it is what is reflected upon, in which case the direction of its activity is centrifugal, and indeed, centrifugal extending into infinity. The I is posited as reality, and, insofar as there occurs a reflection upon whether it possesses reality, it is necessarily posited as *something*, as a quantum.[642] But it is posited as all reality, and thus it is necessarily posited as an infinite quantum, as a quantum that fills infinity.[643]

The centripetal and centrifugal directions of [the I's] activity are therefore both grounded in the same manner in the essential nature of the I; they are both one and the same and can be distinguished only insofar as they are reflected upon as distinct from each other. — (All centrifugal force in the material world is nothing but the product of the I's power of imagination, operating in accordance with a law of reason which brings unity into what is manifold,[644] as will be shown at the appropriate time.)

But that reflection by means of which these two directions can be distinguished from each other is impossible without the addition of some third thing, to which they can be related or which can be related to them. — The demand that all reality ought to be contained in the I (we must always presuppose something that has not yet been established, simply in order to be able to express ourselves, since, strictly speaking, no *demand* — as opposed to *what actually occurs* — has been at all possible until now) is a demand that can be adequately satisfied under our

[I, 275] presupposition: namely, that both directions of the I's activity, the centripetal and the centrifugal directions, coincide and be but one and the same direction.[645] (For the sake of illustration, suppose that one is supposed to explain the self-consciousness of God: this is possible only if one presupposes that God reflects upon his own being. But since, in the case of God, *what is reflected upon* is supposed to be All in One and One in All, and since *what is engaged in reflecting* is likewise supposed to be All in One and One in All, it would be impossible to distinguish in and through God what is reflected upon from what is engaged in reflecting, consciousness and its object.[646] The self-consciousness of God would therefore not be explained, just as it would remain forever inexplicable and incomprehensible for all finite reason, that is, for all rational creatures [*alle Vernunft*] subject to the law of *determination* of what is being reflected upon.[647]) It follows that no consciousness can be derived from the preceding presupposition, [I/2: 408] since the two assumed directions cannot be distinguished from each other.

Now, however, that activity of the I which extends outward into infinity is supposed to be checked at some point and driven back upon itself; consequently, the I is supposed to fail to fill infinity. As has been frequently noted, *that* this occurs, as a *factum*, is something that can simply not be derived from the I, though it can certainly be shown that this must occur *if* any actual consciousness is supposed to be possible.

The demand made by the reflecting I in its present function — namely, that the I that is thereby being reflected upon ought to fill infinity — remains and is by no means limited by the check in question.[648] The question whether the I that is reflected upon actually fills infinity [also] remains, along with the answer: namely, that it does not actually fill infinity, but is, instead, limited at C; and only now is it possible to make the required distinction between the two directions [of the I's activity].

That is to say, in accordance with the demand of the absolute I, its activity (which is, to this extent, centrifugal) is supposed to extend outward into infinity; but this activity is reflected[649] at point C and thus becomes centripetal. Since any two things that are supposed to be distinguished from each other must be related to a third thing,[650] the distinction [between the centrifugal and centripetal directions of the I's activity] becomes possible by their being related to this original demand for an infinitely outgoing [activity in a] centrifugal direction. This is because what is now [I, 276] encountered in reflection is a centrifugal direction [of the I's activity] in accord with the demand in question, as well as [an activity in] a centripetal direction (a second direction, reflected by the check) in conflict with the centrifugal one.[651]

This also explains why this [activity in the] second direction is considered to be something foreign and is derived from a principle posited in opposition to the principle of the I.

With this, we have fulfilled our assigned task. The I's original striving for overall causality [*einer Kausalität überhaupt*] has been genetically derived from the law of the I that requires the I — just as surely as it is supposed to be an I at all — to reflect upon itself and to demand that, in this reflection, it discover itself to be all reality. This necessary reflection of the I upon itself[652] is the ground of all of its proceeding beyond itself,[E] and the demand that it fill infinity is the ground of its striving for overall causality[F 653]; and both [the I's necessary reflection upon itself and the demand that it fill infinity] are grounded solely in the absolute being of the I.[654]

[E] *proceeding beyond itself* [Emphasis added in *SW*.]
[F] *striving for causality as such* [Emphasis added in *SW*.]

This also allows us to discover, within the I itself, the ground of the possibility of an influence of the Not-I upon the I, which was also required. The I posits itself [I/2: 409] purely and simply, and it is thereby complete in itself[655] and closed off from any external impression. But if it is supposed to be an I, it must also posit itself as self-posited;[G] and by means of this new act of positing, which is related to the original act of positing, the I opens itself (if I may express myself in this manner) to an external influence.[656] Simply by repeating the act of positing, the I posits the possibility that something might be present in the I that is not posited by the I itself. Both types of positing are conditions for the influence of the Not-I. Without the first act of positing, the I would engage in no activity that could be limited; without the second, this activity would not be limited for the I, which would not be able to posit itself as limited. Consequently, the I originally stands in a reciprocal relationship with itself, and this is what first makes possible an external influence within the I.[657]

In this way, we have also finally discovered the point of union we have been [I, 277] seeking between the absolute, the practical, and the intelligent natures of the I. — The I demands that it contain within itself all reality and that it fill infinity. This demand is necessarily grounded upon the Idea of the purely and simply posited infinite I, and this is the *absolute* I we have been discussing. (Here, for the first time, the meaning of the proposition, *the I posits itself purely and simply*, becomes completely clear. This proposition by no means applies to the I that is given in actual consciousness, for the latter never exists purely and simply; instead, its state is always either directly or indirectly grounded in something external to the I. Instead, the proposition in question refers to an Idea of the I, an Idea that must necessarily underlie the I's practical and infinite demand, but which is unobtainable for our consciousness and can therefore never appear immediately within consciousness, though it can indeed appear there indirectly, in philosophical reflection.[658])

It is also included in the concept of the I that it must reflect upon itself in order to determine whether it actually includes within itself all reality.[659] This reflection is grounded upon that Idea [of the absolute I], which therefore accompanies it into infinity; and, to this extent, the I is *practical*[660] and not absolute, because it is precisely by means of this tendency[661] toward reflection that it proceeds beyond itself. Nor is this I [which must reflect upon itself in order to determine if it includes all reality] the theoretical I, because nothing grounds its reflection other that this Idea [of the purely and simply posited infinite I], an Idea that stems from the I itself and is completely abstracted from any possible check or impetus, which is why no actual[662] reflection occurs. — This is the origin of the series of what *ought* to be and is given purely through the I: that is, the series of what is *ideal*.

If reflection is directed at this check,[663] and if the I therefore considers its out- [I/2 410] going activity to be limited, this produces an entirely different series, the series of what is *actual*, which is always determined by something other than the I alone. — And to this extent the I is *theoretical* or an *intellect*.

[G] *as self-posited* [Emphasis added in *SW*.]

If the I possesses no practical power, then no intellect is possible. As has already been indicated numerous times, if the activity of the I extends only to the point of the check[664] and does not continue beyond any possible check, then there is in [I, 278] and for the I nothing that checks it, no Not-I. Conversely, if the I is not an intellect, then no consciousness of its practical power is possible, nor is any self-consciousness whatsoever possible. As was just shown, this is because it first becomes possible to distinguish different directions [of the I's activity] only by means of the foreign direction, arising from the check or impetus. (Here we are still abstracting from the fact that, in order to be able to attain to consciousness, the practical power must first pass through the intellect and acquire the form of representation.[665])

With this, we have grasped and exhaustively described the entire essential nature of finite rational creatures [*Naturen*], which includes the following moments: original Idea of our absolute being; striving to reflect upon ourselves in accordance with this Idea;[666] limitation, not of this striving, but rather, of our *actual existence*,* which is first posited through this limitation, a limitation that occurs by means of a principle posited in opposition [to the I], through a Not-I, or through our finitude as such; self-consciousness and, more particularly, consciousness of our practical striving; ensuing determination of our representations; determination of our actions, that is, of the direction of our actual sensible power (both without freedom and with freedom) in accordance with these representations; constant expansion of our limits, into the infinite.

Let me add the following, important remark, which should by itself be sufficient to place the *Wissenschaftslehre* in its proper light and to make the actual teachings [I, 279] of the same completely clear. According to the explication just provided, the [I/2: 411] principle of life and consciousness,[667] the ground of its possibility, is indeed contained in the I; but from this there arises no actual life, no empirical life in time (and any other kind of life is, for us, purely and simply unthinkable). If such an actual life is to be possible, then what is required in addition is a specific check upon the I by a Not-I?[668]

According to the *Wissenschaftslehre*, therefore, the ultimate ground of all reality for the I is an original reciprocal interaction between the I and something or other external to it, about which the only thing that can be said is that it must be posited in complete opposition to the I. Nothing is introduced into the I as a result of this interaction; nothing foreign is imported. Everything that can ever develop within the I, extending into infinity, arises purely from the I itself and in accordance with its own laws.[669] What is posited in opposition to the I does nothing more than set the I in motion so that it can act. In the absence of such a first

---

* In a consistent stoicism, the infinite Idea of the I is taken to be the actual I; absolute being is not distinguished from actual existence. This is why the stoic sage is all-sufficient and unlimited. All the predicates that pertain to the pure I or to God are applied to the stoic sage. According to stoic morality, it is not the case the we ought to become like God; instead, we ourselves are God.[670] The *Wissenschaftslehre* carefully distinguishes between absolute being and actual existence, and it posits the former as the ground only in order to be able to explain the latter. The way to refute stoicism is to show that it cannot explain the possibility of consciousness. This is also why the *Wissenschaftslehre* is not atheistic, as stoicism must be if it proceeds consistently.

mover outside itself, the I would never have acted; and since the essential nature of the I consists entirely in acting, it also would also not have existed. But nothing else pertains to this [first] mover other than that is supposed to be a mover, a force posited in opposition [to the I], as well as being a force that is only felt as such.[670]

From this it follows that the I is dependent with respect to its existence, but that it is purely and simply independent with respect to the determinations thereof. Thanks to its absolute being, the I contains an eternally valid law governing these determinations,[671] as well as the intermediate power [*Mittelvermögen*] to determine its empirical existence in accordance with these laws.[672] The point at which we find ourselves when we activate for the first time this intermediate power of freedom does not depend upon us; but the series we will traverse from this point on, into all eternity, depends, in its entirety, completely on us.[673]

[I, 280]   The *Wissenschaftslehre* is therefore *realistic*. It shows that it is purely and simply the case that the consciousness of finite creatures cannot be explained unless one assumes the presence of a force posited utterly in opposition to them, a force that is, with respect to the empirical existence of such finite creatures, completely independent of them.[674] But the *Wissenschaftslehre* asserts no more than this: namely, that there is such a force posited in opposition, a force that is merely felt[675] but not cognized by the finite being.[H] The *Wissenschaftslehre* promises to derive from the determining power of the I all the possible determinations of this force, or of this Not-I, that can ever — into infinity — appear within our consciousness;[676] and, just as surely as it is the *Wissenschaftslehre*, it must actually be capable of deriving these determinations.

Despite its realism, however, this science is not transcendent, but remains in its innermost depths *transcendental*.[677] To be sure, it explains all consciousness on

[I/2: 412] the basis of something present independently of all consciousness; but it does not forget that, even in providing such an explanation, it proceeds in accordance with its own law; and insofar as it reflects upon the fact that it does so, then this independent existence, insofar as it is supposed to exist for the I (in the concept of the I) becomes, in turn, a product of the I's own power of thinking and thereby becomes something dependent upon the I.[678] Yet the possibility of this new explanation of that previous explanation presupposes, yet again, actual consciousness, the possibility of which again presupposes that "something" upon which the I depends. But even if it is the case that precisely what was first posited as something independent has now become dependent upon the I's thinking, what is independent is nevertheless not eliminated[I] thereby, but merely posited further out. And one could continue in this manner into the domain of the unlimited without ever annulling what is posited as independent of the I. — With respect to its ideality, everything is dependent upon the I; with respect to its reality,[J] however, the I is itself dependent. But nothing is real for the I without also being ideal. The real ground and ideal ground are therefore one and the same

---

[H]   merely *felt* but not *cognized*. [Emphasis added in *SW*.]

[I]   Reading, with *SW*, *aufgehoben* for *hoben*.

[J]   With respect to its *ideality*, everything is dependent upon the I; with respect to its *reality* [Emphasis added in *SW*.]

in the I, and this reciprocal interaction between the I and the Not-I is, at the same time, a reciprocal interaction of the I with itself.[679] Insofar as it does not reflect [I, 281] upon the fact that it itself posited this limiting Not-I, the I can posit itself as limited by the Not-I; insofar as it does reflect upon this fact, it can posit itself as limiting the Not-I.[680]

The fact that the finite mind must necessarily posit something absolute outside itself (a thing in itself) and yet, conversely, must recognize that what it has posited outside itself exists only *for the finite I* (that it is a necessary noumenon[681]) constitutes that circle which the finite mind can expand infinitely, but from which it can never escape.[682] A system that takes no account whatsoever of this circle is a dogmatic idealism, since, in fact, it is only this circle that limits us and makes us into finite beings.[683] A system that fancies it has escaped this circle is a transcendent, realistic dogmatism.[684]

The *Wissenschaftslehre* occupies precisely the middle-ground between these two systems and is a Critical idealism, though one could also call it a real-idealism or an ideal-realism.[685] — Let us now add a few words on this topic, in order to make everything as understandable as possible. We said that the consciousness of finite creatures is inexplicable unless one assumes the presence of a force independent of such creatures. — For whom is this inexplicable? And for whom is it supposed to become explicable? And who in the world is it that then explains this? It is these finite creatures themselves. As soon as we say "explain," we have already entered the domain of finitude, inasmuch as all *explaining* (in contrast with grasping [I/2: 413] something all at once) is a continual process of progressing from one point to the next. Explaining is something finite, and the act of limiting or determining is the very bridge one traverses [when engaged in explaining], a bridge the I possesses within itself.[686] — With respect to its being and determination, the force posited in opposition [to the I] is independent of the [practical activity of the] I, though the practical power of the I, or its drive[687] toward reality, nevertheless strives to modify this force. But the Not-I is dependent upon the ideal activity of the I, upon its theoretical power. The Not-I exists *for the I* only insofar as it posited *by the I*; otherwise, it does not exist for the I. This force possesses independent reality only [I, 282] insofar as it is related to the practical power of the I.[688] Insofar as it is related to the I's theoretical power, it is comprised within the I, contained within its sphere, and subject to its laws of representation. Moreover, how can the Not-I ever be related to the practical power except by means of the theoretical power? And how can it ever become an object of the theoretical power except by means of the practical power? Here we have another confirmation of the following proposition — or rather, here this proposition shows itself in its full clarity: no ideality, no reality, and vice versa. Consequently, one can also say that the ultimate ground of all consciousness is a reciprocal interaction of the I with itself, by means of a Not-I that has to be viewed in various ways.[689] This is the circle from which the finite mind cannot escape, nor can it wish to escape from it without disavowing reason and longing for its annihilation.

The following objection may be of some interest: If, in obedience to the previously mentioned laws [of representation], the I employs its ideal activity to posit a

Not-I as the explanatory ground of its own limited state, thereby assimilating the Not-I to itself, does it not then indeed posit (in a determinate, finite concept) this Not-I itself as a limited Not-I? Suppose that the object in question = A. Yet the activity of the I in positing this Not-I is itself necessarily limited, since it is directed at a limited object. But the I can never limit itself; hence it cannot limit itself in this case. Consequently, insofar as the I limits A (which is certainly supposed to be assimilated to the I), then the I must itself be limited by some B, which is still completely independent of the I and is not assimilated to it. — We concede all this and would only remark that this B can also be assimilated, in turn, to the I, which is something our opponent will concede, while adding from his side that in order for it to be possible for the I to assimilate B to itself, the I must again be limited by some independent C, and so on ad infinitum. The result of this investi-

[I/2: 414] gation would then be as follows: We could never in all eternity indicate to our
[I, 283] opponent a single moment in which an independent reality outside the I would not be present for the I's striving. He, however, would also never be able to indicate to us a moment in which this independent Not-I could not be represented, and in this way made dependent upon the I. Where then does this leave our opponent's independent Not-I or his thing in itself, which is what his argument was supposed to demonstrate? Obviously, it is at once nowhere and everywhere. It is there only insofar as one does not possess it, and it escapes as soon as one wishes to apprehend it. The thing in itself is something for the I, and hence something *in* the I which nevertheless should *not* be *in the I*. Hence the thing in itself is something contradictory, which is nevertheless the object of a necessary Idea, something that must lie at the basis of all of our philosophical thinking and has done so from time immemorial, as well as underlying all the acts of a finite mind — although one was not clearly conscious of this nor of the contradiction it harbors. The entire mechanism of the human mind and of all finite minds is grounded upon this relation of the thing in itself to the I.[690] To wish to alter this relation would be to annul all consciousness and, along with it, all existence.

All apparent objections to the *Wissenschaftslehre*, which confuse those who do not think very carefully, arise solely from the inability to master and to retain the Idea just indicated. One can grasp this Idea incorrectly in two different ways: [1.] Either one reflects solely upon the fact that, since the thing in itself is an Idea, it must surely lie within the I, in which case — assuming that one is also a resolute thinker — one becomes an idealist and dogmatically denies that there is any reality outside us. Alternatively, one clings to one's feelings, and thus denies what is clearly evident, contradicting the argument of the *Wissenschaftslehre* through a decree of healthy common sense (with which, understood correctly, the *Wissenschaftslehre* is in close agreement) and, since one has failed to grasp its meaning, accuses this science itself of idealism. [2.] Or else one reflects solely upon the fact that the object of this Idea is supposed to be an independent Not-I, in which case one becomes a transcendent realist — or, if one happens to have

[I, 284] grasped a few of Kant's thoughts, albeit without having mastered the spirit of his entire philosophy, one then, from that transcendent standpoint which one has still never rejected, accuses the *Wissenschaftslehre* of transcendentism,[691] unaware that with one's own weapons one slays only oneself. — One should do neither of these things; one should reflect exclusively upon neither the one nor the other [aspect of the thing in itself]; instead, one should reflect simultaneously upon both and oscillate inwardly between these two determinations of this Idea, which are posited in opposition to each other. This, however, is a task for the *creative power of imagination*. All human beings share this power, since without it they [I/2: 415] would also never have possessed a single representation. However, it is by no means the case that most human beings have free control over this power of creative imagination and are able to employ it to create something purposefully; nor, should the longed-for image suddenly appear before their soul at some fortunate moment like a bolt of lightning, are they able to hold it fast, investigate it, and imprint it indelibly for any [future] use they may freely choose to make of it. It is this power that determines whether one philosophizes with or without spirit.[692] The *Wissenschaftslehre* is the kind of philosophy that can be communicated only through the spirit and by no means through the mere letters. This is because its fundamental Ideas are ones that everyone who studies it must produce within himself by means of his own creative power of imagination, and it cannot be otherwise in the case of a science that goes back to the ultimate grounds of human cognition, inasmuch as the operation of the human mind proceeds from the power of imagination and the power of imagination can be grasped only by the power of imagination.[693] It is for this reason, to be sure, that it will remain impossible for a person whose facility is already slumbering or dead and beyond any hope of recall to penetrate this science.[694] But the basis for this impossibility should by no means be sought in this science itself, which, if it is grasped at all, is grasped easily; instead, it should be sought in such a person's own inability.*

Just as the Idea in question is the internal foundation-stone of the entire structure, so too is it the external basis for the security of this structure. It is [I, 285] impossible to philosophize concerning any object whatsoever without happening upon this Idea — and with it, upon the proper terrain of the *Wissenschaftslehre*. Every opponent must do battle — though perhaps blindfolded — within its domain and with its weapons, and it will always be an easy matter to remove the blindfold from his eyes and allow him to catch sight of the field upon which he is standing. Consequently, the *Wissenschaftslehre* is completely justified, by the very nature of this matter, in declaring in advance that it will be misunderstood by many people and not understood at all by even more, but also that it will remain [I/2: 416] sorely in need of improvement in all its parts — not merely in its present, extremely incomplete presentation, but even following the most complete presentation that might be possible by any individual — even though, with respect to its fundamental features, it will never be refuted by any person or in any age.

---

* The *Wissenschaftslehre* is supposed to be exhaustive of the entire human being, and it can therefore be grasped only with the totality of all one's powers. It can never become a universally endorsed [*allgemeigeltende*] philosophy so long as, in the case of so many human beings, the development of one of their mental powers is sacrificed to the advantage of another power, sacrificing the power of imagination to the advantage of the power of understanding or the power of understanding to the advantage of the power of imagination — or sacrificing both powers to the advantage of memory. For this reason, the *Wissenschaftslehre* will for a long time have to remain confined to a narrow circle, a truth that is as unpleasant to utter as it is to hear, but which is nevertheless the truth.

§ 6. Third Theorem

In the Striving of the I There Is Posited at the Same Time an Opposed Striving of the Not-I, which Counterbalances that of the I

Let us begin with a few words concerning method. In the theoretical part of the *Wissenschaftslehre* we were concerned exclusively with *cognizing*, but here, in the practical part, we are concerned with *what is cognized*. In the theoretical part we asked, *how* is something posited, intuited, thought, etc.? Here, in the practical part, we are asking, *what* is posited? Hence, if the *Wissenschaftslehre* is supposed to include a metaphysics,[695] that is, a putative science of things in themselves,[696] [I, 286] and if such a science were to be demanded of it, then anyone who makes such a demand would have to be referred to the practical part of the *Wissenschaftslehre*. As will become ever more obvious, it is this practical part alone that deals with an original reality; and if someone should ask the *Wissenschaftslehre*, How then are things in themselves constituted?, the *Wissenschaftslehre* could respond only as follows: They are constituted as we are supposed to make them.[697] It is by no means the case that such an answer renders the *Wissenschaftslehre* transcendent; this is because here too [i.e., in Part III] everything to which we call attention is something we discover within and draw from ourselves, inasmuch as something occurs *in us* that can be completely explained only by means of something *outside us*. We know that this is something we think and that we think it in accordance with the laws governing our mind, and we also know that it is for this same reason that we can never escape from ourselves and can never speak of the existence of an object apart from a subject.

The I's striving is supposed to be infinite and is never supposed to exercise causality. This is thinkable only under the condition of an opposed striving,[698] which counterbalances the striving of the I, i.e., which possesses the same quantity of inner force. The concept of such an opposed striving and of the equilibrium that ensues is already implicit in the concept of striving and can be analytically developed from it.[699] Without these two concepts, the concept of striving contradicts itself.

[I/2: 417] 1.) The concept of striving is the concept of a cause that is not a cause. But every cause presupposes *activity*. Everything that strives possesses force. If it possessed no force, then it would not be a cause, which contradicts what was just said.

2.) Insofar as striving is, as such, an activity, it necessarily possesses a determinate quantity of its own. It aims to be a cause. Yet it does not become a cause; accordingly, it does not achieve its goal and becomes *limited*.[700] Were it not limited, it would become a cause and would not be a striving, which contradicts what was said above.

3.) What strives is not limited *by itself*, since the concept of striving implies that it aims to possess causality. Hence, if it limited itself, it would not be [I, 287] engaged in striving. It follows that every striving must be limited by a force posited in opposition to that striving.[701]

4.) The force posited in opposition must also be a striving; i.e., it must, first of all, aim to exercise causality. If it did not aim at this then it would have no point of contact in common with what is posited in opposition to it.[702] Secondly, it must not exercise any causality; for if it did, then it would completely annihilate the striving of what is posited in opposition to it [i.e., the I], inasmuch as it would annihilate its force.[703]

5.) Neither of the two opposed strivings can exercise causality. If either of them were to exercise causality, then the force of the striving posited in opposition to it would thereby be annihilated, and the two opposed forces would no longer be striving in opposition to each other. Consequently, these two forces must counterbalance each other.[704]

§ 7. Fourth Theorem

The Striving of the I, the Opposed Striving of the Not-I, and the Equilibrium between Them Must Be Posited

A.) The striving of the I is posited as such.

1.) In accordance with the universal law of reflection,[705] the striving of the I is, as such, posited as *something*;[706] consequently, it is not posited [I/2: 418] as an *activity*, as something in motion, as agility, but instead as something stabilized and posited as fixed [*festgeseztes*].[707]

2.) It is posited as a *striving*. Since striving aims to exercise causality, it must, with respect to its character,[K] be posited as causality. But the causality in question cannot be posited as affecting the Not-I, for in that case what would be posited would be real efficacious activity and not striving. Hence, the striving of the I could only revert into itself and could produce only itself. But a self-productive striving that is fixed, determinate, and definite is called a *drive* [*Trieb*].[708]

(The concept of a drive includes the following components: 1.) a drive is grounded in the innermost essence of that to which it is attributed and is therefore produced by the latter's exercise of causality upon [I, 288] itself,[L] through its being-posited by itself; 2.), for precisely the same reason, a drive is something fixed and enduring; 3.) a drive is directed at exercising causality beyond itself, and yet, insofar as it is supposed to be nothing but a drive, it can exercise no such causality all by itself. — It follows that a drive lies only in the subject and that, in accordance with its nature, it does not proceed beyond the circumference of the same.)

If a drive is supposed to be posited, it must be posited *in this way.* And, if it is supposed to be contained within the I and if any consciousness is to be possible, then this drive must be posited (whether this immediately occurs with or without consciousness), since,

---

[K] with respect to its distinctive character [As emended in *SW*, on the basis of Fichte's own marginalia.]

[L] upon itself, i.e., through its [Addition in *SW*, based on Fichte's own marginalia.]

according to what was said above,[709] consciousness is grounded upon a manifestation of striving.

B.) The striving of the I cannot be posited unless an opposed striving of the Not-I is [also] posited, inasmuch as the striving of the I aims to exercise causality, even though it possesses none; moreover, the ground of its lack of causality does not lie within itself, since in that case the striving of the I would not be a striving at all, but would be nothing. Consequently, if the striving of I is posited, the opposed striving in question must be posited outside the I; and it must be posited, once again, purely as a striving, since otherwise the striving of the I — or, as we now recognize it to be, the drive [of the I] — would be suppressed and could not be posited.

C.) The equilibrium between the striving of the I and the opposed striving of the Not-I must be posited.

Here we are not trying to demonstrate that an equilibrium must be maintained between the two, since this has already been shown in the preceding §. Instead, we are only asking, *What* is posited in and through the I when this equilibrium is posited?

[I/2: 419]

[I, 289]

The I strives to fill infinity. At the same time, it possesses the law and the tendency requiring it to reflect upon itself.[710] The I cannot reflect upon itself unless it is limited — and indeed, limited^M with respect to its *drive* — by its *relation or connection to that drive*.[711] Suppose that the drive [of the I] is limited at point C, then the *tendency toward reflection* is *satisfied* at point C, even though *the drive toward real activity* is *limited*. In this case, the I limits itself[712] and is posited in reciprocal interaction with itself. By means of its drive [to fill infinity], the I is driven further beyond itself; by means of reflection, it is brought to a halt and brings itself to a halt.

The union of these two [that is, of drive and reflection] results in the manifestation of a *compulsion*, of an *inability* [eines *Zwanges, eines Nichtkönnens*]. An inability includes the following: a.) a continued striving, since otherwise what I am unable to do would be nothing *for me* and would in no way pertain to my sphere; b.) a limitation of actual activity, and hence an actual activity itself, since what does not exist cannot be limited; c.) what does the limiting does not lie (i.e., is not posited) *in me*,^{N} but *outside me*, since otherwise no striving would be present [in me], and in that case what would be present [in me] would be only an absence of *willing* [*Nicht-wollen*] and not a lack of *ability* [*Nicht-können*]. — Every manifestation of an inability is therefore a manifestation of an equilibrium.

The manifestation within the I of an inability is called *a feeling*.[713] *Activity* (I feel, I am the feeling subject, and the activity in question is that of reflection) and *limitation* (I *feel*, I am in a state of being passively affected and am not active) are intimately united in feeling, in which a compulsion is present. Now this limitation necessarily presupposes a drive to continue further.[714] That

---

^{M} unless it is limited. [Addition in *SW.*]
^{N} does not lie *in me*. [Emphasis added in *SW.*]

which wants nothing else, needs nothing more, or comprises nothing further is not limited^O — limited *for itself,* as goes without saying.

Feeling is purely *subjective.* To be sure, in order to *explain* feeling (which is, of course, a theoretical action) we require *something that limits.*[715] But insofar as feeling is supposed to be present in the I, something that limits is not required for a deduction of feeling, that is, for a deduction of the *representation* or *act of positing* such a thing as feeling in the I.[716]

(Here we encounter crystal-clear evidence of what lies beyond the grasp of so many philosophers who, despite their alleged adherence to the Critical philosophy, have not yet freed themselves of their transcendent dogmatism: namely, evidence *that* and *how* the I is able to develop solely from itself everything that is ever supposed to be present in the I and is able to do so without ever proceeding beyond the I or breaking out of its circle, which must necessarily be the case if the I is supposed to be an I. — A feeling is present in the I. This feeling is a limitation [I, 290] of a drive; and, if it is supposed to be capable of being posited as a determinate feeling and distinguished from others (though granted, at this point we still lack any insight into how this is possible[717]), this feeling must be a limitation of a determinate drive,^{P} which must be distinguished from other drives. The I must [I/2: 420] posit some ground for this limitation, and it must posit it outside itself. It can posit this drive only as limited by something posited in complete opposition to it. *What* is supposed to be posited as the object is, therefore, obviously contained in the drive in question. If, for example, the drive is determined as Y, then the object [that limits it] must necessarily be posited as Not-Y. — However, since all the functions of the mind operate with necessity, one is not conscious of this, one's own acting, and one must [therefore] necessarily assume that one has received from outside that which one has, in fact, produced oneself, by means of one's own force and in accordance with one's own laws. — This way of proceeding nevertheless possesses objective validity, since it is the uniform procedure of all finite reason, and there neither is nor can there be any kind of objective validity other than the kind indicated. At the basis of the claim concerning some other type of objectivity there lies a demonstrably crude and palpable deception.[718]

To be sure, it seems that we have broken through this circle in our investigation, since, for the purposes of explaining striving as such, we have assumed a Not-I, which is completely independent of the I and strives in opposition to it.[719] The ground of the possibility and legitimacy of this way of proceeding is as follows: Everyone who engages with us in the present investigation is himself an I, an I that has itself long engaged in the actions here deduced and has therefore long engaged in positing a Not-I (a Not-I which, as the present investigation should convince him, is his own product[720]). He has necessarily already completed the entire work of reason, and now he freely determines himself to go through this same calculation once again, as it were, in order to observe the same process he himself once completed, but [to observe this process] in another I, an I [I, 291] that he voluntarily situates at the point from which he himself once proceeded and upon which he conducts an experiment. The I that is to be investigated

^{O} is *not* limited [Emphasis added in *SW.*]
^{P} of a *determinate* drive [Emphasis added in *SW.*]

will itself eventually arrive at the point presently occupied by the observer; both I's will then be united, and, with this union, the assigned circuit will be completed.[721])

§ 8. Fifth Theorem

Feeling Must Itself Be Posited and Determined[722]

[I/2: 421] In preparation for the supremely important investigation that is now to be undertaken, let us begin with a few general remarks.

1.) The I harbors an original striving to fill infinity. This striving is in opposition to all objects.[Q]

2.) The I contains a law requiring it to reflect upon itself as filling infinity.[723] Yet it cannot reflect upon itself — and indeed cannot reflect upon anything whatsoever — if what it reflects upon is not limited. Obedience to this law, or, which amounts to the same thing, satisfaction of the drive to engage in reflection, is therefore *conditioned* and is dependent upon the *object*. Without an object, this drive of the I to reflect upon itself cannot be satisfied, and it can therefore be described as a drive *toward the object*.[724]

3.) The limitation that occurs by means of a feeling simultaneously satisfies and fails to satisfy this drive.[725]

    a.) The limitation *satisfies* the drive. The I is purely and simply supposed to reflect upon itself and to do so with absolute spontaneity. It is therefore satisfied with respect to the *form* of the action.[726] The feeling therefore includes something that refers to the I and can be ascribed to it.[727]

    b.) The limitation *fails to satisfy* the drive [of the I to reflect upon itself] with respect to the *content* of the action.[728] The I is supposed to be posited as filling infinity, and yet it is posited as limited. — This too is necessarily present in the feeling.

    c.) However, the positing of this non-satisfaction is *conditioned* by the I's proceeding beyond the boundary posited for it by the feeling in question. Something must be posited beyond the sphere occupied by the I, something that also pertains to infinity, to which, accordingly, the drive of the I also extends. This must be posited as not determined by the I.[729]

[I, 292]

We will be investigating how it is possible for the I to proceed beyond itself in this way, and hence how the positing of this non-satisfaction — or, what amounts to the same thing, the positing of a feeling — is supposed to be possible.

[I/2: 422] I.) Just as surely as it reflects upon itself, the I *is* limited; that is to say, it fails to fill infinity, though it nevertheless strives to fill it. We said that it *is* limited; i.e., it is limited for a possible observer, but it is not yet limited for itself. We ourselves wish to be this observer, or, which means the same thing, instead of positing the I,

---

[Q] This striving is in opposition to satisfaction in any *individual* object. [As emended in *SW*, on the basis of Fichte's marginalia.]

we will posit something that is only observed, something lifeless — to which, however, there is also supposed to pertain something which, according to our presupposition, pertains to the I. Accordingly, let us posit an elastic ball = A and assume that it is impacted by another ball, in which case:

a.) One posits in the first ball a force that will manifest itself just as soon as the power posited in opposition to it is removed and will do so without any external contribution, a force which therefore possesses the ground of its efficacy solely within itself. — This force is present; it strives within itself and upon itself to manifest itself; it is a force directed within and upon itself. It is, therefore, an inner force, since anything of this sort is called an inner force. It is an immediate striving to exercise causality upon itself, which however, because of some external resistance, exercises no causality. [730] What is present within this body itself [the first elastic ball] is an equilibrium between striving and some indirectly present counter-pressure, and this is what we have previously called a *drive*. A drive is therefore posited in the indicated elastic ball.

b.) The same thing is posited in the resisting body B [the second elastic ball] — an inner force, which resists the reaction and resistance of A. Hence, B is itself restricted by this resistance, though it still possesses its ground solely [I, 293] within itself. — A force and a drive are posited in B, just as they were posited in A.

c.) If the force of either of these two balls were to be increased, then that of the one posited in opposition to it would be weakened. If its force were to be weakened, then that of the opposing ball would be increased. The stronger one would manifest itself fully, and the weaker one would be driven completely out of the stronger one's sphere of efficacy. At present, however, they counterbalance each other completely, and the point at which they come into contact is the point of their equilibrium. Were this point to be shifted in the least, the entire relationship would then be annulled.

II.) This is the situation with an object that strives without reflection (which we call "*elastic*"). What is to be investigated here, however, is an *I*, and we will now see what may ensue from this.

A drive is an inner force that determines itself to exercise causality. A lifeless body therefore exercises no causality whatsoever except *outside* itself.[731] This causality is supposed to be arrested by some resistance. Consequently, under [I/2: 423] this condition [of an equilibrium of forces], nothing arises as a result of its self-determination. This is precisely what happens in the case of the I as well insofar as it aims to exercise causality outside of itself, and this is all that can happen if it *merely* demands to exercise external causality.

But the I, just because it is an I, also exercises causality upon itself — namely, that of positing itself, or the capacity for reflection. The drive [of the I] is supposed to determine *the force of the striving subject* itself; consequently, insofar as this force is supposed to manifest itself *in the striving subject itself* (as reflection is supposed to do), *some* [*internal*] *manifestation* must *necessarily follow* from the determination of this drive. Otherwise, no drive would be present, which contradicts our assumption. Consequently, the I's action of reflecting upon itself follows necessarily from the drive.[732]

(This is an important proposition, which sheds the clearest light upon our inquiry.[R]

[I, 294]

1.) The original *duality* [*Zweifach*] of the I, which was displayed above[733] — the duality of striving and reflection — is hereby inwardly united. All reflection is grounded in striving, and no reflection is possible in the absence of striving. — Conversely, if there is no reflection, then there is no striving *for the I* and hence no striving *of the I*, and indeed, no I at all. One necessarily implies the other; reflection and striving reciprocally interact with each other.

2.) Here one gains more precise insight into the fact that the I must be finite and limited. No restriction, no drive — in the transcendent sense; no drive, no reflection — transition to the transcendental; no reflection, no drive, and no limitation and nothing that limits, etc. — in the transcendental sense.[734] So proceeds the circuit of the I's functions and the internally interlinked reciprocal interaction of the I with itself.

3.) The meaning of *ideal* and *real* activity also becomes quite clear at this point, as well as how they are to be distinguished from each other and where the boundary between them lies. Considered as a drive, a drive grounded exclusively in the I itself, the original striving of the I is at once *ideal* and *real*. It is directed at the I itself and strives through its own force; and it is also directed at something outside the I, though there is [as yet] nothing pesent to be distinguished from the I. This original force [*Kraft*] is, as it were, divided by that limitation that annuls its *outward* direction, but not its *inward* one. The remaining force, the one that reverts into the I, is the *ideal* one. The *real* force[735] will be posited at the appropriate time.[736] — And thus, here yet again, we encounter in its fullest light the proposition: no ideality, no reality, and vice versa.[737]

[I/2: 424]

4.) The *ideal* activity will soon reveal itself to be the *activity of representing*.[738] Hence, in relation to this activity the drive in question is called the *drive to representation*. This drive is, accordingly, the first and highest manifestation of the [I's original] drive,[739] and it is by this means that the I first comes to be an intellect. Moreover, it must necessarily behave in this manner if any other drive is ever to attain *to consciousness* or occur within the I *as an I*.

5.) This also most clearly implies the subordination of the theoretical to the practical. It follows that all *theoretical* laws are grounded upon *practical* laws, and since there is indeed but one practical law, all of these theoretical

[I, 295]

[R] [The following five numbered remarks are all contained in a single paragraph beginning with the words "This is an important proposition," a paragraph which is enclosed in parentheses. In the interests of clarity, this paragraph has been broken up into six paragraphs.]

laws are grounded upon one and the same practical law,[740] from which it follows that there is the most complete system in the entire human being [*im ganzen Wesen*]. Therefore, if this drive itself should perhaps allow itself to be heightened, then insight will be heightened as well, and vice versa. This also implies the absolute freedom of reflection and abstraction, even in the theoretical domain, as well as the possibility of *dutifully* directing one's attention to something and withdrawing it from something else, without which no morality whatsoever is possible. Fatalism is [thereby] destroyed from the ground up, for fatalism is basedf on the claim that our acting and willing^S are dependent upon the system of our representations,[741] whereas what now been show is that, on the contrary, the system of our representations depends upon our drive and our will, which is also the only way to refute fatalism in a thoroughgoing manner. — In short, this system produces *unity* and *coherence* in the entire human being, something that so many [other] systems fail to do.)

III.) The I is unable to attain to consciousness of itself as such by means of this reflection upon itself, since it never becomes immediately conscious of its own acting.[742] Yet it is still present as an I — for a possible observer, as goes without saying. Here lies the boundary separating the living I from the lifeless body, which can, however, still harbor a drive. — Something is present, something *for which* something could be present, despite the fact that it is not yet present *for itself.* But there is necessarily present for it [that is, for the living body] an inner, driving force, which, however, is merely *felt*, since no consciousness whatsoever of the I — and hence, no relation to the I — is possible [in this case]. This is a condition that cannot very well be described; but it can be felt, and in regard to it each person must be referred to his own self-feeling. (The philosopher may not refer others to their own self-feeling with regard to the fact *that* this occurs — since, on the supposition that there is an I, this is something that must be strictly demonstrated — but only with regard to *what* is present in this self-feeling.[743] To [I, 296] postulate the presence of a certain feeling means that one is not proceeding in a thoroughly well-grounded manner. To be sure, this feeling [of an inner, driving [I/2: 425] force] will subsequently become recognizable, albeit through its consequences and not through itself.)

We just said that this is what distinguishes what is living from what is lifeless. The feeling of force is the principle of all life and marks the transition from death to life. To be sure, if this feeling is all that is present, then life remains quite incomplete, even though it is already sundered from dead matter.

IV.)

a.) This force is felt as something *driving.* As was just said, the I discovers itself to be driven, and indeed, to be driven *beyond and outside itself.* (Though

---

^S willing and acting [As emended in *SW*, on the basis of Fichte's marginalia.]

we do not at this point possess any insight into where this *beyond*, this *outside itself*, comes from, this will soon become clear.[744])

b.) Just as was previously the case, this drive[745] must *affect what it is able to affect*. It does not determine the *real* activity; that is to say, it exercises no causality upon the Not-I. But it can determine the *ideal* activity, which is dependent solely upon the I itself, and it must determine this ideal activity, just as surely as it is a drive. — Hence it proceeds beyond the [intuited object of the] ideal activity and posits something as the object of the drive; i.e., it posits it as what the drive would produce if it exercised causality.[746] — (It has been demonstrated *that* this production on the part of the ideal activity must occur, but *how* this might be possible is something into which we cannot yet obtain insight and is a question that presupposes a number of other investigations.[747])

c.) The I is at this point conscious neither of this act of production nor of the subject engaging in this act. Consequently, at this point nothing whatsoever arises from the act of production — neither a *feeling* of the object of the drive (something that is by no means possible) nor any *intuition* of this object. Nothing whatsoever ensues from this productive act. From this it follows that all we have to do in order to open the way to the transition that ensues is to explain how the I could feel itself *to be driven toward something with which it is unacquainted*.

[I, 297]

V.) The drive is supposed to be *felt* and to be felt as a drive, that is, as something that does not exercise causality. And yet, at last insofar as it drives the I to produce its object by means of ideal activity, the drive in question exercises causality after all, though it is not felt as a *drive* in this respect.

Insofar as the drive aspires to real activity it is not noticeable and cannot be felt, for it exercises no causality. Hence it is not felt as a drive in this respect either.

[I/2: 426] Let us combine these two points: no drive can be felt unless an ideal activity is directed at the object of that drive, and the ideal activity cannot be directed at an object unless the real activity is limited.

When we combine these two points, we obtain the I's reflection upon itself as *limited*. But since the I is not conscious of itself in this reflection, it is nothing but a *feeling*.

With this, the feeling [in question] has been completely deduced. It includes: [1.] a feeling of force, which has not yet expressed itself;[748] [2.] an object of this feeling, which also does not express itself; and [3.] a feeling of compulsion or inability. And this feeling of compulsion is the manifestation of the feeling that was supposed to be deduced.

§ 9. Sixth Theorem

Feeling Must Be Further Determined and Delineated

I.)

1.) The I now feels itself to be limited. That is to say, it is limited *for itself* and not merely for an external observer, as was previously the case or as is the case with a lifeless elastic body. The I's activity is annulled *for itself — for itself,* we said. This is because, even though, from our higher point of view, we can certainly see that it is the I itself that has exercised its absolute activity to produce outside itself an object of the drive, this is not some- [I, 298] thing that the I we are investigating is able to see.

Complete annihilation of activity contradicts the character of the I.[749] Consequently, just as surely as it is an I, the I must restore the activity in question, and indeed, restore it *for itself.* That is to say, it must at least place itself in a position from which it would be able to posit itself as free and unlimited[750] — if only in the course of some future reflection.

According to our deduction of this activity,[751] this restoration of the I's activity occurs absolutely spontaneously, purely as a consequence of the I's [I/2: 427] own nature, without requiring any special stimulus. The action in question, which will soon be confirmed to be an act of reflecting upon the I that is engaged in reflecting, [and therefore] an interruption of one action in order to posit another in its place,[752] is an action that occurs with absolute spontaneity. In this case, the I acts purely and simply because it acts. According to the preceding description, the I also acts when it feels, but it does so unconsciously. This action [involved in feeling] is now supposed to be replaced by another action, one that makes consciousness at least possible. In engaging in this action, the I acts purely and simply because it acts.

(Here lies the boundary between sheer life and intelligence, just as we previously observed the boundary between death and life. The con- sciousness of the I follows exclusively from this absolute spontaneity. — It is by means of absolute freedom and not by means of any law of nature nor as a consequence of any such law that we raise ourselves to [the standpoint of] reason — not by means of any *transition,* but by means of a *leap.* — This is why philosophy must necessarily start with the I: namely, because the latter cannot be deduced. And this is also why the project of the materialists — namely, to explain the manifestations of reason on the basis of laws of nature — will remain eternally unachievable.[753])

2.) It is immediately clear that the required action, one that occurs purely and exclusively through absolute spontaneity, can be nothing else but an action of the ideal activity.[754] But every action, just as surely as it is an action, has an object. The action we are now considering, which is supposed to be [I, 299] grounded purely and exclusively in the I and to depend exclusively upon the I with respect to all its conditions, can [therefore] have as its object only something present in the I. But there is [at this point, according to the preceding,] nothing present in the I but a feeling. Consequently, the action in question is necessarily directed at a feeling.

This action [of reflection] occurs absolutely spontaneously, and to that extent it is, for a possible observer, an action of the I. The action in ques- tion is directed at a *feeling*; that is to say, it is directed, first of all, at the *reflecting subject* engaged in the preceding reflection, the one that consti- tuted feeling. — Activity is directed at activity. The subject that was, in that [prior] reflection, engaged in reflecting — that is, the *feeling subject* — is consequently *posited as an I.* The I-hood [*Ichheit*] of the subject that is presently engaged in reflecting — an I-hood that does not appear as such within the consciousness of that subject — is transferred to the feeling subject.[755]

According to the preceding line of argument, the I is that which determines itself. It follows that the feeling subject can be posited as an I only insofar as it is determined to engage in feeling solely by a *drive*, and therefore by the I, and hence is so determined through itself. That is to say, it can be posited as an I only insofar as it feels *itself* and *its own force within itself.*[756] — Only the feeling subject is the I, and nothing pertains to the I but a drive, since it is the drive that produces the feeling or the reflection. Whatever lies beyond this boundary is excluded — assuming that something might lie beyond it — , and we indeed know that something does lie beyond that boundary: namely, the *externally directed* drive. One should take careful note of this, since what is excluded must be addressed at the appropriate time.[757]

[I/2: 428]

In this way, therefore, what is *felt* in and for the present reflection [upon the feeling I] is likewise an I. This is because the *feeling subject* is an I only insofar as it is determined by itself, i.e., only insofar as it feels itself.

II.) In the present reflection,[758] the I is posited as an I only insofar as it is at the same time both the *feeling subject* and *what is felt* and thus interacts reciprocally with itself. It is supposed to be posited as an I; therefore, it must be posited in the manner just described.

[I, 300]

1.) In feeling, the *feeling subject* is posited as *active*, since it is engaged in reflecting. To this extent, what is felt in this same feeling is *passively affected*; it is the object of reflection. — At the same time, whenever a feeling occurs the feeling subject is posited *as passively affected*, insofar as it feels itself *driven*, and, to this extent, what is felt — namely, the drive — is *active*; it is *that which drives*.

2.) This is a contradiction, and, as such, it must be resolved, and this can be accomplished in only one way. — The feeling subject is *active* in relation to *what is felt* and is, in this respect, *nothing but* active. (The feeling subject is not conscious of being driven to engage in reflection; original consciousness pays no attention whatsoever to the drive to reflection, though of course we attend to it in our philosophical investigations. This drive to reflection occurs in that which is [in this case] the object of the feeling subject[759] and is not distinguished from it in [that subject's] reflection upon feeling.) And yet this same feeling subject is also supposed to be *passive* in its relation to a drive. The drive in question is the externally directed drive, which is what actually drives the feeling subject to produce a Not-I by means of its ideal activity. (To be sure, it is also active in this function, but, just as before, in the case of its passivity, the feeling subject does not reflect upon its own activity. For *itself*, in its reflection upon itself, it is compelled to act, despite the fact that this seems to involve a contradiction,[760] one that will, however, be resolved at the appropriate time.[761] This is the source of the felt compulsion to posit something as actually present.)

3.) Thanks to the drive to reflect upon the reflecting subject [which is engaged in feeling], *what is felt* is *active*. In this same relation to the reflecting subject, what is felt is also *passive,* since it is an object of [a second act of] reflection. But there is no reflection upon the latter [passive] aspect of this [I/2: 429] relation, since the I is posited as a unity, as precisely one and the same. That is, the I is posited as *feeling itself,* and there is no additional reflection upon this reflection as such. Consequently, the I is now posited as passive in another relation: namely, insofar as it is *limited*; and, to this extent, what limits it is a Not-I. (Every object of reflection is necessarily limited; it pos- [I, 301] sesses a determinate quantity. In the course of reflection, however, this limitation is never derived from the act of reflection itself. This is because there is no reflection upon this reflection itself while one is engaged in reflecting.)

4.) Both [the I that is engaged in feeling and the I that feels the I that is engaged in feeling] are supposed to be one and the same and are supposed to be posited as such. Nevertheless, one is posited as active in relation to the Not-I, whereas the other is posited as passively related to it. In the former case, the I produces a Not-I by means of ideal activity; in the latter, it is limited by the Not-I.

5.) This contradiction can be easily resolved. The productive I was itself posited as *passively affected,* as what is felt in [this second act of] reflection. Accordingly, the I is *for itself* always *passive* in relation to the Not-I. It is by no means conscious of its own activity, nor can it become conscious of it. — It is for this reason that the reality of the thing seems to be felt, though, in fact, all that is felt is the I.

(Here lies the ground of all reality [*Realität*]. As has now been established, reality — whether of the I or of the Not-I[762] — becomes possible for the I only through the relation of feeling to the I. — Anything possible only by means of its *relation to a feeling* — without the I's becoming conscious of *its own intuition of this feeling* or being capable of becoming conscious of it — and which *therefore seems to be felt, is believed.*[763])

Concerning reality as such, whether that of the I or that of the Not-I,[T] there is only *a belief.*)

§ 10. Seventh Theorem   [I/2: 430]

Drive Itself Must Be Posited and Determined

Just as we have now determined and clarified "feeling," so must "drive" now be determined, since it is connected to feeling. This clarification will advance our inquiry and gain us ground in [our consideration of] the practical power.[764]

[T] *Concerning reality as such,* whether that of the *I* or that of the *Not-I* [Emphasis added in *SW.*]

1.) As we know, to say that a drive is posited means that the I reflects upon it. But the I is able to reflect only upon itself and upon what is for and in the I — upon what is, as it were, accessible to the I. For this reason, the drive in question must already have presented itself within the I — and, indeed, must have produced [*bewirkt*] something in the I; and *to the extent that the I has already been posited as an I by means of the reflection just described*, this drive must also have made itself present within the I.

[I, 302]

2.) The feeling subject is posited as I. The felt, original drive determined this subject to proceed beyond itself and to produce something, if only by means of its ideal activity. Now, however, what this original drive is directed at is by no means the merely ideal activity, but *reality*,[765] and therefore the I is determined by this drive to bring forth *a reality outside itself*. — But since the I's striving is never supposed to possess causality, it cannot adequately satisfy this determination to bring forth a reality outside itself; instead, it is supposed to be counterbalanced by the opposed striving of the Not-I. Consequently, insofar as it is determined by the [original] drive, the I is *restricted* by the Not-I.

3.) The I has a constant tendency to reflect upon itself just as soon as the condition for any reflection — namely, a limitation — is present. This condition is satisfied in the case we are now considering; consequently, the I must necessarily reflect upon this, its own [limited] state. — In this reflection, as always, the subject engaging in reflecting forgets itself[766] and is therefore not conscious of engaging in this act of reflection. Moreover, since this reflection occurs in consequence of a sheer stimulus [*Antrieb*], it contains not the least manifestation of freedom and becomes, as was the case above,[767] a sheer *feeling*. The question is simply this, What kind of feeling?

4.) The object of the reflection in question is the I, the I that is driven — driven by a stimulus lying within itself, and therefore driven without any free choice and spontaneity — and is therefore active within itself in the ideal sense [*idealiter*]. — But this [same] activity of the I is directed at an object that the I is unable to *realize*, qua thing, and which it is not even able to *present* [*darstellen*] by means of its ideal activity.[768] It is therefore an activity that *has no object whatsoever*; and yet it is an activity that *is irresistibly driven toward such an object*,[769] an activity that is merely *felt*. Such a determination within the I is called a *longing* [*Sehnen*],[770] a drive toward something with which one is utterly unacquainted, a drive that reveals itself purely through a *need* [*Bedürfniß*], through a *feeling of discomfort*, through a *void*: a drive that seeks satisfaction without indicating where such satisfaction is to be found.[771] — The I feels a longing within itself; it feels itself to be needy.

[I/2: 431]

[I, 303]

5.) Both feelings — the feeling of *longing*, which was just derived, and the previously indicated feeling of *limitation and compulsion* — must be distinguished from and related to each other. — This is because the drive is supposed to be determined; but the drive reveals itself by means of a certain *feeling*, and therefore it is this feeling that has to be determined. It can be determined, however, only by another kind of feeling.[772]

6.) Were the I not restricted in the first feeling, no *sheer longing* could be present in the second; instead, what would be present would be *causality*, since the I would then be able to produce something outside itself, and its drive would not be limited to determining the I itself purely inwardly.[U] Conversely, were the I not to feel itself as *longing,* then it could not feel itself as *restricted,* because it is only by means of the feeling of longing that the I proceeds beyond itself — only by means of this feeling of longing, [a feeling that exists] in and for the I, is anything first posited that is supposed to exist outside the I.[773]

(This longing is important, not only for the practical part, but for the entire *Wissenschaftslehre.* Only by means of longing is the I *driven outside itself — within itself;* only in this way does an *external world* reveal itself *within the I* itself.)

7.) Limitation and longing are now synthetically united; neither is possible without the other. No limitation, no longing; no longing, no limitation. — And yet, each is also posited in complete opposition to the other. In the feeling of limitation, the I is felt only as *passively affected;* in the feeling of longing, it is also felt as *active.*

8.) Both feelings are grounded in a drive within the I, and indeed in *one and the same* drive. The drive of that I which is limited by a Not-I, and which becomes capable of possessing a drive only thereby, determines the power of reflection, and from this there arises a feeling of compulsion. This same drive determines the I to proceed beyond itself by means of [its] ideal activity and to produce something outside itself. Since the I is limited in this [I, 304] respect, there consequently arises a *longing,* from which there arises *a feeling* [I/2: 432] *of longing,* since the power of reflection is thereby posited as necessarily engaging in reflection [upon the longing that has arisen within the I]. This raises the question, How can one and the same drive produce something so opposed to itself?[774] This is made possible precisely by means of the different forces [of the I] to which this drive is addressed.[775] In its first function, it is directed exclusively at the sheer power of reflection, which only apprehends what is given to it.[776] In its second function, this drive is directed at that absolute, free striving, which is grounded in the I itself, a striving that is bent upon creation and that actually does create something by means of ideal activity — though we have not yet advanced far enough to recognize this product or to be able to recognize it.

9.) It follows that longing is the *original, completely independent* manifestations of the I's striving. It is *independent,* because it takes no account whatsoever of any limitation, nor is it arrested by any limitation.[777] (This remark is important, for it will eventually become evident that such longing is the vehicle for all practical laws,[778] all of which must be derivable from this original longing.)

[U] purely *inwardly* [Emphasis added in *SW.*]

10.) As a result of the limitation [of the I's original drive], there arises at the same time within longing a feeling of compulsion, a feeling that must be grounded in a Not-I. The object of striving (which is what the I that was determined by the drive would actually achieve, were it to possess causality, and which one could provisionally call the *ideal*) is in complete conformity and congruence with the striving of the I. In contrast, however, that object which could be posited (and which will certainly also be posited) by relating the feeling of limitation to the I is in conflict with the I. Consequently, these two objects are themselves posited in opposition to each other.

11.) Since there can be no longing without a feeling of compulsion, and vice versa, the I is synthetically unified in both cases: it is one and the same I. Nevertheless, the I is in obvious conflict with itself in these two determinations; it is simultaneously *limited* and *unlimited, finite* and

[I, 305]

infinite. This contradiction must be eliminated; therefore, we will now proceed to clarify it and to resolve it in a satisfactory manner.

12.) As we have said, longing aims to produce something outside the I. It is unable to accomplish this; indeed, so far as we can see, the I is utterly unable to accomplish this in either of its determinations.[779] — Nevertheless, this externally directed drive must affect what it is able to affect. It is, however, able to exercise an effect upon the ideal activity of the I; it can determine this activity to proceed beyond itself and to produce something. — This productive ability,[780] which will soon be genetically deduced, is not in question here. However, the following question must be answered, a question that presses itself upon anyone who has been

[I/2: 433]

thinking along with us: Why indeed did we not draw this inference earlier, since we originally proceeded from an externally directed drive?[781] The answer is as follows: Unless it has first limited itself,[782] the I cannot direct itself *beyond itself effectively* [*gültig*] and *for itself* (for this is all that we are discussing here, having previously made this same inference in the case of a possible observer of the I[783]). This is because there is for the I no distinction between what is internal and what is external [to the I] prior to such limitation. This limitation of itself occurs by means of the *self-feeling*[784] we have deduced. This is because the I is equally incapable of directing itself beyond itself unless the external world somehow reveals itself to the I *within itself.* This, however, is something that first occurs by means of longing.

13.) The question is as follows: *What* will be produced by means of the ideal activity of the I as determined by longing and *how* will this be accomplished?[785] — There is within the I a determinate feeling of limitation = X. — In addition, there is within the I a longing that aims at reality. But reality manifests itself for the I only by means of feeling; hence longing aims at a feeling. Feeling X, however, is not the feeling for which it longs, for in that case the I would not feel itself to be either *limited* or *longing* — indeed, it

[I, 306]

would not feel at all; or rather, it would instead feel the opposed feeling, the feeling posited in opposition to X. That is to say, it would feel -X. The object (which we wish to call −X as well) that must be present if feeling −X rather than feeling X is to be present in the I would have to be produced. Such an object would be the ideal. — Now if, on the one hand,[V] object X (the ground of feeling X, the feeling of limitation) could itself be felt, in that case it would be easy to posit −X simply by positing it in opposition to X. But this is impossible, since the I never feels an object, but only itself, whereas the object can be produced only by means of ideal activity.[786] — If, on the other hand,[W] the I itself could somehow give rise within itself to feeling −X, then it would itself be capable of immediately comparing the two feelings, in order to take note of their differences and to exhibit these differences in their objects, as the grounds of the feelings in question. But the I is unable to give rise to any feeling within itself; for if it could, then it would be exercising causality, which, however, it is not supposed to be able to do. (This recalls the assertion made in the theoretical *Wissenschaftslehre*: The I cannot limit itself.[787]) — The task,[788] therefore, is nothing less than this: to infer immediately from the feeling of limitation (a feeling that is by no means capable of being determined any further) the object of that longing which is posited in complete opposition to this feeling of limitation. This would mean that the I, guided only by the first feeling [of limitation], is supposed to produce the object of the feeling of longing and to do so by means of [its] ideal activity.

14.) The object of the limitation is something real. The object of the feeling of [I/2: 434] longing possesses no reality, though it is supposed to obtain reality in consequence of this longing, since the latter aims at reality. These two feelings are posited in opposition to each other, since through one of the them the I feels itself to be limited, whereas through the other it strives to proceed beyond this limitation. What the one is, the other is not: for the moment, this, and nothing more, is all that can be said about both of them.

15.) Let us advance more deeply into our inquiry. — According to what was said above, the I has posited itself as an I by means of free reflection upon the feeling [of limitation] and has done so in accordance with the following foundational principle: that which posits itself and which is both determining and determined at the same time is the I.[789] — Accordingly, in this reflection (which has manifested itself as a feeling of self), the I has *determined* itself, has completely circumscribed and limited itself. In this [I, 307] reflection it is *absolutely determining*.

16.) It is *this* activity [of reflection] at which the outgoing drive is directed, which therefore becomes, in this respect, a drive toward *determining* or *modifying* something external to the I: namely, that same reality which has already been given to the I by means of feeling as such. — The I was at the same time what is determined and what is engaged in determining. To say that it is driven by the externally directed drive means that it is

[V] *if, on the one hand* [Emphasis added in *SW*.]
[W] *On the other hand* [Emphasis added in *SW*.]

supposed to be that which is *engaged in determining* [*das bestimmende*]. But all determining presupposes a determinable matter [*einen bestimmbaren Stoff*]. — The equilibrium[790] must be maintained; hence, reality remains always what it was: namely, *reality*, something that can be related to feeling. For reality as such, that is, as sheer *matter*, no modification whatsoever is thinkable, other than annihilation and total annulment. But the existence of such matter is a condition for life. What is not alive can contain no drive, and no drive of what is living can be directed at the annihilation of life. It follows that the drive that manifests itself in the I [in this case] is by no means directed at matter as such, but instead, at a certain *determination of matter*. (One cannot say, at a *different matter*. Matter [*Stoffheit*], materiality, is purely and simply simple; instead, one should say that this drive aims at *matter with different determinations*.[791])

17.) It is *this* determination by means of the drive that is felt as a *longing*. Hence longing by no means aims at the production of matter as such; instead, what it aims at is the modification of matter.

18.) As is self-evident, the *feeling* of longing was impossible without reflection upon the determination of the I through the indicated drive [to determination]. This reflection was impossible without *limitation* of the drive, and indeed, of the drive toward determination [*Bestimmungstrieb*] in particular, which is the only drive that manifests itself in longing. But every limitation of the I is merely felt. The question is, What kind of feeling might this be, by means of which the *drive to determining* is felt as limited?[792]

[I/2: 435]

[I, 308]

19.) All determining occurs by means of ideal activity. Hence, if the requisite feeling is supposed to be possible, an object must already have been determined by this ideal activity,[793] and this act of determining must have been related to the feeling in question. — This raises the following questions: 1.) How is the ideal activity supposed to arrive at the possibility and actuality of this act of determining? 2.) How is this act of determining supposed to be able to relate itself to feeling?[794]

We answer the first question as follows: We have previously discovered[795] a determination of the I's ideal activity by means of a drive, a drive that must operate continuously, to the extent that it is able to do so. By means of this ideal activity and in consequence of this determination, the I must posit, as *the ground of [its] limitation*, an object — and, moreover, an object that is completely determined by itself.[796] But for precisely this reason, the I cannot be conscious of this object, nor can it become so. This indicates that there is within the I a drive toward sheer determination, in accordance with which the ideal activity must, first of all, at least strive to *determine* the object that has been posited. — We cannot say *how* the I is supposed to determine the object in consequence of this drive, but we know at least this much: that, in accordance with this drive, which is grounded in its innermost nature, the I is supposed to be that which *engages in an act of determining*, to be that which, in this same act, is *purely, exclusively, and simply active*. But even if we abstract from that

feeling of *longing* with which we are already familiar and the simple presence of which is sufficient to decide our question, can we or can we not
say, on purely a priori grounds, that this drive toward determination can
exercise causality and achieve satisfaction?[797] The possibility of any longing depends upon the limitation of this drive, upon the possibility of
which, in turn, the possibility of any feeling depends — upon which
depends the possibility of any life, consciousness, and spiritual existence
whatsoever. It follows that, just as surely as the I is an I, the drive toward
determination exercises no causality. Yet, just as was previously the case
with striving as such,[798] the reason it exercises no causality cannot lie
within this drive itself, for in that case it would not be a drive. Instead, the
ground of its failure to exercise causality must lie in a counter-drive
[*Gegentriebe*] of the Not-I *to determine itself*. That is to say, the ground of
this failure must lie in the causal efficacy of the Not-I, which is utterly
independent of the I and of its drive — a drive of the Not-I which goes *its
own* way and directs itself according to *its own* laws, just as does the drive   [I, 309]
of the I.[799]

Consequently, if there is an object, and if the determinations of this
object exist in themselves, i.e., if these determinations are produced by
the inherent inner causal efficacy of nature (as we will assume provisionally and hypothetically, but which will soon be realized *by the I*), and if,
in addition and as we have demonstrated, the ideal (intuiting) activity of
the I is driven outward by the drive toward determination: if all this is
indeed the case, then it is and must be the I that determines the object.
In this act of determination, the I is guided by the drive and aims to   [I/2: 436]
determine the object in accordance with the drive. At the same time,
however, the I is subject to the influence of the Not-I, and for this reason
it is limited by the actual constitution [*Beschaffenheit*, that is, by the
properties or attributes] of the thing and is, to a greater or lesser degree,
not able to engage in determining the object in accordance with the
drive toward determination.

The I is limited by this restriction of the drive [to determination]. As is
the case with every limitation of striving, and in the same manner, there
arises a feeling, which in this case *is* a feeling of the limitation of the I — a
limitation produced not by *matter*, but by its *constitution*. And, with this,
we have at the same time answered our second question, concerning how
the restriction of the act of determining is able to relate itself to a
feeling.[800]

20.) Let us further explicate and more rigorously demonstrate what was just said.

a.) As was noted above,[801] the I determines itself absolutely spontaneously.
It is this activity of determining to which the drive that is now to be
examined[802] addresses itself and which this drive impels outward.
If we wish to gain a thorough acquaintance with the determination
of this activity of determining by the drive in question, then, before
doing anything else, we must become thoroughly familiar with *this
activity itself*.

[I, 310]

[I/2: 437]

b.) The activity in question was engaged purely and solely in *reflecting*. It determined the I just as it found it, without altering anything in the I. One might therefore say that it was engaged solely in *forming images* [*bloß bildend*].[803] This drive neither can nor should introduce anything into the I that is not already present therein; accordingly, it simply drives the activity in question to copy [*zum Nachbilden*] what is there, as it is.[804] It drives the activity only to intuit the thing, and by no means to modify it through real causal efficacy. All that is supposed to happen is that a determination should be produced within the I as it exists in the Not-I.

c.) Nevertheless, there is *one* respect in which the I that was reflecting upon itself must have [already] possessed within itself the criterion for this act of reflecting;[805] for this act [of reflection] was directed at that which was *(in a real sense [realiter]) simultaneously determined and engaged in determining*, and it posited it as I.[806] That something of this sort was present did not depend upon the I, insofar as the I was considered to be engaged only in reflecting.[X] Why did the I not reflect upon less than this? Why did it not reflect only upon what is determined or only upon what is engaged in determining? Why did it not reflect upon more than this? Why did it not extend the scope of its object? The reason for this could not have come from outside the I, since the reflection in question occurred absolutely spontaneously. It follows that the I must have contained purely within itself that which pertains to every reflection: namely, the limitation of its object.[807] — That this was the case is also evident from another consideration. The I was supposed to be posited. That which is "simultaneously determined and engaged in determining" was posited as I. The reflecting subject contained this criterion within itself and carried it into its act of reflection; this is because the reflecting subject is itself that which is simultaneously determined and engaged in determining, *inasmuch as it engages in reflection with absolute spontaneity.*

Does the subject engaged in reflecting perhaps also possess such an inner law of determination for determining the Not-I, and if so, what is this law?

It is easy to answer this question on the basis of grounds that have previously been specified. The drive [toward determination] addresses itself to the reflecting I, just as it is. It can add nothing to the reflecting I, nor can it subtract anything from it; the I's inner law of determination remains the same. Everything that is supposed to be an object of the I's reflection and of its (*ideal*) act of determining must be "simultaneously determined and engaged in determining" (*in a real sense*), and this is equally true of the Not-I that is to be determined.[808] The subjective law of determination is therefore as

[X] only as *engaged in reflecting* [*als reflectierende*]. [Emphasis added in *SW.*]

follows: *something is supposed to be simultaneously determined and* [I, 311] *engaged in determining, i.e., determined through itself.* The drive toward determination aims to discover this to be the case, and it can be satisfied only on this condition. — It demands *determinacy,* complete *totality* and *wholeness,* which consists only in this characteristic feature [that is, in self-determination]. That which, *insofar as it is determined,* is not at the same time *that which is engaged in determining,* is, to that extent, an *effect*; and, by means of the boundary drawn by reflection, this effect is excluded from the thing as something *foreign* and is explained on the basis of *something else.* That which, *insofar as it is engaged in determining,* is not at the same time *what is determined,* is, to that extent, a *cause,* and the act of determining is related to *something else* and thereby excluded from the sphere posited for the thing by means of reflection. But a thing is a thing — and the same thing — only insofar as it is reciprocally related to itself.[809] This characteristic feature is transferred from the I to the thing by means of the drive toward determination. This is an important remark.

(This can be illustrated by the most ordinary examples. Why is sweet or bitter, red or yellow, etc., a *simple* sensation, one that cannot be further dissected into further sensations?[810] Or why is this a sensation persisting for itself and not merely a component of another sensation? The reason for this must obviously lie within the I *for which* it is a simple sensation. The I must therefore contain a priori a law of *limitation* as such.[811])

d.) The distinction between the I and the Not-I always remains, despite this sameness of the law of determination [in both cases]. If what is reflected upon is the I, then the subject engaged in reflecting and what is reflected upon are equivalent, one and the same: it is what is determined and what is engaged in determining. If what is reflected upon is the Not-I, [I/2: 438] then the I and Not-I are posited in opposition to each other, since the subject engaged in reflecting is, as is self-evident, always the I.

e.) At the same time, this provides us with a strict proof that what the drive toward determination aims at [in this case] is not real modification, but only an ideal determining, a determining for the I, a copying. Whatever is to be an object of this drive toward determination must, with respect to its reality,[Y] be determined [I, 312] completely by itself, and thus there remains nothing else for a real activity of the I to do; indeed, such a real activity of the I would openly contradict the determination of this drive. If the I were to modify anything with respect to reality of the object of this drive toward determination,[Z] then this would mean that what is supposed to be given is not given.[812]

Y *with respect to its reality* [*realiter*] [Emphasis added in *SW.*]
Z *with respect to the reality of the object of this drive toward determination* [Emphasis added in *SW.*]

21.) The question is simply this, How and in what way is what is determinable supposed to be given to the I? And by answering this question we will once again delve more deeply into the synthetic connection between the actions that are to be displayed here.

The I reflects upon itself as what is simultaneously determined and engaged in determining, and to this extent it limits itself (since it extends precisely as far as that which is both determined and engaged in determining extends). But there is no *limitation* without *something limiting*. This limiting something, which is posited in opposition to the I, cannot be somehow produced by the ideal activity (as was postulated in the theoretical part); instead, it must be given to the I and lie within it. And something of this sort can indeed be found within the I: namely, that which is excluded from the I in this reflection, as was indicated above. — The I posits itself as an I only insofar as it is *what is determined and what is engaged in determining*, but it is both of these only in an ideal respect. Its striving for real activity is, however, limited; to his extent, this striving is posited as an internal, confined, and self-determining force (that is, as simultaneously determined and engaged in determining), or, since it does not manifest itself,[813] as intensive matter.[814] The I reflects upon the latter, as such, and accordingly, by means of positing in opposition, it is transferred outside the I, and what is originally and in itself *subjective* is transformed into something *objective*.[815]

a.) At this point the origin of the law that the I cannot posit itself as determined without positing a Not-I in opposition to itself becomes fully clear.[816] In accordance with this law, with which we are now sufficiently familiar, we could have begun with the following inference: if the I is supposed to determine itself, then it must necessarily posit something in opposition to itself. But since we are now in the practical part of the *Wissenschaftslehre*, and hence must always focus our attention upon drive and feeling, we had to derive this law itself from a drive.[817] — The drive [toward determination], which is originally directed outward, affects what it can; and since it is unable to affect the real activity [of the I], it can it least affect [its] ideal activity, an activity which, by its very nature, can by no means be limited; and thus the drive [toward determination] drives the ideal activity outward. From this there arises an act of positing in opposition, and in this way — by means of this drive and in it — all of the determinations of consciousness — including, specifically, consciousness of the I and the Not-I — are connected with one another.[818]

b.) What is subjective is transformed into something objective; and conversely, everything objective is originally something subjective. — It is not possible to provide a fully adequate example of this, since what we are here discussing is something that is *determinate as such or in general* [*einem bestimmten überhaupt*] and is nothing more than this:

[I, 313]

[I/2: 439]

something determinate. Nothing of this sort can ever be present within consciousness, and we will soon see why.[819] Just as certainly as it is supposed to be present within consciousness, everything determinate is necessarily something *particular.* What was just asserted can be established quite clearly in consciousness by means of the same type of illustration employed above.

For example, let us assume something *sweet, sour, red, gold,* or the like. Such a determination is obviously something purely *subjective,*[AA] and we trust that no one who so much as understands these words will dispute this point. Sweet or sour, red or yellow: what these are supposed to be is something that is purely and simply indescribable; instead, it can only be felt. Nor is this anything that can be communicated to others through any description; instead, if another person is ever to become acquainted with my sensation,[820] he must relate this object[821] to his own feeling.[822] All one can say is that *there is in me the sensation of bitter or sour,* etc., and nothing more. — And yet, assuming that the other person relates this object to his feeling, how do you also know that what arises within him is an acquaintance with *your* sensation? How do you know that he senses in the same way as you? How do you know, for example, that sugar makes precisely the same impression upon his taste that it makes upon yours? To be sure, you call what ensues within you when you eat   [I, 314] sugar "*sweet,*" and he, along with all your fellow citizens, also call it "sweet" along with you. But this is no more than an agreement concerning the word. For how do you know that what you call "sweet" is precisely the same for him as it is for you? This is a question that must remain eternally unanswerable, for this is a matter that lies within the domain of what is purely subjective and is in no way objective. This same matter first passes into the domain of objectivity with the synthesis of sugar and a determinate[BB] taste, a taste that is, *in itself subjective,* but that is objective only *by virtue of its determinacy as such.* — All our cognition proceeds exclusively from   [I/2: 440] such subjective relations to feeling. Without feeling, no representation whatsoever of a thing outside of us is possible.[823]

You now immediately transfer this determination *of yourself* to something *outside yourself.* Compelled to do so by laws that have now been sufficiently displayed in the *Wissenschaftslehre,* you make what is actually an accident of your own I into an accident of a thing that is supposed to exist outside of you: namely, *matter, which is supposed to be extended in and to fill space.* You should already long since have at least suspected that this matter itself might perhaps only be something present within you, something purely subjective, since, without any further ado and without, for instance, the additional occurrence of any new feeling of this matter, you are able to transfer to it something that is, according to your own understanding, purely subjective.[CC] You are able to

---

[AA] purely subjective [Emphasis removed in *SW.*]

[BB] First through the synthesis of sugar with a determinate, etc. [As emended in *SW,* on the basis of Fichte's marginalia.]

[CC]   — such as sweet, red, etc. [Addition in *SW,* on the basis of Fichte's own marginalia.]

do this, moreover, because such matter — that is, matter apart from the subjective element that is to be transferred to it — does not exist at all for you and is therefore nothing else whatsoever for you but the bearer you require for that subjective element that is to be transferred from you [to it]. — Inasmuch as you transfer this subjective element to this bearer of the same, the latter is undoubtedly in you and present for you. Now were this matter originally present outside you and had it entered you from without in order to make possible the synthesis you have undertaken [of your subjective feeling with matter], then it must somehow have entered you by way of *the senses*. The senses, however, provide us only with something subjective, of the sort indicated above. Matter as such by no means pertains to the senses; instead, it can be produced [*entworfen*] or thought only by means of the productive power of imagination. Someone unskilled in abstraction might raise the following objection: Though matter is certainly neither seen nor heard nor tasted nor smelt, it can be apprehended by the sense of touch (*tactus*). But this sense announces itself only by means of a sensation of resistance, of an inability, which is something subjective. It is to be hoped that *that which resists* is not felt but only *inferred*. The sense of touch is concerned only with the surface, which always announces itself by means of something subjective — which announces, for example, that this surface is rough or smooth, cold or warm, hard or soft, etc. The sense of touch does not, however, penetrate to the interior of the body in question. In the first place, why do you spread over an entire, broad surface this warmth or coldness, which you feel (along with the hand, with which you feel it),[824] rather than positing it at a single point?[DD] Secondly, how do you come to assume, in addition, that this body possesses, between its surfaces, an interior, which is something you surely do not feel? It is obvious that this occurs by means of the productive power of imagination.[825] — Yet you nevertheless consider the matter in question to be something objective, and you are correct in doing so, since you are all in agreement concerning the presence of matter; and you have to agree upon this point, since the production of the same is grounded in a universal law governing all reason.[826]

[I, 315]

[I/2: 441]

22.) The drive [toward determination, i.e., the drive to representation] was directed at that activity of the I which is engaged in reflecting upon itself, that activity through which it determines itself *as an I*, and it is directed at this activity *as such*. Consequently, it is expressly implied in determination by this drive that it is the *I* that is supposed to determine the thing[827] — and, accordingly, that the I is supposed to reflect upon itself while engaging in this act of determining. The I must reflect; that is to say, it must posit itself as the subject engaged in determining. — (We will return to this reflection.[828] Here we are considering it only as an aid for advancing our inquiry.)

[DD]   in the single point, which you feel? [As emended in *SW*, on the basis of Fichte's marginalia.]

23.) The activity of the I is a single activity [*ist Eine*], and it cannot address [I, 316] itself simultaneously to several objects. This activity is supposed to determine the Not-I, which we will call X. The I is now supposed to reflect upon itself *as engaged in this act of determining* and, as goes without saying, it is supposed to do so by means of this same activity. This is impossible unless the action *of the subject engaged in determining* (that is, the action of the subject engaged in determining X) becomes interrupted. Since the reflection of the I upon itself occurs with absolute spontaneity, so too must this interruption occur spontaneously. The I interrupts the action of determining [object X] and does so with absolute spontaneity.

24.) The I is therefore limited as it engages in determining, and from this there ensues a *feeling*. The I is *limited*, since the drive toward *determining* extends outwards without any determination; in other words, it extends into the infinite. — This drive contained within itself, as such, a rule requiring it to reflect upon what it had really [*realiter*] determined[EE] by itself and to reflect upon it as one and the same [i.e., as determined by the I]. However, it contained no rule requiring that this reality upon which it reflects (in this case, object X) must proceed to point B, or to point C, etc. This act of determining is now interrupted at a determinate point, which we will call C. (What sort of limitation this might be is something that will become evident at the appropriate time; but one should avoid thinking of it as a limitation in space. What we are discussing here is a limitation of the intension [*der Intension*],[FF, 829] — for example, the sort of limitation that distinguishes what is sweet from what is sour and similar limitations.[830]) *A limitation* of the drive toward determination is therefore present, as a condition for a feeling.[831] Present as well is a *reflection* upon this limitation, as another condition for a feeling. This is because, insofar as the free activity of the I interrupts the act of determining the object, the latter activity is [re]directed at determining and limiting the entire scope [*Umfang*] of the object, which acquires a scope of its own in precisely this way. In this case, however, the I is not conscious that it is acting freely; consequently, it ascribes the limitation to the thing. — What is present is a feeling of the limitation of the I by the *determinacy* of the thing, or a feeling of something *determinate* and *simple*.[832]

25.) We will now describe the reflection that occupies the place of that act of [I/2: 442] determining which is interrupted and announces its interruption by means of a feeling. — The I is supposed to posit itself in this reflection as [I, 317] an I, that is, as what determines itself in this action. It is clear that what is posited as a product of the I[833] can be nothing else than an intuition of X, an image[834] of the same, but by no means X itself[835] — a conclusion that is evident on the basis of theoretical principles,[836] as well as on the basis of

---

EE *really* determined [Emphasis added in *SW*.]
FF a limitation of what is intensive [*des Intensiven*] [As emended in *SW*.]

what was said above.[837] This intuition or image of X is posited as a freely produced product of the I,[838] which means that it is posited as *contingent*, as the sort of thing that does not necessarily have to be as it is, but could also have been different.[839] — Were the I to be conscious of its freedom in the act of forming images (by reflecting, in turn, upon the reflection in which it is presently engaged), then the image would be posited as contingent *in relation to the I*. No such reflection occurs, and therefore this image has to be posited as contingent *in relation to another Not-I*, with which we have, until now, been entirely unacquainted.[840] Let us provide a more complete explication of what we have just asserted in general terms.

In order for it be subject to the law of determination,[841] object X must be determined by itself (simultaneously determined and engaged in determining). And, according to our postulate,[842] it satisfies this condition. In addition, and by means of the feeling that is present, X is supposed to extend to C and no further; but it is also supposed to be determined up to point C. (The meaning of this assertion will soon become evident.[843]) Insofar as it is engaged in an act of ideally [*idealiter*] determining[GG] or intuiting, there is no basis whatsoever within the I for this determination. Hence the I possesses no law governing this determination. (Does this mean that the self-determining subject proceeds only so far? We shall see that, on the one hand, this self-determining subject, considered purely in itself,[844] proceeds further, into infinity.[845] If, on the other hand, a distinction should also be supposed to be present in the thing, then how does this distinction enter into the ideal I's[846] sphere of efficacy? How does such a distinction become accessible to the I, since the latter has no point of contact whatsoever with the Not-I, and indeed is ideally active[HH] only insofar as it has no such point of contact and is not limited by the Not-I? — To express this in a popular fashion: Why is *sweet* something *other* than and posited in opposition to *sour*? Both are, as such, something *determinate*. But beyond this general characteristic, what is the basis for distinguishing them? This basis cannot lie solely in the ideal activity, since no concept of either of the two feelings is possible. Yet the basis for this distinction must nevertheless lie, at least partially, within the I, since this is a distinction that exists *for the I*.)

[I, 318]

Consequently, the ideal I[847] hovers with absolute freedom over and within the boundary.[848] Its boundary [= C] is completely indeterminate. Can it remain in this condition? By no means, since, according to our postulate, it is now supposed to reflect upon itself in this intuition and therefore posit itself in this intuition as *determined*, since all reflection presupposes determination.

[I/2: 443]

[GG] *ideally* determining [Emphasis added in *SW.*]
[HH] *ideally* active [Emphasis added in *SW.*]

We are certainly familiar with the overall rule of determination: namely, something is determined only insofar as and to the extent that it is determined by itself. It follows that, in this act of intuiting X, the I must itself posit the boundary of its intuiting. It must determine itself to determine point C as precisely the boundary point, and X would therefore be determined by the absolute spontaneity of the I.

26.) However (and this is an important argument), X is the kind of thing that determines itself by the law of determination as such, and X is the object of the postulated intuition only insofar as it determines itself. — To be sure, until now we have considered only the *internal* determination of X's nature. But the *external* aspect of this limitation follows immediately from the internal one. X = X only insofar as it is simultaneously determined and engaged in determining, *and X extends just so far as it remains both determined and determining* — up to [the boundary] C, for example. If the I is supposed to limit X correctly and in accordance with the object [*Sache*], then it *must* limit X at C, in which case one could not say that the limitation occurs with absolute spontaneity. These two claims[849] contradict each other, which makes it necessary to introduce a distinction.

27.) The limitation[II] [of X] at C is, however, only *felt* and not *intuited*. What is freely posited is supposed to be only *intuited* and not *felt*. But there is no   [I, 319] connection between feeling and intuition. Intuition *sees*, but it is empty;[850] feeling *refers to reality*, but it is *blind*.[851] — Yet X is supposed to be truly limited and is supposed to be limited in precisely the way it is limited.[852] A unification or synthetic connection is therefore required between feeling and intuition. Let us now investigate this connection further, and, by doing so, we will arrive unawares at the point we are seeking.[853]

28.) What was required is this: the intuiting subject is supposed to limit X through absolute spontaneity, and yet do so in such a way that X appears[854] to be limited only by itself. This requirement will be satisfied if the ideal activity, by means of its absolutely productive power, posits a Y lying beyond X (at points B, C, D, etc., since the determinate boundary point can neither be posited by the ideal activity itself nor immediately given to it[855]). — Since it is posited in opposition to something determined internally, Y must satisfy the following requirements: (1) Y must itself be something;[856] i.e., it must, in accordance with the law governing   [I/2: 444] any determining whatsoever, be simultaneously determined and engaged in determining. (2) Y is supposed to be posited in opposition to — or to limit — X; insofar as X is engaged in determining, Y it is not related to X as determined [by X], and insofar as X is determined, Y is not related to X as engaged in determining [X], and vice versa. It is not supposed to be possible to grasp X and Y together nor to reflect upon them as upon a single object. (It should be noted that what we are here discussing is not a relative determination or limitation. X and Y are indeed related to

---

[II] from A to C [Addition in *SW*, on the basis of Fichte's marginalia.]

[I, 320]

each other in this way; but what we are now discussing is the internal determination of X and Y, with respect to which they are not related to each other in this manner. Every possible point of X is reciprocally related to every other point of X, and the same is true of Y. But every point of Y is not reciprocally related to every point of X, and vice versa. Each of them is something, but each is something different. This makes it possible, for the first time, for us to pose and to answer the following question: *What are X and Y?* The entire Not-I is something even apart from positing in opposition; but it is not any determinate, specific something, and the question, *What is this or that?*, here makes no sense at all,[JJ] since this a question that can be answered only by positing [something else] in opposition.

This is what the drive [toward determination] determines the ideal activity to do, and from the previously indicated rule[857] it is easy to deduce the law governing the required action [on the part of the ideal activity]: namely, X and Y are supposed to exclude each other reciprocally. Insofar as this drive [toward determination] is directed only at the ideal activity, as is here the case, we can call it *the drive toward reciprocal determination* [*Wechselbestimmung*].

29.) Boundary point C is posited only by means of a feeling; consequently, Y (which lies beyond C, since it is supposed to commence precisely at C) can also be given only through its relation to this feeling. This feeling alone is what unites both [X and Y] at the boundary. — It follows that the drive toward reciprocal determination is at the same time directed at a feeling.[858] *Ideal activity and feeling* are therefore internally united in this drive [toward reciprocal determination], in which the entire I is one. — To this extent, we can call the drive in question *the drive to change as such* [*den Trieb nach Wechsel überhaupt*]. — It is this drive that manifests itself through *longing*; the object of longing is *something else*, something *posited in opposition* to what is present.

Ideality and the drive toward reality are inwardly united in longing. Longing is directed *toward something else*, which is possible only on the presupposition of a preceding determination by means of ideal activity. Also present in longing is the drive toward reality (as limited), since this drive is *felt* but is neither thought nor presented. This shows how an *externally directed* drive, and hence the presentiment of an external world, can appear within a feeling. This is possible because the feeling in question is modified by the ideal activity, which is free of any limitation. In addition, this shows how a theoretical function of the mind can be traced back to the practical power of the same,[859] something that must be possible if a rational being is ever supposed to constitute a complete whole.

[I/2: 445]

[I, 321]

30.) Feeling is something that does not depend upon us, since it depends upon a limitation, and the I is unable to limit itself.[860] But now a feeling posited in opposition to this first feeling is supposed to be present. The

---

[JJ] in the absence of positing in opposition [Addition in *SW*, on the basis of Fichte's marginalia.]

question, however, is whether the external condition,[861] under which alone such a second feeling is possible, is also present. This must be the case. If this condition is not present, then the I does not feel anything *determinate*; it feels *nothing whatsoever*, and therefore it is not alive and is not an I, which contradicts what is presupposed by the *Wissenschaftslehre*.

31.) A feeling of something *posited in opposition* is the condition for the satisfaction of the drive [to reciprocal determination]; consequently, *longing* is *the drive toward a change of feeling* as such. What is longed for is now determined, but only by the predicate that it should be *something other*[KK] for feeling.

32.) The I, however, cannot feel two different ways at once, for it cannot be simultaneously *limited at C* and *not limited at C*. For this reason, its altered state cannot be *felt as* an altered state. Consequently, the other [state] would have to be intuited[LL] solely by the ideal activity, intuited as something other and posited in opposition to the present feeling. — Both intuition and feeling would therefore necessarily be simultaneously present in the I and would be synthetically united in one and the same point.

In addition, the ideal activity is unable to displace or to produce any feeling; consequently, this activity can determine its object only as *not* being **[I, 322]** what is felt and as capable of acquiring all determinations except those present in the [present] feeling. In this manner, the thing in question always remains determined only negatively for the ideal activity, and what is felt remains likewise undetermined by the ideal activity. The only means of determination that can be imagined [*erdenken*] [in this case] is a negative determining that continues into infinity.[862]

(And this is indeed the case. What, for example, is the meaning of *sweet*? To begin with, this is something that is not related to vision, hearing, etc., but only to *taste*. What taste is is something you must already know by means of sensation and can call to mind only by means of the power of imagination, albeit only obscurely and in a negative fashion (in a synthesis *of everything that is not taste*). In addition, among all the things that **[I/2: 446]** are related to taste, sweet is what is not *sour, bitter*, etc., nor is it any of the many other determinations of taste that you may be able to enumerate. But even if you had also made an inventory of all the sensations of taste with which you are acquainted, new and previously unfamiliar ones could always still be given to you, of which you would then judge: these are not *sweet*. The boundary between sweet and all the other sensations of taste with which you are familiar thus remains forever infinite.)

The only question remaining is the following: How does the ideal activity become aware that the state of the feeling subject has undergone alteration? — We may provisionally say that it discovers this through the satisfaction of longing, by means of a feeling[863] — a circumstance from which many important results will ensue.

KK something that changes [*ein wechselndes*] [As emended in SW.]
LL be *intuited* [Emphasis added in SW.]

§ 11. Eighth Theorem

Feelings Themselves Must Be Capable of Being Posited in Opposition to Each Other

1.) By means of its ideal activity, the I is supposed to posit object Y in opposition to object X; it is supposed to posit itself as altered. But it posits Y only
when prompted to do so by a feeling, and indeed, by *another* feeling.[864] —
Ideal activity is dependent solely upon itself, and not upon feeling. Feeling
X is present within the I, and in this case, as has been indicated,[865] the
ideal activity is incapable of limiting the object or of specifying *what* it is.
In accordance with our postulate,[866] another feeling, Y, is now supposed to
arise within the I, and the ideal activity is now supposed to determine X; that

[I, 323]   is, it is supposed to be able to posit X in opposition to a determinate Y. This
alteration and change in feeling is therefore supposed to be capable of
influencing the ideal activity. The question is, How is this supposed to occur?

2.) For an observer outside the I, these feelings themselves are *different*, but
they are [also] supposed to be different for the I itself; that is, they are supposed to be posited [by the I] as opposed to each other. This is something
that can be accomplished only by the ideal activity. Consequently, both

[I/2: 447]   feelings must be posited. But in order for them *both* to be capable of being
posited, they must be synthetically united — even as they are also posited
in opposition to each other. Hence we must answer the following three
questions: (a.) How is a feeling posited? (b.) How are feelings synthetically
united by means of positing? (c.) How are they posited in opposition to
each other?

3.) A feeling is posited by means of ideal activity, and this can be conceived
of only in the following way: The I reflects upon a limitation of its drive,
but it does so without any self-consciousness.[867] From this there arises,
first of all, a self-feeling.[868] The I reflects further upon this reflection
[upon a limitation of its drive] and posits itself as what is, in this reflection, simultaneously determined and engaged in determining.[869] As a
result, feeling itself becomes an ideal action, inasmuch as the ideal activity
is transferred thereto.[870] The I feels, or, more correctly, *senses something*:
namely, matter.[871] — This is the same reflection that was discussed above,[872]
the feeling by means of which X first becomes an object. By means of
reflection upon *feeling*, feeling becomes *sensation*.[873]

4.) Feelings are synthetically united *by means of ideal positing*. The ground of
their relation[874] can be nothing else but the ground for reflecting upon
both feelings. This ground of reflection was as follows:[875] In the absence of
such a reflection, the drive toward reciprocal determination[876] could neither be satisfied nor posited as satisfied; and if this drive is not satisfied,
then there is no feeling, and consequently, no I at all. — The synthetic unifying ground [*Vereinigungsgrund*] of reflection upon both feelings thus lies
in the fact that no reflection upon *either of the two* — as a single feeling —
is possible without reflection upon them *both*.

The condition under which it would be impossible to reflect upon an individual feeling will soon become evident. — Every feeling is necessarily [I, 324] a limitation of the I; hence, if the I is not limited, then it feels nothing, and if it cannot be *posited* as limited, then it cannot be posited as feeling. From this it follows that, if *two feelings* were to be related to each other in such a way that the *one* were limited and determined *only through the other*, then neither the one nor the other could be reflected upon without reflecting upon both. This is because nothing can be reflected upon without reflecting upon its limit, but in the case we are considering one feeling is always the limit of the other.

5.) If [two] feelings are to be related to each other in this manner, then each of them must include something that refers to the other. — And we have actually discovered such a relationship. We have indicated a feeling that is connected with a longing[877] and hence with a drive toward *alteration*. In order for this longing to be completely determined, this *other* [feeling], *which is what is longed for*, must [also] be indicated. Such a different feeling [I/2: 448] has now been postulated.[878] Considered in itself, this second feeling may determine the I as it will. Insofar as it is something longed for, and insofar as it is what is longed for,[MM] it must be related to the first feeling, and, with regard to the first feeling, this second one must be accompanied by a feeling of *satisfaction* [*Befriedigung*]. The feeling of longing cannot be posited without positing a [feeling of] satisfaction at which this longing aims; and the satisfaction cannot be posited without presupposing a longing that is satisfied. The boundary [between these two feelings] lies where the longing ceases and the satisfaction begins.

6.) The only question remaining is the following: How does satisfaction reveal itself in feeling? — Longing arose from the impossibility of determining [feeling X], since no limitation [of X by another feeling] was present. Ideal activity and the drive toward reality[879] were thus united in longing.[880] The following ensues just as soon as another feeling arises: (1.) The required determination, the complete limitation of X, becomes possible and actually occurs, since both the drive [toward alteration] and the force it requires are present. (2.) From the very fact that this occurs, it follows that [I,325] another feeling is present. Within a feeling in itself, qua limitation, there is no difference whatsoever, nor can there be. But because something that was impossible without an alteration of feelings has now become possible, it follows that the state of the feeling subject has been altered.[881] (3.) *Drive* and *action*[882] are now one and the same; the determination for which the drive yearned is [now] possible and actually occurs. The I reflects *upon this [new] feeling* and reflects *upon itself* as engaged in feeling. That is to say, it reflects upon itself as simultaneously what is engaged in determining and what is determined [by this feeling], and thus as completely at one

[MM] and is the *determinate* [feeling] that is longed for [As emended in *SW*, on the basis of Fichte's marginalia.]

with itself.[883] Such a determination of feeling can be called *approval* [*Beifall*]. The feeling in question is accompanied by approval.

7.) The I cannot posit this concurrence of drive and action without distinguishing them from each other. But it cannot distinguish them from each other without positing something in which they are opposed to each other. The feeling preceding the current one is precisely such a thing, which is therefore necessarily accompanied by [a feeling of] *disapproval* [*Misfallen*] (the opposite of approval, a manifestation of disharmony between drive and action). — Not every longing is necessarily accompanied by disapproval, but when a longing is satisfied this produces disapproval of the preceding feeling: it becomes weak, insipid.

8.) Objects X and Y, which were posited by the ideal activity, are now no longer determined merely by means of opposition, but are also determined by the predicates "producing *disapproval*" and "*producing approval.*" This sort of determining is carried forward into the infinite, and the inner determinations of things[884] (determinations that are related to feeling) are nothing other than degrees of what produces disapproval or approval.[885]

[I/2: 449]   9.) Until now, this harmony or disharmony, this approval or disapproval (as a coincidence or non-coincidence of two different things, but not as a feeling), has been present only for a possible observer, and not for the I itself. But both of these feelings are also supposed to be present for the
[I, 326]   I itself, and they are both supposed to be posited by the I[886] — though we do not yet know whether this occurs in a purely ideal fashion, by means of intuition, or by means of a relation to feeling.

10.) When anything is supposed to be either ideally posited or else felt, it must be possible to indicate a drive directed toward it. Nothing exists within the I unless there exists within the I a drive [directed toward it].[887] Hence it must be possible to indicate a drive directed toward the harmony in question.[888]

11.) Something is "in harmony" when it can be considered to be reciprocally determined and engaged in determining. — However, what is in harmony is not supposed to be one thing, but instead a harmonizing dyad [*Zweifaches*]. The relationship would therefore be as follows: A in itself must, as such, be simultaneously determined and engaged in determining. And the same is true of B. Now, however, another specific determination (the determination "to what extent"[NN, 889]) is supposed to be present in both A and B, with respect to which A is what is engaged in determining to the extent that B is posited as what is determined, and vice versa.

12.) Such a drive [toward harmony] is contained in the drive toward *reciprocal determination*.[890] — The I determines X by means of Y and vice versa.[891] Let us attend to the I's acting in both of these determinations. Each of

---

[NN] *"how far"* [Emphasis added in *SW*. There is no closing parenthesis in Fichte's text following the opening parenthesis preceding "the determination." In *SW*, the closing parenthesis is inserted at the end of no. 12, below.]

these actions is obviously determined by the other, since the object of each is determined by the object of the other. — One could call this drive *the drive toward reciprocal determination* of the I through itself, or one could call it the drive toward absolute *unity* and completeness of the I within itself.[892] (We have now completed the circuit: [1.] the drive toward determination — to begin with, determination of the I; [2.] then, by means of the former, [the drive toward] determination of the Not-I; [3.] [the drive toward] self-determination of the Not-I by means of reciprocity, since the Not-I is a manifold,[893] and therefore nothing particular can be determined completely in and through itself; [4.] by means of this same reciprocity, the drive toward reciprocal determination of the I through itself. There is therefore a reciprocal determination of the I and Not-I, and, thanks to the unity of the subject,[894] this reciprocal determination must be transformed into a reciprocal determination of the I by itself. With this, and in accordance with the previously established schema,[895] the I's modes of acting have now been enumerated and exhausted. This con-   [I, 327] firms the completeness of our deduction of the chief drives of the I, for this rounds off and concludes the system of drives.)

13.) That which is in harmony with and determined reciprocally through itself is supposed to include both the drive and the action [of the I]. (a.) Each of these should be capable of being viewed in itself as simultaneously determined and engaged in determining. A drive of this sort would be   [I/2: 450] one that produced itself absolutely, an absolute drive, a drive for drive's sake. (To express this as a law — which is precisely how, for the sake of determination, it must be expressed from a certain standpoint of reflection[896] — , this is a law for law's sake, an absolute law or categorical imperative: *you purely and simply ought.*) It is easy to see where what is *undetermined* lies in the case of such a drive, inasmuch as this is a drive that drives us outward into the realm of what is undetermined, without any goal. (The categorical imperative is purely formal and has no object.) (b.) To say that an *action* is simultaneously determined and engaged in determining is to say that it occurs because it occurs and simply for the sake of acting, i.e., that it occurs with absolute self-determination and freedom. Such an action contains within itself its total foundation [*Grund*], along with all the conditions for such acting. — In this case too, it is also immediately obvious where what is undetermined lies: there is no action without an object. Consequently, this action must simultaneously provide itself with its object,[897] which is impossible.

14.) The *drive* [toward harmony with itself] and the [I's] *acting* must now be related to each other as reciprocally determining each other. Such a rela-tionship requires, first of all, that the acting in question *can be considered to be produced*[898] by the drive. — This acting is supposed to be absolutely free, and hence by no means determined irresistibly by anything, and therefore also not determined by the drive. But this acting can neverthe-less be so constituted that it can be considered to be either determined by the drive or not determined by it. The question that must now be answered is this: *How* does this harmony or disharmony manifest itself? But the answer to this question will prove to be self-evident.[899]

[I, 328]

Secondly, such a relationship between drive and acting requires that the *drive* be capable of being posited as determined by the action. — Two things posited in opposition to each other cannot be simultaneously present in the I. Drive and action, however, are here posited in opposition to each other. Consequently, just as surely as an action occurs, the drive is interrupted or limited, and from this there arises a *feeling*. The action is directed at the possible ground of this feeling, at positing and realizing it.[900]

Now if, in accordance with the preceding requirement, *the acting* is determined by *the drive*, then *the object* is determined by the drive as well: it is in conformity with the drive and is what is demanded by it. The drive is now (ideally[OO]) determinable by the action, and we can conclude that it is the type of drive that is directed at this action.

Harmony is present, and from this there arises a feeling of *approval*, which is in this case a feeling of *satisfaction*,[901] of total completion (which, however, lasts but a moment, on account of the necessary return

[I/2: 451]

of longing[902]). — If, however, the action is not determined by the drive, the object is *opposed to*[PP] the drive and there arises a feeling of *disapproval*, or dissatisfaction, a feeling of the division of the subject within itself. — Even in this case, the drive is still determinable by the action, albeit only negatively: it is not the sort of drive that is directed at this action.

15.) The acting we are discussing is, as always, a merely ideal acting, something occurring only by means of representation. Even our sensible efficacy in the sensible world, in which we *believe*,[903] is accessible to us only indirectly, by means of representation.[904]

[OO] *ideally* [Emphasis added in *SW*.]
[PP] opposed to [Emphasis removed in *B* and *SW*.]

III
OUTLINE OF WHAT IS DISTINCTIVE OF THE *WISSENSCHAFTSLEHRE* WITH REGARD TO THE THEORETICAL POWER

Outline of What is Distinctive of the *Wissenschaftslehre* with Regard to the Theoretical Power[1]

[I/3: 141]
[I, 331]

As a
Manuscript for His Listeners

by

JOHANN GOTTLIEB FICHTE

Jena and Leipzig
Christian Ernst Gabler
1795

[I, 331]
[I/3: 143]

§ 1. The Concept of the Particular in the Theoretical *Wissenschaftslehre*²

For the purpose of establishing the theoretical *Wissenschaftslehre*, we began (in the *Foundation of the Entire Wissenschaftslehre*) with the proposition "the I posits itself as determined by the Not-I."ᴬ We have examined how and in what manner something corresponding to this proposition could be thought to be originally present in a rational being. After separating and setting aside everything impossible and contradictory, we found what we were seeking; that is, we discovered the only possible way in which something corresponding to the proposition in question could be conceived to be present in a rational being. For just as it is certain that this proposition should now be considered valid and that it can be considered valid only in the way already shown, it is also certain that this proposition must be originally present in our mind as a *factum*.³ The *factum* thereby postulated was the following: Upon the occasion of a check⁴ upon the original activity of the I (a check or impulse that remains completely inexplicable and incomprehensible at this point), the power of imagination, which oscillates between the original direction of the I's activity and the [opposing] direction arising from reflection,⁵ produces something [namely, a representation] composed of both directions. Since nothing can be found in the I that the I has not posited within itself (a conclusion that follows from the very concept of the I), the I must posit this *factum* within itself. That is, it must originally explain this *factum* to itself; it must completely determine and ground it.⁶

A theoretical *Wissenschaftslehre* is, as such, a system of those facts [*Tatsachen*] which appear in the mind of a rational being in the course of this original explanation of the *factum* in question, and this original explanation comprises reason's theoretical power. — I intentionally said, "the *original* explanation of this [I, 332] *factum*." This *factum* is present in us without any conscious participation on our part. It is explained — again without any conscious participation on our part — solely by and in accordance with the laws and nature of a rational being, and the various elements distinguished in the course of this explanation constitute new facts. Reflection is turned upon this original *factum*, and this is what I call the "original explanation" [of this *factum*]. The conscious, scientific explanation that we undertake when we engage in transcendental philosophizing is some-[I/3: 144] thing totally different. In this latter type of explanation, reflection is directed upon the original explanation of the first *factum* in order to establish this first explanation scientifically.

In the "Deduction of Representation"⁷ we have already indicated briefly the general way in which the I posits this *factum* within itself. There we were concerned with explaining this *factum as such or in general*, and we abstracted completely from the explanation of any particular *factum* pertaining to the concept of representation. That is, we disregarded its explanation as a particular *factum*.⁸

ᴬ But an *infinite* universal [Emphasis added in *SW.*]

This was only because we did not — and could not — go into every detail of this explanation. Had we done so, we would have found that no *factum* of this sort can be completely determined merely as a *factum* as such or in general; it is completely determinable only as a *particular factum*, one that always is and must be determined by another *factum* of the same type. Consequently, the theoretical *Wissenschaftslehre* can be complete only if it is also [concerned with what is] *particular*. Therefore, if we are to proceed consistently in accordance with the rules of the *Wissenschaftslehre*, our presentation of the theoretical *Wissenschaftslehre* must necessarily become a presentation of what is particular in the theoretical *Wissenschaftslehre*.[9] This is because any such presentation must ultimately arrive at a point where one *factum* of this sort is determined by another *factum* of the same sort, which has been posited in opposition to it.[10]

A few more words of explication concerning this point: Kant starts by presupposing the existence of a *manifold*,[11] for possible absorption into the unity of consciousness. Given the standpoint he adopted, this is the only assumption with which he could have begun. Kant thereby established what is particular for the theoretical *Wissenschaftslehre*. This is all that he wished to establish, and thus he [I, 333] was justified in proceeding from the particular to the general. It is indeed possible to explain in this manner a collective universal, a whole constituted from previous experience and unified by the same laws. But an infinite universal,[B] an experience that continues infinitely, can never be explained in this way. No path leads from the finite to the infinite. There is, however, is a path leading in the opposite direction, from undetermined and undeterminable infinity to finitude, by means [I/3: 145] of the power of determining. (It follows that everything finite is a product of the activity of determining). The *Wissenschaftslehre*, which is supposed to encompass the whole system of the human mind, has to follow this path and descend from the universal to the particular. It must prove that a *manifold* is given for possible experience. This proof will proceed as follows: Whatever is given must be *something*; but it is something only insofar as there is also something else — which is also something, though a different something. As soon as such a proof becomes possible we enter the realm of what is particular.[12]

The *method* of the theoretical *Wissenschaftslehre* has already been described in the *Foundation*,[13] and it is simple and easy. The thread of the argument proceeds according to the following principle (which is here regulative throughout): *nothing pertains to the I except what it posits within itself.* We begin with the *factum* derived above, and then we observe how the I might be able to posit this *factum* within itself. This positing is a *factum* as well, and it must also be posited by the I within itself, and so on, until we arrive at the highest theoretical *factum*: namely, that *factum* through which the I (consciously) posits itself as determined by the Not-I. The theoretical *Wissenschaftslehre* thus concludes with its own foundational principle. It reverts into itself and is therefore complete.

There may well prove to be characteristic distinctions among the facts [*Tatsachen*] [I, 334] we are supposed to derive. Such distinctions would justify us in introducing divisions among these facts and within the science which they establish. In

---

[B] the proposition *the I posits itself as determined by the Not-I.* [Emphasis added in *SW*.]

accordance with the synthetic method, however, such divisions will be introduced only where there is an obvious basis for doing so.

[I/3: 146]   The actions through which the I posits something within itself are in this case *facta*, because, as we have just said, they are objects of reflection [for the philosopher]. However, it does not follow from this that they are what are usually called "*facta* of consciousness," or that one actually becomes conscious of them as facts of (inner) experience. If consciousness exists, then this is itself a fact, and it must be derived like any other fact. Furthermore, if particular determinations of this consciousness exist, then these must also be derivable and must constitute what are, properly speaking, the *facta* of consciousness.

On the one hand, it is clear from what was just said that, as has been often remarked,[14] the *Wissenschaftslehre* should not be reproached if some *factum* it has established cannot be encountered in (inner) experience. The *Wissenschaftslehre* makes no such claim; it merely proves the necessity of thinking that something corresponding to a certain thought is present in the human mind. If we are not conscious of the *factum* in question, the *Wissenschaftslehre* also explains why we could not be: namely, because it is one of the grounds for the possibility of any consciousness whatsoever. — On the other hand, it is also clear from what has been said that anything actually established by the *Wissenschaftslehre* as a fact [*Tatsache*] of inner experience is not established by appealing to the testimony of experience, but is established instead through its deduction. If such a deduction is correct, then a *factum* exactly of the sort that has been deduced will certainly be found in experience. If no such *factum* is to be met with in experience, then the deduction is certainly incorrect. And if this turns out to be the case, the philosopher, for his part, will do well to go back and ferret out the false inference that he must have made somewhere along the line. As a science, however, the *Wissenschaftslehre* is completely unconcerned with experience

[I, 335] and purely and simply does not take it into account. The *Wissenschaftslehre* would have to be true even if there were no experience whatsoever (though, of course, in the absence of experience a *Wissenschaftslehre in concreto* would also be impossible, but that does not concern us here). Furthermore, it would be certain a priori that all possible future experience would have to conform to the laws established by the *Wissenschaftslehre*.

[I/3: 147]   ## §2. First Theorem: The Indicated *Factum* Is Posited through Sensation, or, Deduction of Sensation

I.

The conflict between those directions of the I's activity that have been posited in opposition to each other (a conflict described in the *Foundation of the Entire Wissenschaftslehre*[15]) is distinguishable within the I itself. As surely as this conflict is present within the I, the I must posit it within itself, and therefore it must first be distinguished [from the I]. To say that the I posits this conflict means, first of all, that *the I posits this conflict in opposition to itself.*

Up until now, that is, until this point in the reflection [necessarily engaged in by the I], nothing at all has been posited in the I. As yet, the I contains nothing except what pertains to it originally: namely, *pure* activity. At this point, therefore, to say that the I posits something in opposition to itself means that it posits something *not as pure activity* — and this is all it can mean. Accordingly, the condition of the I when it is in a state of conflict would be posited as the opposite of its pure condition; it would be posited as a mixed activity, an activity that conflicts with and destroys itself. — Such an action of the I is purely antithetical.

We will here leave entirely unexplored the question of how, in what manner, and by means of what power the I is able to posit anything at all, since this entire doctrine [viz., the portion of the theoretical *Wissenschaftslehre* that deals with what is particular] is concerned solely with the products of the I's activity. — If, however (as was already mentioned in the *Foundation of the Entire Wissenschaftslehre*), this conflict should ever be posited within the I, and if anything further were to follow from it, then the mere *positing* of this conflict as such would mean that the oscillation of the power of imagination between two direc- [I, 336] tions of activity posited in opposition to each other would have to cease. Yet traces of this former oscillation would have to remain as a *something*, a possible *matter* [*Stoff*].[16] We can already see how this could occur, even though we do not yet see the power through which it would occur. — What the I has to do is posit this *conflict* of directions posited in opposition to each other, or (which here amounts to the same thing) posit this conflict of opposing forces. It must not posit either one of these forces alone, but must posit them both and must posit them *in conflict* — that is to say, in opposed but perfectly counterbalanced activity. But perfectly [I/3: 148] counterbalanced opposing activities cancel each other out and nothing remains. Nevertheless, something is supposed to remain and to be posited. What remains, therefore, is *a static matter* [*ein ruhender Stoff*] — something that *possesses force*, but which, on account of the conflict in question, cannot express this force in activity, a *substrate* of force. (One can convince oneself of this at any time by making the experiment with oneself.) But the important point is that this substrate remains not as *something that was posited in advance*, but rather as the *sheer product of the unification of activities posited in opposition to each other*. As will become clearer and clearer, this is the foundation of all matter, as well as the foundation of all possible enduring substrata within the I (and nothing lies outside the I).

II.

The I is supposed to posit this conflict *within itself*. Hence it must *posit* itself as *identical* with this conflict; it must relate the conflict to itself, and for this to be possible the conflict must contain within itself something that can serve as the basis for its relation to the I. But as we have just remarked, the only thing that pertains to the I at this point is pure activity. Pure activity is as yet the only thing that can be related to or equated with the I. Consequently, pure activity must provide the ground we are seeking for the relation [between the pure I and the conflict between the opposite directions of its activity]. The pure activity of the I must therefore be found within this conflict itself — or, to be more precise, the pure activity must be *posited* within this conflict, introduced into it synthetically.

But the activity of the I when it is embroiled in conflict has just been posited as an activity that is *not pure*. However, we now see that this same [conflicted] activity must also be posited as *pure* activity in order to make possible its relation to the I.[17] This activity [embroiled in conflict] is consequently *posited in opposition*

[I, 337] *to itself.* This is impossible and contradictory, unless some third thing is posited as well, in which this activity is at once equal to itself and posited in opposition to itself. *Such a third thing must therefore be posited as the synthetic unifying link.*[18]

What such a third thing would be, however, is *an activity that opposes all the activity of the I* (an activity of the Not-I). Such an activity would completely suppress and annihilate the conflicted activity of the I[19] by counterbalancing it. Accordingly, if the required relationship [between the pure I and the suppressed or "conflicted" activity] is to be possible, and if the contradiction that mitigated against such a possibility is to be resolved, then an *activity* of this sort, one completely opposed to the activity of the I, must be posited.

The contradiction in question is actually resolved in just this way, and it thereby becomes possible for the conflicted activity of the I to be posited in opposition to

[I/3: 149] itself. This activity is pure and is to be posited as such (if we abstract from the opposing activity of the Not-I, which irresistibly suppresses it). This same activity is not pure, but rather objective (if it is posited in relation to the activity posited in opposition to it). It is therefore either pure or not pure only under a certain condition, and this condition can be posited or not posited.[20] As soon as it is posited that this is the sort of condition that can be either posited or not posited, it is also posited that the activity of the I can be posited in opposition to itself.

The action here described is simultaneously *thetic, antithetic,* and *synthetic.* It is *thetic,* insofar as it posits outside of the I a purely and simply imperceptible activity posited in opposition to the I. (We will later consider *how* the I could do this; all that we have shown here is *that* this occurs and must occur.) The same action is *antithetic,* insofar as, by positing or not positing a certain condition, it posits

[I, 338] one and the same activity of the I in opposition to itself. It is *synthetic,* insofar as, by positing the activity posited in opposition *as* a contingent condition,[21] it also posits this activity as one and the same [as the action that posits it].

III.

Only now does it become possible to establish the relation we were seeking between the conflicted activity and the I. Only now is it possible to posit this conflicted activity as something pertaining to the I. Only now can this activity be

---

* In opposition to Reinhold, Aenesidemus states that the entire representation (not merely its form) is related to the subject.[22] This is quite correct; what is related [to the subject] is the entire representation. But it is also true that the ground of this relation is provided only by its form. It is precisely the same in our present case. We must not confuse the ground of the relation with what is related. In order to be sure that this does not occur in the course of our deductions we must be on guard against it from the start.

appropriated by the I. It is posited in the I because and insofar as it can be thought of as pure activity as well, and this is because it would be pure if it were not impinged upon by the activity of the Not-I, and because it is objective (and thus not pure) only when it is conditioned by something totally alien, something that does not lie within the I at all but is posited in utter opposition to the I. — It is important to note (and must not be lost sight of) that this [conflicted] activity is related to the I, not merely to the extent that it is posited as a pure activity, but also to the extent that it is posited as objective. This [conflicted] activity is thus related to the I *following* the synthesis and along with everything united in the I by this synthesis. The purity posited in this activity is merely the *ground of the relation*. But this [conflicted] activity is also *what is related* [to the pure activity of the I]. For the [conflicted] activity is posited as pure, in the sense that it would be pure activity were it not affected by the activity posited in opposition to it. Now, however, it is posited as *objective* activity, *because* it actually is affected by the [I/3: 150] opposing activity [of the Not-I].*

In this relationship the activity posited in opposition to the I is *excluded*. The activity of the I can now be regarded either as pure or as objective, for the same condition is posited in either case. In the first case, it is posited as something from which one must abstract; in the second, as something upon which one must reflect. (This condition is, to be sure, *posited* in either case, and we are not here concerned with how and by means of what power this is accomplished.) As will [I, 339] become clearer and clearer, here lies the ultimate reason [*Grund*] why the I goes beyond itself and posits something outside itself. For here, for the first time, something disengages itself from the I (if I may so express myself), something which, by means of further determination, will gradually transform itself into a universe with all its characteristic features.

The relationship that has now been derived is called *sensation* [*Empfindung*] (in other *words, finding-within-oneself* [*Insichfindung*]). (Only what is foreign is *ever found*; what was originally posited in the I is always present.) What is *sensed* is that activity of the I which has been canceled and annihilated. Insofar as it is suppressed, this activity is sensed (found *in the I*) [*ist* empfunden[23]] and is something foreign; and this is because this activity cannot originally be suppressed, nor can it be suppressed by the I itself. This activity is sensed (found *in the I*) [*ist empf*unden] and is something *within* the I only under the condition that another activity is posited in opposition to it; but if this opposing activity were to vanish, the suppressed activity would itself be pure activity. The sensing subject [*das Empfindende*] is, of course, the I that (in the action we have derived) is engaged in *relating* [these activities to each other]. Understandably enough, [I/3: 151] this I, to the extent that it *senses, is not itself sensed*, and we are therefore not at all concerned with it at this point. Whether, how, and through which particular mode of action this [sensing] I is posited [as such] is something that will have to be examined in the following section. Nor are we here concerned with the opposing activity of the Not-I, which is excluded in sensation. Like the relating I, this activity [of the Not-I] is not sensed, since it must be excluded if sensation is to be possible at all.[24] We will see later how and through which determinate mode of action this opposing activity is posited.[25]

We should not be disturbed by this remark that some things have to be left completely unexplained and undetermined at this point. This merely serves to confirm something that was said about the synthetic method in the *Foundation of the Entire Wissenschaftslehre*:[26] namely, that only the intermediate links would be united by this method, leaving the extremes (in this case, the sensing I and the activity of the Not-I, which was posited in opposition to the I) un-united and requiring further syntheses.

[I, 340]

§3. Second Theorem: The Sensing Subject Is Posited through Intuition, or, Deduction of Intuition

In the preceding § sensation was deduced as an action of the I, through which the I appropriates and relates to itself something foreign, which it has discovered within itself. We became acquainted with both this action itself *(sensation)* and the object of this action *(what is sensed)*. However, the *sensing subject* (the I engaged in this action) and the activity of the Not-I (which, in sensation, is excluded and posited in opposition to the I) remained unknown and, according to the rules of synthetic logic, had to remain unknown. With all that we now know about the synthetic method, we can expect that our next task will be to [I/3: 152] unite synthetically these excluded extremes — or, should this prove impossible, at least to introduce between them some intermediate link.

Our starting point here is the following proposition: According to what has already been said, sensation is in the I. Now, since nothing pertains to the I except what it posits within itself, the I must originally posit sensation within itself; that is to say, it must appropriate [*zueignen*] sensation. We have not yet deduced this positing of sensation. Though we have seen in the previous section how the I posits within itself what is sensed and have seen that sensation is precisely this act of positing, we have not yet seen how the I posits the sensation itself within itself, or how the I posits itself as the sensing subject.[27]

I.

In order to show this, we must first be able to distinguish the activity of the I in sensing (the act of appropriating what is sensed by positing it in opposition to the I) from what is thereby appropriated or sensed.

According to the previous section, what is sensed is an activity of the I, an activity that is considered to be embroiled in conflict with an opposing and equal force, which cancels and destroys it. What is sensed is regarded as a non-activity, [I, 341] which, nevertheless, could and would be an activity were it not for the force posited in opposition to it. What is sensed is therefore regarded as *static* activity, as matter [*Stoff*] or the substrate of force.

Consequently, the activity posited in opposition to this activity must be posited as an activity that is not suppressed or hindered by any opposing force. It must be posited as an actual activity, an actual acting.

II.

An actual activity of this latter sort is now supposed to be posited in the I, but the hindered and suppressed activity which opposes this real activity must (in accordance with the previous section) also be posited in the I. This is self-contradictory unless the two activities (the actual as well as the suppressed activity) can be related to each other by synthetic unification.[28] Accordingly, before we can begin to establish the desired relation between the activity in question and the I, [I/3: 153] we must first relate this [actual] activity to the [suppressed] activity that opposes it. For otherwise, though we would certainly have established a new *factum* in the I, we would have thereby displaced and lost the previously established *factum*. We would, therefore, have gained nothing and would not have advanced a single step.

Both the indicated actual activity of the I and the suppressed activity must be related to each other. But according to the rules of synthesis this is possible only if the two are united, or (what amounts to the same thing) if some determinate, third thing is posited between these two — a third thing which is at the same time activity (of the I) and passive affection (suppressed activity).

This third thing is supposed to be an activity of the I. It must therefore be posited purely and simply by the I alone; it must be an act that is grounded in the I's mode of action. Consequently, it must be a positing; indeed, it must be a determinate positing of something determinate. The *real ground* of this third thing should be the I.

It follows from the above description that this third thing is also supposed to be a passive state of the I. It must be a determinate and limited positing. However, [I, 342] the I cannot limit itself (as has been sufficiently shown in the *Foundation*). Accordingly, this limitation must come (albeit indirectly) from outside the I, from the Not-I. It follows that the *ideal ground* of this third thing (the reason why it has any quantity at all) should be the Not-I.

This third thing is supposed to be both [the actual and the suppressed activity of the I] at once; the distinction just made should not correspond to separate elements within this third thing. This *factum* [that is, the "third thing" we are now looking for] must be capable of being regarded as something that is purely and simply posited by the I, even with respect to its *specific, determinate* character; and it must also be capable of being regarded as posited by the Not-I, even with respect to its *being*. Its ideal and real grounds are supposed to be intimately united, to be one and the same.

In order to become completely familiar with this *factum*, we now wish to consider it provisionally in its relation to both the actual and the suppressed activities — both of which must be possible. This *factum* is an action of the I, and [therefore] it must be capable of being regarded as something grounded, in all of its specific determinations, purely and exclusively in the I. At the same time, it must be capable of being regarded as a product of an action of the Not-I and as grounded in the Not-I with respect to all of its determinations. — Consequently, the determinate way in which the I acts should not, as it were, determine the determinate way in which the Not-I acts; on the contrary, each should proceed alongside the other in complete independence, each grounded in itself in accordance with its own laws. And yet they must be in the closest harmony. Each should be exactly what the other is, and vice versa.

[I/3: 154]   When one considers that the I is engaged in positing and that the activity that is supposed to be grounded purely and simply in the I must therefore be one of positing, then one can see at once that the act in question must be one of *intuiting* [*ein Anschauen*]. The I observes [*betrachtet*] a Not-I, and this act of observation is all that pertains to the I at this point. In this act of observation, as such, the I posits itself and does so completely independently of the Not-I. It engages in observation entirely on its own and without the slightest external compulsion.[29] On its own and conscious of its activity, the I posits one distinguishing property

[I, 343] [*Merkmal*] after another within its consciousness. But it posits these as copies of something present outside of the I. — These copied properties are supposed to be actually encountered in this external things, and not merely because they were posited in consciousness. Instead, they are supposed to occur completely independently of the I and in accordance with their own laws, which are grounded in the thing itself. The Not-I does not produce the intuition in the I; nor does the I produce the properties [*Beschaffenheit*] of the Not-I. The I and Not-I are supposed to be completely independent of each other, and yet in the closest harmony. If there were any way to observe the Not-I in itself, except by means of intuition, and if there were any way to observe the intuiting subject in itself,[30] in the mere act of intuiting and without any relation to the intuited Not-I, they would be found to be determined in the same way. — We will soon observe that the human mind really does try to do this, though naturally only by means of intuition and in accordance with the laws of intuition. But it does so unconsciously, and this is precisely the source of the harmony that was demanded.

It is certainly remarkable that those persons who believed themselves able to recognize things in themselves did not notice this simple point, which becomes obvious with the least reflection upon consciousness, and that it did not occur to them to inquire concerning the ground of this assumed harmony — a harmony that is obviously only presupposed, but neither is nor can be perceived. We have now deduced the ground of all cognizing. We have shown why the I is and must be an intellect:[31] namely, because it has to resolve a contradiction *within itself,* a contradiction between its own activity and its own state of being passively affected. It must resolve this contradiction *originally* (and it must do so unconsciously, and it must do this as a condition for the very possibility of any consciousness). It is clear that we could not have shown this had we not proceeded beyond all consciousness.[32]

The following remark is intended to clarify what has already been deduced, to shed some light on what is to come, and to facilitate a clear understanding of our
[I, 344] method. In our deductions we are always concerned only with the products of the
[I/3: 155] indicated action of the human mind and not with this act itself. In each of the following deductions, the act that produced this first product is itself, in turn, made into a product by means of a new act, which is directed at the first act. In each deduction something is established, without any further determination, to be an acting of the mind; then, in the subsequent deduction, this same acting is posited and further determined.[33] Thus, to take our present case, the intuition we

have just deduced synthetically must have already been present as an acting in the preceding deduction. The action indicated in that preceding deduction was the following: the I posited its own conflicted activity [i.e., the activity distinguished by a conflict of directions] as active insofar as it imagined a certain condition to be absent, but it posited this same activity as suppressed and static insofar as this condition was imagined to be present. In both cases, however, this conflicted activity was posited within the I. The intuition we have just derived is obviously an action of this sort. In itself and qua action, intuition is grounded entirely in the I. This follows from the postulate (in the previous section) that the I must posit anything that is to be found within it. Intuition posits within the I something that is not supposed to be established by the I at all, but is instead supposed to be established by the Not-I; that is, it posits the impression [*Eindruck*] that has occurred.[34] As an action, intuition is entirely independent of this impression, just as the impression is entirely independent of intuition. They run parallel to each other. Perhaps I can make this clearer by means of the following image: The original pure activity of the I is modified and is, as it were, given shape or form [*gebildet*] by the check or impetus [provided by the Not-I], and, to this extent, this activity is by no means ascribable to the I. Another free activity[35] now tears the first activity, just as it is, free from the encroaching Not-I. It then observes and examines the activity it has thereby torn away from the Not-I and observes what it contains. However, it cannot consider what it observes to be the pure shape of the I; instead, it can only take it to be only an image [*Bild*] of the Not-I.[36]

III.

Following these preliminary investigations and hints, our actual task is even clearer.

The I's action in sensation is supposed to be posited and determined. We may express the same thing in a more popular manner by asking, How does the I [I, 345] manage to engage in sensing? What mode of acting makes sensation possible?

This question forces itself upon us because, according to what was said above, sensing would appear to be impossible. The I [in sensation] is supposed to posit something foreign within itself. This foreign element is a non-activity, a state of being passively affected [*Leiden*], and the I is supposed to posit this *within itself* by means of activity. The I must therefore be active and passively affected at the same time, and only on the assumption of such a unification is sensation possible. [I/3: 156] Accordingly, we have to indicate something in which activity and passive affection are so closely united that a certain activity would be impossible without a certain state of passive affection, and vice versa — something in which passive affection can be explained only by activity, and vice versa, something in which activity and passive affection are each incomplete when considered apart from the other. They must be so intimately united that activity necessarily leads to a state of passive affection and a state of passive affection necessarily leads to activity, for such is the nature of the synthesis required above.

No activity in the I can be related to a state of passive affection in such a way that it *produces* this state or posits it as produced by the I. This is because in such a case the I would simultaneously posit something within itself and annihilate it, which is self-contradictory. (The activity of the I cannot be directed at the content [*Materie*] of the state of passive affection.) However, the activity of the I can ascribe a limit to the state of passive affection and determine it in that way. Moreover, this is an activity that is impossible without a state of being passively affected, since (as was just said) the I cannot cancel out a part of its own activity; only something outside the I can do that. Consequently, the I can posit no limit, unless what is supposed to be limited is provided from without. The *act of determining*[37] is, therefore, an activity that is necessarily related to a state of passive affection.

Similarly, were passive affection to consist merely in the *limitation of activity*, then it would necessarily be related to activity and would be impossible without it. No activity, no limitation of activity; and there could therefore be no passive

[I, 346] affection of the sort indicated. (If there is no activity in the I, then no impression whatsoever is possible. The type of effect produced [by any impression] is thus by no means grounded solely in the Not-I, but is grounded in the I as well.)

From this it follows that the third factor we were seeking in order to make possible the synthesis [of the I's activity and state of being passively affected] is *limitation*. Sensation is possible only to the extent that the I and the Not-I reciprocally limit each other, and it is possible only at the boundary they share. (This boundary is the actual point of union between the I and the Not-I. This boundary is all they have in common, nor could they have anything else in common, since they are supposed to be posited in total opposition to each other. Beyond this common point their ways part. From this point, the I becomes an intellect only by freely crossing this boundary and thereby transferring something from itself to what is supposed to lie on the other side of the boundary. Considered from another point of view, the I becomes an intellect by absorbing into itself something that is supposed to pertain to what lies on the other side of this boundary. The results are the same in either case.)

[I/3: 157]

IV.

The third factor, the one that resolves the contradiction and makes possible sensation as a union of activity and being passively affected is therefore limitation.

To begin with, limitation permits the *sensing subject* to be related to the I, or (to express this in a more popular manner) the sensing subject is the I and can be posited as such [only] insofar as it is limited in and by sensation. Only insofar as it can be posited as limited is the sensing subject the I, and only to this extent is the I engaged in sensing.[38] Were the I not limited (by something positing in opposition to it), then sensation could not be attributed to it at all.

As we observed in the previous §, the I limits itself in sensation. It excludes something from itself as foreign to the I, and in doing this it posits itself within

[I, 347] certain restrictions, on the other side of which is supposed to lie not the I, but something posited in opposition to the I. The I *is* now limited (perhaps for an intellect outside of the I).

What is supposed to be posited now is the *sensation itself*. This means that sensation is first supposed to be posited in relation to one of the previously indicated elements [involved in sensing], namely, the act of excluding. (Sensation also includes an act of relating, but that is not what presently concerns us.) The I is supposed to be posited *as limited*. It is not supposed to be limited only in the eyes of some possible intellect outside of itself; it is supposed to be limited *for itself* as well.

Insofar as the I *is* limited, it extends only *up to* the boundary. Insofar as it posits itself as limited, it necessarily goes beyond this boundary: it extends to the boundary itself, to the boundary *as such*. And since a boundary is nothing apart from two elements posited in opposition to each other, the I also extends to what lies beyond the boundary in question.

The I is posited as limited as such. First of all, this means that, insofar as the I is enclosed within a boundary, it is *posited in opposition* to an I that is not limited by this determinate boundary. Consequently, such an unlimited I must be *posited* in order to make possible the postulated act of positing in opposition.

The I is unlimited and absolutely unlimitable insofar as its activity depends only upon itself and is grounded solely within itself, and thus it is unlimited and unlimitable only insofar as it is *ideal* (to employ the expression that we have constantly employed). Such a purely ideal activity of this sort is posited, and it is posited as extending beyond the limitation. (Appropriately, our present synthesis meshes with the synthesis established in the previous §. There too, the sensing subject had to posit the curbed activity as an activity — that is, as something that would be an activity in the absence of the Not-I's resistance and were the I dependent solely upon itself, in which case this same activity would be posited as   [I/3: 158] an ideal activity. Here as well, this same curbed activity is posited as an activity, but it is posited only indirectly. It is not posited by itself; instead, it is posited along with the activity that precedes the check — which is equally necessary, if our explication is to advance and to cover new ground.)

The limited activity is posited in opposition to the unlimited, ideal activity. Hence, to the extent that the former activity is supposed to be limited, this [second]   [I, 348] limited activity is not ideal and is not dependent upon the I; instead, it is dependent upon the Not-I, which is posited in opposition to the I. We will call such a [limited, non-ideal] activity one that is directed at *what is actual*.

It is clear that the activity of the I (considered simply as an action in its own right and quite apart from whether it is curbed or not) would thereby be considered to be posited in opposition to itself; that is, it would be viewed as directed either at what is ideal or at what is real. The activity of the I extending beyond that boundary (which we will call C) is a purely ideal activity and in no way real, whereas the real activity does not extend beyond this boundary at all. The activity that lies inside the limitation — that is, between A [the I itself, as the starting point of activity] and C — is both ideal and real. It is ideal insofar as it is posited (by virtue of the previous positing) as having its ground solely within the I, and it is real insofar as it is posited as limited.

It is furthermore clear that this entire distinction originates from the act of positing in opposition: if no real activity were posited, then no ideal activity would be posited as ideal, for there would be no way of distinguishing it. If no ideal activity were posited, then no real activity could be posited either. Ideal activity and real activity reciprocally determine each other. Thus, here again (and, thanks to this application, this point is now somewhat clearer) we have the proposition: ideality and reality are synthetically united. If nothing is ideal, then nothing is real, and vice versa.

It is now easy to show how what is supposed to happen next must occur, that is, to show how the terms posited in opposition to each other are, in turn, synthetic-ally united and related to the I.

What is supposed to be related or attributed to the I is the activity lying between A and C. Since it is limited, this activity could not be related to the I, for the I does not limit itself. But this same activity is also ideal, and, as such, it has its ground solely within the I (by virtue of the previously indicated positing of ideal activity as such). This ideality — which, as will be shown at the proper time, is freedom or spontaneity — is the ground of the relation [between this conflicted activity and the I]. The activity in question is limited only insofar as it depends [I, 349] upon the Not-I, which is excluded [from the I] and regarded as something for-eign. And yet, for reasons stated in the previous section, this activity is [also] [I/3: 159] ascribed to the I, not merely insofar as it is an ideal activity, but also, and explicitly, insofar as it is a real, limited activity.

To the extent that it is limited and excludes from itself something foreign (which is all that we have been concerned with so far, and not with the question concerning how this activity also absorbs this foreign thing into itself) the activity that was just related to the I is obviously the previously derived sensation.[39] We have therefore accomplished part of what was required.

Since we are now sufficiently familiar with the rules governing the synthetic way of proceeding, there will be no temptation to confuse that to which, in the action now deduced, some *relation* or *reference* is made [*das Bezogene*] with *the subject responsible for this relating* [*dem Beziehenden*]. We will now characterize the latter, to the extent that this is possible and necessary at this point.

The activity of the relating subject obviously extends beyond the boundary in question and pays no heed whatsoever to the Not-I; on the contrary, it excludes it. Consequently, this activity is purely ideal. But that to which this activity relates is also purely ideal, namely, the same ideal activity of the I. It is therefore impossible to distinguish the relating subject [the subject responsible for the relation] from that to which it relates. Even though the I was just supposed to be posited and related to something else, this something else is nevertheless by no means present for reflection within this relationship. The I acts. This is something we can see from our present standpoint of scientific reflection, and any other intellect, were it to observe the I, would see this as well. But, from its present standpoint, the I itself cannot see that it is acting (though at some future point it may well be able to see this). This is why it forgets itself in the object of its activity. Here we have an activity that appears to be nothing but a state of passive affection, which is what we were seeking. The name of such an action is *intuition*, a silent, unconscious contemplation, which loses itself in its object. *What is intuited* is the I that is engaged in sensing. Similarly, *the intuiting subject* is also the I, which, however, neither reflects upon its own act of intuiting nor — insofar as it is engaged in intuiting — is capable of doing so.

Here for the first time a substrate for the I enters consciousness: namely, that [I, 350] pure activity which is posited as existing even in the absence of any foreign influence, but which is posited only in consequence of what is opposed to it, and is therefore posited by means of reciprocal determination. The *being* of such a pure activity is supposed to be independent of any foreign influence upon the I, but it cannot be posited without such a foreign influence.[40]

V.

Sensation must be posited: that is the task of this §. But sensation is possible only insofar as the sensing subject attends to something that is sensed and posits it within the I. Consequently, what is sensed must also be capable of being related to [I/3: 160] the I by means of this intermediary concept [*Mittelbegriff*] of limitation.

It is true that what is sensed has already been related to the I in sensation (see above), but what has to be posited now is the sensation itself. Sensation has just been posited by means of an intuition, from which, however, what is sensed was excluded. This is obviously insufficient. Sensation must also be capable of being posited as appropriating to itself what is sensed.

This appropriation [*Zueignung*] of the relationship [between sensation and what is sensed] is supposed to be made possible by the intermediary concept of limitation. If limitation is not posited, then the requisite relation is impossible, since it is made possible only by means of the concept of limitation.

When something contained in sensation is excluded and posited as limiting sensation, it then follows that this same something is itself limited by the I, as something that does not pertain to the I. Yet when we consider it from a higher point of view, we can see that this excluded something — precisely because it is the object of this act of limiting — is once more included *within the I*. Since the I limits it, it must certainly be contained in the I.

We must now adopt this higher standpoint, in order to posit as an action this limiting of the I, an action by means of which what is limited (namely, what is sensed) necessarily enters the I's own sphere of activity; and in doing so we will, as was required, thereby posit the sensing subject. To be sure, we will not posit this sensing subject directly in the I (which was how it was just posited); nevertheless, we will posit it as the sensing subject. We will determine its mode of acting, characterize it, and distinguish it from all of the other [I, 351] activities of the I.

By recalling what was said on this subject in the course of the deduction of sensation, we can immediately become precisely acquainted with this act of limiting, by means of which the I appropriates what is sensed. What was sensed was related to the I by positing an activity in opposition to the I, an activity that was posited solely as a [contingent] condition — that is, as something that could be either posited or not posited. As always, what does or does not engage in this act of positing is the I. Thus, for the sake of this relationship [between sensation and what is sensed], not only was something attributed to the Not-I, but something was also indirectly attributed to the I: namely, the ability to posit or not to posit something. It is important to notice that what is supposed to be ascribed to the I in this case is neither the ability to posit nor the ability not to posit, but rather, the ability *to-posit-or-not-to-posit*. Consequently, the positing of a particular something must occur in the I at the same time as the non-positing of this same something, and these acts of positing and non-positing must be synthetically united. This must occur, and it certainly does occur in every case in which something is [I/3: 161] posited as a contingent condition, no matter how much those whose knowledge of philosophy is limited to a scanty acquaintance with logic may complain about logical impossibility and incomprehensibility whenever they encounter a concept of this type. Such a concept is produced by the power of imagination and must be grasped by the power of imagination, without which there would be no logic nor any logical possibility at all.

This synthesis proceeds as follows: First, something is sensed. This is possible only if the Not-I is posited as a purely contingent condition for the possibility of what is sensed. (Here we are not yet concerned with *how* this act of positing occurs.) However, this act of positing is impossible unless the I is engaged in simultaneously positing and not positing. From this it follows that an act of this sort necessarily occurs in sensing, as a mediating link between the elements [I, 352] involved. What we have to show is how the act of sensing occurs; therefore, we have to show how an act of positing and non-positing can occur.

To begin with, the activity involved in positing and non-positing is, with respect to its form, obviously an ideal activity. It proceeds beyond the boundary [between I and Not-I] and is therefore not curbed by it. The I must posit within itself everything that is supposed to be in the I: this is the ground of our deduction of the activity in question and, along with it, of sensation as a whole. The activity in question is therefore grounded solely within the I. But if it is only this [that is, if it is only grounded solely within the I] and nothing more, then it is a mere non-positing and not a positing; it is nothing but pure activity.

But the activity in question is supposed to be an act of positing as well; and of course it is an act of positing, because it does not by any means, as it were, cancel or diminish the activity of the Not-I as such. The activity in question leaves this activity [of the Not-I] as it is and merely posits it as lying beyond the range of the I. On the other hand, however, just as surely as a Not-I is a Not-I, it never lies beyond the range of the I. Either it is posited in opposition to the I, or else it does not exist at all. Hence the activity with which we are here concerned is an activity that does posit a Not-I as such, but is free to posit it wherever it wishes. The I is limited, since it has to posit a Not-I as such; but it is also not limited, because, by means of its ideal activity, it can posit this Not-I as far beyond itself as it wishes. (Suppose C to be the determinate boundary point [between the I and Not-I]. The activity of the I that we are here examining posits C as the boundary point as such, but it does not leave this boundary at the point determined for it by the Not-I. Instead, it moves it farther away, into the domain of what is unlimited. Hence this activity of the I does indeed posit a boundary as such [*eine Grenze überhaupt*] for the I; and yet this same activity — insofar as it is precisely this activity of the I — posits no boundary for itself since it places this boundary at no determinate point. Among all the points that are possible, there is none beyond which this boundary could not be — and, indeed, would not have to be — extended. This is because an ideal activity is directed at this boundary, an activity that possesses within itself the ground of this limitation. But the I contains no ground for limiting itself. As long as the activity in question continues to operate, it has no [I/3: 162] boundary. Were it ever to cease — and at the proper time we will show under what conditions it does in fact cease — the same Not-I, with the same undiminished [I, 353] and unrestricted activity, would still remain.) Accordingly, the action of the I in this case is an *act of limiting* by means of ideal (free and unrestricted) activity.

We wished to provide a provisional characterization of this activity in order not to allow the indicated incomprehensibility to persist for long. In accordance with the rules of synthetic method, however, we should have immediately determined this activity by means of positing in opposition. We will now do just that and will thereby make ourselves completely intelligible.

For the sake of the present synthesis, something that is simultaneously *posited* and *not-posited* must be posited in opposition to the act of positing and non-positing, and this positing in opposition is supposed to determine both [what is posited and what is not-posited]. According to the preceding inquiry, the activity of the Not-I was already something of this sort. The activity of the Not-I is simultaneously posited and not-posited; that is to say, as the I extends the boundary [between itself and the Not-I] it simultaneously extends its own real activity. The I posits the activity of the Not-I, but it does so ideally, by means of its own activity. This is because if there were no such presupposed activity of the Not-I, and if no such activity were posited, then no boundary would be posited either. In the very act of extending the boundary, however, the I posits a boundary; and the boundary of the Not-I is altered as the boundary of the I is altered. In this entire process of extension, however far we may imagine it to extend, the boundary is always posited by both the I and the Not-I. But each of these posits this boundary in a different manner, and in this way the I and the Not-I are posited in opposition to each other; and in order to determine the nature of this opposition we must posit this boundary in opposition to itself.

The boundary [between the I and Not-I] is either *ideal* or *real*. Insofar as it is ideal, it is posited by the I; insofar as it is real, by the Not-I.

But even to the extent that this boundary is posited in opposition to itself, it still remains one and the same, and these opposing determinations are synthetically united in it. This boundary is real only insofar as it is posited by the I — and therefore, only insofar as it is also ideal. It is ideal (that is, capable of being extended by the I's activity) only insofar as it is posited by the Not-I — and therefore only insofar as it is real.

In this way, the activity of the I that proceeds beyond the fixed boundary C [I, 354] itself becomes simultaneously real and ideal. This activity is real insofar as it is directed at a point posited by something real; it is ideal insofar as it does so on its own accord.

In this manner, what is sensed can now be related to the I. The activity of the [I/3: 163] Not-I is and remains excluded [from the I]. This is because, so far as we can now see, as the boundary is extended into infinity it is precisely the Not-I that is pushed outward along with it. But a product of the Not-I can be related to the I, and the product in question is that limitation of the I which serves as the condition for the ideal activity that has now been described.

In this relationship, this product of the Not-I [that is, the limitation of the I] is supposed to be related (as to the I) to the ideal action directed at the Not-I, and this same ideal action is supposed to be responsible for relating them in this way. There is therefore [in this case] no difference between the relating subject (which, in accordance with the synthetic method, should not be posited at this point anyway) and that to which it is related (which, in accordance with the same method, must of course be posited here). Hence, no relation to the I occurs at all, and the action thereby deduced is an *intuition*, in which the I loses itself in the object of its activity. *What is intuited* is an ideally grasped product of the Not-I, which is extended by means of intuition into an unconditioned realm. Here for the first time we discover a substrate for the Not-I. The *intuiting subject* is, as we have said, the I — an I which, however, does not reflect upon itself.

VI.

Before we proceed to the most important part of our present inquiry, a few preparatory words and a summary of the whole are in order.

What was supposed to occur has by no means yet occurred. The sensing subject is posited by means of intuition; what is sensed is also posited thereby. But if, as was demanded, the *sensation* is supposed to be posited [as well], then the sensing subject and what is sensed must not be posited separately, but in synthetic unity with each other. This could occur only in consequence of extremes that have yet to be united. Such extremes were in fact present in the preceding inquiry, though we have not yet called explicit attention to them.

[I, 355]

In order to posit the I as limited and in order to appropriate this limit to the I, we first required an ideal, unlimited, and (so far as we could see) unlimitable activity [of the I] posited in opposition to the limited activity [of the I]. If the relationship demanded [between the sensing subject and what is sensed] is to be possible, this unlimited activity must already be present within the I as an unlimited activity, which is supposed to determine another activity (namely, the limited activity) by means of its opposition to it. How and upon what occasion does the I engage in an action of this sort? — This question must still be answered.

[I/3: 164]

What is sensed is supposed to lie beyond the determinate border [between the I and Not-I]. In order for it to be possible for what is sensed to be encompassed by and posited within the I, we assumed that there is an activity that, so far as we could see, extended the boundary without limit. What proves *that* such an act occurs is that otherwise the required relation [between the sensing I and what is sensed] would be impossible. But the question remains, Why should this relation, along with the action that is a condition for it, occur at all? Suppose that it could subsequently be shown that these two activities were one and the same: in that case it would follow that in order to be able to limit itself the I would have to extend the limit, and in order to be able to extend the limit, it would have to limit itself.[41] The sensation and the intuition would thereby be intimately united, and one would be impossible without the other; moreover, in sensation, inner intuition (the intuition of the sensing subject) and outer intuition (the intuition of what is sensed) would also be intimately united.

The rigorous form to which we have adhered until now has been indicated with sufficient clarity to allow anyone to easily employ it in order to test our reasoning. Without binding ourselves to this rigorous form, let us now, for the sake of clarity in this important and decisive, though complex, investigation, pursue a more natural path. We will now attempt to answer the pressing questions [I, 356] that have been raised, with the expectation that the results of this effort will determine what is to be undertaken next.

A.) From where does the ideal, unlimited activity, which is supposed to be posited in opposition to the real, limited activity, come? Or, if we are still not yet able to answer this question, can we still not distinguish additional characteristics of this ideal activity?

The limited activity is supposed to be determined as such by its opposition to the unlimited activity and is therefore supposed to be related to it. But nothing can be posited in opposition to what is not posited. Consequently, the possibility of the desired relationship *presupposes* not only the limited [real] activity but also the unlimited, ideal activity, which is what we are actually concerned with here. This ideal activity is a condition for the relationship [between the limited and unlimited activities]. However, this relationship (at least as considered from our present point of view) is not a condition for this [unlimited, ideal] activity. If the relationship is to be possible, the ideal activity must already be present in the I.

Leaving aside the question of its origin and the particular occasion that gives rise to this ideal activity, it is nevertheless clear that no boundary point C exists for this ideal activity. It is not directed at such a boundary point, nor is its direction determined by such a point. It proceeds completely freely and independently into an unlimited realm.

Because it is opposed to the limited activity, this ideal activity has to be expressly [I/3: 165] posited as unlimited. This necessarily means that it must be posited as *not* limited *with respect to C;* for nothing is limited which does not have a determinate boundary, and therefore the limited activity must necessarily be posited as limited with respect to the determinate boundary point C. (Whether the unlimited activity may perhaps be limited with respect to another point, one lying beyond C, remains completely undetermined by its opposition [to the limited activity] and is supposed to remain so.)

From this it follows that, in the relationship just described, the determinate boundary point C^C is related to the unlimited activity. Since the unlimited activity is supposed to be given prior to the relationship, C must actually lie in this [unlimited ideal] activity itself. In order for C to be capable of being related to the ideal activity, this activity must necessarily come into contact with C. And yet, as

---

^{C} The *determinate* boundary point C [Emphasis added in *SW.*]

may here seem to be the case, this ideal activity comes into contact with C as if by
[I, 357] accident, without being originally directed toward C.

In the act of relating, point C is posited within the unlimited ideal activity at the place where it occurs, and it is posited there without the slightest freedom. This point of incidence is determined; the activity of relating is concerned only with explicitly positing this point *as* the point where C occurs. In addition, insofar as it is engaged in the activity of relating, the ideal activity is posited as *going beyond point C*. This, in turn, is impossible unless the point in question is posited as lying completely within the [circumference of this unlimited ideal] activity, (inasmuch as this activity is supposed to extend beyond it) and posited as a point beyond which this activity extends. Accordingly, point C is carried along within the [unlimited ideal] activity throughout its entire range. A boundary point is posited wherever this [unlimited ideal] activity is reflected upon, but it is posited only experimentally and ideally, in order to measure its distance from the first fixed and immovable point [C]. However, this second, ideal point can never be firmly established, since this [unlimited ideal] activity is supposed to be one that *goes* beyond — an activity that is supposed to go on and on and never be limited. Instead, this second, ideal point is continually hovering and floating away [*fortschwebend*], and it does this in such a way that within the entire range of this activity no point can be posited (ideally) with which this [second] ideal point would not have come into contact. As certainly, therefore, as this ideal activity extends beyond the boundary point [C], this second, ideal point must itself be extended endlessly (until we may perhaps once again arrive at a new boundary).

But what is the activity that extends this point? Is it the presupposed [unlimited] ideal activity, or is it the activity involved in relating? Prior to the relationship [between the limited real activity and the unlimited ideal activity] it is obviously not the ideal activity that extends this boundary point, for prior to this relationship no boundary point is present for the ideal activity. However, the very act of relating already presupposes extension [beyond the boundary point], for this is the basis or ground of the acts of distinguishing and relating [the two activities]. Therefore, the boundary point and its extension are synthetically posited[42] precisely in and by means of the relation [between them]. As we know, all relating is grounded solely in the I; consequently, the boundary point and its extension are also posited by means of an ideal activity, albeit by a different one.

[I/3: 166]   In order to clarify what follows, let us enumerate the actions of the I we have discovered so far: (1.) an action whose object is the ideal activity and (2.) an action
[I, 358] whose object is the real, limited activity. Both of these first two actions must be simultaneously present in the I; consequently, they must be one and the same, even though we as yet have no insight into how this is possible. (3.) An action that transfers the boundary point from the real to the ideal activity and follows it there. This last action introduces a distinction within the ideal activity itself: namely, a distinction between the ideal activity extending up to point C (up to which point the ideal activity is completely pure) and the ideal activity that goes beyond C and is supposed to extend the boundary thereby. The importance of this will become evident later. — We will not further characterize these actions at this point, since a complete characterization of them will not be possible until later.

To avoid confusion with what follows, we will use letters to designate these determinate activities, which have been posited in opposition to each other and related to each other: the ideal activity proceeding from A through C into the realm of the unlimited, and the real activity proceeding from A to the boundary point C.

B.) As we have just seen in more detail, the I cannot posit itself as limited without at the same time proceeding beyond the boundary [between itself and the Not-I] and distancing itself from it. As it proceeds beyond this boundary, however, the I must at the same time posit itself as limited by it. As has been established, this is self-contradictory. Now it is true that we have said that the I is limited and unlimited in entirely opposite respects and with reference to entirely opposed kinds of activity. It is limited insofar as its activity is real and unlimited insofar as it is ideal. It is also true that we have posited these two kinds of activity in opposition to one another. We have done this, however, only insofar as they are limited and unlimited and not on the basis of any other distinguishing feature, and hence our explanation is circular. The I posits the real activity as limited and the ideal activity as unlimited. Fine, and which activity does it posit as real? The limited one, and it posits the unlimited activity as ideal. If we cannot escape from this circle and indicate some ground for distinguishing between real and ideal activity — a ground that has nothing to do with limitation — , then the requisite distinction and relation [between the unlimited ideal and limited real activities] is impossible. We intend to discover such a ground of distinction, and this is the [I, 359] goal of our present inquiry.

Let us provisionally advance the following proposition, the truth of which will soon be confirmed: The I can in no way posit itself *for itself* without limiting itself and thus proceeding beyond itself.

The I is originally posited through itself; that is to say, it is what it is for any intel- [I/3: 167] lect outside of itself. Its nature [*Wesen*] is grounded in itself, and this is how we must think of the I *if* we are going to think of it at all. Moreover, for reasons expounded in the "Foundation of Practical Knowing,"[43] we can ascribe to the I a striving *to fill* infinity, as well as a tendency to *comprehend* it [*dieselbe zu umfassen*], that is, to reflect upon itself as infinite. Both tendencies pertain to the I just as surely as it is an I at all.[44] But no action of the I springs from this mere tendency — nor can it.

Suppose that the I's striving carries it to point C and that its striving to fill infinity is curbed and interrupted at point C. This, of course, is posited from the standpoint of a possible intellect outside the I, an intellect that observes the I and has posited its striving in its own consciousness. What happens in the I when its striving is interrupted? The I was also striving at the same time to reflect upon itself; but it could not do so, because everything that is reflected upon must be limited, and the I was unlimited.

The I is limited at point C. Consequently, along with its limitation at C the I also reflects upon itself. It turns back upon itself and discovers itself; it feels *itself* — but it obviously feels nothing outside of itself as of yet.

This reflection of the I upon itself is an action of the I (as we can indeed see from our standpoint, and as any intellect outside of the I would also be able to see). This act is grounded in the necessary tendency [of the I to reflect upon itself] and on the additional condition [that the I's original striving to fill infinity is curbed]. But what does this reflection mean for the I itself? In it, the I discovers itself for the first time; it first comes into being *for itself*. The I cannot assume that the ground for anything else is present within the I prior to its

[I, 360]   own existence. Consequently, this self-feeling is, for the I, only a state of being passively affected. The I does not *engage in reflecting* for itself; instead, it *is* reflected upon by something outside itself. We see it engaging in acting and doing so with necessity — partly because the I can act at all only insofar as it acts in accordance with the laws of its own nature, and partly, and with regard to the specific point [C], its action is made possible only by a condition external to itself. By no means does the *I itself* see itself acting; instead, it is only passively affected.

[I/3: 168]   The I now *exists* for itself, and it exists because and insofar as it is limited. Just as surely as it is an I and is supposed to be limited, it must posit itself as limited, and this means that it must posit in opposition to itself something that limits it. This necessarily occurs as a result of an activity that proceeds beyond boundary C and comprehends what is supposed to lie beyond this boundary as something posited in opposition to the striving I. What kind of an activity is this — first, for the observer and, second, for the I?

Both the form and the content of this activity are grounded solely in the I. The I *posits* something limiting because it *is* limited and because it must posit everything that is supposed to lie within itself. The I posits this *as* something limiting, and hence as something posited in opposition [to the I], as Not-I. It does this because it must explain its own *limited state*. One should not therefore, even for a moment, think that this opens the way for the I to penetrate the thing in itself (something with no relation to any I). We begin with the presupposition that the I is limited. — Does this limitation possess a ground in itself (that is, apart from any relation to some possible intellect)? How is this ground constituted? How could I possibly know this? How can I give a rational answer to this question when I am enjoined to abstract from all reason? For the I (that is, for all reason), *this limitation possesses a ground*, because for the I every limitation presupposes something limiting. And for the I as well, the ground of this limitation does *not* lie within the I itself, but instead, in something posited in opposition to the I. Otherwise, the I would harbor contradictory principles and would therefore

[I, 361]   not exist at all. What is posited in opposition is posited as such by the I in accordance with the laws of reason; it is a product of the I.

(Our argument proceeds as follows: The I is limited and must necessarily be limited if it is ever to be an I. In accordance with the laws of its own nature, it must posit this limitation as well as posit its ground in something limiting [the I]. This limiting something is, accordingly, the I's own product. — Should someone have so entangled himself in transcendent dogmatism that he cannot free himself from it, even after all that has been said, he might argue against us more or less as follows: "I concede that this whole way of reasoning is the way in which the I explains things. But what arises in the I in this way is merely the representation of the thing. Of course, this representation is a product of the I, but the thing itself is not. I, however, am not concerned with the way the I explains things but rather with how things really are — in themselves. You maintain that the I must be limited. *This limitation — considered in itself* and entirely apart from the I's reflection upon it, which does not concern me here — *must have some ground*, and this ground is precisely the thing in itself." Our reply to the transcendent dogmatist is that his explanation is exactly the same as that of the I on which we are reflecting. [I/3: 169] Just as surely as his inference conforms to the laws of reason, he himself is that I. He needs only to reflect upon this circumstance in order to see that he is still — albeit unknowingly — caught up in the same circle in which we knowingly find ourselves. If, in his manner of explanation, he cannot free himself from those laws of thinking which govern his own mind, then he will never escape from the circle we have drawn around him. But if he does free himself from the laws of thinking, then his objections will, once again, present no danger to us. This § will show clearly why he continues to insist on a thing in itself, even after he has conceded that we possess no more than a representation of it.)

What is the action in question for the I? It is not for the I what it is for an observer, because the grounds upon which the observer judges this action are not present for the I. For the observer, this action occurred entirely within the I with respect to [I, 362] both its form and its content. It occurred because the I had to engage in reflection, and it had to engage in reflection in consequence of its own purely active nature (with which such an observer is familiar) — particularly since it is actively engaged in reflecting. The I has by no means yet posited itself for itself as reflecting, nor even as active; instead, according to what was said above, it is only passively affected. Consequently, it is by no means conscious of its own acting, nor can it become so. Indeed, were it to be possible for the product of this acting to appear to the I, it would appear to it to be something that is present without any help from the I.

(It is impossible to have, from the moment of its inception, an original consciousness of what has here been deduced — to catch oneself, as it were, in the act. This is because, in order to reflect upon its own determinate manner of acting, the mind must already have attained a much higher level of reflection. But we can perhaps perceive something similar [to such an original self-consciousness] when we initiate what we might call a new series within consciousness — when, for instance, we awaken from a deep sleep or a faint, particularly when we are in an unfamiliar place. On such occasions, our consciousness always begins with the I. We first seek and discover ourselves, and then, in order to orient ourselves, we turn our attention to the things around us. We ask ourselves, "Where am I? How did I get here? What was the last thing that happened to me?" We ask these questions in order to attach our present series of representations to others which have come to an end.)

C.) For the observer, the I has now proceeded beyond the boundary point C, while still retaining the constant tendency to reflect upon itself. Since the I cannot reflect without being limited, but cannot limit itself, it is clear that the requisite [I/3: 170] reflection [upon itself beyond point C] will be impossible unless the I is once again limited at some possible point D, lying beyond point C. But since the demonstration and determination of this new boundary would lead us too far into

matters that do not pertain to the present §, we must here content ourselves with
[I, 363]   the following postulate (which we are totally warranted in making): If what proceeds beyond C is an I, then it must posit or reflect upon its act of proceeding
beyond C. In making this assertion, however, we have no desire to absolve ourselves of the obligation to indicate (at the proper time) the condition under which
such a reflection is possible.

Merely by virtue of the very act of proceeding beyond and outside itself, the I
produced (for a possible observer) a Not-I, and it did so without any consciousness. The I now reflects upon its own product, and in this reflection it *posits* this
product *as* Not-I, and it posits it simply as such, absolutely and without any further determination. Once again, this positing occurs unconsciously, because the I
has not yet reflected upon itself. — We will not linger over these actions of the I,
since they are completely incomprehensible at this point, and since we will
encounter them again at the appropriate time, albeit along an opposing path.*

The I must reflect anew upon this product of its second action: that is, upon
any Not-I posited as such, though, yet again, it cannot reflect without a new limitation, which will be exhibited at the proper time. — In feeling, the I is posited as
passively affected; therefore, the Not-I, which is posited in opposition to the I,
must be posited as active.

The Not-I (which is posited as active) is, in turn, reflected upon, and this too
must occur under the previously indicated condition.[45] Only now have we arrived
at our new area of inquiry. As we have always done before, we will [first] consider
things from the point of view of a possible observer, because we can observe
nothing from the point of view of the I that is under investigation. Such an
observer's point of view is very advantageous in inquiries of this sort, which go
beyond the ordinary ways of thinking and which seem to the inexperienced
thinker to be transcendent inquiries.

An active Not-I is posited in and through the I (though, as has frequently been
noted, the I does this unconsciously). A new activity of the I is directed at this
active Not-I; in other words, it is reflected upon. We can reflect only upon what is
[I, 364]   limited; consequently, the activity of the Not-I is necessarily limited — and limited
as activity — because and insofar as it is posited *in action*. However, the range
[*Umfang*] of its sphere of efficacy is not limited — limited, for instance, in such a
[I/3: 171]   way that it could extend only as far as E or F, and no further (as one might prema-
turely assume). Indeed, how could we be supposed to become acquainted with
such a "range," when there is as yet no space? The Not-I does not remain *active*;
instead, it comes to rest. The expression of its force is curbed, and all that remains
is a mere substrate of this force[46] — something that is asserted here simply in
order to make ourselves understandable, though it must be thoroughly deduced
later. — (From our present point of view, we can assume that the activity of the
Not-I is curbed solely by the reflecting activity of the I, that is to say, in and by
means of this act of reflecting. At the proper time, we will place the I itself in a
position to make this same assumption. At this point, however, the I is conscious
of this activity neither directly nor indirectly — i.e., by means of deduction — and

---

* Here we catch a passing glimpse of points we still have to investigate.

is therefore unable to explain this curbing [of the activity of the Not-I] on the basis of [its own] activity. Instead, it will derive this curbing [of the activity of the Not-I] from the opposing force of another Not-I, which is posited in opposition to the first Not-I, as we shall see at the proper time.)

Insofar as the I is engaged in reflecting, it does not reflect upon this very act of reflecting. It cannot simultaneously act upon an object and upon its own acting. Consequently, it is not conscious of the activity in question; instead, it forgets itself entirely and loses itself in the object of this activity. Here again, therefore, we encounter that first and original outer intuition which we described above (though it has not yet been posited *as* outer).[47] As yet, however, no consciousness whatsoever arises from this intuition — not only no self-consciousness (that is clear enough from what was said above), but not even any consciousness of the object.

In the course of our previous derivation of sensation, we discussed the conflict between the opposing activities of the I and the Not-I, which were supposed to annihilate each other reciprocally. From our present standpoint, this now [I, 365] becomes perfectly clear. No activity of the I could be destroyed if the I had not already passed beyond what we can imagine to be its first and original range (the area lying between A and C in our presentation) and entered the sphere of efficacy of the Not-I (viz., the area from C to infinity). Furthermore, there would be no Not-I and no activity of the Not-I if the I had not posited them; both are products of the I. — The activity of the Not-I is annihilated when one reflects *upon the fact* that this activity was something previously posited, something that is now being canceled by means of reflection in order to make reflection possible. The activity of the I is annihilated when one reflects *upon the fact* that the I does not in turn reflect upon its act of reflecting — in which it is, of course, active. Instead, the I loses itself in this act of reflection and transforms itself, as it were, into the Not-I — a point that will be subsequently be further confirmed. — In short, we [I/3: 172] have now arrived precisely at the point from which we began in the preceding § and in the entire portion of the theoretical *Wissenschaftslehre* concerned with what is particular: namely, we have arrived at that conflict which is supposed to be present within the I for a possible observer. But this conflict has not yet been reflected upon [by the I itself], and is therefore not yet present in the I for the I. Consequently, no consciousness whatsoever can be derived from what has been established so far, even though we now have available all the conditions for its possibility.

VII.

With respect to the possibility of reflecting upon itself, the I is now for itself what, at the beginning of our inquiry, it was for a possible external observer. This observer was confronted with an I, that is, with something perceptible, which was supposed to be thought of as an I. He was also confronted with something else, a Not-I, as well as with a point of contact between the I and the Not-I. By themselves alone, however, these two perceptions would not have supplied him with a

[I, 366]   representation of the limitation of the I, unless he had reflected upon both. He was therefore supposed to be engaged in reflection, because only insofar as he was so engaged was he an observer, and this same observer has since witnessed all of the actions that must necessarily ensue from the nature of the I.

By means of these same actions, the I itself has now arrived at the point occupied by the observer from the start. The I's sphere of efficacy (which is posited *for the observer*) contains the following things (which are also present as products of the I itself): a perceptible I (which can be perceived because it is limited), a Not-I, and a point of contact between the two. The I has only to engage in reflection in order to make precisely the same discovery that only the observer could make until now.

Even at the beginning of all its activity, the I originally reflected upon itself. It did so of necessity, as we have already observed. — The I possessed within itself a general tendency to reflect. Because of the limitation [of the I], the condition for the possibility of reflecting was added as well, following which the I necessarily engaged in reflection. From this there arose a feeling, and from this feeling there arose everything else we have derived. The tendency to reflect continues without end; hence, it is always present within the I, and the I can therefore reflect upon its first reflections themselves, as well as upon everything that has resulted from these reflections, because the condition that makes reflection possible is present — which is to say, because the I is limited by something that can be regarded as Not-I.

[I/3: 173]   The I does not *have to* engage in reflection in this case (as we assumed in the case of the first reflection), because what conditions the reflection that has now become possible is not unconditionally a Not-I, but may also be regarded as something contained within the I. — What limits the I is the Not-I, which is produced by means of something contained within the I. One might object that, since it is supposed to be limited by means of its own product, the I is in this way supposed to be able to limit itself. This has repeatedly been explained to be the sharpest contradiction of all, and all our previous reasoning has been based on the necessity of avoiding this contradiction. In the first place, however, this Not-I is not completely and absolutely the product of the I, because it was posited only under the condition that the I was limited by the Not-I. In the second place, and for the precisely the same reason, the I does not consider the Not-I to be its own

[I, 367]   product, inasmuch as it posits itself as limited by the Not-I. As soon as it recognizes the Not-I as its own product, it posits itself as not limited by it.

If, however, what we have posited within the I is really supposed to be present within the *I, then* the I has to reflect.[48] This is why we postulate the occurrence of this act of reflection and have the right to do so. — If, merely for the purpose of making ourselves understood, we may be permitted for a moment to entertain a transcendent thought, we might say the following: Perhaps we are affected by a multitude of influences, but if we do not reflect on this fact then we do not know it, and, in a transcendental sense, there would in this case be no influences at all upon us — as an I.^D

---

^D *as an I.* [Emphasis added in *SW.*]

For the reasons previously indicated, the required reflection occurs abso-lutely spontaneously. The I reflects purely and simply because it reflects. Not only is the tendency to engage in reflection grounded in the I, so too is the action of reflection itself. It is true that this action of reflection is *conditioned* by something outside the I (that is, by an impression received by the I), but it is not *necessitated* thereby.

In considering this [action of] reflection, we can direct our attention toward two things: toward the I that is thereby *reflected upon* and toward the I that *is engaged in reflecting*. Our inquiry is divided into two parts, which will probably give rise to a third (as the synthetic method would lead one to expect).

A.) We have until now been able to attribute nothing to the I except feeling. The I is a feeling subject and nothing more. Consequently, when we say that the I that is reflected upon is limited we mean that it feels itself to be limited, or that there is present in the I a feeling of limitation, a feeling of inability or compulsion. It will now become clear how this is possible.

Insofar as the I posits itself as limited, it proceeds beyond the boundary: this is a canonical principle.[49] Consequently, the I necessarily posits the Not-I at the same time [that it posits itself as limited], though it does so without being conscious of its acting. An intuition of the Not-I is united with this feeling of compulsion; but [I/3: 174] this is a mere intuition, in which the I forgets itself in what it intuits.

The intuited Not-I and the I that is felt and that feels itself must be synthetically united. This occurs by means of the boundary. The I feels itself to be limited and [I, 368] posits the intuited Not-I as the source of its limitation. Or, expressed in more eas-ily understood terms: I see something, and at the same time I have a feeling of compulsion that I cannot immediately explain. Yet this feeling of compulsion should be explained. I therefore relate what I see to my feeling of compulsion and say that what I see is the ground of the compulsion I feel.

However, the following question could still cause some difficulty: How does it happen that I feel compelled at all? Of course I explain this feeling[E] to myself on the basis of the intuited Not-I. But I cannot engage in intuiting if I am not already engaged in feeling. It follows that this feeling has to be explained independently of the intuition. But how? It is precisely this difficulty that will force us to connect the present synthesis (which is incomplete and impossible when taken by itself) to another. It will force us to invert the preceding proposition and assert that I am as incapable of feeling a compulsion without intuiting [as I am of intuiting with-out feeling]. Accordingly, intuition and feeling are synthetically united. Neither is the ground of the other; instead, they reciprocally ground each other. In order to facilitate this discussion in advance, let us leave matters just as they are and address at once the question just raised, [namely: how does it happen that the I feels itself to be compelled at all?].

The I originally seeks to determine the constitution or attributes [*Beschaffenheit*] of things entirely on its own. It purely and simply demands causality. This demand is resisted when it is directed at reality (and can therefore be called real activity),

---

[E] *I of course explain this feeling* [Emphasis added in *SW*.]

and, as a result of this resistance, another tendency that is originally grounded in the I is satisfied: namely, the tendency of the I to reflect upon itself. From this there arises a reflection upon a determinate, given reality. Insofar as this reality is already determined, it can be grasped only by the ideal activity of the I, that is, by the activity of representing or copying. Now suppose that both the activity *directed at* the attributes of a thing and the activity that *copies* these attributes that are determined without the participation of the I are posited as [activities of the] I — and that they are posited as [activities of] one and the same I (and that this occurs absolutely spontaneously). In that case, the real I is posited as limited by the intuited attributes of the thing, that is, by the very attributes that would have [I, 369] been posited in opposition to the I's activity if it had continued; consequently the entire I, when synthetically unified in this manner, feels itself to be limited or compelled. — Feeling is the most primordial interaction of the I with itself, and even precedes the Not-I, since a Not-I must, of course, be posited in order to [I/3: 175] explain feeling. (As goes without saying, we are here speaking of a Not-I that is *in* the I and *for* the I.) The I strives toward infinity; it reflects upon itself, and in doing so it limits itself.[50] This was all derived above, and from it a possible observer might infer a feeling on the part of the I. But the I has as yet no feeling of itself [*Selbstgefühl*]. Both the limited I and the limiting I, synthetically united by absolute spontaneity, are posited — and posited as the same I. This is what we have now derived, and from this there arises, for the I, a feeling, a feeling of itself, in which the I's activity and state of being passively affected are internally united in a single state.

B.) We are also supposed to reflect upon the I that is, in this action [by means of which a feeling arises], engaged in feeling. This reflection also occurs necessarily and with absolute spontaneity. As we will show in what follows, however, this act of reflection is not merely postulated; instead, it is accomplished with synthetic necessity, as the condition for the possibility of the previously postulated reflection. Here we are less concerned with this reflection itself than with its object, insofar as it is its object.

The reflecting I that engaged in this action [of reflection] did so with absolute spontaneity, and its acting was grounded solely in the I; it was an ideal activity. The I must therefore reflect upon this activity as an ideal activity and posit it as extending beyond the boundary and proceeding endlessly — unless it is limited in the future by another reflection. But according to the laws of reflection, the I can reflect only upon what is limited, even if it is limited merely and solely by the very act of reflection. Consequently, just as surely as it is an object of reflection, this act of reflecting is something limited. Given the unlimitedness [of the action of reflecting], which must be preserved, it is immediately obvious what the limitation in question will be. — This activity cannot be reflected upon qua activity (since, as we have already learned, the I is never immediately conscious of its own [I, 370] acting). Instead, this activity is reflected upon as a substrate, and thus as a product of an absolute activity of the I.

It is immediately evident that the I which posits this product forgets itself in the act of positing and therefore intuits this product without being conscious of its own act of intuiting.

Insofar, therefore, as the I reflects in turn upon the absolute spontaneity of its own reflecting in that first act in which it was engaged, an unlimited product of its own activity is posited as such. — We will later become better acquainted with this product.[51]

This product is supposed to be posited as a product of the I; therefore, it must necessarily be related to the I. It cannot be related to the intuiting I, for (according to what we said above) this intuiting subject has not yet been posited. [I/3: 176]

At this point, the I is posited only insofar as it feels itself to be limited; hence, the product in question would have to be related to this aspect of the I.

But the I that feels itself to be limited is posited in opposition to the I that freely produces something, and indeed, produces something unlimited. The I that is engaged in feeling is not free; it is compelled. The productive I is not compelled; it produces freely.

This, of course, is how things must be if any relationship and synthetic unity [between the limited or real and the unlimited or ideal activities of the I] is to be possible and necessary. Hence, we have only to exhibit the ground of the requisite relationship.

The ground in question must be free or absolute activity.[52] Such activity does not pertain to the limited I; hence, it is difficult to see how the two [i.e., the free and the limited activities of the I] could be united.

We need only advance a single step further in order to obtain the most surprising result — one that will put an end to age-old confusions and install reason in its rightful place forever. — It is the I itself that is supposed to be responsible for this relation — that is, to be the subject engaged in relating [*das beziehende*]. The I necessarily proceeds beyond the limitation, and does so purely and simply on its own, without any reason [*Grund*] for doing so and in opposition to external reasons [which oppose its doing so]. In going beyond this limitation, the I appro- [I, 371] priates this product and freely makes it its own. — The ground of the relation [between the ideal and real activities of the I] and the subject engaged in relating are therefore one and the same.

The I itself never becomes conscious of this action, nor could it ever become conscious of it. The essence of this act is absolute spontaneity, and as soon as this action is reflected upon, it ceases to be spontaneous. The I is free only when it acts. As soon as it reflects upon its action that action ceases to be a free action; indeed, it ceases to be an action at all and becomes a product.

As we shall soon see in more detail, the entire distinction between ideality and reality, between representation and thing, arises from the impossibility of any consciousness of a free action.

Freedom or (what is the same thing) the immediate acting of the I is, as such, the point of union between ideality and reality. The I is free, inasmuch as and because it posits itself as free or sets itself free, and it posits itself as free or sets itself free inasmuch as it is free. Determination and being are [here] one and the same. What acts and what is acted upon are [here] one and the same. Simply in determining itself to act, the I engages in this act of determining; and insofar as it is engaged in acting, it determines itself.

The I cannot posit itself as free by means of reflection. This is a contradiction. We would never arrive at the assumption that we are free simply by pursuing the path of reflection. Yet the I appropriates something as a product of its own free activity, and to this extent it posits itself, at least indirectly, as free.*

[I/3: 177]

[I, 372]   C.) According to the first synthesis, the I is limited insofar as it feels itself, and to this extent it posits itself as limited. According to the second synthesis, the I is free and posits itself (at least indirectly) as free, in that it posits something as a product of its own free activity. These two specific determinations of the I (that is, its limitation in feeling and its freedom in producing) are posited in utter opposition to each other. But perhaps the I could posit itself as free or as determined in two quite different respects, and, in this way perhaps, its identity would not be canceled. In both syntheses, however, the I is expressly required to posit itself as limited, because and insofar as it posits itself as free, just as it is equally required to posit itself in both syntheses as free, because and insofar as it posits itself as limited. From this it follows that the I must be free and limited in one and the same respect. This is obviously self-contradictory, and this contradiction must be resolved. — But first let us delve more deeply into the meaning of the propositions that have now been presented as posited in opposition to each other.

1.) The I is supposed to posit itself as limited because and insofar as it posits itself as free. — The I *is* free only insofar as it acts. We must therefore provide a preliminary answer to the question, What is *action*? On what basis do we differentiate between action and non-action? All action presupposes some force. To say that an action is absolute is to say that this force is determined solely in and through itself — that it receives its direction solely from and through itself. Consequently, this same force previously had no direction. It was not posited in action, but was instead posited as a static force, as a mere striving to exert force.[53] Accordingly, just as it is certain that the I is supposed to posit itself as totally engaged in acting (for the moment, the specific action in question is that of reflection), it is also certain that it must posit itself as not acting. The determination to act presupposes stasis. — In addition, [in the case of an absolute action] this force provides itself with a direction; that is, it provides itself with an object toward which it proceeds. The force in question provides itself with its own object; but insofar as it does this, it must also already possess that with which it is supposed to provide itself. This object must therefore already have been given to it, and the force must be related to this object as passively affected by it. It follows from this that self-determination to act necessarily presupposes a state of being passively affected. — Here again, we find ourselves entangled in new difficulties, which, however, will shed the clearest light on our entire inquiry.

[I/3: 178]

[I, 373]

---

* The common sense proofs for freedom are therefore quite correct and completely in accord with the workings of the human mind. — Diogenes *moved* in order to prove the disputed possibility of motion. In doing so, he proved this only to himself, for his demonstration did not, of course, put errant speculation back in its place. Similarly, should you seek to reason away someone's freedom, and should your likely-sounding reasons really succeed in raising doubt concerning this matter, he can always demonstrate his freedom on the spot by actually producing something that can be derived only from his own free acting.

2.) The I is supposed to posit itself as free because and insofar as it posits itself as limited. That the I posits itself as limited means that it posits a limit or boundary for its activity. (This does not mean that it produces this limitation; rather, it only posits the limitation as something posited by an opposing force.) Accordingly, in order to be limited the I must already have acted; its force must already have acquired a direction, and indeed, a direction determined by the I itself. All limitation presupposes free acting.

Let us now apply these foundational principles to the present case.

For itself, the I is still something compelled, forced, and limited, inasmuch as it proceeds beyond the boundary and posits a Not-I, which it then intuits, without being conscious of itself in this intuition. From the higher standpoint at which we have now situated ourselves, we know that this Not-I is the product of the I and that the I must reflect upon the Not-I, as upon its own product. This reflection occurs necessarily and with absolute spontaneity.

One and the same I cannot, in one and the same activity, simultaneously produce a Not-I and reflect upon it as its product. Consequently, just as surely as the requisite second activity is supposed to pertain to the I, the I must limit and interrupt its first activity. Moreover, this interruption of its first activity must likewise occur with absolute spontaneity, since this entire action occurs spontaneously. Furthermore, absolute spontaneity is possible only on this condition. The I is supposed to determine itself absolutely spontaneously; but nothing pertains to the I except activity. Consequently, it must limit one of its own actions, and (again because nothing pertains to it except activity) it must do so by means of another action which is posited in opposition to its first action.

In addition, the I is supposed to posit its product (the opposed and limiting [I, 374] Not-I) *as* its product. The I posits the Not-I as its product and raises it to a higher level of reflection precisely by means of that action whereby (as was just said) it interrupts its act of producing. The lower, first level of reflection is thereby interrupted. All that we are now concerned with is the transition from the first to the second level of reflection, that is, with the point of union between the two. As we [I/3: 179] know, however, the I is never immediately conscious of its own acting; consequently, it can posit what is required [namely, the Not-I] as its own product only indirectly, by means of a new reflection.

By means of this new act of reflection, the Not-I must be posited as a product of absolute freedom. The distinguishing feature of such a product is that it could also be something else and could also be posited as such. The intuiting power[54] oscillates between various specific determinations and posits only one from among all those that are possible, and in this way the product obtains the distinctive character of an *image* [Bild].[55]

(In order to make ourselves understood, let us take as an example an object with various distinguishing properties, despite the fact that it is still too early to speak of such an object. — In the first intuition — that is, in the productive intuition — I am lost in an object. The first thing I reflect upon is myself; I discover myself, and I distinguish between myself and the object. But everything in the object is still confused and intermingled; it is nothing more than an object. I then reflect upon the individual distinguishing properties of this object — for example, upon its shape, its size, its color, etc. — and I posit these within my consciousness. As I consider each individual property of this sort, I am, to begin with, doubtful and uncertain. I base my observation upon an arbitrary schema of shape, size, and color that approaches the shape, size, and color of my object. I look more closely, and only then do I determine more closely my original schema: let us say, for example, I determine that the shape is that of a cube, the size is that of a fist, and the color is dark green. By means of this transition from an unspecified product of the free power of imagination to the complete determination [of

[I, 375]   this product] in one and the same act, what appears within my consciousness becomes an image and is posited as such. It becomes *my* product, because I must posit it as absolutely determined by my own spontaneous activity.)

Insofar as the I posits this image as a product of its activity, it necessarily posits in opposition to it something that is not a product of this activity; that is, it posits this image in opposition to something that is no longer determinable but is instead completely determined and is determined only by itself, with no contribution from the I. This is the *actual thing*, to which the I that is engaged in forming an image[56] directs its attention as it drafts its image and which must necessarily hover before it as it is engaged in forming this image. This actual thing is the product of the I's first action (the action that has now been interrupted), but it is impossible to posit it as such in this relationship.

The I copies the actual thing. This thing must therefore be contained in the I and accessible to its activity; that is to say, it must be possible to indicate some ground of

[I/3: 180]   the relationship between the thing and its image (which are posited in opposition to each other). The ground of the relationship in question is a completely determined yet unconscious intuition of the thing. All the distinguishing features of the object are completely determined in and for such an intuition; and to this extent the intuition can be related to the thing, and the I remains passively affected in this intuition. Nevertheless, this intuition is also an action of the I and can therefore be related to the I that is actively engaged in forming images. Hence, the I engaged in forming images has access to the intuition; the I determines the image that it forms in accordance with the determinations it discovers in this intuition. (Or, if you prefer — though the meaning is the same — the I freely peruses the determinations present in the image, enumerating and taking note of them.)[57]

(This mediating intuition[58] is of the greatest importance. Consequently, even though we will return to it later, let us immediately add a few remarks concerning it.

The mediating intuition is here postulated by means of a synthesis [of image and object], which must necessarily be present if any image of an object is to be possible. But the question still remains, from where does this intuition come? — Can this intuition not also be derived from somewhere else, since we are in the

[I, 376]   sphere of the actions of the rational mind, a sphere in which all actions are interconnected like the links of a chain? Of course it can. — Originally, the I produces the object. It is interrupted in this process of production, so that it can reflect upon the product of the same. What happens to the interrupted action as a result of this interruption? Is it completely annihilated and eradicated? This cannot be the case, since, were this action to be destroyed, then the entire thread of consciousness would be broken by this interruption, and no consciousness could

ever be deduced. Moreover, we were expressly required to reflect upon the product of this action, and that too would be impossible were the action to be completely canceled. And yet, it cannot possibly remain an action, because anything
at which an action is directed is, to that extent, not an action. But the product of
this action — namely, the object — must remain. What the interrupting action
[of reflection] is directed at, therefore, is this object; and, precisely because this
action is directed at this object and because it interrupts the first action, it
thereby makes this object into *something* — that is, it makes it into something
established and fixed.

Another question: Does this interrupting action, which we know to be directed
at the object, continue to exist as an action or not?

The I spontaneously interrupted its own action of producing in order to reflect
upon the product [of this action], and thus it interrupted its action of producing
in order to posit a new action in its place and — with specific reference to the
point at which we have now arrived in our inquiry — in order to posit this product [of this action] *as its own*. The I cannot simultaneously be engaged in acting
within two different relationships; consequently, the action directed at the object
is itself interrupted while an image is being formed. This first action is present
merely as a product; it is, after all, an immediate intuition directed at the object,   [I/3: 181]
and it is posited as such. Consequently, precisely the same intuition that was just
posited as a mediating factor here reveals itself as such [a mediating factor] — but
now from another angle.

This intuition is unconscious for exactly the same reason that it is present:
namely, because the I cannot act in two different ways at once and hence cannot
reflect on two objects simultaneously. In the present context, the I is regarded as
positing its product *as* such; that is, it is posited as engaged in forming images.
For this reason, it cannot simultaneously posit itself as immediately engaged in   [I, 377]
intuiting the thing.

This [mediating] intuition is the ground of all the harmony we assume to exist
between things and our representations of them.[59] As we have said, we draft an
image spontaneously, and it is easy to explain and to justify how we are able to
view this image as our own product and to posit it within ourselves. But this
image is also supposed to correspond to something outside us — to something
that was neither produced nor determined by this image, to something that exists
independently of the image and in accordance with its own laws. It is by no means
easy to see what right we have to make such a claim, or even to see how we could
ever come to make this claim in the first place, unless we at the same time possess
an immediate intuition of the thing. If we convince ourselves that such an immediate intuition is necessary, we will not be able to resist for very long the conviction that the thing [which is immediately intuited] must lie within ourselves,
since we cannot act directly upon anything except ourselves.)

As we have just seen, the I is completely free while engaged in forming images.
The image possesses the specific character that it does because the I determines
the image in one way rather than another (which, of course, it could also have
done in this regard). Because it is freely determined, the image can be related to
the I and can be posited *within* the I as its product.

However, this image is not supposed to be empty. It is supposed to correspond to a thing outside the I, and it must therefore be related to this thing. We have just indicated how the I gains access to the thing, thus making possible the relationship between the two: namely, by means of an immediate intuition of the thing, an intuition that must be presupposed. Insofar as it is related to the thing, the image is completely determined: it has to be precisely *this* image and not some other one, because the thing is completely determined, and the image is supposed [I, 378] to correspond to it. This complete determination is the ground of the relation [I/3: 182] between the image and the thing. Not the slightest difference now remains between the image and the immediate intuition of the thing.

In saying this, we are obviously contradicting what was said before; for anything that must necessarily be what it is and can be nothing else is not a product of the I, nor can it be posited in the I or related to it. (In any case, as has been frequently remarked, the I is not immediately conscious of its freedom in forming images. However, we have shown that, insofar as the I posits the image, it posits it as its own product, since it also posits this image as capable of possessing other possible determinations. This conclusion cannot be overturned by any subsequent operation of reason. If, however, the I immediately relates precisely this image to the thing, then it no longer posits this image as its own product. The I is no longer in the same situation as before, and there is no connection between its previous situation and its present one, except for a connection that might be imposed by a possible observer, who thinks of the I that is acting in both situations as one and the same I. What previously was only an image is now a thing. Of course, it must be a simple matter for the I to return to its previous level of reflection. Yet again, however, this will facilitate no connection [between the image and the thing]; what was previously only a thing will now be an image once again. If, while engaged in this operation, the rational mind did not proceed according to a law, which it is our present task to discover, then there would arise a lasting doubt about whether there are only things and no representations of them, or only representations and no corresponding things. Sometimes we would consider what is present in us to be a mere product of our power of imagination, and sometimes we would consider it to be a thing that affects us without any participation on our part. Such wavering uncertainty really does arise if one forces someone unaccustomed to such inquiries to concede that the representation of a thing may be found only within himself. One moment he admits it, and the next [I, 379] moment he will declare, "But it is, nevertheless, outside of me!" And then the very next moment he may perhaps once again think that it is supposed to be inside him, until he is once again forced to situate it outside himself. He cannot rescue himself from this difficulty, and this is because, even if he has always obeyed the laws of reason in all his theoretical proceedings, he possesses no scientific acquaintance with these laws and cannot provide an account of them.)

The Idea [*Idee*] of the law we are seeking would be as follows: An image must not be possible at all without a thing, and a thing must not be possible (at least in the respect that here concerns us: that is, possible as something for the I) without [I/3: 183] an image. In this way, the image and the thing would be synthetically connected, and neither could be posited without positing the other.

The I is supposed to relate the image to the thing. We have to show that this relationship is impossible unless the image *as such* (that is, as a free product of the I) is presupposed. If the requisite relationship is the only thing that makes the thing possible at all, then by corroborating the last assertion, we will have succeeded in proving that the thing is not possible without the image. — Conversely, The I is supposed to produce the image freely. It must be shown that this is impossible unless the thing is presupposed, and it will thereby have been demonstrated that no image is possible without a thing (a thing for the I, as goes without saying).

Let us first discuss the relationship of the image (completely determined, of course) to the thing. They are related to each other by the I. The I, however, is not immediately conscious of this act [of relating], and it is therefore not easy to see how the image could be distinguished from the thing. Consequently, the I must be present within consciousness, at least indirectly. This would make it possible to distinguish the image from the thing.[60]

That the I is indirectly present within consciousness means that the object of the I's activity (that is, the unconscious product of this activity) is posited as a freely produced product — that it is posited as capable of being something else, as contingent.

The thing is posited in this way insofar as the completely determined image is [I, 380] related to it. A completely determined image — that is, a property (the color red, for example) — is present, and, if the requisite relationship is to be possible, the thing must be present as well. This image and this thing are supposed to be synthetically united by an absolute action of the I.[61] The thing is supposed to be determined by the property. Consequently, the thing must not be determined by this property prior to this absolute action nor independently of it; instead, the thing must be posited as something to which this property can either pertain or not pertain. A thing's set of properties is posited as contingent for the I only because an acting is posited. But precisely because its set of properties is contingent, the thing reveals that it is presupposed to be a product of the I — a product to which nothing pertains except being. The free action [of the I] and the necessity that such an action occur provide the sole basis for the transition from what is undetermined to what is determined, and vice versa.

(We will attempt to make this important point even clearer. — In the judgment "A is red," "A" occurs first. A is posited, and insofar as A is supposed to be A, the proposition A = A is valid in this case. Qua A, A is completely determined by itself — with respect, for instance, to its form, its magnitude, its position in space, etc. (as one can imagine in the present case). Note that this is true, despite the fact [I/3: 184] that nothing at all pertains to the thing we were just discussing, since it is still utterly indeterminate nothing, that is, pertains to it beyond the fact that it is a thing, which is to say, beyond the fact that it *is*. "*Red*" is what occurs next in the judgment. Red is also something completely determinate: it is posited as excluding all other colors, as not yellow, not blue, etc. — This is precisely what happened above, and thus we here have an example of what we mean by "the complete determination of the property" or, as we have also called it, "the image."[62] — Now what is the relation between [object] A and the color red prior to this judgment?

Obviously, this remains undetermined. Any colors, including red, could pertain to A. What is undetermined becomes determined only as a result of the judgment, that is, only as a result of the synthetic action accomplished by the power of imagination of the person judging, and this action is expressed in the copula "*is*."

[I, 381] When the predicate "red" (= "not-yellow," "not-blue," etc.) is applied to A, A is thereby deprived of all those possible colors (yellow, blue, etc.) that might have pertained to it. — Just as surely as an act of judgment occurs at all, A has to be something undetermined. If A were already determined, then no judgment would be passed and no action would occur.)

The result of our inquiry is the following proposition: *If the reality of a thing* (qua *substance) is presupposed, all the properties of that thing are posited as contingent. Hence they are indirectly posited as products of the I.* In this case, therefore, what the I is attached to is the set of the thing's properties [*die Beschaffenheit im Dinge*].

In order to secure a better overview, let us sketch here the systematic schema that must guide us in discovering the final solution to our question. The validity of this schema was demonstrated in the *Foundation of the Entire Wissenschaftslehre*, in the course of discussing the concept of reciprocal interaction.[63] — The I posits itself as totality; that is to say, it determines itself.[64] This is possible only if the I excludes from itself something by means of which it is limited. If A is the totality, then B is what is excluded. — But just as surely as B is excluded, it is also posited. B is supposed to be posited by the I, which can posit A as the totality only on this condition. Consequently, the I must also reflect upon B as something posited. But in that case A is no longer the totality. When B is posited, A is itself excluded from the totality (which is how we expressed it in the *Foundation*). Consequently, what is posited is A + B. — A + B must in turn be reflected upon in their *unity* with one another. Otherwise, A and B would not be united. By means of this act of reflection, A + B is itself limited; hence it is posited as the totality, and, in accordance with

[I/3: 185] the previously indicated rule, something must be posited in opposition to it. — Insofar as A + B is posited as the totality through the indicated act of reflection, it is equated with that A (in this case, the I) which is posited absolutely as the totality. That is to say, A + B is, in the sense with which we are now familiar, posited and absorbed into the I. To this extent, B is posited in opposition to the totality and, since B is here contained in A + B, B is posited in opposition to itself,

[I, 382] inasmuch as it is partly united with A (contained in the I) and partly opposed to A (posited in opposition to the I). According to the formula stated and demonstrated above, A + B is determined by B. — "A + B determined by B" must now be reflected upon as such, that is, insofar as A + B is determined by B. — But since B is supposed to be determined by B, then that A which is synthetically united with B must also be determined by B. Furthermore, since B and B are supposed to be synthetically united, that A which is united with the first B must also be synthetically united therewith.[65] This contradicts our first proposition, according to which A and B are supposed to be posited purely and simply in opposition to each other. This contradiction can be resolved only if A is posited in opposition to itself, which would mean that A + B is determined by A, as was required in the explication of the concept of reciprocal interaction. But if the required synthesis is to be possible, then A cannot be posited in opposition to itself. From this it follows that A must be simultaneously equal to itself and posited in opposition to itself, and hence there must be some action of the absolute power of the I (the power of imagination) which unifies A absolutely. — Guided by this schema, let us new resume our inquiry.

If A is the totality and is posited as such, then B is excluded. — To the extent that it drafts an image with absolute freedom, oscillating between several possible ways of freely determining it, the I indirectly posits itself as I and limits itself. The image is not yet determined, but it is becoming determined, and the I is caught up in the action of determining. What we are here referring to is the same state [of the I] that was fully described above. Let us call it A (= the inner intuition engaged in by the I while it is freely forming images[66]).

Insofar as the I acts in this manner, it posits the completely determined property in opposition to the freely oscillating image and indirectly posits it in opposition to the I itself, which is engaged in freely forming this image. We have already shown above how the completely determined property is included in and apprehended by the I. This act of positing the property in opposition [to the image and thus in opposition to the I] occurs by means of the immediate intuition of the thing, in which, however, the I is not conscious of itself. This [I, 383] determinate [property] is not posited as I; instead, it is posited in opposition to the I and hence excluded from it. Let us call it B.

B is posited, and consequently A is excluded from the totality. — The I posits the property as something determinate, and it cannot posit itself as free in this action of forming images (as it is supposed to do), unless it posits the property in this manner. Consequently, just as surely as the I is supposed to posit itself as freely forming images, it must reflect upon the determinacy of the property [B]. (Here [I/3: 186] we are not concerned with the synthetic union of several characteristic features [*Merkmale*] in a single substrate. Nor, as will become immediately evident, are we concerned with the synthetic union of these characteristic features with the substrate. Instead, what we are concerned with is the complete determinacy of the representing I when it apprehends a characteristic feature. As an example of such a characteristic feature one might imagine the shape of a body in space.) By positing a determinate property, the I is excluded from the totality. That is to say, the I is no longer self-sufficient; it is no longer determined by itself, but instead by something posited completely in opposition to itself. Its state (that is, the image it contains) can no longer be explained solely on the basis of the I, but only by something outside the I. Consequently, what is posited as the totality is A + B, or A determined by B (externally determined pure intuition). (With regard to these present distinctions in general, and particularly with regard to the ones we are currently making, it is important to note that nothing whatsoever corresponding to each of these individual distinctions could occur within consciousness. The actions of the human mind described here do not occur in the soul separately, nor do we claim that they do. Everything we are now establishing occurs in synthetic unity. We are advancing steadily along the synthetic path, inferring the presence of one link from the presence of the others. An example of the sort of intuition here deduced would be the intuition of any pure geometrical form — of

[I, 384] a cube, for example. But such an intuition is impossible. One cannot imagine a cube without at the same time imagining the space in which it is supposed to be suspended and then describing its limits. At the same time, the proposition "the I cannot posit a limit without at the same time positing something limiting, which is excluded by this limit" is here demonstrated in sensible experience.)

A + B *must be reflected upon and indeed must be reflected upon in this connection with one another.* That is, the property [B] must be reflected upon *as a determinate* [property]. Otherwise, the property would not be present in the I, nor would the requisite consciousness of it be possible. We are therefore driven beyond our present standpoint by something that is itself included within this standpoint (just as the I that is the object of our inquiry is similarly driven): this is precisely the essence of synthesis. Here lies that X of which we have often spoken and which testifies to the incompleteness [of our inquiry]. — Like every act of reflection, this one too occurs absolutely spontaneously. The I reflects purely and simply because it is an I. For reasons that have frequently been cited, the I is not conscious of the spontaneity of its own action.

[I/3: 187] Nevertheless, the object of its reflection (insofar as it is such) thereby becomes the product of that spontaneity and must therefore display the characteristic feature of any product of the I's free action: namely, *contingency*. But this product cannot be contingent insofar as it is posited as *determinate* and is reflected upon as such. It must, therefore, be contingent in some other respect, as will immediately become evident. — In consequence of the contingency that pertains to it, it becomes a product of and is absorbed into the I. In this way, the I once again determines itself, and this is not possible unless it posits something (namely, a Not-I) in opposition to itself.

(Let me at this point make a general remark, for which the groundwork has already been laid, but which would not have been clear before now. The I reflects freely. This is an action of determining, which, precisely for that reason, is itself determined.[67] The I, however, cannot reflect or posit a limit without at the same time absolutely producing something else as a limiting agent. Hence, *determining* and *producing* always go together, and this is the basis of the identity of consciousness.)

[I, 385] What is posited in opposition is *necessary* in relation to a determinate property. In relation to what is posited in opposition to such a property itself, such a property is *contingent*. Moreover, like the property itself, that which is posited in opposition to it is posited in opposition to the I. Consequently, like the property itself, what is posited in opposition to this property is also a Not-I, but a *necessary* Not-I.

According to the above explication, however, the property in question, as something determinate, and *insofar* as it is determinate (that is, something to which the I relates merely passively) must be excluded from the I. And the I, when and insofar as it reflects upon something determinate (as is the case here), must exclude this determinate thing from itself. In the present reflection the I also excludes from itself another Not-I, considered as something that is both determinate and necessary. Therefore, both the determinate property in question and what is posited in opposition to it must be related to each other and synthetically united. The ground for uniting them is that, in relation to the I, both Not-I's are one and the same.[68] The ground for distinguishing them from each other is that the property [one of the Not-I's] *is contingent* and could be different, but the substrate [the other Not-I] is, as such, necessary in relation to the property. — Both are united; that is, they are necessary and contingent in relation to each other. The property must have a substrate, but this property does not have to pertain to this substrate. Such a relationship of synthetic unity between what is contingent and what is necessary is termed a relationship of *substantiality*. — (B is posited in opposition to B. The latter B is by no means included in the I. — A + B is determined by B. Though the image that is absorbed into the I — and which is, in itself, completely determined — may always be as determined as one could wish for the I, in relationship to the thing [that is, to its substrate] the property that is expressed in this image is contingent. This property might also not have pertained to this thing.) [I/3: 188]

The B that was excluded in the previous operation must now be reflected upon. We recognize this B as the necessary Not-I, as opposed to the contingent Not-I, which is contained in the I.[69] It immediately follows from this reflection that A + B, which was previously posited as the totality, can no longer be the totality; that is, it can no longer be the unique content of the I, and, to that extent, it could be contingent. A + B must be determined by something necessary. *First of all*, the [I, 386] property, the distinguishing feature, the image (or whatever one wishes to call it) must be determined by the necessary Not-I. This property was posited as a contingent feature of the thing, which was itself posited as something necessary. Hence, the property and the thing are posited in complete opposition to each other. As surely, however, as the I is supposed to reflect upon them both, they must be united in this I, which is one and the same. This is accomplished by the absolute spontaneity of the I. The union in question is solely a product of the I. This union is posited; that is to say, *a product is posited by the I.* — But the I is never immediately conscious of its own acting; it is conscious of it only in and through the product of this acting. Consequently, the union of the property and the thing must itself be posited as contingent. Moreover, since everything contingent is posited as originating through acting, this union must be posited as originating through acting. — That which is, with respect to its existence, contingent and dependent upon something else cannot be posited as acting. Only that which is necessary can be so posited. In and by means of reflection, the concept of acting (which actually lies only in the subject engaged in reflecting) is transferred to what is necessary,[70] and what is contingent is thereby posited as the product of what is necessary, as an expression of the free activity of the latter. Such a synthetic relationship is called a relationship of *causal efficacy*; and the thing in question, viewed as containing within itself a synthetic union of what is necessary and what is contingent, is the *actual* thing.

At this supremely important juncture we will add a few remarks:[71]

1.) The indicated action of the I is obviously one accomplished in intuition by the power of imagination. This is because, on the one hand, the I, in this action, unites things posited in utter opposition to each other (which is the task of the power of imagination), while on the other hand, in so acting, the I transfers to the object of its acting something lying within the I (which is a characteristic feature of intuition).

2.) Accordingly, the so-called category of causal efficacy [*Wirksamkeit*] here reveals itself as originating solely in the power of imagination. And so it is: nothing can enter the understanding except by means of the power of imagination. Here we can already foresee what alterations the understanding will make in this product of the power of imagination. It was because the power of imagination transfers its own *free* acting to the thing that we posited the thing as *acting freely* and not in accordance *with any* rules. (Hence, until the understanding comprehends and grasps its own mode of acting, the thing, along with all of its possible modifications, is posited within consciousness as *fate*.) What is lacking is any conformity *to law*. If the constrained understanding is directed at a thing, then that thing will behave in accordance with a rule, just as does the understanding.

[I, 387]

[I/3: 189]

3.) For Kant, the categories were originally generated *as forms of thinking*, and, from his point of view, this was quite correct.[72] But in order to make possible the application of these categories to objects, Kant needed the schemata produced by the power of imagination.[73] For Kant, therefore, as well as for us, the categories are worked up by the imagination and are accessible to it. According to the *Wissenschaftslehre*, the categories arise *together with the objects*, and, in order to make the objects possible at all; they arise from the power of imagination itself.

4.) Maimon and the *Wissenschaftslehre* say the same thing about the category of causal efficacy, but he calls this procedure of the human mind a deception.[74] We have already seen elsewhere[75] that we cannot call something a deception if it conforms to the laws of rational beings and is, according to these laws, purely and simply necessary and unavoidable — unless, that is, we want to cease to be rational beings. The real point of contention, however, is the following: Maimon would say, "I am prepared to concede that there are a priori laws of thinking, as you have shown." (This is in fact a large concession, for how can there be present in the human mind a mere law without any application, an empty form without matter?) "But even if I concede the existence of these laws," Maimon would continue, "only the power of imagination can apply them to objects. Hence, in applying these laws to objects, both the object and the law must be present in the power of imagination at the same time. How then does the power of imagination gain access to the object?" This question can be answered only as follows: The power of imagination must itself produce the object (as is demonstrated in the *Wissenschaftslehre* on the basis of arguments quite independent of the present problem). — The error lies in thinking that the object is supposed to be something other than a product of the power of imagination. It is true that this error is confirmed by a

[I/3: 190]

[I, 388]

literal interpretation of Kant, but it is in complete contradiction to his *spirit*. To maintain that the object is not a product of the power of imagination is to become a transcendent dogmatist and to depart completely from the spirit of the Critical philosophy.

5.) Maimon doubted merely the applicability of the law of causal efficacy,[76] though, in accordance with his own principles, he could have doubted the applicability of all a priori laws. — This is what Hume did when he observed that you yourselves are the ones who contain the concept of causal efficacy within yourselves and transfer it to things, and this is why your knowledge possesses no objective validity.[77] Kant concedes him this premise, not only for the concept of causal efficacy, but for all a priori con- [I/3: 191] cepts. But Kant rejects Hume's conclusion by proving that an object can exist only for some possible subject. This dispute never touched upon the question of how — that is, by means of what power of the subject — that which is in the subject is transferred to the object. Maimon demonstrates that only the power of imagination can apply the law of causal efficacy to objects, and from this he concludes that our cognition possesses no objective validity and that the application of the laws of our thinking to objects is therefore a mere deception. The *Wissenschaftslehre* concedes him his premise — not only for the law of causal efficacy, but for all a priori laws. However, by means of a more detailed determination of the object (one already contained in the Kantian determination of the same), the *Wissenschaftslehre* shows that it is for precisely this reason that our knowledge possesses objective validity and that it could possess such validity only under this condition. — Skepticism and Criticism thus continue along their monotonous paths, each remaining forever true to itself. Only in a very improper sense can it be said that the Critical phi- [I, 389] losopher refutes the skeptic; instead, he concedes everything the skeptic demands and usually even more. He merely limits the demands that the skeptic — like, for the most part, the dogmatist — makes concerning cognition of the thing in itself, and he accomplishes this by showing such demands to be unfounded.)

As we observed above, what we now recognize to be an expression of the otherwise free activity of the thing and to be completely determined thereby is [I/3: 192] posited in and determined for the I. Accordingly, the I itself is indirectly determined by the thing. It ceases to be an I and itself becomes a product of the thing, because what fills and stands in for the I is a product of the thing. It is by means of these expressions of itself that the thing affects the I, which is, therefore, no longer an I at all (that which is self-posited); instead, in this determination, it is the I that is posited by the thing. ([Hence one speaks of] the effect of the thing upon the I, or the "physical influence" of the Lockeans and those more recent eclectics who piece together an incoherent whole from completely heterogenous parts of the Leibnizian and Lockean systems. From the present standpoint — but only from this standpoint — such talk is entirely justified.) — This is what we discover when we reflect upon "A + B determined by B."

This is impossible; hence, "A + B determined by B" must again be posited in the I or, in accordance with our formula, "determined by A."

First of all, A (i.e., the effect the thing is supposed to produce in the I) is posited as contingent with respect to the I. Consequently, an I that necessarily exists in and through itself (the I in itself) is posited in opposition to this effect within the I and posited in opposition to the I itself, to the extent that the I is determined by this effect. What is necessary (the I in itself) is here posited in opposition to what is contingent in the I, just as what is necessary in the Not-I (the thing in itself) was previously posited in opposition to what is contingent in the Not-I.

[I, 390]   Moreover, just as was the case with the thing in itself, this necessary I is a product of the I itself. What is necessary is substance; what is contingent is an accident thereof. — Both the contingent I and the necessary I must be posited as synthetically united, that is, as one and the same I. But what is contingent and what is necessary are posited in absolute opposition to each other; consequently, they can be united only by an absolute activity of the I. As before, the I is not immediately conscious of this activity; instead, it transfers it to the object of reflection and thereby posits a relationship of causal efficacy between the two: the contingent I is the effect of the reflecting activity of the absolute I. What is contingent is an expression of the I and, to this extent, is something actual for the I.[78] The fact that what is contingent is supposed to be an effect of the Not-I is completely abstracted from in this act of reflection, for something cannot at the same time be an effect of the I and an effect of what is posited in opposition to it, the Not-I. The thing and its expression are thereby excluded from and posited in complete opposition to the I. — Both the I and the Not-I necessarily exist in themselves and completely independently of each other. Through its own activity and force, each

[I/3: 193]   expresses its independence. Since we have not yet subsumed this activity and this force under any laws, they are still completely free.

We have now deduced how we come to posit an active I in opposition to an active Not-I and come to regard them as completely independent of each other. To this extent, the Not-I exists as such and is determined by itself. For the Not-I, the fact that the I entertains a representation of the Not-I is something contingent or accidental. Similarly, the I exists and acts through itself, and, for the I, it is contingent that it has representations of the Not-I. The expression of the thing within the realm of appearance is a product of the thing, but this same appearance is a product of the I, inasmuch as it exists for and is comprehended by the I.

The I cannot act unless it has an object; therefore, the causal efficacy of the Not-I is posited by the causal efficacy of the I. The Not-I can exercise an effect, but it cannot affect the I unless the I exercises an effect as well. When we posit a causal efficacy of the Not-I *for the I* we simultaneously posit the causal efficacy of the

[I, 391]   I. The expressions of both forces are therefore necessarily synthetically unified, and the ground of their unification (which we previously called their "harmony"[79]) is something that must be demonstrated.

Like every unification we have indicated so far, this one occurs absolutely spontaneously. That which is freely posited is characterized by contingency; consequently, the present synthetic unity must also be contingent. — Acting was transferred above [from the I to the Not-I]; consequently, it has already been posited and cannot be posited again. What remains, therefore, is the contingent unity of acting, that is, the accidental encounter of the causal efficacy of the I and the causal efficacy of the Not-I *in some third thing, which neither is nor can be anything more than that in which the I and the Not-I encounter one another* [*Zusammentreffen*]. We will call this third thing *a point*.

§ 4. The Intuition Is Determined in Time; What Is Intuited Is Determined in Space

According to the previous §, the intuition is supposed to be found within the I, as one of its accidents. Consequently, the I must posit itself as the intuiting subject; it must determine the intuition with respect to itself. This proposition is postulated in the theoretical part of the *Wissenschaftslehre* in accordance with the following foundational principle: nothing pertains to the I except what it posits within itself.

We will here follow the same plan of inquiry as in the previous §, with the differ- [I/3: 194] ence that there we were speaking of *something*, namely, an intuition, whereas here we are speaking only of a *relationship*, that is, of a synthetic unification of intuitions posited in opposition to each other. Thus, whereas in the preceding section we reflected upon a single component [*Glied*], what we will have to reflect upon here are two opposing components in their connection with each other; hence, what was there something singular will here always be something threefold.[80]

I.) Intuition, in the sense determined above (that is, the synthetic unification of [I, 392] the causal efficacies of the I and the Not-I through their contingent encounter at a single point) is posited and absorbed into the I. In other words, *the intuition is posited as something contingent* (in the sense with which we are now sufficiently familiar). — Note that nothing that has ever been established in intuition may be altered; instead, everything must be carefully retained. The intuition merely becomes *further* determined, while all of those specific determinations which have previously been posited remain.

As an intuition, intuition X is posited as contingent. This means that another intuition is posited in opposition to this first intuition [= X] — not another object, another specific determination [of X], or something of that sort, but rather (and this is very important!) another completely determined *intuition* = Y. In contrast to the first intuition, X, this second intuition, Y, is necessary; in contrast to Y, X is contingent. To this extent Y is completely excluded from the I that intuits X.

X, being an intuition, necessarily occupies a single point; so does Y, qua intuition, but it occupies a point posited in opposition to the first point and completely distinct from it. What the one is the other is not.

The question is simply this: What is the necessity that is attributed to intuition Y in relation to intuition X, and what is the contingency attributed to X in relation to Y? The answer is as follows: If intuition X is supposed to be united with its point, then intuition Y is necessarily synthetically united with its point. The possibility of synthetically unifying X with its point presupposes the unification of intuition Y with its point, but not vice versa. The I posits that another intuition could be posited at that point where X is posited. But if X is to be posited as an intuition of the I, then it is purely and simply the case that nothing but Y can be posited at the point where Y is posited.

[I, 393]   Only insofar as the contingent character of this synthesis is posited can X be posited as an intuition of the I. And only insofar as the necessity of a similar synthesis [Y] is posited in opposition to the contingency of X can the contingency of this synthesis itself be posited.

[I/3: 195]   (There remains, of course, a far more difficult question: How else can point X be determined and determinable, except by means of intuition X? And how else can point Y be determined, except by means of intuition Y? Until now, the point in question has been nothing more than the point of encounter between the causal efficacies of the I and the Not-I. It is this synthesis, and it alone, that makes intuition possible. This is precisely how this point was presented in the previous §. It is now clear that, if point X is to be posited as a point at which another intuition could be posited, and if, in contrast, point Y is to be posited as a point at which no other intuition could be posited, then both points must be separable from their respective intuitions, and it must be possible to distinguish these points from one another independently of these intuitions. To be sure, we cannot yet see *how* this is possible, but we can see *that* it must be possible if any intuition is ever to be attributed to the I.)

     II.) If A is posited as the totality, then B is excluded. If A is the image that is supposed to be freely determined, then B is the property that is determined without the participation of the I. — According to the previous §, a specific object X is excluded [from the I] in intuition X, insofar as X is supposed to be an intuition at all. Similarly, in Y, the intuition that is posited in opposition to X, [a specific object Y is also excluded from the I]. Both objects are determined as such; that is say that in intuiting these objects the mind is forced to posit them exactly *as* it posits them. This determinacy must remain, and there is no question of changing it.

     But any existing relationship between these two intuitions must necessarily also exist between their objects. From this it follows that object X must be *contingent* in relation to object Y, and object Y must be *necessary* in relation to object
[I, 394] X. The determination of X necessarily presupposes that of Y, but not vice versa.

     Both objects, *simply insofar as they are objects of intuition*, are completely determined, and their requisite relationship to each other cannot be based on this determinacy. Instead, it must be based on some determinacy that is still completely unknown: namely, a determinacy through which something becomes, not an object of intuition in general, but an object of an intuition that can be distinguished from all other intuitions. This requisite determination does not pertain to the object's *inner* determination (insofar as the proposition A = A applies to it); instead, it is an external determination of this object. Since it is impossible for an intuition to be posited in the I without the requisite distinction [between it, as contingent, and another necessary intuition], and since this same [external]
[I/3:196] determination is a condition for the requisite distinction, it follows that the object in question is an object of intuition only on the condition of such determinacy,

and moreover, that such determinacy is the exclusive condition for all intuition. For the time being, we shall call this unknown something, which is supposed to determine the object, O; we shall call the way in which Y is determined by this unknown something z; and we shall call the way in which X is determined by it v.

The reciprocal relationship between all of these terms is as follows: X must be posited as capable of being either synthetically united or not united with v, and hence v must be posited as capable of being synthetically united either with X or with any other object. Y, on the other hand, must be posited as necessarily syn-thetically united with z, if X is supposed to be united with v. — *Inasmuch as* v is posited as something which either is or is not *to be united* with X, Y is necessarily posited as *united* with z. From this it immediately follows that any possible object can be united with v — any object, that is, except Y, since Y is already inseparably united [with z]. Similarly, X can be united with any possible O except z, which is inseparably united with Y. Hence X is purely and simply excluded from z.

X and Y are totally excluded from the I, which completely forgets and loses itself in their intuition. Consequently, the relationship between X and Y (which is what we are discussing here) cannot in any way be derived from the I; instead, [I, 395] this relationship must be *attributed to the things themselves*. This relationship does not appear to the I to be dependent on its freedom, but instead to be determined by the things. — The relationship in question was as follows: since z is united with Y, X is purely and simply excluded from z. As applied to the things, this relation-ship must be expressed as follows: Y excludes X from z and thereby determines X negatively. If Y extends to point d, then X is excluded up to that point; if Y extends to point c, X is excluded only that far, etc. Since, however, the sole reason why X cannot be united with z is that it is excluded from z by Y, and since this exclusion obviously remains in force only so long as the reason for it continues to pertain, then it follows that X definitely begins where Y ceases to exclude it or comes to an end. X and Y are therefore continuous.

This act of excluding as well as this continuity are possible only if X and Y pertain to a common sphere (with which, of course, we are still completely unacquainted) and if they encounter each other at a *single* point within this sphere. The positing of this sphere constitutes the synthetic unification of X and Y in the requisite relationship. Consequently, such a common sphere is produced by the absolute spontaneity of the power of imagination.

III.) If the B that was excluded [from the I, considered as the totality] is reflected upon, then A is thereby excluded from the totality (i.e., from the I). B, however, was absorbed into the I precisely by means of reflection; hence, B is itself posited as united with A qua totality (insofar as this totality is contingent). Therefore, another B, in relation to which the first B is contingent, must be excluded or pos-ited in opposition to [the first] B, and this second B must be considered to be something necessary. We will apply this general principle to the present case.   [I/3: 197]

As we have shown, Y is now determined as synthetically united with an O, which is still completely unknown; similarly, X is at least *negatively* determined in relation to and by means of O. X cannot be determined by O in the same way that Y is; instead, it must be determined in an opposing way. X is therefore excluded [I, 396] from determining Y.

Insofar as both X and Y are united with or absorbed into the I (as happens in this case), they must be posited as contingent *in this respect as well*. This means, first of all, that a necessary X and a necessary Y (in relation to which the present X and the present Y are both contingent) are posited in opposition to the X and Y that are absorbed into the I, following the procedure deduced in the previous §. This necessary X and this necessary Y are the substances to which the contingent X and Y pertain as accidents.

Without dwelling any longer on this step in our inquiry, let us proceed at once to the synthetic unification of what is now posited as contingent and what is posited as necessary in opposition to what is contingent, a synthetic unification that was also deduced above. This synthetic unification is as follows: the Y that was absorbed into the I (and was to that extent contingent) is an appearance, a result or expression of force Y, a force that was necessarily presupposed. The same is true of X; indeed, both [the contingent] Y and [the contingent] X are expressions *of free* forces.

Whatever relationship exists between Y and X qua appearances must also exist between the forces they express. Consequently, the expression of force Y is completely independent of the expression of force X. On the other hand, however, the expression of force X depends upon and is conditioned by the expression of force Y.

I asserted that X is *conditioned* by Y; that is to say, the expression of force Y does not determine the expression of force X *positively*. Nothing deduced so far would lend the slightest support to the claim that the expression of force Y positively determines the expression of force X. The reason why the expression of X has precisely the character it has and not some other specific character is not to be found in the expression of Y. However, the expression of force Y does determine the expression of force X *negatively*, since the reason why X *cannot* express itself in a certain specific way among all those that are possible is to be found in Y.

This appears to contradict what was said above. It is expressly posited that both X and Y are supposed to express themselves by means of free, purely and simply unrestricted causal efficacy. But, according to the preceding inference, the expression of X is supposed to be conditioned by the expression of Y. For the moment, we can explain this only negatively: X, no less than Y, produces an effect purely and simply because it produces an effect. Accordingly, the causal efficacy of Y is not, as it were, the condition for the causal efficacy of X as such and with respect [I, 397] to its form. Our proposition should by no means be taken to mean that Y affects or influences X, that it forces and drives X to express itself. — Moreover, in the [I/3: 198] manner in which it expresses itself, X is completely free, as is Y, and this is why Y cannot condition and determine the way in which X produces an effect. Y cannot determine the content of X. It is therefore important to ask what possible relationship could nevertheless remain [between Y and X], which would enable the causal efficacy of the one to condition the causal efficacy of the other.

Both Y and X are supposed to be synthetically related to a completely unknown O. This is because, as we have shown, just as surely as an intuition is supposed to be appropriated by the I, Y and X are necessarily related to each other in a certain way only in respect of their relationship to O. Consequently, each must be independently related to O. (This is the same sort of inference I could make if I did not know whether A and B were of a specific size, but knew that A was bigger than B. From this I could infer that A and B must, in any case, each have their own determinate magnitude.)

O must be something that leaves the free causal efficacy of both [force] X and [force] Y unimpaired; for both are supposed to operate freely (as was expressly required) and are supposed to be synthetically united with O in, during, and without detriment to their exercise of free causal efficacy. Everything at which the causal efficacy of a force is directed (in other words, every object of a force, for this is the only kind of synthetic unification with which we are as yet acquainted) necessarily limits — through its own resistance — the causal efficacy of the force in question. Consequently, O can possess no force, no activity, nor any intensity; it can have no effect at all. It follows that O possesses no reality whatsoever; it is nothing. — What O may yet turn out to be is something we shall perhaps see later. The relationship established above was as follows: Y and z are synthetically united, and, as a result, X is excluded from z. As we have just seen, this synthetic unification of Y with z is something that occurred by means of the free, undisturbed causal efficacy of Y's own inner force. Nevertheless, z is in no way the product of this causal efficacy itself; instead, z is merely necessarily united with [I, 398] the force in question. Therefore, it must always be possible to distinguish z from a product of [force] Y's causal efficacy. In addition, it is precisely through this unification that the causal efficacy of [force] X and of its product is *excluded* from z. From this it follows that z is Y's *sphere of causal efficacy.* — And, according to what was said above, z is *nothing but this sphere.* In itself, z is nothing; it possesses no reality, and nothing can be predicated of it except what has already been deduced. — Moreover, z is *purely* and *exclusively* Y's sphere of causal efficacy. This is because, by being posited as such, [force] X, along with every possible object of X, is excluded from Y. Y's sphere of causal efficacy and z are one and the same; they are equivalent. z is nothing more than this sphere, and this sphere is nothing other than z. If Y exercises no causal efficacy, then z is nothing; and Y exercises no causal efficacy if z does not exist. Y's causal efficacy *fills* z; that is to say, it excludes from z everything that does not pertain to Y's causal efficacy. (We should not yet think of any [spatial] extension, for none has yet been demonstrated; nor should [I/3: 199] extension be introduced surreptitiously, merely by employing the term.)

If z extends to points c, d, e, etc., then X's causal efficacy is excluded as far as c, d, e, etc. But the sole reason that X's causal efficacy cannot be united with z is that it is excluded from z by Y. From this it follows that there is a necessary continuity between the spheres of efficacy of X and Y and that they encounter one another at a single point. The power of imagination unites both spheres of efficacy and posits z and -z, or, as was determined above, v = 0.[81]

Yet the causal efficacy of X is supposed to be excluded from z without any detriment to X's freedom. But if the filling of z by Y involves the negation or cancellation of anything in X — if, that is, it makes impossible some expression of X's force, an expression that would, by itself, be possible — then this exclusion [of X from z] does not occur without detriment to X's free causal efficacy. Consequently, the filling of z by the causal efficacy of X must *by no means be a possible expression of X*. X must include no tendency whatsoever to fill z. X contains within itself the

reason why z is not included within its sphere of causal efficacy; or rather, there is nothing in X that could be the ground of its having z within its sphere of efficacy.
[I, 399]   Otherwise, X would be restricted rather than free.

Y and X thus encounter one another contingently at a single point, a point at which absolute opposites are joined in absolute synthetic unity (see above). This encounter occurs without any reciprocal influence or encroachment between Y and X.

IV.) A + B is supposed to be determined by B. Until now, only B has been determined by B, though A has also been determined by B indirectly. Previously, A referred to what is in the I, and since there is nothing in the I but intuition, this means that the I itself is determined by the Not-I, and that what is in the I, what constitutes the I, is itself indirectly a product of the Not-I. Let us now apply this to the present case.

X is a product of the Not-I, and, with respect to its sphere of efficacy, it is determined in the I. The same is true of Y. Both are determined absolutely freely by themselves. In consequence of their contingent encounter, they both determine the point of this encounter as well, a point to which the I is only passively related.

This, however, is not the way it should be, nor can it be so. Just as surely as the I is an I, it must freely produce this determination. — We previously offered the following general solution to this difficulty: All reflection upon something qua substance (that is, as something enduring and causally efficacious) — which, once it has been posited as substance, is, of course, necessarily and synthetically related to its product and henceforth inseparable from it — is dependent upon the absolute freedom of the I. The present difficulty is resolved in the same manner: Whether the I does or does not wish to reflect upon Y and X as upon something *enduring* and *simple* is something that depends upon the absolute freedom of the
[I/3: 200]   I. Of course, if the I does reflect upon X and Y, then, in accordance with this rule, it has to posit Y in and as filling z, the sphere of its causal efficacy; and it has to posit C as the boundary point between the two spheres of causal efficacy [z and v]. But the I does not have to reflect upon Y and X; instead, it could, with absolute freedom, posit anything else as substance in their place
[I, 400]   In order to make this quite clear, one may imagine the spheres [of efficacy] z and v to be connected at point C (which is, in fact, how they have been posited). Instead of positing Y in sphere z, the I can posit a and b therein and make z into the sphere of efficacy for both a and b by dividing it at point g. Suppose that what is now a's sphere of efficacy is called h. If so, the I is also not compelled to posit as an indivisible substance in h; instead, it could posit e and d and then divide that point e into f and k, and so on, ad infinitum. However, according to the previously deduced rule, once the I has posited an a and a b, it must then assign them spheres of causal efficacy, which encounter each other at a single point.

For reasons that have already been indicated more than once, the I *must actually posit* this contingency of Y, as well as the contingency of Y's sphere of causal efficacy for the I, and do so *by means of the power of imagination*.

Consequently, O is posited as something *extended, connected,* and *infinitely divisible*; that is to say, O is *space*.

1.) *The power of imagination distinguishes space from the thing that actually occupies it*, and it accomplishes this (as it should) by positing the possibility of completely different substances with completely different spheres of causal efficacy occupying space z. In doing this, it projects an empty space. But it projects this empty space only experimentally and in passing, in order immediately to fill it again with whatever substances and attendant spheres of causal efficacy it pleases. Consequently, there is no empty space at all, except while the power of imagination is engaged in making the transition from filling the space with A to filling it with b, c, d, etc., as it chooses.

2.) The infinitely smallest part of space is still space, that is, something that possesses continuity; it is not a mere point or the border between determinate places in space. It is space, because something can be posited in it; moreover, insofar as space itself is posited, the power of imagination actually does posit something in it: namely, a force that necessarily expresses itself and cannot be posited at all without being posited as expressing itself (in conformity with the synthesis of free causal efficacy, which was dealt with in the previous §[82]). According to the synthesis [I, 401] undertaken in the present §, however, this force cannot express itself unless it has a sphere for its expression, one that is nothing but this sphere of its expression.

3.) Consequently, intension and extension [*Intensität und Extensität*] are [I/3: 201] necessarily and synthetically unified; one must not claim to deduce the one without the other. Every force necessarily fills a place in space. (Force does not fill space itself, because *it does not exist in space*; in itself, force is *nothing at all* unless it is expressed. Force fills space through its necessary product, which is the unifying ground of intension and extension.) Moreover, space is nothing other than what has been or will be filled by this product.

4.) The internal determinations of things relate solely to feelings (of greater or lesser approval or disapproval[83]) and are quite inaccessible to the theoretical power of the I. One feels, for example, that things are bitter or sweet, rough or smooth, heavy or light, red or white, etc. Apart from such internal determinations (which must here be completely ignored), things can be distinguished from each other only by the space they occupy. Consequently, the space a thing occupies pertains to it in such a way that it is attributable to the thing (and by no means to the I), but is nevertheless not part of the thing's inner nature.

5.) Space, morever, is everywhere the same. This is why it is impossible to distinguish and to determine anything on that basis, unless some thing (= Y) has already been posited in a certain space. The space in question can then be determined and characterized by Y, and it can now be said of X that it occupies a *different* space — different, obviously, from the space occupied by Y. All specific determinations of space presuppose a space that is filled and thereby determined. — If you were to posit A in infinite empty space, it would remain as undetermined as it was before. You could not tell me

[I, 402]

where A is, because you would have no determinate point by means of which you could measure it or from which you could orient yourself. The place occupied by A is determined by nothing except A, and A is determined by nothing but the place in space it occupies. Consequently, all [spatial] determination is purely and simply impossible unless you posit such a determination. This is an absolutely spontaneous synthesis [of a point in space with something that fills it]. — To express this same point in sensible terms: any intellect that had in view a point from which and a point toward which A was moving would be able to observe A as continually moving through space; you, however, would not notice this movement, because, for you [who posited A alone in infinite space], there would be no such points, but only boundless, empty space. For you, therefore, A would always remain in its place, just as certainly as it remains in space, since it occupies its place absolutely because you posit it there. Now posit B beside A. B is determined, and if I ask you where it is you will answer, "beside A." And I will be satisfied with this answer, unless, of course, I go on to ask,

[I/3: 202]

"but where is A?" If, next to B, you posit C, D, E, etc., etc., etc., then you have determined the *relative* positions of all these objects. Fill up as much space as you will: this filled space will still remain finite. In no way can it be related to infinite space. With space it will always be as it was with A; that is to say, it is determined only because you have determined it by means of your absolute synthesis. — This seems to me to be an obvious remark, from which one should long since have discovered the ideality of space.

6.) The characteristic feature of the object of a *present* intuition is that we posit it by means of the power of imagination in a space — indeed, in an *empty* space. But, as we have shown, this is impossible unless we presuppose a space that has already been filled. — We thereby obtain a dependent succession of spatial fillings, and, for reasons that will be presented later, this succession can always be traced back ad infinitum.

V.) The freedom of the I was supposed to be re-established by positing the I as free to join z to Y or to a, b, c, etc., by means of which the Not-I (the determination of

[I, 403]

Y and X in space) was also supposed to be posited as contingent. O revealed itself to be space only when this freedom was posited. We have therefore ascertained the type of contingency involved, and this remains. The question is whether the difficulty in question[84] has thereby been satisfactorily resolved.

It is true that the I is absolutely free to posit Y, X, or a, b, c, etc. in space. If, however, the I is supposed to reflect upon X qua substance (and that is the assumption with which we began), then, in accordance with the rule presented above, *it must necessarily* posit Y as a determinate substance and as determined by space z. Hence the I is not free under this condition. Neither, moreover, is the I free to determine the place of X. In this respect too, the I is determined, since it must posit X next to Y. Consequently, given the assumption stated at the beginning of this § [namely, that the I is reflecting on X as a substance], the I remains determined and compelled. It must, however, be free, and this abiding contradiction has to be resolved. It can be resolved only in the following way: Y and X must both be determined and posited in opposition to each other in some manner other than through their determination and determinability in space, since both Y and X were previously separated from their space and hence posited as existing on their own and as distinguished on their own from anything other than themselves. Y and X must [therefore] also possess additional characteristic features, by virtue of which the proposition A = A applies to them — for example, X may be red, Y yellow, etc. But the rule that determines place is not related in any way to these characteristic features, nor does this rule imply that what is determined in space is Y, qua something yellow, and that what is spatially determinable by Y is X, qua something red. Instead, this rule applies to Y insofar as it is determined, and only in this respect does it apply to Y. Similarly, the rule that determines place applies to X insofar as it is determinable, and in no other respect. This rule states [I/3: 203] that the object of the intuition that is supposed to be posited must necessarily be something determinable and cannot be something already determined. It also states that something determined must be posited in opposition to what is determinable, and, to this extent, what is determined cannot be what is determinable. This leaves entirely undecided the question of whether X, qua something that is otherwise determined by its inner characteristic features — or Y, qua something determined by its inner features — is determined or determinable in space. This [I, 404] gives freedom its latitude. It must posit something determinable in opposition to something determined. But from among things that are in other respects posited in opposition to each other it can choose to treat whichever ones it chooses as determined and whichever ones it chooses as determinable. Whether X is determined by Y or vice versa depends entirely upon this spontaneity.

(It makes no difference which spatial series one describes: whether one moves from A to B or from B to A, or whether one posits B beside A or A beside B; for things in space exclude each other *reciprocally*.)

VI.) The I can make whichever [of these opposed things] it wishes determined or determinable, and, in the manner just indicated, it posits this, its own freedom by means of the power of imagination. The I oscillates between determinacy and determinability; it assigns this pair of characteristics to a pair of things, or else it assigns neither to either (which amounts to the same thing). However, just as it is certain that an intuition and an object of an intuition are supposed to be present, so is it also certain (according to the rule with which we began) that I make *one* of these two things — which are determined in themselves — into *something spatially determinable*.

No reason can be given why the I posits as determinable precisely X or Y or anything else that is possible. Nor should there be any reason for this, for this occurs absolutely spontaneously. This spontaneity expresses itself as contingency. But one must note carefully wherein such contingency actually lies.

Something determinable is freely posited. According to the rule, its determinability is, as such, necessary, and, as an object of intuition, it must be something determinable. Consequently, the contingency of what is determinable consists in its *being-positing* or *being-there*.[85] The positing of the determinable thing becomes an accident of the I. In contrast, the I itself is posited as substance, in accordance with the rule introduced in the previous section.

VII.) At this point in our overall synthetic procedure, the I and the Not-I are posited in complete opposition to each other and as independent of each other, just as they were posited in the previous §. The inner forces within the Not-I operate with absolute freedom. They fill their spheres of causal efficacy, encounter each other contingently at a single point, and (without detriment to the freedom of either) thereby reciprocally exclude each other from their respective spheres of causal efficacy — or, as we now know, from their respective spaces. — The I posits as substance whatever it chooses; it, so to speak, distributes space among substances in any way it wishes. With absolute freedom, the I determines by itself what it wishes to make determined in space and what determinable; that is, it freely chooses the direction in which it wishes to traverse space. In this way, all connection between the I and the Not-I is canceled; they are connected by nothing other than empty space. This space, however, is completely empty and is supposed to be nothing more than the sphere in which the Not-I freely posits its products *realiter* and in which the I (with similar freedom) posits its products *idealiter*, as fabricated [*erdichtete*] products of a Not-I. Consequently, the empty space in question limits neither the I nor the Not-I, nor does it join them to each other. This explains the opposition posited between the being of the I and the being of the Not-I, as well as their independent being-there, but it does not explain the requisite harmony between them. Space is rightly called the form of outer intuition[86] — that is, the subjective condition that makes outer intuition possible. If there is no other form of intuition, then the requisite harmony between the representation and the thing — and hence any relationship between the two — is impossible, and consequently it is also impossible for the I to posit them in opposition to each other. Let us continue along our path, along which we will undoubtedly encounter this additional form of intuition.

VIII.)

[I, 405]

[I/3: 204]

1.)   Y and X are both products of the free causal efficacy of the Not-I, which is completely independent of the I, and this is true of them in all their possible relationships and connections to each other, including their relationship to each other in space. *For the I*, however, Y and X are not products of the Not-I's free causal efficacy; in fact, they are nothing at all for the I, unless the I, from its side, exerts a free causal efficacy of its own.

2.)   The causal efficacy of both the I and the Not-I must be reciprocal; that is, the expressions of both must encounter each other at a single point — namely, the point of the absolute synthesis of both through the power of imagination. The I *posits* this point of union by means of its absolute power, and it posits it as *contingent*. This means that *the encounter of the causal efficacies of these opposites* is contingent, as was seen in the preceding §.

[I, 406]

3.) Such a point must be posited if either Y or X is to be posited. To say that an object is posited means that it is synthetically united with such a point, which occurs by synthetically uniting the causal efficacy of the object with that of the I.

4.) With respect to the determinacy or indeterminacy of Y or X, the I freely oscillates between opposing directions. This means that it is the spontaneity [I/3: 205] of the I alone that determines whether Y or X is synthetically united *with the point* and *thereby with the I.*

5.) This freedom of the I, as determined in this manner, must be posited by the power of imagination. The *sheer possibility* of a synthesis of the point with the causal efficacy of the Not-I must be posited. This is possible only if the *point* in question can be posited apart from *the causal efficacy of the Not-I.*

6.) Such a point, however, is nothing but a synthesis of the causal efficacies of the I and the Not-I. Hence, it cannot be separated entirely from the causal efficacy of the Not-I without disappearing completely. Consequently, only the determinate X is separated from the point, and an indeterminate product, which could be a, b, c, etc. (i.e., a Not-I as such), is synthetically united with it. This is accomplished so that the point can retain its deter- [I, 407] minate character as a synthetic point. (It is clear for reasons already stated that this is how it must be. The encounter of X with the causal efficacy of the I, as well as with the point that must now be investigated, was supposed to be contingent and to be posited as such. This clearly means that X must be posited as capable of being united or not united with the causal efficacy of the I and with the point now under investigation — and the same would hold for any possible Not-I in X's place.)

7.) According to everything we have presupposed, the I is actually supposed to unite the point in question with X synthetically. For there is supposed to be an intuition of X, which, according to the previous §, is not even possible *as such* (i.e., qua mere intuition) without this synthesis. This synthesis occurs absolutely spontaneously and without any determining ground, as has already been proven. By uniting X with this point, however, anything else that might otherwise be possible is excluded from this point; for the point in question is the point of union between the I and a force in the Not-I — a force which, as a substance, is posited as an independent, unitary, and freely operating force. Various [other] possible forces are thereby excluded.

8.) This act of composition [*Zusammensetzen*] is actually supposed to be a *positing* together [*Zusammen*setzen], and it is supposed to be posited as such; that is, it is supposed to occur by means of the absolute spontaneity of the I. Furthermore, this positing is supposed to bear the stamp of such spontaneity: namely: *contingency*. But it is not supposed to bear this stamp in any of the respects indicated above; instead, it has to bear it within itself, since this synthesis actually occurs and everything else is in fact excluded. It must therefore be posited as accompanied by this particular stamp and characteristic feature [namely, contingency]. This, however, is possible only if one posits this act of composition in opposition to another, necessary synthesis of a specifically determined Y with some point — but not with X's point, since everything else is excluded from this point by the synthesis. Y must be united with *another* point, one that has been *posited in opposition* to Y. Let us call this point c, and the point with which X is united point d.

[I/3: 206]

[I, 408]

9.) Point c, like point d, is a point of synthetic union of the causal efficacies of the I and the Not-I. However, c is posited in opposition to d in the following way: In the case of d, the union is regarded as dependent upon freedom (it could be different); in the case of c, however, the union is regarded as necessary (it cannot be posited as capable of being otherwise). (The synthetic action is finished, completely over; it is no longer under my control.)

10.) The contingency of the synthetic unification with d must be posited; and therefore, the necessity of the union with c must also be posited. It follows that both c and d must be posited in this relationship as necessary and contingent with respect to one another. If the synthetic union with d is to be posited, then the unification with c must be posited as having already occurred. The converse, however, is not the case. When the unification with c is posited, that with d is not posited as having already occurred.

11.) According to our postulate, the synthesis with d is supposed to occur. If this synthesis is posited as such, then it is necessarily posited as *dependent*, that is, as conditioned by the synthesis with c. The converse, however, is not the case; c is not conditioned by d.

12.) In addition, the synthesis with c is supposed to be exactly what the synthesis with d was: namely, an arbitrary, contingent synthesis. If it is posited as such, another synthesis with b must again be posited in opposition to it as necessary, in which case c would be dependent upon and conditioned by b, but not vice versa. Moreover, like c and d, b is a contingent synthesis, and thus, insofar as b is posited as such, another, necessary synthesis with a is posited in opposition to it. Consequently, b would be related to a in precisely the same way that c is related to b and d is related to c, and so on, ad infinitum. In this way we obtain a series of points considered as the points of synthetic unification for the causal efficacies of the I and the Not-I in intuition. Each of these points is

[I, 409]

dependent upon another determinate point, which is not, conversely, dependent upon it. And each point has another determinate point which is dependent upon it, but upon which it itself is not dependent. In short, we have a *temporal series*.

13.) According to the preceding explication, the I posited itself as utterly free to unite with this point whatever it wished: that is, [anything included in] the entire, infinite Not-I. The point thereby determined is only contin-

[I/3: 207]

gent and not necessary. It is only dependent, and there is no other that depends upon it. It is called the *present* point.

14.) Suppose we abstract from the synthetic unification of a specific point with the object, and hence from the entire causal efficacy of the I (which is united with the Not-I only through this point). If we make this abstraction, then it follows that things — regarded in themselves and independent of the I — are *simultaneously* in space (that is to say they can all be synthetically united with one and the same point). However, they can be perceived in time only sequentially, *one after another* — in a successive series, each member of which is dependent upon another, which is not dependent upon it.

In this connection we still have the following remarks to make.

a.) There is no *past* for us at all, except insofar as it is thought of in the *present*. What was yesterday (one must here express oneself in a transcendent manner in order to be able to express oneself at all) *is not*. It exists only insofar as I am currently thinking *that it* was yesterday. The question, Has time really passed? is therefore perfectly similar to the question, Is there a thing in itself or not? Of course time has passed, if you posit it as having passed. And whenever you raise this question, you posit a past time. If you do not posit a past time, you do not raise this question; and consequently, no time has passed for you. This remark is very easily understood and should long since have led to correct ideas concerning the ideality of time.

b.) Yet there must necessarily be a past for us. For only if there is a past can there be a present, and only if there is a present is consciousness possible. In this context, let us repeat the proof of this, the final point that was supposed to be presented in this §. — Consciousness is pos- [I, 410] sible only on the condition that the I posit a Not-I in opposition to itself. Understandably, this positing in opposition is possible only if the I directs its ideal activity at the Not-I. This activity is an activity of the I and not an activity of the Not-I only insofar as it is a free activity — that is, only insofar as it could have been directed at any other object instead of this one. If consciousness is to be possible, this [ideal] activity must be posited in this manner, and that is how it is posited. The characteristic feature of the present moment is that any other perception could have occurred within it. This is possible only if there is another moment in which no perception can be posited other than the one that is posited. This is the characteristic feature of the past moment. Consciousness is therefore necessarily [I/3: 208] consciousness of freedom and of identity. It is consciousness of identity, because every moment (just as surely as it is a moment) must be attached to another moment. Perception B cannot be a perception unless it is presupposed that the same subject has another perception, A. Should A now disappears and the I be supposed to proceed to perception C, then B must at least be posited as a condition of C, and so on, ad infinitum. The identity of consciousness depends upon this rule, and, strictly speaking, only two moments are required for this identity. — There is no *first* moment of consciousness at all, only a *second* one.

c.) Of course, a past moment — indeed, any possible past moment — can be raised again to consciousness. It can be represented and raised to present consciousness, posited as having occurred in *the same subject* — so long as one reflects that a different perception *could have occurred* in the past moment in question. This moment is then posited in opposition to another moment, which preceded it. And *if* a certain determinate perception is to be posited in the former moment [namely, in that originally past moment, which has now been raised to consciousness], then the perception that occurred at the moment prior to it was the only perception that could have occurred. This explains why we can always go back just as far as we wish, unconditionally and endlessly.

[I, 411]

d.) A determinate quantity of space always exists *simultaneously*; a quantity of time always exists *successively*. That is why we can measure one only by means of the other. We measure space by the time required to traverse it, and we measure time by the space we or any other regularly moving body (for example, the sun, the hand of a clock, a pendulum) can traverse during that time.

Concluding Remark

In the *Critique of Pure Reason*, Kant begins his reflections at a point at which time, space, and the manifold of intuition are already given as present in and for the I. We have now deduced these a priori, and thus they are now present for the I. With this, we have established the distinctive character of the theoretical portion of the *Wissenschaftslehre*, and for the moment we take leave of our reader, who will find himself situated at precisely the point where Kant begins.

APPENDIX

"The Zurich *Wissenschaftslehre*"

(February–April 1794)

J. K. Lavater's Transcription of the First Five lectures

Jens Baggesen's Notes on the Zurich *Wissenschaftslehre*

Concluding Lecture: *Concerning Human Dignity*
(privately printed, April 1794)

J. G. Fichte

"PROLEGOMENA" TO THE ZURICH LECTURES ON
WISSENSCHAFTSLEHRE

February 1794
As Transcribed by J. K. Lavater[1]

ONE

[Monday, February 24, 1794]
Philosophy

Reinhold calls philosophy the science of whatever is determined purely by the power of representation.[2]

This is a definition of theoretical philosophy, but not of philosophy as a whole.

On one point everyone is in agreement: philosophy is supposed to be a science. What is in dispute is only the object of this science.

The concept of science is itself undetermined and undeveloped. This is the source of the conflict: essential, characteristic features of this concept have been overlooked and other, contingent ones have been considered essential.

Science as such has to be considered with respect to its *form*.

Form is the relationship of the parts of a science to the whole of that science, and of its whole to these parts. Science also has to be considered with respect to its *content*, that is, its *inner content*.

A.
Form.

Every science has a *foundational principle* [*Grundsatz*], on the basis of which all the propositions [of that science] are proven, and which itself stands in need of no proof.

Everything present within a science must be precisely determined and derived from its foundational principle, whether immediately or mediately.

Concatenation of all the propositions into a single whole [*an Einen*] is what makes a science into a system.

This connection and concatenation of various propositions into a *single whole* has been considered to be the *essence* of science.

One [thereby] determines the *how* of the presentation; the *what* thereof remains undecided. But *form* can be no more than a *means*, not the *end* [of science].

B.
[*Content*]

Science must also be considered with respect to its content.

Is there a [proper] *content* of science, insofar as it is *science*?

Or is it the case that all that is needed in order for something to become a science is purely [IV/3: 20] and simply a certain composition [*Beschaffenheit*] of our representations? [3]

Example

A fabrication [*Erdichtung*] can be *coherent* in itself and completely consistent, and yet still not be called a science.

Systematic form does not constitute the essence [of science].

We must therefore also seek out the distinguishing feature of science with respect to its content.

*

Only what one *knows* can become the content of a science, and only insofar as one knows it.

The content of science is therefore *that which is certain.*

No science can ever arise from anything uncertain.

It follows that systematic form is nothing more than a contingent means toward achieving this end, [that is, certainty]. What is essential is what is *certain*, to which is then added *form*, the systematic element, without which that which is certain is not called a science.

A person who possesses isolated cognitions of something possesses *knowledge*[4] of it. Science itself presupposes the combination of all the propositions. It aspires to be a whole.

What makes science into a science does not lie in the propositions themselves, but in the relationships between the propositions.

*

The prerogative that mathematics arrogates to itself: namely, that it is the only certain science, is one that should be shared by all the sciences. A = B, B = C; therefore, A = C. It comes down to relationships of equivalence. In a *science*, all the propositions are derived from *a single* foundational principle; that is to say, they are traced back to a relationship of equivalence with this foundational principle.

The foundational principle alone is immediately certain.

What is equivalent to *it* is therefore certain as well.

The foundational principle is certain in itself; the derived propositions are certain because they are equivalent to it.

Systematic method is therefore not the end, but only a means.

*

One knows everything that attains to our consciousness, and one is certain of this.

*

[IV/3: 21] The definition of knowing is the definition of consciousness.

*

A definition should indicate the genus of what is to be defined, as well as the characteristic feature [*Merkmal*] that distinguishes it [and constitutes its specific difference].

*

There can be no characteristic feature that distinguishes the highest genus.

*

Consciousness cannot be defined, though it can certainly be *described*. The task of philosophy is to seek out and to exhaust the individual types of consciousness.

*

To say that philosophy is a science is to say that it produces cognition that obtains certainty through the *object* of this cognition.

*

Every thing is equivalent to itself: A = A.

*

Things posited in opposition to each other are not equivalent to each other with respect to any single characteristic feature; A.)(–A
   Two things that are equivalent to a third thing are themselves equivalent: A = B. B = C. C = A.

*

We require a *foundational principle*, which must obtain its certainty in some other way [other than through such inferential equivalences].

*

What then is the source of this certainty of the grounding principle and of those that are equivalent to it?   [IV/3: 22]

*

If we had a science that could ground both the validity of all *foundational principles* and the validity of all *relations of equivalence*, and if this science were philosophy, we would then have discovered the definition of philosophy.

*

Philosophy would be science itself [*die Wissenschaft an sich*], the science of science as such — or *Wissenschaftslehre*.[5]
   a) To say this is not yet to maintain that any such science is either present or possible.
   b) At this point — that is, until it has been proven through its realization — this definition remains arbitrary. The reality of a definition is proven through the reality of the corresponding thing.
   c) One might ask whether this [definition of philosophy] accords with linguistic usage. Answer: A determinate definition is better than an indeterminate one — which is no definition at all.
   d) The word *philosophy* can hardly be retained. It will become unusable.[6]
   The nation that discovers this *science par excellence* will be authorized to name it. Hence philosophy, which is what we are seeking, is science *par excellence*: *Wissenschaftslehre*.

*

The *Wissenschaftslehre* furnishes all the sciences with their foundational principles and proves the validity of the relations of equivalence within these sciences.

*

II.

Tuesday, February 25, 1794
More precise determination of philosophy and of its relationship to logic.

We said that philosophy is the science of science as such.

All the characteristic features of philosophy must be contained in this concept [of the science of science]. It follows that these characteristic features must be developed from this [IV/3: 23] concept.

The *Wissenschaftslehre* is the science of any science whatsoever.

The object of the *Wissenschaftslehre* is therefore science as such.

*

Every science must have a foundational principle that is completely certain.

*

The *Wissenschaftslehre* has to ground or serve as the foundation of the chief foundational principle of every possible science.

*

a) The *Wissenschaftslehre* has to establish what it means for something *to be certain*, and it has to show *how* it is possible for something to be certain.

b) The *Wissenschaftslehre* has to establish those propositions which are supposed to be the foundational principles of other sciences, and it has to prove these propositions.

It follows that every actual as well as every future science must be related exclusively to the *Wissenschaftslehre*.

If *everything* the human mind is ever able to encounter is grounded upon the foundational principle provided by the *Wissenschaftslehre*, and if everything within the *Wissenschaftslehre* can be traced back to a single foundational principle and can in this manner be demonstrated to be either true and certain or else false and groundless, then this is an external criterion for the correctness of the *Wissenschaftslehre*.

Objection.

(which, to be sure, can be answered fully only by philosophy as a whole)

A sharply delineated boundary must be drawn between the universal *Wissenschaftslehre* and [each] special science. Such a boundary is difficult to determine. For example, the foundational principles of mathematics and of pure natural science must be contained in the *Wissenschaftslehre*. But if these modes of inferences were not sharply distinguished from each other, then everything would be *Wissenschaftslehre*, and there would be no special sciences.

As we will see, all sciences are grounded upon *facts* [*Tatsachen*], which in the case of *Wissenschaftslehre* are F/Acts [*Tathandlungen*]. We will see too that the sole task of every science is to develop those facts that are proper to it, and that it strays into a foreign domain when it develops any other facts.

[IV/3: 24]   It is the task of every science to develop[7] facts.

The universal *Wissenschaftslehre* includes *the* F/Act that underlies and grounds all other facts.

*

The very same things that are, in the particular sciences, facts, are, in the *pure* sciences, *F/Acts*.[8]

Thus, if a universal *Wissenschaftslehre* is supposed to deal with *the* F/Act that makes possible all other facts and F/Acts, it would then, in developing this first F/Act, which precedes all others, have to indicate and enumerate all these additional facts and F/Acts, while leaving the *further development* of these *particular* facts to the *particular* sciences.

Example.

Geometry obtains from the *Wissenschaftslehre* the concepts of *space* and a *point*; therefore, the *Wissenschaftslehre,* as such, is obliged to develop both of these intuitions (that of space and that of a point) from the F/Act that is expressed by its foundational principle.

*

Geometry comes into being by means of my I's free action of moving a point in space along a line.

No geometry comes into being simply from space and a single point.

"*I* am *I.*" This is [asserted by] *philosophy*.

"*A is A.*" This is [asserted by] *logic*.

*

Every science possesses a foundational principle, the certainty of which must be obtained from the *Wissenschaftslehre*.

*

Insofar as the *Wissenschaftslehre* has to indicate what is certain as such, in can be called material philosophy or *Wissenschaftslehre* of inner content.   [IV/3: 25]

*

The *Wissenschaftslehre* has two distinguishing features:

1) it is certain [and thus possesses content].
2) it is able, by establishing relations of equivalence, to reduce all its propositions to a single principle.

As a science, the *Wissenschaftslehre* must possess systematic form.

*

The validity of the systematic way of proceeding, that is, of proceeding *by means of relations of equivalence*, must be demonstrated, and the conditions of this validity must be established.

The *Wissenschaftslehre* must *legitimate* systematic *form* for the other sciences, and to this extent it is called *formal philosophy,* or the *Wissenschaftslehre of forms*.

The goal of the present *lecture* is to develop the concept of the *Wissenschaftslehre*.

*

When one talks about a *material Wissenschaftslehre* and a *formal Wissenschaftslehre,* this does not mean that there are two different parts of the *Wissenschaftslehre*.

Instead, it means only this: that the power of understanding is able to think of these [two aspects of *Wissenschaftslehre*] apart from each other.

In the *Wissenschaftslehre* itself, form is determined by content.

*

However, there actually exists a science that deals with the *purely formal aspect* of all the sciences, and this science is called *logic*.

*

What then is logic? How is it distinguished from the formal *Wissenschaftslehre*?

In the same way that form is distinguished from content.

A = A. This means that, if A exists, then A = A.

A = B.

B = C.

Therefore, C = A.

Or [instead of asserting that A is equal to A, one can also assert that] A is posited *in opposition*
[IV/3: 26] to A. I.e., A is equal to B, and B is therefore posited in opposition to A.

Even if there are no objections to be raised against this form, the existence of A cannot be demonstrated by purely formal means. How is it then that I come to say, "A *is*"? Does A exist? This is a question concerning the content of the proposition.

No philosophical proposition is correct purely by virtue of its form. In philosophy, the correctness of the mere form follows immediately from the reality of the inner content. This anyway is how things *ought to be* in philosophy! This is what philosophy *ought to* accomplish! Let us say that *A* is the *I*.

This is what is asserted by the form [of this proposition]. *I* am *I* — the form of this proposition is already *material*.

This must be valid for all propositions! (This proposition is mentioned here only as an example).

Logic asserts, "if *A* exists, then A = A."

Philosophy asserts," *because* A exists, then A = A."

Philosophy posits unconditionally.

Logic posits a second term, on the condition that a first one is posited.

[1.]

Logic cannot posit what is *primary* [*das* Erste].

The *Wissenschaftslehre* has to posit something primary.

2.

Nor can logic prove the legitimacy of its *relations of equivalence*.

Logic does not prove the proposition:

A = B

B = C

C = A.

That is to say, logic does not prove that two things equal to a third thing are themselves equal. This must therefore be proven elsewhere.

Consequently, this must be proven by the *Wissenschaftslehre*, which is charged with proving everything.

The *Wissenschaftslehre* is therefore distinguished from logic by the fact that the former proves the legitimacy of the relations of equivalence exhibited within logic, and indeed of all
[IV.3: 27] relations of equivalence. *Logic*, in contrast, presupposes that all of this has been proven.

3.

Logic indicates [*angiebt*] the condition for conditioned relations of equivalence, but logic does not demonstrate [*erweist*] this condition.

The concept of a *body* is equivalent to the sum of all intuitions of bodies. The *Wissenschaftslehre* demonstrates this by showing *how* we could have constructed [such] concepts.

This is the task of the universal *Wissenschaftslehre*.

This leads us to a cognition of the relationship of logic to universal *Wissenschaftslehre*.

Philosophy provides the *form*, along with the *inner content*. *Logic* ignores this *content* and exhibits the mere *form*, as valid for all possible content subsumed under this highest content.

The *Wissenschaftslehre* asserts that "*I am I*."

Logic asserts that "A = A."

Logic is authorized to subordinate A = A to *I* = *I*, because every possible A is something in the *I*. If "*I am I*" is proven, then it is true that A = A.

Logic is an abstract science, since it abstracts from all content, including the particular determinate contents of *Wissenschaftslehre*.

Logic is related to the *Wissenschaftslehre* in the same way every *abstractum* is related to its *concretum*.

2. [sic!]

Logic possesses only a *negative* validity, whereas the *Wissenschaftslehre* possesses a *positive* validity.

Anything that sins against logic cannot be true.

Whatever is in accordance with logic *can* be true.

Logic is correct with respect to its *form*, but perhaps it cannot signify anything real [*Reelles*].

*

Logic can never answer the question concerning whether something corresponds to a concept. *Logic* is therefore related to the *Wissenschaftslehre* in the same way every *negative* cognition is related to a *positive* one.   [IV/3: 28]

*

Logic is neither the *fundamental doctrine* [*Grundlehre*] nor a *portion* [of the same]; instead, logic is the *daughter* of philosophy.

Logic is a distinct science, which continues to exist *for itself*; and, like every possible science, it is grounded upon the universal *Wissenschaftslehre*.

What distinguishes logic from all the other sciences is this: that it has no proper *content* (in the philosophical sense) of its own, and is therefore the most singular science possible.

The *object* of logic is the mere *form* of all the sciences — a form, moreover, that is not grounded in logic itself, but is exhibited [there] only in order to facilitate an easier overview.

*

Logic is called the *doctrine of reason* [*Vernunftlehre*]. This name can no longer be retained.

Reason does not compare or assert equivalences; it *posits*.[9]

Logic is the *doctrine of relations of equivalence* [*Gleichungslehre*].

III.

Wednesday, February 26, 1794
The concept of the Wissenschaftslehre, continued.

The *Wissenschaftslehre* has to establish the foundational principles and the validity of all forms. These are its externally identifiable characteristic features. It is itself supposed to be a *science*, and its *inner* determinations follow from this requirement.

*

[I.]

Every science must have a foundational principle; hence the *Wissenschaftslehre* must also have a foundational principle.

This foundational principle is not supposed to be demonstrated within the *Wissenschaftslehre* itself. (No science can demonstrate its own foundational principle.) Nor can the foundational principle of the *Wissenschaftslehre* be demonstrated in any other science.

Every other science must either be derived from the *Wissenschaftslehre* [or not derived therefrom]. But [, in the first case,] since this other science is itself based upon the *Wissenschaftslehre*, there would arise a circle in the proof [if one tried to obtain from that sci-
[IV/3: 29]   ence the grounding principle of the *Wissenschaftslehre*].

It is equally impossible that this foundational principle could be included in another science, one not derived from the *Wissenschaftslehre*, for in that case the *Wissenschaftslehre* would no longer be *Wissenschaftslehre*. Instead, the *Wissenschaftslehre* would be the science that would demonstrate this foundational principle.

*

All our knowledge must ultimately come to an end in something immediately certain, and this is what is supposed to stand at the summit of a *Wissenschaftslehre*.

*

[1.]

The foundational principle of the *Wissenschaftslehre* cannot be proven in any way whatsoever. Yet, since it must nevertheless be certain, this principle must be *certain* immediately and in itself; and, if the meaning of this principle is not to remain ambiguous, it must be adequately determined through itself.

2.

The certainty, not merely of all the propositions contained in the *Wissenschaftslehre* itself, but also of all the propositions that could appear in any science whatsoever, must be derivable from this foundational principle.

The foundational principle of the *Wissenschaftslehre* would be the supreme *condition of all knowing*, and no knowledge would be possible without presupposing this principle.

(This would be merely the negative [criterion for any possible knowledge].)

[Expressed positively,] this foundational principle must also be that principle to which it is possible to trace back all possible knowing, the principle from which everything can be derived.

Two Remarks

1. It has not yet been asserted purely and simply that there is any such principle or that there must be one. All that has been claimed is this: if a *Wissenschaftslehre* is to be possible, then there must be such a principle.

Should there be such a principle, then there is also a firmly established system in the human mind. But is there such a system? For the time being, it is not yet possible to claim this. That there is such a foundational principle is something that cannot be demonstrated on the basis of any principle obtained from outside the *Wissenschaftslehre*.

[IV/3: 30]   The only way to demonstrate that there is such a firmly established system of the mind is to establish this [foundational] principle itself. — Only the *Wissenschaftslehre*, which is itself made possible by this principle, only the actual realization [of this principle as the supreme foundational principle of all human knowledge], can make it clear that such a principle is possible.[10]

The only way to refute those skeptics who ask whether such a foundational principle is possible is to establish the *Wissenschaftslehre* itself. The *Wissenschaftslehre* demonstrates its own possibility only through itself.

Second remark

Whether a certain proposed proposition is this universal foundational principle is also something that cannot be demonstrated prior to the completion of the entire doctrinal structure [of the *Wissenschaftslehre*].

Such a foundational principle should possess the following characteristic features:

[1.] It should be certain in itself, *immediately* and without any proof; it should be clear without any explanation.

(Many things that are completely certain and clear to the child are by no means certain and clear to the philosopher, nor do they need to be so for him. The philosopher *knows* less than the child. The child knows that there are bodies outside him, and to him this clear. Yet this is not certain for the philosopher. It is something he only *believes*.)

It does not yet follow from the mere fact that someone *has the opinion* that a proposition is immediately *certain* and *clear* that it is the foundational principle we are seeking.

[2.] The second characteristic feature of the universal foundational principle we are seeking is this: *Everything must be derivable from this principle.*

If there is a system in the human mind, then there can also be a foundational principle from which this system can be derived.

Whether a proposed proposition is a foundational principle of this sort is something that can be demonstrated only by attempting to apply it to all possible sciences. This foundational principle can therefore be discovered only by means of an experiment [*durch Versuche*].

Everything we know pertains either to the *I* or to the *Not-I*. Consequently, we could never attain to a level of cultivation at which there could be additional instances of knowing other than [those that pertain either to] the *I* or the *Not-I*.

(If this universal foundational principle satisfies these negative and positive [criteria],[11] then this would answer the objection of the skeptics — namely, the objection that no secure universal foundational principle can be established, since we cannot foresee the degree to which human beings may be cultivated [in the future].)

II.

Every science must possess systematic form; hence, the *Wissenschaftslehre* must possess systematic form as well.

To say that the form of the *Wissenschaftslehre* is determined [*bestimmt*] can mean two different things:

a.) [First of all, it can mean that] the form of the individual propositions is determined:
affirmatively — I am I;
negatively — I am not Not-I.
But from where does the *Wissenschaftslehre* obtain the form of these individual propositions?   [IV/3: 31]

The *content* of the individual propositions determines the *form* of the same. The proposition concerning the *I* ["I am I"] must be positively affirmative.

The *content* determines the form of this proposition, and the form determines the content.

Is this then a circle? This is how it is supposed to be!

The first principles of the *Wissenschaftslehre* are purely and simply true. It follows that in the *Wissenschaftslehre* we do not need logic in order to determine the form of the individual propositions [of the *Wissenschaftslehre*.]

b.) [Secondly,] "the form of the *Wissenschaftslehre* is determined" can also mean "what is determined is the relation of the individual propositions to one another, the order and derivation of the same."

From where does such determination come? Once again, it comes from the *Wissenschaftslehre* itself. In the *Wissenschaftslehre*, every proposition determines the position of the one that follows it.

The first two principles of the *Wissenschaftslehre* establish the logical principles of *identity* and contradiction on the basis of something real: namely, the *I* and the *Not-I*.

Unless one assumes a third principle, however, these first two principles will contradict one another (which they are not permitted to do, since the principle of contradiction has already been proven to be valid).

*

I am I.
The *Not-I is not I.*
The *Not-I* is posited in opposition to the I.
The *I* exists [*ist*] purely and simply.
The *Not-I* is *nothing*.
Each restricts the other — if one adds to this the concept of quantity and limitation.[12]

Every proposition in the *Wissenschaftslehre* therefore determines the position of the one that precedes it and the one that follows it.

Consequently, the form of the whole determines itself.

The form of a *Wissenschaftslehre* cannot be incorrect [simply] because it contradicts logic. Logic imposes no law upon the *Wissenschaftslehre*; instead, [the *Wissenschaftslehre* can be called incorrect only] if it contradicts or annuls itself.

Whatever one may mean by "philosophy," any science that still recognizes any higher law above itself is not the highest and first science.

Logic cannot be an Elementary Philosophy,[13] because logic is a science of mere form, and [IV/3: 32]   there can be no form without content (since the form is only abstracted from the content).

Consequently, there must always be a higher science, from the content of which logic has abstracted [its form]. (Reinhold's Elementary Philosophy would therefore not be the first [science], but rather the third — logic, and [then] *Elementary Philosophy*, if, that is, the latter depends upon logic.)[14]

The principle of contradiction, along with the content of the same, was long present in the *Wissenschaftslehre*, even prior to logic.

The *Wissenschaftslehre* is therefore determined through itself, just as much with respect to its inner content as with respect to its form. It is a purely and simply unconditioned science.

What it contains is what exists purely and simply, *because* it is.

It is *so*, because it is so.

*

The human mind is not restricted by anything outside itself.

It restricts itself. It gives itself its own law.

It is enclosed within a circle that it itself has drawn around itself.

IV.

Thursday, February 27, 1794
The relationship of the Wissenschaftslehre *to geometry.*

Two more remarks.

a.) [First general remark.] The *external* relationship between the *Wissenschaftslehre* and mathematics, and, in particular, between the *Wissenschaftslehre* and geometry (which is the basis of all mathematics), still remains to be indicated (the *inner* relationship between them depends, *per se*, on the *Wissenschaftslehre*).

Kant conceded to geometry the exclusive possession of *demonstration* [*Demonstration*], [IV/3: 33] because geometry could construct its concepts, which the *Wissenschaftslehre*[15] is unable to do.

All his followers said the same thing.

From this, all the skeptics, and Maimon[16] in particular, have drawn certain conclusions to the detriment of philosophy and the value of the same.

*

If our explanation of the *Wissenschaftslehre* should confirm itself by actually establishing the *Wissenschaftslehre*, and if it should therefore also succeed in providing geometry — as a science grounded upon this universal science — with a foundation, with respect both to the foundational principle of geometry and to the form and system of that science: if this should be the case, then it would be remarkable that a derived science [such as geometry] should possess some essential feature [such as being able to construct its concepts] that *the* science from which it is derived does not possess, and that the *Wissenschaftslehre* should hand over to geometry something that could not be found in the *Wissenschaftslehre* itself.

*

For Kant, to *demonstrate* [*domonstrieren*] something means (in accordance with the etymology of the word) to make something visible [*vorweisen*] in a sensible representation by dissecting or analyzing [*durch Zerlegung*] the latter, and one can do this *only* when the concept in question is supported by a sensible presentation [*Darstellung*] — that is to say, when one [IV/3: 34] can construct it.[17]

I draw a line by moving a point forward in space. I then construct a second line in another direction, and then a third in yet another direction. These three lines intersect to enclose a space. They form a triangle, which has come into being by means of construction. These three lines produce three angles.

To demonstrate [the truth of this proposition] thus means to show [*nachweisen*] by means of intuition that three angles arise from three lines.

These three lines intersect one another at three points. I call the inclination with respect to each other of the lines intersecting at a point *arbitrary*: here we have three points of contact and therefore three angles. The demonstration of this is grounded upon the preceding construction.

But from where does geometry obtain this power of construction?

Three elements are required for the very first [geometrical] construction, which is the construction of a line. Only these elements can bring a line into being.

First of all, geometry requires a *point, through which* it draws [its line]; [second, it requires] *the space within which* it draws [its line]; [and third, it requires] the free and spontaneous self-activity [*freien Selbsttätigkeit*] of the power of imagination, which draws [the line in question]. It obtains all three of these from the *Wissenschaftslehre*, and hence the possibility of all construction (and therefore the possibility of demonstration as well) is grounded upon the *Wissenschaftslehre*.

It will become evident in the *Wissenschaftslehre* that one of these three requirements — namely, sheer space — is an original sensible intuition, which first makes possible all pure and empirical intuitions.[18]

It will also become evident that the *I* is originally an intuition as well, though not a sensible one; instead, it is an *intellectual* intuition.[19]

The *Wissenschaftslehre* is therefore in possession of intuition from the start, just as much as geometry.

Moreover, all the intuitions of geometry are grounded in the intuitions of the *Wissenschaftslehre*.

Finally, it will also become evident [first of all] that the intuition of space is likewise produced by means of the activity of the power of imagination — though not produced freely, as is the case with geometrical intuition, but with necessity — and therefore that this intuition [of space] is constructed. It will also become evident that the *Wissenschaftslehre* is also in possession of a construction, which, however, is unique [*welche die Einzige ist*].

[But] the *Wissenschaftslehre* cannot demonstrate anything on the basis of this construction [of sheer space], because the latter is infinite and consequently exceeds our power of apprehension, and because the further elaboration — that is, the limitation of this construction (namely, space) — is assigned to geometry.

Thus, secondly, the possibility of all demonstration is grounded in the *Wissenschaftslehre*, even if the demonstration in question does not occur within the *Wissenschaftslehre* itself.

[IV/3: 35]   But why is it that no error can have occurred in this case? — Why is such a demonstration true? Why is what can be established on the basis of an originally constructed pure intuition (intuition a priori) certainly contained in such a demonstration? That is to say, why is it that there can be a correct demonstration?

[For the following reason:] because this [that is, what is established by means of construction in pure intuition,] is something that I myself, in the act of constructing, have first put there by means of the free self-activity of my own power of imagination. This, for example, is why the three indicated lines enclose a space: because I myself have enclosed a space by means of three lines — and thus it is by virtue of my own action [that they enclose this space]. The enclosed space exists in consciousness because the action of enclosing the space occurred in consciousness. — But the validity of this inference presupposes an answer to a still higher question: *namely*, why does consciousness contain what I have placed in it?

This is a question geometry cannot answer.

Geometry presupposes that this question has been answered in the *Wissenschaftslehre*.

What I have placed in consciousness is there because *I* am I.

Every demonstration is therefore based upon two facts. The first is my construction by means of the power of imagination — either the construction of space, which occurs in the *Wissenschaftslehre*, or an arbitrary construction within space, which occurs in geometry itself. The second fact is the fact that "*I am I*" [which is exhibited] in the *Wissenschaftslehre*. "I, the subject engaged in demonstrating, am [also] the subject who is engaged in the act of constructing," and this must be the case in any derived science, which is what geometry is supposed to be.

*

Now that we have become acquainted with the method of demonstrative proof, let us employ this in order to seek out the method of proof employed within the *Wissenschaftslehre*, a method of proof with which we are still unacquainted. This will then allow us to provide a correct and determinate account of the characteristic differences between these two methods of proof.

*

All certainty proceeds (like [our certainty concerning] space in particular) from some fact. (In the broadest sense, *fact* is the *genus* and *F/Act* is the *species*.)[20]

Something *is* what it is, because I have made it.

Now this action of *making*, upon which the proof in question is based, is an action that occurs either with *freedom* or with *necessity*.

*

In the first case [i.e., if the action of making occurs freely], I am immediately conscious of my acting, since everything that occurs freely is — in *this acting* — *certain* for the acting subject.   [IV/3: 36]

In the second case, that of [an act of making that occurs with] necessity, one must engage in *reflection* in order to become conscious of this acting, since what occurs with necessity is not ordinarily [recognized as] an acting, but rather as a state of being passively affected [*ein Leiden*].

The actions — that is to say, the constructions — that occur in geometry are of the *first* sort; the actions — that is to say, the *concepts* — that occur in the *Wissenschaftslehre* are of the *second* sort.

Finally, the activity of the acting subject is directed either at something outside the acting *I* or else it is directed at the acting *I* itself. In the first case, the *I* becomes all the more readily conscious of its action (that is, of its acting), because it becomes conscious of the product of its acting, which could not exist independently of this acting. In this case, the *action* and its *product* are noticeably distinct from each other, and the latter announces the presence of the former.

In the second case, the acting subject and what is acted upon are *one and the same* (because the acting subject is operating upon itself), and, once again, this makes it more difficult to distinguish them and to become conscious of the acting.

Geometry is an illustration of the first kind [of acting]. In geometry, reason produces intuitions in something outside the *I*, namely, in space.

With respect to all the propositions it must prove, the *Wissenschaftslehre* is an illustration of the second kind [of acting].

In the *Wissenschaftslehre*, reason produces concepts within the I itself. The [distinctive] character of the method of proof employed in the *Wissenschaftslehre* follows from the following two characteristic features of the actions [involved] in a *Wissenschaftslehre*: first, that they are necessary actions, and second, that they are actions directed at the *I* itself. In *geometry*, the *acting* is beyond any *doubt*. One is immediately conscious of the action in question, and the demonstration that serves as a proof simply has to show *what* is produced [by this action].

In the *Wissenschaftslehre*, this situation is reversed. One is immediately conscious of the attributes [*Beschaffenheit*] of *what* is produced — for example, that everything that can be sensed must be in space and time, or that every determinate sensation must have a cause. What one is not conscious of, however, is the spontaneous self-activity that is associated with [and produces] these attributes.

In this case, therefore, what the proof has to show is not *that* something is so, but rather, that it is so by virtue of a [necessary] action of our mind — or, as Kant puts it, that the propositions in question are true a priori.

In *geometry*, the action is *given*. and what must be sought is the *product* of the same. In the *Wissenschaftslehre*, the *product* is given, and what must be sought is the action by virtue of which it is present. Geometry asks, *quid facti*? *Wissenschaftslehre* asks, *quid juris*?[21]

Thus, with respect to its inner and essential nature, the method of proof employed in the *Wissenschaftslehre* is precisely the opposite of the one employed in geometry, and the external differences between geometry and the *Wissenschaftslehre* follow from this [inner difference in their methods of proof].

If, therefore, the *Wissenschaftslehre* includes only *one* undoubted fact, which grounds the [IV/3: 37] entire science, and if what must be demonstrated is that all the other facts [established in this science] are indubitable, then the only way to prove this is by showing that even this first fact could not be a fact unless all the others were facts as well.

Just as surely as this first fact is a fact, then the others that follow from it must be facts as well.

The quality of these other facts, as facts, is derived from the quality of the first one, as a fact. Consequently, *philosophical proofs* are *deductions* [*Deduktionen*], and a deduction is the sort of proof that is here being analyzed and explicated. That is to say, a deduction is a proof that proceeds by means of relations of equivalence, as does demonstration [*Demonstration*] as well; but a deduction should not show merely that something is, but should also show that it is a *fact*.

The foundational principle of all demonstration is as follows: Because a certain action has occurred within consciousness, an action which, in itself, was not necessary, then consciousness must be modified in a certain manner, if it is to remain *one and the same*.

In contrast, the foundational principle of deduction is as follows: Because consciousness is one and the same, then a certain action must necessarily have occurred.

This explication must make it clear that the *Wissenschaftslehre* is and must be fully the equal of geometry with respect to the precision of its proofs and that demonstration has no advantage whatsoever over deduction in this respect.

For those incapable of sustained attentiveness, however, demonstration does indeed have a great advantage with respect to comprehensibility [*Faßlichkeit*]. This is because it has lying before it something that has been established in a sensible intuition, and it proceeds from this intuition and returns to it again and again. The path of demonstration is short, and it always keeps its intuition close by and right before its eyes. Once it has finished [a demonstration], geometry introduces a new intuition, with which it proceeds in the same manner.

The science of geometry thus includes resting places, and it consists of parts that are externally related and are utterly and most certainly abstract.

In contrast, the path of deduction proceeds forward in an unbroken line, and it is not a short path.

[IV/3: 38]   One of the fixed endpoints of this path is also nothing but a point, and the other is always pending. All the preceding points must remain constantly present.

*

V.

Friday, February 28, 1794

[b)] Second general remark.

The *Wissenschaftslehre is not the system [of the human mind], but is the presentation [Darstellung] of that system, achieved by means of reflection.*

According to everything that has been said so far, the aim of the *Wissenschaftslehre* is nothing less than this: to ascertain the universal and necessary determinations of *the entire system of the human mind.*

Yet this science is not this system *itself,* but is merely a presentation of it.

However, insofar as this is what the *Wissenschaftslehre* (that is, the presentation of the system of the human mind) is, and insofar as the *Wissenschaftslehre* itself is not this necessary, original, and universal system, there is also required, in addition to that highest F/Act which the *Wissenschaftslehre* ascertains to be the ground of this system, a specific action of *reflection* upon this *highest F/Act* on the part of the philosopher.

With this act of reflection, we are, so to speak, conducting an experiment with ourselves.

If this experiment is undertaken correctly, and if our presentation of this original system (that is, the system in the human mind) is therefore correct, then it follows that the system in question, which is the object of this science, has existed without any help from the philosopher from the beginning of the human race and of all other minds, just as the nature of electricity has existed from the beginning of the physical world, even though it was only in recent times that such a thing was suspected and that experiments were made with it and it was treated scientifically. Electricity has always operated in accordance with its own laws, even when we were unfamiliar with these laws, and it would always have continued to act in accordance with them, even if we had never noticed them, or even if what we now consider to be the laws of electricity were not the laws of electricity.

So too in the case of the human mind: if it operates in accordance with necessary laws, then it has always acted in accordance with these same laws, and it will continue to do so, even if our presentation [of these laws and of the system in question] were to be utterly incorrect. If the human mind contains within itself a system, then this system is certainly correct, universally valid, incontrovertible, infallible, etc. It surely possesses all the properties we demand from our *Wissenschaftslehre*. This however (that is, our *Wissenschaftslehre*) is not the system [of the human mind] but is only the presentation of the same. As philosophers, we are not the legislators of the human mind, but only its historians.²²

If our presentation is correct, then everything that is valid regarding what is being presented will certainly be valid in this presentation.   [IV/3: 39]

If, on the other hand, our presentation (which is based on an experiment) were to be incorrect, if the way we proceeded in erecting our system were to be incorrect, then the results would necessarily be incorrect as well.

But how do we intend to prove that our *way of proceeding* is correct?

*

This reflection upon ourselves, this self-observation by means of which we intend to bring into existence a science of our *I*, is itself an act of our mind, and indeed a particular act of the same, and it is [therefore] subordinated under the highest act of the mind, the one we wish to establish as the foundation of the system. Nevertheless the validity of these reflections (or of our reflective way of proceeding) is itself also something that is examined and proven in the course of our *Wissenschaftslehre*.

This does indeed constitute a genuine circle in [our] manner of proof. Right from the start, we assume the validity of proceeding in this reflective manner and in accordance with certain rules, and then, on the basis of the presumed validity of this way of proceeding and by means of the same, we prove the validity of this way of proceeding and of its rules.

There is no way to avoid this circle. This is because the *Wissenschaftslehre* is supposed to be the highest science of all; and therefore it can be preceded by no higher science, within which the validity of our way of proceeding in the *Wissenschaftslehre* could be proven. Such a higher science would, in turn, have to presuppose an even higher one, within which the validity of this higher science's way of proceeding was proven, and so on, ad infinitum.

But one should not allow oneself to be frightened by this circle. This very circumstance — namely, that an unbiased investigation results in precisely those same rules, the validity of which has been presupposed from the start — provides an excellent *test* — a test, I say — of the correctness of our way of proceeding.

It is one of the prerogatives of genius to be led by an obscure feeling of necessity to the correct path leading to clear insight into the ground of this necessity.²³

But one must not wish to remain with this obscure feeling, but rather to illuminate it to the greatest extent possible. A circle always remains; but if, after tracing the circumference of this circle, one arrives at the very same point from which one started, then this is a proof of the correctness of my circle, and even provides a mechanical test of the instrument by means of which this circle was inscribed.

From this, to be sure, it follows with certainty *that the most precise investigation of all human knowledge must ultimately conclude at a single point, one that cannot be proven, but must be accepted purely on the basis of faith or belief.* But it is necessary to add that the philosopher is [IV/3: 40] not permitted to defend this point by appealing to any external ground of belief.

Everything one can possibly know or claim to know is based upon the doctrine that applies to all knowing; consequently, to foist upon [the *Wissenschaftslehre*] such an [external] foundation, which would necessarily have to be derived [within the *Wissenschaftslehre* itself], would be to replace an infinitely small and unavoidable circle with one that is both enormous and entirely avoidable.

Afterwards, of course, I can examine my path of reflection by testing it, that is, by retracing this same path several more times, in the same way one reviews and examines the same calculation several times. One has calculated correctly when one always gets the same result; alternatively, instead of descending from the universal to the particular, I can proceed in the reverse direction, from the particular to the universal.

[Additionally,] I can reflect once again upon my reflection itself, and then I can reflect in turn upon this act of reflecting [upon my reflection].

I can draft for myself particular rules regulating the particular manner of this reflection, and other similar things. Yet [in the first case, that is, when I check my results by repeating the process of reflection or trying to reverse the direction of the same] the possibility always remains that every time I repeat my examination I may always err in the same way — or that when I proceed in the reverse direction I may once again have erred in very same way — and therefore the same result that I always obtain is not necessarily correct. In the second case [in which I design for myself specific rules governing my own process of reflection], the particular logic I have designed will always still continue to obtain its validity from the results of the *Wissenschaftslehre*,[24] and therefore the most that can be insured by means of all these repeated efforts is a very high degree of *probability*, but never *certainty* concerning the correctness of my results.

From this one can judge what one ought to think about the conflict between, on the one hand, the skeptics — who call attention to the uncertainty of human knowledge and the weakness of human understanding, as well as to the fact that human reason and all the sciences are necessarily capable of infinite improvement — and, on the other, the systematic thinkers, who claim universal validity and infallibility for their philosophy.

Both sides are right, but they fail to understand each other and are talking about entirely different things.

Philosophy, that is, the entirely correct and complete presentation of the necessary system of reason, is certainly universally valid and infallible — just as infallible, for example, as the rule of multiplication that states that one of the factors must be added to itself just as many times as the other factor contains units. But no philosopher can prove either to himself or to others that *his* representation [of this necessary system of reason] is actually correct and complete; the most he can accomplish is to make this very highly probable to [IV/3: 41] himself and to others.

Similarly, [in the case of multiplication,] it can be no more than very highly probable to the person doing this calculation that he has actually added the one factor to itself as many times as the other contains units. The *Wissenschaftslehre* is not merely the arithmetical rule; it is the calculation itself. — No one can guarantee that he has not made an error of calculation.

If this distinction between the first, necessary F/Act — that is, consciousness — and an entirely different fact — that is, the arbitrarily initiated reflection of the philosopher[25] upon this first F/Act — had been made earlier, then both the objections of the skeptics concerning the arrogant presumption of the systematic philosophers and the complaints of the latter concerning the obstinacy of the skeptics, would long since have ceased.

In this [original] act of reflection the *I* represents itself. It proceeds from itself. It externalizes itself. Insofar as it is represented, the *I* becomes Not-I, just like everything else that is represented. Consequently, the philosopher's action regarding the *I*, even that of the best, most perspicuous, and most intuitive [*unmittelbarsten*] philosopher, is based upon an act of representing. It follows that the highest action of the philosopher is that of reflection, or of reflective understanding.

In the course of philosophizing, all the actions of the *I* become merely represented. By no means, however, does it directly follow from this that *what* is represented is also nothing but an act of representing. Therefore, I am not permitted to conclude that the act of representing is, as such, the highest action of the *I*. (It is indeed the highest action of the person engaged in philosophizing, but not of the human being as such.) What the latter may be will be revealed by the investigation.

Representing is certainly the highest action of the cognizing I (which we mention here only provisionally and historically[26]); that is, it is the highest action of the I considered as an intellect.

All cognizing is related to a *Not-I*. Consequently, insofar as the *I* itself is supposed to be cognized within the *Wissenschaftslehre*, it is a *Not-I*, of which the absolute I has a representation. — The manner in which the *Wissenschaftslehre* proceeds is, therefore, purely theoretical. The *I* is represented. But from this it does not follow that the I must be represented merely *as representing*, merely as an *intellect*. Other determinations may well be found in the I. There is no disputing that the philosophizing and reflecting *I*, the I that as the subject[27] of the *Wissenschaftslehre*, is engaged purely in representing. But the represented I, the I that is the object of the *Wissenschaftslehre*, could well be something more.

J. G. Fichte

EXCERPTS FROM THE ZURICH
LECTURES ON *WISSENSCHAFTSLEHRE*

February or March 1794
As Transcribed by Jens Baggesen[28]

Wissenschaftslehre

The self-positing of the I means *its absolute presentation* [*Darstellung*]. Expressed historically, this mean: the I presents [*stellt sich dar*] inasmuch as it presents itself.[29]

———————

The I is the highest reality, without which no other reality could exist.
    Being purely and simply.
    The I exists for the I. — I am (for myself). — Everything that is exists, but only for the I.
    The theoretical portion of the *Wissenschaftslehre* goes no further than this.
    This theory[30] is therefore purely egoistic — and it cannot be otherwise. If it goes beyond this, it becomes Spinozism.[31]

———————

§ II.

Second foundational principle: a Not-I is posited in opposition to a Not-I

    1. The *Not-I* is not I: −A is not = A.
    The power purely and simply to posit [something] in opposition to something that has been purely and simply posited.
    NB. The I is what it is purely and simply by means of its own positing — the Not-I, however, is what the previously posited I is not. Its determination depends upon the I, but not vice versa.
    In itself, the Not-I* is absolutely nothing (for the I) — it exists only in representation.
    Logical principle: [obtained,] as was the case with the first [principle], by abstraction from the material [or content of the proposition, "the I posits the Not-I in opposition to itself"]:
    What is posited in opposition is not the same [as the subject that posits it in opposition].
Not-I is not I.†

———————

Wissenschaftslehre.
                              Attempt at an Improved Table of Categories

Quantitatas qualitiva — intensiva[32]
Reality
Negation
Limitation

———

* Category of negation. [Baggesen's footnote.]
    † What is posited in opposition is not the same: principle of contradiction, or the principle of positing in opposition. [Baggesen's footnote.]

Mathematical Categories

Quantitas quantitiva — extensiva[33]
Unity
Multiplicity
Universality

Qualitas quantitiva — relativa[34]
Substance and Accident
Cause and Effect
Action and Passivity

Dynamic Categories

Qualitas quantitiva modalis[35]
Possibility — Impossibility
Existence [*Dasein*] — Non-being [*Nichtsein*]
Necessity — Contingency

[I/2: 83]
[I, 412]

CONCERNING HUMAN DIGNITY

===============

DELIVERED AT THE CONCLUSION OF HIS
PHILOSOPHICAL LECTURES[36]

================

BY J. G. FICHTE

================

[I/2: 85]   1794

The author
dedicates these pages to his patrons and friends,
not as an inquiry,
but rather as an outpouring of enraptured feeling
following inquiry,
and in memory of those blissful hours he has spent with them
in a common striving for truth.

We have now completed our survey of the human mind or spirit [*Geist*]. We have laid a foun- [I/2: 87]
dation upon which can be erected a scientific system which will be an accurate presentation of
that system which is *originally present* within every human being. In conclusion, let us conduct a brief overview of the whole.

Philosophy teaches us to seek everything within the I. It is through the I that the dead,
formless mass [*Masse*] first acquires order and harmony. *Regularity* proceeds from the human
being alone; it surrounds him and extends to the boundary of his observation. As he expands
this boundary, order and harmony are expanded as well. His observation assigns to each of the [I, 413]
infinitely different things its proper place, so that no thing can take the place of another; it
introduces unity into infinite difference.[37] Human observation is what holds together the
celestial bodies and makes them into *one* organized body. Thanks to it, the planets move along
their allotted paths. From the lichen to the seraphim, this immense hierarchy owes its existence to the I. The system of the entire mental world[38] is [also] contained in the *I*, and man is
justified in expecting that the laws he gives to himself and to this entire world must be valid for
that world and in expecting that this same law will eventually be universally recognized. The I
harbors within itself the sure guarantee that order and harmony will forever continue to
spread outward from it into those regions where there is now neither order nor harmony, the
sure guarantee that the cultivation of the universe will continue to advance along with the
cultivation of human beings. Thanks to the human being, everything that still lacks form and
order will resolve itself into the most beautiful order, and what is already harmonious will
become ever more harmonious, in accordance with laws that are still to be developed.[39] He
will introduce order into turmoil and design into universal devastation. Thanks to him, decay
will become regeneration, and death will be summoned to a new and splendid life.

Such is the human being, considered merely as an observing intellect; but what is he
originally, when we think of him in terms of his active, practical power?

The human being does not simply *introduce* a *necessary* order into things, he also endows
them with an order he has freely *chosen*. Nature awakens in the presence of the human being,
and in his sight it prepares itself to receive from him a new and more beautiful creation. Even
the human body is the most spiritual one that could be made from the surrounding matter.[40]
In his atmosphere, the breeze becomes gentler, the climate milder, and nature rejoices in
anticipation of being transformed by him into a shelter for and caretaker of living beings. The
human being commands raw material to organize itself in accordance with his ideal and to
provide him with what he needs. For him, what was previously cold and dead waxes into
nourishing grain, refreshing fruit, and stimulating grapes; and it will wax into something else [I, 414]
for him just as soon as he commands it do so. — Animals are improved around the human [I/2: 88]
being; under his intelligent eye they shed their wildness and receive from the hand of their
master healthier nourishment, which they repay with willing obedience.

In addition to this, souls too become more refined around the human being. The more of a
human being one is, the deeper and wider will be one's influence upon other human beings;
and humanity will never fail to recognize anything that bears the true stamp of humanity.[41]
Every human heart and every human mind opens itself to any pure outpouring of humanity.
Around the higher human beings, others form a circle, in which those with the greatest degree
if humanity are nearest the center. Their spirits strive and struggle to unite and to constitute
but a single spirit in many bodies. They all share one understanding and one will, and they
stand before us as co-workers on the great, the only-possible, project of the human species.[42]
The higher human being powerfully propels his own age to a higher level of humanity, which
then looks back and is astonished to see the gulf it has traversed. With the arms of a giant, the
higher human being tears what he can grasp from the almanac of the human species.

Shatter the hut of clay in which he lives! With respect to his existence, the human being is
purely and simply independent of everything outside himself. He exists purely and simply

through himself. And even in this hut of clay, he already possesses a feeling of this existence — in those exalted moments when time, space, and all that is not he himself vanish for him, moments when his spirit forcefully tears itself free of his body and then, just as freely, returns to it, in order to pursue those goals that he can accomplish only by means of the body. — Divide the last two adjacent particles of dust that now surround him! He will *still* exist; and he *will* exist because he will *will* to do so. Through himself, and by virtue of his own energy, he is eternal.

[I, 415]   Hinder and frustrate his projects! — You may be able to delay them, but what are thousands and thousands of years in the almanac of humanity? — No more than a gentle morning dream once we have awakened. He will continue to exist, and he will continue to *act efficaciously*. What seems to you to be his disappearance is simply an expansion of his sphere [of efficacy]; and what seems to you to be death is his ripeness for a higher life. The *colors* and *external forms* of his projects can vanish for him; his *project* remains the same, and at every moment of his existence he is constantly drawing something new from outside himself into his own circle. And he will continue to do so, until everything has been incorporated into this circle — until everything material bears the stamp of his influence, and until all spirits constitute one with his own.

This is the human being. This is anyone who can say to himself, "*I am a human being.*"

[I/2: 89]   Should he not stand in sacred awe of himself and shudder and quake before his own majesty! — This is anyone who can say to me, "*I am.*" — You, wherever you may live, you, who simply bear a human countenance — whether you may still be living very much like an animal, planting sugarcane beneath the slave driver's lash — or whether you may find yourself on the coast of Tierra del Fuego,[43] warming yourself before a flame you did not kindle until it goes out, and then crying bitterly because it will not remain lit by itself — or whether you may seem to me to be the most wretched and depraved of villains: you are nevertheless what I am, for you can say to me "I am." For this reason, you remain my companion and my brother. It is certain that I too once stood upon that rung of humanity where you now stand — for it *is* a rung of human-ity, and there is no skipping any of the rungs along this ladder. Perhaps I stood there without the ability to be clearly consciousness that I was doing so, or perhaps I passed over it so quickly

[I, 416]   that I had no time to become conscious of my own state, but I surely stood there. And, though it may take a million years, or a million times a million years — what is time? — , you too will surely someday stand on that rung upon which I stand *now*, and someday you will surely occupy a rung from which I can influence you and you can influence me. You will someday be drawn into my circle, and I will be drawn into yours, and I will recognize you as my co-worker on my great project.[44] — This is what everyone who is an I is for me, who is [also] an I. Should I not tremble before the majesty contained in the image of the human being and before the divinity that, though perhaps concealed in darkness, inhabits the temple that bears this stamp?

In the presence of such thoughts, earth and heaven, time and space, and all the limitations of sensibility vanish for me. Should not the individual vanish for me as well? I will not lead you back to the individual.

All individuals are included in the one great unity of pure spirit.[*][45] Let this be the final word with which I commend myself to your memory — as well as the memory to which I commend you.

---

[*] Even if one is unfamiliar with my system, it is impossible to consider this thought to be Spinozistic, at least not if one wishes to survey the course of this meditation as a whole. For me, the unity of pure spirit is an *unreachable ideal*, a final end, but one that will never become actual.

Endnotes

I. *Concerning the Concept of the Wissenschaftslehre, or of so-called "Philosophy"*

1. This is the title page of the first, 1794 edition. The title page of the second, 1798 edition (published in Jena and Leipzig by Christian Ernst Gabler) omits the description of Fichte as "designated regular professor of philosophy at the University of Jena" and replaces the declaration "as a manuscript for the use of his listeners" with the phrase "second, improved and augmented edition." The main differences between the two editions is that the second edition adds a new, second Preface and omits the Third Part of the first edition ("Hypothetical Division of the *Wissenschaftslehre*"). The second edition also includes scores of smaller changes and additions, all of which are included in the footnotes of this translation.

2. *Aenesidemus, or Concerning the Foundation of the Elementary Philosophy Propounded in Jena by Professor Reinhold, including a Defense of Skepticism against the Pretensions of the Critique of Reason* was an anonymously published treatise, which appeared in 1792. Its author was a former classmate of Fichte's, G. E. Schulze, Professor of Philosophy at Halle. Fichte's first public announcement of his new philosophical project came in his review of *Aenesidemus*, which appeared in the *Allgemeine Literatur-Zeitung* in February of 1794, just as Fichte was beginning his Zurich lectures on what he was by this point calling "the *Wissenschaftslehre*" (*RA, GA*, I/2: 41–67; *SW*, I, pp. 3–25; *EPW*, pp. 59–77). For further information on this topic, see Breazeale, "The *Aenesidemus* Review and the Transformation of German Idealism," Ch. 2 of *TWL*.

3. Salomon Maimon was an eccentric, self-taught philosopher, whose *Versuch über die Transcendentalphilosophie* (1790) was recognized by Kant himself as containing some of the most trenchant criticisms of his new transcendental philosophy. Fichte was an admirer of this and other writings by Maimon, with whom he corresponded for several years. As he wrote to K. L. Reinhold in a letter of March–April 1795, "my respect for Maimon's talent knows no bounds. I firmly believe that he has overturned the entire Kantian philosophy as it has been understood until now by everyone, including you, *and I am prepared to prove it*" (*GA*, III/2: 275; *EPW*, pp. 383–4).

4. *Zum Range einer evidenten Wissenschaft*. For Fichte, the word *evident* usually has the sense of "self-evident." This complaint recalls the subtitle of Kant's *Prolegomena to any Future Metaphysics*: namely "That Would Put Itself Forward as a Science."

5. That is, the Kantian philosophy, which Fichte very frequently refers to simply as "the Critical philosophy." In order to preserve the technical meaning of this adjective in such contexts, it is here capitalized.

6. That is, the unexpected invitation from the University of Jena to begin lecturing on the *Wissenschaftslehre* in the Summer Semester of 1794.

7. Regarding Fichte's reception of the third *Critique*, see Breazeale, " 'The Summit of Kantian Speculation': Fichte's Reception of the *Critique of the Power of Judgment*." *Anuario Filosófico* 52 (2019): 113–44.

8. K. L. Reinhold was a distinguished philosopher who immediately preceded Fichte as "extraordinary professor" at the University of Jena. Reinhold was influential, first as a

popularizer of Kant's philosophy, in his *Letters on the Kantian Philosophy* (1786–87), and then as the first philosopher to propose a thoroughly systematic revision of the same, which he called "Elementary Philosophy" or "Philosophy of the Elements" and presented and developed in a series of treatises published between 1789 and 1791. The most striking features of Reinhold's Elementary Philosophy were its effort to derive all of Kant's conclusions from a *single foundational principle* and its identification of this principle as "the principle of consciousness" (viz., in consciousness, the subject distinguishes representations from both the subject and the object and relates them to both). According to Reinhold, the power of representation (*Vorstellungsvermögen*) is the most fundamental cognitive power of the human mind, from which he proposed to derive the powers identified by Kant (intuition and understanding). Fichte fully (albeit inaccurately) expected his audience at Jena to consist largely of adherents of Reinhold's *Elementarphilosophie*, which is surely one of the reasons he so strongly emphasizes the importance of grounding any adequate system of philosophy in a single foundational principle — even if, in Fichte's version, this same principle is immediately connected to two further foundational principles. Regarding Reinhold's achievement, see Breazeale, "Between Kant and Fichte: Karl Leonhard Reinhold's 'Elementary Philosophy,'" *Review of Metaphysics* 35 (1982): 785–821.

9. Viz., the First and Second Introductions (1797) to *VWL* (*GA*, I/4: 183–269; *SW*, I, pp. 419–518; *IWL*, pp. 1–105).

10. The "specific points" in question concern the aim [*Absicht*] and nature [*Wesen*] of the present work.

11. "My aim is always to promote *genetic* insight, and that is why I go back to the original operation of the human mind" (Fichte, *VLM, GA*, II/4: 154).

12. The task of such "critique" is to determine what metaphysics is and how it should proceed, a task that has to be accomplished prior to metaphysical inquiries.

13. At the time he was writing this (1798) Fichte had produced two, perhaps three "versions" of the foundational portion of his system: the one presented in 1794-95 (*GWL* and *GEWL*), the one presented three times in his lectures between 1796 and 1799 (*WLnm*), and the "Zurich lectures" from the winter and spring of 1794.

14. On this point, see especially *GA*, I/4: 209–16; *SW*, I, pp. 453–63; *IWL*, pp. 36–46.

15. The author in question is C. F. Nicolai. See Nicolai, *Beschreibung einer Reise durch Deutschland und die Schweiz im Jahre 1781*, Vol. 11 (Berlin, 1796), as cited in *FiG*, I, p. 322.

16. The hostile review to which Fichte here refers was an anonymous review of Kant's *Critique of Pure Reason*, which appeared in the January 19, 1782, issue of the *Göttingische Anzeigen von gelehrten Sachen*, a journal Fichte believed to be particularly hostile to his own writings as well.

17. Early in 1797 Fichte fulfilled this intention when he published, in the *Philosophische Journal einer Gesellschaft Teutscher Gelehrte*, the first (and only) installment of the *Annalen des philosophischen Tons*, in which he responded to two critical reviews of GNR (*GA*, I/4: 293–321; *SW*, II, pp. 459–89; *EPW*, pp. 341–54 [excerpt]).

18. The two reviews (which are not translated here) are J. S. Beck's omnibus review of *BWL* and *GWL*, published in February 1795 in the *Annalen der Philosophie und des philosophischen Geistes* and an anonymous review of F. W. J. Schelling's *Ueber die Möglichkeit einer Form der Philosophie überhaupt*, which appeared in the January 9, 1795, issue of the same journal. Note that Fichte here seems to treat this anonymous review of Schelling's book as a review of the *Wissenschaftslehre*.

19. The "celebrated veteran of philosophical literature" to whom Fichte refers is K. L. Reinhold, whose (temporary) conversion to the standpoint of Fichte's *Wissenschaftslehre* was made

public in a long and laudatory omnibus review of *BWL, GWL, GEWL*, and *VWL*, published in the *Ällgemeine Literatur-Zeitung* in January 1798.

20. That is to say, the Kantian or "Critical" system.

21. Less than a year before he wrote these words, Fichte had devoted a lengthy section of the Second Introduction to *VWL* to a detailed defense of his frequently reiterated claim that the *Wissenschaftslehre* and Kant's Critical philosophy share precisely the same "spirit." See *GA*, I/4: 221–44; *SW*, I, pp. 221, 468–91; *IWL*, pp. 51–76.

22. This is a reference to Fichte's *Attempt at a New Presentation of the Wissenschaftslehre* (a revised version of his lectures *WLnm*), which had begun to appear serially in the *Philosophisches Journal* in 1797. Unfortunately, Fichte was forced by events in Jena to discontinue publication following the appearance the two Introductions and Chapter One.

23. That is, how do I know the *necessary* and *sufficient* conditions for positing such a connection between two propositions?

24. The indicated distinction between "dogmatism" and "dogmaticism" was proposed by Schelling in the fifth of his *Philosophical Letters on Dogmatism and Criticism*, which appeared in the *Philosophisches Journal einer Gesellschaft Teutscher Geleherten*, Band 5, Heft 5 (1795).

25. Jacques Etienne Montgolfier, who, with his brother Joseph, invented the hot-air balloon in 1783.

26. *Der erste Satz aller Wissenschaftslehre*. Presumably, the phrase "all *Wissenschaftslehre*" here designates not a number of different systems (different *Wissenschaftslehren*), but rather, the single system of *The Wissenschaftslehre*, considered with respect to *all* its parts, as in the title of *GWL, Foundation of the Entire [gesammte] Wissenschaftslehre*.

27. "The reality of a definition is proven through the reality of the corresponding thing" (Fichte, *ZV, GA*, IV/3: 22; below, p. 441).

28. The term translated here as "experiment" is *Versuch* ("attempt," "try"). The "experimental" character of the *Wissenschaftslehre* is a frequent theme of Fichte's early writings. See *GWL, GA*, I/2: 269, 353, 365 (below, pp. 212, 290, 302); *GEWL, GA*, I/3: 148 (below, p. 385); *ZV*, IV/3: 38 (below, pp. 452–3); and *WLnmK, GA*, IV/3: 339; *FTP*, p. 101; and *VWL, GA*, I/4: 209; *IWL*, p. 37.

29. *erörtern*. In the Transcendental Aesthetic of *KrV*, Kant employed the term *Erörterung* ("explication" or "exposition") rather than "deduction" as the title for his analyses of space and time. See *KrV*, A22/B37 ff.

30. It is this "form" that determines the relationship between propositions and hence what can be properly inferred from each of them. Since the form of science is everywhere the same (as determined by the *Wissenschaftslehre*) there cannot be different kinds or modes of inference in the various sciences.

31. Fichte has now identified all the issues that will be discussed in the following sections of this short work: § 4 examines the *Wissenschaftslehre*'s claim to have "exhausted"—that is, to have exhaustively described and delimited—all human knowledge; § 5 examines the boundary between the *Wissenschaftslehre* and the various particular sciences; § 6 considers the relationship between the *Wissenschaftslehre* and formal logic; and § 7 investigates the relationship of the *Wissenschaftslehre* to its proper object, the necessary actions of the human mind.

32. "'Popular philosophers' are those who resolve every difficulty easily and without any effort or reflection, merely with the aid of what they call their own 'healthy common sense'" (Fichte, *EVBG, GA*, I/3: 34; *SW*, VI, p. 302; *EPW*, p. 153).

   Popular-Philosophie was a distinct movement associated with the German Enlightenment in the latter portion of the eighteenth century. As the name suggests, the "popular philosophers" generally worked outside the academy and cultivated an urbane and accessible, non-systematic literary style. They tended toward moderate skepticism and philosophical eclecticism, but were perhaps best known for their unyielding defense of "healthy common sense." For a succinct account of this movement, see Lewis White Beck, *Early German Philosophy: Kant and his Predecessors* (Cambridge, MA: Harvard University Press, 1969), pp. 319–24; and Frederick C. Beiser, *The Fate of Reason: German Philosophy from Kant to Fichte* (Cambridge, MA: Harvard University Press, 1987), pp. 165–92.

33. *durch weiteres Zurückschliessen.* That is, if one continued to seek higher principles from which the proposition in question (the one that does not belong to the present, completed system of human knowledge) could be inferred.

34. This is one of the passages (mentioned by Fichte in his Preface to the second edition), which were omitted from the second edition in order to avoid further controversy. The controversy provoked by this particular remark centered on objections raised by Fichte's brilliant student, Johann Friedrich Herbart. See the draft of Herbart's October 1, 1795, letter to Fichte, *GA*, III/2: 411–15, in which he outlines his objections.

35. It is important to keep in mind the restriction just noted. Fichte is certainly not making the absurd claim that there could be no particular sciences in the absence of *his* actual philosophical system, but rather, that there could be no such sciences in the absence of that system of the necessary activities of the human mind which is the *object* of the *Wissenschaftslehre*. See the following §.

36. The "otherwise admirable philosophical author" responsible for this objection to the footnote in the first edition is Salomon Maimon. See Maimon, "Ueber den Gebrauch der Philosophie zur Erweiterung den Erkenntniss," *Philosophisches Journal einer Gesellschaft Teutscher Gelehrten*, 2. Band, 2. Heft (1795), p. 13.

37. On this topic, see Fichte's unpublished 1794 lectures on "The Difference between the Spirit and the Letter in Philosophy" (*UGB, GA*, II/3: 315–42; *EPW*, pp. 192–215), as well his 1794 essay "On Stimulating and Increasing the Pure Interest in Truth" (*GA*, I/3: 83–90; *SW*, VIII, pp. 342–52; *EWP*, pp. 223–32).

38. The term "pragmatic history" can be traced back to Polybius. It was subsequently employed by, among others, Kant and Maimon. But Fichte uses this term in very different and distinctive way (derived from Ernst Platner, the first volume of whose *Philosophischen Aphorismen* served as the textbook for the lectures on "Logic and Metaphysics" that he delivered every semester throughout his career in Jena, beginning in the winter semester of 1795–96): namely, to designate an a priori *genetic* account. The difference between a "pragmatic history of the human" and a mere "historical" (or "journalistic") treatment of the same is that, whereas the latter simply chronicles "what has happened" (*data*), the former offers an a priori account of *how* and *why* it *had* to happen the way it did and therefore *become* what it *is*, and it explains this in terms of the constitutive *acts* of the human mind (*genesis*) (see *VLM, GA*, II/4: 222). For Fichte, therefore, a "genetic account" of the necessary acts of the human mind is the same thing as a "pragmatic history of the human mind." For a full discussion of Fichte's adoption and use of this term, see Breazeale, "A Pragmatic History of the Human Mind," Ch. 4 of *TWL*.

39. On the distinction between proof and derivation, see Kant *KrV*, A735/B765.

40. That is to say, the *Wissenschaftslehre* can provide an *exhaustive account or description* of representation as a necessary action of the intellect.

41. This is an obvious allusion to K. L. Reinhold's Elementary Philosophy, which did indeed take "representation" as its supreme concept and starting point. In his letter of March–April 1795, Fichte wrote as follows to Reinhold: "You, like Kant have given humanity something it will retain forever. He showed that one must begin with an

investigation of the subject; you showed that that investigation must proceed from a single first principle." In a later letter to Reinhold (July 2, 1795), Fichte conceded that "I acknowledge that your Principle of Consciousness is, at any rate, an announcement of the unity of speculative reason—something about which I do not at all disagree" (*GA*, III/2: 346; *EPW*, p. 400).

42. *Vorstellungsvermögen.* This is the term employed by Reinhold to name that power of the mind that he considered to underlie the powers discussed by Kant in *KrV*, the powers of intuition and understanding. One of the main objectives of the Jena *Wissenschaftslehre* was to demonstrate that this is *not* the most fundamental power of the mind after all.

43. This brief, untitled announcement, which was obviously intended to promote interest in Fichte's "public" lectures on *Morality for Scholars,* was distributed on its own and also published at the end of the first edition of *BWL.*

44. Fichte here refers to his "lectures" (that is, semester long lecture courses) on the *Wissenschaftslehre* in the plural because at this point he still intended to deliver one set of private lectures on "theoretical" and another on "practical" *Wissenschaftslehre,* a plan he soon abandoned, in order, as he put it, "not to make myself sick from studying" (Fichte to his wife, Johanna, May 20, 1794; *GA*, III/2: 113).

45. This declaration appeared on the title pages of the first editions of both *GWL* and *GEWL*, but was omitted from later editions of both.

46. During the summer semester of 1794 (his first at Jena), Fichte delivered his private lectures on the foundations of the *Wissenschaftslehre* five mornings each week from 6 to 7 a.m. He also delivered a very well-attended weekly series of public lectures on "Morality for Scholars" Friday afternoons at 6 p.m.

47. Fichte continued this series of public lectures into the following, winter semester of 1794–95. The first five were published as *EVGB* (*GA*, I/3: 25–68; *SW*, VI, pp. 291–346; *EPW*, pp. 144–84) and some of the later, unpublished ones were posthumously published as *UGB* (*GA*, II/3: 315–42; *EPW*, pp. 192–215).

II. *Foundation of the Entire Wissenschaftslehre*

1. This is a translation of the title page of the original, 1795 edition [= *A*]. An authorized second edition, published early in 1802 by the Tübingen publisher, J. G. Cotta appeared in a single volume along with *Outline of What is Distinctive of the Wissenschaftslehre with Regard to the Theoretical Power* and was described on the title page as a "new unaltered edition," but without the note "a manuscript for the use of his students" [= *B*]. A few weeks later, in 1802, a second, unauthorized new edition of *GWL* was published in Jena by the publisher of the first edition, C. E. Gabler [= *C*]. This edition included numerous corrections and additions made by Fichte himself before he withdrew his authorization for Gabler's new edition. It also retained on the title page the remark "a manuscript for the use of his students," with the additional note: "second, improved edition."

2. This preface was published in July 1795 along with the second installment of *GWL*, which consisted of Part Three of the same. In *B*, this Preface is re-titled "Forward to the First Edition."

3. This is an allusion to J. S. Beck's sarcastic and dismissive review of *BWL* and the first installment of *GWL*, published anonymously in February 1795 in Halle in the *Annalen der Philosophie und des philosophischen Geistes von einer Gesellschaft gelehrter Männer* (rpt. in *FiR*, I, pp. 264–78). Some of the more critical passages from Beck's review were reproduced by Fichte himself as an appendix to the second edition of *BWL* (*GA*, I/2: 169–72).

4. "The author of this treatise has been convinced by his reading of the modern skeptics—especially Aenesidemus, but also Maimon's excellent writings—of something that even before this seemed to him to be very likely: namely, that philosophy itself has not yet been elevated to the rank of a self-evident science, despite the efforts of the most perspicacious men. The author believes that he has discovered the reason for this. He also believes that he has discovered an easy way to satisfy fully all the quite well-founded demands made by the skeptic upon the Critical philosophy, and he believes he can do so in a manner that will reconcile the conflicting claims of the dogmatic and Critical systems, just as the conflicting claims of the various dogmatic systems were reconciled by the Critical philosophy." (Fichte, *BWL, GA*, I/2: 109; above, p. 152).

5. A reference to Fichte's unexpected call to Jena in the first months of 1794, which caused him to modify his plan to devote a year or more to developing and expounding his new system. Instead, he had to do this in his private lectures at Jena, beginning in May of 1794. ("Private" lectures were open only to tuition-paying students, whereas "public" lectures, such as Fichte's own *EVBG*, were free and open to everyone.)

6. In addition to hostile reviews in professional journals, Fichte's new philosophy was openly reviled by many of his colleagues, including some of those at Jena. As one of those colleagues, F. K. Forberg, wrote on March 18, 1795: "The parties at Halle [viz., J. S. Beck, J. A. Eberhard, and L. H. Jakob] have now formally opened their campaign [against Fichte]. Until now, all the Kantians and Anti-Kantians have become opponents of the Fichtean philosophy. Everywhere one hears ridicule concerning the foundational principle factory that appears to have been officially established in Jena. Other than Schiller, no significant person has yet declared himself for the Fichtean philosophy" (*Fragmente aus meinen Paperien* [1795], as cited in *FiG*, 1, p. 253).

7. *Nachbeterei.* This was one of Fichte's terms of abuse for the "so-called Kantians" who opposed the *Wissenschaftslehre*. See, the footnote below, *GA*, I/2: 335n., below, p. 273n. (a note cited by J. S. Beck in his harsh review), in which Fichte describes Kant's followers as mere *Nachbeter* or "parrots."

8. *ob ächte Philosophie, oder Schwärmerei, und Unsinn. Schwärmerei*, in this context, means irrational, enthusiastic speculation unbound by the laws of the understanding. Fichte's colleague at Jena, K. C. E. Schmid, in the Preface to his own *Grundriß des Naturrechts* (1795), was obviously referring to Fichte when he criticized certain unnamed "schwärmische Weltreformatoren," who promote the "creative imagination" to the detriment of reason and the laws of the understanding. *Unsinn* or "nonsense" was a term employed by Beck, in his review of *BWL* and the first installment of *GWL*, to describe the contents of Fichte's system. This passage is included in the selections from J. S. Beck's review that Fichte appended to the second edition of *BWL* (*GA*, I/2: 170). [*K*, p. 14.]

9. At the time he wrote this Preface Fichte was living in a country estate in Oßmannstedt, where he had sought refuge following the tumultuous events in Jena during the spring of 1795, which culminated in students throwing stones through his window and nearly injuring his elderly father-in-law. (For details concerning these events, see *EPW*, pp. 24–8.) Fichte did not lecture at all during the summer semester of 1795.

10. "The literalist [*Buchstäbler*] clarifies nothing for himself; instead, he learns it by heart and then repeats it. He grasps nothing with his powers of imagination and understanding, but rather with his memory alone. There are many things floating in his memory that do not belong to him but are utterly foreign. 'So and so said.' 'In this or that book it says': this is the ultimate and highest ground of demonstration we can expect from him. It is very much to philosophy's disadvantage and explains in particular the poor reputation that it enjoys even among honest men, that every great man is followed by others who are not nearly so great and who transform results that were originally proposed with spirit and

that can be grasped only by means of spirit into a catechism that can be — and quickly is — learned by heart" (Fichte, *UGB, GA,* II/2: 339; *EPW,* pp. 212–13).

11. This promise remained unkept, in the sense that Fichte never appears to have been satisfied with any of the subsequent versions of the foundational portion of his system, which he subsequently expounded in lectures in Jena, Berlin, Erlangen, and Königsberg, none of which were published during his lifetime. These include the so-called *Wissenschaftslehre nova methodo* [*WLnm*], upon which he lectured three times at Jena between 1796 and 1799; the unfinished *Neue Bearbeitung der Wissenschaftslehre* (Fall 1800); the *Darstellung der Wissenschaftslehre von 1801/02;* three different series of lectures on the *Wissenschaftslehre* delivered privately in Berlin in 1804; new lectures on *Wissenschaftslehre* in Erlangen (1805) and Königsberg (1807); four more complete sets of lectures on the *Wissenschaftslehre* from Fichte's final Berlin period (1810, 1811, 1812, and 1813); and the unfinished Berlin *Wissenschaftslehre* of 1814, suspended by Fichte's death in January of that year.

12. This is a reference to Parts One and Two of *GWL,* which were originally issued in fascicles to those attending Fichte's private lectures on "theoretical philosophy" during the Summer Semester of 1794 and were then privately circulated among Fichte's students and their acquaintances. These fascicles were subsequently bound together and issued by the Tübingen publisher Christian Ernst Gabler in September 1794 as the "first installment" of *GWL.* Similarly, the fascicles constituting Part Three were first distributed individually to students attending Fichte's private lectures on "practical philosophy" during the Winter Semester of 1794/95 and then bound together, along with this Preface, and issued by Gabler as the "second installment" of *GWL* in the late summer of 1795.

13. I.e., Part Three, "Hypothetical Division of the *Wissenschaftslehre*" (*BWL, GA,* I/2: 150–2; not in *SW;* above, pp. 189–90). This section, in which Fichte provides a very brief description of the "three absolutes" of his system, but does not further explain nor defend them, was omitted entirely from the second ed. of *BWL,* published in 1798.

14. "The I posits itself purely and simply; it is at once subject and object. But this is not an adequate description of the I. It is no more than a formula, and, for those who do not breathe life into it by an inner intuition they themselves produce, it remains an empty, dead, and unintelligible figure of speech" (Fichte, *VSSW, GA,* I/3, 254; *SW,* II, p. 442; *EWP,* p. 323).

15. "I do not know whether I can yet claim to have provided a clear presentation of these matters, but I do know that, if I had the requisite time, I could achieve greater clarity—as much clarity as could ever be desired. Taking into account my public lectures, I have to fill at least three printer's sheets every week, quite apart from my other endeavors" (Fichte to Goethe, June 21, 1794; *GA,* III/2: 143; *EPW,* p. 379).

16. "I would particularly like to repeat my request to let words remain words. I would ask you not to judge the individual parts too strictly before you have obtained an overview of the whole, and not to seek to construct such an overview by combining the individual parts, but rather, to seek to understand the individual parts from the perspective of the whole. My mind is so constructed that I must grasp the whole either all at once or not at all, and this explains the faulty organization of my writings" (Fichte to K. L. Reinhold, August 29, 1795, *GA,* III/2: 384; *EPW,* p. 406).

17. Another reference to Beck's review of *BWL* and Parts One and Two of *GWL,* which includes the following passage: "The reviewer first took up the *Foundation of the Entire Wissenschaftslehre* and was delayed for a good while by the thought that the author wished to parody the frivolous manner in which many up-and-coming philosophers of our day philosophize, in order to make this more obvious. In the end, however, the fact that the book was meant as a guide for lectures, as well as the precedents just mentioned, finally

forced the reviewer to conclude that the author was completely in earnest about his intention to reform philosophy" (*GA*, I/2: 171).

18. This reference to having worked through his system "three times" presumably refers to the following: (1) the lengthy manuscript written in Zurich during the Winter of 1793/94, *EM*, in which one can observe Fichte's initial "discovery" of some of the central themes and theses of his new system, even if he had not yet hit upon a name for the same; (2) the series of private lectures he delivered in Zurich during the first months of 1794, now baptized "*Wissenschaftslehre*"; and (3) the lectures on "theoretical" and "practical" philosophy that he delivered in Jena during the Summer Semester of 1794 and Winter Semester of 1794/95 (that is, the text of *GWL*). Though they consider this interpretation, the authors of *K* maintain instead that the three versions in question are (1) the Zurich lectures, (2) the Jena lectures of theoretical philosophy during the Summer Semester of 1794 (i.e., the "first installment" of *GWL*, and (3) the second installment of the same, consisting of Fichte's lectures on practical philosophy during the winter semester of 1794/95). [*K*, p. 19.]

19. *ächter durchgeführter Kriticismus*. Like Kant himself, Fichte generally employs the term "Criticism" or "Critical philosophy" as a synonym for transcendental idealism or "the Kantian philosophy" generally. In order to indicate this technical sense of the term, it is here capitalized throughout, as is the related term "the Critical philosophy."

   This passage may well have been influenced by Fichte's acquaintance with a passage from the manifesto for the new *Philosophisches Journal einer Gesellschaft Teutscher Geleherten* published in May 1795 by his colleague F. I. Niethammer, in which he maintained that none of the current versions of the Critical philosophy had succeeded in the task of securing all knowledge by means of a single universally valid foundational principle. It may have also been influenced by an article in the same journal in 1795 by Paul Anselm Feuerbach, which argued that Kant's Critical philosophy is simply incompatible with any system allegedly grounded upon a highest, absolute principle. [*K*, p. 20.]

   Fichte's point is that what matters is not what label is assigned to his philosophy but whether it is founded on self-evident principles and is successful in its goal of providing an exhaustive a priori account — or "pragmatic history" — of the necessary operations of the human mind.

20. *Ketzereien*. Though this term may seem overly strong, one should recall that Fichte was dismissed from his position at Jena in 1799 as a result of being charged with "atheism." For discussion of this event, see the editors' introductions to *IWL*, *EPW*, and *FAD*.

21. Despite this reference to the *Ostermesse* (i.e., the annual Easter Book Fair in Leipzig, which occurred on April 26 in 1795), the second installment of *GWL* did not actually appear until the end of July 1795.

22. This is the forward to the authorized second edition of *GWL*, advertised on the title page as "new, unaltered edition" and published in 1802 by the Tübingen publisher Johann George Cotta. It therefore appears only in *C*.

23. The "new presentation" in question was a revised version of the foundational portion of his entire system, based upon the lectures entitled "Foundations of Transcendental Philosophy (*Wissenschaftslehre*) *nova methodo*" [*WLnm*], which Fichte first delivered at Jena in the Winter Semester of 1796/97 and then repeated the following two Winter Semesters. He began publishing a revised version of these lectures in installments in the *Philosophisches Journal einer Gesellschaft Teutscher Gelehrten* in 1797 under the title *Attempt at a New Presentation of the Wissenschaftslehre* (*VWL*, *GA*, I/4: 183–281; *SW*, I, pp. 419–534; *IWL*, pp. 2–118). Unfortunately, this project was interrupted by the Atheism Controversy and only two Introductions and Part One of the same were ever published. When he arrived in Berlin in 1799, one of Fichte's first endeavors was to resume the project of revising for publication his lectures on *WLnm*. He announced the new presentation

not only in this 1802 Preface to *GWL* but even earlier, in an 1800 "Announcement to the Public" (*GA*, I/7: 153–64; *IWL*, pp. 186–201). It is unclear precisely to which version Fichte is referring in this Forward, since he abandoned his efforts to revise for publication his lectures on *WLnm* sometime in the winter of 1800/01 and began work instead on an altogether new version, the *Wissenschaftslehre* of 1801/02, which he prepared for publication but never actually published.

24. This promise was to remain unmet.

25. *Grundsatz*. Christian Wolff employed the term *Grundsatz* or "foundational principle" as a German translation of *axiom*, and *Lehrsatz* as a translation of *theorem*. It was important to Fichte to present his own system in a manner comparable to that mathematics, in keeping with his ambition to construct a system that would be "just as evident as geometry" (Fichte to J. F. Flatt, November/December 1793, *GA*, III/2: 21; *EPW*, p. 366.) Accordingly, *GWL* begins with three "first" or "foundational" principles — i.e., "axioms" — and then derives therefrom eleven "theorems." [*K*, p. 23.] Fichte is explicitly indebted to K. L. Reinhold for the notion that a truly "scientific" system of philosophy must always proceed from a single, indemonstrable (i.e., "unconditioned") but self-evidently certain *Grundsatz*. See his acknowledgment of his debt to Reinhold on this point in *RA* (*GA*, I/2: 62; *SW*, I, p. 20; *EPW*, p. 73).

26. "To say that human knowledge in its entirety is supposed to be exhausted means that one has to determine, unconditionally and purely and simply, not only what a human being is capable of knowing at his present level of existence, but what he is capable of knowing at any possible and conceivable level of his existence." (Fichte, *BWL*, *GA*, I/2: 129; above, p. 172).

27. "If the principle from which the *Wissenschaftslehre* begins could be proven, then it would — precisely for this reason — not be the foundational principle. Instead, the highest principle from which the principles in question were demonstrated would be the starting point. — That from which the *Wissenschaftslehre* proceeds can neither be grasped through concepts nor communicated thereby; it can only be directly intuited" (Fichte, *GG*, *GA*, I/5: 350n.; *SW*, V, p. 180n., *IWL*, pp. 145–6n.).

"In the *Wissenschaftslehre*, 'to determine' means the same as 'to restrict', and indeed, 'to restrict to a certain *region* or *sphere* within our *knowledge*.' But the absolute foundational principle embraces the entire *sphere* of our knowledge. This principle is valid in relation to any consciousness whatsoever" (Fichte, *WLnmH*, commentary on § 1 of *GWL*; *GA*, IV/2: 32–3; *FTP*, p. 118).

28. See Fichte's discussion of the need for an absolutely first, utterly unconditioned foundational principle or *Grundsatz* in *BWL*, as well as the discussion of his debt to Reinhold in the editor/translator's introduction to *EPW*. As Fichte explains (*GA*, I/2: 273 and 282; below pp. 215 and 224), "to determine" a proposition is to *restrict* or to *limit* its validity; hence, "any positing whatsoever of quantity, whether of reality or of negation, is called 'determination.'" The point is that the absolutely first foundational principle has unlimited validity and applies to all our knowledge — here taking *Wissen* in a broad sense, which includes practical knowledge (of moral obligation, e.g.) as well as theoretical cognition. [*K*, pp. 25–8.]

29. *Tathandlung* is a somewhat obscure legal and theological term adopted by Fichte as an apt, technical term to designate the original character of the I as both an activity (of self-positing) and the product of that same activity (the I that is posited). The term *Tat* means "deed" or "achievement" and the term *Handlung* "action." The term *Tathandlung* is here employed in contrast to the ordinary term for a mere "fact" or "state of affairs" (*Tatsache*). *Tathandlung* designates the original and unconditioned self-positing of the I, which, in Fichte's view, has no existence or "nature" apart from its own original and spontaneous

"positing" of the same, an act (or "F/Act") that can be derived from no higher one. As Fichte explains a few pages later (*GA*, I/2: 259; below, p. 203): "The I *is*, and it *posits* its being and does so by means of its own sheer being. — It is both the acting subject and the product of the act, what is active and what is produced by means of the activity. Action and deed [*Handlung und Tat*] are one and the same, and this is why the '*I am*' is the expression of a F/Act and also the only such expression that is possible." What the term *Tathandlung* is intended to emphasize is that the I is, from the start, both a "doer" and a "knower," neither a purely "theoretical" nor a purely "practical" entity, but always already *both at once*. For further discussion of this important term see the Editor's notes on "Fichte's Technical Vocabulary," above, p. 103.

30. As Fichte explains in § 8 of *GWL* below (*GA*, I/2: 424; below, p. 353), "to reflect" means "to direct one's attention to something," whereas "to abstract" means "to withdraw one's attention from something else." Obviously, these two actions always accompany one another, inasmuch as one must abstract from *other* objects of reflection in order to reflect upon any specific one.

    In the "First Introduction" to *VWL*, which was published in 1797, Fichte emphasizes that transcendental philosophy begins with an act of *abstracting* entirely from everything but one's own I while simultaneously *reflecting* upon what remains within consciousness following this act of global abstraction. Another name for such "reflection" is "attentiveness" or *Aufmerksamkeit*. See *GA*, I/4: 188–91; *SW*, I, pp. 425–9; *IWL*, pp. 11–14.

31. *Tatsache des Bewußtseins*. This was a phrase popularized by K. L. Reinhold and others, who sought to ground their systems upon appeals to what they claimed to be the "immediate facts of consciousness." Indeed, Reinhold maintained that his own foundational principle, the "Principle of Consciousness," which asserts that in every state of consciousness the subject distinguishes the representation from and relates it too both the representing subject and the object represented, is ultimately grounded upon and confirmed by an immediate "fact of consciousness." Here Fichte implicitly contrasts such an approach with his own, which seeks to explain these same "facts" of consciousness in terms of something even higher: the original self-productive activity of the I. (See *RA*, *GA*, I/2: 48–9; *EPW*, p. 65.) As Fichte pointed out in a published "Private Letter" in 1800, "whereas psychology teaches us about the facts of consciousness, what the *Wissenschaftslehre* is talking about is what one finds to be the case when one discovers oneself!" (*GA*, I/6: 387n.; *SW*, V, p. 394 n.; *IWL*, p. 174n.)

32. The "rules" in question are the laws of general logic, including the principle of identity, the principle of opposition, and the principle of sufficient reason (or "grounding principle," *Satz des Grundes*). Here, in Part One of *GWL*, these three logical laws or principles will be derived from, respectively, the first, second, and third foundational principles of the entire system.

33. See *GA*, I/2: 148–9; *SW*, I, pp. 79–80; *EPW*, pp. 132–3.

34. What Fichte is pointing out here is that, no matter which "fact of consciousness" one may begin with, one can always think away (or "abstract from") all its empirical determinations; but one cannot abstract from self-identity as a fact of empirical consciousness: A = A. [*K*, pp. 39–40.] As Fichte will note, there is an intimate connection between one's inability to think of anything without presupposing the principle of identity and one's capacity to think away or abstract from every object of consciousness *except* the pure I itself.

35. This is the proposition or principle that Fichte will later identify as the "principle of identity." See *GA*, I/2: 283; below, p. 225.

36. *Ohne allen weitern Grund*. The term *Grund* means (among other things) "ground," "basis," "cause," or "reason." The claim here is that human beings possess the ability to posit some

things, including the principle of identity, freely or spontaneously — that is, for no "reason," or on the basis of no external "ground."

37. "jener Satz sei schlechthin, d.i., *ohne alle weitern Grund*, gewiß: und indem man dieses ohne Zweifel mit allgemeiner Bestimmung, tut schreibt man sich das Vermögen zu, *etwas schlechthin zu setzen*." The term *"Vermögen"* (often translated as "faculty," but here translated consistently as "power") here refers to an innate capacity of the human mind, in this case, its ability to "posit something purely and simply." "To posit" (*setzen*) X is simply to assert or affirm or declare. To do so *"schlechthin"* — "purely and simply" — is to engage in an act of positing that possesses no ground or basis or reason beyond itself. For Fichte, the name for the ability or power to posit something purely and simply is *Vernunft* or "reason" (see *GA*, I/2: 373-4; below, p. 309). Such an act (or F/Act) satisfies the requirement of a "free" action in the negative, Spinozistic sense: i.e., it is nether produced by nor grounded in anything beyond itself. For this reason, the term *schlechthin* is sometimes translated as "absolutely," a translation that is here avoided as potentially misleading (though Fichte does indeed sometimes treat *schlechthin* and *absolut* as synonyms). Instead, *schlechthin* is here almost always translated as "purely and simply." Finally, note the implicit connection made in this passage between a principle or *proposition* (*Satz*) and the act of *positing* (*setzen*) the same.

38. See the following point 5.

39. Concerning the meaning of the formula "A = A," see Fichte's 1800 review of C. G. Bardili's *Grundriss der Ersten Logik*, in which he contrasts his understanding of this formula with Bardili's as follows:

"Had you grasped merely the first pages of the *Wissenschaftslehre* with a sense for the transcendental, then you would immediately have noticed that Bardili makes an entirely different use of the formula 'A=A' than occurs in these first pages. You would already have realized that in the *Wissenschaftslehre* this formula does not represent the mere *repetition* of A (as an act of thinking) — which could never furnish a single, continuous thread of consciousness, but would instead provide a new self-subsistent consciousness at every moment. Instead, in the *Wissenschaftslehre*, the copula contains a reflection *upon the posited-being of the first A occuring within consciousness*, and hence a consciousness that reverts into itself, i.e., self-consciousness — which is precisely that act by means of which the I comes into being. You would have realized that one does not arrive at the foundation of all consciousness by means of even the purest thinking and that it is by no means the case that such pure thinking stands above the I, but rather (if I may so express myself), that the I signifies *intellectual activity* [*Intelligieren*] par excellence, of which *thinking, intuiting*, and *willing* are only sub-species, which are not themselves posited purely and simply, but must instead be derived from the I. You would have noticed that Bardili does not even succeed in grasping *thinking* as an *act*, rather than simply as something *given*, as pure *being*-thought" (*Rezension Bardili*, *GA*, I/6: 447; *SW*, II, p. 501).

40. *festgesetz*. This term is here employed as a synonym for *gesetz*, and it seems to be employed in the same manner later in *GWL* (*GA*, I/2: 289–90; below, p. 230). [*K*, p. 50.]

41. This paragraph anticipates and presupposes Fichte's thesis that anything "given" to the I must be "posited" by the I — that every *datum* is originally a *factum* (something made). See *GA*, I/2: 364; below, p. 301. [*K*, pp. 51–2.]

42. *absoluten Setzen*. This is an example of Fichte describing as "absolute" positing what he had previously described as "purely and simply" positing.

43. *Durch dieses Operation*: that is, by means of the I's act of positing itself purely and simply. Fichte probably picked up this Latin term as a synonym for action or activity from Reinhold, who used it to refer to the "Operations of the Mind." Fichte also employs the

term "operation" in this sense in his July 2, 1795, letter to Reinhold (*GA*, III/2: 344) and in *GEWL* (*GA*, I/3: 182; below, p. 414). [*K*, p. 68.]

44. "Regarding the 'A = A' of the *Foundation* [*of the entire Wissenschaftslehre*]: This is a judgment connected with an original *act of self-reverting*. — It is very clear that reflection upon oneself is a condition for any reflection upon A. I do not believe that the present presentation [of the *Wissenschaftslehre*] can be any more illuminating [on this point]. And yet, just look how this guidance has been misunderstood! At that time I did not yet realize the thoroughly unphilosophical and dogmatic character of the age with which I had to deal" (Fichte, *NBWL*, *GA*, II/5: 338).

45. "It should by no means be held against a philosophical system that its object, considered as the explanatory ground of experience, must lie beyond experience; for this is true of every philosophy and is required by the very nature of philosophy" (Fichte, *VWL*, *GA*, I/4: 190; *SW*, I, p. 428; *IWL*, p. 14).

46. Though Fichte does not explain what these "essential conditions" are, they would appear to be those features of an "action" which permit empirical consciousness to recognize judging as an action. Such conditions (or grounds) are as follows: In every act there must be an acting subject and a product of the action, and this is the case in the act of judging, as well as in that of representing. A condition for the possibility of action is that there be present a *distinction* between the acting subject and the product of its action. [*K*, pp. 62–3.]

47. *Bedingungen.* The "conditions" in question here must not be confused with what was described above, in point (a.), as the "conditions for being an action within empirical consciousness." Instead what Fichte appears to be referring to now are the empirical determinations of consciousness, in contrast with the non-empirical or "pure" determinations of the same. "Pure activity" or "the pure I" is always "non-empirical." [*K*, p. 68.]

48. *Das ich setzt sich selbst.* See the long, informative discussion of this controversial phrase in *K*, pp. 69–76.

49. "The rational being *is* only insofar as it *posits* itself *as being*, i.e., only insofar as it is conscious of itself. All *being*, that of the I as well as that of the Not-I, is a determinate modification of consciousness; and without some consciousness there is no being. Whoever claims the opposite assumes a substratum of the I, something that is supposed to be an I without being one, and thereby contradicts himself" (Fichte, *GNR*, *GA*, I/3: 324; *SW*, III, p. 3; *FNR*, p. 4).

50. According to Fichte, every "activity" has a "product" and is inseparable from the same. "Acting" is therefore "making." As will become clear in Part Two, the product in question is made possible by the (unconscious) operation of the productive power of imagination, which Fichte describes as the "absolute power of production." See *GA*, I/2: 361 and 443; below, pp. 298–9 and 371. [*K*, p. 79.]

51. "All that remains after abstraction has been completed (i.e., after we have abstracted from everything we can) is the *abstracting subject* itself, that is, the *I*. This I is what remains, and it is this *for itself*. It is therefore a subject-object. The I that remains after abstraction has been completed is the I with its original character, the I in its purity. I would rather not call this a *fact* [*Tatsache*], since the I does not remain left over in the manner of something found, that is, as an *object*. Instead, I would prefer to call it a *F/Act* [*Tathandlung*], if it is to have a name that bears some analogy with customary philosophical terminology — to which the previous presentation of the *Wissenschaftslehre* [= *GWL*] remained all too faithful, thereby exposing itself to the distortions of the literalists" (Fichte, *VSSW*, *GA*, I/3: 259; *SW*, II, p. 448; *EPW*, p. 328).

   As described at the beginning of § 1, "this foundational principle [of the *Wissenschaftslehre*] is supposed to express that *F/Act* which neither appears nor can appear among the empirical determinations of our consciousness, but instead lies at the basis of all consciousness and alone makes consciousness possible." Though he had previously described this foundational principle, the "I am," as based upon or expressing a fact of consciousness, Fichte now maintains that this principle is actually based upon something deeper still, something underlying empirical consciousness (and, in particular, underlying all empirical consciousness of the "fact" that "A = A"): namely, upon a purely self-referential or self-productive activity, which he calls the "pure I" or the "F/Act." (We cannot distinguish the I from the *Tathandlung*; these are identical expressions. It is not that the I is brought into being by the F/Act and then acts on its own. On the contrary, it is sustained by a *Tathandlung* at every moment of consciousness — which is not to say that the I itself is conscious of this. The pure I, the *Tathandlung*, is not and cannot be an object of empirical consciousness, except in the special sense that the philosopher is able to *infer* or to *postulate* its reality from the facts of empirical self-consciousness.) The transition from *Tatsache* to *Tathandlung* occurs in point 5; above. [*K*, p. 80.]

52. Despite this claim, Fichte nevertheless sometimes uses the term *Tathandlung* in the plural and speaks of additional F/Acts on the part of the I. See, e.g., *ZV, GA*, IV/3: 23–4; below, p. 442, where he states that the *Wissenschaftslehre* is grounded on several F/Acts. As an example, he suggests that geometry is based on a specific *Tathandlung* of the I underlying intuitions of space and time, but derivable from and based on the highest F/Act of self-positing. See too *GNR*, in which Fichte seems to treat the three foundational principles of *GWL* as grounded upon three distinct *Tathandlungen* (*GA*, I/3: 336; *SW*, III, p. 25; *FNR*, p. 25). [*K*, p. 33].

53. This is the only occurrence of this term in Fichte's writings. The opposite of the "formal subject" would be the I as "material subject." Hence the contrast is between the I as substance (formal subject), which is the I that posits itself purely and simply, and the I that as engaged in representation and posits for itself its own accidents (the existing I or material subject, which is never posited purely and simply). For Fichte, this relation of the formal to the material I is the original relationship from which the logical relation of subject and predicate is derived.

    In *EM* Fichte defines the "absolute subject" as "a subject that can never in turn become a predicate" (*GA*, II/3: 170). Cf. the later remark "The absolute I of the first foundational principle is not *something; (it possesses no predicate,* nor can it have one); it is purely and simply *what* it is, and this cannot be clarified any further" (*GA*, I/2: 271; below, p. 210). To be sure, the essence of the I cannot be exhausted by any predicate; on the other hand, it has the task of determining itself by means of predicates ad infinitum (see *GA*, I/2: 277 below, pp. 219–20).Therefore, it is not merely permissible; it is urgently necessary to think of the I as substance (*GA*, I/2: 300; below, p. 239). In § 1 we are still abstracting (though only temporarily) from finitude and no specific *use* is yet made of the category of limitation, which Fichte derives from that of substance. [*K*, p. 83.]

54. The essence or "essential nature" (*Wesen*) of anything, the I included, is simply *what* that thing is. In the case of the absolute I, its "essence" is to posit itself purely and simply, and what it posits in this way, when reflected upon, is reflected upon *as constituting* the I's own essence. The I is, after all, only what it posits itself to be. Hence the being (*Sein*) and the essence (*Wesen*) of the I are posited as one and the same — in and by means of a unique F/Act or *Tathandlung*.

55. *und das Ich ist demnach für das Ich schlechthin, und notwendig. Was für sich selbst nicht ist, ist kein Ich.* To say that the I exists "for itself" is simply to say that it is "self-conscious."

    "Everything that exists does so only for the I, and the I itself exists only for the I. One can by no means speak of an existence [*Bestehen*] of the I other than for itself, for this would be purely and simply incomprehensible, and one could make no sense whatsoever of it" (Fichte, *VLM, GA*, II/4: 341).

56. Fichte was probably familiar with this topic in the version discussed by Leibniz in his July 6, 1811 letter to Jacobi — a passage translated and quoted by Jacobi on p. 161n. of his 1787

edition of *David Hume über den Glauben*, a work with which Fichte was quite familiar. [*K*, p. 85.]

57. "What then is the worst misfortune that can befall him? It is what one ordinarily calls 'death.' But what is death, this most terrible and widely feared thing that can befall us on earth? Death is an appearance like any other appearance. But no appearance can affect the I. Only if one thinks that it can affect the I is there anything fearful about death. But anyone who feels his own self-sufficiency will find it physically impossible to think that death can affect the I. For such a person, death is nothing more than the end of a particular series of appearances. He does not know what will come after the end of this series, and that is the least of his worries. What he does know is that *he* will exist. It is impossible for him to think that he will not exist, for the I is that from which he cannot abstract. To try to think of oneself as nonexistent is pure nonsense" (Fichte, *UGB*, *GA*, II/3: 332; *EPW*, p. 207).

58. "Everything that exists does so only for the I, and the I itself exists only for the I. One can by no means speak of a continual existence [*einem Bestehen*] of the I other than for itself, for this is something that purely and simply cannot be understood and from which not the least can be made" (Fichte, *VLM*, *GA*, II/4: 341).

59. "Just as certainly as a human being possesses reason, he is his own purpose, that is to say, he does not exist because something else ought to exist; instead, he exists purely and simply because *he* ought to exist. His sheer being is the ultimate purpose of his being, or (which amounts to the same thing) it is contradictory to inquire concerning any purpose of man's being: he is *because* he is. This quality of absolute being, or being for its own sake, is the characteristic feature, the determination or vocation of every human being, considered purely and solely as a rational being" (*EVBG GA*, I/3: 29; *SW*, VI, pp. 295–6; *EPW*, p. 148).

60. "'*I posit myself as positing myself*': This presupposes that something has already been posited, something that can only be inferred and grasped by means of thinking. But what we are describing here is immediate consciousness, and the I consists in this harmony.

   "'*I posit myself purely and simply*': This means that I am conscious of myself, first as the object of consciousness, and then again as the subject, i.e., the subject who is conscious. What is discovered and its discoverer are here one and the same. The I is the same as immediate consciousness.

   "'*I am*': in this context, *to be* means to be the object of a concept. In contrast, *becoming* signifies an *acting*, and this *acting*, this activity, considered in a *state of repose* [*als ruhend*], is a concept, a being, a determinate being, which the I portrays as a *fact*, as a concept, as something discovered.

   "Here [in *WLnm*] we began with the F/Act and arrived at the fact; but the method of the book [*GWL*] is just the reverse.

   "'*In a state of repose*' means that I discover the I as something *posited*, as a product, as something discovered.

   "One must begin with being and infer self-positing therefrom, and vice versa. Similarly, one must infer the intuition from the concept, and vice versa. Both must be present together. A state of repose must be connected with the intuition of an activity. I obtain the concept only by means of the intuition, and I obtain the intuition only by means of the concept, for both occur simultaneously in the free act of self-reverting activity. Nothing precedes this act: no *something in itself* is presupposed as the ground of this act" (Fichte, Commentary on § 1 of *GWL*, *WLnmH*, *GA*, IV/2: 33; *FTP*, pp. 118–19).

   "In the printed *Wissenschaftslehre* [i.e., in *GWL*] we proceeded from the concept to the intuition, whereas the path followed here [in *WLnm*] is just the reverse" (Fichte, Commentary on § 1 of *GWL*, *WLnmK*, *GA*, IV/3: 349; *FTP*, p. 118).

61. *Die Erzählung*. This term, which might also be translated as "narrative" or "tale," or "account," is an anticipation of Fichte's familiar description of the transcendental philosopher as a "pragmatic historian" of the human mind (*BWL, GA*, I/2: 147; above, p. 186; and *GWL, GA*, I/2: 365; below, p. 302.)

62. In this context, "originally" means "a priori." "The foundational determinations [*Grundbestimmungen*] of consciousness, which is what philosophy deals with, is the Kantian a priori, i.e. what is original" (Fichte, *SB, GA*, I/7: 211; *SW*, II, p. 353; *CCR*, p. 63).

63. Though he employs this subject-object formula frequently in *WLnm* and *VWL*, it first appeared in *VSSW*, in the spring of 1796, immediately prior to Fichte's first lectures on *WLnm*. See *GA*, I/3: 259; *SW*, II, p. 448; *EPW*, p. 328.

64. "Logic does not provide the foundation for the *Wissenschaftslehre*; it is, instead, the latter that provides the foundation for the former. It is purely and simply the case that the *Wissenschaftslehre* cannot be demonstrated from logic. Prior to the *Wissenschaftslehre*, one may not presuppose the validity of a single proposition of logic — including the law of contradiction. On the contrary, every single logical proposition, as well as logic in its entirety, must be demonstrated from the *Wissenschaftslehre*. What has to be shown is that the forms established within logic actually are the forms of a particular content in the *Wissenschaftslehre*.

"Neither is the *Wissenschaftslehre* conditioned and determined by logic; instead, it is logic that is conditioned and determined by the *Wissenschaftslehre*. The *Wissenschaftslehre* does not somehow obtain its form from logic. It possesses its form within itself and establishes it for a possible [subsequent] free act of abstraction. The *Wissenschaftslehre* is the condition for applying logic; the forms established by the *Wissenschaftslehre* may not be applied to any content not already contained in the *Wissenschaftslehre*. These forms do not necessarily have to be applied to the entire content they contain within the *Wissenschaftslehre*, for in that case no particular science [of logic] would arise, and we would instead have nothing but a repetition of portions of the *Wissenschaftslehre*. Nevertheless, these logical forms must necessarily be applied to a portion of the content of the *Wissenschaft*, to a content included within the content of the latter. If this condition is not met, then the science produced thereby is nothing more than a castle in the air.

"Finally, the *Wissenschaftslehre* is necessary — not, to be sure, as a clearly thought-out and systematically established science, but rather as a natural predisposition. Logic, on the other hand, is an artificial product of the freedom of the human mind. No knowledge nor science whatsoever would be possible without the *Wissenschaftslehre*; without logic, all of the sciences could still have come into being, only somewhat later. The former is the exclusive condition for all the sciences; the latter is a highly beneficial discovery for securing and facilitating scientific progress" (Fichte, *BWL, GA*, I/2: 138–9; above, p. 180).

65. As previously mentioned, "to determine" a proposition is "to limit it." Fichte's point is that the validity of the principle of identity is limited to the sphere of what is posited in and by the I; i.e., it does not apply to things in themselves. The I as "substance" (see below, § 4) is that domain or "sphere" within which every A is posited. [*K*, p. 92.]

66. *Handlungs*art. The I's distinctive "manner of acting" is what was previously called a F/Act or *Tathandlung*. [*K*, p. 92.]

67. That is, given by the form of the preceding inference from being-posited to being.

68. *Realität*. In contrast with many previous philosophers, including Spinoza, Leibniz, and Kant, who identified a thing's "reality" with its "essence" and distinguished "reality" from "actuality" (*Wirklichkeit*), Fichte generally understands reality to be the same as existence (*Existenz*), which he always interprets as "actuality" or *Wirklichkeit* — a term closely

related to "acting" or "having an effect" (*wirken*). Ordinary existence (which is what is derived in § 3), is therefore understood as a limitation of a greater reality, the original activity of the I qua *Tathandlung*. In striking contrast to Kant's effort to derive the categories of the understanding from the forms of judgment, Fichte's project is to derive them from the mind's various *modes of acting*. Here he derives the qualitative category of "reality" from the I's unconditioned positing of itself. [*K*, pp. 92–3.]

69. A "thing" is what is posited within the I as a *product* of the I's own activity (though, of course, it is not recognized to be such by the empirical subject or "finite I"). As such, it is something static and lifeless. [*K*, p. 94.]

70. "My respect for Maimon's talent knows no bounds. I firmly believe that he has completely overturned the entire Kantian philosophy as it has been understood until now by everyone, including you. No one noticed what he had accomplished; they looked down upon him from their heights. I believe that future ages will mock us bitterly" (Fichte to Reinhold, March–April 1795; *GA*, III/2: 275; *EPW*, 383–4).

71. In his *Versuch über die Transzendentalphilosophie* (1790) and again in his *Streifereien im Gebiete der Philosophie*, I (1793), Maimon challenged the strategy of Kant's transcendental deduction of the pure categories of the understanding and maintained that before raising the *quid juris* concerning our right to apply *any* of the categories (including the category of *reality*), one must first answer the *quid facti* concerning the actual application and applicability of a priori categories to the a posteriori manifold of intuition. According to Maimon, Kant simply cannot answer this question, since, unlike Leibniz, he distinguishes sharply between the powers of sensibility and understanding as two utterly independent sources or "roots" of human cognition. Maimon therefore accuses Kant of begging the central question against Hume's skepticism, inasmuch as he assumes precisely what Hume denies: namely, that we do — *as a matter of fact* — experience the "necessary connection" of impressions. See *Versuch über die Transzendentalphilosphie* (Berlin: Christian Friedrich Voß und Sohn, 1790), pp. 62–73; *Essay on Transcendental Philosophy*, trans. Nick Midgley, Henry Somers-Hall, Alistair Welchman, and Mertin Reglitz [NY: Continuum, 2010], pp. 37–43.

    Fichte owed a triple debt to Maimon for: (1) his insight that Kant had not refuted Humean skepticism; (2) his reference to Leibniz, who treated the distinction between sensibility and understanding as a quantitative rather than a qualitative one; and (3) his argument against realism: namely, that no heterogeneous "thing in itself" could conceivably produce a representation in us. [*K*, pp. 95–6.]

72. How reality can be "transferred" from subject to object will be one of the chief issues addressed in Part Two, below.

73. This is apparently how Kant interpreted the Cartesian *cogito*. See *KrV*, B422n. Descartes, however, explicitly rejects such a "syllogistic" interpretation of his claim and asserts (in his response to the second set of objects to the *Meditations*) that the "I think" is a foundational concept obtained through direct insight into oneself.

74. " 'I think' presupposes 'I.' Thinking is only one determination of the I, only one portion of the actions of which I am capable. I do not merely think, but I also feel and will. Everything is contained in the I. Nevertheless, I cannot arrive at a determinate concept of the I without having obtained the concept of myself as such; consequently, consciousness of myself as such precedes all consciousness of myself as engaged in thinking" (Fichte, Student transcript of *VLM*, *GA*, IV/1: 220–1).

75. I.e., the first principle of Reinhold's Elementary Philosophy, also known as "the principle of consciousness": in consciousness, the subject distinguishes both the subject and the object from the representation and relates it to them both.

76. Reinhold "goes considerable farther" than Descartes because "representing" is a higher and more encompassing mental act than merely "thinking." But, for Fichte, there is a still higher (and even more original) act of the I: namely, *positing*.

77. "Both distinguishing and relating can become objects of representation, and they are such within the context of the Elementary Philosophy. However, they are not representations to begin with, but only ways in which the mind must necessarily be thought to act if it is to produce a representation. Of course, it undeniably follows from this that representation is not the highest concept for every conceivable operation of our minds" (Fichte, *RA*, *GA*, I/2: 48–9; *SW*, I, p. 9; *EPW*, pp. 64–5).

78. Spinoza denies the presence of "pure consciousness" within finite human beings, whereas for Fichte, all empirical consciousness is simply a determination of "pure" or original consciousness. See above, point 6, where Fichte explains that all empirical activity is a determination of the original, pure activity of the I — i.e. the *Tathandlung*. (See too *GA*, I/2: 383 below, p. 318): "the more a determinate individual is able to think himself away, the more his empirical consciousness approximates pure consciousness." In contrast, as Fichte proceeds to explain, Spinoza assigns "pure consciousness" only to his absolute principle (God or nature) and treats empirical, human consciousness simply as one of the infinitely many necessary modes of this single substance. For a detailed discussion of Fichte's acquaintance with and interpretation of Spinozism, see Breazeale "Fichte's Spinoza: 'Common Standpoint,' 'Essential Opposition,' and 'Hidden Treasure,'" *Internationales Jahrbuch des Deutschen Idealismus/International Yearbook of German Idealism* 14 (2018): 103–38.

79. "Even without being familiar with my system, it is impossible to consider this thought [viz., that *all individuals are included within the one great unity of spirit*] to be Spinozistic, at least if one surveys the entire movement of this meditation. The unity of pure spirit is for me an *unobtainable ideal*, an ultimate goal, which, however, will never be actual" (Fichte, *Über die Würde des Menschen* [*Concerning Human Dignity*, 1794], *GA*, I/2: 89n.; *SW*, I, p. 416n.; below, p. 460n.).

80. "To be precise, the *Wissenschaftslehre* […] or transcendental idealism — understood as the system that moves within the circumscribed territory of the subject-objectivity of the I, as finite intellect, and its original limitation through *material feeling* and *conscience* — is able to deduce completely the sensible world within this circumscribed area, but it absolutely does not embark upon any exploration of the original restriction itself" (Draft of a letter from Fichte to Schelling, December 27, 1800, *GA*, III/4: 405; *PRFS*, p. 48).

81. See Maimon, *Ueber die Progressen der Philosophie*, first published in 1792 as an independent contribution to a Prize Essay contest sponsored by the Berlin Royal Academy and cited by Fichte from Maimon's *Streifereien im Gebiete der Philosophie* (1793), in which *Ueber die Progressen* was reprinted, pp. 32–9. Fichte never wavered in his agreement with Maimon's claim that Leibniz's philosophy, correctly understood, is really the same as Spinoza's.

82. See *GA*, I/2: 256 below, pp. 200–1. As in § 1, Fichte's strategy in § 2 is to begin with a "*fact of empirical consciousness*" (in § 1 this was the proposition "A = A," whereas in § 2 it is the proposition "–A is not A") and then seek out the original *power* and resulting *act* of the mind that underlies and makes possible the "fact" in question.

83. "This proposition establishes the absolute act of positing in opposition as such" (Fichte, Commentary to §§ 2 and 3 of *GWL*, *WLnmK*, *GA*, IV/3: 358; *FTP*, p. 136).

84. That is to say, if we assume that the principle of contradiction can be derived analytically from the principle of identity (as most formal logicians do assume). Fichte rejects such a derivation because he is concerned with the I's *act* of positing something in opposition to itself, an action that cannot be derived analytically from the I's original act of self-positing.

Note that what Fichte describes as the "true meaning" of this second foundational principle does not become completely clear until much later, namely, in § 5 (*GA*, I/2: 390; below, p. 324). [*K*, p. 112.]

85. Recall how, in § 1, Fichte moved from the Principle of Identity, "A = A," to something in the I that underlies and makes possible this logical principle: namely, X, which is supposed to make possible the transition implicit in the hypothetical judgment, *if* A is posited, *then* A is posited. The point of this paragraph is that the Y that allegedly underlies the proposition "–A is not = A" would be identical to the previous X, if "–A is not = A" could be obtained from "A = A" by mere *analysis*.

86. Viz., in § 1. See I/2: 256–7; above, p. 201, where X stands for the necessary connection between "if" and "then" in a hypothetical judgment.

87. *Förmlichkeit*. This is a translation of the scholastic term *formalitas*, which could also be translated as "being formed" or "having some form." The transcendental unity of consciousness is the "form of form itself," inasmuch as it is the necessary condition for "forming" both intuitions and concepts. [*K*, pp. 112–13.]

88. That is to say, under what condition is –A posited? What is the ground or basis for positing –A? Fichte's claim here is that there are *no* such conditions. Positing in opposition — like positing as such — occurs "purely and simply" because it occurs; i.e., it is *unconditioned*.

89. Fichte can perhaps be faulted for not making clear to his readers the important difference between the kind of *qualitative* negation discussed in § 2 and the more familiar type of *quantitative* negation that is the topic of § 3. [*K*, p. 113.] In fact, he does not clarify this distinction until much later (*GA*, I/2: 351; below, pp. 289–90), where he writes as follows: "Just as a Not-I was previously posited in opposition to the I as such, as a *quality* posited in opposition [to the I], so now there is posited in opposition to what is subjective something objective, and this is accomplished through the mere exclusion of the latter from the sphere of what is subjective, and thus purely through and by means of *quantity* (of limitation, determination), and this way of proceeding involves a quantitative antitheses, just as the preceding one involved a qualitative antithesis."

90. Fichte appears to employ these two terms, *Gleicheit* and *Identität*, as synonyms, the meaning of which he also expresses by the mathematical symbol for equality, "=."

91. If the I that posited A were not identical to the I that posits –A and were it not to posit for itself this identity, then it could not *recognize* that –A is in fact the opposite of A, since it would not know it had posited A. [*K*, p. 114.]

92. "The Not-I is also derived in a different manner in § 2 of the book [= *GWL*], in which the absolute act of positing in opposition is supposed to be established by means of the logical principle "–A is not = A." Everyone will immediately concede this principle in itself, but how do I know that it is true? From experience? This is not sufficient, for how could this principle be known from experience? This act of positing –A in opposition to A is absolute — *because* I posit something in opposition and must do so" (Fichte, Commentary on §§ 2 and 3 of *GWL*, *WLnmH*, *GA*, IV/2: 42; *FTP*, pp. 135–6).

93. But –A is conditioned with respect to its *what* (or "content"), conditioned by the fact that –A must be the *opposite* of a previously posited A.

94. "One cannot posit acting without also positing a state of repose, nor something determinate without something determinable, nor an I without a Not-I. This the origin of the unity of acting as well as of the unity of consciousness" (Fichte, Commentary on §§ 2 and 3 of *GWL*, *WLnmK*, *GA*, IV/3: 358; *FTP*, p. 136).

95. "If something is supposed to be *absolutely* posited in opposition, then the question arises: in opposition to what? To nothing else but the I, since this is what is immediately posited. This *absolute* act of positing in opposition is *absolute* and therefore cannot be learned from experience; but it first appears within experience in the form of something posited in

opposition [to the I's self-positing], and only then does experience become possible" (Fichte, Commentary on §§ 2 and 3 of *GWL*, *WLnmH*, *GA*, IV/2: 42; *FTP*, p. 136). See *GA*, I/2: 271; below, p. 214: "The opposite of everything that pertains to the I must pertain to the Not-I, by virtue of sheer positing in opposition."

96. "Had we postulated anything here [in *WLnm*], it would have been a general cognition of the transition from the I to what is represented. That this cognition must be determined objectively is something established in intuition. From this necessary determinacy we deduced determinability, and from determinability we deduced the Not-I. The portion of the compendium [i.e., *GWL*, § 2] corresponding to this section [of *WLnm*] proceeded in the diametrically opposite direction. It began with the act of positing the Not-I in opposition [to the I], and this opposition was posited as absolute (§ 2). The act of determining was then derived from this act of positing in opposition (§ 3). Both paths are correct, since the necessary determinacy of the I and the necessary being of the Not-I bear a reciprocal relationship to each other. One can proceed from either to the other. Either path is possible. But our present path [in *WLnm*] has this advantage: that the determinacy of the I is also what links the I with the Not-I" (Fichte, Commentary on §§ 2 and 3 of *GWL*, *WLnmK*, *GA*, IV/3: 358; *FTP*, p. 135).

97. "Something is restricted only by means of positing [something] in opposition to it. It follows that the I must necessarily posit what restricts it as something posited in opposition, something outside itself, a Not-I" (Fichte, *VLM*; *GA*, II/4: 85).

98. In this case, X is the empirical and a posteriori "heterogeneous" element encountered within the I, which then becomes the basis for positing a representation of an "external" object, as explained in Parts Two and Three. See *GA*, I/2: 405; below, pp. 336–7. [*K*, p. 118.]

99. Fichte employs two words for "object" — "*Objekt*" and "*Gegenstand*" — interchangeably, though in *GWL* he generally prefers the latter. Note the etymological relationship between *Gegenstand*, "that which stands opposite or over against [the I]" and *Gegensetzen*, "to posit in opposition."

100. "I am" is a *material* proposition because of its determinate *content*; it indicates *what* exists: namely, the I. [*K*, p. 118.]

101. *Satz des Gegensetzens*. This is Fichte's name for the logical principle traditionally known as the principle of [non-]contradiction. The point of this new name is to emphasize that this formal, logical principle has roots in the I's materially real activity of positing something in opposition to itself.

   "What is posited in opposition to itself is not the same: principle of contradiction, or principle of being posited in opposition" (Fichte, *ZV*, *GA*, IV/3: 47; below p. 456). "The two first principles of the *Wissenschaftslehre* establish the logical principles of identity and contradiction on the basis of something real: namely, the I and the Not-I" (Fichte, *ZV*, *GA*, IV/3: 31; below, p. 448).

102. Reality is "being"; its opposite, negation, is "non-being." The Not-I possesses no reality in itself; instead, reality must be "transferred" to it from the I (see *EM*, *GA*, II/3: 92). The opposition between "negation" and "reality" is a *qualitative* opposition (see I/2: 309, 325, and 351; below, pp. 247–8, 264, 288). [*K*, p. 119.]

103. "This is intended only to clarify what occurs within us. The older method [of *GWL*] continues in this manner and merely *analyzes* [what occurs within us]" (Fichte, Commentary on §§ 2 and 3 of *GWL*, *WLnmK*, *GA*, I/3: 358; *FTP*, p. 136).

   "'To prove' means the same as 'to establish within intuition.' We can analyze only what occurs within us, what is already in us" (Fichte, Commentary on §§ 2 and 3 of *GWL*, *WLnmH*, *GA*, IV/2: 42; *FTP*, p. 136).

104. "Instead of 'insofar as' it would have been better to say, 'if the Not-I is posited'" (Fichte, Commentary on §§ of *GWL*, *WLnmH*, *GA*, IV/2: 42; *FTP*, p. 136).

"The Not-I is supposed to appear as a certain quantity or sphere of our activity. But this is not possible unless its opposite, the I, also appears within consciousness at the same time; and within this identity, the I must be posited simultaneously along with the Not-I, since the Not-I is indeed nothing. But what is posited and what is posited in opposition thereto nullify each other, and this, therefore, is a contradiction" (Fichte, Commentary on §§ 2 and 3 of *GWL*, *WLnmH*, *GA*, IV/2: 42; *FTP*, p. 136).

"This 'insofar as' already includes within itself what is to be derived. To this extent, 'insofar as' means 'quantity' or 'sphere.' One could say that if the Not-I is posited then the I is not posited. Yet both the Not-I and the I are now supposed to appear within consciousness, and within one and the same consciousness; for without an I, the Not-I posits nothing. One cannot understand an opposite without positing its opposite as well" (Fichte, Commentary on §§ 2 and 3 of *GWL*, *WLnmK*, *GA*, IV/3: 358; *FTP*, p. 135).

105. I.e., the I = I, the I qua F/Act. The identity in question = self-identity.

106. The distinction between the I and the Not-I (insofar as *both* are posited in the I) is a *quantitative* not a *qualitative* one (cf. the following, third foundational principle). Hence, the *limited* I, which is posited in opposition to the limited Not-I. [*K*, p. 122.]

107. "Now since the things that have been posited in opposition to each other are now supposed to continue to exist alongside each other, the I must possess the power — in one and same act of consciousness — to posit things that are, in this same act of consciousness, posited in opposition to each other, since neither is possible apart from the other. The I thus possesses the power to proceed synthetically" (Fichte, Commentary on §§ 2 and 3 of *GWL*, *WLnmK*, *GA*, IV/3: 359; *FTP*, p. 137).

108. The point seems to be that the I qua consciousness is the unlimited I, within which both the limited I and limited Not-I are posited. This I qua consciousness will be described in Part Two as the I qua *substance*, and the limited I that is posited within this substance (in opposition to the limited Not-I) will be described as an *accident* of this substance. The I qua freedom is, in contrast, the I that posits the I qua substance. [*K*, pp. 121–3.]

109. "The philosopher is not a mere observer; instead, he conducts experiments with the nature of consciousness and turns to himself for answers to his specific questions. This is a system for independent thinkers; it cannot be grasped merely through reading and study. Everyone must produce it within himself, particularly since no fixed terminology will be introduced" (Fichte, *WLnmK*, *GA*, IV/3: 339; *FTP*, p. 101).

"But insofar as this is what the *Wissenschaftslehre* (that is, the presentation of the same) is, and insofar as it is not itself the necessary, original, and universal system, the philosopher also requires, in addition to that highest F/Act, which the *Wissenschaftslehre* ascertains to be the ground of this system [of the human mind], a particular action of *reflection* upon this *highest F/Act*. When we engage in this act of reflection, we conduct, so to speak, an experiment with ourselves.

"If this experiment is undertaken correctly, and if our presentation of this original system (that is, the system in the human mind) is therefore correct, then it follows that the system in question, which is the object of this science, has existed without any help from the philosopher from the beginning of the human race and of all other minds, just as the nature of electricity has existed from the beginning of the physical world, even though it was only in recent times that such a thing was suspected and that experiments were made with it and it was treated in a scientific manner. Electricity has always acted efficaciously in accordance with its own laws, even when we were unfamiliar with it, and it would always have continued to act in accordance with these same laws even if we had never noticed them, or even if what we now consider to be the laws of electricity were not its laws.

"So too in the case of the human mind: if it acts efficaciously according to necessary laws, then it has always acted in accordance with these same laws, and it will continue to do so, even if our presentation [of these laws and of the system in question] were to be utterly incorrect. If the human mind contains within itself a system, then this system is certainly correct, universally valid, incontrovertible, infallible, etc. It certainly possesses all the properties we demand from our *Wissenschaftslehre*. This however (that is, our *Wissenschaftslehre*) is not the system [of the human mind]; instead, it is only the presentation of the same. As philosophers, we are not the legislators of the human mind, but only the historians [*Geschichtsschreiber*] of the same.

"If our presentation is correct, then everything that is valid with respect to what it presents will of course also be valid with respect to it. If, on the other hand, our presentation were not correct (it is based on an experiment), if the way we proceeded in setting up our system were incorrect, then the results would necessarily be incorrect as well" (Fichte, *ZV, GA*, IV/3: 38; below, pp. 452–3).

110. These, of course, are the two concepts previously established in §§ 1 and 2.

111. "'To synthesize' means 'to posit together,' 'to combine' [*zusammensetzen*]; but only things posited in opposition to one another can be posited in combination. It follows that, if these terms are to be combined in a *single* act, then the I must be able to bring opposites — and thereby a manifold — into being within a single act, and such an act must therefore possess a certain scope or range [*einen Umfang*]. This range of this act within which a manifold is combined and through which it becomes possible is called "quantifiability" in the book [= *GWL*]. Consciousness of this act contains that from which a transition is made, that to which it is made, and the acting itself [i.e., the act of transition]. Consciousness is no act [*Akt*]. It is in a state of repose; it contains a manifold, beyond which consciousness is, as it were, led. In consciousness everything is simultaneously united and separated. This is the meaning of 'limits,' 'divisibility,' and 'quantifiability'" (Fichte, Commentary on §§ 2 and 3 of *GWL, WLnmK, GA*, IV/3: 359; *FTP*, p. 137).

112. "What we have referred to here [in *WLnm*] as 'the relationship between determinacy and determinability' is called '*quantity*' (or sometimes '*quantifiability*') in the book [i.e., in *GWL*]. This has given rise to some misunderstanding, for many have taken this to imply that the I is something extended. In fact, all that really possesses *quantity* is the positing subject itself" (Fichte, Commentary on §§ 2 and 3 of *GWL, WLnmK, GA*, IV/3: 358; *FTP*, p. 135).

"What is called *quantity* in § 3 [of *GWL*] is the relationship between determinacy and determinability and refers to the necessary conjunction of two things posited in opposition to each other, which however must be viewed as posited in opposition to each other. *Quantity* thus designates the entire range of activity — the activity of what is determinable and of what is determinate" (Fichte, Commentary on §§ 2 and 3 of *GWL, WLnmK, GA*, IV/2: 41–2; *FTP*, p. 135n.).

113. "It follows that consciousness contains a manifold, which is simultaneously united and separated. This is what was called 'limits' or 'quantifiability' [in *GWL*]. *Divisible* means being capable of being a part of a manifold — and in this case capable of being part of the manifold of consciousness, which includes the I and the Not-I. But this does not mean that the I itself is, in turn, supposed to harbor a manifold, e.g. A, B, C, etc., but only that both together [viz., I and Not-I] are divisible in one and the same consciousness: what the one is, the other is not" (Fichte, Commentary on §§ 2 and 3 of *GWL, WLnmH, GA*, IV/2: 43).

114. "This can give rise to some misunderstanding. I and Not-I are only parts of the manifold. They lie within the same consciousness and cannot be separated from each other; they are *partes integrantes* [integral parts]. Consciousness includes the restricting [as well]:

what the one is, the other is not. But this does not mean that either the I or the Not-I is to be further divided. What this passage should say is that consciousness is divisible into an I and a Not-I" (Fichte, Commentary on §§ 2 and 3 of *GWL*, *WLnmK*, *GA*, IV/3: 359; *FTP*, p. 138).

"Let us posit the I as the highest concept, to which a Not-I is posited in opposition. It is clear that the Not-I cannot be posited in opposition to the I unless this Not-I is *posited*, and indeed, posited within the highest thing of which we can conceive — that is to say, posited within the I. In this case it would be necessary to consider the I in two different respects: as that *within* which the Not-I is posited and as *what* is posited in opposition to the Not-I, and is hence itself posited within the absolute I" (Fichte, *BWL*, *GA*, I/2: 150; above, p. 189).

115. "But it is the task of metaphysics to display this entire system [of the necessary actions of the intellect]. This entire system occurs, as it were, in a single stroke — although in metaphysics this is presented as a continuous series of actions, in which it is always indicated that one action is impossible without the one that succeeds it, and this, in turn, without another action, etc. [....] The *Wissenschaftslehre* commences with the I. It shows that the I cannot posit itself without positing a Not-I in opposition to itself. Inasmuch as both the I and the Not-I are supposed to be posited in opposition to each other, the I posits them both in a single act. Each annuls the other, and yet I am supposed to think of them together. Consequently, each must be restricted by the other; insofar as I am thinking of one, I am not thinking of the other, and vice versa" (Fichte, Student transcription of *VWL*, *GA*, IV/1: 350).

116. I.e., A,1: "Insofar as the Not-I is posited, the I is not posited, for the I is completely annulled by the Not-I" (*GA*, I/2: 268; above, p. 211).

117. "To say that the I and the Not-I are now both 'something' means that we can now ascribe predicates to them, and this occurs only by means of positing in opposition. The only way that anything can be 'something' is by being posited in opposition to something else" (Fichte, Commentary on §§ 2 and 3 of *GWL*, *WLnmK*, *GA*, IV/3: 359; *FTP*, p. 138). "'To be something' means that one can ascribe predicates to it, but only by means of positing in opposition. What the I is, the Not-I is not" (Fichte, Commentary on §§ 2 and 3 of *GWL*, *WLnmH*, *GA*, IV/2: 43).

118. *Das absolute Ich.* Fichte describes the absolute I in two ways in *GWL*; first, under the rubric of substantiality, as the I that can never become Not-I and then, under the rubric of causality, as the autonomous I. He never describes it as "God." [*K*, pp. 128–34.]

119. "Consciousness witnesses acting; everything that can subsequently be posited, all determinability, is included within this act" (Fichte, Commentary on §§ 2 and 3 of *GWL*, *WLnmH*, *GA*, IV/2: 243; *FTP*, p. 138).

120. "No proposition is possible without both content and form. There must be something about which one has knowledge, and there must also be something one knows about this thing. It follows that the initial proposition of all *Wissenschaftslehre* must have both content and form. [...] Should the *Wissenschaftslehre* turn out to have other foundational principles in addition to this absolutely first one, then these others could be only partially absolute, though they must [also] be partially conditioned by the first and supreme principle, for otherwise there would not be one single foundational principle. — Consequently, the 'absolutely first' element in any such additional foundational principle would have to be either its content or its form, and similarly, the conditioned element would have to be either its form or its content. Supposing the unconditioned element to be the *content*, then the *form* of this content would be conditioned by the

absolutely first foundational principle, which, if it is supposed to be the absolutely first foundational principle, must condition something in this second principle. In this case, accordingly, the form of this additional foundational principle would be determined within the *Wissenschaftslehre* itself, determined through it and by means of its first foundational principle. Or supposing the reverse, that the form [of the additional foundational principle] is the unconditioned element. In this case the content of this principle would necessarily be determined by the [first] foundational principle, and hence its form would be indirectly determined by this first principle as well, insofar as it is supposed to be the form of a certain content. Thus, in this second case as well, the form would be determined by the *Wissenschaftslehre*, and indeed, by its foundational principle. — But if an absolute foundational principle, a *Wissenschaftslehre*, and a system of human knowledge as such are to exist, then there cannot be any foundational principle that is determined neither in form nor in content by the absolutely first foundational principle. This is why there can be no more than three foundational principles: one determined absolutely and purely and simply by itself with respect both to its form and its content; one determined by itself with respect to its form; and one determined by itself with respect to its content" (Fichte, *BWL, GA,* I/2: 122; above, pp. 165–6).

"All of this follows upon the establishment of three absolutes: an absolute I, which is governed by laws it gives itself and which can be represented only under the condition of an affection by the Not-I; an absolute Not-I, which is free and independent of all of our laws and which can be represented only as expressing these laws, either positively or negatively, but always to a finite degree; and an absolute power within ourselves to determine ourselves purely and simply according to the effects of both the Not-I and the I, a power that can be represented only insofar as it distinguishes an affection by the Not-I from an effect of the I, or from a law. No philosophy can go beyond these three absolutes" (Fichte, *BWL, GA,* I/2: 151–2; above, pp. 165–66).

121. Note how this formula combines all three of the foundational principles: "I posit," "I posit in opposition," and "I posit a divisible Not-I in opposition to a divisible I." It is vital to recognize that the "absolute" actions (of positing, positing in opposition, and uniting by means of divisibility) described in Part One do not occur *sequentially;* instead, they must occur *simultaneously* in order for any of them to occur at all. [*K,* pp. 137–9.]

"All that has been proven [so far] is that, if the I is to attain to consciousness, then it must posit a Not-I; but it has not been proven that it ought to attain to consciousness" (Fichte, Commentary to §§ 2 and 3 of *GWL, WLnm, GA,* IV/3: 359; *FTP,* p. 138).

122. "The soul of my system is the principle, 'the I posits itself purely and simply.' These words have no meaning nor value unless the I has an inner intuition of itself. In conversation, I have frequently been able to elicit this intuition in people who could not understand me at all, but who then understood me completely. It is said that all operations of the mind presuppose purely and simply that there is an I, as well as something posited in opposition to it — that is, a Not-I. Only through the I and Not-I are any mental operations possible. There is no reason why the I is I and the thing is Not-I; this positing in opposition occurs absolutely. (We do not learn from experience what we should include and *not* include as part of ourselves. Nor is there any a priori foundational principle according to which this can be determined. Instead, this distinction is absolute, and only in consequence of it are all a priori foundational principles and all experience possible.) The unification of the I and Not-I by means of *quantity,* mutual restriction, determination, limitation, or whatever you wish to call it, is also something that occurs absolutely. No philosophy

can go beyond these principles, but *from them all philosophy*, that is to say, the entire operation of the human mind, *must be developed*" (Fichte to Reinhold, July 2, 1795, *GA*, III/2: 344; *EPW*, pp. 398–9).

123. "Concerning this remark, there remains a gap to be filled: namely, we have to provide a *deduction* of our *postulate*, upon which everything that has been established so far rests. The postulate states that *the I appears outside of itself, as it were, and makes itself into an object* [*Objekt*]. But why should and why must it do this?" (Fichte, Commentary on §§ 2 and 3 of *GWL, WLnmH, GA*, IV/2: 43–4; *FTP*, p. 138).

"The path followed in the compendium [i.e., in *GWL*] is the opposite of the one we are following here [in *WLnm*]. In § 2 of the book we started with the Not-I, and, from § 3 on, we progressed to what is determinable, and finally to what is determinate" (Fichte, Commentary on §§ 2 and 3 of *GWL, WLnmH, GA*, IV/2: 41; *FTP*, p. 135n.).

124. Fichte here proposes a new and original interpretation in terms of the category of "limitation" of the *Satz des Grundes*, the logical "principle of grounding," better known in English as "the principle of sufficient reason." The connection or conjunction between the two terms related to each other as "ground" and "grounded" (or ground and consequent) in a judgment such as "if A, then B," or "B, because A," is the same as in the judgment "B *insofar as* A." On this interpretation, the "ground" of such a judgment is the larger *sphere* or *domain* of what it grounds, and the "condition" of a hypothetical judgment determines the boundary of a more limited sphere with this larger one. See *GA*, I/2, 273 and 307; below, pp. 215–6 and 245. [*K*, p. 140.]

125. "The grounding principle or principle of sufficient reason [may be expressed as follows]: 'no two things are positing in opposition to each other unless they are equivalent in some third thing, and no two things are equivalent unless they are posited in opposition to some third thing,' which is the basis of all synthesis" (Fichte, *BWL, GA*, I/2: 148; above, p. 187).

126. Fichte's vocabulary is here plainly modelled on Reinhold's Principle of Consciousness: in consciousness the representation is *distinguished* by the subject from both the subject and the object and *related* to both. [*K*, pp. 138–9.]

127. A "material principle" is one that possesses determinate *content* as well as logical *form*. The material principle to which Fichte here refers is the principle that "the I as well as the Not-I are posited as divisible." The logical principle of sufficient reason is derived from this material principle by abstracting from its content (i.e., from the I and Not-I). [*K*, p. 141.]

128. −X would be posited in −A if A and −A were posited in *complete opposition* to each other. −X is, instead, *that characteristic feature* in which A and not −A are opposed to each other. [*K*, p. 141.]

129. The principle of sufficient reason can be applied only where something is conditioned by something else, and hence only "insofar as" the latter is the "ground" of the former. This is why this principle is limited to the realm of *finite* cognition. [*K*, p. 143.]

130. "It is quite correct to say that anyone who believes he is entitled to ask what is the *ground* on the basis of which *freedom* has determined itself to A rather than to −A thereby proves, by means of circular reasoning, the nothingness of freedom, inasmuch as such reasoning presupposes the nothingness of freedom and, if one understands oneself correctly, the nothingness of any will whatsoever. But the person who makes this objection has, without realizing it, already been drawn by him [i.e., by the dogmatist] into this circle, since he has assumed that freedom could, at the very least, be a cause in the sensible world. The source of this misunderstanding can be eliminated only by returning to what, to this reviewer, seems to be the true spirit of the Critical philosophy, which teaches that the

principle of sufficient reason can by no means be applied to the *act of determining* absolute self-activity through itself (determining itself to engage in *willing*), for this is a single [*Eins*], simple, and completely isolated action. In this case, the act of determining is itself, at the same time, the process of becoming determined, and the determining subject is what becomes determined" (Fichte, *RC*, *GA*, I/2: 10–11; *SW*, VIII, p. 414; *Crev*, p. 294).

131. See *GA*, I/2: 276–8; below, pp. 218–20.
132. Note the differences between Kant's understanding of "synthesis" (as a spontaneous act of connecting or unifying independently given items, such as the intuitions that constitute the manifold of sensibility) and Fichte's very different understanding of synthesis as a creative act on the part of the power of productive imagination, by means of which the I unites two opposing terms in a third term, which it simply posits.
133. An apparent, albeit very inexact, allusion to *KrV*, B 314.
134. See *KrV*, B 19.
135. "A certain school [namely, Fichte himself and his followers] calls the procedure we have just described [by means of which we employ the principle of sufficient reason in order to proceed beyond immediate consciousness of our affections to mediated consciousness of objects], so far as we have been able to describe it, a 'synthesis.' By this term you should understand, at least here, not a *connection* [*Verknüpfung*] of two items that already existed prior to this connecting, but an *attaching* [*Anknüpfen*], an addition of a quite new component, one that first comes to be in this process of being attached to another component, which exists quite independently of it" (Fichte, *BM*, *GA*, I/6: 228; *SW*, II, p. 215; *VM*, p. 40).
136. "Yet this very action of representing, the act of consciousness, is obviously a synthesis, since it involves distinguishing and relating; indeed, it is the highest synthesis and the ground of all other possible syntheses" (Fichte, *RA*, *GA*, I/2: 45; *SW*, I, p. 7; *EPW*, p. 63). The "other syntheses" in question are the ones discussed in Part Two, sections C, D, and E.
137. This occurs at the end of Part Two, when the final, absolute antithesis — namely, that between the finite and the infinite — is "resolved," not by means of a new synthetic ground of connection between the I and the Not-I, but rather, by a *Machtspruch* or "decree" of reason on the part of the I: "let there be no Not-I!" See *GA*, I/2: 301; below, p. 240.
138. "How is it possible [as in Reinhold's *Elementary Philosophy*] to trace all the actions of the mind back to an act of combination? How is *synthesis* thinkable apart from a presupposed *thesis* and *antithesis*?" (Fichte, *RA*, *GA*, I/2: 45; *SW*, I, p. 6; *EPW*, p. 63).
139. In *BWL* Fiche had argued that there can be only *one* system of the human mind (and hence only one true or well-grounded) system of philosophy. See *GA*, I/2: 124–6; above, pp. 167–9.
140. *eine geendete Annäherung zum Unendlichkeit.* This phrase becomes something of a formula in Fichte's Jena writings, along with others, such as "*nach einer vollendeten Annäherung zum Unendlichen*" ("following a completed approximation to the infinite"). Fichte uses "infinity" and "the infinite" as more or less interchangeable terms.
141. See *GA*, I/2: 361, 394, and 403–4; below, pp. 299, 327–8, and 335.
142. *dürfte der Analogie nach.* Just as both antithesis and synthesis have now been linked to a specific form of judgment, so should one — "by analogy" — expect a form of judgment to be associated with the act of absolute positing ("positing purely and simply") or "thesis."
143. Analytic judgments presuppose a "ground of distinction," and synthetic judgments presuppose a "ground of relation or connection."

144. *einen Aufgabe für ein Grund.* Such a third thing or logical ground is, according to Fichte, a requirement of "logical form." A thetic judgment is not analytic but synthetic; hence, like very positive judgment, the judgment "I am I" requires a *third* term, i.e., some *ground* or *basis* for connecting the subject and predicate. In this case however, the third term in question — *and hence the ground of the identity of the I* — is not something that is already *present* but is instead what *ought to be.* The infinite task of the self-positing I is precisely to supply itself with such a ground, i.e. to be totally independent and self-determining, *to be its own ground.* It could achieve this goal, however, only by completely overcoming the Not-I — in which case it could no longer be able to posit itself as an I at all.

145. "Is *absolute* autonomy supposed to be *grounded* [in something else]? That is a contradiction" (Fichte, *RA, GA,* I/2: 55; *SW,* I, p. 14; *EPW,* p. 69).

    "One should never have said 'the human being *is* free,' but rather 'the human being necessarily strives, hopes, and assumes that he is free.' — The proposition 'the human being *is* free' is not true" (Fichte, *EM, GA,* II/3: 183).

146. *in der Idee.* "The object of this Idea, i.e., what arises within us when we think in accordance with the concept of morality [...] can only be an *Idea,* a mere thought *within us,* with no claim that anything in the actual world *outside us* corresponds to this concept. This immediately raises the question, what is this Idea? Or, since Ideas certainly cannot be apprehended [*aufgefaßt*], how and in what way is this Idea to be described? (I am presupposing that one is aware that Ideas cannot be thought immediately, just as, previously, the I as subject-object = X could not be thought. Nevertheless, one can indicate how one ought to proceed in one's thinking in order to grasp Ideas, even if one is, in the end, unable to grasp them — just as we could previously at least indicate that the subject and object were supposed to be thought purely and simply as one. Ideas are *problems* or *tasks* for thinking, and they occur in our consciousness only to the extent that we are at least able to comprehend the task in question)" (Fichte, *SS, GA,* I/5: 74–5; *SW,* IV, p. 65; *SE,* p. 67).

    According to Kant, an *Idee* or "Idea" is a concept that can be thought but not cognized, since we have no sensible intuitions to provide it with determinate content. His examples include the Ideas of "freedom," "immortality," and "God." In order to indicate this rather technical sense of the term, it is always capitalized in this translation.

147. See Kant, *KrV,* A71/B97–A73/B98. Kant's example of an infinite judgment is "the soul is not mortal," which, as he explains, only distinguishes between the sphere of what is mortal and the infinite sphere of what is not mortal, while assigning the soul to the latter sphere (which remains infinite and thus indeterminate).

148. It is important not to confuse the kind of "opposition" discussed here, in § 3, with the opposition between the I and the Not-I discussed in § 2. In the case of the latter, the opposed terms (I and Not-I) contradict one another (hence the need for the third foundational principle); in the case of the former, the limited I and limited Not-I are not contradictories but opposites, both posited without a higher genus (namely, the realm of consciousness as such or the "pure I"), which they have in common. [*K,* pp. 112 and 152.]

149. "Indeterminable," in the sense that the I is not determined by anything outside itself. But it is, of course, precisely the task of any finite I to continue to *determine itself* freely, in accordance with the demands of the pure I (or "pure will"), as revealed through moral duty — and to do so into infinity.

150. Judgments of the first type are *hypothetical,* whereas those of the second type are *thetic* — the prime example of which is, for Fichte, the judgment "I am" (see *GA,* I/2: 277; above, p. 219). [*K,* pp. 148 and 153.]

151. This distinction between "dogmatism" and "Criticism" was introduced by Kant (*KrV,* B xxxv). For Fichte's most sustained and detailed comparison between these two systems,

which he considered to be the only two possible consistent systems of philosophy, see the two 1797 "Introductions" to *VWL*.

152. "The Humean system holds open the possibility that we may someday be able to go beyond the boundary of the human mind, whereas the Critical system shows that the thought of a thing existing *in itself* and independently of any kind of representative power, a thing that is supposed to possess existence as well as certain properties, is a piece of whimsy, a pipe dream, a non-thought. [...] Here, at the foundation of this new skepticism, we can therefore clearly and distinctly recognize that old mischief that was perpetrated with the thing in itself, at least until Kant. [...] It is by no means ingrained in the human mind to think of a thing independent of *any* representational power *at all*; on the contrary, it is downright impossible to do this" (Fichte, *RA, GA, I/2*: 57 and 61; *SW*, I, pp. 17 and 19; *EPW*, pp. 71 and 72–3).

153. Note how Fichte, in § 2 of *BWL*, connects the notions of a system of philosophy, a system of human knowledge, a system of the human mind, and that of a purely and simply posited first foundational principle for philosophy.

154. Fichte employs the term "practical" in the same way as Kant: to refer to *willing* and to *efficacious acting*.

155. See *GA*, I/2: 399, 403, and 410; below, pp. 331, 335, and 341. The "practical law of the I" to which Fichte refers in the preceding sentence is not (yet) the moral law. It is the I's original demand for *unity*.

156. This reference to the dogmatic function of the "feeling of dependence" is probably an allusion to Schulze/Aenesidemus's claim that most people's belief in God is based on an obscure feeling of dependence, just as their belief in external things is grounded in an equally obscure feeling of dependence upon something that conditions their experience, as the external cause of their representations. [*K*, p. 162.]

157. "We can become conscious of all of the intellect's manners of acting (which are supposed to be exhaustively described by the *Wissenschaftslehre*) only in the form of representation, that is, only insofar as and in the manner that they are represented" (Fichte, *BWL, GA*, I/2: 149; above, p. 188).

    "The content of philosophy as a whole is the human mind, in all its operations, activities, and modes of action; philosophy becomes *Wissenschaftslehre* only after it has completely exhausted these modes of action. The philosopher observes the operations of the human mind and thereby freezes and stabilizes what is changeable and transitory within himself" (Fichte, *UGG, GA*, II/3: 324–5; *EPW*, p. 200).

158. "The entire corruption of philosophy and of metaphysics, which is what Kant repudiated, is based upon one's refusal to believe in experience and one's quest for something behind it. A scientific philosophy shows that there is nothing more behind experience and that what comes to be therein are our own perceptions. Hence there is no truth other than that of ordinary human understanding. This is also what philosophy asserts. The difference is that ordinary human understanding asserts this because of its incapacity to doubt it, whereas philosophy asserts it because it has eliminated all doubt concerning this point" (Fichte, Student transcription of *VLM, GA*, IV/1: 194).

159. "The transcendental philosopher must assume that everything that exists does so only *for* an I and that what is supposed to exist for an I can exist only *through* the I. By contrast, ordinary human understanding [*der gemeinen Menschenverstand* = "common sense"] accords an independent existence to both and claims that the world would always continue to exist, even if ordinary human understanding did not. Ordinary human understanding need not take account of the philosopher's claim, nor can it do so, since it occupies a lower standpoint; but the philosopher must certainly pay attention to ordinary human understanding, and his claim remains indeterminate and therefore partially incorrect so

long as he has not shown precisely how *ordinary human understanding follows necessarily* from his claim alone *and can be explained only if that claim is presupposed*. Philosophy must deduce our conviction concerning the existence of the world outside ourselves" (Fichte, *GNR*, *GA*, I/3: 335; *SW*, III, p. 24; *FNR*, p. 24).

160. See *KrV*, B 106.

161. "Mutually grounded," in the sense that there can be no antithesis (§ 2) without synthesis (§ 3) Both actions (that of positing in opposition and that of positing the I and Not-I as divisible) are grounded in the first foundational principle, which "purely and simply posits" the entire sphere or logical space within which the limited I and limited Not-I mutually limit each other. [*K*, p. 17.]

162. What is "present" (*vorhanden*) in the mind is always the product of a preceding act. [*K*, p. 173.] The original and necessary antithetic action of the I, to which this passage refers, should not be confused with the purely *qualitative* opposition of the Not-I as such to the I, which is derived in § 2, but refers instead to the *quantitative* opposition made possible by § 3, the product of which is the opposition contained in the first principle of the theoretical part of the *Wissenschaftslehre* (§ 4).

163. The "precedence" in question here is purely logical (or transcendental) and not temporal.

164. The synthetic concepts which are to be established in Part Two by being derived from the proposition that "the I posits itself as determined by the Not-I" are the Kantian categories of "relation." In § 4 Fichte begins with the third of these categories ("reciprocal determination") and then derives Kant's first two categories of relation ("substantiality" and "causality") as further determinations of the category of reciprocal determination.

165. "This passage does not give any consideration to the question of whether this reciprocal determination is ideal or real" (Fichte, Commentary on § 4 of *GWL*, *WLnmK*, *GA*, IV/3: 381; *FTP*, p. 182).

166. Two sentences earlier Fichte had claimed that the I and Not-I are posited as "restrictable" [*beschränkbar*] by each other, but now he asserts that the I posits the I as "restricted" [*beschränkt*] by the Not-I. As *K* points out (pp. 175–7), these are hardly the same claim, though Fichte seems to think that the second follows analytically from the first. *K* challenges this assumption and argues that the only way I can know that I am *actually* restricted or limited rather than merely *capable* of being restricted by the Not-I is through actual experience, and Fichte himself seems to endorse this conclusion (see *GA*, I/2: 390 and 400; below, pp. 324 and 332). But if so, this raises doubts concerning whether the first principles of both the theoretical and the practical parts of *GWL* are actually derived from the third foundational principle after all.

167. "Here [in *WLnm*] we pay no heed to this reciprocal determination of the I and Not-I; [instead] we have established a reciprocal determination of the I with itself — between its *real* [*reading 'reale' for 'reine'*] and its *ideal* activity" (Fichte, Commentary on § 4 of *GWL*, *WLnmH*, *GA*, IV/2: 67; *FTP*, p. 182).

168. In other words, one is not warranted in claiming that a particular "foundational principle" actually can and does provide the *foundation* of a system until such a system has actually been successfully erected upon it. Fichte makes this same point in *BWL* and in the two 1797 Introductions to *VWL*.

169. "There are several different *methods* of treating a topic synthetically: 1.) One can start with a contradiction and then simply try to resolve it by making certain additional suppositions. This is the *method* that was followed in the instructor's published [*Foundations of the entire*] *Wissenschaftslehre*. It is the most difficult method of all, which is why the latter was not understood by the public nor by some of those who attended his earlier lectures" (Fichte, "A Few Remarks on Synthetic Method," *WLnmH*, *GA*, IV/2: 107–8; *FTP*, pp. 248–9).

170. This is the first occurrence of the term "*Vermögen*," often translated as "faculty." A *Vermögen* is simply a "capacity" or "ability" or "power" to accomplish something.

171. *welches insofern leidend ist. Leidend* is derived from the verb *leiden*, which often means "to suffer," but is used in a more technical sense by Fichte to mean "being passively affected." This is the first occurrence of this important term in *GWL*.

172. Keep in mind that Fichte has just explained that "to determine" anything is to *limit* or *restrict* it. "To limit X" therefore means to remove a certain portion of reality from X and to posit in opposition to X a Not-X, which possesses precisely the quantity of reality that was annulled in X.

173. In order to "determine itself" at all, the I must posit itself as *limitable* or *capable of restriction*, and in order to do this it must posit all reality (which was posited solely in the I in § I) as an *absolute quantum* and posit itself as possessing only a *part* of this absolute quantum of reality. Hence the I can "determine itself" only by restricting its share of the absolute quantum of reality, thereby assigning the remainder to the Not-I. "The topic is not yet how the I can be determined by the Not-I; that the I is determined is presupposed. The I must posit all reality, but it cannot posit it in itself alone, since it is determined. It therefore divides reality and posits a part of it in the Not-I" [*K*, p. 182].

174. This is because a quantity of *negation* is, in this case, equal in *quantity* to the same quantity of *reality*.

175. By speaking of "reality in" the I rather than the "reality of" the same, Fichte is reminding us that reality is here *quantified*. A certain amount of that reality is assigned to and is therefore "in" both the I and Not-I.

176. Namely, the task of determining how it is possible to think of the I as partially *determined* and partially *determining*. See *GA*, I/2: 287; above, p. 228.

177. *was bei Kant* Relation *heisst*. See *KrV*, A80/B106. For Kant, the "categories of relation" include (1) inherence and subsistence; (2) cause and effect; and (3) community or interaction.

178. The "chief difficulty" to which Fichte here refers would appear to be the unsolved problem mentioned above: namely, to understand *how* the I can successfully posit negation in itself and reality in the Not-I.

179. That is to say, we have now "gained a new footing" for the "dialectical" method we have been employing so far, which involves seeking out ways to avoid the fundamental contradiction between the I and the Not-I by introducing new — and ever more complex — intermediate synthetic concepts. A very different "genetic" method will be introduced near the end of Part Two and employed in most of Part Three.

180. The synthetic concept in question is that of reciprocal determination, from which Fichte will now proceed to derive two further synthetic concepts (both subsumed under that of reciprocal determination): *causality* (or causal efficacy) and *substantiality*.

181. To be sure, Fichte is not strictly entitled to claim that both propositions are "contained in" the proposition that the Not-I determines itself. The first of the two opposed propositions — "the Not-I possesses reality in itself" — is contained in that proposition, but the second of the two opposed propositions — "The Not-I possesses no reality whatsoever in itself" — is actually contained in or follows from the first foundational principle, which of course remains valid. [*K*, p. 185.]

182. "Relative" reality is the kind of *quantifiable* reality that is a function of the reality (or nonreality) of something else (§ 3). "Positive" reality (of the type purely and simply posited by the I of itself in § 1) is purely *qualitative* in character and does not depend upon anything else. [*K*, p. 186.]

183. "This activity is pure and is to be posited as such (if we abstract from the opposing activity of the Not-I, which irresistibly represses it). This same activity is not pure, but rather

objective (if it is posited in relation to the activity posited in opposition to it). It is there-fore either pure or not pure only under a certain condition, and this condition can be posited or not posited. As soon as it is posited that this is the sort of condition which can be either posited or not posited, then it is also posited that the activity of the I can be posited in opposition to itself" (Fichte, *GEWL*, *GA*, I/3: 149; below, p. 386).

184. This is the first appearance of this way of characterizing the pure I or F/Act. This theme will be explored in more depth below (*GA*, I/2: 322, 379–80, 393, 397, 401, 406, 418, and 423–4; below, pp. 261, 315–6, 327, 330, 344, 347, and 352). It is even more central to *WLnm* and *VWL*, which *begin* by characterizing the I as a "self-reverting activity." This same self-reverting activity will later, in Part Three of *GWL*, be identified with the "cen-tripetal" activity of the I (*GA*, I/2: 406; below, p. 337).

   "*Self-reverting activity* (I-hood, subjectivity) is the defining characteristic of a rational being. Positing of oneself (reflection upon oneself) is an act of this activity. Let us call this act of reflection A. *It is by means of an act of such an activity that a rational being posits itself.* All reflection is directed at something, B, as its object. What sort of 'something' must the object of the requisite reflection (= A) be? — It is by means of such an act of reflection that a rational being is supposed to posit its own self-positing and have itself as its object. But the defining characteristic of a rational being is self-reverting activity. Hence the ultimate and highest substrate (= B) of its reflection upon itself must also be *self-reverting, self-determining activity*" (Fichte, *GNR*, *GA*, I/3: 329; *SW*, III, p. 17; *FNR*, p. 18).

   "I asked you to 'think of yourself,' and in understanding that last word you also engaged — *in the very act of understanding this request* — in that self-reverting activity that produces the thought of the I" (Fichte, *VWL*, *GA*, I/4: 280; *SW*, I, p. 533; *IWL*, pp. 117–18).

185. *sich selbst vorstellt.* Only when it has a representation (*Vorstellung*) of itself does the I become an object of consciousness.

186. This would appear to be a reference to Salomon Maimon's skeptical critique of Kant's phi-losophy. According to Maimon, the application of the categories of the understanding to the manifold of sensation produces only a "deception" [*Täuschung*] of objective reality, an illusion he attributes to the operation of the power of imagination [*Einbildungskraft*]. See *GA*, I/2: 368 below, p. 305. See too Kant's reference to a *Täuschung* from which we cannot escape in *KrV*, A298/B354, as well as Fichte's own reference to an inescapable but "benefi-cent" deception produced by the power of imagination (*GA*, I/2: 367; below, p. 304).

187. See the previous remark concerning the difference between "relative" (or quantitative) and "positive" (or qualitative) *reality*.

188. *ist für dasselbe Leiden* (Affection überhaupt). K plausibly suggests (p. 189) that Fichte's conception of *Leiden* or "being passively affected" or "affection" may owe something to Spinoza's definition of the same in *Ethics*, III, def. 2. In any case, it should be clear that, for Fichte, being passively affected is a "reciprocally determined" concept, one that is always related to the concept of activity. Thus, in *GEWL*, he defines *Leiden* as "suppressed activ-ity" and "non-activity" (Fichte, *GEWL*, *GA*, I/3: 153–5; below, pp. 389–91).

189. Namely, the contradiction between the proposition that all reality is posited in the I and the proposition that some reality is posited in the Not-I. This is the contradiction that is supposed to be resolved by means of the concept of the I's being passively affected and the ensuing quantification of reality. [*K*, p. 191.]

190. *die Synthesis der Wirksamkeit* (*Kausalität*). Fichte's use of the term *Wirksamkeit* as a syn-onym for Kant's Latinate term, *Kausalität* probably derives from Jacobi, of whose writings Fichte was an avid student. [*K*, p. 191.]

191. The literal meaning of the German word for "cause," *Ursache* is "primordial-subject matter" (*Ur-Sache*).

192. It is difficult to render Fichte's point here in English, but easy enough to explain. After having distinguished the two terms that mutually determine each other in this case as "cause" and "effect," he now proposes to distinguish these concepts, considered separately, from a third concept, which includes both "cause" and "effect," namely, the entire *process* in which a cause produces an effect. The German term "*Wirkung*" is usually translated as "effect," but it is here rendered as "effective cause," to reflect the unity of cause and effect in a single concept. As for Fichte's last point, in a note to the draft of his first book, he had already criticized Kant for his "misuse of the word causality [*Kausalität*] as a synonym for cause [*Ursache*]" (*GA*, II/2: 112).

193. Contrast this with Kant, for whom the categories are a priori rules for determining the pure form of all experience (time).

194. This remained an unfulfilled promise.

195. *Durch Wechselbestimmung*. This is the first appearance of a term that will recur over and over again in what follows: The verb "*wechsel*" means "to change" or "to exchange." Though he occasionally employs *wechseln* to mean "change," Fichte more often employs this term to indicate being involved in a mutual or reciprocal relationship. If two terms or components of a relationship are related to each other in such a way that each determines the other, they are in a relationship of "reciprocal determination."

196. *das Ich bestimmt durch Tätigkeit sein Leiden*. This is the first appearance of the noun "*Leiden*" (see the previous *GA*, I/2: 287; above, p. 228 on the verb *leiden,* in section II, B, *GA*, I/2: 287; above, p. 228).

197. This is the kind of *qualitative* positing in opposition that occurs in § 2, in contrast to the purely *quantitative* opposition encountered in § 3.

198. Namely, the contradiction between the claim that the I is the determining subject and the claim that the I is that which becomes determined.

199. Affection is a quantum of activity in the sense that being passively affected negates the totality of activity (= the totality of reality).

200. The point here is that a quantum can be determined as such only by being posited in opposition to another quantum, and therefore not in opposition to activity as such but rather to activity as the totality or total quantum of reality. [*K*, p. 194.]

201. This X, which is the concept we are seeking, the concept that can "synthesize" the claims that the I *determines itself* and that the I *becomes determined*, is the concept of "substantiality."

202. In other words, thinking is an "accident" of the I's overall being. Fichte here employs the expression "*Arten des Seins*" (kinds of being) for what he will subsequently call "accidents" of the I qua substance. See Kant, *KrV*, B229: "The determinations of a substance, which are nothing else than the particular ways in which this substance exists, are called 'accidents.'"

203. *Realitäten*. As Fichte explains in point 14, below, the "realities" of the I are simply the I's various "ways of acting," since the I is here treated as a substance containing several possible ways of acting (or several "accidents").

204. Somewhat confusingly, Fichte has not yet given a name to this newly discovered synthetic concept, which will soon be revealed to be that of *substance* or *substantiality*.

205. *Die Regeln der Bestimmung überhaupt* are the logical rules of definition, according to which one must provide both the ground of the *connection* between two terms (that is, some shared genus-concept) as well as the ground of the specific *difference* between them. In what follows, the genus concept is "reciprocal determination" and the specific differ-

ence is what distinguishes all particular instances of reciprocal determination from the general concept of reciprocal determination — particular instances, which, to this extent belong to the same genus (qua particular instances of reciprocal determination) and are, in turn, distinguished from one another according to the specific differences between the various instances of reciprocal determination. [*K*, p. 196.]

206. This is the first appearance of the noun "*das Wechsel*," though we previously encountered the compound term *Wechselbestimmung* or "reciprocal determination." Taken by itself, *Wechsel* usually means "change" or "exchange," though Fichte frequently employs this word to designate a mutual or reciprocal relationship between two terms or components. Moreover, in the following portion of Part Two, the term *Wechsel* is very often employed as an abbreviated synonym for *Wechsel-Tun und Leiden*, or "reciprocally-related-acting-and-being-passively-affected."

207. In the case of the synthetic concept of causal efficacy, the order of reciprocal determination proceeds from the cause to the effect; in the case of the synthetic concept of substantiality, the order of reciprocal determination proceeds from the substance to the accident, i.e., from the determining activity to the activity that is determined. Hence, in the case of causal efficacy, what is primary is affection or being passively affected, whereas in the case of substantiality it is activity that is primary. [*K*, p. 196.]

208. As *K* points out (p. 198), Fichte here seems to appeal simultaneously to two rather difference conceptions of the relation of accidents to substance. The main argument of this section has been that the distinction between substance and accident is a quantitative distinction between the totality of reality and a limited quantum of the same, which exists "in" the former. But in speaking of accidents as "in" or "related to" the substance, he seems to be echoing Kant's view (*KrV*, A183/B227) that "all existence and all variation in time can be regarded in relation to what is enduring in all appearances as nothing but determinations of the existence of the latter."

Fichte seems unaware of any incompatibility between these two views, as he continues to defend the former, quantitative or "inherence" view of the relation of accident to substance. "Fichte's concept of substance is simply an ontological formulation of the conviction, which he shares with Kant, that our knowing and acting always remain referred to experience, to the world. This means that there is no solution (as 'ecstasies,' whether in time or at the end of time), but only infinite progress." In other words, Fichte's project is to go from an "externalist" to an "internalist" or from an extrinsic to an immanent conception of substance, which, for the finite I remains forever a *project* and never a fait accompli. [*K*, p. 198.]

209. Fichte here appears to be operating with a Spinozistic concept of substance and accident. Spinoza does not actually employ the term "accident" in the *Ethics*, but, in a letter to Oldenberg (October 1661) he uses the terms "accidents or modifications" to refer to "that which exists in something else and is represented by means of that in which it exists." [*K*, p. 197.]

210. "What is posited in opposition is *necessary* in relation to a determinate property. In relation to what is posited in opposition to it, such a property is *contingent*. Moreover, that which is posited in opposition to it is, like the property itself, posited in opposition to the I. Thus, like the property, what is posited in opposition thereto is also a Not-I, but a *necessary* Not-I.

"According to the above explication, however, the property in question, as something determinate and *insofar* as it is determinate (i.e., something to which the I relates merely passively), must be excluded from the I. And the I, when and insofar as it reflects upon something determinate (as is the case here), must exclude this determinate thing from itself. In the present reflection, the I also excludes from itself another Not-I, considered as

something that is both determinate and necessary. Therefore, both the determinate property in question and what is posited in opposition to it must be related to each other and
synthetically united. The ground for uniting them is that, in relation to the I, both Not-I's
are one and the same. The ground for distinguishing them from each other is that the
property [i.e., one of these two Not-I's] *is contingent* and could be different, but the substrate [i.e., the other Not-I] is, as such, necessary in relation to the property. — Both are
united; that is, they are necessary and contingent in relation to each other. The property
must have a substrate, but this property does not have to pertain to this substrate. Such a
relationship of synthetic unity between what is contingent and what is necessary is
termed a relationship of *substantiality*" (Fichte, *GEWL*, *GA*, I/3: 187; below, pp. 418–9).

211. "Die Substanz ist *aller Wechsel im allgemeinen gedacht*: das Accidens ist *ein Bestimmtes,
das mit einem andern wechselnden wechselt.*" Fichte appears to be employing several
senses of the verb *wechseln* in this sentence, including: "to change," "to exchange," and "to
be reciprocally related." I here follow Philonenko in interpreting "*ein Bestimmtes*" in the
light of the first paragraph of section 14 as "a determinate reality."

  Whereas Kant identifies "substance" with that permanent substratum that underlies all
changes of accidents over time (*KrV*, B225), Fichte here defines it as nothing other than
the totality of all reciprocal activity and hence of all possible accidents (that is to say, the
totality, of all the I's determinate activities and states of passive affection) — a notion of
substance that seems closer to Leibniz's than to Kant's.

212. "The I is simple substance, but how do I know this? Or, more precisely, what is this term
supposed to mean? — Are there then substances in themselves? 'Substance' is indeed no
more than a way of thinking, and apart from the representation of the I there can be no
talk of substance" (Fichte, *VLM*, *GA*, II/4: 341).

213. The point of this rather obscure sentence is that, even if the I itself is the only original
substance, the accidents of this substance, insofar as they are the same and can be combined in a genus-concept (specifically, in the concept of "matter," first understood as an
accident of the I), can also be treated as unchangeable in relationship to *their* accidents.
In this way, the I transfers the category of substance from itself to the Not-I. In fact, Fichte
does not provide such an explanation in *GWL*, but does further develop the concept of
substance — as *matter* — in *GEWL*, § 3, in a deduction that (in stark contrast to Kant's
treatment of the same category) *precedes* the deduction of space of time. [*K*, p. 200.]

214. The two "extremes" to which Fichte here refers are the opposing propositions stated at the
beginning of section D: viz., that the I *actively* determines itself, and that the I is what is
determined and is therefore *affected*. "The middle" (or middle term) in this case would
explain how the I can be at once active and affected. [*K*, p. 201.]

215. We will encounter this "absolute decree of reason" near the end of Part Two (*GA*, I/2: 301;
below, p. 240) and with this we will make the transition from Part Two (the "theoretical"
portion of *GWL*) to Part Three (the "practical" portion of the same).

  "I will begin by describing the task of philosophy as that of answering the following,
familiar question, How can what is objective ever become what is subjective; how can a
being for itself [i.e., a Not-I] ever become something represented [by the I]? No one will
ever explain how this remarkable transformation takes place without discovering a point
where what is objective and what is subjective are not distinct from each other at all, but
are completely one and the same. Our system establishes just such a point and then proceeds from there. This point is 'I-hood' [*Ichheit*] — 'intelligence,' 'reason,' or whatever one
may wish to call it. [...] The first way that what is subjective and what is objective are
unified — or viewed as in harmony with one another — is when *I engage in cognition*. In
this case, what is subjective follows from what is objective; the former is supposed to
agree with the latter. *Theoretical* philosophy investigates how we arrive at the assertion of

such a harmony. — [In the second case,] what is subjective and what is objective are viewed as harmonizing in such a way that what is objective ought to follow from what is subjective; a being ought to ensue from my concept (the concept of an end): *I act efficaciously.* It is the task of *practical philosophy* to investigate the origin of such an assumption of harmony" (Fichte, *SS*, *GA*, I/5: 21; *SW*, IV, pp. 1–2; *SE*, pp. 7–8).

216. A translation of the Greek phrase *hen kai pan*, which became something of a motto for the early German romantics. It is likely that Fichte first encountered this phrase in Jacobi's *Über die Lehre des Spinoza*, 2nd rev. ed. (Breslau: 1785), p. 12, where it is attributed to Lessing and cited as evidence of the latter's covert "Spinozism." For Fichte, in contrast, this is not a theoretical fact about ultimate reality, but is instead a *practical imperative* — and one which can never be fulfilled completely. [*K*, pp. 205–6.]

217. The two types of reciprocal determination to which this title refers are *causality* and *substantiality*. As Fichte will point out later in this section (*GA*, I/2: 304–6; below, pp. 242–4), the "opposition" between the propositions associated with these two different ways of considering the reciprocal determination of the I and the Not-I actually amounts to a "contradiction." Section E of Part Two is an elaborate effort to resolve this contradiction with the resources provided by the (theoretical) principle that the I posits itself as determined by the Not-I. In the end, however, it can be resolved (in Part Three) only in terms of the (practical) principle that the I posits itself as determining the Not-I.

218. This is the principle underlying all of Part Two and was formulated as such in Part Two, B, above. The principle that the I posits itself as determined by the Not-I cannot be annulled without annulling the unity of consciousness, since this principle was introduced precisely in order to avoid any direct contradiction between the I and the Not-I, which would indeed destroy the unity of consciousness.

219. To clarify the "circle" in question here: the principle of causality presupposes that of substantiality, since the I must posit its own state of being passively affected in order to posit any causally efficacious activity on part of the Not-I; and conversely, the principle of substantiality presupposes that of causality, since the I can posit its own state of being passively affected only if the Not-I has already actively produced such a state within the I. [*K*, p. 208.]

"Nothing is accomplished by means of the concepts of *substantiality* and *causality*, taken individuality. They contradict each other; therefore, we must interpose between them the concept of reciprocal interaction, in order to unite them" (Fichte, Student transcript of his lectures on the "Philosophical Science of Right," Fall 1795, *GA*, IV/3: 72).

220. *nicht eben schulgerechter Form.* The following "explanation" is not completely "rigorous" (or in an appropriately "scholastic" form), since it makes use of the concept of time, which has not yet been derived systematically; indeed, this will not occur until *GEWL*. [*K*, p. 209.]

221. "Transcendent idealism would be a system that derives determinate representations from the free and utterly lawless acting of the intellect — which is a completely self-contradictory supposition, since, as just noted, the principle of sufficient reason is quite inapplicable to completely free and lawless acting" (Fichte, *VWL*, *GA*, I/4: 200; *SW*, I, p. 441; *IWL*, pp. 26–7).

Fichte associates "idealism" with the concept of substantiality, inasmuch as this concept attributes all activity (and hence all reality) to the I, and "realism" (or "dogmatism") with the concept of causality, which attributes all activity and reality to the Not-I. The project of the *Wissenschaftslehre* is to steer a middle course between these two extremes, which is why Fichte will later describe his own system, not as "idealism," but as "real-idealism" or "ideal-realism" (*GA*, I/2: 412; below, p. 343).

222. Here Fichte appears to be echoing Kant's claim, in his 1790 essay, *Über eine Entdeckung, nach der alle neue Kritik der reinen Vernunft durch eine ältere entbehrlich gemacht werden soll*

[*"Concerning a Discovery according to which any new Critique of Pure Reason is allegedly made dispensable by an older one"*] that Leibniz's doctrine of the pre-established harmony between body and soul is reducible in principle to an "idealism" according to which "bodies" are simply products of the soul's own representing activity. [*K*, p. 210.]

223. Such idealism, which assigns to the I the power to limit itself purely and simply, is incompatible with the first foundational principle of *GWL*, since the latter assigns to the I the absolute power to "posit itself" as such (or "purely and simply"), but *not* the power to engage in a free and unconditioned act of self-limitation. This is a point that Fichte will emphasize over and over again in what follows. (See *GA*, I/2: 309, 411, and 413; below, pp. 247, 341–2, and 344.) The limitation (or finitude) of the I, first posited in the third foundational principle, is ultimately comprehensible only as conditional upon the presence within and for the I of an involuntary *feeling* of an *Anstoß* or "check" upon its real activity.

224. The I can posit neither its own state of being passively affected nor the activity of the Not-I *schlechthin* or "unconditionally," since the positing of the former is conditional upon and presupposes that of the latter, and vice versa.

225. That is, from the propositions (1.) that the I posits within itself a state of being passively affected and (2.) that the I posits activity in the Not-I. As we have now seen and in accordance with the principle of reciprocal determination, in order to posit either of these propositions, the I must also posit the other. Consequently, these "original propositions" cannot really be posited "purely and simply" (and hence "unconditionally" or "absolutely") after all.

226. Another name for such "independent" activity is "absolute" activity (see *GA*, I /2: 313–4; below, pp. 251–2). Fichte also associates independent or absolute or unconditioned *activity* with independent or absolute *reality* (see *GA*, I/2: 341; below, p. 279). As *K* explains (p. 214), it is necessary to posit such an "independent" activity in both the I and the Not-I, since otherwise the acts of self-determination and becoming determined would be quite incomprehensible. If the I and Not-I are each thought of as determined or determining only "in part" (as they must be, in order to avoid contradiction), then they each must contain a "reality" or "activity" that is not reciprocally determined by the other and is in that sense "independent" or "absolute." Later in Part Two, Fichte will identify this independent activity of the I with the *power of productive imagination*. In Part Three (the "practical" portion of *GWL*), it will be identified with the absolute striving of the I to fill all reality, and we will there learn more about the "absolute" or "independent" reality or activity of the Not-I as well.

227. Once again, Fichte proposes to resolve the contradiction between the independent activity on the one hand and the reciprocally related activity and state of being passively affected on the other in the only way available: that is, by an application of the *Satz des Grundes* or Principle of Sufficient Reason to this distinction. Previously (*GA*, I/2: 272; above, p. 215), this principle was defined as the "the *sheer form of the unification of terms posited in opposition to each other by means of the concept of divisibility*: A is in part = −A, and vice versa." The task of any "explanation" according to such a principle is to discover the "ground" of that respect in which A and −A differ, as well as the "ground" of that respect in which they are the same, and that is precisely what Fichte will attempt to do in what follows.

228. Fichte here introduces a new distinction between the "independent activity" of the I and of the Not-I, understood, first of all, in their *indirect* relation to one another (by means of the reciprocal relationship between partial activity and a partial state of being passively affected in both the I and the Not-I), and secondly, as considered *in themselves* or *an sich*, with no relation, whether direct or indirect, to each other. [*K*, p. 215.] Here, as Philonenko points out, Fichte is anticipating the distinction between the *form* and the *content* of the independent activity (see *OC*, p. 58n.).

229. The first of these propositions may be viewed as an expression of what Fichte will later call "dogmatic qualitative realism," based on the principle of causality, and the second as an expression of what he will call "dogmatic qualitative idealism," based on the principle of substantiality.

230. "The cases before us" here concern the reciprocal relationship of causal efficacy, the reciprocal relationship of substantiality, and the independent activities of the I and the Not-I. As Fichte will go on to explain (*GA*, I/2: 314; below, p. 314), this "first proposition" concerns only the *content* or *matter* of the reciprocal relationships in question. The *form* of the same will be considered in the immediately following section II.

231. "The principle of determination" or *Satz der Bestimmung* is another name, according to Fichte, for the *Satz des Grundes*, the principle of sufficient reason or "grounding principle."

232. That is, it is posited as such in *philosophical reflection* upon the concept of causal efficacy.

233. As Fichte explains below (*GA*, I/2: 368 below, p. 305), this power of the Not-I is something merely "ideal," something that is "merely thought of," a power that possesses being only by virtue of the I's exercise of its power of representation. Hence an "ideal ground" is an explanatory ground of X that is added to X only in thought (or by means of "reflection"). The I's state of being passively affected is the "ideal ground" of its cognition of the activity of the Not-I, which it then posits as the "real ground" of its own passive affection. Nevertheless, as Fichte explains a few pages later (*GA*, I/2: 310; below, p. 248), the Not-I remains a merely ideal ground of the passive affection of the I and possesses no reality apart from representations. [*K*, p. 217.]

     As Fichte had already explained in *RA* (*GA*, I/2: 53; *SW*, I, p. 13; *EPW*, p. 68), "If all that is said [when Kant claims that we must seek out some foundation for the forms of synthetic judgment] is that *we* are required to seek a foundation for these forms and to posit this foundation in our mind (and nothing more is being said), the principle of sufficient reason is at first being employed as merely logically valid. But since what is established thereby exists only as a thought, then one should think that the *logical* foundation of a thought is at the same time its *real* or *existential* foundation."

     Fichte will ultimately conclude that, in the case of the concept of causal efficacy, real and ideal ground are, in fact, one and the same. See *GA*, I/2: 326; below, pp. 264–5.

234. The rule or principle of *reciprocal determination* is subordinate to the *principle of determination* as such, which, according to Fichte is precisely the *Satz des Grundes* or grounding principle.

235. Recall that, for Fichte, "positive reality" is associated with *activity* and "positive negation" with the state of being passively affected (see I/2: 293; above p. 233). Every *quantitative* reciprocal relationship therefore depends upon the *qualitative* opposition between the I's doing and its being passively affected, which is why the discussion of causal efficacy must precede that of substantiality. [*K*, pp. 217–18.]

236. In contrast to a merely *ideal* ground, a *real* ground does not exist merely in thought. Since all reality is supposedly posited in the I, and posited there by the I itself, the I can be described as its *own* real ground. Insofar as the I's state of being passively affected is understood as a "positive negation," it too requires a real and not merely ideal ground. [*K*, p. 218.]

237. Such an inference is valid only insofar as the difference between activity and a state of passive affection is viewed as a purely *qualitative* and not as a merely *quantitative* difference.

238. Fichte is here using the term "speculative" as a synonym for "theoretical." The claim that theoretical or speculative philosophy is concerned exclusively with explaining representation indicates Fichte's debt to K. L. Reinhold's Elementary Philosophy, which *begins*

with what he calls the "principle of consciousness," namely, that in consciousness the subject distinguishes the representation from both itself and the object and relates it to both. According to Reinhold, moreover, the I provides only the *form* of the representation, whereas the *content* of the same is ultimately dependent upon affection by the object, understood as a thing-in-itself. To this Fichte objects as follows, in *RA*:

"Finally, the critic [Aenesidemus, a.k.a., G. E. Schulze] turns to what he takes to be the chief mistake of the Elementary Philosophy and the basis of all its other errors. Thus he writes: 'It is *not* merely something in the representation that is related to the subject and something else that is related to the object; instead, it is the *entire* representation that is related to both subject and object, though related differently to each. The representation is related to the subject in the way every property is related to its subject; it is related to the object in the way every symbol is related to what it symbolizes. Reinhold overlooked this difference in the very manner of relating, and thus he thought that the only way to explain the possibility of relating the representation to two different things was by presupposing two different component parts of the representation itself.' Considered by itself, this is quite correct, though rather than employing Aenesidemus' terms, the reviewer would prefer to say that the representation is related to the object as an effect is related to its cause and to the subject as an accident is related to the substance" (*RA*, *GA*, I/2: 59; *SW*, I, p. 18; *EPW*, p. 72).

239. *Fatum* is "fate." On Fichte's understanding of dogmatic realism, the I can never be anything but an accident of the Not-I (or of the "Absolute") and must therefore lack any genuine freedom of its own. This same criticism of dogmatic realism is one of the main topics of Fichte's two "Introductions" to the *Wissenschaftslehre* or 1797.

240. This expression raises the question: what would constitute a "formal" Spinozism, and is Fichte's own system an example of the same? This was a point of vigorous discussion among Fichte's contemporary critics and followers, some of whom (including Jacobi and Schelling) described the *Wissenschaftslehre* as an "inverted Spinozism." Presumably, a formal Spinozism would be a system that treats the I rather than the Not-I as the only substance, in which case the *Wissenschaftslehre* would be just as "monistic" or "Spinozistic" as Spinoza's own system, but not at all materialistic. [*K*, p. 219.]

241. This is the same system Fichte had already described as "transcendent idealism," an idealism that maintains that the I possesses the ability arbitrarily to posit within itself a diminished sum of reality (see *GA*, I/2: 303; above, pp. 241–2). Such an "idealism" fails to explain why every finite intellect must necessarily posit — as a noumenon or thought-entity — something external to itself as the cause of its state of passive affection (*GA*, I/2: 412; below, p. 342).

242. "Critical idealism is neither materialism nor dogmatism. It is not materialism, which begins with things; nor is it the sort of idealism that begins with mental substance; nor is it dualism, which begins with the mind and the thing in itself, considered as two separate substances. Instead, Critical idealism begins either with their reciprocal interaction as such, or else with accidents of both. (Substance and accident are [for Critical idealism] forms of our thinking, employed in order to explain consciousness.) Critical idealism thereby avoids the necessity of having to deny either of these two. Materialism denies what is mental, while [non-Critical] idealism denies what is material. Nor does this system face the insoluble task of uniting extremes that cannot be united once they have been separated (as in the case of dualism); instead, it discovers the I and the Not-I to be united.

"Nothing in the *Wissenschaftslehre* is more crucial than this interaction of the I and the Not-I [...]. The I is intuitable only in reciprocal interaction with the Not-I. It can be thought of apart from this relationship, but then it is not actual, but is a necessary Idea. The Not-I, on the other hand, cannot even be thought of outside of reason. The I is primary;

the Not-I is secondary, and this is why one is able to think of the I in isolation, but not of the Not-I" (Fichte, *WLnmK*, *GA*, IV/3: 372–3; *FTP*, pp. 164–5).

243. As Fichte will explain below, the I is "practical" when it reflects upon itself in conformity with the Idea that it ought to contain within itself all reality (an Idea ultimately grounded in the absolute self-positing of the I described in §1). See *GA*, I/2: 407–9; below, pp. 238–9.

244. See the discussion of an "infinite judgment," *GA*, I/2: 277; above, pp. 219–20.

245. *Kanon*. This is the Latin term employed by Kant in *KrV* to describe logic as providing rules for the avoidance of error.

246. That is to say, in the context of our current reflection upon the concept of substantiality.

247. As will eventually become clear, the "limited activity of the I" is, in this case, the activity of *representing*. The point here is that, even though *what* the I represents is not dependent upon the I, the fact *that* it is engaged in representing does depend — purely and simply, or absolutely — upon nothing but the I itself. [*K*, p. 223.]

248. Less than a year earlier, in *EM*, Fichte described the power of imagination as "the productive power [*produktive Eigenmacht*] of the soul" and defined the "pure power of imagination" as the [power of the subject "to determine its own being in an accident of itself" (*GA*, II/3: 114). It is *this* independent activity of the I that is supposed to initiate and determine the reciprocal relationship between action and passive affection.

249. According to this account, the reciprocal relationship between the I's activity and its state of passive affection is first *posited* by the I and subsequently *determined*: namely, by positing an independent activity of the I that determines this reciprocal relationship. Recall that the independent activity of the I is first introduced as an activity posited in opposition to the I's state of being passively affected (see *GA*, I/2: 305; above, p. 243).

250. That is to say, we must distinguish the meaning of this new proposition from that of the proposition that an independent activity is determined by reciprocally-related-acting-and-being-passively-affected.

251. The "components" in question are, of course, *activity* and *being passively affected*.

252. In the case of the concept of causal efficacy, we had to posit an "independent activity" *of the Not-I* as the explanatory ground of the reciprocal relationship between activity and being passively affected. Here, in the case of the concept of substantiality, we will posit an independent activity of the I for a similar reason: as the explanatory ground of the reciprocal relationship between activity and being passively affected.

253. In this case, however, the independent activity in question will prove to be an independent activity of the I rather than of the Not-I.

254. Namely, when an independent activity is determined by reciprocally-related-acting-and-being-passively-affected. See *GA*, I/2: 306; above, pp. 244–5. This was the topic of Part One.

255. als begründet *Faktum*. Regarding this term (and the difference between a "*Faktum*" and a "*Tatsache*"), see the "Notes on the Translation" in the Editor's Introduction.

256. That is, in the case that reciprocally-related-acting-and-being-passively-affected is determined by an independent activity. See *GA*, I/2: 306; above, pp. 244–5. This will now become the topic of Part Two.

257. Of course, the presence of an "intelligent observer" is also presupposed in the preceding "first case." The difference is the difference between what Fichte will proceed to describe as "simple reflection" (first case) and "reflection upon the first reflection" (second case). [*K*, p. 225.]

258. The independent activity determines the "form" of the reciprocal relationship in the sense that it determines, first, that the I's state of being passively affected will be posited, and second, that this will produce a transition from the positing of being passively affected to the positing of activity, and vice versa. [*K*, p. 225.]

259. In discussing "The Final Aim of the Natural Dialectic of Human Reason," Kant clarifies his view of the Ideas of Reason, according to which we must regard things in the world "as if" they were created by the Supreme Being, by distinguishing between *heuristic* and *ostensive* concepts. "In this way the Idea is only a heuristic concept and not an ostensive one. Furthermore, it does not indicate what the character of an object is, but rather, how, under the guidance of this concept's, we ought to *search* for this character and its connection to experiential objects as such" (*KrV*, A671/B699). Here Fichte appears to be using this term in a similar manner. We will be proceeding "heuristically" insofar as we consider the reciprocal relationship as a guide for discovering the independent activity operative in this case.

260. The content or material character of the I's activity is determined by *what* the I does: namely, what it does not posit in itself it posits in its other, in the Not-I. It thereby *transfers* the activity posited within itself to this other. This transference is the product of the independent activity of the I, which accomplished this reciprocal relationship. [*K*, p. 226.]

261. The *erstes Grundsatz* to which Fichte here refers is not the absolutely posited foundational principle presented in § 1, but (as Fichte's page reference makes clear), the first of the three fundamental principles guiding the present portion of his inquiry, viz.: "an independent activity is determined by reciprocally-related-acting-and-being-passively-affected."

262. *des nächstvorherghenden Satzes*. This is the proposition examined in section II, 3, a, above, viz: "In the reciprocal relationship of *causal efficacy* an activity is posited in the Not-I by means of a state of being passively affected in the I" (*GA*, I/2: 315; above, p. 254).

263. See *GA*, I/2: 338; below, pp. 282–3.

264. See *GA*, I/2: 345; below, pp. 282–3.

265. See *GA*, I/2: 345; below, pp. 282–3.

266. See Fichte's assertion, in *VKO*, that the Idea of God as legislator of the moral law is based "upon an alienation of what is our own and the transference of something subjective to a being outside of us; and this alienation is the actual principle of religion, insofar as this is supposed to determine the will" (*GA*, I/1: 33; *SW*, V, p. 55; *ACR*, p. 41).

267. See *GA*, I/2: 343; below, p. 281.

268. In the case of the synthetic concept of causal efficacy, the *form* of the reciprocally-related-acting-and-being-passively-affected was previously identified as "positing by means of non-positing, or a transition" (*GA*, I/2: 315; above, p. 254), a form that is supposed to be determined by an activity (of the I) independent of the reciprocally related terms. The *content* of the reciprocally-related-acting-and-being-passively-affected is in this case the I and the Not-I, which is also supposed to be determined by an independent activity, in this case an activity of the Not-I (See *GA*, I/2: 309; above, p. 247).

    In the case of the synthetic concept of substantiality, the *form* of the reciprocally-related-acting-and-being-passively-affected was previously identified as "non-positing by means of a positing" (*GA*, I/2: 317; above, p. 255), and this form is also supposed to be determined by an activity independent of the reciprocally related terms. In the case of substantiality, the *content* of the reciprocally-related-acting-and-being-passively-affected is acting and-being-passively-affected. This content too is supposed to be determined by an independent activity, in this case another activity of the I: "the power of imagination" (*GA*, I/2: 314; above, p. 252). [*K*, pp. 230–1.]

269. Were this X posited in only one of the related components it could not fulfill its assigned function as the *ground* of their relationship.

270. The issue here is this: How can the unity of consciousness be insured if consciousness is understood as constantly in motion? Fichte's answer is that this is possible only if we postulate some underlying continuum in which all these opposed elements are united.

These points are then transformed by the power of imagination into temporal moments. [*K*, p. 231.]

271. This is the claim that the connection between the reciprocally related components (cause and effect, for example) is not grounded upon anything in those components themselves, but solely upon the activity of consciousness in its 'transition' from one component to the other. Kant associates this kind of "idealism" with Hume and quotes his claim that "as we feel a customary connection between the ideas, we transfer that feeling to the objects and this is the work of the power of imagination (*An Enquiry Concerning Human Understanding*, VIII, ii).

272. The *actual* transition — i.e., transition considered as an *activity* of the I — is the basis of the possibility of the transition of the *content* of the reciprocal relationship from one component to the other. [*K*, p. 232.]

273. More specifically, it lies in the power of imagination. See *GA*, I/2: 368–9; below, pp. 305–6, which makes it clear that this absolute activity of transition is ultimately grounded in the first foundational principle of *GWL*. [*K*, p. 232.]

274. In the discussion that follows, Fichte will frequently employ the expressions "activity of the form" and "activity of the content" to refer to those previously posited "independent activities," which are supposed to determine, respectively, the form and the content of the reciprocally-related-acting-and-being-passively-affected.

275. Fichte seems to associate the notions of "circular movement" and "self-reproduction," not simply in the present passage, but also in *GA*, I/2: 359; below, p. 297.

276. This is the movement from (1) The activity of the form (i.e., the independent activity that determines the form of the reciprocally-related-acting-and-being-passively-affected), to (2) the activity of the content (i.e., the independent activity that determines the content of the reciprocally-related-acting-and-being-passively-affected), to (3) the content of the reciprocally-related-acting-and-being-affected, and finally to (4) the form of the reciprocally-related-acting-and-being-passively-affected. *K* suggests (p. 233) that this illustrates the "methodological circularity" of the *Wissenschaftslehre*, to which Fichte had already referred in *BWL* (*GA*, I/2: 131; above, p. 173).

277. The "particular cases" in question are the two synthetic concepts previously identified and discussed: the concept of causal efficacy and the concept of substantiality.

278. "The activity of the form" is just another name for the independent activity that determines the form of the reciprocal relation [*Wechsel*] of causal efficacy. Similarly, "the activity of the content" is the independent activity that determines the content of the same *Wechsel*. The independent activity that determines the form of the reciprocally-related-acting-and-being-passively-affected is an activity of the I, whereas the independent activity that determines the content of the same is an activity of the Not-I.

279. Note how Fichte here treats as synonyms the terms *bestimmt* (determined, determinant), *begründet* (grounded), and *gesetzt* (posited). This is helpful for understanding how he employs the verb "to posit."

280. As will become evident later in this same paragraph, this "not posited being" is the passive affection or "being-passively-affected" (*Leiden*) of the I.

281. See the discussion of the "activity of the content," *GA*, I/2: 319; above, p. 258.

282. See *GA*, I/2: 307 and 319; above, pp. 245–6 and 258. In this case, X is the ground of the relation between the I and the Not-I that is expressed in the concept of causal efficacy, namely, a passive affection of the I.

283. See *GA*, I/2: 311; above, p. 249. The conflict in question has now been somewhat mitigated because the activity of the Not-I has not been confined to a limited domain.

284. The first kind of reflection is the reflection that the independent activity of the I grounds and determines the form of reciprocally-related-acting-and-being-passively-affected and thereby determines its content as well.

285. The second kind of reflection is the reflection that the independent activity of the Not-I grounds and determines the activity of the I.
286. As *K* observes (p. 236), "not positing" does not mean simply failing to posit something; on the contrary, Fichte here employs this expression to mean actively denying, negating, or annulling something.
287. It is a "circular" action in the sense of "reciprocity" or "reciprocal action": what the I does not posit in the I, it posits in the Not-I, and this is why what is posited in the Not-I must not and cannot be posited in the I. [*K*, p. 236.]
288. According to our first foundational principle, the I, qua I, must always posit its own existence. The being of the I is therefore always a "posited being."
289. *der gemeine Menschenverstand.* This term could also be translated simply as "common-sense."
290. As Fichte will proceed to explain, the "ambiguity" or "double meaning" (*Zweideutigkeit*) implicit in the word "to posit" (*setzen*) concerns the difference between *ideal* and *real* positing, the difference between positing something as an object of consciousness (that is, within the I) and positing it as existing apart from the I. For an analysis of this distinction, see Claudio Cesa, "'...ein Doppelsinn in der Bedeutung des Wort Setzens,'" in *Der Grundansatz der ersten Wissenschaftslehre Johann Gottlieb Fichte*, ed. E. Fuchs and I. Radrizanni (Neuried: Ars Una, 1966), pp. 134–44; Paul Franks, "Fichte's Position: Anti-Subjectivism, Self-Awareness and Self-Location in the Space of Reasons," in *The Cambridge Companion to Fichte*, ed. David James and Günter Zöller (Cambridge: Cambridge University Press, 2016), pp. 374–404; and David W. Wood, "The 'Double Sense' of Fichte's Philosophical Language." *Revista de Estud(i)os sobre Fichte* 15 (2017).
291. *der gemeine Menschensinn.* Fichte appears to be using this term simply as a synonym for *gemeine Menschenverstand* (ordinary human understanding or "common sense.")
292. See *GA*, I/2: 309; above, p. 248, where Fichte explains that the "quality" in question is "being-passively-affected," understood as a "negative" quality to which "reality" is posited in opposition.
293. I.e., as a certain quantity of diminished activity.
294. See *GA*, I/2: 308–9; above p. 247. An "ideal ground" is the basis or ground of a knowledge claim. In this case, the passive affection of the I is the basis for the I's claim that the Not-I is the cause of its own passive state of affection and hence the "real ground" of the "quality" in question (being-passively-affected). [*K*, pp. 237–8.]
295. These are Neolatin scholastic terms: *idealiter* means "ideally" or "in an ideal manner," and *realiter* means "really" or "in a real manner."
296. For Fichte's account of the "creation" or production of the *Stoff* of experience, see *GA*, I/2: 440; below, p. 368.
297. The question at issue concerns the difference between a "passive affection" of the I produced by the Not-I, and *consciousness* of the same affection. Only the latter requires an ideal ground.
298. This is the question posed by "common sense" concerning how an ideal ground can ever become a real ground. The new question raised by Fichte is how a real ground can ever become an ideal ground.
299. I.e., the synthesis of the activity of the Not-I and the passive affection of the I. See *GA*, I/2: 324; above, p. 263.
300. The real ground must always be posited as such by the I, and this positing is the ideal ground of the real ground in question.
301. I.e., an inability to abstract from the realm of ordinary experience and from objects of the same.

302. This promise remained unfulfilled. There is no discussion of this topic in either *GWL* or in *GEWL*. [*K*, p. 239.]
303. The first principle of Part Two of *GWL* (which is what Fichte is referring to when he speaks of the "theoretical *Wissenschaftslehre*") is "the I posits itself as determined by the Not-I."
304. That is, Critical idealism is the standpoint of Part Two, the entire "theoretical part" of the *Wissenschaftslehre*.
305. That is, between the activity of the Not-I and the being-passively-affected of the I, or between the activity of the I and the reality of the Not-I.
306. That is, beyond the theoretical portion of the *Wissenschaftslehre*.
307. The "two modes of reflection" in question are: (1) viewing the reciprocal-acting-and-being-passively-affected as determined by an independent activity and (2) abstracting from the independent activity and viewing the reciprocal activity as inherent in the reciprocally-related components themselves. It has now been established that both modes of reflection are incorrect and that the independent activity and the reciprocally-related-acting-and-being-passively-affected are correctly viewed only when viewed together, as a synthetic unity.
308. As Fichte explains near the end of this paragraph, what makes this mutual intrusion possible is the "qualitative opposition" of the two components of the reciprocal-acting-and-being-passively-affected — (1.) acting and (2.) being-passively-affected — , each of which refers to the other. [*K*, p. 242.]
309. The representation of time is required if — and only if — one is concerned with the coming to be and passing away of the *accidents* of an abiding, underlying substrate or substance. This allows us to apply opposed albeit temporally indexed predicates to the same substance without contradiction. [*K*, p. 242.]
310. The power of imagination is not the power of abstraction. It is the latter that is required here, where we are treating the concept of causal efficacy in complete abstraction and isolation from that of substance.
311. Namely, the proposition that the *content* of this reciprocally-related-acting-and-being-passively-affected determines its *form*.
312. I.e., between the I and the Not-I.
313. *Der Anstoß*. This is the first appearance of a term that will be assigned a special, technical meaning in what follows, where it is translated as "impetus" or "check" (and often as both). On this occasion, however, it is being employed in a quite ordinary, non-technical sense, as in the ordinary *Stein des Anstoßes* or "stumbling block."
314. See the previous section, which concluded (*GA*, I/2: 326; above, p. 264) that ideal ground and real ground are the same in the concept of causal efficacy.
315. As Fichte had explained earlier, "positing by means of a non-positing" (positing in the *positive* sense) is what he also calls "transference" or *Uebertragen* (see I/2: 315; above, p. 254). The point here is that the I does not posit the Not-I directly, but only indirectly or mediately, by means of its non-positing of something in itself. Positing in the *negative* sense is the same as what Fichte calls "alienating" or *Entäußern*, a non-positing by means of a positing (*GA*, I/2: 317; above, p. 256).
316. The distinction here is between the kind of positing that occurs "purely and simply," "unconditionally," or "absolutely" (*schlechthin*) and is therefore "direct" or "immediate" (*unmittelbar*) and another type of positing that occurs only by means of and as a result of an act of non-positing. The latter is called by Fichte "indirect" or "mediate" (*mittelbar*) positing.
317. Fichte has not in fact previously discussed the "absolute reality" of the I; instead, he here appears to be referring to his previous discussion of the "absolute activity" of the same

(*GA*, I/2: 287–8; above, p. 228). For Fichte, however, "activity" and "reality" are really one and the same, and the I can be said to possess "absolute reality" only insofar as it is "absolutely active." [*K*, p. 332.]

318. This is evidence against Dieter Henrich's influential claim that it is only in the revised version of the foundational portion of his system—that is, in *WLnm*—that Fichte realizes that the I must not merely "posit itself" but also "posit itself *as* self-positing." (See Henrich, *Fichtes ursprüngliche Einsicht* (Frankfurt am Main: Klostermann, 1967); trans. David Lachterman, "Fichte's Original Insight," *Contemporary German Philosophy* 1 (1982) 15–52). This claim is already fully present here in *GWL*. See too *GA*, I/2: 337; below, p. 274.

319. This is because in mediate or indirect positing there is no "ground of identity" (also called the "ground of connection") nor "ground of distinction" between the two, reciprocally related terms and because such grounds of connection and distinction are required if there is to be any application of the "grounding principle" (principle of sufficient reason). [*K*, p. 245.] See *GA*, I/2: 272; above, pp. 214–5.

320. I.e., "qualitative" idealism.

321. What is at issue here is not a pre-established harmony between ideas and mind-independent things, but rather an "idealistic" harmony between limitations of the I and the ideally posited ground of the same in the Not-I. This is what makes this kind of idealism "consistent" for Fichte. [*K*, p. 245–6.]

322. The question, Why does the I posit something in opposition to itself? has now been answered. It does so, according to the quantitative idealist, simply because it finds itself to be limited.

323. This concept is self-contradictory because Fichte understands "finite" to mean "possessing a ground outside of itself" and hence not absolute. [*K*, p. 246.]

324. The first kind of idealism is "qualitative" because it annuls an activity that is posited entirely (or "in itself") and replaces *acting* with *being-passively-affected*. The second kind of idealism annuls this activity only in part and is hence "quantitative." Qualitative realism, discussed below, supposes something qualitatively different from the I, a thing in itself, as the *cause* of the I's limitation; whereas quantitative realism simply supposes the reality of something in the I but not posited by the I: an impression or limitation of the I qua *substance*. [*K*, p. 247.]

325. Namely, *why* the I posits something in opposition to itself at all. Quantitative idealism explains this by appealing to the fact that the I simply finds itself to be finite and to be determined in a particular manner.

326. Fichte had employed similar language a few months earlier in a footnote to § 4 of *BWL*, in which he compares the possible tasks facing one at any given time to the infinite radii of a circle and then maintains that the actual task we pursue and the course (radii) we travel is "determined by the impression made by the Not-I." But it is noteworthy that in the second, 1798, edition, he altered this passage to read "is something that is *determined by the gradual development of our original limitedness [Begrenztheit]*" (*GA*, I/2: 130n.; above, p. 172n.). In his Platner lectures he also suggested replacing the term "check" or "impetus" (*Anstoß*) with "original limitedness" (*VLM, GA*, II/4: 360).

327. Regarding the "spirit" of Kant's philosophy and the need for "spirit" to understand the same, see, above all, Fichte's 1794 lectures "Concerning the Difference between the Spirit and the Letter within Philosophy" (*GA*, II/3: 315–42; *EPW*, pp. 192–215), as well as his lengthy discussion of the "spirit of the Critical philosophy" in § 6 of the Second Introduction to *VWL*. As for Kant's claim to have established only the propaedeutic to a scientific system of metaphysics or philosophy, see *KrV*, A11/B25. Concerning Fichte's deduction of space and time, there are only hints in *GWL*, see *GA*, I/2: 367 and 440; below, pp. 304 and 368). This, however, is one of the main topics of *GEWL*, see *GA*, I/3: 193ff.; below, pp. 423ff.

328. The synthesis in question is a synthesis of (a) the synthesis of independent activity, and (b) the synthesis of reciprocally-related-acting-and-being-passively-affected. Just as Critical idealism is a synthesis of realism and idealism, Critical quantitative idealism is a synthesis of quantitative realism and quantitative idealism. [*K*, p. 253.]

329. Namely, the sphere of the I.

330. In other words, the I posits itself as limited by the Not-I. More specifically, the I posit itself first as absolute and then as limitable with respect to its quantity by the Not-I. See *GA*, I/2: 286; above, p. 227.

331. See *GA*, I/2: 354 and 361; below, pp. 291 and 199: no subject, no object — and vice versa.

332. The I's act of positing, considered simply as such, is unconditional and occurs, as Fichte puts it "purely and simply" (*schlechthin*) — whether what it posits is the I or the Not-I. (See §§ 1 and 2.) In contrast, mediate or indirect positing posits something determinate and limited, whether that is the limited I or the limited Not-I.

333. *Kein Du, kein Ich; kein Ich, kein Du.* Many scholars, including Reinhard Lauth, cite this passage as evidence that Fichte already introduces his new ground-breaking concept of intersubjectivity in *GWL*. (See Reinhard Lauth, "Nouvelles recherches sur Jacobi," *Archives des Philosophie* 34 [1971], 283.) This, however, seems problematic. Instead, it appears that Fichte is here merely paraphrasing a well-known passage from F. H. Jacobi's 1787 work, *David Hume über den Glauben*, p. 65, in which the term "*du*" quite plainly refers, not to *other I's*, but instead, to *objects of consciousness in general*. There is a similar passage in Jacobi's *Über die Lehre des Spinozas*, 2nd ed., p. 163. The present claim is therefore the same as the one Fichte has just been elaborating: The I cannot posit itself without also positing a Not-I — rather than, more specifically, positing other individual I's. Fichte does not explicitly introduce the latter doctrine until two years later, in *GNR*, and his revolutionary account of intersubjectivity plays no role whatsoever in *GWL*. On this controversial issue, See Klaus Hammacher, "Fichte, Maimon und Jacobi: Transzendentaler Idealismus und Realismus," in *Transzendentalphilosophie als System*, ed. Alfred Mues (Hamburg: Meiner, 1989), pp. 253–4. As Hammacher notes, the use of *du* as a synonym for *gegenständlich Dasein* ("objective existence") was not uncommon at the time.

   Neverthless, some commentators insist that Fichte's celebrated and blazingly original thesis concerning the necessity of "recognition" by another I as a condition for the possibility of self-positing is already present and operative in *GWL*, even though the only evidence for this claim in *GWL* is the present passage. Whatever Fichte may have meant by this sentence, the doctrine of intersubjective recognition in response to a "summons" from another individidual I plays no systematic role whatsoever in *GWL*. Indeed, that was unquestionably one of the major *deficiencies* of this text in its author eyes, since this doctrine is explicitly incorporated into his next presenation of the foundational portion of his system, his 1796/99 lectures on *Wissenschaftslehre nova methodo*.

334. In fact, Fichte offers no such explanation here or elsewhere, though in Part Three he does defend the appropriateness of another term for object, namely, *Gegenstand* (*GA*, I/2: 393; below, p. 327). Nevertheless, he appears to use these two terms, *Objekt and Gegenstand* quite interchangeably.

335. According to "the law of the mediacy of positing" one cannot posit the (limited) I, as subject, without positing in opposition to it a limited Not-I, as object.

336. *selbst dieses Leidens (Affektion, Bestimmung).* This passage indicates why "being-passively-affected," or "passive affection" or even "affection" (and not "passivity") is the most appropriate translation of *Leiden*.

337. *In der folgenden Hauptsynthesis.* That is, in the immediately following synthesis of *substantiality*.

338. That is, by preceding from the positing of the I, which is the "mediating component" between the posited I (subject) and posited Not-I (object). Recall Fichte's earlier remark concerning the distinctive method of this part of his treatise, in which each synthesis succeeds in unifying opposites at their midpoint (*Mittelpunkt*), leaving the two extreme ends unmediated and not united. See *GA*, I/2: 300; above, p. 239.

339. As explained above, the "ideal" reality of the I is its reality insofar as it is posited *as* posited. See *GA*, I/2: 333; above, p. 271.

340. This explanation is "circular" because the quantitative idealist bases the passive affection on the law of mediate positing and bases this law on being-passively-affected.

341. They are both wrong for the following reason: if, in mediate or indirect positing, the being-posited-in-opposition of the components of the reciprocal-acting-and-being-passively-affected is really the same as their reciprocal-acting-and-being-passively-affected, then one cannot begin from either side of the relationship. This synthesis allows us to grasp the relationship of its components to one another, but not the act of synthesis itself. [*K*, p. 257.]

342. See *GA*, I/2: 336; above, p. 274.

343. The previously assigned task is to explain how the reciprocally-related-acting-and-being-passively-affected and the independent activity can be understood as mutually determining each other. See *GA*, I/2: 318; above, p. 257.

344. That is to say, concerning the kind of grounding proposed by critical, quantitative idealism.

345. This is the same activity that was previously described as *Entäusßern* or "alienating."

346. That is to say, it must be excluded from a specific sphere, which must, therefore, first be determinately posited as such, before anything can be excluded (or "alienated") from it.

347. "Objective acting" was previously described as "an activity directed at something in the Not-I, at an *Object*" (*GA*, I/2: 328; above, pp. 267 and 326-7). In § 5 Fiche will identify "objective activity" with the kind of activity that posits an object. "Objective activity" is therefore the same as "objective positing." See *GA*, I/2: 347 and 393; below, pp. 284 and 326-7.

348. B is some determinate property or capacity of something else, A. In the example Fichte is about to provide, in which "a piece of iron" is A, and "movement" is a property B of this piece of iron, whereas the true "substance" is the higher sphere that includes both A and B: the iron plus its movement (as precipitated by a magnet in this instance).

349. As *K* notes (p. 258), Not-A is here "indeterminate" in the same way and sense in which the Not-I is indeterminate: namely, each is determined only as *not* something else (whether A or I).

350. *welches sich fortbewegt*. Note the reflexive form of this verb. Fichte is here referring to the capacity of the iron to move, indeed to "move itself" — albeit in response to something outside itself. As will soon become evident, what he has in mind is a piece of iron that "moves" (or "moves itself") toward a magnet. The question at issue is whether this property of "moving" is part of the complete concept of the iron as a substance. Though Fichte here speaks explicitly of a "piece of iron," in what follows he will usually refer simply to "the iron." But it is vital to keep in mind that he is here not referring to the universal or *general concept* of iron, but rather to *this particular piece of iron* and to the concept of the same. The question is, What essentially pertains to the concept of this piece of iron? More specifically, does the piece of iron's movement in the presence of a magnet pertain to it?

351. Fichte here employs the term *Ding an sich* or "thing in itself" not in the problematic Kantian sense but in the traditional Scholastic sense, which means something "considered as such." In *C*, he amended this potentially misleading passage to refer instead to a "*Ding für sich*." The ordinary but erroneous view of substance to which Fichte refers is the view that what is "essential" is the substance qua A, whereas the properties or accidents of the same are "inessential."

352. Hence the true substance is not "iron" (or "the piece of iron") per se, but is the general concept of iron (the "essence" of the same) along with the indeterminate totality of all its possible determinate accidents or properties. As *K* notes (pp. 259–60), when applied to the I, this means that the absolute I of § I cannot be thought of as a substance, since this requires that the I be thought of as determinable in various ways, something that first becomes possible in § 3, when a limited Not-I is posited in opposition to a limited I. Fichte writes that "insofar as they are posited by means of the concept of mutual limit-ability as both alike and opposed to each other, both the I and the Not-I are, so to speak, something (namely, accidents) contained in the I (understood as a divisible substance) and posited by the I (understood as the absolute, unrestrictable subject, to which nothing is equal nor posited in opposition)." See *GA*, I/2: 279; above, p. 221.

   Applied to the concept of the I in itself, what this means is that any determination of this concept is foreign. The absolute I is to be thought of as our proper nature, as our essence (*essentia*, not *substantia*), not as a substance in Descartes' and Spinoza's sense; it is the I in itself insofar as it is purely alone. The absolute I is self-positing, pure self-relation, pure being with itself, pure identity (A = A). Since Fichte understands substance and accident as concepts that mutually refer to each other, the absolute I is not, for him, a substance, even though it occupies the position traditionally occupied by substance. [*K*, p. 259–60.]

353. See *GA*, I/2: 348–9; below, p. 286.

354. More precisely, the independent activity that determines the form of the reciprocally-related-acting-and-being-passively-affected also determines the activity that determines the content of the same.

355. Both the limited Not-I and the limited I are, in this sense, "accidents" of the I, as are the I's own self-determinations, such as "thinking." As Fichte explained earlier, "Thinking is by no means the essence, but only a particular determination of the being [of the I], in addition to which there are many other determinations of our being." See *GA*, I/2: 262; below, p. 206.

356. See a *GA*, I/2: 334; above, p. 272. The difference between "qualitative" and "quantitative" idealism is that, according to the former, the I annuls something that has been posited in itself, independently of the I, whereas in the case of the latter it annuls merely a determinate quantity that has been posited.

357. See *GA*, I/2: 346–7; below, p. 284.

358. *Das Allumfassende*. As *K* points out (p. 362), this is the term employed by Goethe (*Faust* I, l. 3438) as a name for God, in a passage later cited by Fichte at the conclusion of *UGG* (*GA*, I/5: 356–7; *SW*, V, p. 189; *IWL*, p. 153).

359. This is an implicit criticism of Kant's concept of substance as "that which endures through all the changes of appearances" (*KrV*, B224). As Fichte explains in his 1795 essay, "Von der Sprachfähigkeit und dem Ursprung der Sprache," the understanding of substance as "what *endures*, in contrast with what *changes*" is merely the "*sensible concept of substance*," which he claims was prevalent prior to the *Wissenschaftslehre*. But, he continues, "I explain the concept of *substance* transcendentally, not as *that which endures* but rather as the *synthetic unification of all the accidents*. Endurance is merely a sensible feature [*Merkmal*] of substance, which has been imported into it from the concept of time. The object of our perception is obviously not that which endures but only that which changes. Every external representation arises only when we are passively affected, which is possible only by means of an impression upon our feeling, which effects a change within us. For this reason it is clear that every object of which we are supposed to become conscious must announce itself to us by means of some alternation [of our state]. Something that endures [*Etwas bleibendes*] is therefore not perceptible; instead, we must refer all changes

to something that persists — to an enduring substrate, which, however, is only a product of the power of imagination. The word *'being'* or *'is'* is then applied to this substrate. No action of our mind would be possible without such a substrate, and no language would be possible without a reference to it (*GA*, I/3: 111–12; *SW*, VIII, pp. 219–20; "On the Linguistic Capacity and the Origin of Language," trans. Jere Paul Surber, in Surber, *Language and German Idealism: Fichte's Linguistic Philosophy* [Atlantic Highlands, NJ: Humanities Press International, 1995], p. 131).

360. More precisely, the independent activity that determines the content of reciprocally-related-acting-and-being-passively-affected determines the activity that determines the form of the same.

361. Qualitative realism was previously defined as maintaining that an independently existing Not-I produces an impression upon the I, an impression that drives part of the activity of the I back into itself (see *GA*, I/2: 334; above, p. 273). Elsewhere, Fichte describes this same position as "dogmatic realism" (see a *GA*, I/2: 310, 324, and 328; above, pp. 248, 263, and 267).

362. The *qualitative realist* thinks that the real ground of the I's positing lies not in the I but in the object that affects it.

363. "No matter how often one pretends to the contrary, no person has ever had nor ever can have Aenesidemus' thought of a thing that possesses reality and distinctive properties independently not merely of the human power of representation, but of any and every intellect. *In addition, one always thinks of oneself, of an intellect striving to know the thing.* This was why the immortal Leibniz, who saw a little further than most of those who came after him, necessarily had to endow his thing, or monad, with the power of representation" (Fichte, *RA*, *GA*, I/2: 61; *SW*, I, pp. 119–20; *EPW*, p. 73).

364. I.e., "determine."

365. Here it is important to recall that the "existence" of the Not-I — as encountered, for example, in the previous discussion of causal efficacy — is itself a product of the activity of the I, something posited by the I as independent of itself.

366. See *GA*, I/2: 326; above, pp. 264–5.

367. "The purely formal character of this reciprocally-related-acting-and-being-passively-affected is therefore a *non-positing* by means of a positing" (*GA*, I/2: 317; above, p. 256).

368. As *K* points out (pp. 264–65), this phrase, "*Dinge überhaupt und an sich*" is employed by Kant (*KrV*, B298). "*Dinge überhaupt*" was the German term employed by Christian Wolff to translate the traditional subject of ontology: being or *ens*. See too *KrV*, B304.

369. *bestimmt.* Throughout this discussion, when Fichte speaks of a concept as being *unbestimmt* or *bestimmt* this can be translated accurately either as "indeterminate" or "determinate" or as "undetermined" or "determined." Something is *indeterminate* because it has not been adequately *determined* (or specified), etc. I have employed both translations interchangeably, depending on the context.

370. As was suggested earlier, in the passage in which Fichte first introduces the "piece of iron" as an illustration of the activity of the I (*GA*, I/2: 326; below, p. 265), the iron corresponds to the positing of the I; the movement corresponds to the positing of the object; and the magnet corresponds to the Not-I, posited as the cause of the movement. [*K*, p. 265.]

371. Recall what was said above on this topic: "The *form* of their reciprocity is their mutual encroachment [*Eingreifen*] and being encroached upon; the *content* of the same is the *acting and being-passively-affected* that immediately occurs in both as a result of this encroachment and of this openness to being encroached upon [*Eingreifen lassen*]." (*GA*, I/2: 320; above, p. 259). Obviously, such a "form" is insufficient to determine the *content* of this reciprocal relationship and the *totality* of the same (A or A+B).

372. *in beider Rücksicht*: namely, insofar as the totality is supposed to be (1) the determinately posited sphere of A, and (2) the indeterminate but determinable sphere A + B.

373. *schwebt.* This is the first appearance of this term, which Fichte will later employ to describe the manner which the power of imagination is able to "float" or "hover" or "oscillate" above or between opposing components, thereby unifying them synthetically.

374. This X serves as the ground or reason that determines whether one should start with and proceed from A or A + B. As Fichte will soon explain, X thereby depends upon which of these "totalities" one should reflect, or if one should instead reflect upon both.

375. *Naturlehre.* This was a common name for "physics" in late eighteenth-century German usage. [*K*, p. 266.]

376. Namely, to the magnet that attracts it and sets it in motion.

377. Applying this to the I: If we proceed from the first foundational principle of § 1, then what is essential for the I is its self-positing, and its positing of an object is inessential. In contrast, if we proceed from the third foundational principle of § 3, then both self-positing and object-positing are contingent for the I.

378. "In order to secure a better overview, let us sketch here the systematic schema that must guide us in discovering the final solution to our question. The validity of this schema was demonstrated in the *Foundation of the Entire Wissenschaftslehre*, in the course of discussing the concept of reciprocal interaction. — The I posits itself as totality; that is to say, it determines itself. This is possible only if it excludes something from itself, by means of which the I is limited. If A is the totality, then B is what is excluded. — But, just as surely as B is excluded, it is also posited. B is supposed to be posited by the I, which can posit A as the totality only on this condition. Consequently, the I must also reflect upon B as something posited. But then A is now no longer the totality. When B is posited, A itself is excluded from the totality (which is how we expressed it in the *Foundation*). Consequently, what is posited is A + B" (Fichte, *GEWL*, *GA*, I/3: 184; below, p. 416).

379. The determinability of the totality is supposed to be what determines the reciprocal excluding and being-excluded of the reciprocally related components.

380. This "ground" will be revealed in Part Three.

381. The "absolute ground" would be the purely and simply posited determinate totality (= A), whereas the "relative ground" would be the totality consisting of the absolutely posited ground plus what is excluded therefrom (= A + B). This mention of "*relativer Grund*" is followed by the introduction of the term "*Relation*" as a synonym for *Wechsel*.

382. That is to say, let us apply it to the concept of "substance" or "substantiality."

383. In this paragraph Fichte clarifies the parallels between his previous example (iron and movement) and the absolutely posited I and the object posited by the I.

384. *Unbegrenzt.* This term is here employed as a synonym for *unbestimmt* ("undetermined" or "indeterminate"). The totality A + B is "unlimited" because it is not determined by A.

385. The purely self-positing I is determined or "limited" by the principle of identity, which forbids self-contradiction. [*K*, pp. 46 and 269.]

386. "I posit myself as positing; this presupposes something posited, which can only be inferred and grasped by means of thinking. But this is immediate consciousness, and the I itself consists in just this harmony" (Fichte, *WLnmH*, *GA*, IV/2, 33; *FTP*, p. 118).

387. Compare this to the determination of A by A + B.

388. The phrase "determinate determinability" synthesizes the *content* of reciprocally-related-acting-and-being-passively-affected (= *determinability*) with the *form* of the same (= *relation*, understood as reciprocal excluding and being-excluded). Hence the I of § 1 is not a substance; instead, this would be the *I* of § I as it acts in §2 and §3, first positing the Not-I and then positing the I and Not-I as mutually limiting one another. [*K*, p. 360.]

389. *aus den Ich [...] herausgegangen.* More literally, "going beyond" or "going outside" the I. The I of § 1 first becomes a "subject" when it "goes beyond itself" and posits a Not-I,

which it then, of course, excludes from itself. Only in excluding this *object* from itself does the I posit itself as a *subject* (a finite I).

390. "Unconditioned" or "unconditional" positing occurs solely by means of the *Tathandlung* or "F/Act" of the pure I discussed in § I, where it is claimed that "the I originally posits its own being purely and simply" (*GA*, I/2: 259–60; above, pp. 204–5). Even though unconditioned self-positing is a necessary condition for self-consciousness, it is not yet "for itself" and hence is not a sufficient condition for actual I-hood. The I cannot posit its being for itself "unconditionally," since this presupposes the exclusion of the Not-I (see *GA*, I/2: 260; above, p. 204). Hence both "unconditioned" and "conditioned" positing are required if the I is to posit itself for itself as self-positing. Though every I presupposes the act of unconditioned positing described in § 1, it also presupposes the conditioned relation of substantiality that Fichte is here analyzing, without which there is no actual self-consciousness and "no actual life" (*GA*, I/2: 410–11; below, p. 341). [*K*, p. 270.]

391. *der Forderung widerspricht.* What is requested here is that one think of the piece of iron in motion.

392. This entire paragraph is meant to illustrate the divisibility of the I and the distinction between the "absolute I" and the "I as subject," which has its own "place" only in relation to an object, a Not-I. The presence of a magnet leads to the positing of the I's movement, and thus to a further determination of the originally posited concept of the iron in itself (corresponding to the absolute I of § 1), a determination not essential to the unconditionally posited pure I. Considered on its own or "absolutely," the iron is a "thing in itself," whereas considered "relatively," in its relation to movement, it is conditional upon the presence or absence of a magnet. [*K*, p. 270.]

393. Namely: "*neither the form nor the content* [*of the reciprocal-acting-and-being-passively-affected*] *should determine the other; instead, they should mutually determine each other*" (above, *GA*, I/2: 345; above, p. 283).

394. *erste Moment.* The term "moment" is here used to identify a step or factor in an ongoing process and has no temporal implications.

395. *Gebiete des Grundes.* More literally, "area" or "domain" of grounds, but the meaning of this phrase seems to be very similar to that of Wilfred Seller's well-known term, "space of reasons." *K* relates this phrase to the principle of sufficient reason (*Satz des Grundes*) and Fichte's discussion of the same in § 3, where he maintains that this principle applies only to cases in which different things are posited as either alike or opposed to each other in a certain respect (*GA*, I/2: 273; above, p. 216).

396. What is excluded from the I in this case is the Not-I. See above, § 2. However, what Fichte describes as the "true meaning" of this act of exclusion will become clear only in § 5, in the context of explaining the role of the *Anstoß* of "check" in occasioning the I's positing of its own limits and hence its positing the Not-I. See *GA*, I/2: 355; below, p. 292.

397. See the "Deduction of Representation" with which Part Two concludes.

398. See *GA*, I/2: 347; above, p. 284, where what is excluded from the I is described as "a posited Not-I or an object."

399. *Relation.* See *GA*, I/2: 345–6; above, p. 283.

400. *in der Vollendung eines* Verhältnißes, *nicht aber einer* Realität. This is the first appearance of the term *Verhaltnis*, which seems to mean exactly the same thing as the term *Relation* which Fichte has employed throughout the preceding discussion.

401. Substance has now been revealed to be the same thing as a totality that is determinately determinable. Determinacy and determinability are in this case supposed to be one and the same, which means that substance cannot be distinguished from its accidents. It follows that the absolute I of § I cannot be a substance; instead, as Fichte will proceed

to explain, the I as substance is a product of the productive activity of the power of imagination, the operation of which presupposes the positing of a divisible I and Not-I (§ 3). [*K*, p. 272.]

402. "Is there any philosopher who does not realize that, ever since Locke, there has been a very determinate nominal explanation of substance as *the bearer of accidents*? In the very *Wissenschaftslehre* on which the reviewer claims that Fichte attempts to base his system of religion, we believe that, had he ever even leafed through this *Wissenschaftslehre*, he would have discovered there a very determinate real, genetic explanation of substance: namely, that a substance is supposed to be *the accidents themselves, grasped together in sensible intuition as a unity*" (Fichte, *Friedrich Nicolai's Leben und sonderbare Meinungen*, *GA*, I/7: 448n.; *SW*, VIII, 79–80n.).

403. When one accident gives way to a succeeding one, they must be posited in *opposition* to each other, insofar as it is possible to *distinguish* them from each other. [*K*, p. 273.]

404. In fact, in Part Three Fichte will introduce his own conception of the "bearer" of these accidents, namely "matter" or *Stoff* (see *GA*, I/2: 440; below, pp. 357–8). But for Fichte, this too is a product of the productive power of imagination — in contrast to the traditional notion of substance as a bearer of accidents, independently of any action by the I.

405. See *GA*, I/2: 359; below, p. 297. The "most wonderful power" in question is *produktive Einbildungskraft*, the power of imagination.

406. As Fichte will explain in Part Three, "life" is dependent upon the interaction between the I and the Not-I. See *GA*, I/2: 410–11; below, p. 341.

407. *als eine fortlaufende Zeitreihe.* See *GA*, I/2: 360 and 367; below, pp. 298 and 304.

    "How does a temporal series arise for us — as a series of our representations?

    "Such a series is supposed to: (1) be a continuous series, without any gap, and (2) consist of multiple moments. b is supposed to be a different moment than a, but in what respect? Another object is represented at moment b. It is the former, the temporal series, that supports the moment, and only through this series and in no other way can one moment be distinguished from another.

    "But if a and b are posited in complete opposition to each other, then there is a gap. — There is no line, but rather individual, isolated points — and, indeed, several such points. N.b., these points do not even exist *for me,* but for someone outside of me. Both points must therefore be posited as simultaneously the same and opposed to each other, so that those that are the same will continue to flow forth [*fortlaufe*]. Consciousness advances [*übergehe*] by means of that aspect of these moments that remains the same, and *only* what is posited in opposition, insofar as it has been posited in opposition, constitutes the difference [between moments a and b]. — The thread [of consciousness] continues to be carried forward by means of what remains the same, but what is posited in opposition is distinguished from what preceded it" (Fichte, *VPA*, II/4: 101–2).

408. According to the principle of non-contradiction, accidents posited in opposition to each other can be thought only discursively, one after the other, in a temporal series. They cannot both be ascribed to the same substance at the same time. But if, as Fichte is here attempting to do, one constructs a concept of substance independently of any temporal features (i.e., not as "enduring"), then the only relationship between accidents posited in opposition to each other is that of *exclusion*, in which case they would mutually annihilate one another.

409. We do not yet know *what* these "subjective" and "objective" factors [*eines Subjektiven und Objectiven*] may be, since they are here determined only with respect to their (reciprocally determined) *quantity* and not their *quality.* (In Part Three we will learn that the subjective factor involved in the positing of an object external to the I is, in fact, "feeling.")

In the concept of determinability, what is subjective and what is objective are both distinguished from or posited in opposition to each other and also equated with each other, since they are *both* posited as "determinable."

410. "The concept of determinability" is here a synonym for what was previously described as the "higher sphere" embracing both A and what is excluded from A, namely B. See *GA*, I/2: 340; above, pp. 277–8.

411. See *GA*, I/2: 270; above, p. 313, where "divisibility" is defined as "quantifiability as such."

412. This is a reference to § 1, in which the "category of reality" is applied to the I itself, including everything posited in and by the I. See *GA*, I/2: 261; above, p. 205. The term employed here, "absolute reality," appears to be a synonym for what Fichte had earlier called "reality in itself" (*GA*, I/2: 332; above, p. 271). It is this "absolute" reality of the pure I that is then divided (in § 3) between the limited I and limited Not-I.

413. A "thetic judgment" or "thesis" is one that asserts something purely and simply, without any additional ground or reason.

414. See *GA*, I/2: 351; above, p. 288.

415. *Von einem thetischen Verfahren ausgehen.* See the earlier discussion of the "thetic way of proceeding" (*GA*, I/2: 276–8; above, pp. 219–20), where a thetic judgment is described as "one that posits something that is not equal to anything else nor posited in opposition to anything else, but is simply posited as equal to itself. Such a judgment cannot, therefore, presuppose any ground of connection or any ground of distinction." We are further informed that "the manner in which the human mind proceeds in the case of all thetic judgments is grounded in the positing of the I purely and simply through and by itself."

416. This is a reference to the foundational principle of Part Two: "the I posits itself as determined by the Not-I."

417. The foundational principle of Part Two functions there as a "thesis," even though, in Part One, it, along with the foundational principle of Part Three, were both theorems, rather than theses, since they were both partially derived from the first, utterly unconditioned, foundational principle of § 1: "The I posits itself purely and simply." At the beginning of Part Three we will "break through" the restriction or limitation defining the theoretical portion of the *Foundation* (namely, the restriction implicit in the principle that "the I posits itself as determined by the Not-I").

418. See above, § 2.

419. See above, § 3.

420. The difference is as follows: The "subject in itself" and "object in itself" are both posited purely and simply ("unconditionally" or "absolutely"). Unlike "what is subjective" and "what is objective," they are not posited by means of reciprocal-acting-and-being-passively-affected.

421. I.e., in § 2.

422. That is, the positing of something purely subjective within the I, or the positing of the I itself as a determinate (subjective) quantity. Though *this* thesis presupposes an antithesis, this is not true of the absolute thesis described in § 1.

423. As *K* notes (p. 276) the "content" of the antithesis is the *qualitative* opposition between the components of the relation. This implies that the reciprocal concept of substantiality (based on the third fundamental principle, § 3) presupposes the previously elucidated reciprocal concept of causal efficacy.

424. I.e., thesis, antithesis, and synthesis.

425. Fichte's explicit comparison between the three "acts of the mind" involved in the present synthesis and the three foundational principles laid out in §§ 1–3 strongly suggests that the latter really constitute only *one single* foundational act and are distinguishable from one another only within philosophical reflection. This is an important point, since it

implies that the F/Act or *Tathandlung* or thesis described in § 1 is really not possible apart from the antithesis described in § 2 and the synthesis described in § 3. [*K*, pp. 276–7.]

426. See *GA*, I/2: 350; above, p. 288, where the concept of determinability is associated with "*an absolute act of combining and retaining of factors posited in opposition to each other —* one subjective, the other objective."

427. This is because the theoretical portion of the *Foundation* is concerned purely with the quantitative *relation* between the I and the Not-I and not with the reality of either. See *GA*, I/2: 292; above, p. 232, where Fichte explains that the components in a mere "relation" are related to each other only quantitatively, in such a way the quantity of the one is "relative to" the quantity of the other.

428. "One enters my philosophy by means of what is utterly *incomprehensible*. This makes my philosophy difficult, because the topic can be approached only by means of the power of imagination and not at all by means of the understanding; at the same time, however, this is what guarantees its correctness. Everything *comprehensible* presupposes a higher sphere within which it is *comprehended*, and it is therefore not the highest thing, precisely because it is *comprehensible*. (Does our grasp of even the most humble object proceed from anything other than a function of the imagination, and is our grasp of philosophy the only thing that is supposed to proceed from something else?)" (Fichte to Reinhold, July 2, 1795; III/2: 245–6; *EPW*, p. 399).

429. See *GA*, I/2: 348; above, p. 285.

430. See *GA*, I/2: 288, 304, 325, and 347; above, pp. 229, 243, 264, and 285.

431. *das Zusammentreffen, — Eingreifen beider*. Regarding this "mutual encroachment" of the components of this relationship of substantiality, see *GA*, I/2: 320–1 and 330; above, pp. 259 and 268–9.

432. Here Fichte presupposes the Kantian distinction between a "physical" and a "mathematical" point, according to which the latter is not a part of space but a boundary of the same, whereas the former is the Leibnizian notion of a simple point in space, which consists of an aggregation of such "points." See *KrV*, A438/B467. However, as *K* points out (p. 277), Fichte also seems to accept Salomon Maimon's criticism of Kant's conception of a physical point and to endorse his replacement of the same with Maimon's own (difficult) notion of a physical point as a "differential" or infinitely small point. See Maimon, *Versuch über die Transzendentalphilosophie* (Berlin: Christian Friedrich Voß und Sohn, 1790, pp. 27–8); *Essay on Transcendental Philosophy*, trans. Nick Midgley, Henry Somers-Hall, Alistair Welchman, and Merten Reglitz (New York: Continuum, 2010, pp. 19–21).

433. Fichte here appears to be proposing this description of the boundary between light and darkness as an illustration of the "encroachment" of the I and the Not-I upon each other.

434. "Spirit or mind [*Geist*] as such is what is otherwise called the *productive* power of imagination. The *reproductive* power of imagination repeats something that was already present in empirical consciousness, though it does not repeat it in exactly the same context in which it first appears in consciousness. The reproductive power of imagination is also able to assemble a new whole by combining various other ones; but, strictly speaking, it still remains purely reproductive. The productive power of imagination does not repeat anything; it is, at least from the point of view of empirical consciousness, completely creative — and it creates from nothing" (Fichte, *UGB*, *GA*, II/3: 316; *EPW*, p. 193).

435. The activity just explained is "*an absolute act of combining and retaining factors posited in opposition to each other — one subjective, the other objective — in the concept of determinability*, an absolute act in which they are nevertheless also posited in opposition to each other" (*GA*, I/2; 350; above, p. 288).

436. "Concerning the sheer reciprocal-acting-and-being-passively-affected: if the form of the same (reciprocal exclusion of the components) and its content (the encompassing sphere,

which contains both components as excluding each other) are to become synthetically united, then reciprocal excluding is itself the sphere in which they are included; i.e., the reciprocally-related-acting-and-being-passively-affected consists in the sheer relation, and nothing else is present other than reciprocal excluding, the determinability just described" (*GA*, I/2: 352; above, p. 289).

437. Namely, the independent activity of the productive power of imagination. As was previously established, the principle of reciprocal determination does not apply to independent activity. However, there is a reciprocal relationship between this independent activity and reciprocally-related-acting-and-being-passively-affected.

438. *ein Objectives und Subjectives*. These terms do not necessarily refer to any specific objective or subjective "thing," but rather to whatever may occupy the general spheres of objectivity and subjectivity.

439. The absolute activity of combining and retaining something subjective and something objective in the concept of determinability is supposed to determine the "relation" between the two, reciprocally related components.

440. It is "idealistic" because the reciprocal relation is supposed to be determined solely by the absolute activity of the I. Of course, it is not idealistic insofar as this same activity is, in turn, supposed to be determined by the reciprocal relation between subjective and objective components.

441. "Intellect" [*Intelligenz*] is another name for the limited or restricted I of Part Two, the "theoretical" or cognizing I. § 4 in its entirety may be considered a genetic definition of the productive power of imagination as essential to the operation of the intellect. [*K*, p. 280.]

442. In order to be an "intellect" in the full sense, the power of imagination must not operate blindly, but must be supplemented by the powers of understanding and reason. [*K*, p. 280.]

443. See *GA*, I/2: 293; above, p. 233: In positing its own being, the F/Act or *Tathandlung* of the I is by no means directed at an object, but instead reverts upon itself. Only when the I is itself *represented*, i.e., only when it entertains a representation of itself, does it first become an object of consciousness.

444. See *GA*, I/2: 331–2; above, p. 278.

445. I.e., the absolute, independent activity of the I, which simultaneously posits within the I (as a more encompassing sphere) the coming together (*Zusammentreffen*) of what is subjective and what is objective. See *GA*, I/2: 353; above, pp. 290–1.

446. This term was adopted from contemporary rationalist mechanics, where it was employed as a synonym for "impetus" or "impulse." Fichte employs it in precisely this sense in several works, including *SE*. (See, e.g., the reference to how a ball is "impelled" or *angestoßen* by an original "pulse" or *Stoß* [*SS*, *GE*, I/5: 42; *SW*, IV, p. 25; *SE*, p. 30]) and *BM* (which includes a similar reference to a ball that is *angestoßen* and thus moves in a certain direction, as affected by a certain force or *Kraft* [*BM*, *GE*, I/6: 289; *SW*, II, p. 295; *VM*, p. 104]). The term *Anstoß* does not refer to an action of the I, but to how it is affected — at once thwarted or limited and ("checked") and set in motion ("impelled") by the *Anstoß*. This check or impetus is always something that *happens to* the I. It is an alien force, which, in Fichte's words, "merely sets the I in motion" (*GA*, I/2: 411; below, pp. 341–2). A few sentences later, Fichte calls the *Anstoß* "the first mover", a *force* outside of and opposed to the I, and hence an opposed striving or *Gegenstreben* (*GA*, I/2: 411; below, pp. 347). [*K*, p. 281–4.]

"Upon the occasion of the check upon the original activity of the I (a check or impulse that remains completely inexplicable and incomprehensible at this point), the power of imagination, which oscillates between the original direction of the I's activity and the [opposing] direction arising from reflection, produces something composed of both directions" (Fichte, *GEWL*, I/3: 143; below, p. 382).

"Perhaps I can make this clearer by means of the following image: The original pure activity of the I is modified and, as it were, given shape or form [*gebildet*] by the check or impulse, and, to this extent, this activity is by no means ascribable to the I" (Fichte, *GEWL*, I/3: 155; below, p. 391).

"Even the philosopher explains this act of production by referring to an *impulse* or *check*. This is now quite comprehensible. As we have seen, my *activity is limited*. This original limitation is one that occurs through duty; every other limitation is, in turn, only a *sensible* presentation [*Darstellung*] of the former — that is, a presentation of it by means of the power of imagination" (Fichte, Unpublished Comments on *GEWL* (1794/95 or 1795/96); *GA*, II/4: 360).

Though "check" appears to be the standard English translation of *Anstoß*, it is nevertheless inadequate and misleading, because, unlike, "impetus" or "impulse," it fails to convey the sense of an *Anstoß* as *setting a process in motion*. But "iimpulse" is not perfect either, since it fails to convey the sense of an *Anstoß* as *setting a limit* to the activity of the I. It is therefore important to keep in mind that this term usually has *both* meanings, denoting both a limit to the original activity of the I and the initiator of a series of reflective acts on the part of the I qua intellect. For a detailed discussion of this term and its function, see Ch. X of *TWL*.

447. This is the first description of the I as seeking to "expand" the domain of its activity. As *K* notes (p. 284), this characterization of the I or subject may seem surprising, since it is not the same as the one we have just been considering in our derivation of the concept of substance; instead, we are now explicitly concerned with the *activity* of the I — an activity, says Fichte, that"extends into the domain of what is unlimited, undetermined, and undeterminable, that is, into the infinite" (*GA*, I/2: 357; below, p. 295).

448. Namely, "qualitative" realism, which proceeds from something existing outside the I, and "quantitative" realism, which proceeds from a determination present within the I.

449. See *GA*, I/2: 335–6; above, pp. 273–4.

450. Fichte here employs these terms ("reciprocal-acting-and-being-passively-affected" and "sheer check or impulse") in apposition because, as we have just learned, it is the check or impulse that sets the reciprocal-acting-and-being-passively-affected into motion. Hence, they are inseparable from each other.

451. In this case, what needs to be explained (the *explanandum*) is the previously mentioned "transition from the Not-I to the I," whereas the proposed explanatory ground of this transition (the *explanans*) is the check or impulse.

452. *reflectirt*. Though this is the same verb that Fichte employs to designate the self-reverting intellectual activity of attending to one's own mental acts and states (which is therefore a crucial component of the method of transcendental philosophy), it is here employed in a sense derived from rationalist mechanics, to describe the way a physical force (or ray of light) is "reflected" or undergoes a change of direction. On the other hand, Fichte's intransitive use of the verb "to reflect" to mean "to be driven back into itself" is highly unusual and is probably derived from Leibniz. [*K*, pp. 286–7.] For further discussion of how the I is "driven back into itself" by the impetus or check, see *GA*, I/2: 404–5 and 409; below, pp. 336–7 and 340. To further complicate matters, Fichte often uses the verb *reflectieren* to describe the familiar process of turning one's attention toward an object in order to "reflect upon" it.

453. At last it becomes clear that what conditions the very possibility of the I's act of positing something in opposition to itself (and thereby determining — and positing — itself in

this way) is precisely the "check" upon its original activity and the ensuing "impulse" or "impetus" to engage in the new activity of "reflection."

454. The "chief difference" to which Fichte here alludes is the difference between the "independent activity" and the "reciprocally-related-acting-and-being-passively-affected." Fichte's claim is that this difference is based upon the difference between "combining" and "coming together." [*K*, p. 288.]

455. *Zusammentreffen* (the coming together of components posited in opposition to each other) represents the *realistic* dimension of Fichte's system, and *Zusammenfassen* (the I's act of combining components posited in opposition to each other) represents the *idealistic* dimension of the same. [*K*, p. 288.]

456. It is posited by the power of imagination, as was illustrated by the previous discussion of the boundary between light and darkness. Hence it is by virtue of its power of imagination that the I can "combine" opposing components by positing a boundary where they "come together."

457. This is the position defended by "quantitative idealism" (see *GA*, I/2: 333ff.; above, pp. 272ff.).

458. They are *both* determinable, and hence they are not posited in opposition to each other in that respect; indeed, each is determinable by the other.

459. Namely, in the concept of "determinability," in which the components are synthetically linked as determinable by each other.

460. *ein Widerstand*. In this context, this is a functional synonym for *Anstoß*. Other such synonyms include *Hemmung* (obstruction) and *Schranke* (limit).

461. The boundary in question is "unlimited" and "infinite," in the sense that it can be posited by the infinite activity of the I to lie anywhere within the "infinite" or indeterminate domain of what is Not-I (and thus understood as the predicate of an "infinite judgment" in the Kantian sense). [*K*, p. 291.]

462. As Gueroult explains, it is precisely because the I posits the boundary that it determines itself as infinite (i.e., as going beyond any boundary it can posit). It thus posits itself not as positing the infinite (A + B) but as the *substrate* of the same. (Martial Gueroult, *L'évolution et la structure de la doctrine de la science chez Fichte* [Paris: Société de l'édition, 1930], Vol I, pp. 224–5.) The I is the substrate of the infinite in the sense that the infinite is indeed present in the I but is not identical with its "essence" as an I. [*K*, p. 291.]

463. In the same act through which the I *distinguishes* the infinite action from itself it also *ascribes* this same action to itself.

464. *K* analyzes this paragraph in four steps. It begins with a thesis, which is further developed and grounded as follows: Steps one and two are concerned solely with the relationship between the infinite activity extending beyond the boundary (= A) and the finite limit or boundary itself (= B), disregarding the components that come together at this boundary. (1.) no infinite activity, no restriction (A determined by B); (2.) no restriction, no infinite activity (B determined by A). The final two steps are concerned with the synthetic connection between A and B. (3) is concerned with determinability (A + B determined by A), and (4) is concerned with the determination (A + B determined by B). Note that it is the I that is here posited as finite, whereas the Not-I is posited as infinite. [*K*, pp. 289–90.]

465. Namely, the determinate limit or boundary of the I's activity.

466. Namely, in *GEWL*. See *GA*, I/3: 204ff.; below, pp. 432ff.

467. *in demselben*. This could refer either to the hovering of the imagination or to the conflict within the I.

468. "Finally, a rational being cannot posit itself as acting efficaciously without at the same time positing itself as engaged in representing. It cannot posit itself as having an effect

upon a determinate object without all the while representing that determinate object. It cannot posit any determinate effect as completed without positing the object at which the efficacious action was directed. That is, since the object is posited as annihilating efficacious activity, even while the efficacious activity is supposed to persist alongside the object, there arises a conflict, which can be resolved only by means of the oscillation of the power of imagination between the two, by means of which a *time* arises" (Fichte, *GNR*, *GA*, I/3: 338–9; *SW*, III, pp. 28–9; *FNR*, p. 28).

469. Fichte appears to have adopted the phrase *Vorstellung der Vorstellenden* ("representation of the representing subject") from the following passage in Ernst Platner's *Philosophischen Aphorismen*, I (which was the text he used throughout his tenure in Jena as the basis for his own lectures on "Logic and Metaphysics"):

"§ 154. If it must be conceded that, when it is clearly consciousness of a representation, what the soul is aware of is itself, as the representing subject, as distinct from the represented object, and thus, that, in this case, the soul possesses a representation of which it itself is the object. In this case, it also has to be conceded that the soul perceives itself as an object and that, to this extent, the self-feeling *I* is not empty of all content, but has an actual object. For if no representation is possible without reference to an object, then this is also true of the represention of the representing subject, i.e., the soul's representation of itself.

"§ 155. Anyone who seeks more in this self-feeling than the representation of the representing subject and hopes to derive from this predicates applicable to the soul apart from the power of representing (e.g., non-bodily being, constancy, identity, and the like) is unfamiliar with the source of these predicates" (Platner, *Philosophische Aphorismen*, *GA*, II/4S: 49–50).

470. This, of course, is the foundational principle of Part Two as a whole, which explains the possibility of cognition or of the "theoretical" activity of the I.

471. I.e., the practical power of "striving" (*Streben*), though *K* suggests (p. 298) that the "higher practical power" to which Fichte here refers is not "striving" but "longing" (*Sehnen*), which, is derived prior to striving in Part Three.

472. I.e., in Part Three, below.

473. It is important to note that Fichte is not saying that the Not-I is the product of the absolute and unconditioned self-positing discussed in § 1. The Not-I is posited *only* by the I that "determines itself," but the principle that "the I determines itself" is possible only as an alternative to "the I is determined by the Not-I." It is therefore the task of Part Two to overcome the conflict between these two principles. There can be a Not-I only for an I that is limited but still in some sense "self-determining," i.e., only for a representing or cognizing subject. See *GA*, I/2: 287; above, p. 228. [*K*, p. 299.]

474. "A foundational principle has been exhausted when a complete system has been erected upon it, that is, when the principle in question necessarily leads to *all* the propositions that are asserted [within this system] and when *all* these propositions necessarily lead back to the foundational principle. The negative proof that our system includes no superfluous propositions is that no proposition occurs anywhere in the entire system that could be true if the foundational principle were false — or could be false if the foundational principle were true. [...] Furthermore, the science is a *system* (or is complete) when no additional propositions can be inferred from its foundational principle, and this furnishes the positive proof that the system does not include any more propositions than it should. [...] In order to be able to demonstrate purely and simply and unconditionally that nothing more can be inferred [from this foundational principle] we need a positive criterion. This criterion can only be this: that the foundational principle from which we began is our final result. In that case it would be clear that we could proceed no further

without retracing the path we had already taken" (Fichte, *BWL*, *GA*, I/2: 130–1; above, pp. 172–3).

"The *method* of the theoretical *Wissenschaftslehre* has already been described in the *Foundation*, and it is simple and easy. The thread of the argument proceeds according to the following principle (which is here regulative throughout): *nothing pertains to the I except what it posits within itself.* We begin with the *factum* derived above, and then we observe how the I might be able to posit this *factum* within itself. This positing is a *factum* as well, and it must also be posited by the I within itself, and so on, until we arrive at the highest theoretical *factum*: namely, that *factum* through which the I (consciously) posits itself as determined by the Not-I. The theoretical *Wissenschaftslehre* thus concludes with its own foundational principle. It reverts into itself and is therefore complete" (Fichte, *GEWL*, *GA*, I/3: 145; below, p. 383).

475. This is Fichte's version of the Kantian project: to establish the conditions for the possibility of x and to do so a priori.

476. "In this business [of creating images], the power of imagination is the creator of everything that appears in our consciousness, and, since all consciousness presupposes that of which one is conscious, the power of imagination is the creator of consciousness itself. There is no consciousness whatsoever prior to and independent of this operation of the power of imagination; and there is no consciousness of any determinate something prior to the creation of this determinate something by the power of imagination. This is why this action of the power of imagination, as the ultimate ground of consciousness, cannot — either in general or in some particular instance — be an object or fact [*Tatsache*] of consciousness. Were it to be an object or fact of consciousness, this would be the most certain proof that the power of imagination is not the ground we are seeking and that one must therefore ascend even higher in order to discover this ground, until one has finally come upon something that is not a fact of consciousness" (Fichte, *UGB*, *GA*, II/3: 310).

"I maintain that the productive power of imagination creates the material for representation: it alone shapes everything found within empirical consciousness, and it is the creator of consciousness itself" (Fichte, *UGB*, *GA*, II/3: 316; *EPW*, p. 193).

477. Fichte, like Kant, generally understands a *factum* as *something produced*, such as the celebrated Kantian *Factum der Vernunft* or "fact of reason," which consists in our awareness of moral obligation. Such a *factum* is not a "fact" that is simply given to us, like an empirical fact or *Tatsache*. It is not a *datum given* to us but a *factum* we ourselves have to produce within ourselves. Hence the *factum* to which Fichte is here referring is not the "fact" of the power of imagination itself, but rather, the *product* of this power's synthetic activity of oscillating between opposites, trying to synthesize the infinite and the finite in response to a check upon the activity of the I. [*K*, p. 304.] Every representation is just such a *factum*.

"Philosophy can do no more than *explain facta*; by no means can it produce any *facta* — beyond, that is, the fact [*Tatsache*] of philosophy itself" (Fichte, *GG*, *GA*, I/5: 348; *SW*, V, p. 178; *IWL*, p. 143).

478. Namely, the assertion that the I posits itself as determined by the Not-I.

479. That is, according to the requirement implicit in the first principle of Part Two. It is, after all, supposed to be *an I* that posits itself as determined by the Not-I.

480. "Nothing is easier than to bring forth, *with freedom* and where no necessity of thought prevails, every possible determination in one's mind and to allow one's mind to act arbitrarily, in any manner that might be suggested by someone else; but nothing is more difficult than to observe one's mind in its *actual* — i.e., as described above, in its necessary — acting, or to observe that the mind must act in this determinate way in a particular situation. The first way of proceeding yields concepts without an object, an empty thinking;

only in the second does the philosopher become the observer of a real act of thinking on the part of his mind.

"The former is an arbitrary mimicking of reason's original ways of acting, as learned from someone else, stripped of the necessity that alone gives meaning and reality to these ways of acting; the latter alone is the true observation of reason's way of proceeding. From the former there emerges an empty formulaic philosophy, which believes it has done enough if it simply proves that one can think of something, without being concerned about the object (about the conditions that make such thinking necessary). A real philosophy presents concepts and objects at the same time and never treats one without the other. The aim of Kant's writings was to introduce such a philosophy and to do away with all merely formulaic philosophy" (Fichte, *GNR*, *GA*, I/3: 316–17; *SW*, III, pp. 5–6; *FNR*, pp. 6–7).

481. *Formular-Philosophie*. Fichte often uses this term as a way of contrasting his own version of transcendental idealism with various forms of dogmatism. The *Wissenschaftslehre* is "a system of real thinking" [*System eines reelen Denkens*], because it possesses genuine *content*. This is because the thoughts in question are ones that allegedly correspond to certain original *facta* (and acts) of the human mind. All other types of philosophy lack such content and thus lack "reality." They can therefore be described as possessing nothing but *form* and hence as "purely formal" (or "formulaic") philosophies.

"Yet even if one quite correctly follows this principle [that one cannot abstract from the pure I], it remains entirely possible that one has merely learned the letter of this principle but has failed to grasp its spirit. Perhaps one may employ the formula that expresses this principle because one has accepted it on trust or faith, or perhaps because one has noticed how useful it is for furnishing specific explanations of those things philosophy is supposed to explain. Nevertheless, so long as one has not had the intuition of what is expressed in this formula, then one possesses no more than a formula. And even if such a person were able to expound a philosophy, one that may perhaps possess spirit and life for someone else, *for us* it would still possess neither; for us, it would be no more than a formulaic philosophy" (Fichte, *UGB*, *GA*, II/3: 329; *EPW*, pp. 204–5).

482. Regarding the "popular philosophy" movement in late eighteenth-century Germany, see the editor's footnote no. 32 to Fichte's reference to "popular philosophers" in the first edition of *BWL* (above, pp. 463–4.)

483. "For the purpose of establishing the theoretical *Wissenschaftslehre*, we began (in the *Foundation of the Entire Wissenschaftslehre*) with the proposition that the I posits itself as determined by the Not-I. We have examined how and in what manner something corresponding to this proposition could be thought to be originally present in a rational being. After separating and setting aside everything impossible and contradictory, we found what we were looking for; that is, we discovered the only possible way in which something corresponding to this proposition could be conceived to be present in a rational being. For just as it is certain that this proposition should now be considered valid and that it can be considered valid only in the way already shown, it is also certain that this proposition must be originally present in our mind as a *factum*. The *factum* thus postulated was the following: Upon the occasion of the check on the original activity of the I (a check that remains completely inexplicable and incomprehensible at this point), the power of imagination, which oscillates between the original direction of the I's activity and the [opposing] direction arising from reflection, produces something composed of both directions [namely, a *representation*]. Since nothing can be found in the I that the I has not posited within itself (a conclusion that follows from the very concept of the I), the I must posit the *factum* in question within itself. That is, it must originally explain this *factum* to itself; it must completely determine and ground it" (Fichte, *GEWL*, *GA*, I/3: 143; below, p. 382).

484. Up until this point, our philosophical reflections have been "artificial," because they were freely generated by thinking the proposition "the I posits itself as determined by the I." From now on, however, our reflections will be "real," because they will describe the actual and necessary actions of the I, as it attempts "to explain to itself" or to discover the conditions for the possibility of the *factum* now established. In other words, following the dialectical rigors of pure thinking in the earlier parts of Part Two, Fichte has now embarked upon his projected "pragmatic history of the human mind."

485. The difference between a *datum* (something "given," in the mathematical sense) and a *factum* (an occurrence or happening, the product of an action) is discussed in Aristotle's *Poetics*, 1451b4. For Fichte, a *factum* is something produced by the I; but when we are unaware of this act of production and are aware only of a product of the same, the latter is, for us, not a *factum* at all, but a *datum*. [*K*, pp. 315–16.]

486. "Our portrayal [of the system of the human mind] contains truth only on the condition and only insofar as it is accurate. We are not the legislators of the human mind, but are instead its historians. We are not, of course, journalists, but are instead writers of pragmatic history" (Fichte, *BWL*, *GA*, I/2: 147; above, p. 186). See too the editor's note to this passage in *BWL*.

487. *Nicht blinde sondern experimentirende Wahrnehmung.* During his first years in Jena, Fiche frequently emphasized the "experimental" character of his project. See *GA*, I/2: 353, and 420; below, pp. 290 and 349. See too *GEWL*, *GA*, I/3: 148; below, p. 385; and *VWL*, *GA*, I/4: 209; *SW*, I, p. 454; *IWL*, p. 37.

488. "Philosophy is the systematic history of the human mind's universal modes of acting" (Fichte, *UGB*, *GA*, II/3: 334; *EPW*, p. 208).

489. See *GA*, I/2: 352–3; above, p. 290.

490. See *GA*, I/2: 353; above, p. 290.

491. This is the specific function of the productive power of imagination.

492. "Everyone knows you are a realist, and I am, after all, a transcendental idealist, and an even stricter one than Kant. Kant clings to the view that the manifold of experience is something given — God knows how and why. But I straightforwardly maintain that even this manifold is produced by our own creative power" (Fichte to Jacobi, August 30, 1795, *GA*, III/2: 346; *EPW*, p. 411).

493. See *GEWL* for Fichte's bold and original transcendental deduction of space, time, and the manifold of intuition.

494. See *GA*, I/2: 353; above, p. 290. The power in question is that of productive imagination.

495. How the I can posit itself as determined by the Not-I is explained by the synthetic operation of the productive power of imagination on the occasion of the check or impetus, the product of which is a "representation."

496. Fichte has not previously spoken of the posited identity of "ideality" and "reality." Perhaps what he is referring to here is, instead, the posited identity of the real and ideal ground — as above, where this is described as the foundational claim of transcendental idealism. See *GA*, I/2: 326; above. pp. 254–5. [*K*, p. 321.]

497. "According to the published *Wissenschaftslehre*, ideality and reality are one. NB: the being and the thinking of the I are not, as it were, predicates of the I; instead, the I first comes into being through the union of both. Being and thinking are therefore, if one may express it this way, necessary ingredients of the I. Consciousness as a whole and the I are entirely the same, simply viewed from different sides. Within ordinary consciousness and experience, this is the I; in transcendental philosophy, it is the identity of being and thinking" (Fichte, *WLnmH*, *GA*, II/4: 1798; *FTP*, p. 381).

498. Pure thinking does not require intuition, consciousness does.

499. *Vorstellungsvermögen.* This is a term coined by K. L. Reinhold, who devoted his so-called "Elementary Philosophy" to an analysis of this power, which he claimed underlies Kant's two cognitive powers of thinking and intuition.

500. "An investigation conducted on the basis of pure principles of reason is always transcendental; that is to say, it does not presume to say how things are *in themselves*, independent of a rational being, for it knows that such a question and such a claim is meaningless. [Instead, a transcendental inquiry investigates] how things are for us, for a possible I" (Fichte, *VLM, GA,* II/4: 72).

501. Namely, Salmon Maimon. See Maimon's *Versuch über neuen Logik oder Theorie des Denken, nebst anghängten Briefen von Philalates an Aenesidemus* (Berlin: Ernst Felisch. 1794), pp. xxxv–xxxvi; and *Streifereien im Gebiete der Philosophie* (Berlin: Wilhelm Vieweg, 1793), p. 57.

502. Such skepticism would teach us "to doubt our own being" qua *rational* beings or I's, inasmuch as it challenges the legitimacy of a standard of reality constructed purely in accordance with the laws governing such beings.

 "Maimon and the *Wissenschaftslehre* say the same thing about the category of causal efficacy, but he calls this procedure of the human mind a deception. We have already seen elsewhere that we cannot call something a deception if it conforms to the laws of rational beings and is, according to these laws, purely and simply necessary and unavoidable — unless, that is, we want to cease to be rational beings. The real point of contention, however, is the following: Maimon would say, 'I am prepared to concede that there are a priori laws of thinking as you have shown.' (This is in fact a large concession, for how can there be present in the human mind a mere law without any application, an empty form without matter?) 'But even if I concede the existence of these laws,' Maimon would continue, 'only the power of imagination can apply them to objects. Hence, in applying these laws to objects, the object and the law must be present in the power of imagination at the same time. How then does the power of imagination gain access to the object?' This question can be answered only as follows: The power of imagination must itself produce the object (as is demonstrated in the *Wissenschaftslehre* on the basis of arguments quite independent of the present problem). — The error lies in thinking that the object is supposed to be something other than a product of the power of imagination. It is true that this error is confirmed by a literal interpretation of Kant, but it is in complete contradiction to his *spirit*. To maintain that the object is not a product of the power of imagination is to become a transcendent dogmatist and to depart completely from the spirit of the Critical philosophy" (Fichte, *GEWL,* I/3: 189–90; below, pp. 420–1).

503. See *GA,* I/2: 355; above, p. 292.

504. I.e., insofar as it is a "reflection" of the original activity extending from A to C. Since this original activity of the I extends into the domain beyond any possible check, Fichte will subsequently describe it as "infinite."

505. See *GA,* I/2: 305 and 312; above, pp. 243 and 251.

506. See *GA,* I/2: 305 and 312; above, pp. 243 and 251.

507. "The I acts. This is something we can see from our present standpoint of scientific reflection, and any other intellect, were it to observe the I, would see this as well. But, from its present standpoint, the I itself cannot see that it is acting (though at some future point it may well be able to see this). This is why it forgets itself in the object of its activity. With this we have an activity that appears to be nothing but a state of passive affection, which is what we were seeking. The name of this action is *intuition,* a silent, unconscious contemplation, which loses itself in its object. *What is intuited* is the I that is engaged in sensation. Similarly, *the intuiting subject* is also the I, which, however, neither reflects

upon its own act of intuiting nor — to the extent that it is engaged in intuiting — is capable of doing so" (Fichte, *GEWL*, *GA*, I/3: 159; below, pp. 394–5).

"Intuiting" (*Anschauen*) is therefore simply a more precise name for the synthetic activity of the power of imagination in this case. As Fichte will subsequently express this, intuition is "an oscillation of the power of imagination between two conflicting directions" (*GA*, I/2: 373; below, p. 309).

508. See *GA*, I/2: 375–6; below, p. 311.

509. "According to the previous §, the intuition is supposed to be found within the I, as one of its accidents. Consequently, the I must posit itself as the intuiting subject; it must determine the intuition with respect to itself. This proposition is postulated in the theoretical part of the *Wissenschaftslehre* in accordance with the foundational principle: nothing pertains to the I except what it posits within itself" (Fichte, *GEWL*, *GA*, I/3: 193; below, p. 425).

510. See *GA*, I/2: 351; below, p. 288.

511. What is intuited at this point is the act of intuiting—that is, the activity of the I lying between A and C, an activity that possesses two different directions, which can be synthetically united only by the productive power of imagination (the product of which, in this case, is an "intuition"). [*K*, p. 329.]

512. For the answer to this question, see *GA*, I/2: 378; below, p. 314.

513. In Part Three, Fichte will describe these "inwardly" and "outwardly" directed activities of the I as "centripetal" and "centrifugal." Bear in mind that "reflection" is always a centripetal or inwardly directed activity of the I. In the immediately following passage, Fichte will discuss how an activity of the I is "reflected" (as a result of the check or impetus) and can thus become an object of the I's own "reflection." Here Fichte brings together two quite distinctive senses of the term "reflection," with occasionally confusing results.

514. "Merely by the act of proceeding beyond, as such, the I produced (for a possible observer) a Not-I and did so without any consciousness. The I now reflects upon its product, and in this reflection it *posits* this product *as* Not-I, and posits it as such absolutely and without any further determination. And here again, this positing occurs unconsciously, because the I has not yet reflected upon itself" (Fichte, *GEWL*, *GA*, I/3: 170; below, p. 404).

"In the first intuition, that is, in the productive intuition, I am lost in an object" (Fichte, *GEWL*, *GA*, I/3: 179; below, p. 411).

515. Hence it is ascribed to the Not-I.

516. *Hinschauen* is normally an intransitive verb meaning "to look," as in *auf etwas hinschauen* ("to look at something"). In contrast, Fichte here employs it in an active or transitive sense, meaning something similar to "to place" or "to situate." The idea seems to be that "intuiting," properly understood, is a *productive activity* of the I, by means of which something is produced and situated or placed — that is, posited — beyond the I and in the Not-I.

"The term *intuition* is Kantian, and we employ it in precisely Kant's sense. This term has, however, occasioned discomfort and various misunderstandings. That is to say, in the case of intuition the Kantians always presuppose that the object to be intuited is already present. The intuition of which the philosopher speaks is not something that is there, but is instead a seeing there, a looking toward [*ein Hinsehen, ein Hinschauen*]. The situation is as follows: a painter who wishes to depict something — a rose, e.g. —would be incompetent if, with every brushstroke, he were to think only of this single stroke, for then there would be no whole and no harmony [in his painting]. Instead, the painter projects [*hinwirft*] the entire rose upon the paper; he sees it there [*hinsieht*], and only then does he first see the individual brushstroke. Or, in the case of writing, no one pays attention to how he will make each stroke of the pen, but instead projects upon the paper the entire letter and traces it. Similarly, the philosopher's intuition is no seeing of the thing in itself, but is instead a looking toward [*hinschauen*] a form [*Gestalt*] for us, that is, for all reason" (Fichte, Student transcript of *VLM*, *GA*, IV/1: 205).

517. "Intuition" occurs only when an outgoing activity of the I is "reflected back" to the I by its encounter with a check (*Anstoß*).

518. "The I reflects purely and simply because it reflects. Not only is the tendency to engage in reflection grounded in the I, so too is the action of reflection itself. It is true that this action of reflection is *conditioned* by something outside the I (i.e., by an impression it received), but it is not *necessitated* thereby" (Fichte, *GEWL*, *GA*, I/3: 173; below, p. 407).

"One and the same I cannot, in one and the same activity, simultaneously produce a Not-I and reflect upon it as its product. Therefore, just as surely as the requisite second activity is supposed to pertain to the I, the I must limit and interrupt its first activity. Moreover, this interruption of its first activity must likewise occur with absolute spontaneity, since this entire action occurs spontaneously" (Fichte, *GEWL*, *GA*, I/3: 178; below, p. 411).

519. One is caught up in a circle if, on the one hand, what is intuited (the Not-I) is construed as the product of the activity of the intuiting subject, and, on the other, the intuition is construed as an effect of the Not-I. [*K*, p. 332.]

520. As will be explained below, "stabilization" (*fixiren*) is an act of synthesis and involves the production by the power of imagination of something distinct from both of the activities in opposing directions but "assembled from them both."

521. "If, however (as was already mentioned in the *Foundation of the Entire Wissenschaftslehre*), this conflict should ever be posited within the I, and if anything further were to follow from it, then the mere *positing* of this conflict as such would mean that the oscillation of the power of imagination between two directions of activity posited in opposition to each other would have to cease. Yet traces of this former oscillation would have to remain as a *something*, a possible *matter*. We can already see how this could occur, even though we do not yet see the power through which it would occur. — What the I has to do is posit this *conflict* of directions posited in opposition to each other or (which here amounts to the same thing) this conflict of opposing forces. It must not posit either one of them alone, but must posit them both and must posit them *in conflict* — that is to say, in opposed but perfectly counterbalanced activity. But perfectly counterbalanced opposing activities cancel each other out and nothing remains. Nevertheless, something is supposed to remain and to be posited. What remains, therefore, is *a static matter* [*ein ruhender Stoff*] — something that *possesses force,* but which, on account of the conflict in question, cannot express this force in activity, a *substrate* of force" (Fichte, *GEWL*, *GA*, I/2: 147–8; below, p. 385).

522. See *GA*, I/2: 360; above, p. 298, where reason is identified as the sole power of the mind capable of stabilizing the oscillation of the power of imagination. See too *GA*, I/2: 268; above, p. 211, where Fichte refers to the unconditioned operation of reason as a *Machtspruch* or "decree." Reason is here understood as a fundamentally *practical* power of the I, which demands that all reality should be posited by the I. See *GA*, I/2: 399; below, p. 331.

523. *gleichsam* verständig *wird. Verständig* is from the verb *verständingen*, which means "to inform" or "to notify" and is related to the verb *verstehen,* "to understand." According to Fichte himself, *verständigen* means to orient someone, to place him in the position he is supposed to occupy and divert him from the false position he presently occupies.

In a passage from *EM*, which is cited and examined by *K*, Fichte defines the term *verständig* and explicitly relates it to *Beständigung* and *Bestandigkeit,* meaning "endurance" or "unchangeability." The power of understanding "brings to a halt" the oscillations of the power of imagination. Here Fichte is playing on the sense of "*ständig*" as "enduring" or "unchanging" (in which case "*ver-ständigen*" might mean something like "to make-enduring"). The power of understanding might thus be understood as the power to put things in their proper place and to recognize what endures. [*K*, p. 333.]

"Matter possesses permanence [*Beständigkeit*]; this is what makes it unchanging [*Beständigung*]. 'To make understandable [*verständigen*]' means to orient someone, to place him in the position he is supposed to occupy and divert him from the false position he presently occupies. Understanding is the power of putting things in their proper place: what is unchanging, permanence" (Fichte, *EM, GA*, II/3: 132).

524. "What does it mean *to understand* or *to comprehend*? It means to *posit as stabilized, to determine, to delimit*. I have comprehended an appearance if, through it, I have obtained a complete cognitive whole, which, with respect to all its parts, is grounded in itself, when each part is grounded or explained through all the others, and vice versa. Only in this way is it completed or delimited. — I have not comprehended something so long as I am still trying to explain it, if my view of it is still in *a state of oscillation* and thus not yet fixed —that is to say, if I am still being driven from one part of my cognition to another" (Fichte, *GNR, GA*, I/3: 377; *SW*, III, p. 77; *FNR*, p. 72).

525. This is perhaps a reference to Kant's claims concerning the active character of the power of understanding.

526. "What is actual [*Wirklich*] is what is given by means of receptivity. [...] Actuality [*Wirklichkeit*] follows from an effect [*Wirkung*]" (Fichte, *EM, GA*, II/3: 43).

527. "When one reflects on the object and distinguishes it from the way of acting through which it emerges, this acting becomes a mere *comprehending* [*Begreifen*], apprehending [*Auffassen*], and grasping [*Umfassen*] of something that is given. It becomes this, since (for the reason indicated above) the object appears to be present, not as the result of this acting, but instead, to be present without any contribution from the (free) I. Accordingly, one is correct to call this way of acting, when it occurs with the abstraction just described, a *concept* [*Begriff*] [....] For ordinary human beings and from the point of view of common consciousness, there are only objects and no concepts; the concept vanishes into the object and coincides with it. The discovery of the concept alongside the object was a product of philosophical genius. That is because it required the talent to discover — in and during the acting itself — not only what emerges in the course of such acting, but also the acting as such, a discovery that required the talent to unite these completely opposed directions in a single act of apprehension and thereby to grasp one's own mind in its action. In this way, the domain of consciousness acquired a new territory" (Fichte, *GNR, GA*, I/3: 315; *SW*, III, p. 5; *FNR*, p. 5).

528. This is a reflection that was described above as occurring with absolute spontaneity, unlike the cditioned by the check or impulse.

529. See *GA*, I/2: 372; above, p. 308.

530. This is because this activity of intuiting is not ascribed to the I. See *GA*, I/2, 371; above, pp. 307–8.

531. I.e., determined as limited by the activity of the I that is operative in reflection.

532. In its purely "productive" capacity, the power of imagination produces what is intuited; in its "reproductive" capacity the power of imagination makes possible the determination of what is intuited *as* intuited. What was previously simply "intuited" must now be *understood* as intuited. For this purpose, it must be "apprehended" by the power of understanding, which requires the assistance of the reproductive power of imagination. [*K*, p. 336.]

533. For Fichte, as for Spinoza, all "determination" always involves "negation."

534. The only way we have been able to distinguish one activity from another is in terms of their *directions*. This makes it clear that, in the preceding, when Fichte refers to "opposing

directions," etc., he is always referring to *activities* in opposing directions and not simply to these sheer "directions" on their own.

535. In order to become aware of myself as intuiting, I must determine my activity of intuiting, which can be limited only with reference to what is intuited. What is intuited is the original activity, which is checked at C and then reflected back to A. [*K*, p. 336.]

536. There is no, as it were, second *Anstoß*, which would reflect the original activity of the I back from the indeterminate realm of the infinite, lying beyond C. Nevertheless, this activity must "obscurely" encounter and be reflected by *something* in this realm. Just as the productive activity of the I proceeds into infinity, so the activity that opposes this activity proceeds from the infinite realm of the Not-I. Otherwise the point of the check (= C), would be something fixed and immovable, which could not be extended further by the practical activity of the I. [*K*, p. 337.]

537. As Fichte's addition to C indicates, what he has in mind here is a mere "something," lacking any further determination or qualities, something *thought of* by the I as a cause or substance, as "that which is intuited" and as what underlies "the intuition" of the same. [*K*, p. 337.]

538. "Insofar as the I posits this image as a product of its activity, it necessarily posits in opposition to it something that is not a product of this activity; that is, it posits it in opposition to something that is no longer determinable but is instead completely determined, and is determined only by itself, without any contribution from the I. This is the *actual thing*, to which the I that is engaged in forming an image directs its attention as it drafts its image, and which must necessarily hover before it as it engages in the act of image formation. This actual thing is the product of the I's first action (the action that has now been interrupted), but it is impossible to posit it as such in this relationship" (Fichte, *GEWL*, *GA*, I/2: 179; below, p. 412).

539. See *GA*, I/2: 370 and 373; above, pp. 306 and 309.

540. I.e., in the intuited object.

541. See *GA*, I/2: 374; above, p. 310.

542. Here one should not think of the "thing in itself" as a substance that is passively affected; instead, *Leiden schlechthin* here means something like "being passively affected as purely and simply posited." [*K*, p. 338.]

543. The point is that, from the standpoint of both the intuiting subject and what is intuited, the act of intuition is *conditioned* by something else; hence we cannot distinguish these standpoints by saying that one recognizes such a condition and the other does not.

544. I.e., as having *different* conditions.

545. Only insofar as it is passively affected can the intuiting subject engage in intuiting.

546. Reading, with *K*, *welches* as referring to *anschauens* rather than to the grammatically more plausible *Gefühl* ("feeling"). [*K*, p. 339.]

547. "What emerges in the I's *necessary* acting (although, for the reason indicated, the I does not become conscious of its acting) is something that itself appears to be necessary; the I feels itself to be constrained in its presentation [*Darstellung*] of what emerges in this way. One then says, 'this object possesses *reality*.' The criterion of all reality is the feeling that one must present something *just as* it is presented. We have seen the ground of this necessity: the rational being must act in this way if it is to be a rational being at all. This is why we express our conviction concerning the reality of something by saying, 'just as surely as I live, or just as surely as I exist, this or that exists'" (Fichte, *GNR*, I/3: 315; *SW*, III, p. 3; *FNR*, p. 5).

548. See Kant's use of this term, *KrV*, B68, to describe the I's positing of its own representation, thereby "affecting itself."

549. "Spontaneous self-activity [*Selbsttätigkeit*] designates the power *to have an effect upon oneself*, that is, *to exercise efficacy* in accordance with *the laws of one's own nature and nothing else*. This power can therefore be ascribed to the I." (Fichte, *EM, GA*, II/3: 70).
550. See *GA*, I/2: 377; above, pp. 312–3.
551. See *GA*, I/2: 356; above, pp. 293–4.
552. The "self-reverting" or *in sich zurüchgehende* activity of the I is the activity by means of which "self-affection" occurs.
553. See *GA*, I/2: 373–4 and 378; above, pp. 309–10 and 314.
554. See *GA*, I/2: 294; above, p. 234.
555. See *GA*, I/2: 260 and 366; above, pp. 204–304.
556. See *GA*, I/2: 382; above, p. 319. We are not yet familiar with this law, since we are now considering the power of judgment to be still acting freely.
557. "The second [of the higher powers of cognition] is the power of understanding, or better, the power of judgment (since the power of understanding, considered with respect to its freedom, would be better called the power of judgment, leaving the name 'understanding' applicable only to the stable and dead power of the same). There is great confusion about this in the usual philosophical terminology" (Fichte, *VLM; GA*, II/4: 126–7).
558. I.e., the determination of the intuiting subject, independently of any reciprocal interaction with the object.
559. In his so-called "Platner lectures" on Logic and Metaphysics, Fichte criticizes Platner (a well-known "popular philosopher") for doing just this: inquiring about "the seat of the soul," as if it were a corporeal thing in space and time. See *VLM, GA*, II/4: 66 and 83.
560. "The pure I of the published *Wissenschaftslehre* is to be understood as reason as such, which is something quite different from personal I-hood" (Fichte, *WLnmH, GA*, IV/2: 240).
561. In preparation for a reference to Kant's "Antinomies of Pure Reason," Fichte here provides an example of the thesis of the second antimony: the soul is immoral. [*K*, p. 345.]
562. I.e., the I.
563. As we can now appreciate, the reciprocal relationship of the I with itself must be posited along with the foundational principle of Part Two: the I posits itself as determined by the Not-I. This is as far as the purely theoretical portion of the *Wissenschaftslehre* can go: The I posits or "determines" itself as determined, and in doing so it is simultaneously the determining subject and what is determined. [*K*, p. 345.]

    "Here is deduced, by the I and for the I, that reciprocal interaction, which, from the point of view of the theoretical I, expresses the third foundational principle. The I has now obtained, for itself, a representation of the representing subject" (Geuroult, p. 238).
564. See *KrV*, B349ff. This is Fichte's explanation of the Kantian antinomies, which arise when the I first posits itself as the pure I or as reason itself —and is thereby *determined* —and then takes itself to be identical with the power of imagination —and therefore to be *undetermined*. The solution to the antinomies is to recognize the one-sided, but necessary, character of each of these ways of positing itself. [*K*, p. 345.]
565. Though the title of Part Three of *GWL* is *Grundlage der Wissenschaft des Praktischen*, Fichte refers to it in *GEWL* (which was prepared at the same time as Part Three of *GWL*) as *Grundlage des praktischen Wissens* or *Foundation of Practical Knowing*. See *GEWL, GA*, I/3: 167; below, p. 401.

    "Just as theoretical philosophy has to present that system of necessary thinking according to which our representations correspond to a being, so practical philosophy has to provide an exhaustive presentation of that system of necessary thinking according to which a being corresponds to and follows from our representations" (Fichte, *SS*, *GA*, I/5: 22; *SW*, IV, 3; *SE*, p. 8).

566. Namely, the check upon the I's outgoing activity and the I's own power of productive imagination.

567. *Faktum.* The *"factum"* to which Fichte is here referring is the limitation of the I by the Not-I posited by the intellect in consequence of the check it experiences. See *GA*, I/2: 362; above, p. 299.

568. See *GA*, I/2: 275; above, pp. 217–18.

569. This is the task of section I, below.

570. *in unserer Theorie.* That is, in the theoretical part of the *Wissenschaftslehre,* as presented in Part Two of *GWL.*

571. See *GA*, I/2: 302; above, p. 241.

572. *soll.* The following section is replete with similar "is supposed to be" formulations. This is a reminder of the *hypothetical* of *postulatory* character of the discussion at this point. See *GA*, I/2: 388–91; above, pp. 322–5. [*K*, p. 352.]

573. This is the "major antithesis" to which Fichte referred on the preceding page, the antithesis between the *intelligent* and *absolute* I, between the I as intellect and the purely self-positing I.

574. I.e., "undetermined." The task of Part Three is to explain what it means for the I to *determine* (i.e., to limit) the (until now, "undetermined") Not-I. [*K*, p. 352.]

575. The "proposition is question" is the principle that "the I posits itself as determining the Not-I." In Part Two, the major principle, "the I posits itself as determined by the Not-I," was analyzed as containing two subordinate principles: "The I posits itself as determined" (and in this sense, determines itself) and "the Not-I determines the I" (see *GA*, I/2: 287; above, p. 228). Analogously, the chief major principle of the practical part of the *Wissenschaftslehre,* "the I posits itself as determining the Not-I," also contains two subordinate principles: "the I posits itself as engaged in determining" and "the I determines the Not-I." The first of these subordinate principles is not, however, thematized in Part Three. Nor is there any need to do so, inasmuch as the entire content of Part Three is supposed to be comprised in the "major antithesis" indicated above, *GA*, I/2: 386; above, p. 320. [*K*, p. 352.]

576. I.e., the conclusion that the Not-I is supposed to be determined *immediately* by the absolute I, and hence that the representing I is supposed to be determined *indirectly* by the absolute I.

577. I.e., the Not-I that is considered by the intellect to be responsible for that check or limit that initiates the production of representations, as described at the conclusion of Part Two.

578. "Something can be limited only by what is posited in opposition to it. Therefore, the I must necessarily posit what limits it as something posited in opposition to itself, something outside of itself, a Not-I. — What is outside the I, insofar as it is *in the I*, is its product; and the I has never gone outside itself" (Fichte, *VLM*, *GA*, II/4: 85).

579. *die freilich einen Umweg nimmt.* The reason for this "detour" or "roundabout route" is that the Not-I cannot be annihilated without also annihilating the representing I or intellect, without which self-consciousness (and therefore the I as such) would be impossible. The path in question leads not to the annihilation of the Not-I, but to its ever-closer assimilation to the I, a process in which the Not-I becomes ever more *rational* and hence "I-like." [*K*, p. 155.]

580. See *GA*, I/2: 408; below, p. 339.

581. That is, in the same way in which the absolute (or "infinite" or "pure") I is the ultimate "cause" of those determinations of the Not-I that are posited by the intellect in accordance with its own necessary laws.

582. I.e., according to the second foundational proposition (§ 2): the I posits the Not-I in opposition to itself.
583. "That the I does not posit itself 'in part' means that it posits itself as limited; i.e., the intellect must posit something real in opposition to itself, because the ideal [activity] is supposed to be limited. But the reason for this limitation cannot lie within the ideal [activity] itself, and it must therefore be referred to the real [activity]. This is how we come to posit something in opposition to the I" (Fichte, *WLnmK, GA*, IV/3: 381; *FTP*, p. 182).
584. "'A priori, this is a mere hypothesis.' This proposition is strictly demonstrated in the present version [of the *Wissenschaftslehre, nova methodo*], because ideal and real activity have here been distinguished and separated from each other" (Fichte, *WLnmK, GA*, IV/3: 381; *FTP*, p. 182).
585. "The finitude of a rational being consists in an original limitation of its striving to be everything, to possess all reality in itself and through itself" (Fichte, *VLM, GA*, II/4: 84).
586. "If one were to suppose that the I were not limited and that its drive were an activity, then the I would be an act of self-affection and nothing more. The I would not be constrained, and consequently, no ideal activity would be present; ideal and real activity would coincide. We are unable to think of anything of this sort that would pertain to us; instead, this would describe the self-consciousness of a purely thought-of God" (Fichte, *WLnmK, GA*, IV/3: 376; *FTP*, p. 173).
587. "We cannot yet speak of causality here [in *WLnm*], since the concept of causality has not yet been explicated. In this present version, acting is not inferred from the Not-I; instead, the Not-I is inferred from acting" (Fichte, *WLnmK, GA*, IV/3: 381; *FTP*, p. 182).
588. "Infinity is here assumed only for the purposes of the presentation. In order to explain striving, sheer acting [*ein bloß tätiges*] must be be presupposed" (Fichte, *WLnmK, GA*, IV/3: 381; *FTP*, p. 182).
589. "Where the previous presentation [*GWL*] speaks of 'limits,' the present presentation [*WLnm*] speaks of 'being halted' or 'being constrained.' In this new presentation, however, we do not infer the Not-I from the limited state of the I" (Fichte, *WLnmK, GA*, IV/3: 381; *FTP*, p. 183).
590. "'The *infinite* I.' This is to be made comprehensible in terms of its opposite, that is, by means of the I that is limited by striving" (Fichte, *WLnmH, GA*, IV/2: 67).
591. See *GA*, I/2: 293; above, p. 233.
592. I.e., they are all features of that *Tathandlung* or F/Act introduced in § 1.
593. *ihr wider- oder gegenstehendes.* "The concept of causal efficacy, which is produced with absolute freedom and could be varied ad infinitum under the same circumstances, extends to causal efficacy in the object. The object must therefore be infinitely alterable, in consequence of an infinitely variable concept. One must be able to make of the object whatever one can will to make to make of it. The object is fixed, and thus, by virtue of its constancy, it could indeed *resist* the influence of the I; but the object is not capable of any alteration by itself (it cannot *instigate* any causally efficacious operation); it cannot *act* in opposition to the causal efficacy of the I" (Fichte, *GNR, GA*, I/3: 338; *SW*, III, 28; *FNR*, p. 28).
594. See above, p. xx; *GA*, I/2: 266 and 268; above, pp. 209 and 211.
595. Fichte may here be referring to the schema laid out above (*GA*, I/2: 369; above, p. 306), according to which we are invited to envision the infinitely outgoing activity of the I as a straight line proceeding from point A to point C, passing along the way through point B. In this illustration, C is the point where an actual check upon the activity the I occurs, the ground of which is attributed by the intuiting I to the Not-I. [*K*, p. 363.]
596. *weil die Grenze ins unendlichen immer weiter hinaus gesetzt werden kann.* The task assigned to the finite I is one of endless progress. [*K*, p. 363.]

597. This domain is "infinite," because the boundary between the I and the Not-I is not fixed, but can always be advanced by means of the practical action of the I, as Fichte will go on to explain. [*K*, p. 363.]

598. Recall, from Part Two, that it is by virtue of the power of productive imagination that the I, qua intellect, first posits for itself an (ideal) representation of an object in response to the check or impetus it encounters.

599. *ohne allen Grund.* An action "without any ground or reason" is an *unconditioned* or *absolute* action, one that occurs *schlechthin*, or "purely and simply." Even if such an action occurs in response to a check upon the activity of the I, there is still no basis or ground for its occurrence *as an action* — beyond the nature of the I itself, as is indicated in the immediately following parenthetical remark, which makes it clear that what is "without any ground" is "the act of positing, considered simply as such."

600. As we learned in Part Two, the activity ascribed to the object can only be the activity of the I as reflected by the check, that is, the activity proceeding from C (the point of the check) back toward A (the I). What connects this activity with the infinite, outgoing activity of the I is the power of imagination, which transforms this merely "reflected" activity of the I into an activity on the part of the object, posited as independent of the I, as Not-I. Though the check is *initiated* by something independent of the I, it is the I alone that is responsible for *connecting* these two activities and hence for *positing* the Not-I. And this explains why, in § 2, it was claimed that the act of positing the Not-I in opposition to the I is "unconditioned" with respect to its form (as an act of positing in opposition). [*K*, p. 364.]

601. *schlechthin gleich gesetzt.* See *GA*, I/2: 272; above, p. 215, where Fichte explains that "to posit items that have been posited in opposition to each other as alike, or to compare them, is called *connecting* or *relating* them to each other."

602. "The pure I can be represented only negatively, as the opposite of the Not-I. The characteristic feature of the latter is multiplicity, and therefore the characteristic feature of the former is complete and absolute unity. The pure I is always one and the same and is never anything different. We may therefore express the above formula as follows: a human being is always supposed to be at one with himself; he should never contradict himself. Now the pure I cannot contradict itself, since it contains no diversity, but is instead always one and the same. However, the empirical I, which is determined and determinable by empirical things, can contradict itself. […] The ultimate, characteristic feature of all rational beings is, accordingly, absolute unity, constant self-identity, complete identity with oneself" (Fichte, *VBG*, *GA*, I/3: 29–30; *EPW*, pp. 148–9).

603. Regarding Fichte's idiosyncratic conception of the categorical imperative as the demand that a finite rational being should always be in harmony with itself in determining its will, see the third lecture of *VBG*. See too his December 6, 1793, letter to F. I. Niethammer, in which he writes, "Admittedly, Kant is responsible for the misinterpretation that one has to conceive the moral law to be applied to all rational beings in order to be able to recognize its universality. But for Kant this is supposed to be no more than an empirical test, not a transcendental feature of the moral law. Pure philosophy is acquainted with only *one I*, and this single I ought not contradict itself. There are not several categorical imperatives, but only one" (*GA*, III/2: 20; *EPW*, p. 368).

604. I.e., on the assumption that the absolute activity of the I could actually determine that of the Not-I and that the latter is dependent upon the former. In this case, the resisting activity of the object (= Y) would be transformed by the activity of the I into a different activity (= −Y), an activity in harmony with the absolute activity of the I, and the object would therefore be posited by the I as it *ought* to be, not as it *is actually encountered by the I*.

605. I.e., the demand that all activity be equivalent to the activity of the I.

606. *Alles in Allem.* This is a translation of the famous saying of Anaxagoras, *en panti panta*, later taken up by Plato and then by Paul (I Corinthians 15:28). Fichte may very well have acquired this expression from a passage in the second, 1785 edition of Jacobi's *Über die Lehre des Spinoza*, pp. 291–2. [*K*, pp. 369–70.]

607. See *GA*, I/2: 404; below, p. 336.

608. The terms, *Tendenz* (tendency) and *Streben* (striving), like the terms *Anstoß* (check or impetus) and *Widerstand* (resistance), are borrowed from the technical language of contemporary natural science, according to which every "substance" or thing "strives" to express and maintain itself. [*K*, pp. 372–3.]

    "The I, however, is supposed to be absolute and is supposed to be determined purely and simply by itself; but if it is determined by the Not-I, then it is not self-determined — which contradicts the highest and absolutely first foundational principle. In order to avoid this contradiction, we must assume that the Not-I that is supposed to determine the intellect is itself determined by the I, which in this case would not be engaged in representing, but would instead possesses absolute causality. But such causality would completely annul the opposing Not-I and, along with it, all of those representations that depend upon this Not-I. Consequently, the assumption of such an absolute causality would contradict the second and third foundational principles. It follows from this that we have to represent this absolute causality *as* something that contradicts representation, as something that *cannot be represented*, as a causality that is not a causality. The concept of a causality that is not a causality is, however, the concept of *striving*. Such a causality is conceivable only under the condition of a completed approximation to infinity — which is itself inconceivable. — This concept of striving (the necessity of which has to be proven) provides the foundation for the second part of the *Wissenschaftslehre*, which is called the Practical Part." (Fichte, *BWL*, *GA*, I/2: 150–1; above, pp. 189–90).

    "This striving can be characterized as the totality of *self-activity*. Wherever self-activity is constricted, it must therefore express itself by means of a drive to expand its boundaries" (Fichte, *EM*, *GA*, II/3: 197).

609. "'The conclusion.' Something must be assumed immediately, in advance of all free determination, something in which the I and Not-I are united: a tendency, a striving, a drive" (Fichte, *WLnmK*, *GA*, IV/3: 381; *FTP*, p. 183).

610. I.e., the "major antithesis" of § 4, the contradiction between the I as intellect and the pure I. See *GA*, I/2: 386; above, p. 320.

611. It "annuls itself" because, by being completely determining by the I, the Not-I ceases to be Not-I and becomes I, in which case there is nothing upon which the I could exercise its causality — hence "annulling" itself. [*K*, p. 373.]

612. The "absolute" action in question is that action by means of which the I purely and simply posits a Not-I in opposition to itself. (See above, § 2.) The thesis that the absolute (or pure) activity of the I *directly* determines its objective activity is presupposed by proponents of "intelligible fatalism," a position associated with Fichte's colleague at the University of Jena, C. Chr. E. Schmid. See Fichte's comments on intelligible fatalism in his 1793 review of Leonard Creuzer's *Skeptical Reflections on the Freedom of the Will* (*RC*, *GA*, I/2: 13; *SW*, VIII, 416; *Crev*, pp. 295–6).

613. What Fichte is attempting to do here is to provide a deeper explication of the act of positing something purely and simply in opposition to the I, as introduced in the explication of the second foundational principle in § 2. We are now in a position to see that such an act of positing in opposition presupposes the experience of resistance to an externally grounded activity. The pure, infinitely outreaching activity of the I is "reflected" at point C (the point of the check or impetus) and is transformed into an activity of the

object, directed back toward point A (the I). And then, by means of another "absolute" or unconditioned action, the I's intuiting activity, which is directed from A to C, is "compared" or "connected" with the activity of the object proceeding from C to A. Activites posited in opposition to each other can be connected only by means of the power of productive imagination, which here operates as an independent and absolute power or activity of the I. [*K*, p. 374.]

614. "If, in intellectual intuition, the I *is because* it is and *is what* it is, then it is, to that extent, *self-positing*, absolutely independent and autonomous. The I in empirical consciousness, however, the I as intellect, *is* only in relation to something intelligible, and is, to that extent, dependent. But the I that is thereby posited in opposition to itself is supposed to be not two, but one — which is impossible, since 'dependence' contradicts 'independence' Since, however, the I cannot relinquish its absolute independence, a striving is engendered: the I strives to make what is intelligible dependent upon itself, in order thereby to unify the I that entertains representations of what is intelligible with the self-positing I. This is what it means to say that *reason is practical*. In the pure I, reason is not practical, nor is it practical in the I as intellect. Reason is practical only insofar as it strives to unify these two. This is not the place to show that these are the foundational principles that must underlie Kant's own expositions (granted that he never established them specifically). Nor is this the place to show how a practical philosophy arises when the striving of the intelligent I (which is, in itself, hyperphysical) is represented — that is, when one *de*scends the same steps that one *a*scended in theoretical philosophy" (Fichte, *RA*, *GA*, I/2: 65; *SW*, I, 22–3; *EPW*, 75–6).

"If, in the first place, the I, considered as a representing being, gives itself a law (the law of unconditioned necessity), then it possesses autonomy, and this autonomy, in its connections with the pure I, as posited through intellectual intuition and in abstraction from anything representable, is pure self-determination: it exhibits itself [*es stellt sich selbst dar*]. But if the self-exhibiting and representing I are supposed to be not two, but one and the same substance, then this can be thought of only be conceiving of the self-exhibiting I to be connected to the Not-I as a striving to make itself uniform with the former, and hence as a striving to realize all of those determinations that alone would make possible such harmony — and this is the meaning of the expression, 'reason is practical'" (Fichte, Draft of *RA*, *GA*, II/2: 395).

615. "The main question is whether the feeling of what is purely and simply right [...] can or cannot be derived from anything higher — and indeed, from practical reason. Against anyone who would deny such a possibility, one cannot yet again appeal to a fact [*Tatsache*], for though such a person will concede anything that is an actual fact, it is not a fact that reason is practical, nor that it possesses the power to produce the feeling of what is right. [...] Nor, finally, can one refute this system [of natural benevolence] by appealing to the fact that it provides no ground for assuming the freedom of the will; for such freedom is not a fact of consciousness, but is a mere postulate of the ethical law, a law that is itself assumed to be an effect of practical reason. A system that does not need practical reason can get along very well without freedom. [...] The essential difference between a system of this kind [that is, a system of "intelligible fatalism"] and the Kantian system would be that in the former ethical feeling would indeed be an effect of reason (understood as the power of original laws) — but an effect of *theoretical* reason — and the ethical law would therefore be *conditioned* by the mechanism of our minds and would *necessarily* be applied to every case to which it is applicable. [...] In the Kantian system, in contrast, ethical feeling would be an effect of the kind of reason that would, in this function, stand under no condition other than that of its own essential nature (namely, the condition of absolute unity and hence uniformity) — i.e., it would be an effect of practical reason. The latter,

however, can neither be described as a fact nor postulated in consequence of any fact whatsoever; instead, it must be proven. It must be proven *that* reason is practical. Such a proof, which might well also provide the foundational of *all* philosophical knowledge (with respect to the content of the same), must proceed approximately as follows: The human being is given to consciousness as a unity (as an I). This fact can be explained only by presupposing something in human beings that is simply unconditioned; therefore, we must assume that there is within human beings something purely and simply unconditioned. But what is purely and simply unconditioned is practical reason. And now, for the first time, it may be securely assumed that this ethical feeling — which is, to be sure, given as a feeling — is an effect of that practical reason which has now been demonstrated" (Fichte, *RG, GA*, I/2: 26–9; *SW*, VIII, 432–26; *Grev*, pp. 303–5).

616. " 'Force' is that X in which everything is united — being passively affected and activity, when united, give us force. But how? [...] Force is the *power of a thing to be a cause and to produce an effect*" (Fichte, *EM, GA*, II/3: 85).

617. The striving in question was curbed or restricted by the check or *Anstoß*.

618. This is the same schema introduced at *GA*, I/2: 370; above, p. 306, and applied at *GA*, I/2: 376; above, pp. 311–2.

619. This restriction does not apply to the original self-positing of the I described in § 1, only to those acts of positing that occur in consequence of the check to the infinitely outgoing activity of the I. [*K*, p. 385.]

620. This synthesis will be the topic of § 11, below.

621. "The real controversy between Criticism and dogmatism concerns the *connection between our knowledge and a thing in itself*. In this controversy the skeptics have correctly allied themselves with the dogmatists and with healthy common sense (which certainly deserves to be taken into consideration though not, of course, as a judge, but rather as a witness called to bear testimony). Some future *Wissenschaftslehre* might well be able to settle this controversy by showing the following: that our knowledge is by no means connected directly with things in themselves by means of representations, but is connected with them only indirectly, by means of *feeling*; that in any case, things are *represented* merely as *appearances*, whereas they are *felt as things in themselves*; that no representations would be possible at all without feeling, but that things in themselves can be recognized only *subjectively*, i.e., insofar as they have an effect upon our feeling" (Fichte, *BWL, GA*, I/2: 110n.; above, p. 152n.).

622. Fichte here distinguishes between different *objective* activities of the I. The first, finite objective activity is that of the "theoretical" I, that is, of the I qua intellect, and is directed at an actual object; the second, infinite objective activity of the I is directed at an imagined object, hence at the concept of a goal or at an ideal. [*K*, p. 386.]

623. That is, the distinction between an actual and an imagined object.

624. That is to say, it is determined as a determining activity.

625. See *GA*, I/2: 396; above, pp. 329–30.

626. See *GA*, I/2: 398; above, p. 331.

627. According to the second foundational principle (§ 2), the positing of an *object as such* (the Not-I) occurs (with respect to its form, that is, as an act of positing something in opposition to the I) "purely and simply." But this is not sufficient for the positing of any *determinate, actual object*, which requires a check upon the original outgoing activity of the I and the ensuing "objective" activity attributed to the determinate object in question. [*K*, p. 387.]

"1.) The finitude of a rational being consists in an original restriction of its striving to be everything, to possess within itself and by itself all reality. This restriction pertains, as such, to [every] finite rational being, which is not a rational being apart from such restriction.

"2.) There can be different determinate degrees and types of this restriction. The species of finite rational being is determined by the degree and type of restriction involved, which can be called the *organization* of the rational being in question [...].

"3.) What constitutes the character of humanity as a species of finite rational beings (an empirical concept) is the determinate restriction we assume in the case of ourselves and others like us, which determines our empirical view of the world — a restriction that cannot be explained any further. (This is simply how God has made us).

"4.) What ensues from this manner of restriction as such is valid for the species; what ensues from the employment of freedom is valid for the individual; what ensues from the application of the law of reason is valid for all finite rational beings" (Fichte, *VLM, GA*, II/4: 84–5).

628. See *GA*, I/2: 397; above, p. 330.

629. "This unity — an I which, in determining itself, determines at the same time everything that is Not-I (the Idea of the deity) — is the final goal of this striving. When this goal is represented by the intelligent I as lying beyond itself, this striving is *belief* (belief in God). This striving cannot cease short of its goal; that is, the intellect cannot consider any single moment of its existence in which the goal remains unachieved to be the last (belief in immortality)" (Fichte, *RA, GA*, I/2: 65; *SW*, I, 23; *EPW*, p. 76).

630. "We will continue to exist eternally, since we will have to continue to develop ourselves forever. God wills the attainment of the final end of the ethical law, and thus he must also will that we continue to exist eternally. He is all-powerful and can therefore certainly see to this. This is the ground of our belief in immortality" (Fichte, *VLM, GA*, II/4: 348).

631. "The error of the mystics is that they represent the infinite, which cannot be attained at any time, as something that can be attained in time. The complete annihilation of the individual and the fusion of the latter with the absolutely pure form of reason, or God, is indeed the ultimate goal of finite reason; but this is not possible in any time" (Fichte, *SS*, *GA*, I/5: 142; *SW*, IV, 151; *SE*, p. 143).

632. An apagogic proof proceeds by demonstrating the untenability of the opposite of what one is trying to prove (*reduction ad absurdum*). It is therefore an indirect mode of proof.

633. Fichte appears to have adopted this way of describing his new method from Ernst Platner's discussion of "genetic" definition in § 440 of Part One his *Philosophische Aphorismen*, where he describes such a definition as one that explains *why* something is as it is. Platner then proceeds to show the origin of such a conception in Aristotle and its later development in the writings of Christian Wolff (*GA*, II/4S: 440–1). [*K*, pp. 391–2.]

634. "It is always my intention to facilitate *genetic* insight, and this why I return to the original operation of the human mind" (Fichte, *VLM, GA*, II/4: 154).

635. The "resisting" (*widerstrebenden*) activity in question is that of the Not-I.

636. " 'Let us explain ourselves....' (This is an important point and is recommended reading.) The I sees everything within itself; even when it views something as lying outside itself, the ground for doing so must nevertheless lie within the I" (Fichte, *WLnmK, GA*, IV/3: 382; *FTP*, p. 183).

637. *Verschiedenes*. There can be within the I nothing that is heterogeneous or foreign to the I; the I can contain nothing that is not part of its own self-identity.

638. "Recommended for re-reading. — The I sees nothing but itself; *it* alone is the immediate object. Thus, if the I is now supposed to see something else, something outside itself, it must intuit something else within itself" (Fichte, *WLnmH, GA*, I/2: 68; *FTP*, p. 183n.).

639. See *GA*, I/2: 369; above, p. 306.

640. "First of all, with respect to its form, the task is to think the I at the requisite level of abstraction as something *subsisting* and fixed. [...] (Anyone familiar with the spirit of transcendental philosophy will share our presupposition that this act of thinking of something subsisting must itself be based upon our laws of thinking and that, accordingly, what we are here seeking is only the essence of the I for the I, and by no means the latter's essence in itself, as a *thing* in itself.)" (Fichte, SS, GA, I/5: 44–5; SW, IV, 28; SE, p. 33).

641. "What exists for me exists in and through me. Everything arises in accordance with the laws of my reason. The laws of reason are, at the same time, the laws of the world. It is not the case that reason conforms to the world; instead, it is the world that conforms to reason. The world is a certain way of looking at our own reason" (Fichte, Eschen transcript of VLM, GA, IV/3: 134).

642. I.e., before deriving the necessity of opposed directions of the I's activity — and of hence of real *difference* — within the I itself.

643. In contrast with the sheer Not-I (§ 2), which is purely and simply posited in opposition to the I, some of the features of the I itself are in this case transferred to an external "body" (*Korper*), which is posited as possessing an internal force, which permits it to resist and to check the outgoing, centrifugal activity of the I. [K, p. 397.]

644. See GA, I/2: 291 and 351; above, pp. 232 and 288. As a quantum, the I is capable of limitation and hence "open" to negation by the Not-I.

645. "The I is originally posited through itself; i.e., it is [for itself] what it is for any intellect outside of itself. Its being [*Wesen*] is grounded in itself; and this is how we must think of the I, *if* we are going to think of it at all. Moreover, for reasons expounded in the 'Foundation of Practical Knowing,' we can ascribe to the I a striving *to fill* infinity, as well as a tendency to *comprehend* it [*dieselbe zu umfassen*], that is, to reflect upon itself as infinite. Both tendencies pertain to the I just as surely as it is an I at all. (See GWL, p. 263 [= the present passage].) But no action of the I springs from this mere tendency — nor can it" (Fichte, GEWL, GA, I/3: 167; below, p. 401).

646. The "law of reason" is in this case the law of identity ($A = A$), which requires the I to transfer to the Not-I (which is always something manifold) its own unity, thereby unifying the manifold. [K, p. 403.]

647. According to Fichte, two things can be related to each other only in terms of a ground that is distinct from both, and hence by means of some "third thing." (See GA, I/2: 274; below, p. 217.) In this case, this third thing is the *demand* that the I "fill infinity" and that, in doing so, it *reflect upon itself* in order to determine whether it really does "fill infinity." In the Idea of a "completed infinity" (and hence of the complete assimilation of the Not-I to the I) the centrifugal and centripetal activities of the I finally do indeed "coincide," since there is no longer any check, which is the ground of their distinction.

648. "We are now standing at the limit of all consciousness, and thus, in order to make the transition [from what is indeterminable] to what is determinate, we also require something incomprehensible — a nothing (for finite beings like ourselves, who can think only discursively). We must think of an I that is not limited — an I that is a sheer act of affecting itself, in which no ideal and real activities occur (in separation from each other), but in which these coincide. (See GWL, p. 339 [= the present passage].) From this we proceed to the limited I, whose practical activity is arrested and which, because of this resistance, can never become an activity, but of which activity is only demanded — and which, moreover, possesses a drive with which consciousness is necessarily connected — or through which it first obtains its consciousness" (Fichte, WLnmH, GA, IV/2: 261; FTP, pp, 173–4n.).

"If one were to suppose that the I were not limited and that its drive were an activity, then the I would be an act of affecting itself and nothing more. The I would not be constrained, and consequently, no ideal activity would be present; ideal and real activity would coincide. We are unable to think of anything of this sort that would pertain to us; instead, such a thought would pertain to the self-consciousness of God, which is purely thought. (See the remark within parenthesis on p. 339 of the compendium [= the present passage].)" (Fichte, *WLnmK*, *GA*, IV/3: 376; *FTP*, p. 173).

649. Concerning this *Gesetz der Bestimmung*, see *GA*, I/2: 437, 442–3; below, pp. 364 and 370–1.

650. Hence the demand that the I fill infinity underlies and makes possible the I's theoretical activity of reflecting, which is a condition for the possibility of self-consciousness. Self-consciousness must not, therefore, be understood as a purely theoretical relation of the I to itself, for it is grounded in a practical relation of the I to itself. [*K*, p. 406.]

651. This is a rather different sense of "reflection" than the one that invoked just a page earlier, where "reflecting" was identified as a spontaneous activity of the I. Here, in contrast, "reflection" is described as an automatic consequence of the check, which "reflects" an original activity of the I. [*K*, p. 107.]

652. Namely, to the demand that the I fill infinity, which is in this case the "third thing," which alone makes possible the distinction between the centrifugal and centripetal directions of the I's activity.

653. Though it might appear that Fichte is here referring to a centrifugal direction of the I's activity that occurs independently of the check, this is not the case, as is indicated by the immediately following description of this activity as "foreign." [*K*, p. 405.]

654. This is not a reflection that is *initiated* consciously; it occurs spontaneously, by virtue of the "absolute being" or "essential nature" of the I as such. Such reflection can be *accomplished*, however, only if the I is limited and encounters an activity in the opposite direction, the activity initiated (i.e., "reflected") by the check. [*K*, p. 405.]

655. The demand that the I fill infinity is the basis or ground for its striving for overall causality. This is a demand both of the reflecting I and of the absolute I. The I's centrifugal activity is a manifestation of this demand. In proceeding beyond itself, the I simultaneously "opens itself" to external influence and strives to determine itself as an infinite quantum. [*K*, p. 406.]

656. The "absolute being" [*absolutes Sein*] of the I is equivalent to its "essential nature" [*Wesen*].

657. *in sich selbst vollkommen*: i.e., "complete in itself," without any relation to anything outside of itself. This is a formulation from Plotinus, which Fichte probably obtained from the title of Karl Phillipp Moritz's *Über den Begriff des in sich selbst Vollendenten* (1785). [*K*, p. 406.]

658. The I does not "open itself" to an external influence because it is finite and needy, but because it is required by its own essential nature to reflect on and to obtain knowledge concerning itself (in order to determine whether it actually fills all reality). [*K*, p. 410.]

659. Here Fichte introduces a distinction between the original — or absolute — self-positing of the I, described in § 1, and self-positing *as* self-posited, which makes possible actual consciousness. The second of these two acts of self-positing is the one that opens the I to an external influence, thereby making possible the actions of positing in opposition and positing the reciprocal interaction between the limited I and limited Not-I described in § 3 and Part Two. Hence the "absolute self-positing" of § 1 does not, by itself, lead to actual self-consciousness. [*K*, p. 411.]

"The question concerning what the genuinely spiritual element in man, the pure I, might be like, considered purely and simply in itself, isolated and apart from any relation to anything outside itself, is unanswerable and, taken precisely, harbors a self-contradiction. It is by no means true that the pure I is a product of the Not-I (which is my name for everything thought to exist outside the I, everything distinguished from and posited in opposition to the I). The assertion that the pure I is a product of the Not-I expresses a transcendental [*sic!* should be "transcendent"] materialism, which is completely contrary to reason. It is, however, certainly true (and, at the appropriate place, will be strictly demonstrated) that the I is never conscious of itself nor able to become conscious of itself, except in its empirical determination — which necessarily presuppose something outside the I" (Fichte, *EVBG, GA,* I/3: 28; *SW,* VI, 294–5; *EPW,* p. 147).

660. On the one hand, the "Idea of the I" is indeed present within actual consciousness (as indicated in the immediately following paragraph); on the other, it is present only for the philosopher, in the sense that it is only the philosopher who reflects upon the conditions necessary for the possibility of such an Idea, in order to describe the *genesis* of the same within actual consciousness.

"I would now like to add a few words concerning a most remarkable confusion, namely, the confusion between the I as an intellectual intuition, with which the *Wissenschaftslehre* commences, and the I as an Idea, with which it concludes. As an intellectual intuition, the I contains nothing but the form of I-hood, self-reverting acting, which, to be sure, also becomes the content of the I. [...] The I exists in this form only *for the philosopher,* and insofar as one grasps it in this form one necessarily raises oneself to the level of philosophy. But the I is present as an Idea *for the I* itself, for the I the philosopher is observing. [...] The I as an Idea is identical to the rational being. On the other hand, it is the latter only insofar as this rational being has completely succeeded in exhibiting universal reason within itself, has actually become rational through and through, and is nothing but rational. As such, it has ceased to be an individual, which it was only because of the limitations of sensibility. On the other hand, the I as an Idea is the rational being insofar as it has also completely succeeded in realizing reason outside itself in the world, which therefore also remains posited in this Idea. [...] All that the Idea of the I has in common with the I as an [intellectual] intuition is this: in neither case is the I considered to be an individual. In the latter case, it is not thought of as an individual because I-hood has not yet been determined as individuality; in the former case, on the other hand, it is not thought of as individual because individuality has vanished as a result of a process of cultivation in accordance with universal laws. But these two I's are also posited in opposition to one another, inasmuch as the I, considered as an [intellectual] intuition, contains nothing but the form of the I, and does not include any reference whatsoever to the proper content of the I, which becomes thinkable only when the I thinks of a world. In contrast, the entire content of I-hood is included in the thought of the I as an Idea. Philosophy in its entirety proceeds from the former, which is therefore its foundational concept. From this, it proceeds to the latter, the I as an Idea, which can be exhibited only within the practical part of philosophy. [...] The latter is nothing but an Idea. It cannot be thought of in any determinate manner, and it will never become anything real; instead, it is only something to which we ought to draw infinitely nearer" (Fichte, *VWL, GA,* I/4: 265–6; *SW,* I, 515–16; *IWL,* pp. 100–1).

661. Unlike the "philosophical reflection" mentioned in the preceding paragraph, this act of reflection is not consciously undertaken; instead, it occurs spontaneously, in accordance with the "essential nature" or "law" of the I.

662. The highest practical goal of the I is the realization of the Idea of an I whose consciousness is determined by the I alone and by nothing external to the I. See *GA,* I/2: 277; above, p. 220.

663. *Tendenz.* This term here appears to be a synonym for *Streben* (striving).

664. The mere "tendency" or "striving" to reflect (spontaneously, to be sure, and by no means voluntarily) becomes an "actual" reflection if and only if the infinite practical striving of the I "to fill infinity" encounters a check or impetus.

665. More accurately, reflection is directed not at the check, but at the centripetal activity that is occasioned by the check when the outgoing activity of the I is thereby "reflected" back to the I, which then becomes an intuiting subject. The check itself, as such, does not lie within the I, but is only a theoretical device for explaining the presence within the I of something foreign. [K, p. 416.]

666. " 'If the I possesses no practical power ...' This passage deserves to be re-read, but it needs to be read in the light of the new presentation [i.e., WLnm]. This new version does not repeat what was said in the earlier one concerning the 'check' and the 'direction' [of the I's activity]; instead, it speaks of "constraint" [of the ideal and real activities]" (Fichte, WLnmK, GA, IV/3: 382; FTP, p. 183).

    "In place of the expression *check*, it would be *correct* to say that what we have here is the constraint [Gebundenheit] of the *ideal* and real *activities*" (Fichte, WLnmH, GA, IV/2: 68).

667. The check, that is, the limitedness and finitude of the I, is a condition for the possibility for the "I as intellect" and hence for any self-consciousness. It is in this sense that the essential nature of the I — considered on its own — is deficient and necessarily "open to" external influence. [K, p. 416.]

    "Something that certainly does follow from what has been said here is that we can become conscious of all the intellect's manners of acting (which are supposed to be exhaustively described by the *Wissenschaftslehre*) only in the form of representation, that is, only insofar as and in the manner that they are represented" (Fichte, BWL, GA, I/2: 149; above, p. 188).

668. Again, this is a spontaneous "tendency" toward reflection upon itself, a striving grounded in the essential nature or laws of the I and not a consciously undertaken voluntary activity.

669. According to the *Wissenschaftslehre*, we are not God, but should constantly and endless strive to *become God*. See EM, GA, II/3: 238, where the goal of the I's practical striving toward absolute unity with the Not-I is explicitly described as "oneself becoming God."

670. Namely, the absolute I.

671. " 'According to the explication just provided...' This point would now be expressed as follows: the I is originally self-positing; but were its activity not limited, it would be unable to posit itself. Consequently, the original activity must be limited if reflection is to be possible at all. The Not-I does not impinge upon the I; instead, it is the I that, in the course of its expansion, impinges upon the Not-I" (Fichte, WLnmK, GA, IV/3: 382; FTP, p. 183).

672. "The action indicated in that preceding deduction was the following: the I posited its own strife-torn activity [i.e., the activity distinguished by a conflict of directions] as active insofar as it imagined a certain condition to be absent, but posited it as suppressed and static, insofar as this condition was imagined to be present. In both cases, however, this strife-torn activity was posited within the I. The intuition we have just derived is obviously an action of this sort. In itself and qua action, intuition has its basis entirely in the I. This follows from the postulate (in the previous section) that the I must posit anything that is to be found within it. Intuition posits within the I something that is not supposed to be established by the I at all, but is instead supposed to be established by the Not-I; that is, it posits the impression that has occurred. As an action, intuition is entirely independent of this impression, just as the impression is entirely independent of intuition. They run parallel to each other. Perhaps I can make this clearer by means of the following image: The original pure activity of the I is modified and, as it were, given shape or form [gebildet] by the check or impetus [provided by the Not-I], and, to this extent, this activity is by no means ascribable to the I. Another free activity now tears the first activity, just as

it is, free from the encroaching Not-I. It then observes and examines the activity it has thereby torn away from the Not-I and observes what it contains. However, it cannot consider what it observes to be the pure shape of the I; instead, it can only take it to be an image of the Not-I" (Fichte, *GEWL, GA*, I/3: 155; below, p. 391).

673. As Fichte will go on to explain (*GA*, I/2: 416; below, p. 346, it is the I itself that attributes this opposing "force" or motive power to the Not-I, and it does so in consequence of the check (which is simply a limit to the I's own force, one that succeeds in redirecting — or "reflecting" — this same force back upon the I itself). [*K*, pp. 424–5.]

"No activity in the I can be related to a state of passive affection in such a way that it *produces* this state or posits it as produced by the I. This is because in such a case the I would simultaneously posit something within itself and annihilate it, which is self-contradictory. (The activity of the I cannot be directed at the content [*Materie*] of the state of passive affection.)" (Fichte, *GEWL, GA*, I/3: 156; below, p. 392).

674. This "eternal law" will prove to be the categorical imperative, the moral law, which demands of the I complete self-sufficiency. See *GA*, I/2: 450; below, p. 377.

675. The power in question — the mediating or intermediate power of freedom — can be described as "intermediate" precisely because it "mediates between" the absolute being and the empirical existence of the I. [*K*, p. 425.]

676. "'The ultimate ground of all reality for the I...' Nothing foreign is incorporated into the I. It receives no impressions or images from the world. What is posited in opposition to the I possesses no force that it could transmit to the I; instead, what is posited in opposition to the I is the I's own restriction, and the reason why the I posits something lies within the I itself. — Force does not pertain originally to the Not-I, to which nothing originally pertains but being. The Not-I can initiate nothing; it is capable only of hindering and arresting. The I cannot attain to consciousness if it is not restricted. The ground of this restriction lies outside the I, but the I possesses within itself the ground of activity. I am originally restricted, and a manifold of feelings is also present within me from the start. I can do nothing to alter this fact, which conditions and makes possible my entire being, nor can I go beyond it; this is simply the point at which I find myself. Only if I am provided with an endless time am I then free and able to do whatever I want within this sphere" (Fichte, *WLnmK, GA*, IV/3: 382; *FTP*, pp. 183–4).

677. "As you know, the origin of the content of experience is explained on the basis of an absolute restriction, and it was demonstrated *that* it is absurd to inquire any further concerning the ground of this restriction. The Critical philosophy is therefore realism and not idealism. But it is not a dogmatic realism, and this is the only respect in which it could it be called idealism" (Fichte, *VLM, GA*, II/4: 249).

"I am restricted as such; such restriction constitutes my entire condition (my single and indivisible state for all eternity — where 'eternity' signifies the negation of time), and one may not ask any further questions concerning this restriction. This is my original restriction [*meine erste Beschränktheit*]" (Fichte, *WLnmK, GA*, IV/3: 433; *FTP*, p. 278).

"This restriction marks and constitutes the limit of reason; for it is precisely reason itself that asks questions, but reason comes into being only by means of this very restriction. Consequently, so long as one expects a rational answer, one cannot ask any questions concerning this restriction" (Fichte, *WLnmH, GA*, IV/2:124; *FTP*, p. 278.)

678. "'The *Wissenschaftslehre* is therefore realistic ...' Properly speaking, what is felt is not what is posited in opposition to the I; instead, I feel myself to be restricted, and the existence of what is posited in opposition to me is first inferred in order to explain this restriction. The positive component in things is simply nothing whatsoever other than that aspect of them that is related to our feelings. That something is red is a fact that cannot be derived from anything else, but that objects are in space and time and are related to each

other in certain specific ways is something that can indeed be deduced" (Fichte, *WLnmK*, *GA*, IV/3: 382; *FTP*, p. 184).

679. "If things in themselves, independent of our power of representation, are unable to produce in us *any* determinations *whatsoever,* then we can know very well that they did not produce the determinations actually present in us at the moment" (Fichte, *RA*, *GA*, I/2: 55; *SW*, I, 14; *EPW*, p. 69).

680. "An inquiry on the basis of pure principles of reason is always transcendental. Such an inquiry does not presume to say how things are *in themselves* — that is, independent of any rational beings — , since it knows that such a question and such a claim is nonsensical; but it also knows what these same things must necessarily be for us, that is for any possible empirical I" (Fichte, *VLM*, *GA*, II/4: 72).

681. That is to say, the Not-I must be posited as such, posited by the I in opposition to itself. What is present to the I independently of its own acts is *feeling,* which is unquestionably a state *of the I* — albeit one accompanied by a feeling of necessity.

682. I.e., the possibility of providing a (genetic) "explanation" of how the I first posited something independent of itself as capable of affecting consciousness (which was the earlier description of what Fichte will later describe as the presence within consciousness of "representations accompanied by a feeling of necessity"). See *VWL*, *GA*, I/4: 186–7; *SW*, I: 422–3; *IWL*, pp. 7–8.

683. "We have now deduced the ground of all cognizing. We have shown why the I is and must be an intellect: namely, because it has to resolve a contradiction *within itself,* a contradiction between its own activity and its own state of being passively affected. It must resolve this contradiction *originally* (and it must do so unconsciously — as a condition for the very possibility of any consciousness). It is clear that we could not have shown this had we not proceeded beyond all consciousness" (Fichte, *GEWL*, *GA*, I/3: 154; below, p. 390).

684. "'Despite its realism…' I cannot exist unless I am restricted. But what does this mean? After all, it is by means of my own positing that what restricts me is therefore external to me. In reflecting upon my own consciousness, I gain insight into why I must be restricted.

"I could not be conscious of myself were I not restricted and were there nothing to restrict me. But I posit what restricts me only insofar as I am already conscious of myself, and therefore, only insofar as I am restricted. The possibility of positing A is conditioned by B; but I can posit B only if I am conscious and thus only if I am restricted by C, etc. I am restricted at every point of consciousness; yet I can now reflect upon this fact and can say that my restriction exists only insofar as I posit it" (Fichte, *WLnmK*, *GA*, IV/3: 382–3; *FTP*, p. 184).

685. I.e., something only *thought* and not anything *actual.*

686. "The power of representation exists *for* the power of representation and *by means of* the power of representation: this is the circle within which every finite understanding — that is to say, every understanding we can conceive — is necessarily confined. Anyone who wants to escape from this circle does not understand himself and does not know what he wants" (Fichte, *RA*, *GA*, I/2: 51; *SW*, I, 11; *EPW*, p. 67).

687. "The active, willing, practical subject discovers itself to be restricted. If one were to ask, What is responsible for this restriction? one would become transcendent. I am restricted: this is what is ultimate" (Fichte, student transcript of *VLM*, *GA*, IV/1: 212).

688. "'The fact that the finite mind must necessarily posit…' This circle is all that really limits us. Again and again, whenever we posit something within ourselves that we take to be external to ourselves, we are then forced to seek something else beyond what we have posited, something that is supposed to be independent of us, etc. A person who is not conscious of this law will conclude that our own representations are all that exist. Such a

person is a transcendent idealist; whereas a person who believes that things could exist apart from our representations is a dogmatist" (Fichte, *WLnmK, GA*, IV/3: 383; *FTP*, p. 184).

689. "If the term 'idealism' is supposed to designate a system that derives all consciousness from the purely ideal activity [of the I], then the W.L. is certainly not an idealism. On the contrary, it repudiates such a system as in the highest degree absurd and incapable of explaining that consciousness which we all actually possess. (I also do not know if anyone has propounded such a system. For Berkeley, at least, that deity through whom representations are produced in us was something supremely real.) Nevertheless, many of those who have proposed to refute the *Wissenschaftslehre* appear to have taken it to be such a system. Perhaps they only read the first installment of the same [that is, Parts One and Two of *GWL*] and were so exhausted by this that they did not read the second, in which they would have discovered, right at its apex, a sustained discussion of a certain *striving*, as the first object of any consciousness of what is real and, by means of this, the object of all other real consciousness.

"If dogmatism is a system that proceeds from something real, without any relationship to something ideal, then the W.L. has protected itself against all dogmatism by means of the preceding assertions, and, for anyone who is the least bit self-aware, and so long as he remains self-aware, it has uprooted dogmatism from the ground up.

"In contrast with these systems, the *Wissenschaftslehre* is an ideal-realism or real-idealism; indeed, a transcendental idealism, inasmuch as it claims that this derivation is necessary only for the self-cognizing intellect, whereas the *Wissenschaftslehre* itself explains how and why the thought of the influence [upon the I] of foreign laws of the thing remains valid for ordinary consciousness.

"If, on the contrary, one understands *idealism* to be a system that derives all consciousness from the immanent laws of the intellect, which is neither ideal nor real, but is the unity of both, then the *Wissenschaftslehre* is certainly *idealism* — precisely because it claims that such a derivation is necessary only for a self-cognizing intellect, that is, for ordinary consciousness" (Fichte, *NBWL, GA*, II/5: 366-7).

690. To *explain* something is to *relate it to its ground*. Both the principle of sufficient reason (*Satz des Grundes*) and the category of limitation are derived from the third foundational principle (§ 3). [*K*, p. 419.]

"'As soon as we say explain ...' I explain something (A) by connecting it with something else (B), etc. I cannot grasp everything at once, for I am finite. This is what is called 'discursive thinking.' The finitude of rational beings consists in having to explain things. With respect to its being, as well as with respect to the determinacy thereof, the Not-I is independent of the practical I. But it is dependent upon the theoretical I, for a world is present only insofar as we posit it. When one is acting, one occupies the practical standpoint. For acting, the Not-I possesses independent reality; one can alter and combine objects, but cannot produce them" (Fichte, *WLnmK, GA*, IV/3: 383; *FTP*, pp. 184-5).

691. *Trieb*. Fichte appears to have adopted this locution from Reinhold, who introduced the concept of a "drive" of the I, which could be directed either at the "form" or at the "content" of its representations. [*K*, p. 430.]

692. "'insofar as it is related to the practical power...' That something "is related to the practical power of the I" means that it is treated as a hindrance to that power" (Fichte, *WLnmK, GA*, I/3: 383; *FTP*, p. 185).

693. "'Consequently, one can also say...' This means: [an interaction] between the ideal and the real I" (Fichte, *WLnmK, GA*, I/3: 383; *FTP*, p. 185).

694. "'The entire mechanism of the human mind...' Our grasp of the thing in itself is like our grasp of infinite space: it becomes finite as soon as one wishes to grasp it. The thing in

itself, that is, what actually restricts us, is an Idea — namely, the Idea that I must forever posit myself as restricted" (Fichte, *WLnmK, GA*, IV/3: 383; *FTP*, p. 185).

695. *Transzendentismus.* This term was employed by Fichte's colleague and co-editor of the *Philosophisches Journal*, F. I. Niethammer in the first issue of the same journal to characterize those Kantians who returned to the "old dogmatism," either through "transcendentism" or "hypercriticism." Yet another of Fichte's colleagues, C. C. E. Schmid, in his *Bruchstücke aus einer Schrift über die Philosophie und ihre Principien* (1795) accused the *Wissenschaftslehre* itself of being a transcendent system, inasmuch as it allegedly goes beyond the boundaries of consciousness in positing the pure I or "subject in itself." [*K*, pp. 432–3.]

696. "The new series of things into which we are supposed to be introduced [by the *Wissenschaftslehre*] is the series constituted by the actions of the human mind [*Geist*] itself, and no longer the series constituted by the objects of these actions. These actions are supposed to be represented. But since no representation is possible without an image, images of these actions must also be present. But all images are produced by the absolute spontaneity of the power of imagination, and thus so too are these images. We are acquainted with some of these images — though by no means with the highest actions of the human mind — from Kant's writings, where they are called 'schemata,' whereas the way the power of imagination operates with such images is called by Kant 'schematism.' Transcendental philosophy in its totality ought to be nothing but an accurate schema of the human mind.

"Is there anyone who cannot see that this assigns an entirely new and unforeseen task to the power of imagination, a task it will find to be only slightly easier than it found the task of projecting images at the start of its earthly life? Is there anyone who cannot see that the feelings on which these images are based lie in a deeper region of the human mind, and that the ability to project such images is exactly what we have already described as 'spirit' [*Geist*]? Is there therefore anyone who cannot see that the material of philosophy presupposes spirit for its very possibility, and that all philosophizing that lacks spirit is completely empty and is about absolutely nothing?" (Fichte, *UGB, GA*, II/3: 328–9; *EPW*, pp. 203–4).

697. "It is important to note that what is supposed to be ascribed to the I in this case is neither the ability to posit nor the ability not to posit, but rather, the ability *to-posit-or-not-to-posit.* Consequently, the positing of a particular something must occur in the I at the same time as the non-positing of this same something, and these acts of positing and non-positing must be synthetically united. This must occur, and it certainly does occur in every case where something is posited as a contingent condition, no matter how much those whose knowledge of philosophy is limited to a scanty acquaintance with logic may complain about logical impossibility and incomprehensibility whenever they encounter a concept of this type. A concept of this sort is produced by the power of imagination and must be grasped by the power of imagination, without which there would be no logic nor any logical possibility at all" (Fichte, *GEWL, GA*, I/3: 160–1; below, pp. 395–6.

698. "In our system, one makes oneself into the ultimate basis [*Boden*] of one's philosophy, and that is why it must appear 'baseless" to anyone unable to do this. But we can assure such a person in advance that if he cannot procure this basis for himself and cannot be content with this, then he will be unable to discover such a basis anywhere else. It is necessary that our philosophy confess this quite loudly, so that it might thereby finally be relieved of the unreasonable demand that it demonstrate to human beings from outside something that they have to create within themselves" (Fichte, *SS, GA*, I/5: 43; *SW*, IV, 26; *SE*, pp. 31–2).

699. "*Philosophy,* or what is the same thing, *metaphysics,* arises when one proceeds beyond experience, beyond the circumference of facts, lifts oneself above experience as a whole

and connects it to something that by no means lies within the [realm of] facts or experience: namely, to what grounds experience.

"Facts, *facta*, experience as *such*: these do not pertain to philosophy, since what is grounded is not the ground. Philosophy, or the science of experience, is a *product* of the free power of thinking and is therefore something everyone must generate within oneself" (Fichte, *WLnmH*, *GA*, IV/2: 19; *EPW*, p. 90).

700. Kant defines "ontology" as a science that vainly seeks synthetic a priori cognition of things as such (*KrV*, B303). Fichte's characterization of metaphysics as a putative science of things in themselves is probably derived directly from Maimon's essay. *Über die Progressen der Philosophie* (Berlin: Wilhelm Vieweg, 1793), which was his contribution to prize essay contest concerning the progress of metaphysics since Leibniz. According to Maimon, "the Kantian will answer this question very briefly, as follows: since, according to the Critical philosophy, metaphysics as such (the science of things in themselves) is impossible, it has certainly made no progress" (*Progressen*, p. 3). [*K*, p. 436.]

701. "To begin with, a rational being is — with respect to both the matter and form of all possible cognitions — determined absolutely through itself and through nothing whatsoever outside itself. We here arrive once again — albeit in a more determinate fashion and, to be sure, as the result of a genetic deduction — at something we could otherwise have asserted simply on the basis of the principle of I-hood. Moreover, all the I's cognition is determined by its practical nature [*Wesen*] — as indeed it has to be, since this is what is highest in the I. The only firm and final foundation of all my cognition is my duty. This is the intelligible 'in itself,' which transforms itself by means of the laws of sensible representation into a sensible world" (Fichte, *SS*, *GA*, I/5: 160; *SW*, IV, 173; *SE*, pp. 163–4).

702. Fichte appears to identify "resistance" and "striving in opposition," even though the former would appear to be more passive than the latter. This may perhaps be explained by his conception of natural bodies as analogous to "elastic balls," which respond to external impact by exerting an "opposing-force" of their own, in order to re-establish their spherical shape. [*K*, p. 438.] But note the passage from *WLnm* in which Fichte retracts this characterization of the Not-I and concedes that it is wrong to think of it as striving in opposition to the striving of the I. Instead, he proposes that the Not-I should be viewed merely as a "dam" or "hindrance" to the striving of the I (Fichte, *WLnmK*, *GA*, I/3: 384; *FTP*, p. 185).

703. This claim should not be interpreted *statically*, that is, as if the I's striving could make no progress against the opposed striving of the Not-I. Instead, the "equilibrium" or "counterbalance" in question is constantly being re-established as the I progresses toward its infinitely unobtainable goal. The I does not possess causality in the sense that it can annihilate the Not-I, but it does possess causality in the sense that it can always further determine or "modify" it. [*K*, p. 438.]

704. Recall that the I is to be understood as a *quantifiable* reality. It originally posits itself (§ 1) as possessing unlimited reality, which it is then forced (see § 3) to distribute between the finite I and the Not-I. In order to *reflect* upon itself and determine whether it possesses all reality, the I must be limited, must be a determinate quantity, a "something" (§ 4). At the same time, it continues to posit itself purely and simply as an infinite quantum, filling all reality. [*K*, pp. 438–9.]

705. "'nos. 1–3. The I's striving…' When one considers the I by itself, all one discovers within it is the ground of activity, but no limitation. Considered purely in this manner, the I would become an activity; but no striving would be engendered thereby, for striving is possible only on the assumption of something that limits the activity of the I. Consequently, striving cannot be explained merely through reference to the I" (Fichte, *WLnmK*, *GA*, IV/3: 383; *FTP*, p. 185).

706. Another term adopted from contemporary mechanics. See, for example, J.P. Eberhard's discussion of the "point of contact" between two spheres (*Erste Grunde der Naturlehre* [1753], § 124). This is very likely what Fichte is thinking about in this passage as well. See *GA*, I/2: 422; above, p. 351, where the I and Not-I are described as two "spheres" or "elastic balls" related to — i.e., in contact with — one another. [*K*, pp. 439–40.]

707. "'no. 4.' The Not-I does not approach the I, but vice versa. Therefore, we do not need to assume anything more than the 'being' of the Not-I. Were we to talk about the opposed striving of the Not-I, then we would have to ascribe to the Not-I an inner force or disposition. [...] Consequently, the Not-I should here be represented only as something that merely 'is' [*ein bloßes Seiendes*], and the opposed striving of the Not-I disappears. The I is originally active and manifests its activity as widely as it can. If this activity is arrested at even a single point, this engenders a striving. The Not-I is, in this case, a hindrance, a dam: not a striving in opposition, but something standing in the way" (Fichte, *WLnmK*, *GA*, I/3: 384; *FTP*, p. 185).

708. "'no. 5. Consequently, these two forces must counterbalance each other.' The I can advance only as far as the Not-I permits it to go. Later on we shall see how the I is also able to penetrate the Not-I" (Fichte, *WLnmK*, *GA*, IV/3: 384; *FTP*, p. 185).

709. "According to the laws of reflection, nothing can be reflected upon without being limited — even if it is limited merely and solely by the very act of reflection. Consequently, just as surely as it is itself an object of reflection, this act of reflecting is something limited" (Fichte, *GEWL*, *GA*, I/3: 175; below, p. 408).

710. "'§ 7, no. 1.' What is called 'something' in the book [*GWL*] is in the present exposition [*WLnm*] called 'that which hinders,' i.e., something in a state of being passively affected, to which the ideal activity is related" (Fichte, *WLnmK*, *GA*, IV/3: 384; *FTP*, p. 186).

   "'Something'" means that which is capable of being the object of an ideal activity or intuition — something that constrains the ideal activity and brings it to a halt" (Fichte, *WLnmH*, *GA*, IV/2: 68; *FTP*, p. 186).

711. "The interrupting action [of reflection] is, consequently, directed at this object, and, precisely because this action is directed at the object and because it interrupts the first action, it thereby makes this object into *something* — that is, it makes it into something established and fixed" (Fichte, *GEWL*, *GA*, I/3: 180; below, p. 413).

712. "Activity of this sort is suppressed activity, and in this way it obtains the character of 'being.' Something of this sort, however is a drive, a self-produced striving, which has its foundation within that to which it belongs (see pp. 286–7 of the compendium [*GA*, I/2: 417; above, p. 347]). A drive is an activity that is not any type of activity; it is something that arrests, something that determines the ideal activity, a constant inner disposition to overcome whatever resists (similar to the compression of a steel spring)" (Fichte, *WLnmK*, *GA*, IV/3: 376; *FTP*, pp. 172–3).

   "A drive is a self-produced striving — a continuous tendency toward activity — not an acting, only something that determines the *ideal* activity — only an inner activity, which continually determines itself — not an external, but a suppressed activity, which would become an activity just as soon as the resistance were to recede. *Drive* and *limitation* are one and the same" (Fichte, *WLnmH*, *GA*, IV/2: 60-1; *FTP*, p. 173).

713. See *GA*, I/2: 400 and 410; above, pp. 332 and 341.

714. See *GA*, I/2: 408 and 410; above, pp. 339 and 441.

715. In other words, the I is limited because and insofar as its drive is limited; and its drive is limited because, in order for the I to posit for itself its own infinite striving, it had to posit it as a determinate — that is, as a limited — drive.

716. The I "limits itself" in this case by reflecting upon — i.e., positing — its infinite, real striving as a limited drive and then explicitly positing this limit as its own.

717. "Even at the beginning of all its activity, the I originally reflected upon itself. It did so of necessity, as we have already seen. — The I possessed within itself a general tendency to reflect. Because of the limitation [if the I], the condition for the possibility of reflecting was added as well, following which the I necessarily engaged in reflection. From this there arose a feeling, and from this feeling there arose everything else we have derived" (Fichte, *GEWL*; *GA*, I/3: 172; below, p. 406).

"An original striving is present. This is limited. When I reflect upon this limitation, there arises a *feeling*. But I cannot posit anything *that is limited* (in this case, the I), without [also] positing something that limits it. — I do this only in consequence of a feeling" (Fichte, *VLM*, *GA*, II/4: 61n.).

"The finite rational being possesses the drive and the power to reflect upon itself, but to this extent it is subsumed under the law of its finitude: that is to say, it is able to reflect only upon what is limited and finite. — The first, immediate object of reflection is the I itself, as limited by its own organization. If it reflects upon *a portion* of this state of limitation, *there arises a feeling*. The manner and sum of the I's feelings are determined by its organization. (Our organization is therefore valid only for human beings.)" (Fichte, *VLM*, *GA*, II/4: 85).

"Striving is a striving to posit all reality, a real drive to creation. This is completely suppressed, as such, which means that all reality is now repressed along with it. There is a system of the suppression of this striving, and hence an entire system of what can be felt. Everything, the entire world, is present all at once. If there is an I, then there is a power of reflection, which is succeeded by a material feeling" (Fichte, *VLM*, *GA*, II/4: 56–7).

718. "The *limitation of the drive* precedes everything. From this there ensues a *feeling*" (Fichte, *VLM*, *GA*, II/4: 57).

719. "Feeling is the most primordial interaction of the I with itself, and even precedes the Not-I, since a Not-I must, of course, be posited in order to explain feeling" (Fichte, *GEWL*, *GA*, I/3: 174; below, p. 408).

720. "Recommended for re-reading. Everything that is present in the I and occurs by means of the I can be interpreted as a drive. The ideal activity is a drive for content [*Sachtrieb*], because ideal activity is nothing without objects" (Fichte, *WLnmK*, *GA*, I/3: 384; *FTP*, p. 186).

721. This possibility is explained in § 11, below.

722. This is an allusion to one of Maimon's objections to Kant: namely, that the Kantian account of objectivity is or may be no more than a "deception." Fichte's point is that the deception in question is Maimon's: namely, the deceptive thought that there might be some *other* kind of objectivity. [*K*, p. 446.]

723. This is precisely the "assumption" made by ordinary consciousness, an assumption which it is the task of the *Wissenschaftslehre* to explain. [*K*, pp. 446–7.]

724. "This alteration in the way things appear will become clearer if we raise ourselves to the transcendental standpoint. The world is nothing other than our own inner action (qua pure intellect), made visible to the senses in accordance with comprehensible laws of reason and limited by incomprehensible boundaries, within which we simply find ourselves to be confined" (Fichte, *UGG*, *GA*, I/5: 353; *SW*, V, 184; *IWL*, p. 149).

725. Part Two was previously described as "completing a circuit," in the sense that it concluded with a derivation — for the I itself — of the very principle with which it began ("The I posits itself as limited by the Not-I"). Here in Part Three there is a similar "circuit." § 5 establishes a *factum* consisting in the synthesis of the intelligent I and the absolute I by the "practical I," just as Part Two established the *factum* of the synthesis of the I and the Not-I by the power of imagination. This newly discovered *factum* is subsequently "raised to consciousness" in §§ 6–12 of Part Three — just as the *factum* of the imagination's synthetic

unification of the I and the Not-I was raised to consciousness in the "Deduction of Representation" at the end of Part Two. This "raising to consciousness" is accomplished in five steps, beginning with the derivation of material mechanism (§ 6), and continuing with the derivation of drive itself (§§ 7–8), the drive to representation (§ 8), longing (§ 10), and finally "absolute drive" (§ 11) — at which point the I explicitly posits itself as determining the Not-I. [*K*, pp. 447–8].

726. "Feeling" has already been nominally defined as "the manifestation within the I of an inability" (see *GA*, I/2: 419; above, p. 349), but now it needs to be "deduced," that is, derived genetically as a product of the I's activity. [*K*, p. 448.]

727. See *GA*, I/2: 408; above, p. 339.

728. "§ 8, no. 2 should also be re-read" (Fichte, *WLnmH*, 69; *FTP*, p. 186).

729. "Feeling is grounded in the satisfaction or non-satisfaction of a drive, in part, by means of the original organization (the thing) and, in part, by means of representations as well— representations that are involuntarily related to the drive, or else are related to the *concept* of the drive, as means to its end. This is because agreement or non-agreement with a drive — and not the mere representation of the same — is what produces feeling. There is no such thing as a feeling produced by relating a mere representation to a drive, for if this were the case then one would have to be capable of voluntarily and immediately awakening feelings, which is something one cannot do" (Fichte, *VLM*, *GA*, II/4: 58).

730. The I is satisfied with respect to the *form* of this action, in the sense that it is the *limitation* of this action that makes possible an act of self-reference or reflection on the part of the I. It now becomes possible for the first time for the I actually to distinguish something (the Not-I) from itself. [*K*, p. 449.]

731. "A *representation* is by no means related to the drive; on the contrary, the *limitation of the drive* precedes everything else. From this there arises a *feeling*" (Fichte, *VLM*, *GA*, II/4: 57).

732. "When the drive is not satisfied there arises an obscure *desiring*, a *longing*, which does not arise from a *representation* but rather from a feeling, on account of the natural striving [of the I], which is the foundation of all the operations of the soul" (Fichte, *VLM*, *GA*, II/4: 57).

733. This is because the I can be *dissatisfied* with the finitude of feeling if and only if its activity also proceeds beyond the point of the check. We will see below that this is possible only insofar as the I posits not only a *real* object of intuition but an *ideal* object of its striving.

734. The elastic ball "strives" to expand to its full dimensions but is prevented from doing so by the contiguous presence of (and hence the "check" provided by) the other ball.

735. Though the "lifeless body" or "elastic ball" possesses an inner force directed only at itself, it can only exercise this force and restore its original shape by impacting an external body that has restricted its internal force. [*K*, p. 452.]

736. This constitutes a "genetic deduction" of the previously mentioned drive of the I to reflect upon itself in order to determine if it actually "fills infinity." The "drive to representation" will turn out to be simply a manifestation of the I's original drive to engage in reflection. [*K*, pp. 452–3.]

737. See *GA*, I/2: 408; above, pp. 339–40.

738. The claim that there can be no drive without a limitation is "transcendent," inasmuch as it ignores the fact that both the drive and the limitation must be posited in reflection. Hence the claim that there can be no reflection without a drive can be called the "transition" to the transcendental standpoint expressed in the final claim: no drive without reflection. [*K*, p. 453.]

739. "I ascribe to myself the power to originate a concept purely and simply because I originate it, the power to originate *this* concept just because I do so on the basis of my absolute

sovereignty as an intellect. I also ascribe to myself the power to exhibit this concept through a real act outside the concept. In addition, I ascribe to myself a real, efficacious force capable of producing a being, which is something quite different from the mere power of concepts. The concepts in questions, which are called purposes, are not concepts of cognition, which are *after*-copies [*Nach*bilder] of something given; instead, these concepts are supposed to be models or *advance*-images [*Vor*bilder] of something that is yet to be produced. The real force is supposed to lie outside of these advance images and to exist, as such, for itself. It is only supposed to receive its determination from such images, which are supposed to be observed by cognition" (Fichte, *BM*, *GA*, I/6: 255; *SW*, II, 250; *VM*, p. 69).

740. See *GA*, I/2: 438; below, p. 366.
741. "The I is unlimited and absolutely unlimitable insofar as its activity depends only upon itself and is grounded solely within itself, and thus only insofar as it is *ideal* (to employ the expression that we have constantly employed). Such a purely ideal activity of this sort is posited, and it is posited as going beyond the limitation. [...] The limited activity is posited in opposition to the unlimited, ideal activity. Hence, to the extent that the former activity is supposed to be limited, this [second] limited activity is not ideal and is not dependent upon the I; instead, it is dependent upon the Not-I, which is posited in opposition to the I, and we wish to call such a [limited] activity one that is directed at *what is actual*.

"It is clear that the activity of the I (considered simply as an action in its own right and quite apart from whether it is curbed or not) would thereby be considered to be posited in opposition to itself; that is, it would be viewed as directed either at what is ideal or at what is real. The activity of the I which proceeds beyond that boundary (which we will call C) is a purely ideal activity and in no way real, whereas the real activity does not proceed beyond this boundary at all. The activity that lies inside the limitation, i.e., between A [the starting point of activity] and C, is both ideal and real. It is ideal insofar as it is posited (by virtue of the previous positing) as having its ground solely within the I, and it is real insofar as it is posited as limited.

"It is furthermore clear that this entire distinction originates from the act of positing in opposition: if no real activity were posited, then no ideal activity would be posited as ideal, for there would be no way of distinguishing it. If no ideal activity were posited, then no real activity could be posited either. Ideal activity and real activity reciprocally determine each other. Thus, here again (and, thanks to this application, the point is somewhat clearer) we have the proposition: ideality and reality are synthetically united. If nothing is ideal, then nothing is real, and vice versa" (Fichte, *GEWL*, *GA*, I/3: 157–8; below, pp. 393–4).

742. See *GA*, I/2: 435; below, p. 362.
743. "Are my drive as a natural being and my tendency as a pure spirit two different drives? No, from the transcendental point of view these are one and the same original drive [*Urtrieb*], which constitutes my being, simply viewed from two different sides. That is to say, I am a subject-object and my true being consists in the indivisibility of the two. If I view myself as an *object* completely determined by the laws of sensible intuition and discursive thinking, then what is in fact my one and only drive becomes for me my natural drive, because on this view I myself am nature. If I view myself as a *subject*, then this same single drive becomes for me a pure, spiritual drive, that is, it becomes the law of self-sufficiency. All phenomena of the I rest solely upon the reciprocal interaction of these two drives, which is, properly speaking, only the reciprocal interaction of *one and the same drive with itself.* [...] The two drives are in fact one, but I-hood in its entirety rests on the fact that they appear to be different. The boundary separating them is reflection" (Fichte, *SS*, *GA*, I/5: 125–6; *SW*, IV, 130–1; *SE*, pp. 124–5).

744. The "practical law" in question is the law demanding that the I fill infinity, i.e., that the I ought to be utterly independent or self-sufficient and that everything else should depend upon it. See *GA*, I/2: 286; above, p. 329.

745. Fichte associated philosophical fatalism with dogmatic realism in general and, in particular, with the kind of "Turkish fatalism" defended by Karl Ferdinand Hommel in his *Alexander von Joch beyder Rechte Doctor über Belohnung und Strafe nach Türkischen Gesezen* (1790). Fichte refers to Hommel in the second edition of *VKO*, *GA*, I/1: 139; *SW*, V, 22; *ACR*, p. 14, and in *WLnmK*, *GA*, IV/3: 337; *FTP*, p. 98, as well as in the "First Introduction" to *VWL*, where he writes: "Suppose that someone, such as Alexander von Joch, were to say the following: 'All things are determined by natural necessary; our representations depend upon the properties of things, and our will depends upon our representations. Consequently, our entire will is determined by natural necessity, and our opinion that we possess free will is only a deception'" (Fichte, *VWL*, *GA*, I.4: 199; *SW*, I, 439–40; *IWL*, p. 25).

746. "Insofar as the I is engaged in reflecting, it does not reflect upon this very act of reflecting. It cannot simultaneously act upon an object and upon its own acting. It is, therefore, not conscious of the activity in question; instead, it forgets itself entirely and loses itself in the object of this activity" (Fichte, *GEWL*, *GA*, I/3: 171; below, p. 405). "The I is never immediately conscious of its own acting" (Fichte, *GEWL*, *GA*, I/3: 175; below, p. 408).

747. "The positing of myself as engaged in intuition is a feeling of myself. Obviously, nothing more is present within this feeling of myself other than a feeling. I feel myself, and I feel myself to be limited. I feel myself, and to the extent that I am engaged in feeling, I am not engaged in intuiting or thinking. In this case, I am present for myself only in and by means of feeling" (Fichte, *WLnmK*, *GA*, IV/3: 388; *FTP*, p. 193).

748. See *GA*, I/2: 431; below, pp. 358–9.

749. I.e., the "driving force" mentioned in the preceding paragraph.

750. It has already been established that the ideal activity manifests itself as the drive to representation, through which the I becomes an intellect. Now, however, it becomes clear that the drive to representation is not confined to producing representations of objects on the basis of the check (as explained in the "Deduction of Representation" at the end of Part Two) but also engages in the production of *ideal* representations, representations of objects or states of affairs that *ought to be produced in reality*: concepts of goals or purposes of the I's actions. See *GA*, I/2: 396, 403, and 409; above, pp. 329, 335, and 340. [*K*, p. 462.]

751. See § 10, *GA*, I/2: 433 ff.below, p. 360ff.

752. Since the feeling of force has not manifested itself as such, what is felt by the I is simply a *feeling of compulsion*. [*K*, p. 463.]

753. As explained above, *GA*, I/2: 313; above, p. 251, "The character of the I, however, which can by no means be ascribed to the Not-I, is that of *positing purely and simply and without any ground* (§ 1)."

754. This reference to the I's "free and unlimited positing" should not be understood to imply that the I is no longer finite, since that would, of course, eliminate the possibility of reflection altogether. What Fichte appears to have in mind here is that the I should become capable of making its own limitation into an object of consciousness, that is to say, of *positing* its limitations as such and *in this sense* "limiting itself." [*K*, p. 463.]

755. See *GA*, I/2: 400; above, p. 332.

756. See *GA*, I/2: 441; above, p. 369.

757. "The dogmatists were supposed to establish the transition from being to representing. They have not done this, nor can they, for their principle contains within itself only the ground of a being. It does not contain within itself the ground of what is posited in direct

opposition to being: namely, representing. They make an enormous leap into a world completely alien to their principle" (Fichte, *VWL*, *GA*, I/4: 197; *SW*, I, 437; *IWL*, p. 22).

758. The "ideal activity" of the I is the activity that "reverts into" or is directed back upon itself, the activity of *reflecting*—an activity first made possible by the check upon the original striving of the I. See *GA*, I/2: 423–4; above, p. 352.

759. The spontaneous action in question is directed "at a feeling"; that is to say, it is directed at the reflecting action of the I, which is made possible by the presence of a feeling (on the occasion of a check upon the I's original striving). This spontaneous action is what explicitly posits the "feeling subject" as an I. It is this same spontaneous action that, "in its present function," is engaged in reflecting upon the subject that is engaged in (or is "reflecting upon") feeling. Though I-hood is implicit in this new, spontaneous action, this action itself occurs unconsciously, and the I-hood in question is therefore "transferred" to the feeling subject. [*K*, p. 465.]

760. See the reference to the "feeling of force," *GA*, I/2: 425; above, p. 353.

761. See *GA*, I/2: 445; below, p. 373.

762. In the preceding reflection, the feeling subject lacked self-consciousness, but now it has become united with the subject that reflects upon this feeling subject and hence has become an I. [*K*, p. 465.]

763. The "object of the feeling subject" is in this case the I that is engaged in feeling, in consequence of its drive to reflect upon itself and of the outwardly directed drive.

764. The "contradiction" in question is contained in the notion of being "*compelled* to *act*" [*handelt es gezwungen*], which, for Fichte, is a contradiction in terms. [*K*, p. 466.]

765. See *GA*, I/2: 432; below, p. 360.

766. The reality of the I is conveyed to the I through its feeling of its own force, and the reality of the Not-It is conveyed to the I through its feeling of compulsion. [*K*, pp. 466–7.]

767. "From the standpoint of philosophical argumentation, we cannot say 'there *is* a world.' That which is outside of me is something I can only feel, and in this respect only *believe*. That there are things outside of me is therefore an article of faith. And how does one propose to transform what can merely be believed into something that can be proven, a demonstrable proposition of reason? [...] That there are things outside us is not something we *cognize*; the existence of these things is given to us only *by means of feeling* and in feeling and is therefore purely an object of *belief*" (Fichte, *VSUS*, *GA*, I/3: 112–13n.; *SW*, VIII, 321–2n.).

768. "Drive" was nominally defined as follows: "a self-productive striving that is fixed and determinate and is therefore something definite is called *a drive*" (*GA*, I/2: 418; above, p. 347). What follows is a *genetic* definition of drive, that is, a derivation of drive from striving and limitation.

769. I.e., the original drive aspires to *real* activity. [*K*, p. 468.]

770. This is not meant to imply that the I was previously aware that it was engaging in reflection and then, for some reason, "forgot" this. Instead, Fichte's claim is that the I is simply unable to engage in reflection while at the same time consciously reflecting upon its first act of reflection. In this instance, therefore, to say that the I "forgets itself" means simply that it is not explicitly conscious of the activity of reflecting in which it is engaged. [*K*, p. 469.]

771. See *GA*, I/2: 426; above, p. 347.

772. The I wills a *different reality* (which is what it wishes to "realize" or "make real"), but it is unable to make this a reality, nor can it even form a representation of the reality at which it aims, since every representation refers to a *definite object*. Hence, all that can arise in this case is an utterly indefinite *feeling* of *longing* for something quite unknown. It is

important to recognize that the "longing" in question here is not a longing for any specific object or state of affairs, but for something thoroughly indeterminate—a longing for "something, I know not what." [*K*, pp. 469–70.]

773. "The lower power of desire starts from a drive that is really nothing more than the formative drive of our nature. This drive is directed at the self-sufficient being, in that it requires the latter to unite this [formative] drive with itself synthetically—that is, to posit *itself* as driven. It also manifests itself through longing. Where does this longing lie? It lies not in nature, but in the subject's consciousness, for reflection has now occurred. Longing is directed only at what lies within the natural drive; it aims at a material relationship between my body and the external world" (Fichte, *SS, GA*, I/5: 136; *SW*, IV, 144; *SE*, pp. 137).

774. "When a drive is not satisfied, there arises an obscure *desiring* [*Begehren*], a *longing* [*Sehnen*], which does not arise from a representation but from a feeling. It arises on account of the [I's] natural striving, which is the foundation of all the operations of the soul" (Fichte, *VLM, GA*, II/4: 57).

775. The I spontaneously and necessarily defends itself against any limitation, simply because it is an I. This is because of its original drive to be or to "fill" all reality. Acting in response to a stimulus is the opposite of acting spontaneously. Reason acts in both ways, hence it is both "freedom" and "nature." See below, § 11. [*K*, p. 469.]

776. A feeling (such as longing) can be "determined" or "specified" only by contrasting it with another feeling, in accordance with the principle or law that all determination proceeds by means of negation. In this case, we have two different feelings, the feeling of longing and the feeling of limitation.

777. Actual limitation is therefore the *real ground* of the I's continued state of longing, whereas longing is the *ideal ground* of the I's feeling of limitation. [*K*, p. 472.]

778. That is to say, how can the drive produce in the I such opposed feelings as those of longing and compulsion, which would seem to require that the I be simultaneously active and passive?

779. *an welche er sich richtet.* This depends upon which of the I's two powers or forces—reflection or striving—is *determined* by the drive. [*K*, p. 474.]

780. This is the power of *understanding* (see *GA*, I/2: 374; above, p. 310). The understanding apprehends and grasps the Not-I as something existing in itself and is unaware of the I's role in the production of the Not-I. Consequently, the I feels itself to be constrained by the Not-I. [*K*, p. 474.]

781. "Expressed however one may wish, this weariness with what is transitory, this longing for something higher, better, and unchanging, lies indelibly in the mind of human beings" (Fichte, *AP, GA*, I/5: 474; *SW*, V, 203; *FAD*, p. 100).

782. It is only in *SS* that this "becomes evident," not in *GWL*.

783. I.e., whether determined as a feeling of longing or as a feeling of compulsion (see preceding paragraph).

784. The productive power of the I is its "productive" or "creative" *power of imagination*.

785. See *GA*, I/2: 428; above, p. 356, point 1: the causal effort of the I's "original drive" is always directed "outward," until it is "checked" and thereby restricted. [*K*, p. 477.]

786. Here one must be careful, since, as Fichte frequently notes, the I cannot actually "limit itself." Instead, it can only *discover* itself to be limited (by means of a feeling of compulsion). However, it then spontaneously *posits this same limitation for itself* by means of its finite ideal activity or power of representation. In *this* sense—but *only* in this sense—the I can be said to "limit itself."

787. See *GA*, I/2: 424; above, p. 353.

788. "Both the limited and the limiting I, synthetically united by absolute spontaneity, are posited—and posited as the same I. This is what we have now derived, and from this there

arises, for the I, a feeling, a feeling of itself, in which the I's activity and state of being passively affected are internally united in a single state" (Fichte, *GEWL*, *GA*, I/3: 175; below, p. 408).

789. The question, "what is produced by means of this activity?" will be answered in this paragraph. What is produced is an "ideal" object or goal of the I's acting. But it will require the rest of §10 in order to explain "how" such an ideal is produced by and for the I.

790. There is an object for the I only insofar as it is spontaneously posited as such by the "ideal" or "theoretical" activity of the I, as described in Part Two. This is the sense in which the I can be said to "produce" the objects of experience; but it can do so only upon the occasion of something for which it is not at all responsible and does *not* produce: namely, the check that hinders its original activity and sets in motion both the finite (theoretical) ideal activity of representing and infinite (practical) ideal activity of longing.

791. In fact, no such assertion occurs in Part Two; though, it is certainly implicit in Fichte's critique of "transcendent idealism" in Part Two. [*K*, p. 478.]

792. I.e., the task of explaining *how* the ideal is produced as the object of the feeling of longing.

793. This provides us with a new, more complex understanding of the first foundational principle (§1), one that incorporates the third foundational principle (§3); for we now see that the self-positing of the I must involve its self-determining (and hence its limitation). The first and second foundational principles would therefore be modified to assert that the I is unable to determine itself without simultaneously determining the Not-I. Collectively, the three foundational principles thus constitute an analysis of what is involved in and presupposed by any act of self-determination. [*K*, pp. 478–9.]

794. I.e., the equilibrium or counterbalance between the striving of the I and the striving of the Not-I. See above, § 6.

795. "Now if the causal efficacy of the I is exercised on one and the same object, and if it is therefore regarded at each present moment as conditioned by the preceding moment and, indirectly, by the causal efficacy exercised in all preceding moments: if this is the case, then the state of the object at each moment is likewise regarded as conditioned by all preceding moments, from the first cognition of the object onwards. The object therefore remains the same object, even though it is endlessly altered; that is to say, the substratum brought forth by the imagination in order to connect the manifold in this same object remains the same. This substratum is called 'bare matter' and underlies the accidents, which ceaselessly exclude one another. This is why we can posit ourselves only as altering the form of things, but never the matter, and why we are conscious of our capacity to alter the forms of things ad infinitum but of our incapacity to create or to annihilate those things. It is also why, for us, matter can be neither increased nor diminished and why, from the standpoint of ordinary consciousness (but certainly not from that of transcendental philosophy), matter is originally given to us" (Fichte, *GNR*, *GA*, I/3: 339–40; *SW*, III, 29; *FNR*, pp. 28–9).

796. Answer: the feeling in question would be a feeling of limitation, but of limitation not by the sheer *existence* of matter, but by the particular *constitution* of the same. See *GA*, I/2: 436 and 441; below, pp. 363 and 370. [*K*, p. 482.]

797. I.e., determined as the ground of the limitation of the I's activity. [*K*, p. 482.]

798. The answer to the first question is provided in the immediately following paragraph; the answer to the second is provided in the final paragraph of no. 19, below.

799. See *GA*, I/2: 432; above, p. 360.

800. Of course, Fichte has already observed that what is at the same time determined and determining can *only* be the I. Consequently, the attribution of self-determination to the object will prove to be only provisional, and we will come to see that the self-determination in question was actually *transferred* to the object from the I. See below, no. 20. [*K*, p. 482.]

801. The answer, of course, is that it cannot exercise such causality, and we can assert this "on purely a priori grounds," insofar as the I is supposed to be an I. This is because, in order *to posit itself* as an I (and thus in order *to be* an I), the I must always be *limited*, and hence its drive toward determination must be unable to exercise causality. [*K*, p. 483.]

802. See *GA*, I/2: 404 and 416–18; above, pp. 336 and 346–7.

803. This is how things must appear from the *realistic* standpoint of ordinary consciousness, which remains unaware of the role of the I in the production of this object. [*K*, p. 483.]

804. In other words, our question concerning how the *action* of determining could relate itself to the feeling is answered as follows: this is possible only through the *limitation* of that same action of determining. [*K*, p. 485.]

805. See *GA*, I/2: 427; above, p. 352.

806. I.e., the "drive to representation." See *GA*, I/2: 424; above, p. 353.

807. *bilden*. Though Fichte tends to employ this term primarily in the sense of "forming" or "giving shape to," he here seems to be using it in the more restricted sense of "forming images," and thus as a synonym for *abbilden* ("to copy"). [*K*, p. 485.]

808. "The I originally seeks to determine the constitution or attributes of things entirely on its own. It purely and simply demands causality. This demand is resisted when it is directed at reality (and can thus be called real activity), and, as a result of this resistance, another tendency that is originally grounded in the I is satisfied: namely, the tendency of the I to reflect upon itself. From this there arises a reflection upon a determinate, given reality. Insofar as this reality is already determined, it can only be grasped by the ideal activity of the I, that is, by the activity of representing or copying" (Fichte, *GEWL*, *GA*, I/3: 174; below, p. 408).

809. Interpreting this assertion in the light of the preceding one, this means that the "criterion" in question actually lies — for the I — in the Not-I. [*K*, p. 486.]

810. Now, however, the I posits the Not-I (the object) as also "simultaneously determined and engaged in determining."

811. This claim first becomes clear in point 12, below.

812. "The intuiting power oscillates between various specific determinations and posits only one from among all those that are possible, and in this way the product obtains the distinctive character of an *image*. [...] Insofar as the I posits this image as a product of its activity, it necessarily posits in opposition to it something that is not a product of this activity; that is, it posits in opposition to it something that is no longer determinable but is instead completely determined and is determined only by itself, without any contribution from the I. This is the *actual thing*, to which the I that is engaged in forming an image directs its attention as it drafts its image, and which must necessarily hover before it as it engages in the act of image formation. This actual thing is the product of the I's first action (the action that has now been interrupted), but it is impossible to posit it as such in this relationship.

     "The I copies the actual thing. This thing must, therefore, be contained in the I and accessible to its activity; that is, it must be possible to indicate some ground of the relationship between the thing and the image of the thing (which are posited in opposition to each other). The ground of the relationship in question in this case is a completely determined yet unconscious intuition of the thing" (Fichte, *GEWL*, *GA*, I/3: 179–80; below, pp. 411–2).

813. I.e., only insofar as it is simultaneously determined and engaged in determining.

814. "As affections of myself, sensations are purely and simply nothing extended, but are something simple. Different sensations are not *next* to each other in space, but follow *after* each other in time. But I nevertheless extend them throughout a space. How would it be if, just by means of this extension and immediately along with it, that which is actually nothing but a sensation were to be transformed for me into *something sensible*, and if

consciousness of an object outside me were to originate from just this point?" [Fichte, *BM*, *GA*, I/6: 225; *SW*, 211–12; *VM*, p. 37.]

815. This is just a more specific way of designating what was referred to above as "the law of determination."

816. In order for the drive to be satisfied, there must be not two self-determining substances (I and Not-I), interacting with each other as cause and effect, but only one. So long as a second substance, the Not-I, is conceived of as existing alongside the I, then the I itself must be conceived of as either determined or engaged in determining (but not as both). Hence, as Fichte argues, the reciprocal interaction between the I and the Not-I must be re-conceived as a reciprocal interaction of the I with itself. Were this actually to be the case, however, the I's original drive to determination would indeed be satisfied, but an essential condition for the very possibility of consciousness (opposition from the Not-I) would be eliminated. Hence the activity of the drive in question is always dependent upon its *not* being satisfied. Though the I originally aims at the elimination of the Not-I (or of matter), when it reflects upon the conditions for the very possibility of its existence as an I, it comes to realize that this is impossible: hence the endless striving of the I to *modify* the Not-I. [*K*, p. 489.]

817. I.e., does not exercise causality.

818. *als intensiver Stoff.* "Intensive" is here equivalent to "inner." Matter is a force that does not manifest itself, but operates only *negatively*, by *resisting* the determining activity of the I. This constitutes that "trace" of the opposing directions of activity mentioned near the end of Part Two (see *GA*, I/2: 373 and 376; above, pp. 309 and 313). [*K*, p. 490.]

"If, however (as was already mentioned in the *Foundation of the Entire Wissenschaftslehre*), this conflict [between opposed directions of the I's activity] should ever be posited within the I, and if anything further were to follow from it, then the mere *positing* of this conflict as such would mean that the oscillation of the power of imagination between two directions of activity posited in opposition to each other would have to cease. Yet traces of this former oscillation would have to remain as a *something*, a possible *matter* [*Stoff*]. We can already see how this could occur, even though we do not yet see the power through which it would occur. — What the I has to do is posit this *conflict* of directions posited in opposition to each other, or (which here amounts to the same thing) the conflict of opposing forces. It must not posit either one of them alone, but must posit them both and must posit them *in conflict* — that is to say, in opposed but perfectly counterbalanced activity. But perfectly counterbalanced opposing activities cancel each other out and nothing remains. Nevertheless, something is supposed to remain and to be posited. What remains, therefore, is *a static matter* [*ein ruhender Stoff*] — something that *possesses force*, but which, on account of the conflict in question, cannot express this force in activity, a *substrate* of force" (Fichte, *GEWL*, *GA*, I/3: 147–8; below, p. 385).

"This *matter* is neither my activity nor that of the thing. Instead, it is both. Only insofar as it is *mine* does it become an object of my consciousness" (Fichte's unpublished commentary on *GEWL*, *GA*, II/4: 361).

819. Intensive matter is transformed (by the productive power of imagination) into extensive matter. [*K*, p. 491.]

820. Recall that the I cannot posit itself at all unless it posits itself "as something determinate."

821. In this way, Fichte has managed to provide a "genetic derivation" of the law in question. Positing in opposition has now been derived from the drive; and, in turn, the drive has been derived from positing in opposition. Previously, however, this was accomplished *analytically*, by analyzing the concepts in question. Now, however, it has been accomplished *synthetically* or *genetically*, by deriving the concept of drive from the concrete opposition between opposing forces. [*K*, p. 492.]

"In the present version [*WLnm*], we begin with the immediate object of consciousness, that is, with freedom, and then proceed to display the conditions for the same. Free action is what is most essential to our inquiry. The primary aim of the previous version [*GWL*] was to provide an explanation of representations and the intellect; consequently, free action, striving, and drive were there employed merely as the basis for such an explanation. In the present version, what is practical is the immediate object, and what is theoretical is derived therefrom. Furthermore, the procedure of the present inquiry is predominantly synthetic, whereas that of the former was more analytic.

"What is ideal and what is real accompany each other and remain forever separate. In the book [*GWL*], the ideal is specified first, and the real is then derived therefrom. Here, on the other hand, we begin with what is practical, which is treated in isolation so long as it remains separate from and unrelated to what is theoretical. But as soon as the two come together, they are dealt with in conjunction with each other. Accordingly, the book's division into theoretical and practical parts is here dispensed with entirely. Both versions begin with a reciprocal determination of the I and the Not-I" (Fichte, *WLnmK*, GA, IV/3: 380–1; *FTP*, p. 182). As the conclusion of this passage from *WLnm* makes it unmistakably clear, the real "staring point" of *GWL* is not § 1, but § 3 — or, if one prefers, Part One as a whole.

822. It follows that we are now — finally — in a position to *explain* that act of "positing in opposition" which was first first introduced in § 2. Hence, appearances to the contrary notwithstanding, the three foundational principles introduced in Part One do not describe three distinct acts of positing that occur *prior* to the other acts of the I; instead, they are modes of acting that must operate continuously at every moment of actual, empirical consciousness. [*K*, p. 491.]

823. See below, no. 25.

824. "The determinate character of my limitation manifests itself as a limitation of my practical power (this is the point where philosophy is driven from the theoretical to the practical realm). This determinate limitation is immediately perceived as a *feeling*: sweet, red, cold, etc. (I prefer the name 'feeling' to Kant's 'sensation,' since a feeling becomes a sensation only when it has been related to an object by an act of thinking" (Fichte, *VWL*, GA, I/4: 242–3; *SW*, I, 490; *IWL*, p. 75.)

"The relationship that has been derived here is called *sensation* [*Empfindung*] (in other *words, finding-within-oneself* [*Insichfindung*]). (Only what is foreign is *ever found*; what was originally posited in the I is always present.) What is *sensed* is that activity of the I which has been canceled and annihilated. This activity is sensed (*found* in the I) and is something foreign, insofar as it is suppressed. But this activity cannot originally be suppressed, nor can it be suppressed by the I itself. This activity is sensed (as something *within* the I) insofar as it is suppressed, and it is suppressed only under the condition that another activity is posited in opposition to it; but if this opposing activity were to vanish, the suppressed activity would itself be pure activity" (Fichte, *GEWL*, GA, I/3: 150; below, p. 387).

"*Feeling*: how does it become *sensation*? How does a sensed *object* arise from this, since it is really only something *subjective*? [...] This occurs in part because of the *necessity of external manifestation,* and it occurs in part because of the identity of a single action in different cases. [...] What we are really concerned with, therefore, is whatever it is to which a property is transferred or upon which it is conferred.

"(1.) Feeling. (2.) Sensation as something objective. (3.) Matter as something that possesses a certain set of attributes. The latter is now also supposed to be *sensed*. (Our doctrine claims that it [that is, the material object of sensation] is produced. Consciousness claims that it is sensed. This is, in fact, a confusion.)" (Fichte, Unpublished commentary on *GEWL*, *GA*, II/4: 361.)

Whereas "feeling" is, for Fichte, something purely subjective, "sensation" always involves some reference to an object. Sensation is a feeling *of* something. [*K*, pp. 492–3.]

825. Namely, the object described as "sour" or "sweet," etc.

826. Note how the terms "feeling" (*Gefühl*) and "sensation" (*Empfindung*) are here used interchangeably. In *GEWL*, Fichte introduces a distinction between them.

827. "Only in consequence of a feeling is anything posited: *nihil in intellectu, quod non fuerit in sensibus* [there is nothing in the intellect that was not in the senses]. Feeling is the actual *in itself*, i.e., that which cannot be further explained. [...] Feeling or sensation is the first ground of everything present in the human mind" (Fichte, *VLM*, *GA*, II/4: 89).

"Every representation is based upon a feeling, which becomes possible by means of its relationship to a drive. Feeling is immediate and is by no means based upon representation; on the contrary, representation is based upon feeling" (Fichte, *VLM*, *GA*, II/4: 57).

828. "I never see that a surface is of a certain size. The red color of the table is surely only one thing [*nur Eins*], a simple feeling. Why do I extend this over a surface of a certain size? This is something that must be explained in a very different way" (Fichte, *VLM*, *GA*, II/4: 89).

829. It is the productive power of imagination that is responsible for "extending" the sensed property in space.

830. "A law that is valid for all rational beings. For all rational beings, there is feeling; all of them must posit something outside themselves in accordance with this law. Different feelings: a different, empirically determined world. Same feelings: the same world. Hence, for [all] human beings: the same world" (Fichte, *VLM*, *GA*, II/4: 85).

831. This, of course, is the major principle of Part Three: the I posits itself as determining the Not-I.

832. See below, no. 25.

833. "*Intension* is composed of the quantity of matter, not in space but in time. (Extension is composed of the quantity of matter in space)." (Fichte, *EM*, *GA*, II/3: 81).

834. The interruption of the I's act of determining is therefore accompanied by the feeling of a determinate quality, which must be further determined. This is possible, however, only if what is determined thereby (namely, the limited drive to determination) becomes an object of reflection. But the I is unable to remain fixated upon this object simply by means of its drive to determination; instead, it can accomplish this only by spontaneously determining itself as the perceiving subject. Hence the feeling sought for in no. 18, above, turns out to be a more precise determination of the I's own limitation. [*K*, p. 497.]

835. To say that the drive to determination discovers itself to be limited thus means that it discovers an object that limits itself. [*K*, p. 497.]

836. The move here is from the simplicity of every feeling to the simplicity of the thing. [*K*, p. 497.]

837. Every action has some product. [*K*, p. 497.]

838. "The image is either (1) produced in consequence of a feeling, in order to explain the same, in which case it is supposed to correspond to an object outside us. A sensible image. Or else (2) it is produced by free activity, apart from any feeling and without requiring that anything correspond to it. Representation of fantasy" (Fichte, *VLM*, *GA*, II/4: 66).

839. Hence the sensible image of X already contains reference to object X. The distinction between image and object is therefore a distinction *present within the finite, sensing I* itself. Recall that the object, the Not-I, is present for the I only in consequence of the check on its own outgoing activity and is never given to the I as it is "in itself." The Not-I

can therefore be described as an accident of the I; it is the I in a state of constraint, and the image is the sensible embodiment of this constrained condition (or original "organization") of the I. [*K*, p. 498.]

840. If, in accordance with the first principle of Part Two, the Not-I is supposed to determine the I, then it cannot be produced by the I. [*K*, p. 498.]

841. In this case, the Not-I is simply a "foreign" element within the I, not an object external to it. The latter is subsequently thought of by the I as the cause of this foreign element within itself. Hence there is a certain ambiguity in Fichte's use of the term "Not-I," depending upon the standpoint from which it is described. For the qualitative realist, the Not-I is the object of intuition (the thing); for the quantitative realist, it is the cause of certain representations (produced by the check); and for the quantitative idealist, it is a "foreign" element within the I itself. Thus, when Fichte refers to the Not-I as "produced" by the I, this refers to the idealist's account of the "thing" as posited in order to explain the "foreign" element present within the I itself. [*K*, p. 498.]

842. This is how the Not-I is posited by the philosopher observing the I, not by the I itself, which, as Fichte proceeds to point out, is unaware of its free positing in this case. [*K*, p. 498.]

843. In this case, the Not-I is posited as "contingent" in relation to the determination of the Not-I as such. According to the third foundational principle, the I must be limited; but this principle does not declare that it must be limited in any *particular* manner (having a feeling of "sweet" rather than "sour," for example). Since there is no law determining the necessity of any particular limitation of the I by the Not-I, Fichte can refer to "freedom" in this case: the Not-I could always have been (and be) other than it actually is. [*K*, pp. 498–9.]

844. This "other Not-I" = Y, that Not-I which is posited in opposition to the first object (or Not-I) = X. All we can say about Y at this point is that it is not X (for example, "not sweet"). [*K*, p. 499.]

845. See *GA*, I/2: 407, 437, and 443; above, pp. 339 and 374–5 and below, p. 371.

846. The postulate in question is the postulate that "the I is supposed to posit itself in this reflection as an I, i.e., as that which determines itself in this action."

847. See below, nos. 26–8, for an explanation of *why* object X extends to point C and no further.

848. I.e., considered entirely apart from its synthetic connection to feeling. [*K*, p. 500.]

849. This is because all we can say about any possible object lying beyond boundary C is that it is, for example, "not-sweet," which implies that it might have any of an infinite number of other tastes. [*K*, p. 500.]

850. I.e., the I engaged in reflecting or in entertaining images (representations). The "distinction" [*Unterschied*] that is supposed to be present in the Not-I in this case is, presumably, a *distinct* feeling among the "infinite" number of possible ones (for example, "sour" rather than "sweet").

851. I.e., the ideally active I, the I engaged in *intuiting* the object.

852. As was explained in § 4, such "hovering" or "oscillation" [*Schweben*] is accomplished by the power of imagination.

853. I.e., the claim that object X determines itself and the claim that it is determined spontaneously and freely by the reflecting I.

854. An intuition is a product of the power of imagination, which extends the single point of a simple sensation in both space and time. What is produced in this way is the scope or *Umfang* of the object, but not its *content*, which is provided only by *feeling*. [*K*, p. 501.]

855. It was previously claimed (see, e.g., *GA*, I/2: 374; above, p. 310) that "reality" is a product of the power of imagination. Hence, just as was the case with the terms "thing" and "Not-I," Fichte employs the term "reality" in several different senses. [*K*, p. 501].

856. In other words, object X is supposed to be both limited in itself and limited by the reflecting I.

857. See *GA*, I/2: 445, no. 32; below, p. 373, no. 32.

858. This object only "appears" to the reflecting I to be self-determined; hence, for the transcendental philosopher, the independence of the Not-I is only "apparent."

859. The determinate boundary point of Y can be given only by means of a new *feeling*, and the ideal activity can produce no feelings. Instead, as we have now seen, feeling is engendered only when the original outgoing activity of the I is limited or checked. The indeterminacy of the boundary in question for the ideal activity is what provokes the "hovering" of the power of imagination. [*K*, p. 501.]

860. Y must be another object, posited in opposition to X, since X can be determined only by positing in opposition to X something that is *not* X. [*K*, p. 502.]

861. This is a reference to the frequently invoked "law of determination," which dictates that every object (every "something") must be simultaneously determined and engaged in determining and must therefore be in this sense "self-determined."

862. Though it is directed at the ideal activity, the drive toward reciprocal determination also unites ideal activity and feeling. [*K*, p. 501.]

863. The ideal (or theoretical) activity of the I is, in this case, made possible and provoked by the (practical) drive toward reality, and both are synthetically united in longing. Since the ideal activity is that of the productive power of imagination, Fichte has now accomplished what was previously promised (*GA*, I/2: 361; above, p. 299): namely, he has grounded the I's theoretical power of representation upon a "higher," practical power of the I. [*K*, p. 502.]

864. See *GA*, I/2: 433; above, p. 361.

865. The "external condition" in question here would be an altered state of the world, a new object or new determination of indeterminate but determinable *matter*, and hence a new *feeling* for the I. This, however, is present to the I only as an *ideal* toward which it *strives*.

866. That is to say, the present ideal must be continuously reproduced. [*K*, p. 503.]

867. I.e., the feeling of satisfaction. See *GA*, I/2: 450; below, p. 378.

868. I.e., by a feeling different from the one that prompted the I to posit object X.

869. See above, § 10, no. 28.

870. See *GA*, I/2: 443; above, p. 370.

871. See above, § 8.

872. See *GA*, I/2: 424–5; above, p. 353.

873. See above, § 9.

874. See *GA*, I/2: 427; above, p. 355.

875. See *GA*, I/2: 434; above, p. 362.

876. See *GA*, I/2: 439; above, pp. 366–7.

877. This is the reflection of the I upon matter, by means of which "matter as such" becomes *determinate* matter, a sensible object. But in order for this object to be determined, it has to be posited in opposition to *another* object.

878. *Beziehungsgrund*. According to § 3 (*GA*, I/2: 272; above, p. 215), the "ground of relation" (or "ground of connection") is that feature shared by two opposed terms in which they are the same. In the present case, this ground does not lie in any common feature of the feelings related to each other, but instead, in the satisfaction of the drive toward reciprocal determination, which is described as the ground of reflection upon both feelings, and hence as that in which they are "synthetically united" I/2: 431; above, p. 359.) [*K*, p. 504.]

879. See § 10, no. 30.

880. *der Trieb nach Wechselbestimmung*. See *GA*, I/2: 444; above, p. 372.

881. I.e., the feeling of limitation. See *GA*, I/2: 431; above, p. 358.

882. See *GA*, I/2: 446; above, p. 374.

883. The drive toward reality arises only when the original drive toward determination is checked or interrupted; and thus it arises in *longing*. See *GA*, I/2: 444; above, p. 372. [*K*, p. 505.]

884. See *GA*, I/2: 430 and 440; above, pp. 358 and 377–8.

885. See *GA*, I/2: 445; above, p. 350.

886. The "action" in question here is that of *reflecting*; more specifically, it is that act in which the I reflects upon itself in order to determine if it has actually "filled infinity." See *GA*, I/2: 421; above, p. 350. [*K*, p. 505.] The "drive" that is satisfied is the previously derived "drive to alteration" or for "change as such."

887. Even though the I now has a *feeling* of being completely at one with itself, it is still not truly "at one with itself," since feeling always indicates limitation, and the original drive of the I is to overcome *all* limitations and "fill infinity." Hence the harmony with itself that it feels it such cases is always only temporary and fleeting. [*K*, p. 505.]

888. This is what is referred to in § 19 as the "constitution" [*Beschaffenheit*] of things, that is, their set of determinate properties or attributes.

889. In *BWL* (*GA*, I/2: 109n., above, p. 152n.) Fichte asserts that, whereas things are "represented as *appearances*," they are "*felt as things in themselves*." We now know that the thing in itself is constituted as we are supposed to *make* it (*GA*, I/2: 416; above, p. 346). Consequently, degrees of *reality* are indicated by grades of approval or disapproval. [*K*, p. 506.]

890. See below, no. 13.

891. "Recommended for re-reading. Everything that is present within the I and that happens by means of the I can be explained as a drive. The ideal activity is a drive for content, since ideal activity is nothing apart from objects" (Fichte, *WLnmK*, *GA*, IV/3: 384; *FTP*, p. 186).

892. I.e., this drive aims at harmony or agreement between the drive and the action (of reflecting).

893. *Wie weit?* A is engaged in determining only *to the extent that* B is determined, and B is determined only *to the extent that* A is engaged in determining, and vice versa. [*K*, p. 507.]

894. This is the drive that was described in § 10, no. 28 as directed at ideal activity, the drive that drives ideal activity to reflect upon X and Y as reciprocally determining each other.

895. See above, no. 8.

896. "Man's highest drive is the drive toward identity, toward complete harmony with himself, and — as a means for staying constantly in harmony with himself — toward the harmony of all external things with his own necessary concepts of them. It is not enough that his concepts *not* be *contradicted* (in which case he could be indifferent to the existence or non-existence of objects corresponding to these concepts); instead, there really ought to be something that corresponds to them. All the concepts found within the I should have some manifestation or counterpart in the Not-I. This is the specific character of man's drive" (Fichte, *EVBG*, *GA*, I/3: 35; *SW*, VI, 304; *EPW*, p. 155).

"Man's highest drive is directed at absolute agreement with himself, agreement of his theoretical and practical powers, of head and heart. If I do not practically recognize what I nevertheless recognize theoretically, then I place myself in clear contradiction with myself" (Fichte to Reinhold, August 19, 1799, *GA*, III/2: 386).

897. "The *Wissenschaftslehre* [...] must prove that a *manifold* is given for possible experience. This proof will proceed as follows: Whatever is given must be *something*; but it is something only insofar as there is also something else — which is also something, though a different something. As soon as such a proof becomes possible we enter the realm of what is particular" (Fichte, *GEWL*, *GA*, I/3: 145; below, p. 383).

898. See above, § 1.

899. See the description of the "circle" of the I's actions near the conclusion of Part Two (*GA*, I/2: 322; above, p. 361).

900. That is, from the standpoint of moral consciousness, which (unlike the *Wissenschaftslehre*) is unconcerned with the genetic derivation of this practical law from anything higher and is content to treat this law as a "*factum* of reason." [*K*, p. 511.]

901. Namely, *matter*. [*K*, p. 512.]

902. I.e., "determined."

903. This is manifest through feelings of approval and disapproval.

904. The "ground of a feeling," at which the acting is directed, is an object; and the goal of this acting is to "realize" the intended object by making it *actual* (by modifying matter). [*K*, p. 512.]

905. "The harmony of actuality with the natural drive [in the case of sensible pleasure] does not depend on me insofar as I am a *self*, that is, insofar as I am free. Hence the pleasure that arises from such harmony is a pleasure that tears me away from myself, alienates me from myself, and I forget myself in this feeling. It is an *involuntary* pleasure, and this is indeed its most characteristic feature. The same is the case with its opposite, sensible displeasure or pain. — In the case of the pure drive, the pleasure and the ground of this pleasure are nothing foreign, but instead depend upon my freedom; the pleasure in question is something I could expect to occur in accordance with a rule, whereas I could not expect this in the case of sensible pleasure. The kind of pleasure associated with the pure drive does not lead me outside myself, but rather, back into myself. It is *satisfaction*, and this is something that is never associated with sensory pleasure. It is less arousing than the latter, but more heartfelt, while at the same time it furnishes us with new courage and strength. Precisely because this is something that depends upon our freedom, the opposite of such satisfaction is *annoyance* [*Verdruss*]: inner reproach (nothing similar to which is ever associated with sensible pain, considered simply as such), connected with self-contempt. It would be intolerable to have to feel contempt for ourselves were we not lifted up again by the law's continuing demand upon us, were it not the case that this demand, since it issues from ourselves, re-instills in us courage and respect, at least for our higher character, and were this annoyance not mitigated by the sensation that we are still capable of meeting the demand in question" (Fichte, *SS, GA*, I/5: 138; *SW*, IV, 146; *SE*, p. 139).

904. Longing returns necessarily and endlessly, because even the feeling of satisfaction is, qua feeling, grounded in a *limitation* of the I. Hence the I, so long as it remains an I, can never escape longing, but must strive endlessly to overcome every limitation of itself. [*K*, p. 514.]

905. See *GA*, I/2: 429; above, p. 357.

906. "Now, however, *I* am supposed to have an effect upon that matter, the origin of which was described above. But it is impossible for me to think of this matter as being affected by anything other than something that is itself matter. Consequently, since I do — as I must — think of myself as having an effect upon this matter, I become for myself matter as well; and insofar as I view myself in this manner I call myself a *material body*. I am an articulated body, and the representation of my body is itself nothing but a representation of myself as a cause in the world of bodies and hence only a certain way of viewing my own absolute activity" (Fichte, *SS, GA*, I/5: 28–9; *SW*, IV, 11; *SE*, p. 16).

III. *Outline of What is Distinctive of the Wissenschaftslehre with Regard to the Theoretical Power*

1. This is a translation of the title page of the original, 1795 edition [= *A*]. An authorized second edition, published early in 1802 by the Tübingen publisher, J. G. Cotta, appeared in a single volume along with *Foundation of the Entire Wissenschaftslehre* and was

described on the title page as "new unaltered edition" but without the note "a manuscript for the use of his students" [= B]. A few week later, in 1802, a second, unauthorized new edition of GEWL was published in Jena by Gabler [= C], the changes to which were mainly orthographic and probably made by Gabler himself. It also retained on the title page the remark "a manuscript for the use of his students," with the additional note, "second, improved edition."

2. The title of § 1, *Begriff der besonderen theoretischen Wissenschaftslehre*, would most naturally be translated "Concept of the Particular Theoretical *Wissenschaftslehre*." Part Two of *GWL* was entitled "Foundation of Theoretical Knowledge," but is frequently referred to by Fiche himself in that same work and elsewhere as the "Theoretical Part" of *GWL* or (as in the present passage) simply as the "Theoretical *Wissenschaftslehre*." However, as Fichte will go on to explain in §1 of *GEWL*, the term *besonderen* or "particular" here seems to refer to the distinctive *content* of *GEWL*. As Wilhelm G. Jacobs, editor of a recent edition of *GEWL* argues persuasively: "The title of § 1 does not indicate that we are here concerned with a particular [*besonderen*] part of the theoretical *Wissenschaftslehre*; instead, it indicates that we are here concerned with a discussion of the element of "what is particular" [*des Besonderen*] within theoretical knowledge. The distinctive task of the *Wissenschaftslehre* with respect to the purely theoretical power is to demonstrate that the object of theoretical knowledge must always be something determinate, or, as Fichte says, something particular [*ein besonderer*]" (Editor's introduction to Fichte, *Grundriss des Eigentümlichen der Wissenschaftslehre* [Hamburg: Meiner, 1975], p. ix.)

3. *als Factum.* That is to say, it is certain that there must be some fact about the human mind to which this proposition corresponds or refers. Like Kant, Fichte often seems to use the Latin term "*factum*" to refer specifically to some *product* of the I's cognitive powers (and, more specifically, a product of its productive power of imagination), and he therefore contrasts a *Factum* with a mere *Tatsache* or "fact," in the sense of something purely *given* to the I. (See *GWL, GA*, I/2: 363–4; above, pp. 300–1.) In the present discussion, however, he very often appears to be using these same terms (*Factum* and *Tatsache*) more or less as synonyms. Nevertheless, *Factum* here remains untranslated (*factum*) and *Tatsache* is always translated as "fact."

4. *Anstoß.* Concerning this "check" or "impetus" or "impulse" that restricts the original activity of the I and is the occasion that sets in motion the entire cognitive "mechanism" described in Part Two of *GWL* and continued in *GEWL*, see *GWL, GA*, I/2: 355–6; above, pp. 292–3.

5. Regarding the "oscillation" or "hovering" (*schweben*) of the power of imagination, see *GWL, GA*, I/2: 359–61; above, pp. 297–9.

6. "Re. § I, note well: Everything appearing within consciousness is a *product of the power of imagination.* (What is it that people who wonder so much about this assertion really want? The thing in itself is surely not supposed to exist within us; nor, is it supposed to be, as it were, a 'representation in itself' or the like. Whatever is within us is something that we must surely produce. [...] Even the philosopher explains this act of production by referring to a *check.* This is now quite comprehensible. As we have seen, my *activity is restricted.* This original restriction is the one that occurs by means of duty; every other restriction is, in turn, only a *sensible* presentation of the one occurring by means of duty — that is, a presentation of it by the power of imagination" (Fichte, *Kommentar zum Grundriss des Eigenthumlichen der Wissenschaftslehre, GA*, ll, 4: 360).

(One of Fichte's unpublished notebooks containing his lecture notes on "Logic and Metaphysics" [*VLM*] includes a few pages of fragmentary commentary on the text of the *GEWL*, complete with specific page references to the first edition. These comments, which

Fichte presumably prepared for use in conjunction with his lectures during the winter semester of 1794–95 or 1795–96, are limited to the first few sections of *GEWL*.)

7. This is the concluding section of Part Two of *GWL*. See *GA*, I/2: 369–84; above, pp. 306–19.

8. "[This] is rather preliminary. In transcendental philosophy we deduce things from foundational principles, without reference to the *factum* of consciousness.

"The previous lecture presentation [viz., *GWL*] was *abstract*. That is not to say that it abstracted from experience, but the foundational principles for which I settled there could only furnish something abstract" (Fichte, *Kommentar*, *GA*, II/4: 360).

9. This makes it clear that *GEWL* should be treated as a supplement to Part Two of *GWL*, that is, as belonging to the "theoretical" portion of the first, foundational part of the *Wissenschaftslehre*.

10. "'Determined by another of the same sort.' That is, it *must present itself* to us in this way. We are here within the domain of consciousness, and this entire distinction only arises from the *sensible* manner of representing" (Fichte, *Kommentar*, *GA*, II/4: 360).

11. *ein Mannigfaltiges*, i.e., a *multiplicity* of *particular* representations. Cf. Kant, *KrV*, A77/B103ff. Also see B135: "For through the *I*, as a simple representation, nothing manifold is given. A manifold can be given only in intuition, which is distinct from the I, and it can be thought only through *combination* of the manifold in a single consciousness."

12. "Kant [maintains] *that* it [the manifold of experience] is given. We [maintain] that it *must* be given. And only then [after we have de monstrated the necessity of its being given to us] do we arrive at it" (Fichte, *Kommentar*, *GA*, II/4: 361).

13. See *GWL*, *GA*, I/2: 364–5; above, pp. 301–2.

14. See, e.g., *GWL*, *GA*, I/2: 400; above, p. 332.

15. See Part Three of *GWL*.

16. See *GWL*, *GA*, I/2: 373; above, pp. 309–10.

17. "This is precisely the activity we have been anticipating. It posits [itself], first as *capable* of being pure, and hence as capable of being an activity of the I, and, second as suppressed. [...] It posits something in itself, something that it claims and confesses lies outside it" (Fichte, "[Zum '*Grundriß*' des Eigentümlichen der Wissenschaftslehre]" 1795, *GA*, II/17: 365.)

18. *als synthetisches Glied der Vereinigung.* Such a "third thing" or "intermediate unifying link" must be posited, since otherwise it would not be possible to preserve the *unity* of the I, which would violates the first foundational principle of the *Wissenschaftslehre* (*GWL*, § 1: "I = I").

19. *die Tätigkeit des Ich im Widerstreite.* This is another name for the *real* or *objective* activity of the I, the activity that has been *suppressed* and *counterbalanced* by an opposing activity of the Not-I.

20. "1.) The activity of the I that discovers itself to be in conflict.

"2.) Under a certain condition, this activity is posited as pure.

"3.) This occurs by means of synthetic unification [of the pure activity of the I] with this condition, as [an activity that is] not pure, but is instead *stable* and *static* (excluded by the Not-I).

"4.) Accordingly, an activity of the I is once again posited. The activity we are seeking is the activity responsible for this *unification*." (Fichte, "[Zum '*Grundriß*' des Eigentümlichen der Wissenschaftslehre]" 1795, *GA*, II/17: 365.)

21. A "contingent condition" is a condition for the possibility of X which may or may not prevail. In what follows, it is helpful to keep in mind that Fichte understands "contingent" to mean "dependent upon something else" and hence understands "necessary" to mean "not dependent upon anything outside itself."

22. Regarding Reinhold and "Aenesidemus" (G. E. Schulze), see the Editors Introduction, as well as Fichte's own detailed account of his disagreement with Reinhold and agreement with Schulze on this point in *RA, GA,* I/2: 58–9; *SW,* I, pp. 17–18; *EPW,* pp. 71–2.

23. Fichte here plays upon the meaning of the verb *empfinden* ("to sense" or "to have a sensation"). The particle "*emp*" here means "within" and the stem "*finden*" means "to find" or "to discover."

24. "In section 1 we *comprehended* the [opposed activities of the I which were] in conflict with each other. In order for these to be activities of the I, they would have to be viewed as *pure* activities, which one [of them] was not; [hence the need for] synthetic unification [of the opposed activities]. — What arises from this unification is *what is sensed*, and this is then intuited; i.e., it becomes the object of an activity of the I.

    "The [activity that is] referred to the I is that of intuiting, which is by no means an activity that refers to itself as an activity of the I" (Fichte, "[Zum '*Grundriß' des Eigentümlichen der Wissenschaftslehre*]" 1795, *GA,* II/17: 365).

25. "*Feeling:* How does *it* become *sensation?* How does a sensed *object* arise from *this,* since *it is* really only something *subjective?*

    "This question is answered above: This occurs in part because of the *necessity of external expression,* and it occurs in part because of the identity of a single action in different cases.

    "Here we are within the theoretical domain, and thus we are not really concerned with the necessity of external expression. But we are certainly concerned with the latter transition [that is, with the identity of a single action in different cases]. Thus what we are really concerned with here is whatever it is that a property is transferred to or conferred upon.

    "(1) Feeling. (2) Sensation as something objective. (3) Matter as something that possesses a certain set of properties. The latter is now also supposed to be *sensed.* (Our theory claims that it is produced. Consciousness [claims that] it is sensed. This is in fact a confusion.) How and from where is this matter produced? How can it be sensed? This *matter is* neither my activity nor that of the thing. Instead, it is both. Only insofar as it is *mine* does it become an object of my consciousness.

    "How then is this [matter] indirectly related — and necessarily so — to self-consciousness, that is, to *pure, objective* activity?

    "(a) How is it even possible to explain the form of this objective activity, which nevertheless has to be posited as *our own?* Answer: by positing another [activity].

    "III. This difficulty is overcome" (Fichte, *Kommentar, GA,* II/4: 361).

26. See *GA,* I/2: 275; above, pp. 217–8.

27. "The basis or ground [*Grund*] for positing something *outside of* ourselves becomes evident here. This positing is an explanation.

    "Relation. Sensation. Immediate consciousness of my activity as a limited activity. In this way, and in this way alone, what is objective (i.e., matter) is connected with me.

    "(p. 13 [= the present passage].) Sensation, i.e., the act of sensing, referred to itself, which is obviously an entirely different operation. This operation is now our object.

    "It contains three elements: (1) something that is ascribed or related; (2) something to which it is ascribed, that is, the pure l; (3) something that engages in this act of ascription, as well as this act itself, which we now take as our object [i.e., the finite, cognizing I or 'intellect']" (Fichte, *Kommentar, GA,* II/4: 361-2).

28. "(p. 14 [= the present passage].) *To express this more clearly*: I am what is suppressed, and at the same time I am the *subject who intuits* this suppression — and it is as such that I

become conscious of myself. This is an act of positing in opposition. Where therein lies the *root of self-consciousness*? What is that X upon which *both* of these depend?" (Fichte, *Kommentar, GA*, II/4: 362).

29. "Observation [*Betrachtung*]: The entire activity [of observation] is obviously the same activity that finds itself in conflict, simply posited as active, *pure*, true. It will now be determined more precisely: first, as *posited in opposition*. — This is because synthetic unification occurs precisely by means of opposition; [hence,] the [opposed] components return [...]; and second, as synthetically united. How does this occur? It occurs when and because these opposed elements are related or connected to the condition, and thus relate themselves to this condition. — The condition in question would be that they are supposed to be united, and from this there now arises observation [*Betrachtung*] — but obviously [of] the Not-I, though it was then other." (Fichte, "[Zum '*Grundriß' des Eigentümlichen der Wissenschaftslehre*]" 1795, *GA*, II/17: 366).

30. "Because of the opposed elements contained in this synthesis, *what is engaged in intuiting* [*das anschauende*] is the *power of imagination*, and indeed in this case the reproductive power of imagination, since matter is already present" (Fichte, "[Zum '*Grundriß' des Eigentümlichen der Wissenschaftslehre*]" 1795, *GA*, II/17: 366).

31. *Intelligenz. As an* "intellect, the I is a finite, cognizing subject, one that is always necessarily related to a cognized object or Not-I, by which it posits itself to be determined. This is the I that is considered in detail in Part Two of *GWL*, and this is also the perspective of the I here in *GEWL*.

32. This does not mean that we have *transcended* the realm of consciousness in the manner of the philosophical dogmatist. Instead, Fichte claims to "go beyond all consciousness" in the purely *transcendental* sense, in which consciousness itself is "derived genetically" from its necessary *conditions*, as specified in Part One of *GWL*.

33. "In every successive observation the [same] action is posited again and determined as the product [of this action]. Consequently, in each of the following §§, what was previously an action is always the product [of that action]. The synthetically united elements are always what we were previously seeking, etc. The I does this and that. Hence the same synthetic elements that are here first posited in opposition to each another must already show themselves in the preceding §, though not in a determinate way" (Fichte, "[Zum '*Grundriß' des Eigentümlichen der Wissenschaftslehre*]" 1795, *GA*, II/17: 366).

34. The "impression" in question is the one that occurs in *sensation*.

35. Namely, an act in which the I freely reflects upon its own state.

36. "The entire deduction contains errors, because you [i.e., Fichte himself] did not pay attention to this in the preceding §.—It seems that the action that has now been deduced is inner intuition, and that what is sensed becomes outer intuition.

   "Wait! NB: here there is certainly confusion. That *activity* of the I which is conceived to be in conflict is posited as *static, as stuff or matter* — and it must remain so. No new synthesis should be allowed to contradict what has already been posited. — The I senses *itself*; consequently, what it first intuits is *itself*, and *inner* intuition is purely and simply the first kind of intuition. At the appropriate time, we will discover how outer intuition arises" (Fichte, "[Zum '*Grundriß' des Eigentümlichen der Wissenschaftslehre*]" 1795, *GA*, II/17: 366).

   It is uncertain to precisely which passage in *GEWL* this remark pertains.

37. *das Bestimmen*, viz., the activity of specifying or delimiting the activity of the Not-I. To assign a predicate to something is—in this sense and for Fichte—to "determine" it.

38. "IV. Limitation of activity, as was said—and indeed, limitation in the indicated, determinate meaning of the term (a trivial point).

"Let us now proceed to our main topic. (1) The sensing subject. What does it mean for this subject to ascribe activity to itself?

"The activity it refers to itself is sensation. The intermediate elements have now been completely exhibited. Here we are only obtaining the construction materials. We also wish to *assemble them*.

"Transition. Consciousness of the *sensing subject. — Activity, state of passive affection, and ascribing to them a relationship*, etc. = is X" (Fichte. *Kommentar, GA*, II/4: 363).

39. It is essential to keep this in mind: *sensing* is an activity of the I, and *sensation* is the product of the same.

40. More literally, "its being-posited [*Gesetztsein*] is dependent upon such a foreign influence."

41. As Fichte frequently reminds his readers, the I can never *really* limit itself; however, it can do so "ideally." That is to say, it can and must *posit itself* as limited. But it can do this only insofar as it simply *discovers* itself to be always already limited in a determinate, *real* fashion—a discovery that commences with *feeling*.

42. I.e., they are posited in synthetic unity with one another.

43. That is, in Part Three of *GWL*, though the actual title of that section is "Foundation of the Science of the Practical."

44. See *GWL, GA*, I/2: 408–9; above, pp. 339–40, where Fichte explains that "The I's original striving for overall causality is genetically derived from the law of the I that requires it — just as surely as it is supposed to be an I at all — to reflect upon itself and to demand that, in this reflection, it discover itself to be all reality. This necessary reflection of the I upon itself is the ground of all of its proceeding beyond itself, and the demand that it fill infinity is the ground of its striving for overall causality; and both [the I's necessary reflection upon itself and the demand that it fill infinity] are grounded solely in the absolute being of the I."

45. That is, on the condition that some *limitation* is present in the I, at first in the form of *feeling*.

46. I.e., it is reflected upon merely as "matter as such." See *GEWL, GA*, I/3: 152; above, p. 388.

47. See *GEWL, GA*, I/3: 204; below, p. 432.

48. Just because it is an I, the I must necessarily reflect upon and posit for itself whatever it discovers within itself.

49. *ist Kanon.* "I understand by a canon the sum total of the a priori principles for the correct employment of certain powers of knowledge" (Kant. *KrV*, A796/B825).

50. The I *posits* itself as limited, even though it is not responsible for the fact that it finds itself to be limited.

51. The product in question is *Stoff* — "stuff" or "matter" —, an indeterminate substrate spontaneously posited by the I as underlying all the experienced properties or attributes of the Not-I. For Fichte, the term "*Stoff*" often appears to be interchangeable with "substance" or "matter [*Materie*]." See *GWL, GA*, I/2: 434; above, p. 362.

52. I.e., an activity of the "absolute power of the I," the power of productive imagination. See *GEWL, GA*, I/3: 185; below, p. 417.

53. See above, *GEWL, GA*, I/3: 148; above, p. 385.

54. I.e., the power of productive imagination. See *GWL, GA*, I/2: p. 360; above, p. 298.

55. *des Bildes.* Note the connection between "image" (*Bild*), and "power of imagination" (*Einbildungskraft*) and the verb "to copy" (*nachbilden*). *Bilden* is a key term in the following discussion, where it has the technical meaning of "to form images." (Elsewhere it has usually been translated as "to form or shape," "to develop," or "to cultivate.")

56. *das bildende Ich.* Here Fichte is taking advantage of the double meaning of *bilden*. Not only does this term designate "the I that entertains images," it also designates "the formative or productive I"—hence the I that is somehow responsible for the very images it entertains.

57. "Even though a free being must produce from itself everything that is present within it, something must necessarily appear to be 'given' to such a being. What is the origin of this semblance [*Schein*]? It follows from the very nature of a free being, for a free being arises from a free acting, which is preceded by no consciousness whatsoever. This free acting becomes an object of consciousness and can subsequently be viewed as a product of freedom. Insofar as it becomes an object of consciousness, however, it appears to be something given; and the reason for this lies in the character of the ideal activity, which has to be constrained by something it has not produced. One could also express this point by noting that a free being cannot act at all unless it acts upon something, and this 'something' also comes from freedom. But because this freedom is not itself an instance of acting upon something, it remains in the shadows. This is why an object must necessarily exist for us. See *What is Distinctive of the Wissenschaftslehre*, § 3, VII" (Fichte, *WLnmK, GA*, IV/3: 410; *FTP*, p. 234).

58. *Mittelanschauung*. The intuition produced unconsciously by the "first act" of the I — that is, by the power of imagination — is the ground of the relationship between the *image* and the *actual thing*, thereby "mediating" between them.

59. See *GEWL, GA*, I/3: 154; above, p. 390. The translation here follows the suggestion of Alexis Philonenko in reading *die... wir annehmen* for Fichte's *den... wir annehmen*. A literal translation of Fichte's text would be: "This intuition is the ground of all harmony — a ground we assume [to exist] between things and our representations of them."

60. The only way to distinguish the image from the thing is to recognize the former to be determined by the I — and therefore already be "present" within consciousness.

61. An absolute action is a free or spontaneous action, one grounded entirely in the I. As Fichte goes on to explain, the "absolute action" in question is performed by the productive power of imagination, which freely assigns determinate properties to its objects.

62. Note that the image in question here is an image of the properties of an object, but not of the object itself qua Not-I, substance, or substrate.

63. *Wechselwirkung*. See *GWL, GA*, I/2: 287–90; above, pp. 228–31.

64. The I determines itself *as* totality, rather than as *less* than totality. In either case, it assigns a predicate to, and thereby *determines* — and hence *limits* — itself.

65. We are here supposed to think of two distinct "B's," the first united with the totality and the second excluded from it.

66. *Innere Anschauung des Ich im freien Bilden*. This could also be rendered as "the inner intuition of the I that is engaged in freely forming images." The intuitions in question here — the ones required in order to freely construct an image—are those in which properties are assigned to objects. They are "inner" because they are independent of spatiotemporal (or "outer") features.

67. This action is "determined" or "determinate" (*bestimmt*) because, as an act of reflection, it is determined by its object — in this case, by the I's own state.

68. They are "the same" in the sense that they are *both* excluded from the I and posited as Not-I.

69. The "necessary Not-I" is the substrate or thing, and the "contingent Not-I" is the determinate properties or distinguishing features of this thing (the content of the "image").

70. That is, to the thing or to the substrate of the property in question.

71. This sentence begins with an open parenthesis, which is not closed until the end of remark number 5, below. These parentheses have here been eliminated.

72. See Kant, *KrV*, A84/B116–A130/B169.

73. See Kant, *KrV*, A137/B176–A147/B187.

74. See Maimon, *Streifereien im Gebiete der Philosophie*, p. 53.

75. See *GWL, GA*, I/2: 368–9; above, pp. 305–6.

76. See Maimon, *Versuch über die Transcendentalphilosophie*, p 187.

"The lesson to be drawn from this, therefore, is that all reality — reality *for us*, as goes without saying, since it cannot be understood in any other way in a system of transcendental philosophy — is generated by the power of imagination. One of the greatest thinkers of our age, who, so far as I can see, teaches the same lesson, calls this a *deception* [*Täuschung*] on the part of the power of imagination. But every deception must posit truth in opposition to itself; it must be possible to avoid every deception. Consequently, when it has been proven, as it is supposed to have been proven in our system, that the possibility of our consciousness, of our life, and of our being for ourselves — that is to say, the possibility of our being as an I — is based upon this action on the part of the power of imagination, then this action cannot be eliminated, unless we are supposed to abstract from the I, which is self-contradictory, since the subject engaged in the act of abstracting cannot possibly abstract from itself. Hence, this action on the part of the power of imagination does not deceive us, but provides us with truth, and indeed, the only possible truth. To assume that the power of imagination deceives us is to establish a skepticism that teaches one to call into question one's own being" (Fichte, *GWL*, *GA*, I/2: 368–9; above, pp. 305–6).

77. It is unlikely that Fichte has any specific passage from Hume in mind at this point. Indeed, it is very likely that his acquaintance with Hume's work was based entirely upon his reading of works by Schulze/Aenesidemus, Maimon, Kant, Jacobi, and others

78. *Das zufällige wird bewirktes* […] *und insofern etwas wirklich*. That is to say, what is contingent, including the limited or "contingent" I, is an effect *(Wirkung)* of the absolute I's efficacy *(Wirksamkeit)* and is therefore something actual *(wirklich)*. At this point, Fichte's text contains one play after another on the terms *wirken, bewirktes, wirklich*, etc.

79. See *GEWL*, *GA*, I/3: 154; above, p. 390.

80. "Threefold," because we will be dealing with two opposed elements, plus that which synthetically unites them.

81. The I here posits two distinct spheres of efficacy: sphere z, in synthetic unity with force Y, and an opposed sphere, –z, in synthetic unity with force X, which has v as its sphere of efficacy. Presumably, v = 0 because it is determined by how Y is posited. Y is contingent and X is necessary.

82. See *GEWL*, *GA*, I/3: 188; above, p. 419.

83. See *GWL*, *GA*, I/2: 448–9; above, p. 375.

84. Namely, the "contradiction" between the posited freedom of the I and the determinacy of the substance upon which it is reflecting.

85. *Gesetztsein oder Dasein*. *Dasein* is an ordinary German word for "existence," which literally means "being-there" or "being-present." *Gesetztsein* is a term modeled on *Dasein*. By employing these terms in apposition, Fichte implies that "existing" ("being there") is the same thing as "existing for a subject" ("being posited"), and hence that nothing exists except what is posited to exist, and that what is posited to exist is posited as existing in a particular spatial location.

86. See Kant, *KrV*, B41.

Appendix: *"The Zurich Wissenschaftslehre"*

1. Regarding Fichte's "Zurich lectures," see the Editor's' Introduction, above, pp. 6–14. The complete series, consisting of approximately forty lectures, was delivered between February 24 and April 26, 1794, in the home of K. L. Lavater. Neither Fichte's original manuscript nor either of the two complete copies nor any complete transcript of the same has survived. In 1993, Erich Fuchs discovered, in the Lavater family archives in the Zurich Central Library, a transcript, by Lavater himself, of the first five lectures in this series. The content of these lectures corresponds closely to that of *BWL*, though there is nothing in

the latter corresponding to the discussion of the "constructive methods" of both geometry and philosophy contained in the fourth lecture.

Fuchs published an edition of Lavater's transcript in a slim volume that included, on facing pages, a photomechanical reproduction of the original manuscript, as well as a very brief excerpts from a later portion of the same lecture series, discovered in the private papers of Jens Baggesen, and a long and informative introduction: J. G. Fichte, *Züricher Vorlesungen über den Begriff der Wissenschaftslehre Februar 1794. Nachschrift Lavater. Beilage aus Jens Baggesens Nachlass: Excerpt aus der Abschrift von Fichtes Züricher Vorlesungen*, ed. Erich Fuchs (Neuried: Ars Una, 1996) [= *ZVau*]. Finally, in 1999, both the Lavater transcript and the excerpt from Baggesen's notes were included in *GA* IV/3: 19-41.

2. See Reinhold, *Beyträge zur Berichtigung bisheriger Mißverständnisse der Philosophie*, I (1790), p. 59.

3. That is to say, is it simply the systematic relationship between a set of (represented) propostions that constitutes a "science"?

4. The translation substitutes "*Wissen*" (knowledge) for Lavater's "*Wissenschaft*" (science), in order to preserve the point of Fichte's contrast between possessing isolated bits of knowledge and having "scientific" — i.e., systematic — knowledge of something. In the customary usage of Fichte's time, *Wissenschaft* could indeed be used as a synonym for *Wissen*, but in this case Fichte is clearly drawing a distinction between "knowledge" and "science."

5. This is the very first appearance of the term *Wissenschaftslehre* in any of Fichte's unpublished or published writings and lectures and thus represents, as Fuchs charmingly puts it, "the birthday" of the term (*ZVau*, p. 42).

6. See the corresponding section of *BWL*, where Fichte explains that philosophy — as the mere "love of knowledge" or striving for the same — must be replaced by something else: namely, genuine knowledge or science itself (*GA*, I/2: 117–18; above, p. 162).

7. *entwickeln*. In this case, "to develop a fact" is to make further inferences based upon it and to connect it systematically with other such facts in an attempt to "explain" or draw further implications from it. Fichte would soon replace references to "developing" a fact with references instead to "deriving" or "deducing" a concept therefrom.

8. After arriving in Jena in May of 1794, where he began to elaborate his new system in his "private" lectures on *Foundation of the Entire Wissenschaftslehre*, Fichte no longer referred to a plurality of *Tathandlungen*, but almost always employed the singular term "F/Act" to refer exclusively to the original, spontaneous self-positing (as self-positing) of the I. Presumably, the "pure sciences" to which he here refers are the various parts or branches of the complete *system* of the *Wissenschaftslehre* itself.

9. This passing remark illuminates Fichte's conceptions of both "reason" and "positing." He understands *reason* in a primarily active or practical sense. Reason makes assertions or issues injunctions. *Positing* is asserting, putting something forward. And practical reason — the I — does this *just because it is an I*.

10. The "realization" in question would be the actual, successful *construction* of a complete system of universal philosophy upon the basis of this single foundational principle.

11. *dießes Positivum and Negativum*. This strategy avoids the skeptics' objection because it forecloses the possibility of ever getting beyond the domains of the I and the Not-I.

12. The editors of *GA* IV/3 propose to amend this to read: "if one does not add thereto the concept of quantity and limitation."

13. *Elementarphilosophie* was K. L. Reinhold's name for his systematic version of Kant's Critical philosophy, in which he claimed to derive all of Kant's results from a single foundational principle, the "principle of consciousness" (which asserts that, in consciousness, the subject distinguishes the representation from both the representing subject and object represented and relates it to both). Before settling upon the name "*Wissenschaftslehre*,"

Fichte sometimes referred to his own, improved version of Kant and Reinhold's transcendental philosophy as "my elementary philosophy." Indeed, the title of the manuscript in which he first tried to articulate and to develop some of the basic ideas of his new system was "Personal Meditations on Elementary Philosophy" (*EM, GA*, II/3: 21–226). Even after he had arrived in Jena and was lecturing on the *Wissenschaftslehre*, one of his best students still reported that he was "attending lectures on Elementary Philosophy" (Diary of Johann Smidt, entry for May 26, 1794; as cited in *FiG*, 7, p. 11).

14. The "first science," of course, would be *Wissenschaftslehre*.

15. Note how Fichte here employs the term *Wissenschaftslehre* quite generally, to describe philosophy as Kant understood it, in other words, as a synonym for transcendental philosophy as such and not simply as the name for his own distinctive version of the same ("the *Wissenschaftslehre*"). Regarding Kant's claim that philosophy (and therefore "*Wissenschaftslehre*") cannot construct its concepts, see *KrV*, B762–B765. On the difference between the methods of proof appropriate to philosophy and mathematics, see the "Transcendental Doctrine of Method," Ch. I. "The Discipline of Pure Reason," Sect. I: "the Discipline of Reason in its Dogmatic Use," B741–B766.

16. See Salomon Maimon, *Streifereien im Giebiete der Philosophie*, pp. 15–16, where he notes that mathematics is always able to guarantee the *reality* of its way of proceeding and of the products of such procedures only because it actually *constructs* those products. But since philosophy (as Kant maintains) cannot *construct* its concepts, but can only *analyze* concepts obtained from elsewhere, it has to find some way to build a bridge between the transcendental level and the particular, empirically given contents of experience. But, according to Maimon, it is unable to accomplish this and is therefore unable to answer the *quid facti* concerning the actual application of a priori forms of understanding to particular objects of sensible experience.

17. See Kant *Kritik der Urteilskraft*, § 57 (*Kants gesammelte Schriften*, ed. Königliche Preuißischen Akadamie der Wissenschaften [Berlin: Walter de Gruyter, 1908/13] 5: 342): "concepts of understanding must, as such, be demonstrable at every time; that is to say, the objects that correspond to them must be capable of being given at any time in intuition (pure or empirical), for only in this way can they become cognitions."

18. See § 4 of *GEWL*.

19. Though it featured prominently in Fichte's first published mention of his new systematic strategy (in the Aenesidemus review) and is a focus of much discussion in his later "Introductions" to a new presentation of the *Wissenschaftslehre* (1797), it is noteworthy that this controversial term is completely absent from *BWL, GWL*, and *GEWL*. For speculation concerning the reason for this absence, see the Editor's Introduction, above, p. 18.

20. This way of classifying *Tathandlung* as a species of *Tatsache* is not retained in Fichte's subsequent writings, in which a "F/Act" is almost always distinguished from and posited in opposition to a mere "fact."

21. See Kant, *KrV*, B116: "When teachers of law talk about rights and claims, they distinguish in a legal action the question regarding what is right or legally justified (*quid juris*) from the question concerning fact (*quid facti*)."

22. *Geschichtsschreiber*. Note the very similar version of this claim in *BWL* and *GWL*, to which Fichte there adds the qualifying term "pragmatic" — as in "pragmatic history." See *GA*, I/2:135 and 146; above, pp. 186 and 365.

23. For further discussion of this point, see the second of Fichte's unpublished 1794 lectures "Concerning the Difference between the Spirit and the Letter within Philosophy" (*UGB, GA*, II/3: 336–9; *EPW*, pp. 210–13).

24. *doch immer ihrer Gültigkeit aus den Resultaten über die Wissenschaftslehre erhält*: "über" seems a bit out of place in this phrase, which could be rendered more literally, albeit less intelligibly as "results concerning *Wissenschaftslehre*."

25. *Der willkürlichen Reflexion des Philosophen*. The contrast here is between an act — or F/ Act — which must necessarily occur if consciousness is to be possible at all, and another act — that of philosophical reflection — which must be freely and deliberately undertaken if it is to occur at all. The latter act is *willkürlich* or "arbitrary" in the sense that its occurrence depends entirely upon a free choice by the philosopher.

26. I.e., "factually," or as a simple matter of fact.

27. That is to say, the I that engages in reflection in order to become the subject that is conscious of the acts described within the *Wissenschaftslehre*.

28. Originally published (in part) by Heinrich Fauteck on p. 321 of "Die Beziehung Jens Baggensen zu Fichte," *Orbis Litterarum* [Copenhagen] 38 (1983): 312–37, these two brief texts occupy the front and back of a single sheet (in Baggesen's hand) which is today in the Baggesen Nachlaß in the Royal Library of Copenhagen. Fauteck, however, did not publish the "attempt at an improved table of categories," which appears on the reverse side of the sheet containing this fragmentary transcript of a portion of the Zurich lectures. Both excerpts were included, along with reproductions of the original manuscript pages, in *ZVau*, pp. 184–9. The text itself was subsequently published in *GA* IV/3: 47–8.

    Regarding Fichte's Zurich lectures, Baggesen reported to Reinhold as follows: "I attended only the final three hours of Fichte's course of lectures. He lectures well, in some respects excellently, but far too abstractly and in a dreadfully compressed form. The only person certain of understanding him is Fichte himself, and I predict that in Jena he will be only half understood. Nevertheless, it is just as certain that he will be found interesting. As soon as I receive a copy of this course of lectures, which he has solemnly promised me, I will send it to you — but to you alone — under the seal of friendship. I believe that it is the *non plus ultra* of over-refined speculation and the most abstract metaphysical web that has ever been spun from one I to another — but also nothing more than this. [...] He has five principles that precede the Principle of Consciousness. The highest of these is *I am, because I am*. — *In the I, the Not-I is posited in opposition to the I*, etc." (*FiG*, 1: 75 and 117).

    Baggesen did indeed receive (from Johanna Fichte) the promised copy of Fichte's Zurich lectures, but it too has been lost. Whether the short passages translated here were originally part of that larger manuscript is uncertain, but there is no doubt that they are excerpts from the Zurich lectures, though certainly not from the "prolegomena" to the same. They therefore provide precious, albeit very meager, evidence concerning the contents of at least one of the later lectures in the series, which is consistent with the information concerning the content of the later lectures that is available from other sources, including Fichte's February 1794 letter to Lavater (*GA* III/2: 60–1; *EPW*, pp. 374–5), in which he outlines in advance the plan of his lectures, and Georg Geßner's diary.

29. Fichte had employed this same terminology of "self-presentation" in his personal notes on Elementary Philosophy (*EM*), which he prepared while writing *RA*, but he did not retain it in his subsequent attempts to characterize the self-positing F/Act of the absolute I.

30. That is, the "theoretical part" of the system, as presented in Part Two of *GWL* and supplemented by *GEWL*.

31. Regarding this assertion, see the following remark from Baggesen's September 5, 1794, letter to Reinhold (written after Baggesen had received from Johanna Fichte the promised full transcript of the Zurich lectures). After noting that he had not at first been convinced by Fichte, Baggesen then adds: "Subsequently, and since I have read his new *Wissenschaftslehre* and thought it through, I no longer misunderstand him. He proceeds on both feet, and he leads with the correct one, the practical one, which greatly pleases me. His system appears to be egoistic, and the entire theoretical part actually *is so* as well; and, in my view, this is how it ought to be. But the practical part completely annuls the odious aspect of this egoism. His philosophy as a whole is practical-theoretical. His I is nothing but freedom, and his first principle is the principle of freedom. In my view, the proposition "*I am*" has

a double meaning: "*I exist*" and "*I am I.*" Taken in the former sense, this principle is the principle of consciousness in general; taken in the second sense, it is the principle of freedom. There is certainly no question that his *Wissenschaftslehre* merits study. I have strongly urged him to have it printed as soon as possible" (*FiG*, I: 146).

32. Intensive qualitative quantities.

33. Extensive quantitative quantities.

34. Relative quantitative qualities.

35. Modal quantitative qualities.

36. Delivered April 26, 1794, this is the oration with which Fichte concluded his Zurich lectures. He subsequently had this text privately printed and distributed as a souvenir to those "patrons and friends" who had attended his Zurich lectures.

37. That is to say, it spontaneously applies the pure forms of sensing (intuition) and pure concepts or rules of thinking (understanding) to the manifold of sensations.

38. This is the same system, but now viewed "subjectively" as the system of the *necessary* operations of the human mind — necessary, in Fichte's (and Kant's) view for the possibility of the I itself. We are not yet in the realm of practical/noumenal agency, but still in that of theoretical philosophy, which concerns itself solely with those actions of the mind which are necessary for cognition and the (correspondingly) necessary features of the world.

39. Here Fichte seems to be referring to the domain of aesthetic judgment, the subject of the first part of the Third *Critique*. The concept of "beautiful order" recalls the Kantian conception of "purposiveness without purpose."

40. Fichte's claim is that the human body is uniquely "spiritual" in the specific sense that it is uniquely suited to carrying out the demands of practical reason. See the discussions of the body as a *purposively articulated instrument of the will* in GNR, WLnm, and SS.

41. This "true stamp of humanity" is examined in *GNR*, where it is found to consist in the articulated human body and in human language.

42. That all individual moral agents are only "tools of the moral law" and hence means to the end of reason as such — namely, complete independence from anything outside the I, or the utter self-sufficiency reason itself — is a major theme of *SS*.

43. Kant, an avid reader of ethnographic and travel literature, including Cook's account of his circumnavigation, on several occasions used the example of the "inhabitants of Tierra del Fuego" (along with the "New Hollanders" of Oceana) to suggest that some human beings might not be easily recognizably as "human." In § 67 of the *Critique of the Power of Judgment* he opines that the character of the inhabitants of Tierra del Fuego and New Holland might lead one to call into question his characterization of human beings as ends in themselves — and this might lead one to deny that such people are truly "human" at all. It is this later implication to which Fichte is responding here and elsewhere. See, for example, *EVBG, GA*, II/3: 41; *SW*, VI, p. 311; *EPW*, p. 160.

44. Note that the second lecture of Fichte's *EVBG* concludes with an almost identical passage (*GA*, I/3: 41; *SW*, VI, 311; *EPW*, pp. 160–1).

45. Georg Geßner, who was present at this final lecture, described it as "a very poetic address concerning the *I* — the dignity of human beings — which, however, contained some thoughts that could at least appear to be atheistic" (as cited in *Zvau*, p. 23). It is not implausible that it was the mention of such potentially "atheistic" implications of his address in the discussion following his lecture that led Fichte to append this footnote to the printed version.

Index*

* Certain terms – for example, "I," "Not-I," "activity," and "posit" – occur on nearly every page of the texts translated in this volume. It has therefore been necessary to exercise a certain selectivity in indexing their occurrence.

Printed and bound by CPI Group (UK) Ltd, Croydon, CR0 4YY